Management Accounting

Management Accounting

M.E. Thukaram Rao
Head, Department of Commerce
Sri Sathya Sai University
Brindavan Campus
Bangalore, Karnataka

PUBLISHING FOR ONE WORLD

NEW AGE INTERNATIONAL (P) LIMITED, PUBLISHERS
New Delhi • Bangalore • Chennai • Cochin • Guwahati • Hyderabad
Jalandhar • Kolkata • Lucknow • Mumbai • Ranchi
Visit us at **www.newagepublishers.com**

Published by New Age International (P) Ltd., Publishers
First Edition: 2003
Reprint: 2012

Branches:

- No. 37/10, 8th Cross (Near Hanuman Temple), Azad Nagar, Chamrajpet, **Bangalore** - 560 018.
  Tel.: (080) 26756823, Telefax: 26756820, E-mail: bangalore@newagepublishers.com
- 26, Damodaran Street, T. Nagar, **Chennai** - 600 017. Tel.: (044) 24353401, Telefax: 24351463
  E-mail: chennai@newagepublishers.com
- CC-39/1016, Carrier Station Road, Ernakulam South, **Cochin** - 682 016. Tel.: (0484) 2377004, Telefax: 405
  E-mail: cochin@newagepublishers.com
- Hemsen Complex, Mohd. Shah Road, Paltan Bazar, Near Starline Hotel, **Guwahati** - 781 008.Tel.: (0361) 2
  Telefax: 2543669, E-mail: guwahati@newagepublishers.com
- No. 105, 1st Floor, Madhiray Kaveri Tower, 3-2-19, Azam Jahi Road, Nimboliadda, **Hyderabad** - 500 027.
  Tel.: (040) 24652456, Telefax: 24652457, E-mail:hyderabad@newagepublishers.com
- RDB Chambers (Formerly Lotus Cinema)106A, 1st Floor, S.N. Banerjee Road, **Kolkata** - 700 014.
  Tel.: (033) 22273773, Telefax: 22275247, E-mail:kolkata@newagepublishers.com
- 16-A, Jopling Road, **Lucknow** - 226 001. Tel.: (0522) 2209578, 4045297, Telefax: 2204098
  E-mail: lucknow@newagepublishers.com
- 142C, Victor House, Ground Floor, N.M. Joshi Marg, Lower Parel, **Mumbai** - 400 013. Tel.: (022) 249278
  Telefax: 24915415, E-mail: mumbai@newagepublishers.com
- 22, Golden House, Daryaganj, **New Delhi** - 110 002. Tel.: (011) 23262370, 23262368, Telefax: 43551305
  E-mail: sales@newagepublishers.com

ISBN : 978-81-224-1439-4

₹ 299.00

C-11-09-5888

Printed in India at Mohanlal Printer, Delhi.

PUBLISHING FOR ONE WORLD

NEW AGE INTERNATIONAL (P) LIMITED, PUBLISHERS

4835/24, Ansari Road, Daryaganj, New Delhi-110002

Visit us at **www.newagepublishers.com**

This book is dedicated to

the lotus feet of

BHAGAVAN SRI SATHYA SAI BABA

with whose blessings this book is published.

PREFACE

I have immense pleasure in placing into the hands of my esteemed readers this book on Management Accounting. Although several books are available on the subject, the need for a comprehensive volume covering all the important aspects of Management Accounting has been felt for a long time. My long experience in teaching and the understanding I have acquired over these years have made it possible for me to satisfy this need.

The book is written in a simple and lucid style so that it can be easily understood by the readers. At the end of each chapter, a few standard questions which serve as model questions have been given to enable the students to test their understanding abilities.

In preparing this book, I have derived constant inspiration from my students and colleagues for which I express my gratitude.

In the course of writing this book, I have referred to many standard works of various authors. Some useful definitions and questions from some university and professional bodies have been incorporated in the book.

The book serves the needs of students preparing for examinations of B.Com, B.B.A., B.B.M, M. Com, MBA and other courses in Business Management. It will also be of immense use to the practising managers in the various organisations.

I am extremely grateful to New Age International Publishers, New Delhi for publishing this book so nicely and elegantly.

I shall appreciate receiving comments and suggestions from readers for the improvement of the book.

M.E. Thukaram Rao

CONTENTS

1

NATURE AND SCOPE OF MANAGEMENT ACCOUNTING

INTRODUCTION

The modern business involve several transactions. The efficiency and success of the business depend upon how management of the business deal with such transactions. The transactions which take place in a business can be measured and expressed in terms of money value. Since business is affected by such transactions, they are to be recorded, analysed and reported to management. This helps the management to evaluate the performance of the business. In fact, three branches of accounting have emerged to deal with these aspects. As a first step financial accounting system was developed and it is concerned with money, an economic resource. The American Institute of Certified Public Accountants (A I C P A) defines financial accounting as "the art of recording classifying and summarising in a significant manner and in terms of money, transactions, and events which are in part atleast of a financial character and interpreting the results thereof. "Financial accounting is concerned with preparation of two important statements, viz., income statement and position statement. Through these two statements it furnishes useful information to external parties of a business. However, financial accounting suffers from certain limitations for which reason, cost accounting system was evolved."

While financial accounting is concerned with money as an economic recource, cost accounting is concerned with money as a measure of economic performance. Cost accounting is concerned with classification, collection, recording allocation and control of costs. It consists of systems, methods and techniques which are used to measure, analyse and ascertain the cost of production. It provides useful information to management and profitability of products, departments, process etc.

Management accounting is concerned with presentation of accounting information which helps management in the formulation of policy and to facilitate management in discharging its day-to-day activities. It is the process of identification, measurement, accumulation analysis, interpretation and communication of financial information to facilitate management in planning, evaluating and controlling the activities and accountability of its resources.

NEED FOR MANAGEMENT ACCOUNTING

Modern business are complex in nature. They are large in size and their activities are wide spread. Their ownership is different from management. Instead of owners, the professional managers run and look after the business. Delegation of authority and the decentralisation of decision-making process has necessitated the use of some mechanism of performance, evaluation and responsibility accounting. The functions of planning and decision-making, control and supervision, coordination and staffing are no longer personal. A system of information is needed to help the management to analyse, measure, and check the functioning of each division and unit for their proper coordination to achieve the objectives of the business with utmost economy and efficiency. Even the development of cost accounting does not provide adequate data needed by the management. Management accounting is a system of utilising financial, costing, and other information to assist the management in the performance and evaluation of their functions. The Management Accountant basically collects, analyses, interprets and presents information regarding past activities and current and future events and helps management in decision-making. Thus, management accounting meets the need of the management.

DEFINITION AND CHARACTERISTIC FEATURES OF MANAGEMENT ACCOUNTING

The management accounting team of Anglo-American Council on Productivity defined management accounting as "The presentation of accounting information in such a way as to assist management in the creation of policy and in day-to-day operation of an undertaking."

According to J. Batty, management accounting comprises accounting methods, systems and techniques, which coupled with special knowledge and ability, assist management in its task of maximising profits or minimising losses."

The Institute of cost and Management Accountants, London, has defined management accounting as the "application of professional knowledge and skill in the preparation of accounting information in such a way as to assist management in the creation of policy and in the day-to-day operation of an undertaking".

According to Robert Anthony, "Management Accounting is concerned with accounting information which is useful to management."

Features of Management Accounting

The following are the important characteristic features of Management Accounting.

1. It is a separate branch of accounting which is devised to provide useful data to management in decision-making process.
2. It is based on anticipated events which would take place in future. In simple words it is futuristic in its approach.
3. It is not based on regular or continuous accounting system. Instead it is intemittent in nature. In other words, collection of accounting information for analysis and interpretation is made according to the requirements of the management.
4. It does not follow any prescribed accounting format for reporting. This is because information is provided according to the needs of management.
5. It is only a technique adopted by management to derive information. It cannot take part in executing the decision. In other words it cannot replace management.
6. It is subjective in nature as it is basically depends upon judgement of the person concerned rather than on measurement.
7. It is inter-disciplinary subject as it embraces within itself financial accounting. Cost accounting and financial management. According to J. Batty "management accounting is blending together into a coherent whole, financial accounting, cost accounting and all aspects of financial management."
8. It is not based on any prescribed rules and formats as in the case of financial accounts and cost accounts. It all depends upon informational needs of the management.

9. It is mainly concerned with future events. Its focus is on estimating or forecasting the future based on past results.
10. It is a service function as it provides useful information to various levels of management.

NATURE OF MANAGEMENT ACCOUNTING

The nature of management accounting can be brought out under the following headings:

1. Management Accounting is a branch of knowledge: Though management accounting is considered to be a branch of accounting, in recent time it is regarded as an important branch of knowledge, i.e. a distinct discipline by itself. It is an organised body of knowledge having its own concepts and conventions. However, the principles and rules vary from industry to industry.

2. Management Accounting is a science: Management accounting is a science as it is body of systematic knowledge relating to not only management accounting but relating to a wide variety of subjects such as financial and cost accounting. Statistics, operation research, financial management, auditing, taxation, office management and so on. It is necessary for a management accountant to have intimate knowledge of all these field of study in order to carry on his day-to-day activities. But it is to be emphasised that it is not a perfect science as in the case of natural science.

3. Management Accounting is an art: It is an art as management accountant requires the ability and skill in applying the tools and techniques of management to various management problems. By using the knowledge of management accounting, it is possible for the management accountant to present, analyse and interpret the data.

4. Management Accounting as an extension of Cost Accounting: Some authorities view management accounting as an extension of cost accounting. Management accountant employs most of the techniques of costing, such as standard costing, budgetary control, marginal costing, cost volume-profit analysis inter-firm comparision etc., to assist management in formulation of policy, preparation of plans and controlling the operations. Therefore it is also sometimes said that the management accounting is an extension of the managerial aspect of cost accounting.

5. Management Accounting is a profession: In recent years management accounting has become one of the important profession which has become more challenging. This is evident from two facts. First, the setting up of various professional bodies such as National Association of Accountants (NAA) in U.S.A, The Institute of Cost and Management Accountants, in UK, the Institute of Cost and Work Accountants, in India and similar other professional bodies both in developed and developing countries have increated the growing awareness of Management Accounting profession among people. Secondly a large number of Management Accountants are rendering the professional service to various organisations which is known as "Management Consultancy Service."

OBJECTIVES OF MANAGEMENT ACCOUNTING

The main function of management accounting is to provide useful information to management in maximising profit or minimising loss. This is undertaken by presenting various statements and reports to enable management to formulate right policies. In this regard, management accounting has set before it the following objectives:

1. Planning the activities of the business: Planning is deciding as deviding in advance what is to be done, how and when it is to be done. To undertake this task, management accountant provides information relating to past and helps in estimating future. He also furnishes data relating to alternative course of action so that management can take right decision. The information obtained from management accountant also helps the management to forecast the future. Finaliy management formulates the policy of the business based on facts and figures submitted by management accountant.

2. Controlling the performance of the business: Controlling is a function intended to ensure and make possible the performance of planned activities and to achieve the predetermined goals and results. For this sake, the entire organisation is divided into various segments and each segment is entrusted into the hands of a responsible person. The person in-charge of a segment is responsible for the success or failure of that segment. Further management accounting makes use of techniques such as Budgetary Control and Standard Costing, wherein actuals are compared with targets to know the favourable and adverse variances. In case of adverse variances, the causes are identified and appropriate measures are taken to set right an adverse variance.

3. Useful in organising: Organisation is the process of coordinating the physical, human and momitory resourses. It consists of conscious coordination of people towards a disired goal. It also includes delegation of authority and fixation of responsibility. Management Accounting is concerned with establishing responsibility centres, preparation of budgets, and fixing responsibilities on various persons. A good system of management accounting is helpful in creating an efficient organisational frame work in industries.

4. Motivating employees: Motivation is that function of management by which employees are stimulated to work hard by satisfying their needs, desires and wishes. Management accounting lays down the best alternative method of doing the work. It fixes the targets and on achieving the targets employees are rewarded through incentives.

5. Useful in decision making: Decision-making is concerned with choosing the best course of action from among the alternatives. In business enterprises decisions may relate to expansion or contraction, use of machinery or manual labour, make or buy the components and so on. Management accounting considers the profitability of alternative proposal and their financial implications. The information provided by management accountant helps the management to choose best alternative and to take right decisions.

6. Useful in coordination: Coordination is concerned with the unification, integration, and harmonising of the different activities of the organisation. By preparing budget of various departments, management accounting coordinates the efforts of all the departments. The Management accountant and acts as a coordinator and resolves the problems of various departments.

7. Reporting to management: One of the important objectives of management accounting is to furnish various types of reports to all levels of managements. The technique used is known as Management information system. Through this technique the management accounting appraises the performance of various departments and furnishes up to date information to management on a periodical basis.

8. Facilitates interpretation of financial information: Last but not the least the objective of management accounting is to facilitate management in understanding the financial statements. Some time managerial personnel may not understand the significance of financial statement. Management accountant by using the technique of comparative statement techniques, trend analysis ratio analysis etc., enable management to understand the contents of financial statements. Besides these techniques, statistical techniques such as graphs, charts, averages etc. can also be used to make financial statements more meaningful to management.

SCOPE OF MANAGEMENT ACCOUNTING

The scope of a subject means the areas which fall under its puriew. As for as the scope of Management Accounting is concerned it has a wide scope. The following topics fall under the scope of Management Accounting:

1. Financial accounting: Financial accounting is primarity concerned with recording of transactions in a set of books, posting them into the concerned ledger accounts, preparing trial balance and thereafter in preparing final accounts. The statements prepared under financial accounts forms the basis for analysis and interpretation which serves as a meaningful data for managerial decision making.

2. Cost Accounting: Cost accounting is primarily concerned with collection, analysis allocation apportionment and absorption of overhead with a view to ascertain the cost of production of goods or service. Cost accounting furnishes useful data to management showing areas of inefficiency and the steps to be taken to avoid losses and wastages.

3. Statistical Methods: In order to carry out the functions of management very often management relies on non-quantitative data. Such information is provided by statistical methods and they mainly include sampling techniques, diagrams, graphs, and charts, time series analysis. Index numbers, regression analysis, statistical quality control techniques etc. Thus statistical methods is an integral part of Management Accounting.

4. Operation Research: Modern business is faced with highly complicating problems in decision making process. Operation research techniques offer scientific solution to such problems. Some techniques of operation Research used to solve problems are linear programming, queing theory, waiting line models PERT, CPM, etc.

5. Organisation and Methods: O&M is the name given to any conscious attempt, scientifically applied to improve organisation, simplify and improve method and generally create and maintain an efficient administrative machine. Management accounting is also concerned with improving methods, simplifying the processes and reducing the cost. Management accounting relies on O&M with a view to achieve its objects.

6. Budgetary control: Budgetary control is concerned with [illegible]ation of budgets, comparing actuals with budgets and taking corrective measures to set right adverse deviations. In fact Management accountant acts as a coordination when budgets are prepared for various departments. Hence budgetary control is part and parcel of Management Accounting.

7. Law: Modern business functions within the legal environment. Decisions are also affected by the provisions of some of the important legistation such as companies Act, Foreign exchange Management Act, MRTP Act, and other labour legislation. Hence management accounting relies heavily on law of the country.

8. Taxation: The computation of income tax, sales tax, excise duty, import duty and filing of returns promptly is undertaken under the direct supervision of Management Accountant. So taxation is an important aspect of management accounting.

9. Internal auditing: Internal auditing is concerned with the verification of books of accounts within the organisation. Internal auditing simplifies the task of external auditing. Management Accounting arranges for internal auditing and hence it is a part of Management Accounting.

10. Management information system: Management Accountant prepares various types of reports to meet the different levels of management. The reports are prepared and submitted periodically so as to suit the needs of the management. Based on the reports, management undertakes to exercise control over the business. Hence reporting system serves as a basis for the functioning of management.

11. Capital budgeting and investment decisions: The term capital budgeting refers to long term planning for proposed capital outlay and their financing. It includes raising both long term funds and their utilisation. When current funds are invested in long term activities it results in future benefits. Capital budgeting decisions are very important as they involve large funds, risk and incertainty and they are of an irreversible nature.

FUNCTIONS OF MANAGEMENT ACCOUNTING

Management accounting is entrusted with the functions of classifying, presenting, analysing and interpreting data so as to help management in running the business efficiently and economically. The important functions performed by management accounting are as follows :

1. Recording the data: Though recording of data is originally done under financial accounting, sometimes, to make recording of transactions more meaningful to management, estimates and probabilities are taken into consideration. The management accounting classifies original recorded data into distinct groups, and sub-records are prepared. On the basis of sub-records comprehensive reports are prepared. Management accounting makes use of computers in this regard.

2. Validating the data: The efficient functioning of management depends upon the accuracy and adequacy of the financial data collected from the books of accounts. Management accounting ensures that the management is furnished with accurate and reliable information. Besides furnishing past data management accounting also provides future data based upon predetermined level of activity.

3. Interpretation of data: The recorded and validated data in its raw form may not be useful to management directly. The data requires proper analysis and classification based on their similarities and dissimilarities. This enables management to make decisions and to know its effects or expected results. Hence analysis and interpretation is considered to be an important function of management accounting.

4. Reporting the data: Having analysed and interpreted the data it is to be communicated in the form of reports to various levels of management as and when required. The reports must be promptly prepared and submitted to managers so as to facilitate them to carry out the important functions of coordination, decision-making and controlling.

5. Installation of sound Accounting System: One of the important functions of management accounting is to devise a suitable system of financial and cost accounting system and its installation in the organisation. It is also concerned with modifying and re-modifying the system depending upon the changing economic environment of the business.

6. Providing feed-back reports: The provision of feed-back report helps management in performing control function. The management accounting pin-points the deviation between actual and expected activities and by adopting the principles of selectivity helps management in following the technique of "Mangement by exception."

7. Evaluating the performance of Management: Management accounting is concerned with providing methods and techniques for evaluating the performance of the management in the hight of objectives of the business. Thus it helps in implementing the principle of "Management by objectives."

RELATIONSHIP BETWEEN MANAGEMENT ACCOUNTING AND FINANCIAL ACCOUNTING

The relationship between Management Accounting and Financial Accounting can be studied under the following heading:

Similarities between Management Accounting and Financial Accounting

Management Accounting and Financial Accounting appear to be similar in the following respects.

(*i*) They both study the impact of the business transactions and events of the enterprise.

(*ii*) They both deal with interpretation and reporting of accounting information.

(*iii*) Both the system of Accounting is concerned with providing information for internal and external use.

Dissimilarities

Management Accounting differs from Financial accounting in the following respects:

Financial Accounting	*Management Accounting*
1. It deals with the business as a whole.	1. It deals not only with the business as a whole but also each and every segment of the business.
2. Its main emphasis is external reporting. It may follow the tactics of window-dressing to project better image.	2. Its main focus is internal reporting. The reports provided reflects real situation.
3. It is historical in nature.	3. It is futuristic in its approach.
4. It is more precise being based on actual cost.	4. It may not always be precise and accurate being based on estimates.
5. The accounting information is reported once a year.	5. The reports are furnished periodically depending upon the needs of management.
6. It is governed by the generally accepted accounting principles.	6. It is not based on accounting principles. It is free to formulate its own rules pro-cedures and forms because information is meant only for internal management.
7. It is to prepared compulsorily by higher form of organisations. The preparation of accounts is laid down by the statutes concerned.	7. It is undertaken voluntorily to benefit management.
8. The statements prepared under financial accounts is expressed in monetary terms.	8. The information supplied under manage-ment accounting is both in terms of monetary as well as non-monetary such as quantities of materials, number of working hours, quantities, produced and sold etc.
9. It is objective in nature. It is based on actual measurement.	9. It is subjective in nature as it is based on judgement rather then actual measurement.
10. It is subjected to auditing.	10. It is not possible to verify and audit the transactions.
11. It is independent.	11. It is dependent on Financial accounting.

RELATIONSHIP BETWEEN COST ACCOUNTING AND MANAGEMENT ACCOUNTING

Similarities between Cost Accounting and Management Accounting:

1. Both the branches of accounting are internal to the organisation.
2. Both the branches of accounting assist management in carrying out its functions of planning, decision-making and controlling.
3. Both the branches of accounting use similar techniques such as marginal costing, budgetary control, standard costing etc.
4. There is a great deal of overlapping in their functions.

Dissimilarities:

Cost Accounting	*Management Accounting*
i. The main object of cost accounting is to ascertain and control cost.	1. The main objective of management accounting is to provide useful information to management for decision-making.
2. It is based on both present and future transactions for cost ascertainment.	2. It is concerned purely with the transactions relating to future.
3. Cost accounts has narrow scope as it covers matters relating to ascertainment and control of cost.	3. It has a wide scope in as much it covers the areas of financial accounts, cost accounts, taxation, statistics, law etc.
4. It deals only with monetary transactions, *i.e.*, it covers only quantitative aspect.	4. It deals with both monetary and non-monetary transactions *i.e.*, both quantitative and qualitative aspects.
5. Cost accounts follow a definite principle for ascertaining cost and a format for recording.	5. It does not follow a definite principle and format. Instead, the data to be presented depends upon the needs of management.
6. Cost Accountant occupies a lower position as compared to Management accountant in hierarchy of Management.	6. Management Accountant occupies a higher position in the organisational set-up.
7. Cost accounting techniques are few and includes Marginal Costing. Budgetary control and Standard Costing.	7. Management accounting techniques include apart from the costing technique, other important techniques such as fund flow, cash flow, ratio analysis etc.
8. Cost accounting is concerned with short term planning.	8. Management accounting is concerned both with short term and long term planning. Evaluating the capital investment project is the speciality of Management Accounting.
9. Cost accounting is historical in its approach and it projects the part.	9. Management accounting is futuristic in its approach. It is more predictive in nature when compared to cost accounting.
10. It is independent of Management accounting.	10. It is dependent on Cost Accounting.
11. Cost accounting is concerned merely with assisting in management functions and does not provide for the evaluation of the performance of management.	11. Management accounting is concerned with both assisting management in its functions as well as evaluation of the performence of the management as an institution.

ADVANTAGES OF MANAGEMENT ACCOUNTING

1. Management accounting assists management in the formulation of policy and in performing day-to-day activities of the business Management has to take tactical and strategic decisions to plan for the future. Decisions such as make or buy,

expand or contract, own or lease, modification and diversification of business etc. Through management accounting techniques and by providing relevant accounting data, it is possible for the management to take right decision.

2. Management accounting assists the management in performing the control function effectively. Techniques such as standard costing, budgetary control help management in controlling the operations of business.
3. Management accounting assists management in planning process and thereby attaining the targets of the business.
4. Management accounting helps management in adjusting to the changing economic environment of the business. It enables the business to overcome the seasonal and cyclical fluctuations or to prepare the business to meet such fluctuations.
5. Management accounting facilitaties coordication of activities of various departments and thus helps in attaining the objectives of the business. For this it is necessary to communicate the targets and achievements of various departments to management. Techniques such as budgeting, reporting, interpretation helps management accounting in this regard.
6. Management accounting helps management in the internal organisation of the business. The division of business into various segments, fixation of responsibility, delegation of authority etc. are integral part of management accounting.
7. It helps the management in measuring the performance of business and in evaluating the capital investments in various projects.
8. It provides employment opportunities to Management accountants.

LIMITATIONS OF MANAGEMENT ACCOUNTING

1. Management accounting to a larger extent is based on estimates and probabilities. Hence it is not an exact science. It does not deal with actuals and thus accuracy is not ensured under management accounting.
2. Management accounting is only a tool in the hands of management. It cannot replace management.
3. Management accounting derives its information from financial accounts, cost accounts and other records. The strength and weakness of management accounting, therefore depends upon the strength and weakness of these basic records.
4. The installation of management accounting is a costly affair. Hence only big business establishments alone can think of management accounting. It is outside the purview of small scale enterprises.
5. It is very difficult to get approval of existing accounting staff for the installation of management accounting. Other managerial and lower level managerial personnel resist the installation of management accounting.
6. Management accounting is in its evolutionary stage. The tools and techniques, of management accounting requires refinement, modifications, disending, and reintroduction into the system. It takes a long time to have a full fledged management accounting system in a business.
7. Management accounting is a subject which is based upon various fields of study such as statistics, taxation, law, auditing etc. Lack of understanding or knowledge of any of these discipline will affect the management accountant in finding a solution to the problem.

MANAGEMENT ACCOUNTANT— FUNCTIONS, ROLE, DUTIES AND QUALITIES

Functions of Management Accountant

The term "Management Accountant" has many synonyms. Finance director, financial controller, financial manager, controller are some of the designations given to the person entrusted with the work of management accounting. The management accountant collects and provides accounting, cost accounting, economic and statistical information to the management to assist them in the performance of managerial functions and their evaluations. Through various techniques of recording, analysis, interpretation and presentation he makes the financial, costing and other data active and effective in the performance of management functions, *viz.* planning, decision making and control. The management accountant is forward-looking and therefore he is able to treat economic information and data to make them suitable for use by the management. His functions include the following:

1. To establish, coordinate, and administer plans to facilitate the forecasting of sales, expenses, budgets and standards that will permit profit planning, capital budgeting and financing.
2. To formulate accounting policy and procedures including submission of operating data and special reports and comparing the performance with plans and standards. Comparision of actual and expected performance helps the management in proper fixation of responsibility and in evaluation of functional and divisional heads.
3. To protect the business assets to the extent possible by external controls, internal auditing and insurance coverage.
4. To frame tax policies, and procedures and to supervise and coordinate the reports required by various authorities.
5. To be aware of economic and social forces as also the effect of Governments policies and actions on business activities.

POSITION AND ROLE OF MANAGEMENT ACCOUNTANT

The position or status of Management Accountant differs from concern to concern. It depends upon the policy and pattern of Management. In some organisations he occupies the position of an executive while in others he may be a member of Board of Directors. Generally speaking his position is that of Chief Accountant of the organisation. He works in close coordination with other departmental heads. The position of Management Accountant is exactly like the spokes in a wheel, connecting the rim of the wheel and the hub and in this process receives the information. He processes that information and then returns the processed information back to where it came from.

As regards the role and responsibility of Management Accountant, it can be said that he assists the various levels of management by furnishing useful information. More precisely, the role of Management Accountant can be discussed under the following:

1. Planning: The management accountant helps to:

(*a*) Formulate future plans by providing vital information such as what products are to be sold, condition of the market, prices to be fixed etc.

(*b*) Provides data based on past performance which guides the management for achieving the future goals.

(*c*) Plays an important role in planning the short term budget to the concern.

(*d*) Plans` and prepares the master budget as a whole and presents it to the top management for approval.

2. Controlling: The Management Accountant:

(*a*) Controls the performance of the organisation by preparing performance reports for each responsibility centers.

(*b*) Pin-points the areas that do not conform to plans: and quickly identify weak and troubled spots and draws the attention of the top management to take necessary steps.

3. Organising: Through responsibility accounting system, the Management Accountant represents the design and implementation of accounting system for better definition and consideration.

4. Communicating: The management accountant helps the communication function through budget and performance reports.

5. Motivating: The budgets and performance reports prepared by the management accountant motivates the personnel of the organisation. Budegts, which represent targets motivate managers in achieving the desired goals and the performance reports motivate the personnel.

DUTIES OF MANAGEMENT ACCOUNTANT

1. To serve as the chief accounting officer incharge of the organisation's accounting books, accounting records and forms.
2. To audit all pay rolls and vouchers and have them properly certified.
3. To prepare balance sheet, profit and loss account and other financial statements and reports and furnish to the Managing Director a complete report covering results of the company's operation during the past quarter and fiscal year to date.
4. To supervise the preparation, compilation, filing of all reports, statements, statistics and other data that the law requires or the Managing Director requires.
5. To receive all reports from agents and factory departments that are needed for recording the factory's general operations or for directing or supervising its accounts.
6. To maintain general control over the accounting practices of all subsidiary companies.
7. To supervise the enforcement and maintenance of the classification of accounts and any other accounting rules and regulations that any regulatory body prescribes.
8. To endorse the cheques for deposit or transfer.
9. To approve payment of all vouchers, drafts and other bills payable when required by the Managing director.
10. To prepare a budget showing the factory's future requirements as shown by its accounts and the requirements of the general manager and other officers.

QUALITIES OF MANAGEMENT ACCOUNTANT

1. Knowledge about various branches of study such as Financial Accounting, Cost Accounting, Economics, Statistics, law etc. as management accounting embraces all these field of study.

2. Knowledge of business forecast under anticipated changing environment of business.
3. Ability to appraise management from time to time regarding the current position of the business so that management can review the success or failure of the business.
4. Knowledge of various techniques of management and accounting so that he can prepare and submit reports to enable management to take prompt action to set right adverse conditions.
5. Thorough knowledge about budgeting and forecasting so as to consider alternate proposals under consideration.
6. Knowledge about sources of funds so that best source can be tapped at minimum cost of borrowing.
7. An analytical mind which can see through implications of alternate courses.
8. The ability to understand management structure so that he can submit right report to right managerial level.
9. Ability to get along with all levels of management. The reports prepared and submitted must be free from bias of any type.

INSTALLATION OF MANAGEMENT ACCOUNTING

Installation of Management accounting involves the following steps:

1. Preparation of organisation manual: An organisational manual is a comprehensive book which offers guidance to members of an organisation. It lays down the duties and responsibilities of executives in the organisational hierarchy. It facilitates delegation of authority and fixation of responsibility. Communication process is also facilitated by an organisational mannual.

2. Preparation of printed forms and returns: Management accounting to a large extent involve preparation and submission of reports to all levels of management. To avoid repetitions in preparing reports blank printed forms are made use of. The forms are appropriately filled and submitted to the concerned management.

3. Recruitment of staff: The staff and clerks who will assist management accountant must be recruited and trained.

4. Integration of cost and financial accounting: In order to enable collection and analysis of data it is desirable to classify accounts. As Management accounting uses information from both financial and cost accounting, a system of integration of there two system will help in supplying information promptly to management accounting.

5. Standard costing system: As this is one of the important techniques used by management accountant, a standard costing system is to be devised. This helps in setting up standard cost and in comparing actual costs with standard cost to locate variance. The management accountant can suggest remedial measures to eliminate such adverse variance.

6. Budgetary control system: Budgetary control system not only helps in controlling but also as a tool of coordination. The integration of departmental budgets into a master budget also helps in formulating goals of the organisation.

7. Operation research technique: With the ever charging environment of business the modern business is becoming more complex. It is faced with many challanges and opportunities. Decision making process is becoming more complicating. A system of operation research will help management accountant to solve number of problems faced by the business.

TOOLS AND TECHNIQUES OF MANAGEMENT ACCOUNTING

In order to function efficiently, management accounting makes uses of the following tools and techniques:

1. Financial accounting: Financial accounting provides accounting information to management accountant who in turn rearranages the same for reporting to management. Hence financial accounting is regarded as the backbone of management accounting.

2. Cost Accounting: Cost accounting provides information relating to cost of production. Management accounting compares actual cost with standard cost to know the efficiency of the business.

3. Financial management: Management Accounting makes use of the techniques of financial management such as the extent of trading on equity, proportion of equity, preference share and loan capital, sources of capital, evaluation of alternate investment proposals.

4. Analysis of financial statements: With a view to highlight the performance of business in simple form, management accounting uses a number of techniques of analysis and interpretation. Some such techniques are comparative financial statements, common size statements, find flow statement, cash flow statement, ratro analysis.

5. Cost control techniques: For evaluating the efficiency of business all techniques of costing such as marginal costing, differential costing, budgetary control and standard costing is increasingly used in management accounting.

6. Management information system: Management information system is concerned with furnishing information promptly to the management. This implies reporting all levels of management at appropriate time. Hence, reporting is an integral part of management accounting.

7. Statistical analysis: Of late a large member of statistical techniques are used in management accounting for making financial information more meaningful and to enable comparative study. Some such techniques used are graphs, charts, diagrams, measures of dispersion, correlation and regression analysis, time series analysis etc.

8. Inflation accounting: Thus technique is used for ensuring the maintenance of original capital during the period of rising prices.

ORGANISATION OF MANAGEMENT ACCOUNTING

Organisation of Management accounting system depends upon number of factors such as size of the business, nature of the business, policy and philosophy of management etc. In a medium sized organisation, the Management accountant may function directly under the supervision of a manager. In a large sized business, he may function in liaison with financial controller. He will work as a coordinator of various departments of an organisation. The position of Management Accountant in a large sized concern is shown below:

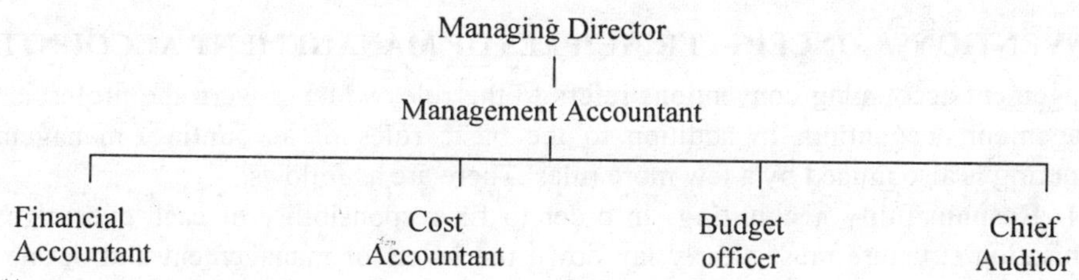

From the above chart it is clear that management accountant is directly responsible to Managing Director as for as accounting department is concerned. He can in turn delegate authority to various persons such as financial accountant (who shall be responsible for preparation of final a/cs) cost accountant (who shall be responsible for ascertaining cost). Budget officer (who shall be responsible for consolideting departmental budget) and Chief Auditor (who shall be responsible for verifying the books of accounts).

MANAGEMENT ACCOUNTING AND FINANCE FUNCTIONS

Finance is the life blood of a business. Collecting and proper utilisation of finds are the two important functions of financial management. Just as other functions of a business such as production, accounting, marketing etc., finance is regarded as a distinct function of the business. Financial management is a separate branch of management which deals with finance function of the business. Though finance function is incharge of finance manager, yet in many countries including India, this function is performaed by the accountant. In some organisations, the accounting and finance function are integrated and is looked after by chief accountant. Where a separate Finance Manager is appointed he has to work in close coordination with Management Accountant. While the Management Accountant furnishes relevant and prompt information, the finance manager based on such information will make decisions. Based on the decisions, the Management accountant has to collect new information and data.

Finance function to a large extent is determined by business environment. Generally speaking, finance is concerned with: (*a*) obtaining finds at the lowest cost and (*b*) making optimum use of these funds. The two major sources of obtaining funds are (*a*) Debt and equity and the two major uses or applications of finance are providing for: (*a*) Fixed assets and (*b*) working assets. The role of Management Accountant in raising funds are to plan for raising funds through equity shares and preference shares. He must also plan for bonus shares and right shares. Regarding loan capital, the funds may be collected through (*a*) debentures (*b*) financial institutions and (*c*) other sources. Debentures may be open or mortgage, naked or simple, redeemable or irredeemable, registered or bearer, first or second, convertible or non-convertible depending upon the financial requirement of a company. Regarding financial institutions, the long term finance is provided by the financial institutions such as IFCI, ICICI, IDBI. Insurance corporations. Miscellaneous sources include (*a*) Lease financing (*b*) Hire purchase finance (*c*) Discounting of bills (*d*) Public deposits (*e*) Trade credit (*f*) Internal source of financing (*g*) retained earnings etc.

Management accountant should ensure that the funds are obtained at the lowest cost and the same are used in the optimum manner, so as to maximise the value of the firm. The funds should be utilised for getting the maximum benefit of the firm and to ensure that there is financial discipline in the organisation.

CONVENTIONS/CONCEPTS/PRINCIPLES OF MANAGEMENT ACCOUNTING

Management accounting conventions refers to the rules which govern the profession of management accounting. In addition to the basic rules of accounting, management accounting is also guided by a few more rules. There are as follows:

1. Responsibility accounting: In order to fix responsibility of each executive the organisation structure must clearly lay down the levels of management and define the duties and responsibilities of each and every person. The process of preparing reports on the basis of level of management or according to the segments of the organisation is known as responsibility accounting. It indicates not only the results of the segment but also the person responsible for such result. Thus according to this convention for every transaction involved, some one is held responsible.

2. Management by exception: This convention is applicable at the time of reporting information to management. According to this convention normal deviation between standard and actual performance is not reported. Instead only significant variances alone are reported to management for taking corrective measures. This is to facilitate management not to be over burdened with too many information but to present only important information.

3. Principle of key areas: In every business enterprise though there are many departments found, only some departments are considered to be most important. The success or future of the entire business depends upon the efficient functioning of such key departments. According to this convention, management accountant must furnish detailed information of such key areas when desired by the management.

4. Matching cost with revenue: Matching of cost with revenue enables to know the actual profit of the business. If the matching principle is not carried out properly it leads to unrealistic profit. According to thus convention, Management Accountant should be alert in matching cost with revenue so as to avoid misleading profit.

5. Preparation of Reports in conformity with objective: According to this convention, accounting records and reports must be free from bias or prejudice. This will facilitate analysis and interpretation of reports according to the prevailing situation.

6. Flexibility: According to this convention, the accounting records, reports, statements relating to past and present must be designed to meet the needs of the business as a whole or to solve a specific problem depending upon the need.

7. Control-at-source accounting: According to this convention costs are to be controlled at the point of incurrence. Control over materials, labourers and other costs are to be exercised to establish cost consciousness in the organisation. This involves preparation of cost sheets of different segments, process, products and in designing the cost accounting system so as to facilitate effective control all over the organisation.

8. Accounting for inflation: According to this convention profit is said to be actually earned provided that capital is maintained in real terms. The convention provides that money value does not remain stable because of inflation. Hence the need for inflation accounting.

9. Use of return on capital employed: The success of business depends upon how best the capital is employed. This can be known by the technique of "Return on capital employed. Management accounting will reveal how effectively the resources are utilised for improving the business."

10. Integration: According to this convention, management information system should be integrated so as to furnish maximum information at minimum cost.

11. Recovery of overheads: According to this convention, overheads are to recovered on the most equitable basis. The overheads are to be recovered by products "on the basis of benefits received for fixed costs or responsibilities incurred for variable costs."

12. Controllable and uncontrollable cost: According to this convention, responsibility is to be fixed by classifying cost into controllable and uncontrollable by management or the department concerned.

13. Forward looking approach: According to this convention management accountant has to anticipate the problem and prevent their recurrence. This is possible through the techniques of budgetary control and standard costing.

14. Appropriate method: According to this convention management accounting must be equipped with appropriate method of collecting, classifying, and presenting information as per the requirements. Mechanisation could be followed in this regard.

15. Personal contact: According to this convention the reports and statements should not replace personal contacts. The management accountant can control cost and perform other functions such as coordination, communication, motivation etc., by means of personal contacts.

QUESTIONS

Simple Questions

1. Define Management Accounting.
2. State the similarities between management accounting and financial accounting.
3. State the similarities between management accounting and cost accounting.
4. List out any four tools and techniques of Management Accounting.
5. State the objectives of Management Accounting.
6. State the limitations of Management Accounting.
7. State any two differences between Management Accounting and financial accounting.
8. State any two differences between Management Accounting and Cost Accounting.
9. Name the concept of management accounting.

Short Answer Questions

1. Explain briefly the functions of Management Accountant. *(Bangalore University, B. Com., April 2000)*
2. Distinguish between Financial Accounting and Management Accounting. *(Bangalore University, B. Com., April 2000)*
3. "Management Accounting is bothering more than the use of financial information for management purposes." Explain this statement. *(Bangalore University, B. Com., November 1999)*
4. "Management Accounting Serves as a tool of management." Discuss. *(Bangalore University, B. Com., November 1998)*
5. Explain the scope of Management accounting. *(Bangalore University, B. Com., November 1997)*
6. "Management accounting has been evolved to meet the needs of management." Discuss. *(Bangalore University, B. Com., April 1995)*
7. "Management accounting is the adoption and analysis of accounting information and its diagnosis and explanation in such a way as to assist management." Elucidate. *(C. S. Inter, December 2000)*
8. What is the role of a management accountant in the management process? *(C. S. Inter, June 1999)*
9. Mention two major sources of finance and two major applications of finance. Explain the role of a management accountant in raising and utilising the finance. *(C. S. Iner, June 1999)*
10. Enumerate the functions of a management accountant. Show how he assists the management in exercising effective control over the business. *(C. S. Inter, December 1999)*
11. Management accounting is concerned with accounting information which is useful to management. *(C. S. Inter, December 1998)*
12. "The emphasis of" financial accounting and management accounting differ significantly." Examine it with appropriate examples. *(C. S. Inter, December 1997)*
13. "The subject of management accounting is very important and useful for optimum utilisation of resources. It is an indispensable discipline for corporate management." Elucidate this statement. *(C. S. Inter, June 1997)*
14. "There is an intimate relationship between management accounting" and "finance function." Elucidate. *(C. S. Inter, June 1996)*

15. Discuss management accounting as an effective tool of financial control. *(C. S. Inter, June 1994)*
16. What is management accounting? Discuss its usefulness for decision making and control. *(C. S. Inter, December 1992)*

Long Answer Questions

1. How does management accounting differ from financial accounting. *(S. V. University, B. Com., April 1999)*
2. Discuss in detail the functions of management accounting. Explain the nature and Scope of management accounting. *(S. V. University, B. Com., October 1999)*
3. Define Management accounting and explain clearly the need and importance of Management accounting. *(S. V. University, B. Com., April 1997)*
4. Who is Management Accountant? What are his functions and duties? *(S. V. University, B. Com., October 1997)*
5. Define management accounting. State its features and limitations. *(University of Mysore, B. Com., April 1994)*
6. Explain the meaning of Management accounting its scope, utility and limitations. In what respects it differ from financial accounting. *(University of Mysore, B. Com., October 1993)*
7. What is Management accounting? How does it differ from cost and financial accounting. *(University of Mysore, B. Com., April 1993)*
8. Explain the meaning and functions of management accounting. Also state its limitations. *(University of Mysore, B. Com., October 1991)*
9. "Management accounting is an extension of managerial aspects of financial accounting and cost accounting." Elucidate. Discuss the use of management accounting as a tool of decision making and exercising control. *(C. S. Inter, December 1991)*
10. What do you understand by Management accounting? What are its advantages? State the methods and techniques of management accounting. *(University of Mysore, B. Com., October 1994)*
11. Explain the meaning and functions of Management accounting. Also state its limitations. *(Kuvempu University, B. Com., November 1991)*
12. Explain in detail the meaning, scope and objectives of Management accounting. *(Kuvempu University, B. Com., November 1992)*
13. What is management accounting? How does it differ from cost accounting and financial accounting. *(Kuvempu University, B. Com., April 1993)*
14. "Management accounting is a coherent whole of financial accounting, cost accounting and all aspects of financial management." Examine this statement. *(Kuvempu University, B. Com., April 1994)*
15. Explain how the management accounts help in removing the limitations of financial accounting in the context of information needs of different levels of management. *(Kuvempu University, B. Com., October 1992)*
16. "Management accountancy is concerned with accounting information which is useful for management." Discuss and also distinguish between financial accounting and management accounting. *(Himachal Pradesh University, B. Com., April 1995)*
17. Define Management accounting. Discuss the main advantages and limitations of Management accounting. *(Himachal Pradesh University, B. Com., September 1994)*
18. Discuss the principal functions of Management Accountancy and show how does it help in solving management problems in key areas in business? *(Himachal Pradesh University, B. Com., September 1993)*
19. What is the usefulness of accounting information for management? State the duties and responsibilities of management accountant. *(Himachal Pradesh University, B. Com., April 1992)*
20. What is the nature of management accounting? What is the difference between financial accounting and management accounting. *(Guru Nanak Dev. University, B. Com., April 1999)*
21. Explain the meaning and objectives of Management Accounting. How does it differ from financial accounting. *(Guru Nanak Dev. University, B. Com., October 1997)*
22. Explain the various conventions of Management Accountancy.

2

FINANCIAL STATEMENTS

INTRODUCTION

The statements which are prepared from accounting information are known as financial statements. They are the end products of accounting process in an enterprise. Under accounting process, it firstly consists of recording the transactions in the books of prime entry and then posted in ledger accounts. At the end of the accounting period the balances are extracted and from these balances, final accounts are prepared. The final accounts or financial statements as they are sometimes called as, disclose the profitable and financial position of the business. A business functions with a view to attain two important objectives, *viz.*, profitability and solvency. Unless a business earns sufficient profits to pay off its debts and pay a reasonable rate of return on capital employed it can not survive. The profitability position is revealed by income statement or profit and loss account. Similarly, the financial strength or solvency position is revealed by position statement or balance sheet. Based on these statements valuable decisions are taken by management and other parties interested in business.

DEFINITION OF FINANCIAL STATEMENTS

Financial statement refers to formal and original statements which are prepared to disclose financial health of the business in terms of profits, position, and prospects as on a certain data. They summarise the overall results of a business by means of grouping and classification process. They provide a systematic collection of financial data in a logical and consistent way.

In the words of John N. Myer, "The financial statements provide a summary of the accounts of a business enterprise, the balance sheet reflecting the assets, liabilities and capital as on a certain data and the income statement showing the results of operations during a certain period." According to this definition financial accounts are the end products of accounting process.

According to Robert N. Anthony, "Financial statements, essentially, are interim reports, presented annually and reflect a division of the life of an enterprise into more or less arbitrary accounting period—more frequently a year. According to this definition, financial statements are a form of reports which helps management in decision making process. Such reports are prepared periodically to enable management to carry out its day-to-day functions."

Kohler in his book Dictionary for Accountants defines financial statements as "A balance sheet, income statement, fund statement or any other supporting statement or other presentation of financial data derived from accounting records." This definition identifies the package of financial statements.

OBJECTIVES OF FINANCIAL STATEMENTS

According to A I C P A, "financial statements are prepared for the purpose of presenting a periodical review or report on the progress by the management." The main object of financial statement is to provide information for decision making for all those who are interested in the affairs of the business enterprise. The various class of people who look forward to the financial statements are the management, investors, prospective investors, creditors etc. However it is to be emphasised that financial statements can not be tailor-made to suit all categories of persons who are interested in the business. There has to be some compromise in the preporation of financial statements. There can be preparation of only one financial statement to meet the requirements of shareholders. But it must give such significant and material information which is beneficial to the other parties as well particularly those who make decisions for the future. For example, an investor is interested in knowing the amount of dividend his shares are going to earn and also the market value of such shares. Similarly, a supplier of goods on credit is interested to know whether the amount due to him will be paid say within a month. Such needs of various parties can be satisfied by a single set of financial statements. The precise objects of financial statements as envisaged by Accounting Principles Board (APB) of America are as follows:

1. To provide reliable financial information about economic resources and obligations, *i.e.*, inflow and outflow of cash.
2. To provide the net result, *i.e.* profit or loss of an enterprise arising from its activities.
3. To provide financial information that assist in earning capacity of the business.
4. To provide other needed information about changes in economic resources or obligations, such as change in working capital, fund flows etc.
5. To provide other information related to financial statements to others who are in need of it.

NATURE OF FINANCIAL STATEMENTS

Financial statements are prepared to portray the results and financial position of an enterprise. They reflect the totality of recorded facts, accounting principles and personal judgements. According to American Accounting Association "Every corporate statement should be based on accounting principles which are sufficiently uniform, objective and well understood to justify opinions as to the condition and progress of business enterprise. Its basic assumption is that the purpose of financial statement is to furnish information that is necessary for the formation of dependable judgements." The nature of financial statements can be explained under the following points:

1. Recorded facts: The term recorded facts means those transactions which are recorded in the books of accounts. Such transactions relate to cash in hand, bills receivable, debtors, creditors, fixed assets, sales, purchases, wages, capital etc. There transactions are recorded on historical basis. Those facts which are not part of accounting books are not shown in financial statements, whatever may be its relative importance to the business.

2. Accounting conventions: These relate to accounting principles which are applied as a long standing practice. For example, the convention relating to conservatism, a provision is made for anticipated loss but not for anticipated profit. Accounting conventions are used for valuation of inventory, allocation of expenses between capital and revenue, valuation of assets etc.

3. Postulates: Postulates relate to assumptions which accountant makes while adopting conventions. One such assumption is relating to continuation of business even beyond the period which is covered by financial statements. This assumption is known as "going concern of the business." According to this assumption, assets are valued at its cost less depreciation. In the absence of this assumption, assets would have been valued at realisable value which may be negligible. Another assumption relate to stability in the value of money over a period of time and some accountants do not value assets on the basis of change in the value of money. A third assumption relates to realisation postulate. According to this assumption there has a time gap between production and sale. The revenue is earned only when sales are effected.

4. Personal judgement: The application of conventions or postulates depend upon the personal judgement of the accountant. For example, the method of Depreciating an asset, the method of valuation of stock, making provision for doubtful debts, the method of amortisation of fixed assets etc., depend upon the personal judgement of the accountant. However, the personal judgement of the Accountant is checked by the consistency principle.

5. Accounting standards and guiding notes: Accounting standards and guiding notes help to a large extent in preparing financial statements. Certain accounting standards such as disclosure of accounting policies. Revenue recognition, accounting for fixed assets etc., are compulsory in nature.

REQUISITES, ATTRIBUTES OR ESSENTIAL REQUIREMENTS OF FINANCIAL STATEMENTS

In order to serve its objectives meaningfully, financial statements must possess the following attributes.

1. Relevance: The financial statements must be relevant for the purpose for which they are meant for. Irrelevant and unwanted information should be avoided but at the same time material facts must necessarily be disclosed.

2. Accuracy: Financial accounts must disclose accurately the profitability, position and prospects of the business. Inaccurate information not only misleads the public but also attracts fines and penalties. Inaccurate information defeats the very purpose for which financial statements are prepared. There should not be any personal prejudice and window dressing of financial statements.

3. Comparability: The financial statements prepared must not only facilitate inter-firm comparision but also intra-firm comparision. Comparision of essential data over a period of time sets a trend which guides management in formulating policies and taking decisions. Inter-firm comparision facilitates the strength and weakness of the firm in the industry.

4. Promptness: In order to facilitate the functioning of the management, there should be quick preparation and prompt submission of the report to all those executives who depend on it. Any delay in presentation of information through financial statements make it difficult to take prompt action to set right adverse results of the business.

5. Generally accepted principles: Financial statements meets the requirements of wide variety of people. As such it is to be accepted and understood by everyone who is interested in it. For this reason financial statements are to be prepared according to "generally accepted accounting principles." The reliability and confidence of financial statements also depends upon the extent to which such principles are applied in preparing the financial statements.

6. Consistency: The personal judgement of accountants sometimes distort the financial statements. As far as possible unformity must be maintained while preparing financial statements. The rules and procedures should not be changed frequently unless the situation demand for a charge. Comparability of statements to a large extent depends upon consistency. For example, if different methods of labour turnover is used to measure the extent of labour turnover it will be difficult to compare, as result differ from method to method.

7. Authenticity: To make financial statement reliable it should be certified by an independent and qualified person known as auditor. A statement which is authenticated by an auditor will be acceptable by all without giving room for doubt and unreliability.

8. Compliance with law: The financial statements must be prepared as per the requirements of statute. In our country section 211 of the companies Act 1956 lays down the provisions relating to preparation of financial statements. when financial statements are prepared according to the legal requirements it increases the confidence of public besides not subjected to any fines and penalties.

IMPORTANCE OF FINANCIAL STATEMENTS

Financial statements are prepared to serve the needs of wide variety of people. The beneficiaries of financial statements are as follows:

1. The management: The facts and figures provided by financial statements enable management to formulate the policies as well as to discharge their day-to-day activities of the business. A comparative study of financial statements over a period of time helps management to know the trends and modify the policies accordingly so as to avoid unfavourable situations.

2. The shareholders: Shareholders are the owners of the share capital of the company. They are interested in knowing the profitability and future prospects of the company. Financial statements serve as a guide to shareholders in this respect.

3. Creaditors and suppliers: Creaditors provide loan facilities to the companies and suppliers supply goods on credit basis. They are interested in knowing the liquidity position of the business. The ability to repay debts is revealed by financial statements.

4. Tax authorities: Tax calculations are based on income earned by the business. Both direct and indirect taxes are based on facts and figures shown by financial statements. Whereas net profit is the basis for paying income tax, sales figure constitutes the basis for paying sales tax and valorem duty.

5. Employees and Trade Unions: The wage fixation policy, payment of bonus to employees etc., are determined on the basis of net profit as revealed by income statement of the organisation.

6. Customers: Customers are primarily interested in the price of goods and services. The cost of production, profit margin, selling price as revealed by the income statement guides the customer in selecting the suppliers.

7. Financial analyst: A financial analyst has to advise his client as to in which company, the amount can be invested. Prospective investors unable to understand financial statement may seek the advise of the financial analyst for his expert advise. Thus financial statements are more important to financial analysts.

8. Stock exchange: All those company which list their securities with the stock exchange must furnish then financial statements with stock exchanges. Based on this, the stock exchange will quote the price of shares for the benefit of shareholders and others.

9. Regulatory authority: The regulating authority of the companies such as company law board, the Registrar of joint stock companies, etc. are also interested in the financial statements of companies. Based on the performance, they can amend the statute depending upon the prevailing environment of the companies.

10. Press: Economic and Commercial Journals and newspapers report the performance, position and prospects of various companies for the benefit of prospective investors. Financial statements constitute the basis for press in such reporting.

11. Trade Associations and chamber of commerce: Trade associations and chamber of commerce collect financial statements of various companies and supply the required information to their members.

12. Government: The Government is interested in the financial statements of companies with a view to formulate policies relating to taxation, price, wage, income and national plans.

13. General public: General public is interested in the financial statements of companies so as to know the extent of social responsibility of business towards the society.

LIMITATIONS OF FINANCIAL STATEMENTS

Financial statements suffer from the following limitations:

1. Interim reports: Financial statements are essentially interim reports but not the final report of the profitable and financial position of the business. In other words they reflect the progress and position of the business at frequent intervals during its life. But the exact result and financial strength of a business can be known exactly only when the business is either sold or liquidated.

2. It reveals only quantitative information: Financial statements portrary only quantitative data which can be measured in terms of value. But there are many aspects which are qualitative and not capable of expressing in terms of money value. Such aspects may relate to harmonious relationship between employees and management, reputation of management, the efficiency of employees etc., which are equally important to a business. Financial statements do not disclose all these particulars because they can not be measured in respect of money value.

3. Historical data: Financial statements are prepared on the basis of past data. They don't take into consideration the future events. So it may not be more useful for decision making.

4. It is based on accounting concepts and conventions: Financial statements are prepared on the basis of certain accounting concepts and conventions. This makes financial statements unrealistic. For example, according to going-concern concept fixed assets are shown at its cost price not at realisable value. Similarly, according to the convention of conservatism, only anticipated losses are provided for but not for anticipated profits. This distorts the profit disclosed by profit and loss account.

5. Personal judgement: The preparation of financial statements are influenced by personal judgement of accountant. Such instances relate to choice of method of depreciation, mode of amortisation of fixed assets, treatment of deferred revenue expenditure; the method of pricing material issues. The personal judgement of accountant often distorts the true picture of the business.

6. Window dressing: Financial statements may not always reveal the accurate information about the business. In order to project better image in the mind of public, the management may resort to window dressing thereby revealing misleading picture of the business.

RECENT TRENDS IN PRESENTING FINANCIAL STATEMENTS

Preparation of financial statements by joint companies in India is governed by section 211 of the Companies Act. In order to make the financial statements more understandable by a layman, it is supported by other information. Such additional information include the following:

1. Summarised profit and loss a/c and balance sheet: In recent times companies are following vertical form of preparing financial statements instead of preparing them under traditional two sided P & L a/c and balance sheet.

2. Highlights: To enable readers to understand the financial report, knowadays important information such as sales, production, profit, capital projects, fixed assets, share capital and other landmarks are furnished at the top of the report. By going through these highlights people can make out the progress and performance of the company.

3. Cash flow statements: Preparation of cash flow statements has become compulsory in recent times. It provides the in-flow and out-flow of cash and thereby net changes in cash resulting from operations and investments in business.

4. Accounting ratios: Ratios establish relationship between various aspects of the business. This helps to understand more easily as ratios are not voluminous as in the case of other information contained in the financial statements.

5. Accounting policies: Some companies disclose the accounting policies on the basis of which accounts are prepared. This is again to enable people to understand financial statements in a better way.

6. Use of charts, graphs, diagrams: Use of charts, graphs, and diagrams are very commont in recent times while publishing financial statements. They not only attract the attention of viewers but also help them to grasp the meaning of data. They have lasting impression when compared to presenting information in the form of figures.

7. Use of schedule: In order to make the final accounts of companies more compact, the Companies Act has prescribed various schedules. The financial statements are supported by these schedules and they relate to capital, reserves and surplus, secured and unsecured loans, current liabilities, fixed assets, current assets, miscellaneous expenses etc.

8. Impact of price level changes: At prices do not remain stable, financial statements prepared on historical basis do not reflect the effect of change in price level on profitability and financial position of the business. Hence in recent time, some companies are disclosing the effect of change in price level through a supplementary statement in addition to financial statements.

9. Rounding off the figures: Following the recommondation of Sachhar Committee which has given an option for the companies to round off the figures to the nearest thousand, or hundred or ten rupees, some companies knowadays portrary rounded figures to facilitate easy understanding.

BASIC FINANCIAL STATEMENTS OR PACKAGES OF FINANCIAL STATEMENTS

According to Accounting Principles Board, (APB) statement no. 4, the following are the important components or packages of financial statements.

1. Income statement
2. Position statement
3. Statement of changes in retained earnings.
4. Statement of changes in financial position.
5. Schedules and Accounting Policies.

The above statements are generally referred to as "basic financial statements. In addition to the above list we may add yet another component, *viz*., miscellaneous statement."

1. Income Statement or Profit and Loss Account

The income statement and profit and loss account are not different but are interchangeably used. Whereas in U.S.A. income statement is a popular usage, in U.K. it is more commonly referred to as profit and loss a/c. According to AICPA terminology, income statement is defined as "a statement which shows the principal elements, the positive and negative, in the derivation of income or loss, the claims against income and the resulting net income or loss of accounting unit." In simple words, an income statement shows revenue and expenses of a business for an accounting period. It matches revenue with costs. If the revenue exceeds the cost it implies the profitability of business and of cost exceed revenue it implies the loss suffered by the business. The same view has been expressed by Haray & Guthmann when he wrote that "the statement of profit or loss is condensed and classified record of gains and losses causing changes in the owners interest in the business for a period of time." By far income statement is considered to be most important among all financial statements.

FORMAT OF PROFIT AND LOSS ACCOUNT

Though schedule VI part II of the Indian Companies Act lays down the contents and other data to be included in an income statement it is silent about the proforma according to which an income statement is to be prepared. However there are two methods which could be followed for preparing an income statement, *viz*., (*a*) Multi-step income statement and (*b*) Single-step income statement.

1. Multi-step Income Statement: This method involves the following steps:

1. *Ascertainment of gross-profit*: From sales and other operating revenues the cost of goods sold is deducted to get gross profit (gross loss in case cost of goods sold exceeds sales).
2. *Ascertaining operating profit*: From gross profit other operating expenses such as administration. Selling and distribution expenses are deducted to get operating profit.
3. *Ascertainment of Net Profit before Tax* (*NPBT*): To the operating profit other non-operating incomes are added and therefrom other non-operating expenses are deducted. The resultant figure is known as net profit before tax.

   Non-operating incomes arise from secondary activities as for example, interest, rent, devidend received by a company whose main business is not to deal with finance, property and investment.

4. *Ascertainment of Profit after Tax* (*PAT*): The provision for tax is deducted from the net profit before tax. The result is net profit after tax.
5. *Ascertainment of Net Profit* (*NP*): Other extra ordinary gains or losses such as gain or loss on the sale of investment, loss by fire etc., are respectively added and deducted to arrive at final figure of net profit.

A proforma of Multi-stage income statement is shown below:

PROFORMA OF MULTI-STEP INCOME STATEMENT

	Net Sales			××
Less:	Cost of goods sold			××
	Gross profit			××
Less:	Office and Administration expenses:			
	Office Salaries	××		
	Office Insurance	××		
	Office Rent	××		
	Taxes	××		
			××	
Less:	Selling expenses:			
	Sales Manager's Salaries	××		
	Salesmen's Salaries	××		
	Advertisement	××		
	Travelling	××		
			××	
				××
	Operating profit			××
Add:	Other revenues:			
	Interest and Dividends	××		
	Rent Received	××		
		××		
Less:	Interest paid	××		
				××
	Net profit before tax			××
Less:	Provision for income tax			××
	Net profit after tax			××
Add:	Gains from sale of Investment			××
	Net profit			××

2. Single Step Income Statement: As multi-step income statement involves many steps it is often confusing. So many businesses use 'single-step' income statement. The following steps are involved under this method.

(*a*) To collect all items of income whether operating or non-operating at one place.

(*b*) To show all deductions from the total income as calculated in step (*a*). The difference shows net profit or net loss.

The proforma of single-step income statement is as follows:

PROFORMA OF SINGLE STEP INCOME STATEMENT

Income:			
	Sales		××
	Dividend on Investment		××
	Interest on Debentures		××
	Royalties		××
	Miscellaneous		××
			××
Less:	Expenses		
	Cost of goods sold	××	
	Selling and distribution expenses	××	
	Office and Administration expenses	××	
	Interest on Debentures	××	
	Provision for Tax	××	
	Loss on sale of Asset	××	××
		Net profit	××

Elements of Income Statement

1. Cost of goods sold: Cost of goods sold, otherwise known as cost of sales represent the cost incurred in manufacturing or purchasing the goods that have been sold to customers. The method of calculating it depends upon the nature of the business, *i.e.*, whether the business is trading or manufacturing concern. In case of trading business it is calculated as under:

Opening stock of Finished goods			××
Add:	Total purchases	××	
Add:	Carriage on purchases	××	××
			××
Less:	Purchase returns	××	
Less:	Closing stock of finished goods	××	××
	Cost of goods sold		××

In case of manufacturing business it is calculated as under:

Direct Materials Cost		××
Direct labour cost		××
Direct expenses		××
	Prime cost	××
Factory overheads		××
	Factory cost	××
Office and Administration overhead		××
	Cost of production	××
Add: Opening stock of Finished goods		××
		××
Less: Closing stock of Finished goods		××
	Cost of goods sold	××

However in financial accounts selling expenses are also included in the "cost of goods sold."

Cost of goods sold can also be calculated by using the following formula:

$$\text{Cost of goods sold} = \text{Sales} - \text{Gross profit}$$

Where gross profit is not given but its percentage to sales is given, cost of goods sold can be calculated by using the following formula:

$$\text{Cost of goods sold} = \text{Sales} - \frac{\text{Sales} \times \text{G.P.\%}}{100}$$

2. Operating Income: Operating income is generated from carrying on business on a day-to-day basis. Generally, sales constitutes operating income.

3. Operating expenses: Expenses which are incurred in carrying on business on a regular basis is known as operating expenses. They are also known as routine expenses and they facilitate the smooth and continuous operations of the business. Examples of operating expenses are office and administrative expenses, selling and distribution expenses, finance expenses.

4. Non-operating income and expenses: Non-operating incomes and expenses are those transactions which are not directly related to main activities of the business. Examples of such incomes and expenses are dividend, interest, rent, commission, loss or gain from sales of securities etc.

5. Net operating profit: It represents the income earned from main activities of the business. The difference between gross profit and operating expenses is known as net operating profit. Since it is the result of the main activities of the business, it is most important element of income statement for managerial planning and decision making.

Problem 1: Following is the profit and loss account of well-balanced limited for the year ended 31st March 1996. You are required to prepare vertical income statement for purpose of analysis:

To Opening stock	7,00,000	By Sales:		
To Purchases	9,00,000	Cash	5,20,000	
To Wages	1,50,000	Credit	15,00,000	
To Factory expenses	3,50,000		20,20,000	
To Office salaries	25,000	*Less:* Returns	20,000	
To Office rent	39,000			20,00,000
To Postage and telegram	5,000	By Closing stock		6,00,000
To Directors fees	6,000	By Dividend on Investment		10,000
To Salesmen's Salaries	12,000	By Profit on sale of furniture		20,000
To Advertising	18,000			
To Delivery expenses	20,000			
To Debenture Interest	20,000			
To Depreciation on:				
Office furniture	10,000			
Plant	30,000			
Delivery Van	20,000			
To Loss on sale of Van	5,000			
To Income tax	1,75,000			
To Net profit	1,45,000			
	26,30,000			26,30,000

(*University of Bombay, B. Com., April 1998*)

Solution:

WELL BALANCED LTD.
INCOME STATEMENT FOR THE YEAR ENDED 31ST MARCH 1996

Particulars			
Sales: Cash		5,20,000	
Credit		15,00,000	
		20,20,000	
Less: Returns		20,000	
			20,00,000
Less: Cost of goods sold:			
Opening stock		7,00,000	
Add: Purchases		9,00,000	
Add: Wages		1,50,000	
Add: Factory expenses		3,50,000	
Add: Depreciation on plant		30,000	
		21,30,000	
Less: Closing stock		6,00,000	
			15,30,000
Gross profit			4,70,000
Less: Operating expenses:			
(*A*) Office and administrative expenses:			
Office Salaries		25,000	
Office Rent		39,000	
Postage		5,000	
Directors fees		6,000	
Depreciation on office furniture		10,000	
		85,000	
(*B*) Selling and Distribution expenses:			
Salesman's Salaries	12,000		
Advertisement	18,000		
Delivery expenses	20,000		
Depreciation on Delivery Van	20,000		
		70,000	
(*C*) Financial expenses:			
Debenture interest		20,000	
			1,75,000
Operating profit			2,95,000
Add: Non-operating income:			
Dividend on investment		10,000	
Profit on sale of furniture		20,000	
			30,000
			3,25,000
Less: Non-operating expenses:			
Loss on sale of Van			5,000
Net profit before Tax			3,20,000
Less: Income tax			1,75,000
Net profit after tax			1,45,000

Problem 2: The following particulars are obtained from the books of Dream Flower Co. Ltd. for the year ended 31st, March 2001. Prepare the income statement in the vertical form:

Opening stock	12,000	Sales	15,00,000
Closing stock	17,000	Purchases	10,00,000
Carriage inwards	20,000	Carriage outwards	42,000
Salaries	75,000	Debenture Interest	20,000
Interest paid	30,000	Loss on sale of machinery	30,000
Rent	20,000		
Telephone charges	12,400	Interest received on investments	25,000
Depreciation on assets	32,000	Advertisement	50,000
Dividend paid	25,000	Interest on Bank Deposits	14,000
Taxes @ 50%		Transfer to general reserve	11,000
		Wages paid	3,000

Solution: **Dream Flower Co. Ltd.**

INCOME STATEMENT FOR THE YEAR ENDED 31ST MARCH 2001

	Sales			15,00,000
Less:	Cost of goods sold:			
	Opening stock	12,000		
Add:	Purchases	10,00,000		
Add:	Carriage Inwards	20,000		
Add:	Wages	3,000		
		10,35,000		
Less:	Closing stock	17,000		
				10,18,000
	Gross profit			4,82,000
Less:	Operating expenses:			
(*A*)	Administrative expenses:			
	Salaries	75,000		
	Rent	20,000		
	Telephone charges	12,400		
	Depreciation on Assets	32,000		
			1,39,400	
(*B*)	Selling and Distribution Expenses:			
	Carriage outwards	42,000		
	Advertisement	50,000		
			92,000	
				2,31,400
				2,50,600
Add:	Operating income			Nil
	Operating profit			2,50,600
Add:	Non-operating Income:			
	Interest on Investments		25,000	
	Interest on Bank deposits		14,000	
				39,000
				2,89,600

Less:	Non-operating expenses:		
	Interest on Debentures	20,000	
	Loss on sale of Machinery	30,000	
			50,000
	Profit before Tax		2,39,600
Less:	Tax at 50%		1,19,800
	Profit after Tax		1,19,800
Less:	Appropriations:		
	Transfer to General Reserve	11,000	
	Dividends paid	25,000	
			36,000
	Profit transferred to Balance sheet		83,800

POSITION STATEMENT OR BALANCE SHEET

A Balance sheet may well be described as a statement of assets and liabilities including capital amount. It reveals the assets and liabilities and capital amount as on a period of time. It highlights the assets possessed by a business and sources of funds (from owners and creditors) used in purchasing of such assets. It discloses the financial position of the business. It records only periodic change rather than continuous one. In this sense it is static where as business is dynamic.

A Balance sheet is often discribed as a statement of equality as it equalises assets and liabilities by placing assets on right hand side and liabilities and capital on the left hand side. In the words of Howard and Upton "the balance sheet is a statement which presents property's value owned by the enterprise and the claims of creditors and owners against these properties."

Yet another view about balance sheet is to consider it as a statement of sources and uses of funds. The equality at both sides of Balance sheet can better be expressed as sources and uses or application of funds. The liability side indicates the various sources from which funds are collected and the asset side indicates the uses of funds. In this sense, the relationship of the two sides of balance sheet is rightly called as 'identity' and not 'equality'. The sources and uses of funds thus indicates the financial position of the business. For this reason a balance sheet is considered as snapshot of financial position of a business as on a given data.

FORM OR PROFORMA OF A BALANCE SHEET

Part I of schedule VI of the Companies Act 1956 lays down the proforma of balance sheet according to which all Joint Stock Companies have to prepare their balance sheets. A balance sheet can be prepared either in horizontal form or vertical form. These are shown below:

PROFORMA OF HORIZONTAL OR TRADITIONAL BALANCE SHEET

Share capital:		**Fixed Assets**	
Authorised capital	××	Goodwill	××
Issued and paid up		Land	××
capital	××	Buildings	××

Reserves and Surplus		Plant and Machinery	××
Capital Reserve	××	Furniture and Fixtures	××
General Reserve	××	Patents, Trade mark,	
Share premium	××	and Designs	××
Secured loans		Vehicles	××
Debentures	××	**Investments**	
Loans and advances	××	Investment in Government	
Unsecured loans		or trust securities	××
Fixed deposit		Investment in shares	××
Loans and advances from			
Subsidiaries	××	**Current Assets Loans**	
Short-term loans and		**and Advances**	
advances	××	(*A*) **Current Assets:**	
Current Liabilities and		Interest accured on	
provisions		Investment	××
(*A*) **Current Liabilities**		Stores and spare parts	××
Sundry creditors	××	Loose Tools	××
Unclaimed dividends	××	Stock in Trade	××
Interest accrued but		Work in progress	××
not due on loan	××	Sundry Debtors	××
(*B*) **Provisions**		Cash on hand	××
Provision for Tax	××	Bank balance	××
Proposed Dividend	××	(*B*) **Loans and Advances:**	
Provident fund	××	Advances and loans	
Insurance and		to subsidiaries	××
pension for staff	××	Advances recoverable	
Other provisions	××	in cash or hand	
		(Rates, Insurance etc.)	××
		Bills of exchange	××
		Miscellaneous expenses	
		not written off	
		Preliminary expenses	××
		Expenses including	
		Commission, or brokerage	
		or underwriting of	
		shares or debentures	××
		Discount allowed on issue	
		of shares or debentures	××
	××		××

PROFORMA OF VERTICAL FORM OF BALANCE SHEET

I. Sources of Funds	
(1) Shareholder's Fund	
(*a*) Capital	××
(*b*) Reserves and Surpluses	××
(2) Loan funds	
(*a*) Secured loans	××
(*b*) Unsecured loans	××
Total	××

II. Applications of Funds:			
(1) Fixed Assets			
Goss Assets	××		
Less: Depreciation	××		
Net Assets	××	××	
(2) Investments		××	
(3) Current assets, loans and advances:			
(*a*) Stock		××	
(*b*) Sundry Debtors		××	
(*c*) Cash and Bank balance		××	
(*d*) Other current assets		××	
(*e*) Loans and advances		××	
		××	
Less: Current liabilities and provisions		××	
Net current assets		××	××
(4) (*a*) Miscellaneous expanditure to the extent not written off			××
(*b*) Profit and loss a/c			××
Total			××

ELEMENTS OF BALANCE SHEET

1. Current assets: Assets which are readily converted into cash during a period of only year are known as current assets. Of course current assets are classified on the basis of their use and not on the basis of time. Assets which are acquired for selling in the course of business are to be treated as current assets. The following are examples of current assets:

(*a*) Cash in hand and at Bank
(*b*) Sundry Debtors
(*c*) Bills Receivables
(*d*) Stock of raw materials, work in progress and finished goods
(*e*) Marketable securities
(*f*) Prepard expenses and so on

2. Fixed assets: There are the assets, which are used for conducting the operations of the business and not for reselling to earn a profit. Examples of Fixed assets are:

(*a*) Land and Building
(*b*) Plant and Machineries
(*c*) Furniture and Fixture
(*d*) Trucks and Automobiles etc

3. Intangible assets: Assets which cannot be seen or touched are known as intangible assets. They dont exist physically in the business. Examples of such assets are:

(*a*) Patents and Trade marks
(*b*) Licence and copy right
(*c*) Good will

4. Other assets: The rest of the assets which do not fall under any of the above categories are known as other assets. Such assets are tangible in nature but are not directly used in the business. Examples of such assets are:

(*a*) Investments (excluding govt. securities and other marketable securities)
(*b*) Debenture redemption fund
(*c*) Any other fund created for redeeming a contingent liability

5. Deferred expenditure: Expenses which are not of recurring nature and which do not arise out of current operations of a business is known as deferred expenditure. Such expenses benefit the business over years. These expenses are therefore written off over a period of time and is a charge on future profit. That portion of deferred expenses which are not written off to P & C a/c is shows on the asset side of the balance sheet under the heading 'miscellaneous expenditure'.

6. Current liabilities: These are the obligations which are to be met on demand or within a period of one year. Even long term liabilities which become payable within a period of one year is also taken as current liabilities. Examples of current liabilities are as follows:

(*a*) Sundry creditors
(*b*) Bills payable
(*c*) Short term public deposits
(*d*) Bank overdraft
(*e*) Provision for tax
(*f*) Unclaimed dividends

7. Long term liabilities: There liabilities become payable over a long period of time say between 2 to 8 years. Examples of such liabilities are as follows:

(*a*) Loan on mortgage
(*b*) Debentures
(*c*) Bank loan
(*d*) Loans from specialised financial institutions.

8. Net worth: The difference between total assets and current and long term liabilities is known as net worth.

9. Other related elements:

(*a*) Liquid assets: There are the assets which are converted into cash when desired without any loss. According to this meaning all current assets excepting stock can be converted into cash in the normal course of dealing by the business without loss. Hence :

Liquid assets = Current assets – Stock

(*b*) Working capital: The excess of current assets over current liabilities is known as working capital. Expressed in the form of an equation:

Working Capital = Current Assets – Current liabilities

(*c*) Capital employed: Capital employed may relate to total or gross capital or net capital employed. Gross capital employed is taken to mean the total assets of a business whereas net working capital is the difference between total assets and current liabilities. Expressed in the form of an equation:

Net Capital employed = Total assets – Current liabilities

Or

Capital employed = Fixed assets + Working Capital

Problem 3: Following is the balance sheet of Mahavir Ltd. as on 31st March 1999:

Share capital	3,00,000	Good will	40,000
Share premism	10,000	Land	1,60,000
General Reserve	1,20,000	Plant	88,000
P & C a/c	34,000	Furniture	6,000
11% Debentures	1,00,000	Trade Investment	1,60,000
Bank loan	70,000	Accounts Receivable	1,40,000
Bank overdraft	40,000	Inventories	1,20,000
Sundry creditors	1,20,000	Prepard expenses	10,000
Provision for Taxation	20,000	Cash at Bank	80,000
		Preliminary expenses	10,000
	8,14,000		8,14,000

Prepare the above balance sheet in vertical form for showing the following:

1. Fixed Assets
2. Intgible Assets.
3. Fictitions assets
4. Quick Assets.
5. Current assets
6. Net worth.
7. Long term liabilities
8. Quick liabilities.
9. Working capital.

(*University of Bombay, B. Com., October 1999*)

Solution: **Vertical Balance Sheet of Mahavir Ltd. as on 31-3-1999**

Sources of Funds:			
I. Shareholder's Funds:			
(*A*) Share capital			3,00,000
(*B*) Reserves and surplus:			
Share premium		10,000	
General Reserve		1,20,000	
P & C a/c		34,000	
		1,64,000	
Less: Fictitions assets		10,000	
			1,54,000
II. Long term liabilities:			
Secured:			
11% Debentures		1,00,000	
Bank loan		70,000	
			1,70,000
Total Fund employed			6,24,000
Application of Funds			
I. Fixed Assets:			
Good will		40,000	
Land		1,60,000	
Plant		88,000	
Furniture		6,000	
			2,94,000
II. Trade Investments			1,60,000
III. Working capital:			
(*A*) Current assets:			
Accounts receivable	1,40,000		
Cash at bank	80,000		
Quick Assets	2,20,000		

Add:	Non-quick Assets			
	Inventories	1,20,000		
	Prepard expenses	10,000		
			3,50,000	
Less:	Current liabilities:			
	Sundry creditors	1,20,000		
	Provision for tax	20,000		
	Quick liabilities	1,40,000		
Add:	Non-Quick liabilities:			
	Bank overdraft	40,000		
			1,80,000	
				1,70,000
	Total fund employed			6,24,000

Problem 4: Given below is the Balance sheet of TY Ltd.

Share capital	3,75,000	Good will	62,500
Capital reserve	4,000	Land	1,14,500
General reserve	60,205	Premises	1,25,000
Debenture redemption fund	84,000	Plant	93,758
P & C a/c	37,554	Furniture	16,650
5% Debentures	1,57,500	3% G.P Notes	76,400
Sundry creditors	36,950	Stock	1,17,815
Proposed Dividend	18,750	Debtors	1,01,971
Provision for Taxation	10,000	Cash	60,140
		Advance tax	13,675
		Preliminary expenses	1,550
	7,83,959		7,83,959

Rearrange the balance sheet in vertical form and calculate the following:
1. Current assets 2. Quick assets 3. Intangible assets 4. Fictitions assets 5. Fixed assets 6. Fixed liabilities 7. Proprietors' fund 8. working capital 9. Total funds employed 10. Secured loans 11. Owned funds.

(University of Bombay, B. Com., April 1995)

Solution:

Balance Sheet as on 31- December 1994

Sources of Funds

(1)	Shareholders funds		
	(*A*) Share capital		3,75,000
	(*B*) Reserves and Surplus:		
	Capital Reserve	4,000	
	General Reserve	60,205	
	Debenture Redemption fund	84,000	
	P & C a/c	37,554	
		1,85,759	
Less:	Preliminiary expenses	1,550	
			1,84,209
(2)	Loan funds		
	5% Debentures		1,57,500
	Total sourees of funds		7,16,709

Applications of Funds

(1) *Fixed Assets:*			
Goodwill		62,500	
Land		1,14,500	
Premises		1,25,000	
Plant		93,758	
Furniture		16,650	
			4,12,408
(2) *Investments:*			
3% G. P. Notes			76,400
(3) *Working Capital:*			
Current Assets:			
Stock		1,17,815	
Debtors		1,01,971	
Cash and Bank		60,140	
Advance tax		13,675	
		(*A*) 2,93,601	
Current liabilities			
Creditors	36,950		
Proposed Divident	18,750		
Provision for Tax	10,000		
		(*B*) 65,700	
Working Capital (*A* – *B*)			2,27,901
Total fund Employed			7,16,709

(1)	Current Assets	2,93,601
(2)	Quick Assets C A = Stock – Advance Tax 2,93,601 = 1,17,815 – 13,675	1,62,111
(3)	Intangible assets	62,500
(4)	Fictitions assets	1,550
(5)	Fixed Assets	4,12,408
(6)	Fixed Liabilities	1,57,500
(7)	Proprietors funds	5,59,209
(8)	Working Capital	2,27,901
(9)	Total funds employed	7,16,709
(10)	Secured loans	1,57,500
(11)	Owned funds	5,59,209

Problem 5: The accountant of a company submits the following financial statements for 1994:

Trading and profit and loss a/c for the year ended 31st December 1994.

To opening stock	35,000	By sales	8,30,000
To purchases	7,50,000	By closing stock	80,000
To Gross profit	1,25,000		
	9,10,000		9,10,000
To Depreciation	18,000	By Gross profit	1,25,000
To other expenses	37,000	By Interest	5,000
To Tax provision	20,000		
To proposed Dividend	8,000		
To Net profit	90,000		
	1,30,000		1,30,000

Balance Sheet as at 31st December 1994

Share Capital	1,50,000	Cash	24,000
Bank overdraft	19,000	Stock	80,000
Creditors	13,000	Debtors	69,250
Depreciation provision	27,875	Land and Building	46,075
Tax provision	20,000	Machinery	64,300
Proposed Dividend	8,000	Prepard expenses	750
P & C a/c	90,000	Good will	10,000
		Preliminary expenses	3,500
		Loan	30,000
	3,27,875		3,27,875

Rearrange the above in a form suitable for analysis. *(University of Bombay, B. Com., October 1995)*

Solution:

Income Statement for the year ended 31-12-94

Sales		8,30,000
Less: Cost of sales:		
Opening stock	35,000	
Add: Purchases	7,50,000	
	78,500	
Less: Closing stock	80,000	
Gross profit		705,000
		1,25,000
Less: Operating expenses:		
Depreciation	18,000	
Other expenses	37,000	
		55,000
Operating net profit		70,000
Add: Non-operating Income		
Interest		5,000
Net profit before Tax		75,000
Less: Tax provision		20,000
Net profit after Tax		55,000
Less: Proposed Dividend		8,000
Profit transferred to balance sheet		47,000

Balance sheet as at 31-12-94

Sources of Funds			
(1) Shareholders Funds			
(*a*) Share capital		1,50,000	
(*b*) Reserves and Surplus:			
P & C a/c	90,000		
Less: Preliminary expenses	3,500		
		86,500	
Net Worth			2,36,500
(2) Loan funds			Nil
Total source of funds			2,36,500

Applications of Funds

(1) *Fixed Assets:*			
Good will		10,000	
Land and Building		46,075	
Machinery		64,300	
		1,20,350	
Less: Depreciation provision		27,875	
			92,500
(2) *Working capital:*			
Current assets loans and Advances			
Cash		24,000	
Stock		80,000	
Debtors		69,250	
Prepared expenses		750	
Loans		30,000	
		2,04,000	
Less: Current liabilities and provisions:			
Creditors	13,000		
Bank OD	19,000		
Tax provision	20,000		
Proposed dividend	8,000		
		60,000	
			1,44,000
Total Application of funds			2,36,500

Problem 6: From the following Horizontal balance sheet extracted from the books of Moon Light Co. Ltd. as on 31st, December 2000, Redraft the same in vertical form:

Share Capital			*Fixed Assets*	
Paid-up capital			Building	150,000
60,000 Equity shares			Machinery	2,00,000
of Rs. 10 each		6,00,000	Motor Vehicles	30,000
Reserves and Surplus			Furniture	5,000
General Reserve	2,50,000			3,85,000
Additors driving the year	50,000		*Less*: Dep.	81,000
		3,00,000		3,04,000
P & C a/c		17,116		
Current Liabilities			Investment	2,88,950
Trade creditors		36,858	**Current Assets**	
Unclaimed dividend		6,526	Stock	1,48,680
Managing Directors			Book Debts	2,23,380
Remuneration		6,500	Cash on hand	72,240
Provisions			**Loans and Advances**	
Provision for taxation		60,000	Interest on Investment	2,750
Proposed dividend		24,000	Advance payment	
Staff provident fund		39,000	of Tax	50,000
		10,90,000	Accuret	10,90,000

Solution:

Vertical Form

Balance Sheet of Moon Light Co. as at 31-12-2000

I. Sources of Funds			
(1) Shareholders funds			
(*a*) Capital		6,00,000	
(*b*) Reserves and Surplus		3,17,116	9,17,116
Total			9,17,116
II. Application of Funds			
(1) Fixed Assets			
(*a*) Gross block		3,85,000	
Less: Depreciation		81,000	
			3,04,000
(2) Investments			2,88,950
(3) Current assets and loans and advances:			
(*a*) Inventories		1,48,680	
(*b*) Sundry debtors		2,23,380	
(*c*) Cash at hand		72,240	
(*d*) Loans and advances		52,750	
		4,97,050	
Less: Current Liabilities and Provisions			
(*a*) Liabilities	49,884		
(*b*) Provisions	1,23,000		
		1,72,884	
Working capital			3,24,165
			9,17,116

3. STATEMENT OF RETAINED EARNINGS

A statement of retained earnings is in fact a part of income statement or profit & loss a/c. In fact it is an extension of profit and loss a/c which reveals how the profit of the company have been utilised to meet various contingencies and the balance amount transferred to balance sheet. As this statement involves appropriating the income towards reserves and dividend it is also known as profit and loss appropriation a/c. However, on the credit side it starts with the opening balance of profit and to it is added profit earned during the current year. The term 'retained earnings' means the accumulated excess of earnings over dividends and losses.

4. STATEMENT OF CHANGES IN FINANCIAL POSITION

It is a statement which reveals the financing and investing activities of a company. It is also known as a 'statement of changes in financial position' during an accounting period. The statement discloses change in working capital. In order to know the change in financial position of a business between two period two different statements, known as fund flow statement and cash flow statement are prepared.

The fund flow statement reveals as to how working capital (*i.e.*, fund) is acquired and spent. Cash flow statement reveals a change in cash position between two accounting period. It helps to know the inflow and outflow of cash in a business.

5. SCHEDULES AND ACCOUNTING POLICES

Sometimes various schedules are prepared to supplement the information contained in profit and loss a/c and balance sheet. Such schedules relate to cost of goods sold, schedule of fixed assets, schedule of investment etc., and are attached to relevant statements.

Accounting policies followed for valuation of stock, depreciation etc., are mentioned as a foot note to the balance sheet. There help the readers to understand the financial statements in a better way.

QUESTIONS

Simple Questions

1. Define financial statement.
2. List out the objectives of financial statements.
3. Mention the various packages of financial statements.
4. What do you mean by multi-step income statement?
5. What do you mean by single-step income statement?
6. How do you ascertain cost of goods sold in case of a trading business?
7. How do you ascertain cost of goods sold in case of a manufacturing business?
8. What is "operating income"? Give an example.
9. What is operating expense? Give an example.
10. What are non-operating incomes and expenses?
11. What is net operating profit?
12. What is a current asset? Give examples.
13. What is a fixed Asset? Give examples.
14. What is an intangible asset? Give examples.
15. What is deferred expenditure? Give examples.
16. What is a current liability? Give examples.
17. What do you mean by long term liability? Give examples.
18. What is net worth?
19. What is liquid asset?
20. What is working capital?
21. What do you mean by capital employed?
22. What is statement of retained earnings?

Short Answer Questions

1. Explain the nature of financial statements.
2. Explain the attributes of financial statements.
3. Explain the importance of financial statements.
4. State the limitations of financial statements.
5. State the recent trends in presenting financial statements.

Long Answer Questions

1. Explain the packages financial statements.

Exercise 1: The following details have been obtained from the books of Mercury Co. Ltd. prepare an income statement in the vertical form for the year ended 31-12-2001.

Balance on 1-4-2000		Dividend paid	30,000
Raw materials	80,000	Sale of scrap	2,500
Work-in-progress	30,000	Purchases	89,000
Finished goods	50,000	Loss on Sale of shares	23,000
Balance on 31-3-2001			
Raw materials	90,000	Manufacturing expenses	75,000
Work-in-progress	40,000	Selling expenses	21,000
Finished goods	38,000	Office expenses	30,500
Sales	3,40,000	Interest paid	7,500

Answer: Profit 22,250.

Exercise 2: From the following particulars prepare an income statement in a vertical form:

Opening stock	1,72,058
Closing stock	1,48,680
Sales	10,83,947
Purchases	5,00,903
Manufacturing expenses	3,59,000
Interest on Investment	11,294
Establishment charges	26,814
General charges	31,078
Directors fees	1,800
Depreciation on fixed assets	10,000
Managing Directors Remuneration	6,500

Answer: Profit Rs. 7,45,268.

Exercise 3: From the following balances ascertain:

(*a*) Current assets (*b*) Fixed assets (*c*) Current liabilities and provisional (*d*) Long term debt (*e*) Shareholders funds.

Equity share capital	3,00,000	Furniture	10,000
Buildings	2,00,000	Machinery	1,50,000
Stock	50,000	Bills receivable	20,000
Debtors	1,00,000	General reserve	20,000
P & L a/c (cr.)	75,000	Bank overdraft (Permanent)	50,000
Provision for Tax	30,000	12% Debentures	1,00,000
Loan from Managing Director	90,000	Cash in hand	10,000
Cash at Bank	40,000	Unclaimed dividends	15,000
Preliminary expenses	70,000	15% Investements	90,000
Creditors	50,000	Bills payable	10,000

Answer: (*a*) Current assets Rs. 2,20,000
(*b*) Fixed Assets Rs. 3,60,000
(*c*) Current liabilities and provisions Rs. 10,5,000
(*d*) Long term debt Rs. 2,40,000
(*e*) Shareholders funds Rs. 3,95,000

Exercise 4: From the following details prepare a balance sheet in a vertical form:

36,900 equity shares of Rs. 10 each fully paid-up	3,69,000
10% cum, preference share capital	80,000
Capital reserve	71,000
Share premium a/c	10,000
P & L a/c (cr.)	24,910
Bank OD (secured by mortgage on land and buildings)	50,000
Creditors	20,000
O/s Managerial Remuneration	1,800
Provision for income-tax	26,190
Proposed dividend on pref. shares	9,600
Advance payment of income-tax	6,000
Cash at bank	5,000
Cash on hand	1,000
Debtors	47,500
Stock	40,000
Investments	1,80,000
Furniture	14,400
Buildings	68,600
Freehold land	3,00,000

Solution: Sources and Applications of funds Rs. 6,04,910.

3

ANALYSIS AND INTERPRETATION OF FINANCIAL STATEMENTS

INTRODUCTION

Financial statements prepared in an organisation conveys the financial information in absolute terms which may not be readily understood by everyone. Moreover these statements do not disclose all the relevant and required information. Further, financial statements suffer from certain inherent limitations. In order to obtain relevant and material information for knowing the strength and weakness of an organisation, analysis and interpretation of financial statements is felt necessary. Analysis and interpretation of financial statement refers to a systematic and constant effort to determine the significance and meaning of the financial statements to enable forecasting profitability, solvency, and prospects of future earning. It is designated to be the last of the four major steps of accounting which involves presentation of information that aids business managers and a large mumber of external parties such as investors, creditors, security analysts, Government and so on.

MEANING, DEFINITION AND IMPORTANCE OF ANALYSIS AND INTERPRETATION OF FINANCIAL STATEMENTS

Analysis of financial statement refers to the art of applying various tools to know the behaviour of the accounting information. It is defined by Metcalf as the "Process of evaluating the relationship between component parts of a financial statement to obtain a better understanding of a firm's position and performance." According to Kennedy and Muller, "Analysis and interpretation of financial statements are an attempt to determine the significance and meaning of the financial statements data so that the forcast may be made of the prospects for future earnings, ability to pay interest and debt maturities and profitability of a sound dividend policy." In the words of Myers, "Financial statement analysis is largely a study of relationship among various financial factors in a business as disclosed by a single set of statements and a study of the trends of these factors as shown in a series of statements." Analysis of financial statements may be compared to x-raying the financial position to diagnose the financial strength and weakness of the business.

Interpretation of financial statements refers to evaluating the performance of the business. According to F. Wood, "To interpret means to put the meaning of a statement in simple terms for the benefit of a person." It may be defined as critical examination of financial statements for a given period.

Differences between Analysis and Interpretation of financial statements

Analysis and interpretation though used synonymously, are not same. They differ in the following respects:

1. The term analysis is used in narrow sense. Whereas the term interpretation is used in a broad sense to include analysis.

2. Analysis is the first step whereas interpretation follows analysis.
3. Analysis implies classification of facts or data in a logical order. It involves splitting the complex data into various simple elements. Whereas interpretation implies explaining the meaning and significance of the facts or data so classified.

However it can be concluded that analysis and interpretation are complementary to each other. Analysis without interpretation is useless and interpretation becomes difficult without analysis.

IMPORTANCE OF ANALYSIS AND INTERPRETATION

The importance of analysis and interpretation of financial statements may be outlined under the following points:

1. Any decision taken on the basis of intution may prove to be wrong. To avoid wrong decision making it is always desireable to analyse and interpret the quantitative data. Decisions based on analysis and interpretation which is done systematically will never prove to be wrong and misleading.
2. All people may not possess knowledge and experience of understanding the financial statements in its raw-form. It can be easily understood even by layman when they are analysed and interpreted.
3. Analysis and interpretation is necessary to verify the correctness and accuracy of the decision made which must have been taken on the basis of intution.

STEPS INVOLVED IN ANALYSIS AND INTERPRETATION OF FINANCIAL STATEMENTS

Analysis and interpretation is one of the important functions of management accountant. It is not only interesting but a significant function of management accountant. In fact it may be regarded as an art as it requires good understanding and experience in this regard. The following steps are involved in the process of analysing and interpreting financial statements :

1. Analysis: Generally information presented in financial statements relate to individual accounts or group balances of many accounts. This leads to lack of homogenity and uniformity. In order to facilitate easy interpretation of information, the data is to be rearranged and reclassified. This process of methodical arrangement of presented data is known as analysis of financial statements. In this process it involves splitting of total items into various component parts. For example, if the short term solveney position of a business is to be known, it is necessary to know the current assets and current liabilities. The component of current assets can be known by analysing the asset side of the balance sheet and segregate current assets from various other components of balance sheet. Similarly, the current liabilities can be known by segregating it from other components of liability side of the balance sheet. In this way analysis includes regrouping or reclassifying of data into homogenous and comparable component parts.

2. Comparision: After division of facts into various components and sub-components, the second step involved is the comparision of figures. This step involves measuring the magnitude of the figures and knowing the extent of relationship between them. Only then it is possible to interpret the analysed data.

3. Study of trend: Having analysed and compared the magnitude of figures, the next step is to observe the data over a period of time. This study reveals the trend and the trend analysis helps in formulating a rational judgement about the performance of a business.

4. Interpretation: The process of drawing conclusions about the financial condition of a business is known as interpretation of financial statements. On the basis of findings a rational judgement is made when submitted in the form of report.

5. Criticism: Closely associated with the step of interpretation is the criticism. It may take two forms.

(*a*) **Criticism as to the form:** This goes to suggest whether the financial statements prepared is according to the law laid down by an Act. In India, the final accounts of Banking companies are to be prepared along with supportive schedules and according to the prescribed mode as required by Banking Companies Act.

(*b*) **Criticism as to reliability:** This goes to suggest that the information furnished is reliable or not. To know the reliability of accounts it is to be ensured that (*i*) Whether adequate provision is made for depreciation (*ii*) Assets are valued on a sound basis (*iii*) Deferred expenditure is gradually written off and so on.

PROCEDURE OF ANALYSIS AND INTERPRETATION

The procedure involved in the process of analysis and interpretation may be outlined as under:

1. As the technique and tools of analysis depends upon the object of analysis and interpretation, at the outset the purpose and extent of analysis is to be determined.
2. To study all data presented in financial statement for a clear understanding.
3. Collect additional information if need be for proper interpretation.
4. Divide and sub-divide the components according to their resemblences.
5. Use proper tools for analysis such as comparative statements, trend analysis etc., depending upon the purpose of interpretation.
6. Interpret the data and draw conclusions therefrom.
7. Prepare report incorporating the conclusions drawn.

Objectives of Analysis and Interpretation of Financial Statements

The objectives of financial statement analysis are as under:

1. To highlight the present and future earning capacity and the profitability of the concern.
2. To show the efficiency of the concern as a whole and department-wise.
3. To determine the solvency of the firm, both short term and long term.
4. To facilitate inter-firm and intra-firm comparisions.
5. To help in preparation of budgets.
6. To help in assessing the long term liquidity position of funds.

Types of Analysis and Interpretation of Financial Statements: Financial analysis is classified on the basis of materials used and modus operandi of the analysis. This is shown below:

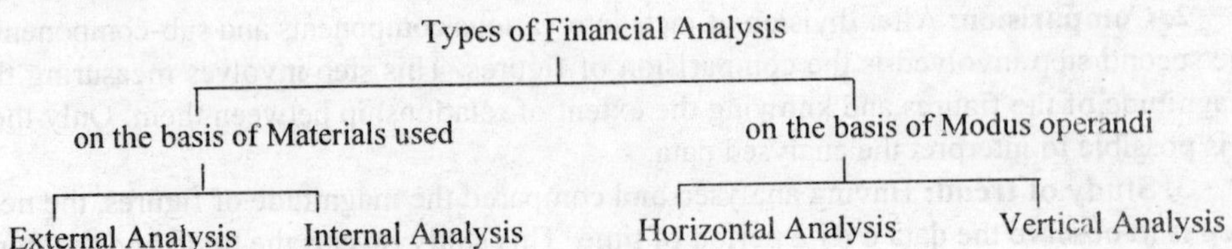

1. External analysis: Such type of analysis is made by outsiders who have no access to the books of accounts. They constitute investors, creditors, credit agencies and government agencies. As they dont have access to the books of accounts they have to depend on the published accounts for the purpose of analysis. However government regulation requiring auditing of accounts has made published accounts more reliable and dependable. As compared to internal analysis, external analysis is not done in detail and hence it serves limited purpose.

2. Internal analysis: It is done by those parties in the business who have access to books of account. Such parties can be designated as Accountant, Financial analyst. Some times it can also be done by employees to know the performance of the business. Internal analysis is done in more detail when compared to external analysis.

3. Horizontal analysis: When financial analysis is done for number of years, it is known as horizontal analysis. Such analysis sets a trend wherein the figures of various years are compared with one standard year known as base year. Based on the trend prevailing it is possible to make decision and form a rational judgement about the progress of the business. This type of analysis is also known as dynamic analysis as it measures the change of position of the business over a member of years.

4. Vertical analysis: When analysis is made for data covering one year's period it is known as vertical analysis. This type is also known as static analysis as it measures the state of affairs of the business as on given period of time. This type of analysis is useful in comparing the performance of several firms belonging to the same industry or various departments belonging to the same company.

Limitations of Financial Analysis

1. Because of the inflationary trend, the financial statements based on historical costs cannot be taken as an indicator for future forecasting and planning.
2. Analysis of financial statements is a tool which if used by an unskilled analyst may lead to faulty conclusions.
3. Financial statements are only interim reports and cannot be taken as final as the ultimate result of the business can be known only when the business is closed down. So analysis of these statements will not serve as conclusive evidence of the performance of the business.
4. The reliability of analysis depend upon the accuracy of the figures used in the financial statements. The analysis is distorted when the financial statements are manipulated by the accountant.
5. The results derived from analysis may be differently interpreted by different users.
6. The analysis of one year's statement will have limited use. Unless analysis is done for number of years it is not possible to compare so as to arrive at a meaningful conclusion.
7. When different firms belonging to same industry use different accounting procedures and policies the comparision will be difficult. This will not provide a reliable basis to know the performance of the industry as a whole.
8. A large number of tools are available for analysis and interpretation. Accordingly the results vary depending upon the type of tool used by the Accountant.

Tools or Techniques or Methods of Financial Analysis

For analysing the financial data and interpreting them in a systematic manner, a number of techniques or tools are available. These are as follows:

1. Comparative financial statements.
2. Common-size statement analysis.
3. Trend analysis.
4. Average analysis.
5. Ratio analysis.
6. Fund flow analysis.
7. Cash flow analysis.

1. Comparative Financial Statements: These are statements indicating the direction of movement with respect to financial position and operating results. They are very useful to the analyst because they contain not only the data appearing in a single statement but also information necessary for the study of financial and operating trends over a period of years. Comparative statements may be made to show:

(*a*) Absolute data (money values or rupee amounts).
(*b*) Increases or decreases in absolute data in terms of money values.
(*c*) Increases or decreases in absolute data in terms of percentages.
(*d*) Comparisions expressed in ratios.
(*e*) Percentage of totals.

The comparative financial statements as the name itself suggests enable comparision of financial information for two or more years placed side by side. From this it is possible to appraise, the performance, position and efficiency of business. The importance of comparative financial statement is recognised by the Indian Companies Act 1956. It makes obligatory for all companies to prepare the final accounts of companies by presenting current years as well as previous years figures.

The more common types of comparative statements are (*a*) Comparative Balance Sheet (*b*) Comparative income statement (*c*) Comparative statement of working capital and (*d*) Comparative statement of Manufacturing costs.

A comparative balance sheet is prepared to know change of Assets liabilities and capital of the business on two different dates. The changes may relate to an increase or decrease in any of the items. It contains columns for (*a*) Absolute data for the previous year (*b*) For absolute data for the current year (*c*) Changes in the items of Balance Sheet (*d*) Change in items of Balance Sheet expressed in percentages.

Similarly a comparative income statement is prepared to compare all items of profit and loss a/c and thus to know the increase or decrease in the items. By looking into the changes in expenditure and revenues it is possible to know the operating efficiency of the business.

Problem 1 (Comparative Income Statement): The following are the income statements of Swadeshi Cotton Mills for the years 2000 and 2001. Prepare comparative income statement and comment on the profitability of the company.

	2000	*2001*		*2000*	*2001*
To opening stock	85,000	2,00,000	By Sales less Returns	10,00,000	12,00,000
To purchases less returns	5,00,000	5,50,000	By closing stock	2,00,000	2,25,000
To Wages	60,000	80,000	By Income received from Investment	12,000	15,000

To Salaries	42,000	64,000	By Dividend received	5,000	7,500
To Rent, rates and insurance	35,000	40,000			
To Depreciation	40,000	60,000			
To Selling expenses	12,000	12,000			
To Discount allowed	5,000	7,000			
To Loss on sale of plant	–	8,000			
To Interest paid	12,000	14,000			
To Net profit	4,26,000	4,12,500			
	12,17,000	14,47,500		12,17,000	14,47,500

Solution:

Comparative Income Statement

		2000	*2001*	*Absolute change*	*Percentage Increase or Decrease*
Net	Sales	10,00,000	12,00,000	+ 2,00,000	+ 20%
Less:	Cost of goods sold (see working note)	4,45,000	6,05,000	+ 1,60,000	+ 35.9%
	Gross profit	5,55,000	5,95,000	+ 40,000	+ 5.41
Less:	Operating expenses:				
	Salaries	42,000	64,000	+ 22,000	+ 52.38%
	Rent, rates, insurance	35,000	40,000	+ 5,000	+ 14.29%
	Depreciation	40,000	60,000	+ 20,000	+ 50.%
	Selling expenses	12,000	12,000	–	–
	Discount allowed	5,000	7,000	+ 2,000	+ 40%
		1,34,000	1,83,000	49,000	+ 36.56%
	Operating profit	4,21,000	4,12,000	– 9,000	– 2.14%
Add:	Non-operating income:				
	Income from investment	12,000	15,000	+ 3,000	+ 25%
	Dividend received	5,000	7,500	+ 2,500	+ 50%
		17,000	22,500	+ 5,500	+ 32.35%
Less:	Non-operating expenses:				
	Loss on sale of plant	–	8,000	+ 8,000	+ 100%
	Interest paid	12,000	14,000	+ 2,000	+ 16.67%
		12,000	22,000	+ 10,000	+ 83.33%
Net	Profit	4,26,000	4,12,500	– 13,500	– 3.17%

Working Note:

Calculation of cost of goods sold:

		2000	*2001*
	Opening stock	85,000	2,00,000
Add:	Purchases	5,00,000	5,70,000
Add:	Wages	60,000	80,000
		6,45,000	8,30,000
Less:	Closing stock	2,00,000	2,25,000
Cost of goods sold		4,45,000	6,05,000

Interpretation:

1. Gross profit has shown an increase in 2001 but it is not commensurete with the increase in sales. The reason is increased cost of goods sold in 2001.
2. Among operating expenses the salary and depreciation have increased substantially. This is responsible for reduction in operating profit.
3. The total non-operating expenses is less in 2001 when compared to non-operating income in both the years.
4. Net profit decreased in 2001 when compared to 2000.

Problem 2: Following income statements of South India Metal Co. Ltd. are given for the years ending 2000 and 2001 prepare a multi-stage comparative income statement and interpret the changes.

Income statement

	2000	*2001*		*2000*	*2001*
To Cost of goods sold	9,00,000	9,50,000	By Sales	15,25,000	17,00,000
To Administration expenses	93,250	95,980	By Dividends	7,500	6,200
To Selling expenses	1,90,000	2,09,000	By profit from		
To Interest period	8,000	7,000	sale of land	6,000	8,000
To Loss on sale of machinery	2,500	800			
To Income tax	85,000	1,68,000			
To Net profit	2,59,750	2,83,420			
	15,38,500	17,14,200		15,38,500	17,14,200

Solution:

Comparative Income Statement

		2000	*2001*	*Increase or Decrease*	*Percentage change*
Sales		15,25,000	17,00,000	+ 1,75,000	+ 11.47%
Less:	Cost of sales	9,00,000	9,50,000	+ 50,000	+ 5.5%
	Gross profit	6,25,000	7,50,000	1,25,000	
Less:	Operating expenses:				
	Administration	93,250	95,980	+ 2,730	+ 2.93%
	Selling	1,90,000	2,09,000	+ 19,000	+ 10%
		2,83,250	3,04,980	+ 21,730	+ 7.67%
	Operating profit	3,41,750	4,45,020	1,03,270	
Add:	Non-operating Income:				
	Interest and Dividend	7,500	6,200	– 1,300	– 17.33%
	Profit from sale of land	6,000	8,000	+ 2,000	+ 33.33%
		13,500	14,200	+ 700	+ 5.18%
	Total Income	3,55,250	4,59,220	+ 1,03,970	
Less:	Non-operating expenses:				
	Loss on sale of Machinery	2,500	800	– 1,700	– 68%
	Income tax	85,000	1,68,000	+ 83,000	+ 92.9%
		87,500	1,68,800	81,300	+ 92.69%
	Net profit	2,67,750	2,90,420	+ 22,670	

Interpretation:

1. The increase in sales is to the extent of Rs. 1,75,000, while cost of sales increased by a sum of Rs. 50,000. The gross profit is increased by Rs. 1,25,000. This is a good indication of profitability.
2. Non-operating expenses is very high (Rs. 81,300), when compared to non-operating income (Rs. 700). This is responsible for decrease in profit.
3. Tax has gone up in 2001 by Rs. 83,000, which is also responsible for decrease in net profit.

Problem 3: From the following income statements extracted from the books of Aravind Parimal Works for the year 2000 and 2001 prepare comparative income statement and interpret the results of the business.

Income Statement (Rs. 000)

	2000	*2001*		*2000*	*2001*
To Opening stock	40.0	92.3	By sales	510.0	725.0
To Purchases	210.0	280.0	By closing stock	98.5	105.0
To Wages	25.0	32.0	By Discount	5.0	–
To Salaries	20.5	22.0	By Interest on investment	5.5	8.0
To Rent, rates and taxes	17.8	18.1	By Interest on bank deposit	5.0	7.2
To Selling expenses	5.8	6.1			
To Distribution expenses	3.2	3.9			
To Loss on sale of investment	–	10.0			
To Interest paid	7.0	7.5			
To Depreciation	35.0	40.0			
To Net profit	250.7	326.82			
	615.0	838.72		615.00	838.72

Solution:

Comparative Income Statement

		2000	*2001*	*Absolute change (Increase or Decrease)*	*Percentage change*
Net Sales		5,10,000	7,25,000	+ 2,15,000	+ 42.16%
Less:	Cost of goods sold (See working note)	1,76,500	2,99,300	+ 1,22,800	+ 69.58%
	Gross profit	3,33,500	4,25,700	+ 92,200	+ 27.65%
Less:	Operating expenses:				
	Salaries	20,500	22,000	+ 1,500	+ 7.32
	Rent, Rates, and Taxes	17,800	18,100	+ 300	+ 1.69
	Selling expenses	5,800	6,100	+ 300	+ 5.17
	Distribution expenses	3,200	3,900	+ 700	+ 21.88
	Depreciation	35,000	40,000	+ 5,000	+ 14.29
	Total operating expenses	82,300	90,100	+ 7,800	+ 9.48
		2,51,200	3,35,600	84,400	+ 18.17%
Add:	Operating Income:				
	Discount	500	–	– 500	– 100%
	Operating profit	2,51,700	3,35,600	+ 83,900	+ 33.33%

Less:	Non-operating expenses and losses:				
	Interest paid	7,000	7,500	+ 500	+ 7.14%
	Loss on sale of Investment	–	10,000	+ 10,000	
		7,000	17,500	+ 10,500	+ 150
		2,44,700	3,18,100	+ 73,400	+ 30.0%
Add:	Non-operating Incomes:				
	Interest on Investment	5,500	8,000	+ 2,500	+ 45.45%
	Interest on Bank Deposits	500	720	+ 220	+ 44.00%
	Total Non-operating incomes	6,000	8,720	+ 2,720	+ 45.33%
	Profit before tax	2,50,700	3,26,820	+ 76,120	+ 30.36
Less:	Tax @ 50%	1,25,350	1,63,410	+ 38,060	+ 30.36
	Profit after tax	1,25,350	1,63,410	+ 38,060	+ 30.36

Working Note:

Calculation of cost of goods sold

	2000	*2001*
Opening stock	40,000	92,300
Add: Purchases	2,10,000	2,80,000
	2,50,000	3,72,300
Add: Direct Wages	25,000	32,000
	2,75,000	4,04,300
Less: Closing stock	98,500	1,05,000
Cost of goods sold	1,76,500	2,99,300

Interpretation :

1. Though sales have increased by 42.16%. the gross profit increase is only by 27.65%. This is on account of rise in the cost of goods sold *i.e.*, 69.58%.
2. Operating expenses have increased only marginally, *i.e.*, by 9.48% which is justified with the increase in sales.
3. There is a considerable increase in non-operating income by 45.33%. This is partly responsible for increased percentage of net profit.
4. Profitability has increased in 2001 as compared to 2000 *i.e.*, by 30.36%.

Problem 4: Khaitan Fans Ltd. submitted the following particulars for the year ended 31.3.2001. Prepare a comparative income statement for the year ended 31st March 2001 for the first four quarters.

1. Sales for the first four quarters is estimated as Rs. 2,50,000, Rs. 2,10,000, Rs. 3,00,000 and Rs. 3,60,000.
2. Selling expenses are 2% and Distribution expenses are 25% of the selling expenses.
3. Cost of goods Sold-Fixed cost Rs. 40,000 fixed per quarter and variable expenses 12 1/2% of selling price.
4. Rent per quarter is Rs. 10,000 and in the last quarter an increase of 5%.
5. Administrative expenses for the first quarter is 37,250 and thereafter 5% increase of the preceding quarters expenses.
6. At the beginning of the second quarter the company borrowed a loan of Rs. 2,50,000. @ 9% and the interest is payable quarterly.
7. Rate of Tax is 25% for the first 2 quarters and 20% of the next two.

Solution:

Calculation of cost of goods sold

Working Note:

	I Qr	*II Qr*	*III Qr*	*IV Qr*
(1) *Fixed cost*	40,000	40,000	40,000	40,000
Add: Variable cost				
$12\frac{1}{2}$% on sales	31,250	26,250	37,500	45,000
Cost of goods sold	71,250	66,250	77,500	85,000
(2) *Rent*	10,000	10,000	10,000	10,000
Add: Increase of 5% in the last	–	–	–	500
quarter	10,000	10,000	10,000	10,500
(3) *Administrative Cost:*				
Ist quarter	37,500			
IInd quarter				
$37{,}500+\left(37{,}500\times\frac{10}{100}\right)$		41,250		
IIIrd quarter				
$41{,}250+\left(41{,}250\times\frac{10}{100}\right)$			45,375	
IVth quarter				
$45{,}375+\left(45{,}375\times\frac{10}{100}\right)$				49,912
(4) *Selling Cost:*				
2% on sales				
Ist quarter	5,000			
$\left(\frac{2}{100}\times 2{,}50{,}000\right)$				
IInd quarter		4,200		
$\left(\frac{2}{100}\times 2{,}10{,}000\right)$				
IIIrd quarter			6,000	
$\left(\frac{2}{100}\times 3{,}00{,}000\right)$				
IVth quarter				7,200
$\left(\frac{2}{100}\times 3{,}60{,}000\right)$				
(5) *Distribution Cost:*				
25% of Selling cost				
I Quarter	1,250			

$\left(\frac{25}{100} \times 5{,}000\right)$

II Quarter — 1,050

$\left(\frac{25}{100} \times 4{,}200\right)$

III Quarter — 1,500

$\left(\frac{25}{100} \times 6{,}000\right)$

IV Quarter — 1,800

$\left(\frac{25}{100} \times 7{,}200\right)$

(6) Interest on loan:

II Quarter, III Quarter, IV Quarter: $2{,}50{,}000 \times \frac{9}{100} \times \frac{3}{12} = 5{,}625$

Comparative Income Statement

		I Qr	II Qr	III Qr	IV Qr
	Sales	2,50,000	2,10,000	3,00,000	3,60,000
Less:	Cost of goods sold	71,250	66,250	77,500	85,000
	Gross profit	1,78,750	1,43,750	2,22,500	2,75,000
Less:	Operating expenses:				
	Rent	10,000	10,000	10,000	10,500
	Administrative cost	37,500	41,250	45,375	49,912
	Selling cost	5,000	4,200	6,000	7,200
	Distribution cost	1,250	1,050	1,500	1,800
		53,750	56,500	62,875	69,412
	Operating profit	1,25,000	87,250	1,59,625	2,05,588
Less:	Non-operating expenses:				
	Interest paid	–	5,625	5,625	5,625
	Profit before Tax	1,25,000	81,625	15,4,000	1,99,963
Less:	Tax	31,250	20,406	30,800	39,993
	Profit After Tax	93,750	61,219	1,23,200	1,59,970

Problem 5 (Comparative Position Statement): Following are the Balance Sheets of a company for the years 1997 and 1998. Prepare a comparative balance sheet and explain the financial position of the concern.

Balance Sheet as on

	1997	*1998*		*1997*	*1998*
Share capital	3,00,000	4,00,000	Land and Buildings	1,85,000	1,35,000
Reserves and surplus	1,65,000	1,11,000	Plant and Machinery	2,00,000	3,00,000
Debentures	1,00,000	1,50,000	Furniture and Fixtures	10,000	12,500
Long term loan	75,000	1,00,000	Other Fixed assets	12,500	15,000
Bills payable	25,000	12,500	Cash at Bank	10,000	40,000

Creditors	50,000	60,000	Bills Receivable	75,000	46,000
Other current liabilities	2,500	5,000	Debtors	1,00,000	1,25,000
			Stock	1,25,000	1,75,000
	7,17,500	8,48,500		7,17,500	8,48,500

(Osamania University, B. Com., October 1999)

Solution:

Comparative Balance Sheet for the years ending 31st Dec. 1997 and 98

	1997	*1998*	*Increase/ Decrease (Rs.)*	*Increase/ Decrease (%)*
Assets:				
Fixed Assets:				
Land and Building	1,85,000	1,35,000	– 50,000	– 27.03
Plant and Machinery	2,00,000	3,00,000	+ 1,00,000	+ 50
Furniture and Fixture	10,000	12,500	+ 2,500	+ 25
Other fixed Assets	12,500	15,000	+ 2,500	+ 20
Total Fixed Assets	4,07,500	4,62,500	+ 55,000	+ 13.49
Current Assets:				
Cash of Bank	10,000	40,000	+ 30,000	+ 300
Bills Receivable	75,000	46,000	– 29,000	– 39
Debtors	1,00,000	1,25,000	+ 25,000	+ 25
Stock	1,25,000	1,75,000	+ 50,000	+ 40
Total Current Assets	3,10,000	3,86,000	+ 76,000	+ 24.52
Total assets	7,17,500	8,48,500	+ 1,31,000	+ 18.26
Liabilities:				
Equity share capital	3,00,000	4,00,000	+ 1,00,000	+ 33
Reserves and Surplus	1,65,000	1,11,000	– 54,000	– 32.73
Total	4,65,000	5,11,000	– 46,000	– 11.61
Debentures	1,00,000	1,50,000	+ 50,000	+ 50
Long term loans	75,000	1,00,000	+ 25,000	+ 33
Total				
Bills payable	25,000	22,500	– 2,500	– 10
Creditors	50,000	60,000	+ 10,000	+ 20
Other current liabilities	2,500	5,000	+ 2,500	+ 100
Total	2,52,500	3,37,500	+ 85,000	+ 33.60
Total capital and liabilities	7,17,500	8,48,500	+ 1,31,000	+ 18.26

Interpretation:

1. There is an increase in Fixed Assets in the year 1998 compared to 1997. This is as compared to long term liabilities and Share Capital which shows an increase of 75,000 (50,000 + 25,000) and Rs. 1,00,000 respectively. The company has bought fixed assets out of long term finds. The working capital is not affected.
2. Current assets show an increase of 24.52%. Whereas current liabilities show an increase of Rs. 10,000 (i.e., 12.9%). The liquidity position is therefore considered to be good.
3. Reserves and surplus has decreased by 32.73%. The company might have utilised the reserve for the issue of bouns shares or for the payment of dividend.

Problem 6: The following are the balance sheets for the year 1991 and 1992. Prepare comparative balance sheet and comment on the financial position.

	1991	*1992*
Liabilities:		
6% preference shares	30,000	30,000
Equity Share Capital	40,000	40,000
Reserves	20,000	24,500
Outstanding Tax	10,000	15,000
Sundry creditors	15,000	20,000
Bills payable	5,000	7,500
Debentures	10,000	15,000
	1,30,000	1,52,000
Assets:		
Land	10,000	10,000
Buildings	30,000	27,000
Plant	30,000	27,000
Furniture	10,000	14,000
Stock	20,000	30,000
Debtors	20,000	30,000
Cash	10,000	14,000
	1,30,000	1,52,000

(*S. V. University, B. Com., April 1999*)

Solution:

Comparative Balance Sheet

	1991	*1992*	*Absolute change*	*Percentage change*
I. *Assets*:				
(1) Current Assets:				
Stock	20,000	30,000	+ 10,000	+ 50%
Debtors	20,000	30,000	+ 10,000	+ 50%
Cash	10,000	14,000	+ 4,000	+ 40%
Total Current Assets	50,000	74,000	+ 24,000	+ 48%
(2) Fixed Assets:				
Land	10,000	10,000	–	–
Buildings	30,000	27,000	– 3,000	– 10%
Plant	30,000	27,000	– 3,000	– 10%
Furniture	10,000	14,000	+ 4,000	+ 40%
Total Fixed Assets	80,000	78,000	– 2,000	– 2.50%
Total Assets (1 + 2)	1,30,000	1,52,000	+ 22,000	+ 16.92
II. *Liabilities*:				
(1) Current liabilities:				
Creditors	15,000	20,000	+ 5,000	+ 33.33%
Bills payable	5,000	7,500	+ 2,500	+ 50
O/s Tax	10,000	15,000	+ 5,000	+ 50
Total Current liabilities	30,000	42,500	+ 12,500	+ 41.66%

(2) Long term loans:				
Debentures	10,000	15,000	+ 5,000	+ 50%
	10,000	15,000	+ 5,000	+ 50%
(3) Shareholders Funds:				
Preference Share Capital	30,000	30,000	–	–
Equity Share Capital	40,000	40,000	–	–
Reserves	20,000	24,500	+ 4,500	+ 22.5%
Total Shareholders Funds	90,000	94,500	+ 4,500	+ 5%
Total of liabilities (1 + 2 + 3)	1,30,000	1,52,000	+ 22,000	+ 16.92

Working Notes:

$$\text{Calculation of percentage change} = \frac{\text{Absolute change}}{\text{Amount of previous year}} \times 100$$

$$\text{For example}: \frac{\text{Change in Current Asset}}{\text{Total Current Asset in 1991}} \times 100$$

$$= \frac{24,000}{50,000} \times 100 = 48\%$$

Similarly other percentages are calculated.

Interpretation:

As there is slight raise in current assets over current liabilities (48% – 41.66% = 6.33%). the financial position can be stated as satisfactory. The company has not shown much change in other aspects. It is still to make effort to gain further in its financial position.

Problem 7 (Comparative Position Statement in Vertical Form): Following are the Balance Sheets as on 31 December 1997 and 1998 of M/s Gautami Ltd.

	1997	*1998*		*1997*	*1998*
Equity Share Capital	1,00,000	1,50,000	Land and Building	80,000	75,000
General Reserve	60,000	10,000	Plant and Machinery	42,000	85,000
P & L a/c	5,000	30,000	Furniture and Fittings	7,000	6,000
Bank O.D	–	65,000	Investments	6,000	12,000
Mortgage loan (Secured on plant)	–	40,000	Stock	27,500	94,500
Provision for tax	10,000	15,000	Sundry Debtors	46,500	77,250
Sundry creditors	30,000	20,000	Cash	2,000	7,250
Bills payable	10,000	30,000	Preliminary expenses	4,000	3,000
	2,15,000	3,60,000		2,15,000	3,60,000

You are required to prepare:

1. Comparative Financial statements in vertical form and to.
2. Offer your comments there on.

(*University of Bombay, B. Com., October 1999*)

Solution:

Comparative Balance Sheet

	1997	*1998*	*Absolute change*	*Percentage change*
Sources of Fund:				
(1) Shareholders fund:				
Equity share capital	1,00,000	1,50,000	+ 50,000	+ 50%

(2) Reserves and surplus:				
General reserve	60,000	10,000	– 50,000	– 83.33%
P & L a/c	5,000	30,000	+ 25,000	+ 5%
	65,000	40,000	– 25,000	+ 38.46%
Less: Preliminary expenses	4,000	3,000	1,000	– 25%
	61,000	37,000	– 24,000	– 39.34%
(3) Long term loan:				
Mortgage loan	–	40,000	+ 40,000	–
Total funds employed (1 + 2 + 3)	1,61,000	2,27,000	66,000	41%
Application of funds:				
Fixed Assets:				
Land and Buildings	80,000	75,000	– 5,000	6.25
Plant and Machinery	42,000	85,000	+ 43,000	+ 102.39%
Furniture and Fittings	7,000	6,000	– 1,000	14.29
(*A*)	1,29,000	1,66,000	37,000	28.68
Trade Investments (*B*)	6,000	12,000	6,000	100%
Current Assets:				
Stock	27,500	94,500	67,000	243.64
Debtors	46,500	77,250	30,750	66.13
Cash	2,000	7,250	5,250	262.5
(*C*)	76,000	1,79,000	1,03,000	135.53%
Current liabilities and provisions:				
Bank overdraft	–	65,000	+ 65,000	–
Sundry creditors	30,000	20,000	– 10,000	– 33.33%
Bills payable	10,000	30,000	+ 20,000	+ 200%
Provision for tax	10,000	15,000	5,000	+ 50%
(*D*)	50,000	1,30,000	80,000	+ 16.0
Working capital	26,000	49,000	23,000	88.46
Total Funds employed	1,61,000	2,27,000	66,000	+ 41

Interpretations:

1. During the year 1998 the bouns shares of Rs. 50,000 are issued by capitalising general reserves. Also new machines were purchased which was financed through mortgaged loan.
2. Increase in current assets is partiy through the plouging back of profits in business and partly by bank overdraft and bills payable.
3. Proprietors funds in proportion to total assets have been reduced as during the year mortgage loan was taken.

Problem 8: From the following data prepare comparative balance sheets in vertical form as at 31-3-1998 and 31-3-1999 of M/s APJ Ltd.

	1998	*1999*		*1998*	*1999*
Share capital	70,000	80,000	Building	55,000	80,000
P & L a/c	20,000	20,000	Machinery	43,000	50,000
Debentures	20,000	30,000	Stock	25,000	5,000

Other secured loans	10,000	20,000	Debtors	15,000	10,000
Creditors	10,000	3,000	Cash	2,000	15,000
Bank O.D	8,000	4,000			
O/s Expenses	2,000	3,000			
	1,40,000	1,60,000		1,40,000	1,60,000

Also offer your comments.

(*University of Bombay, B. Com., April 1999*)

Solution: **Comparative Balance Sheet as at 31st March 1998-99**

	1998	*1999*	*Absolute change*	*Percentage change*
Sources of Funds:				
(*A*) Shareholders fund:				
Share capital	70,000	80,000	+ 10,000	+ 14.29
P & L a/c	20,000	20,000	–	–
	90,000	1,00,000	+ 10,000	11.11%
(*B*) Loan Funds:				
Debentures	20,000	30,000	+ 10,000	+ 50%
Other secured loans	10,000	20,000	+ 10,000	+ 100%
	30,000	50,000	+ 20,000	+ 66.67%
Total Funds (*A* + *B*)	1,20,000	1,50,000	30,000	25%
Application of Funds:				
(*A*) Fixed Assets:				
Building	55,000	80,000	+ 25,000	+ 45.55%
Machinery	43,000	50,000	+ 7,000	+ 16.28
	98,000	1,30,000	+ 32,000	+ 32.65%
(*B*) Current Assets:				
Stock	25,000	5,000	– 20,000	– 80%
Debtors	15,000	10,000	– 5,000	– 33 1/3%
Cash	2,000	15,000	+ 13,000	+ 650%
	42,000	30,000	– 12,000	– 28.57%
(*C*) Current liabilities:				
Creditors	10,000	3,000	– 7,000	– 70%
Overdraft	8,000	4,000	– 4,000	– 50%
O/s expenses	2,000	3,000	+1,000	+ 50%
	20,000	10,000	– 10,000	– 50%
Working capital (*B* – *C*) = *D*	22,000	20,000	– 10,000	– 50%
Total funds *A* + *D*	1,20,000	1,50,000	30,000	+ 25%

Interpretation:

1. Long term funds and building both show increase but not machinery.
2. Current liabilities and current assets show significant decline implying less commercial activity.
3. The above factors collectively indicate that the company is in process of operation.

Problem 9: The following are the balance sheets of Hindustan Ltd. for the years ending 31st March 1993 and 1994.

	1993	*1994*
Equity share capital	4,00,000	6,60,000
Pref. share capital	2,00,000	3,00,000
Reserves	40,000	60,000
P & L a/c	30,000	40,000
Bank O.D	1,00,000	1,00,000
Creditors	80,000	1,00,000
Provision for taxation	40,000	50,000
Proposed dividend	30,000	50,000
	9,20,000	13,60,000
Fixed assets less depreciation	4,80,000	7,00,000
Stock	80,000	1,00,000
Debtors	2,00,000	2,50,000
Bills Receivable	40,000	1,20,000
Prepaid expenses	20,000	24,000
Cash in hand	80,000	1,06,000
Cash at Bank	20,000	60,000
	9,20,000	13,60,000

Prepare the comparative Balance sheet and study its financial position.

(*S. V. University, B. Com., April 1998*)

Solution: **Comparative Balance Sheet as on 1993 and 1994**

	1993	*1994*	*Absolute change*	*Percentage change*
Assets:				
(1) Fixed assets less depreciation	4,80,000	7,00,000	+ 2,20,000	+ 45.83%
(2) Current assets:				
Stock	80,000	1,00,000	+ 20,000	+ 25%
Debtors	2,00,000	2,50,000	+ 50,000	+ 25%
Bills Receivable	40,000	1,20,000	+ 80,000	+ 200%
Prepaid expenses	20,000	24,000	+ 4,000	+ 20%
Cash in hand	80,000	1,06,000	+ 26,000	+32.5%
Cash at Bank	20,000	60,000	+ 40,000	+ 200%
	4,40,000	6,60,000	+ 2,20,000	+50%
Total Assets (1 + 2)	9,20,000	13,60,000	+ 4,40,000	+ 47.83%
Liabilities:				
(1) Shareholders funds:				
Equity share capital	4,00,000	6,60,000	+ 2,60,000	+ 65%
Pref. share capital	2,00,000	3,00,000	+ 1,00,000	+ 33 1/3%
Reserves and Surplus				
Reserve	40,000	60,000	+ 20,000	+ 50%
P & L a/c	30,000	40,000	+ 10,000	+ 33 1/3%
	6,70,000	10,60,000	+ 3,90,000	+ 58.2%
(2) Current liabilities:				
Bank O.D	1,00,000	1,00,000	–	–
Creditors	80,000	1,00,000	+ 20,000	+ 25%
	1,80,000	2,00,000	+ 20,000	+ 11.1%

(3) Provisions:				
Provision for taxation	40,000	50,000	+ 10,000	+ 25%
Proposed Dividend	30,000	50,000	+ 20,000	+ 66.67%
	70,000	1,00,000	+ 30,000	+ 42.86%
Total liabilities (1 + 2 + 3)	9,20,000	13,60,000	+ 4,40,000	+ 47.83%

Interpretation:

1. Working capital has increased by Rs. (2,20,000 – 20,000) 2,00,000.
2. The raise of shareholders fund 58.2% (Rs. 3,90,000) was utilised to raise the fixed Assets 45.83% (Rs. 2,20,000) and utilised for working capital also.
3. The dividend payable to shareholders also has increased which will increase public confidence.

Problem 10 (Comparative Income Statement and Position Statement): From the following financial statements of Vaibhav Ltd. prepare comparative financial statements in vertical form.

Revnue Statement

	31-12-95	31-12-96		31-12-95	31-12-96
Cost of goods sold	6,00,000	7,50,000	Sales	8,00,000	10,00,000
Administrative expenses	30,000	40,000			
Selling expenses	20,000	20,000			
Net profit	1,50,000	1,90,000			
	8,00,000	10,00,000		8,00,000	10,00,000

Balance Sheet

	31-12-95	31-12-96		31-12-95	31-12-96
Equity share capital	4,00,000	4,00,000	Land	2,00,000	2,40,000
9% Pref. share capital	3,00,000	3,00,000	Building	6,00,000	5,40,000
General Reserve	2,00,000	2,45,000	Stock	2,00,000	3,00,000
Tax payable	1,00,000	1,50,000	Debtors	2,00,000	3,00,000
Creditors	2,00,000	2,75,000	Cash	1,00,000	1,40,000
17% Debentures	1,00,000	1,50,000			
	13,00,000	15,20,000		13,00,000	15,20,000

Briefly comment on the difference between the stated net profit of 1996 and the increment in general reserves on 31-12-96 assuming that no amount is paid towards tax in 1996.

Also Ascertain the quantum of cash gross profit of 1996, assuming that no depreciation is provided on Land. *(University of Bombay, B. Com., October 1997)*

Solution:

Comparative Income Statement

	31-12-95	*31-12-96*	*Absolute change*	*Percentage change*
Sales	8,00,000	10,00,000	+ 2,00,000	25%
Less: Cost of Sales	6,00,000	7,50,000	+ 1,50,000	25%
Gross profit	2,00,000	2,50,000	+ 50,000	+ 25%
Less: Operating expenses:				
Administration expenses	30,000	40,000	+ 10,000	+ 33 1/3%
Selling expenses	20,000	20,000	–	–
	50,000	60,000	+ 10,000	+ 20%
Net operating profit	1,50,000	1,90,000	+ 40,000	26.67%

Comparative Balance Sheet

	31-12-95	31-12-96	Absolute change	Percentage change
Sources of Funds:				
(*A*) Shareholders funds:				
Equity share capital	4,00,000	4,00,000	–	–
9% pref. share capital	3,00,000	3,00,000	–	–
	7,00,000	7,00,000		
(*B*) Reserves and surplus:				
General reserve	2,00,000	2,45,000	+ 45,000	+ 22.5%
	9,00,000	9,45,000	+ 45,000	+ 5%
(*C*) Long term liabilities:				
17% Debentures	1,00,000	1,50,000	+ 50,000	+ 50%
Total funds employed	10,00,000	10,95,000	+ 95,000	+ 9.5%
Applications of Funds:				
(*A*) Fixed Assets:				
Land	2,00,000	2,40,000	+ 40,000	+ 20%
Building	6,00,000	5,40,000	– 60,000	– 10%
	8,00,000	7,80,000	– 20,000	– 2.5%
(*B*) Currents Assets:				
Stock	2,00,000	3,00,000	+ 1,00,000	50%
Debtors	2,00,000	3,00,000	+ 1,00,000	50%
Cash	1,00,000	1,40,000	+ 40,000	40%
	5,00,000	7,40,000	+ 2,40,000	+ 48%
(*C*) Current liabilities:				
Tax payable	1,00,000	1,50,000	+ 50,000	50%
Creditors	2,00,000	2,75,000	+ 75,000	+ 37.50%
	3,00,000	4,25,000	1,25,000	41.67%
Working Capital (*B* – *C*) = *D*	2,00,000	3,15,000	1,15,000	41.67%
Total funds employed (*A* + *D*)	10,00,000	10,95,000	+ 95,000	+ 9.5%

Interpretation:

1. Net profit for the year 1996 has increased by 45,000.
2. There is no change in the capital structure of the company.
3. Value of building has decreased by Rs. 60,000 indicating the loss in the value of building. Alternatively it may taken to mean depreciation on building.

Problem 11: Circle and Square are carrying on partnership business. Their position as on 31st March 1995 and 1994 is as follows:

I. The Summarised Balance Sheet

	1995	1994		1995	1994
Capital a/cs.	71,750	59,500	Fixed Assets	52,500	43,750
Bank loan	14,000	10,500	Investments	3,500	1,750
Sundry creditors	38,500	35,000	Stock	21,000	17,500
			Sundry debtors	31,500	26,250
			Loans and advances	14,000	14,000
			Cash and bank balance	1,750	1,750
	1,24,250	1,05,000		1,24,250	1,05,000

II. Summarised Income Statement

		1995	*1994*
Net Sales		42,000	38,500
Less:	Cost of Sales	31,500	29,750
	Gross Margin	10,500	8,750
Less:	Operating expenses	8,750	7,000
	Net profit before Tax	1,750	1,750

(*University of Bombay, B.Com., April 1995*)

Solution:

Comparative Income Statement

		1994	*1995*	*Absolute change*	*Percentage change*
Sales		38,500	42,000	+ 3,500	+ 9.09
Less:	Cost of sales	29,750	31,500	– 1,750	+ 5.88
	Gross margin	8,750	10,500	1,750	+ 20%
Less:	Operating expenses	7,000	8,750	1,750	+ 25
	Net profit	1,750	1,750	–	–

Comparative Balance Sheet

	1994	*1995*	*Absolute change*	*Percentage change*
Sources of Funds:				
Capital a/cs.	59,500	71,750	+ 12,250	+ 20.59%
Loan funds	10,500	14,000	+ 3,500	+ 33.33%
Total funds employed	70,000	85,750	+ 15,750	+ 22.50%
Application of funds:				
Fixed Assets (*A*)	43,750	52,500	+ 8,750	+ 20%
Investments (*B*)	1,750	3,500	+ 1,750	+ 100%
Current Assets:				
Stock	17,500	21,000	+ 3,500	+ 20%
Debtors	26,250	31,500	+ 5,250	+ 20%
Loans and advances	14,000	14,000	–	–
Cash and bank	1,750	1,750	–	–
	59,500	68,250	+ 8,750	+ 14.71%
Current Liabilities:				
Creditors	35,000	38,500	+ 3,500	+ 10%
Working Capital (*C*)	24,500	29,750	+ 5,250	+ 21.43%
Total funds employed (*A* + *B* + *C*)	70,000	85,750	+ 15,750	+ 22.50%

Interpretation:

1. There is an increase in partners capital as well as loans in the firm. This is utilised in financing fixed assets.
2. There is no change in profit in 1995 as compared to 1994 which means that additional capital is used in financing working capital requirements of the business.
3. Cost of sales equals operating expenses. Again both cost of sales and operating expenses equals (1,750 + 1,750 = 3,500) sales. Thus there is no absolute increase in the profit.

2. Common-Size Financial Statement Analysis: They are comparative statements that give only the percentages for financial data without giving the rupee value. They are also known as 100 per cent statements because each statement is reduced to the total of 100 and each individnal item is stated as a percentage of the total of 100. Each percentage shows the relation of the individual items to its respective total. The common size financial statements are most valuable in making comparisions between the firms in the same industry. The two common-size financial statements usually prepared are: (*a*) Common-size income statement and (*b*) Common-size balance sheet.

Computation of Common-size statements

1. In case of common-size income-statement, total net sales are stated as 100 per cent. In case of position statement either total assets or total of liabilities and capital is taken as 100.
2. The quotient of each item is found out by dividing individual money amount by the total amount in the statement. This is expressed in the form of percentage.

Illustration: If the selling expense in any particular year of a business is Rs. 60,000 and its net sales is Rs. 6,00,000 for that year, the above two steps may be illustrated as follows:

$$\frac{\text{Selling expenses}}{\text{Net Sales}} \times 100$$

$$= \frac{60,000}{6,00,000} \times 100 = 10\%$$

This denotes that selling expenses for that particular year is 10% of net sales or they amount to Rs. 10 for every Rs. 100 worth of sales.

Other items can also be incorporated in the statements in the same manner and similar conclusions can be drawn.

Problem 12 (Common-size Income Statement): Prepare common-size income statement in vertical form from the following income statement and briefly comment thereon.

P & L a/c for the year ended 31-3-99

To Cost of Sales	4,91,400	By Gross Sales	8,26,200
To Administrative expenses	81,000	Less Returns	16,200
			8,10,000
To Selling and distribution expenses	1,62,000	By Non-operating income	8,100
To Non-operating expenses	10,800		
To Tax provision	36,450		
To Proposed Dividend	7,000		
To Retained Earnings	29,450		
	8,18,100		8,18,100

(*University of Bombay, B. Com., October 1999*)

Solution:

Common-Size Income Statement

	Amount	*Percentage*
Sales	8,26,200	102
Less: Sales Returns	16,200	2
Net sales	8,10,000	100
Less: Cost of sales	4,91,400	60.67%
Gross profit	3,18,600	39.33%

Less: Operating expenses:			
Office & Adm. expenses	81,000		10%
Selling and Distribution expenses	1,62,000		20%
		2,43,000	
Net operating profit		75,600	9.33%
Add: Non-operating income		8,100	1%
		83,700	10.33%
Less: Non-operating expenses		10,800	0.133%
Net profit before Tax		72,900	9%
Less: Tax provision		36,450	4.50%
Net profit after Tax		36,450	4.50%
Less: Proposed Dividend		7,000	0.86%
Balance transferred to B/S		29,450	3.64%

Interpretation:

1. Operating expenses are high for a given cost of sales. This must be under check.
2. Non-operating expenses are high compared to non-operating income.
3. Rate of Dividend declared is very less (0.86%).

Problem 13: The following figures relate to the activities of R. R. Ltd, Mumbai for the year ending 31st march 1995.

Sales	7,50,000
Purchases	3,75,000
Opening stock	70,000
Closing stock	80,000
Administration Expenses:	
Salaries	37,000
Rent	12,000
Postage and Stationary	5,000
Provision for taxation	50,000
Selling and Distribution expenses:	
Salaries	18,000
Advertising	6,000
Commission on sales	7,500
Discount	2,000
Non-operating expenses:	
Interest	5,000
Loss on sale of assets	11,500
Non-operating income:	
Profit on sale of investments	9,500

You should study the income statement of the concern with the help of common-size statement.

(S. V. University, B. Com., October 1998)

Solution: **Common-Size Income-Statement of R. R. Ltd. for the year ended 31-3-1995**

		Amount	*Percentage*
Sales		7,50,000	100%
Less: Cost of goods sold:			
Opening stock	70,000		
Add: Purchases	3,75,000		
	4,45,000		

Less: Closing stock	80,000		
		3,65,000	48.67%
Gross profit		3,85,000	51.33%
Less: Operating expenses:			
Administration expenses:			
Salaries	37,000		
Rent	12,000		
Postage and stationary	5,000		
		54,000	7.20%
		3,31,000	44.13%
Selling and Distribution expenses:			
Salaries	18,000		
Advertising	6,000		
Commission on sales	7,500		
Discount	2,000		
		33,500	4.47
Operating profit		2,97,500	39.66%
Less: Non-operating expenses:			
Interest	5,000		0.67
Loss on sale of assets	11,500	16,500	1.53
		2,81,000	37.46%
Add: Non-operating Income:			
Profit on sale of investment		9,500	1.27%
Profit before Tax		2,90,500	38.73%
Less: Provision for Tax		50,000	6.67%
Profit after Tax		2,40,500	32.06

Interpretation:

1. Total operating expenses is 1/4th of cost of goods sold (*i.e.*, 87,500: 3,65,000). This is a satisfactory position.
2. Total Non-operating income is less than total non-operating expenses. This is not a satisfactory position.
3. Profitable percentage of 32.06% is considered to be good percentage.

Problem 14 (Common-Size Balance Sheet): Following are the Balance sheets of Vinay Ltd. for the year ended December 1996 and 1997.

Liabilities	*1996*	*1997*	*Assets*	*1996*	*1997*
Equity capital	1,00,000	1,65,000	Fixed Assets (Net)	1,20,000	1,75,000
Pref. capital	50,000	75,000			
Reserves	10,000	15,000	Stock	20,000	25,000
P & L a/c	7,500	10,000	Debtors	50,000	62,500
Bank O.D	25,000	25,000	Bills receivable	10,000	30,000
Creditors	20,000	25,000	Prepaid expense	5,000	6,000
Provision for Taxaction	10,000	12,500	Cash at Bank	20,000	26,500
Proposed dividend	7,500	12,500	Cash in hand	5,000	15,000
	2,30,000	3,40,000		2,30,000	3,40,000

Prepare a common-size balance sheet and interpret the same. (*Osmania University, B. Com., March 1999*)

Solution: **Common-size Balance Sheet of Vinay Ltd. for the year 1996 and 1997.**

	1996		*1997*	
	Rs.	*%*	*Rs.*	*%*
Assets				
Fixed Assets (Net) (*A*)	1,20,000	52.17	1,75,000	51.47
Current Assets:				
Stock	20,000	8.70	25,000	7.35
Debtors	50,000	21.74	62,500	18.38
Bills Receivable	10,000	4.34	30,000	8.82
Prepaid expenses	5,000	2.17	6,000	1.78
Cash at Bank	20,000	8.70	26,500	7.79
Cash in hand	5,000	2.18	15,000	4.41
Total (*B*)	1,10,000	47.83	1,65,000	48.53
Total Assets (*A* + *B*)	2,30,000	100.00	3,40,000	100
Liabilities:				
Capital and Reserves: (*A*)				
Equity capital	1,00,000	43.58	1,65,000	48.53
Preference capital	50,000	21.74	75,000	22.05
Reserves	10,000	4.34	15,000	4.41
P & L a/c	7,500	3.26	10,000	2.95
Total (*A*)	1,67,500	72.82	2,65,000	77.94
Current liabilities: (*B*)				
Bank overdraft	25,000	10.87	25,000	7.35
Creditors	20,000	8.70	25,000	7.35
Provision for taxation	10,000	4.35	12,500	3.68
Proposed dividend	7,500	3.26	12,500	3.68
Total (*B*)	62,500	27.18	75,000	22.06
Total liabilities (*A*) + (*B*)	2,30,000	100	3,40,000	100

Interpretation:

1. Current Assets increased from 47.83% to 48.53%. Whereas current liabilities decreased from 27.18% to 22.06%. The liquidity position is reasonably good.
2. Fixed assets increased from Rs. 1,20,000 to Rs. 1,75,000. They were purchased from the additional share capital issued.

Problem 15: Following are the Balance sheets of 'S' Ltd. for the year ending December 31, 1992 and 1993.

Liabilities	*1992*	*1993*
Equity share capital	40,000	60,000
Reserves and surplus	31,200	35,400
Debentures	5,000	10,000
Mortgage	15,000	25,500
Sundry creditor	25,500	11,700
Other current liabilities	700	1,000
	1,17,400	1,43,600
Assets:		
Land and Building	27,000	17,000
Plant and Machinery	31,000	78,600

Furniture and Fixtures	900	1,800
Other fixed assets	2,000	3,000
Long term loans	4,600	5,900
Cash in hand	11,800	1,000
Sundry Debtors	20,900	19,000
Inventory	16,000	13,000
Prepaid Expenses	300	300
Other current assets	2,500	4,000
	1,17,400	1,43,600

Analyse the financial position of the company with the help of common-size balance sheet.

(*S. V. University, B. Com., October 1999*)

Solution: **Comparative common-size Balance Sheets of 'S' Ltd. as on 31-12-92 and 31-12-93**

	1992		*1993*	
	Amount	*%*	*Amount*	*%*
Assets:				
(1) Fixed Assets:				
Land and Buildings	27,000	23%	17,000	11.84%
Plant and Machinery	31,000	26.40%	78,600	54.74%
Furniture and Fixtures	900	0.77%	1,800	1.25%
Other Fixed Assets	2,000	1.70%	3,000	2.08%
Total Fixed Assets	60,900	51.87%	1,00,400	69.91%
(2) Investments:				
Long term loans	4,600	3.92%	5,900	4.11%
(3) Current Assets:				
Cash in hand	11,800	10.05%	1,000	0.70%
Sundry Debtors	20,900	17.80%	19,000	13.23%
Inventory	16,000	13.63%	13,000	9.05%
Prepaid expenses	300	0.26%	300	0.21%
Other current assets	2,900	2.47%	4,000	2.79%
	51,900	44.21%	37,300	25.98%
Total Assets (1 + 2 + 3)	1,17,400	100%	1,43,600	100%
Liabilities:				
(1) Shareholders funds:				
Equity share capital	40,000	34.07%	60,000	41.78%
Reserves and Surplus	31,200	26.58%	35,400	24.65%
	71,200	60.65%	95,400	66.43%
(2) Long term Debts:				
Debentures	5,000	4.25%	10,000	6.96%
Mortgages	15,000	12.78%	25,500	17.76
	20,000	17.03%	35,500	24.72%
(3) Current liabilities:				
Sundry creditors	25,500	21.72%	11,700	8.15%
Other current liabilities	700	0.60%	1,000	0.70%
	26,200	22.32%	12,700	8.85%

Interpretation:

1. There is drastic fall in the working capital. In the year 1992 it was 21.89 (44.21 – 22.32) and in the year 1993 it was 17.13% (25.98 – 8.85).
2. The liquid assets also have come down which has adversely affected the business.
3. Fixed Assets have increased in 1993, the increase being 18.04% (69.91 – 51.87). This raise in fixed assets is financed partly by raising shareholder's funds and long term loans and partly by diversion from working capital, *i.e.*, 4.57%. The latter is not acceptable.
4. Reserves and Surplus have diminished in 1993, i.e., from 26.58% to 24.65%. This is not a welcome sign.

Problem 16 (Common-size Balance sheet–Vertical Method): Prepare a common-size balance sheet of M/s Ram Ltd. in vertical form from the following information and comment on it.

Balances as on 31.3.1999

	Rs.
Land and Building	6,00,000
Plant and Machinery	5,00,000
Equity capital	5,00,000
Preference capital	2,00,000
Stock	2,40,000
Debtors	2,00,000
Cash and Bank	55,000
Miscellaneous current assets	5,000
Profit and loss a/c (cr. balance)	2,00,000
General reserve	1,00,000
Sundry creditors	80,000
Bills payable	60,000
Miscellaneous current liabilities	60,000
Debentures	4,00,000

(*University of Bombay, B. Com., October 1999*)

Solution: **Common-size Balance Sheet as on 31-December 1999**

	Amount	*Percentage*
Sources of Funds:		
I. Shareholders funds:		
(*A*) Share capital–Equity	5,00,000	35.71%
–Preference	2,00,000	14.29%
(*A*)	7,00,000	50%
(*B*) Reserves and Surplus:		
P & L a/c	2,00,000	14.29%
General Reserve	1,00,000	7.14%
(*B*)	3,00,000	21.43%
II. Long term loan:		
Debentures	4,00,000	28.57
Total funds employed (*A* + *B* + *C*)	14,00,000	100%

Application of funds:		
(*A*) Fixed Assets:		
Land and Building	6,00,000	42.86%
Plant and Machinery	5,00,000	35.71%
(*A*)	11,00,000	78.57%
(*B*) Current Assets:		
Stock	2,40,000	17.14%
Debtors	2,00,000	14.29%
Cash and Bank55,000	55,000	3.93%
Miscellaneous current assets	5,000	0.36%
(*B*)	5,00,000	35.71%
(*C*) Current liabilities:		
Sundry creditors	80,000	5.71%
Bills payable	60,000	4.29%
Miscellaneous current liabilities	60,000	4.28%
(*C*)	2,00,000	14.28%
Working capital $(B - C) = D$	3,00,000	21.43%
Total funds employed $A + D$	14,00,000	100%

Interpretation:

1. Proprietors funds constitute 71.43% (50 + 21.43%) of total fund employed.
2. Fixed assets which constitute 78.57% are financed by proprietor's funds indicate sound financial position.
3. Currents assets are higher than current liabilities.

Problem 17 (Common-size Income and position statement): Shiv Leela Ltd. furnishes you with the following financial statement.

Balance sheet as on 31st March 1999

Share capital:				
Equity	1,00,000	Building	2,00,000	
12% preference	50,000	Less Depreciation	15,000	
				1,85,000
Reserves and Surplus	35,000	Short term Investments		40,000
10% Debentures				
(Secured by Mortgage)	50,000			
Bills payable	15,000	Stock		35,000
Creditors for goods	20,000	Debtors		30,000
Outstanding expenses	10,000	Bank		10,000
Provision for taxation	10,000			
Proposed Dividend	10,000			
	3,00,000			3,00,000

Profit and Loss a/c for the year ended 31-3-1999

To Opening stock	30,000	By sales	3,00,000
To Purchases	1,80,000	By closing stock	35,000

To Expenses:		
Administration	25,000	
Selling	30,000	
Financing	5,000	
To Depreciation	150,000	
To Provision for Taxation	10,000	
To Proposed Dividend	10,000	
To Balance a/c	30,000	
	3,35,000	3,35,000

You are required to:

1. Convert the above into common-size statements in vertical form.
2. Comment on above briefly.

(University of Bombay, B. Com., April 1999)

Solution: **Common-size Income Statement for the year ended 31st March 1999**

			Amount	*Percentage*
Sales			3,00,000	100%
Less: Cost of goods sold				
Opening stock	30,000			
Add: Purchases	1,80,000			
	2,10,000			
Less: Closing stock	35,000			
			1,75,000	58.33%
Gross profit			1,25,000	41.67%
Less: Overheads:				
Administrative (25,000 + 15,000)		40,000		
Selling		30,000		
Financing		5,000		
			75,000	25.60%
Net profit before tax			50,000	16.67%
Less: Income tax			10,000	3.33%
Net profit after tax			40,000	13.34%
Less: Dividend			10,000	3.34%
Retained Earnings			30,000	10.00%

Interpretation:

1. Gross profit is quite high as compared to overheads. This shows efficiency of business.
2. When compared to sales, cost of goods sold is 58.33% which indicates high profitability.

Common-size Balance sheet for the year ended 31st March 1999

	Amount	*Percentage*
Sources of Funds:		
(1) Shareholders funds:		
Equity share capital	1,00,000	42.55%
12% preference share capital	50,000	21.28%
Reserves and Surplus	35,000	14.89%
	1,85,000	78.72%

(2) Loan funds:			
10% Debentures		50,000	21.28%
Total funds		2,35,000	100%
Application of funds:			
(1) Fixed Assets:			
Buildings	2,00,000		
Less Depreciation	15,000		
		1,85,000	78.72%
(2) Current Assets:			
Short term investments		40,000	17.02%
Stock		35,000	14.89%
Debtors		30,000	12.77%
Bank		10,000	4.26%
		1,15,000	48.94%
(3) Current liabilities:			
Creditors		20,000	8.51%
Bills payable		15,000	6.38%
Outstanding expenses		10,000	4.26%
Taxation		10,000	4.26%
Dividend		10,000	4.25%
		65,000	27.66%
Working capital (2 – 3) = 4		50,000	21.28%
Total funds (1 + 4)		2,35,000	100%

Interpretation:

1. Investment of proprietors funds is very high.
2. Fixed Assets are very high compared to current assets.
3. Current Ratio is high and it shows sound financial position.

TREND ANALYSIS OF TREND RATIOS

Trend ratios can be defined as the index numbers of the movements of the various financial items on the financial statement for a number of periods. It is a statistical device applied in the analysis of financial statements to reveal the trend of the items with the passage of time. They provide a horizontal analysis of comparative statements and reflect the behaviour of various items with passage of time. The trend ratios are the useful analytical device for management since by substitution of percentages for large amounts, the brevity and readability is achieved. It can be graphically presented for a better understanding by the management. They are very useful in predicting the behaviour of the various financial factors in future. Sometimes trends are significantly affected by external causes over which the organisation has no control. Such factors are Government policies, economic conditions, change in income and its distribution etc.

Points to be considered in calculation of trend ratios:

(*i*) The accounting principles and practices followed should be constant throughout the period for which analysis is made.

(*ii*) Trend ratios should be calculated only for items having logical relationship with one another.

(*iii*) There should be financial statement for a number of years.

(*iv*) Take one of the statements as the base with reference to which all other statements are to be studied but the selected base statements should belong to a normal year.

(*v*) Every item in the base statement should be stated as 100.

(*vi*) Trend Ratios of each item in other statement is calculated with reference to same item in the base statement by using the following formula.

$$\frac{\text{Absolute value of item in the statement under study}}{\text{Absolute value of the same item in base statement}} \times 100$$

Problem 18: From the following data, calculate trend percentage (taking 1995 as base).

	1995 *Rs.*	*1996* *Rs.*	*1997* *Rs.*
Sales	50,000	75,000	1,00,000
Purchases	40,000	60,000	72,000
Expenses	5,000	8,000	15,000
Profit	5,000	7,000	13,000

(*Osmania University, B. Com., March 1999*)

Solution:

Statement Showing Trend Percentages

Particulars	*1995* *Rs.*	*1996* *Rs.*	*1997* *Rs.*	*Trend percentages (Base 1995)*		
				1995	*1996*	*1997*
Purchases	40,000	60,000	72,000	100	150	180
Expenses	5,000	8,000	15,000	100	160	300
Profit	5,000	7,000	13,000	100	140	260
Sales	50,000	75,000	1,00,000	100	150	200

Problem 19: From the following data, calculate trend percentages (1995 as the base).

	1995 *Rs.*	*1996* *Rs.*	*1997* *Rs.*
Cash	200	240	160
Debtors	400	500	650
Stock	600	800	700
Other current asset	450	600	750
Land	800	1,000	1,000
Buildings	1,600	2,000	2,400
Plant	2,000	2,000	2,400

(*Osmania University, B. Com., October 1998*)

Solution: **Statement Showing Trend Percentages (Base year 1995)**

Assets	*1995*	*1996*	*1997*	*Trend percentages*		
	Rs.	*Rs.*	*Rs.*	*1995*	*1996*	*1997*
Fixed Assets:						
Land	800	1,000	1,000	100	125	125
Building	1,600	2,000	2,400	100	125	150
Plant	2,000	2,000	2,400	100	100	120
Total	4,400	5,000	5,800	100	114	132
Current Assets:						
Cash	200	240	160	100	120	80
Debtors	400	500	650	100	125	163
Stock	600	800	700	100	133	117
Other current assets	450	600	750	100	133	167
Total current assets	1,650	2,140	2,260	100	130	137

Problem 20: Calculate Trend percentages from the following information extracted from the financial statements of different entities. Give your appropriate comments on each statement.

(*a*) *Assets:*	*1992*	*1993*	*1994*	*1995*
	Rs.	*Rs.*	*Rs.*	*Rs.*
Fixed Assets	2,11,696	2,08,694	2,04,580	1,84,122
Investments	20,000	15,000	10,000	9,000
Cash in hand	41,680	30,472	20,346	18,312
Sundry Debtors	1,85,040	1,31,346	85,750	77,175
Stock	1,31,474	1,34,684	1,45,172	1,30,655
Prepaid expenses	1,690	3,236	2,440	2,196
	5,91,580	5,23,432	4,68,288	4,21,460
Liabilities:				
Sundry creditors	1,40,712	1,32,684	1,17,410	1,05,669
Liability for expenses	5,640	4,094	2,490	2,240
Share capital	4,45,228	3,86,654	3,48,388	3,13,551
	5,91,580	5,23,432	4,68,288	4,21,460

(*b*)	*1994*	*1995*	*1996*	*1997*
	Rs.	*Rs.*	*Rs.*	*Rs.*
Sales	9,880	13,640	16,400	18,040
Cost of Sales	8,810	12,490	14,970	16,460
Expenses	50	130	80	100
Indirect expenses	200	370	500	540
Tax	450	190	390	450
Profit	?	?	?	?

(*University of Bombay, B. Com., October 1999*)

Solution: **Statement Showing Trend Percentages**

Particulars	*Amount (Rs.)*				*Trend percentages*			
	1992	*1993*	*1994*	*1995*	*1992*	*1993*	*1994*	*1995*
Assets:								
Fixed Assets	2,11,696	2,08,694	2,04,580	1,84,122	100	98.58	96.64	86.97
Investments	20,000	15,000	10,000	9,000	100	75.00	50.00	45.00

Cash in hand	41,680	30,472	20,346	18,312	100	73.11	48.81	43.93
Sundry Debtors	1,85,040	1,31,346	85,750	77,175	100	70.98	46.34	41.71
Stock	1,31,474	1,34,684	1,45,172	1,30,655	100	102.44	110.42	99.38
Prepaid expenses	1,690	3,236	2,440	2,196	100	191.48	144.38	129.94
	5,91,580	5,23,432	4,68,288	4,21,460	100	88.44	79.15	71.24
Liabilities:								
Share capital	4,45,228	3,86,654	3,48,388	3,13,551	100	86.84	78.25	70.42
Sundry creditors	1,40,712	1,32,684	1,17,410	1,05,669	100	94.29	83.44	75.10
Liability for expenses	5,640	4,094	2,490	2,240	100	72.59	44.15	39.72
	5,91,580	5,23,432	4,68,288	4,21,460	100	88.48	79.15	71.24

Interpretation:

1. Share capital has reduced to 70.42% which means it includes redeemable preference shares which is redeemed in instalments.
2. During the last four years no new fixed assets were purchased.
3. Compared to the year 1992, the investments to the extant of 55% was sold to raise funds in the year 1995.
4. Cash and stock position has gone down to about 50% in 1995 compared to the year 1992.
5. It seems that company has reduced its operation. This is evident by the redemption of shares.

(*b*) **Trend Percentage**

Particulars	*Amount (in Rs.)*				*Trend percentage*			
	1994	*1995*	*1996*	*1997*	*1994*	*1995*	*1996*	*1997*
Sales	9,880	13,640	16,400	18,040	100	138.06	165.99	182.59
Less: Cost of sales	8,810	12,490	14,970	16,460	100	141.77	169.92	186.83
Gross profit (*A*)	1,070	1,150	1,430	1,580	100	107.48	133.64	147.66
Less: Expenses:								
Expenses	50	130	80	100	100	260	160	200
Interest expenses	200	370	500	540	100	185	250	270
Tax	450	190	390	450	100	42.22	86.67	100
Total (*B*)	700	690	970	1,090	100	98.57	138.57	155.71
Net profit (*A* – *B*)	370	460	460	490	100	124.32	124.32	132.43

Problem 21: Calculate the Trend percentages from the following figures of X Ltd. taking 1995 as the base and interpret them.

(*Rs. in Lakhs*)

Year	*Sales*	*Stock*	*P B T*
1995	1,881	709	321
1996	2,340	781	435
1997	2,655	816	458
1998	3,021	944	527
1999	3,768	1,154	672

(*Bangalore University, B. Com., October 2000*)

Solution: **Statement Showing Trend percentage (Base year 1995)**

Year	*Sales*		*Stock*		*Profit before Tax*	
	Amount	*Trend percentage*	*Amount*	*Trend percentage*	*Amount*	*Trend percentage*
1995	1,881	100	709	100	321	100
1996	2,340	124	781	110	435	136
1997	2,655	141	816	115	458	143
1998	3,021	161	944	133	527	164
1999	3,768	200	1,154	162	672	209

Interpretation:

1. The sales have continuously increased in all the years upto 1999. The percentage in 1999 is 2000 as compared to 100 in 1995. The increase in sales is quite satisfactory.
2. The figure of stock have also increased from 1995 to 1999. This implies the increased production capacity of the business.
3. Profit before tax has substantially increased. In the five year period it has more than doubled. The comparative increase in profit is much higher in 1998 and 1999 as compared to that in 1997.

Problem 22 (Calculation of missing information using trend percentages): On the basis of the following balances as at 31st December 1995 extracted from the books of Alpha Ltd. You are required to:

(*a*) Calculate trend statement for the year 31st December 1995, 1996 and 1997.

(*b*) Give your interpretation on the same.

Base Year

Particulars	*Balance as on 31-12-95*	*Trend as on 31-12-95*	*Balance as on 31-12-96*	*Trend as on 31-12-96*	*Balance as on 31-12-97*	*Trend as on 31-12-97*
Fixed Assets	1,60,000	100	?	150	?	200
Less: Depreciation						
Provision	60,000	100	?	150	?	250
Net Fixed Assets	1,00,000	100	?	150	?	170
Current Assets:						
Stock	3,00,000	100	?	120	?	140
Debtors	4,50,000	100	?	120	?	160
Bank Balance	1,00,000	100	?	80	?	110
Short term advance	?	?	?	?	?	?
Total current Assets	10,00,000	100	?	110	?	130
Less: Current liabilities	3,00,000	100	?	120	?	144
Working capital	?	?	?	?	?	?
Capital employed	?	?	?	?	?	?
Debentures	4,00,000	100	?	75	?	50
Net worth	?	?	?	?	?	?

(*University of Bombay, April 1998*)

Calculation of Trend statements as on December 1995, 1996, 1997

	31.12.95		31.12.96		31.12.97	
	Rs.	*Trend*	*Rs.*	*Trend*	*Rs.*	*Trend*
Fixed Assets	1,60,000	100	2,40,000	150	3,20,000	200
Less: Depreciation						
Provision	60,000	100	90,000	150	1,50,000	250
Net fixed Assets	1,00,000	100	1,50,000	150	1,70,000	170
Current Assets:						
Stock	3,00,000	100	3,60,000	120	4,20,000	140
Debtors	4,50,000	100	5,40,000	120	7,20,000	160
Bank Balance	1,00,000	100	80,000	80	1,10,000	110
Short term advance	1,50,000	100	2,20,000	146.67	1,90,000	126.67
Total current Assets	10,00,000	100	12,00,000	120	14,40,000	144
Less: Current liabilities	(–)3,00,000	100	(–)3,30,000	110	(–)3,90,000	130
Working capital	7,00,000	100	8,70,000	124.29	10,50,000	150
Capital employed	8,00,000	100	10,20,000	127.50	12,20,000	152.50
Less: Debentures	4,00,000	100	3,00,000	75.00	2,00,000	50
Net worth	4,00,000	100	7,20,000	180	10,20,000	225

QUESTIONS

Simple Questions

1. What is meant by financial analysis?
2. Distinguish between 'analysis' and 'interpretation' of financial statements.
3. What is meant by external analysis of financial statements?
4. What is meant by internal analysis of financial statements?
5. What is meant by horizontal analysis of financial statements?
6. What is meant by vertical analysis of financial statements?
7. List out the various methods of financial analysis.
8. What is meant by comparative statements?
9. What is a common-size statement?
10. What is trend analysis?

Short Answer Questions

1. "Decisions taken on the basis of financial statements may not be regarded as final and accurate"– Comment.
2. Write an analytical note on comparative income statement and state the procedure of computing them.
3. "The significance of financial statements lies not in their preparation but in their analysis and interpretation"– Comment.
4. Write an analytical note on common-size statements and state the procedure of computing it.
5. Briefly analyse the importance of "Trend percentages" as a tool of financial analysis and state the procedure of computing it.
6. Explain the procedure of financial statement analysis.
7. State the limitations of financial analysis.

Exercise 1 (Comparative Financial Statements): Balance sheet of RT Ltd, as on 31st December 1994 and 1995 is given below:

	1995	*1996*		*1995*	*1996*
Preference share capital	–	4,00,000	Fixed Assets	7,00,000	10,00,000
Equity share capital	5,00,000	5,00,000	Investments (at cost)	1,00,000	1,20,000

Reserves and surplus	1,35,000	1,71,500	Stock	1,50,000	1,80,000
12% Debentures	2,00,000	–	Debtors	2,36,000	2,44,000
Bank O.D	50,000	80,000	Cash	24,000	2,500
Sundry creditors	1,50,000	1,25,000			
Provision for taxation	75,000	1,20,000			
Proposed dividend	1,00,000	1,50,000			
	12,10,000	15,46,000		12,10,000	15,46,000

Prepare a comparative financial statement.

(University of Bombay, B. Com., October 1996)

Exercise 2: The Balance sheets of Santhosh Ltd. is as follows:

	1993 (Rs.)	*1994 (Rs.)*
Liabilities:		
Equity share capital	2,00,000	2,50,000
10% pref. share capital	2,00,000	1,50,000
Reserve fund	80,000	1,00,000
P & L a/c	1,00,000	1,50,000
12% Debentures	2,00,000	3,00,000
Creditors	1,00,000	1,20,000
Bank O.D.	50,000	20,000
	9,30,000	10,90,000
Assets:		
Buildings	3,00,000	3,20,000
Machinery	1,50,000	1,80,000
Furniture	40,000	35,000
Investments	1,00,000	1,50,000
Stock	1,50,000	2,00,000
Debtors	1,00,000	1,20,000
Cash at Bank	90,000	85,000
	9,30,000	10,90,000

You are required to comment on the financial position of business with the help of comparative Balance sheet Technique. *(Bangalore University, B. Com., April 1996)*

Exercise 3: From the following profit and loss account and balance sheet of Radha industries, prepare a comparative income statement and a comparative balance sheet.

Profit & loss A/c (Rs. in lacs)

	1992 Rs.	*1993 Rs.*		*1992 Rs.*	*1993 Rs.*
To Cost of goods sold	500	640	By sales	700	900
To Operating expenses:					
Administrative expenses	20	20			
Selling expenses	30	40			
To Net profit	150	200			
	700	900		700	900

Balance sheet as on 31st December (Rs. in lacs)

	1992	*1993*		*1992*	*1993*
Bills payable	50	75	Cash	50	70
Tax payable	100	150	Debtors	300	450
Sundry creditors	150	200	Stock	100	200
Debentures	100	150	Land	100	120
Pref. share capital	300	300	Buildings	200	180
Equity share capital	200	200	Machinery	250	225
Reserves	200	250	Furniture	100	80
	1,100	1,325		1,100	1,325

(*University of Madras, B. Com., September 1994*)

Exercise 4 (Common-size Financial Statements): From the following particulars prepare a common-size income statement and interpret changes in 1996 as compared to 1995.

(*Amount in lakhs of Rs.*)

	1995	*1996*
Net Sales	600	800
Cost of goods sold	400	500
Gross profit	200	300
Operating expenses	40	50
Operating profit	160	250
Non-operating income	20	25
Non-operating expenses	30	40
Net profit	150	235

(*Bangalore University, B. Com., April 2001*)

Exercise 5: The profit and loss account of a company is given below:

P & L A/c

	1997	*1998*		*1997*	*1998*
To Cost of goods sold	600	750	By Net sales	800	1,000
			By Non-operating Income	50	100
To *Operating expenses:*					
Administration expenses	30	40			
Selling expenses	40	50			
To Non-operating expenses	30	40			
To Net profit	150	220			
	850	1,100		850	1,100

You are required to prepare a common-size income statement and interpret the changes.

(*Bangalore University, B. Com., April 2000*)

Exercise 6: Following are the two Balance Sheets on two different dates rearrange them in vertical form and prepare common-size statements.

	1993	*1994*		*1993*	*1994*
Equity share capital	2,25,000	2,62,500	Good will	45,000	35,250
General Reserve	15,000	22,500	Machinery	67,500	1,43,250
Capital Reserve	–	18,750	Building	75,000	56,250
P & L a/c	13,500	20,250	Long term Investment	7,500	26,250

Creditors	33,000	48,750	Stock	63,750	58,500
Provision for Tax	21,000	24,000	Debtors	45,000	67,500
Proposed Dividend	20,250	24,750	Bank	12,750	21,000
			Bills Receivable	11,250	13,500
	3,27,750	4,21,500		3,27,750	4,21,500

(University of Bombay, B. Com., October 1998)

Exercise 7: Following are the Balance sheets of Shanti & Co. and Sheela & Co. as on 31.12.1999.

Liabilities:	*Shanti & Co.* *Rs.*	*Sheela & Co.* *Rs.*
Equity share capital	3,00,000	1,50,000
Preference share capital	1,75,000	1,30,000
Reserves and Surplus	1,20,000	1,20,000
Debentures	4,55,000	2,50,000
Creditors	25,000	9,000
Bills payable	30,000	15,000
	11,05,000	6,74,000
Assets:		
Land	3,00,000	2,00,000
Building	3,00,000	1,20,000
Machinery	2,00,000	1,50,000
Investments	80,000	44,000
Debtors	1,70,000	1,40,000
Cash	55,000	20,000
	11,05,000	6,74,000

Compare the financial position of the two companies with the help of common-size Balance sheets are comment. *(Bangalore University, B. Com., April 2000)*

Exercise 8: The summarised Balance sheet of two companies are as follows:

Balance sheet as on 31.3.1998

	Top Ltd.	*Ten Ltd.*		*Top Ltd.*	*Ten Ltd.*
Equity share capital	1,20,000	3,50,000	Fixed Assets	2,45,000	4,10,000
10% Pref. shares capital	1,00,000	50,000	Current Assets	2,90,500	3,32,800
Reserves	1,40,000	56,000	Preliminary expenses	10,000	6,000
15% Debentures	50,000	50,000			
Current liabilities	1,35,500	2,42,800			
	5,45,500	7,48,800		5,45,500	7,48,800

Revenue Statement for the year 31.3.1998

	Top Ltd. *(Rs.)*	*Ten Ltd.* *(Rs.)*
Sales	10,00,000	12,00,000
Less: Cost of sales	6,00,000	8,00,000
	4,00,000	4,00,000
Less: Operating expenses (including interest)	1,40,000	2,05,000

Less: Non-cash operating expenses (Depreciation)	10,000	20,000
	2,50,000	1,75,000
Less: Taxes	1,00,000	70,000
Less: Dividend	70,000	75,000
Retained earnings	80,000	30,000

Prepare:

(*a*) Common-size balance sheet (in vertical form).

(*b*) Common-size income statement (in vertical form).

(*c*) Comment in brief.

(*University of Bombay, B. Com., April 1998*)

Exercise 9: From the following financial statements of loyal limited prepare common-size financial statements and give your comments on them.

P & L a/c for the year ended 31-3-1996

To Opening stock	4,00,000	By sales	20,00,000
To Purchases	12,00,000	By closing stock	6,00,000
To Wages	2,50,000		
To Factory overheads	2,50,000		
To G. P. cld.	5,00,000		
	26,00,000		26,00,000
To Administrative expenses	75,000	By G. P. bld.	5,00,000
To Selling and Distribution expenses	50,000	By Dividend	30,00
To Depreciation	65,000		
To Interest on Debentures	20,000		
To Net profit cld.	3,20,000		
	5,30,000		5,30,000
To Preference dividend	15,000	By Balance bld.	2,00,000
To Provision for tax (1996)	1,05,000	By Net profit bld.	3,20,000
To Surplus to Balance sheet	4,00,000		
	5,20,000		5,20,000

Balance sheet as on 31-3-1996

Equity share capital	10,00,000	Good will	5,00,000
Pref. share capital	5,00,000	Plant and Machinery	5,00,000
General Reserve	1,00,000	Land and Building	8,00,000
P & L a/c Balance	4,00,000	Furniture	1,00,000
Provision for Tax	1,05,000	Stock	5,00,000
Bills payable	1,95,000	Bills Receivable	80,000
Bank overdraft	1,00,000	Debtors	2,00,000
Creditors	5,00,000	Bank	2,20,000
	29,00,000		29,00,000

(*University of Bombay, B. Com., October 1997*)

Exercise 10 (Trend Analysis): From the following information interpret the results of operations of a manufacturing concern using Trend ratios-use 1995 as base.

(*Amount in lakh of Rs.*)

Particulars	*1995*	*1996*	*1997*	*1998*
Net sales	100	95	120	130
Cost of goods sold	60	58.90	69.60	72.80
Gross profit	40	36.10	50.40	57.20
Operating expenses	10	9.70	11.00	12
Net operating profit	30	26.40	39.40	45.20

(*Bangalore University, B. Com., April 2001*)

Exercise 11: Calculate Trend percentages.

	1994 Rs.	*1995* Rs.	*1996* Rs.
Sales	50,000	75,000	1,00,000
Purchases	40,000	60,000	72,000
Expenses	5,000	8,000	15,000
Profit	5,000	7,000	13,000

(*Osmania University, B. Com., March 1998*)

Exercise 12: Pass and Fail are partners of a firm carrying on business.

(*i*) **Their position as on 31st December 1992, 1993 and 1994 are as follows:**

	1994	*1993*	*1992*		*1994*	*1993*	*1992*
Partners capital a/c	4,00,000	3,40,000	3,00,000	Fixed Assets	4,00,000	3,60,000	2,80,000
General Reserve	1,00,000	1,00,000	1,00,000	Current Assets:			
Secured loans	60,000	60,000	50,000	Stock	1,60,000	1,50,000	1,35,000
Unsecured loans	1,60,000	1,80,000	1,40,000	Debtors	2,00,000	1,60,000	1,40,000
Sundry Creditors	1,60,000	90,000	45,000	Loans and advances	1,00,000	80,000	60,000
				Bank	20,000	20,000	20,000
	8,80,000	7,70,000	6,35,000		8,80,000	7,70,000	6,35,000

(*ii*) **Summarised Income Statement for the year ended**

	31-12-94 Rs.	*31-12-93* Rs.	*31-12-92* Rs.
Sales	40,00,000	36,00,000	30,00,000
Less: Cost of sales	28,00,000	24,00,000	20,00,000
Gross profit	12,00,000	12,00,000	10,00,000
Less: Expenses	8,00,000	8,00,000	7,00,000
Net profit	4,00,000	4,00,000	3,00,000

Work out trend percentages and give your interpretation on the same.

(*University of Bombay, B. Com., October 1995*)

4

RATIO ANALYSIS

INTRODUCTION

Ratio analysis is the process of determining and interpreting numerical relationship based on financial statements. It is the technique of interpretation of financial statements with the help of accounting ratios derived from the balance sheet and profit & loss account. It involves the comparision of existing ratios against standards established. The standards may be set by management as goals expressed in the budgets (i.e., budgetary standard) or may be historical figures showing performance of the same concern in the past (*i.e.* historical standard) or may be figures reflecting the performance of other companies (*i.e.*, industrial or market standard.)

Meaning of Accounting Ratios

A ratio is simply one number expressed in terms of another, it is an expression of relationship spelt out by dividing one figure by another. It is the quotient of two arthmetical numbers obtained from financial statements. Wixon, Kell and Bedford in their book 'Accountant's Handbook' define ratio, as "an expression of the quantitative relationship between two numbers. According to J. Batty the term accounting ratio is used to describe the significant relationship which exists between figures shown in a balance sheet and profit and loss account in a budgetary control system or any other part of accounting organisation.

Nature of Accounting Ratios

Ratios are indicators, sometimes they serve as pointers but not in themselves powerful tools of management. The ratios help to summarise the large quantities of financial data and to make qualitative judgement about the firm's financial performance.

Thorough ratios are indicators, too much reliance should not be put on the figures arrived at by the ratios. They can not be taken as the final result regarding good or bad financial position of the business. They are at best symptoms and there is always a need to investigate the facts revealed by them further. Hence ratios alone are not adequate for taking a financial decision. Infact, it must be used for what they are financial tools. Quite often ratios are looked upon as ends in themselves rather than as means to on end. The value of a ratio should not be regarded as good or bad among themselves. It may be an indication that a firm is weak or strong in a particular area but it must never be taken as a powerful tool of management.

Ratios as a matter of fact tools of quantitative analysis and it is quite possible that quantitative factors may override numerical aspects with the consequence that the conclusions from the ratio analysis may get distorted. In a way ratios are an attempt to delve in past as financial statements, (from which ratios are derived), are historical documents. But in a modern business, it is more important to have an idea of the probable happening in future rather than, those in the past. These factors emphasise that ratios themselves are not powerful tools of management.

Mode of Expressing Accounting Ratios

Accounting ratios can be expressed in various ways, such as:

(*a*) Pure ratio, say ratio of current assets to current liabilities is 2: 1, or

(*b*) a rate, say current results are 2 times current liabilities

(*c*) a percentage, Say, current assets are 200% of current tiabitites.

Each method of expression has a distinct advantage over the other. The analyst will select that method which best suits his convenience and purpose. There are certain accounting ratios which can be best expressed if stated as a pure ratio, *eg*., debt-equity ratio, current ratio etc. Some other ratios can be best expressed as a rate only, *eg*. stock turnover ratio, debtors, turnover ratio etc. While some others can most advantageously be expressed as a percentage only eg. gross profit ratio, operating ratio etc. Ratios are expressed in such a way that the first appears as the numerator and the second as the denominator.

Interpretation of Ratios

The significance of Ratio analysis lies in proper interpretation of the related items calculation by ratios as a step of ratio analysis is a simple task and it is a clerical work. Interpretation of ratios which is the ultimate step is difficult process and requires knowledge, intelligence and skill. The following are the various ways of interpreting accounting ratios.

(1) Single absolute ratio: A Ratio taken in isolation may not convey much meaning. If it is expressed in relation to another aspect it may prove to be more useful. For example if current ratio is less than one, it may reveal the insolvency position of the business, *i.e.*, current assets are not sufficient to pay current liabilitites sometimes a single ratio may fail to show the exact financial position of business.

(2) Group ratios: When group of ratios are calculated and interpreted they convey better idea about the business operation and efficiency for example, in addition to calculating current ratio, *i.e.*, current asset to current liabilities if liquid ratio, *i.e.*, liquid asset to liquid liabilities, is also used, it throws better light on the business.

(3) Historical comparision—Under this method of interpretation, the ratios of current period is companed with ratios of past year or years. Comparision of ratios over a period of time gives better indication and sets a trend which again reflects the performance and position of the business. However, care must be taken to ensure that there is no change in accounting policy and procedure during the period of comparision.

(4) Inter-firm comparision—Under this method, the ratios of one firm is compared with ratios of other firm belonging to the same industry. But this method may prove to be ineffective when different firms use different accounting policies and procedure.

(5) Projected ratios—Sometimes ratios can be calculated based on estimated financial statements. In which case they constitute standard ratios. The actual ratios are compared with standard ratios. The variance in ratios indicate the success or failure of the business.

Uses or Utility of Ratios

Ratio analysis is one of most important tools of analysing and interpreting the financial statements. It helps in understanding the financial health and trend of a business. Its past performance enables to forecast the future state of affairs of the business. It reveals the symptoms of a business as in the case of a patients temperative. Blood pressure or pulse beat which indicates the symptoms of disease in a patient. The utility of ratio analysis can be explained under the following headings:

(1) Utility to management: Management of a business uses ratio analysis in: (*a*) formulating the policies, (*b*) in making decisions, (*c*) Evaluating the performance, (*d*) in knowing the trends of the business, (*e*) in planning and forecasting the future, (*f*) communicating, (*g*) controlling.

(2) Utility to shareholders and investors: An investor would assess the financial position of a business before he invests his money in it. All investors are interested in the safety, security and profitability of their investments. Ratios enable the prospective investors to select best companies to invest their finds. The shareholders of a company uses ratios to evaluate the performance and future prospects of the company. By reviewing the operational effeciency, they are able to make out the price of their shares in the stock market.

(3) Utility to Creditors: Creditors and suppliers who supply goods on credit basis are interested in the solvency and liquidity position of the company. This can be known by looking into current ratio and acid-test ratio.

(4) Utility to employees: Employees are interested in the performance of business as their fringe benefits are related to the profits earned by the company. Profitability ratios such as gross profit ratio, net profit ratio etc. can be used by them in order to claim increased wages and other benefits.

(5) Utility to Government: The Government uses ratio analysis with a view to study the cost structure and thereby implement price control measures to protect the interest of the customers.

Limitations:

1. Usefulness of ratios depends upon the abilities and intentions of the persons who handle them. It will be affected considerably by the prejudice of such persons.
2. Ratios are worked out on the basis of money value only. They do not take into account the real values of various items involved.
3. Historical values are considered in working out the ratios. However, the effects of changes in the price levels of various items are ignored and to that extant the comparison and evaluation of proposals through ratios become unrealistic.
4. One particular ratio in isolation is not sufficient to analyse investment proposals or liquidity analysis. A group of ratios are to be considered simultaneously to arrive at the conclusion.
5. Ratio analysis is only a technique for making judgement and not a substitute for judgement.
6. Ratios are only symptoms, they may indicate what is to be investigated, only a careful investigation will bring out the correct position.
7. Liquidity ratios can mislead since current assets and liabilities can change quickly. Their utility becomes more doubtful for firms with seasonable business.
8. If there is window dressing in financial statements, ratios derived therefrom will

not serve the purpose. Outsiders cannot make out the window dressing of a business.

9. Financial statements buffer from inherent limitations which make ratios inaccurate. Ratios calculated on the basis of past statements need not necessarily constitute true indicator of future.

Types of Ratios—A Traditional Basis of Classification of Ratios

Accounting ratios may be classified according to the following bases:

(1) Classification on the basis of statements: This include the following:

(*a*) *Balance sheet or position ratios*: They deal with realtionship between two items or group of items which are taken from the balance sheet such as current ratio, debt-equity ratio, etc.

(*b*) *Profit and loss account or revenue ratios*: These are the Ratios which are calculated out of the figures appearing in the profit and loss account. They are also known as operating ratios. Some ratios derived from profit and loss account, are gross profit ratio, expense ratio, operating profit ratio etc.

(*c*) *Position-cum-revenue ratios*: These ratios are also known as consolidated or combined or complex ratios or inter-statement ratios. They portrary the relationship between items one of which is a part of the balance sheet and the other of the revenue statement. Examples of such ratios are, return on total resources, return on capital empolyed, turnover of debtors etc.

(2) Classification on the basis of time: On the basis of time ratios are classified into :

(*a*) Structural ratios, *i.e.*, ratios computed from data refering to the same point of time; *eg*., ratios of a particular month or year.

(*b*) Trend ratios, *i.e.*, ratios compared between the items referred to different period of time.

(3) Classification on the basis of nature: On the basis of nature of ratios, it is classified into:

(*a*) *Primary ratios*: It measures the size of profit in relation to capital employed, *e.g*., operating profit to capital employed.

(*b*) *Secondary ratios*: Also referred to as supporting ratios, brings to light strategic facts in the profit earning structure, *e.g.* stock velocity, debtors velocity, expense ratios etc.

(4) Classfication according to functions: Ratios are grouped in accordance with certain tests which they are intended to subserve from the view point of various parties having a financial interest in on enterprise. There tests are:

(*a*) *Financial ratios*: Financial ratios include liquidity and solvency ratios. Ratios indicating the liquidity position of the firm are current ratio, quick-ratio, absolute liquidity ratio, solvency ratios include proprietory ratio, debt-equity ratio, capital gearing ratio.

(*b*) *Profitability ratios*: Profitability ratios would cover gross profit ratio, net profit ratio, return on capital employed.

(*c*) *Market Test Ratio*: Market test ratios comprise of divident yield, fixed dividend cover, price earning ratio, etc.

For the sake of clear understanding we classify ratio into the following types:

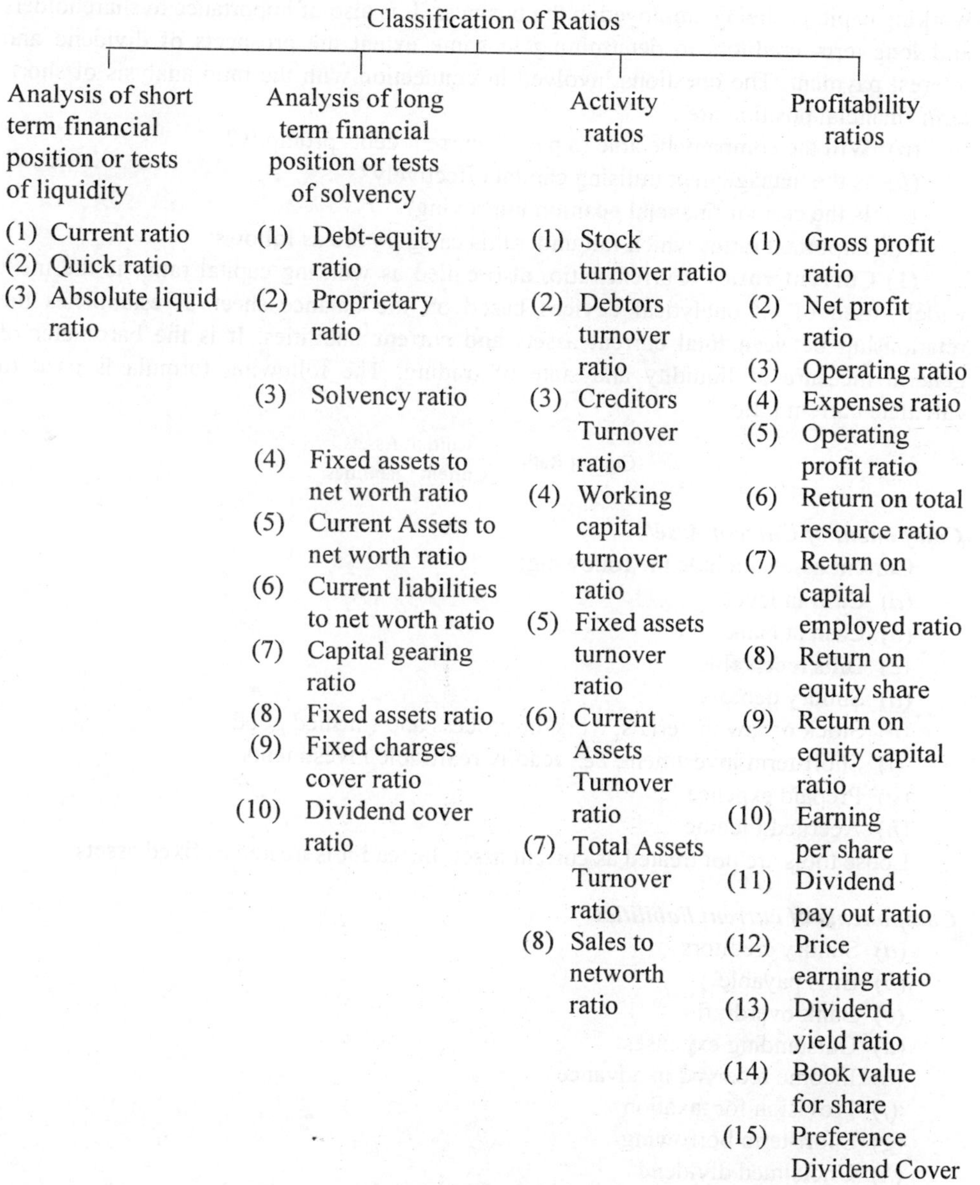

(I) ANALYSIS OF SHORT-TERM FINANCIAL POSITION OR TESTS OF LIQUIDITY

The liquidity ratios are used to test the short term solvency position or liquidity position of the business. It enables to know whether short-term liabilities can be paid out of short-term assets. This ratio also indicates whether a firm has adequate working capital to carry out routine business activity. Though commercial Banks and other short-term creditors are Primarily concerned with the analysis of short-term financial position or test of liquidity, it is a valuable aid to management in checking the efficiency with which working capital is being employed in the business. It is also of importance to shareholders and long-term creditors in determining to some extent the prospects of dividend and interest payment. The questions involved in connection with the ratio analysis of short-term financial position are :

(*a*) Will the company be able to pay its current debts promptly?
(*b*) Is the management utilising capital effectively?
(*c*) Is the current financial position improving?

The important ratios which fall under this category are as follows:

(1) Current ratio—Current ratio, also called as working capital ratio, is the most widely used of all onalytical devices based on the balance sheet. It establishes the relationship between total current assets and current liabilities. It is the barometer of general measure of liquidity and state of trading. The following formula is used to calculate current ratio:

$$\text{Current Ratio} = \frac{\text{Current Assets}}{\text{Current Liabilities}}$$

Component of Current Assets

Current assets include the following:

(*a*) Cash in level
(*b*) Cash at bank
(*c*) Bills receivable
(*d*) Sundry debtors
(*e*) Stock of raw materials, work-in-process and finished goods
(*f*) Short-term investment, *i.e.*, readily realisable investments
(*g*) Prepaid expense
(*h*) Accrued Income

Loose tools are not treated as current asset. Instead it is treated as fixed assets.

Components of current liabilities

(*a*) Sundry creditors
(*b*) Bills payable
(*c*) Bank overdraft
(*d*) Outstanding expenses
(*e*) Income received in advance
(*f*) Provision for taxation
(*g*) Short-term borrowing
(*h*) Unclaimed dividend
(*i*) Proposed dividend

Current assets are those assets which are expected to be converted into cash within a year. Current liabilities are those liabilities which are payable within one year:

Significance of current ratio

1. It indicates liquidity position of the business
2. It denotes the adequacy of working capital
3. It discloses, over or under capitalisation
4. Margin of safety for short-term creditor

Standard current ratio

A current ratio of 2: 1 is considered ideal as a rule of thumb. It means the current assets must not only be equal to current liabilities but should leave a comfortable margin of working capital after paying off the current debts. But in actual practice 1: 1 ratio is found acceptable than 2: 1. A high ratio, *i.e.*, more than 2: 1, say, 3: 1 indicates under trading and the same also indicates one of the signs of over capitalisation. Conversely, a low ratio indicates over trading or under capitalisation of business.

Limitations of current ratio

(*a*) Current ratios differ among various industries and also between manufacturers and retailers in the same line of business.

(*b*) All current assets are treated alike but they are not equally or readily realisable in cash to meet the demand of the total current liabilities.

(*c*) The credit given to the debtors and available from the creditors in a particular business can affect the position of this ratio. If these periods are different the desirable ratio would also differ.

(2) Quick ratio or acid test ratio or liquid ratio: It is a refinement of the current ratio and a second testing device for the working capital position. It is concerned with the relationship between liquid assets and liquid liabilities. The following formula is used:

$$\text{Quick Ratio} = \frac{\text{Quick Assets}}{\text{Quick Liabilities}}$$

Components of quick assets: The assets which are converted into cash without loss within a short period of time say, 1 year is known as quick assets. Quick assets include all current assets except stock and prepaid expenses.

Components of quick liabilities: The liabilities which become payable within a short period of time, say 1 year is known as quick liabilities. It includes all current liabilities except bank overdraft and cash credit as they more or less constitute permanent arrangement and renewed periodically.

Interpretation of quick ratio: A quick ratio of 1:1 is usually considered to be ideal. This ratio is a more rigorous test of liquidity than the current ratio and when used in conjuction with it, gives a better picture of the firm's ability to meet its short-term debts out of short-term assets. However, care must be exercised in placing too much reliance on 100% acid test ratio without further investigation. This is so because the interpretation of the acid test ratio, depends on circumstances. For example, a seasonal business which seeks to stabilise production will tend to have a weak acid-test ratio during its period of slack sales, and probably a powerful one during the period of heavy selling.

(3) Absolute liquidity ratio or cash position ratio: This ratio establishes a relation between absolute liquid assets to quick liabilities. The following formula is used:

$$\text{Absolute Liquidity Ratio} = \frac{\text{Absolute Liquid Assets}}{\text{Quick Liabilities}}$$

Components of Absolute liquid assets: Absolute liquid assets include (*a*) cash in hand, (*b*) cash at bank, (*c*) Marketeable securities, (*d*) temporary investments. The following assets are not included in absolute liquid asset—(*a*) closing stock, (*b*) prepaid expenses, (*c*) outstanding income, (*d*) sundry debtors, (*e*) bills receivable.

Interpretation:

The ideal absolute liquid ratio is 1: 2. It means if the ratio is 1: 2 or more than this the concern can be taken as liquid. If the ratio is less than the standard of 1: 2, it means the concern is not liquid.

Problem 1: The following is the Balance sheet of Super Star Company Ltd. on 31st Dec., 1995. Calculate the liquidity group ratios and comment upon the same.

Equity share capital	10,00,000	Land and Building	7,00,000
Profit and loss a/c	1,50,000	Plant and Machinery	17,50,000
General reserve	3,00,000	Stock	10,00,000
Bank over draft	20,00,000	Sundry debtors	5,00,000
Sundray creditors	5,00,000	Bills receivable	50,000
Bills payable	2,50,000	Cash at Bank	2,00,000
	42,00,000		42,00,000

(Osmania University, B.Com., March 1996)

Solution: Current ratio = $\frac{\text{Current Assets}}{\text{Current Liabilities}}$

$$\frac{17,50,000}{27,50,000} = 0.636$$

Current Assets:

Stock	10,00,000
Sundry Debtors	5,00,000
Bills received	50,000
Cash at Bank	2,00,000
	17,50,000

Current liabilities:

Bank overdraft	20,00,000
Sundry creditors	5,00,000
Bills payable	2,50,000
	27,50,000

Interpretation:

The current ratio is 0.636: 1. Which is much below the standard ratio if 2: 1

(2) Quick ratio = $\frac{\text{Quick Assets}}{\text{Quick Liabilities}}$

$$= \frac{7,50,000}{7,50,000} = 1$$

Quick Assets:

Sundry debtors	5,00,000
Bills receivable	50,000
Cash at Bank	2,00,000
	7,50,000

Quick liablities:

Sundry creditors	5,00,000
Bills payable	2,50,000
	7,50,000

Interpretation:

The quick ratio is 1:1 and the standard ratio is also 1:1. So it can meet its current obligation (except bank overdraft)

(3) Absolute liquid ratio = $\dfrac{\text{Absolute liquid Assets}}{\text{Liquid Liabilities}}$

$= \dfrac{2,00,000}{7,50,000} = 0.26$

Interpretation:

The absolute liquid ratio is 0.26:1 and the standard ratio is 1:2. It means the liquidity position of the company is not satisfactory.

Problem 2: The following particulars are extracted from the books of Bright star so as on 31-12-2001. Calculate absolute liquid ratio.

	(Amt. 000)
Good will	50
Plant and machinery	400
Investment	200
Marketable securities	150
Bills receivable	40
Cash in hand	45
Cash at Bank	30
Stock	75
Bank O D	70
Sundry creditors	60
Bills payable	90
O/s expenses	30

Solution: Absolute liquid ratio $= \dfrac{\text{Absolute liquid Assets}}{\text{Liquid liabilities}}$

$= \dfrac{2,25,000}{1,80,000} = 1.25$

Absolute liquid assets

Marketable securities	1,50,000
Cash in hand	45,000
Cash at Bank	30,000
	2,25,000

Liquid liabilities:

Sundry creditors	60,000
Bills payable	90,000
O/s expenses	30,000
	1,80,000

Interpretation:

The ratio of 1.25 is higher than the standard ratio of 1.2. Hence the liquidity position is satisfactory.

(II) ANALYSIS OF LONG-TERM FINANCIAL POSITION OR TESTS OF SOLVENCY

When an organisation's assets are more than its liabilitites is known as solvent organisation. Solvency indicates that position of an enterprise where it is capable of meeting long obligation. The long-term debt is contributed by debenture holders, financial institutions, other suppliers selling goods on instalment basis. All such creditors are interested in the security of loan as well as the interest due thereon. As such long term solvency ratios denote the ability of the organisation to repay the loan and interest thereon. The following ratios are used to indicate solvency position of a concern.

(1) Debt-equity ratio or external-internal equity Ratio: Debt-equity ratio expresses the relationship between debt and equity. Debt here is taken to mean long-term and short-term debt and equity means owners or shareholders funds. In other words, this ratio indicates the relaionship between external equities, *i.e.*, outsiders funds and internal equities *i.e.*, shareholders finds. The following formula is used:

$$\text{Debt-equity ratio} = \frac{\text{Debt}}{\text{Equity}}$$

OR

$$\frac{\text{External equities}}{\text{Internal equities}}$$

Components of Debt: It comprises of long term as well as short term debt.

Components of Equity: It consists of shareholders funds, reserves and accumulated profit. However, if there is any accumulated losses or fictitors assets, they are deducted from shareholders finds.

Often a question would arise as to treatment of preference share capital as a part of shareholders finds. While some accountants are of the opinion that it must be treated as internal equity; others are of the view that it is an external equity as a fixed rate of dividend is paid on them. Further redeemable preference share may have to be paid during the life time of the company. If preference shares are redeemable it can be treated as external equity and irredeemable preference share is treated as internal equity. Similarly, there is a difference of opinion as to treatment of current liabilities. Some accountants are of the opinion that current liabilities are payable within a short-period of time and hence they do not constitute a long-term debt. As such no interest becomes payable on such current liabilities. But some other accountants feel that current liability is an outside debt and therefore it is a part of external equity. It is suggested that current liability is to be included in the long-term liabilities.

Interpretation:

The standard debt-equity ratio is 2: 1. It means for every 2 shares there is 1 debt. If the debt is less than 2 times the equity, it means that creditors are relatively less and the financial structure of the business is sound. If the debt as more than 2 times the equity. The state of long-term creditors are move and indicates week financial structure..

Problem 3: The comparative figures of X Ltd. and Y Ltd. are given below:

	X Ltd.	*Y Ltd.*
Total assets	2,00,000	3,00,000
Total liabilities	40,000	1,00,000
Owner's equity	1,60,000	2,00,000

Calculate Debt-equity ratio for each company and comment. (*Bangalore University, B.Com., Nov. 1995*)

Solution: Debt-equity Ratio $= \frac{\text{Debt}}{\text{Equity}}$

X Ltd. $= \frac{40,000}{1,60,000} = 0.25$

Y Ltd. $= \frac{1,00,000}{2,00,000} = 0.50$

Interpretation:

In the case of X Ltd. it is less dependent on debt (as its borrowed capital is 25%) and dependent more on equity. In the case of Y Ltd. borrowed capital as 50% and equity fund is 50%. Y Ltd. is cosidered to be more satisfactory in terms of capital structure.

(2) Proprietory ratio or net worth ratio: This ratio establishes the relationship between the proprietors fund, (equity + preference + capital reserves + free reserves + undistributed profits) and total assets. It is also called as net worth to total assets ratio. The following formula is used:

$$\text{Proprietory Ratio} = \frac{\text{Proprietor's Fund}}{\text{Total Assets}}$$

or

$$= \frac{\text{Capital employed}}{\text{Total liabilities}}$$

Interpretation:

Higher the proprietory ratio, stronger the financial position and vice-versa. A ratio of 0.5: 1 is considered ideal.

Problem 4:

Given: Total assets Rs. 8,00,000

Proprietor's equity Rs. 4,00,000

Calculate proprietory ratio *(Bangalore University, B.Com., November, 1992)*

Solution: Proprietory Ratio $= \frac{\text{Shareholders funds}}{\text{Total Assets}}$

$$= \frac{4,00,000}{8,00,000} = 0.5$$

(3) Solvency ratio: It expresses the relationship between total assets and total liabilities of a business. It is expressed as a proportion and the following formula as used:

$$\text{Solvency Ratio} = \frac{\text{Total Assets}}{\text{Total Liabilities}}$$

Interpretation:

No standard ratio is fixed in this regard. It may be compared with similar, such organisations to evaluate the solvency position. Higher the solvency ratio, the stronger is its financial position and *vice-versa.*

(4) Fixed Assets to net worth ratio: It is obtained by dividing the depreciated book value of fixed assets by the amount of proprietors funds. It is calculated by applying the following formula:

$$\text{Fixed Assets to Net Worth Ratio} = \frac{\text{Net Fixed Assets}}{\text{Net worth or proprietor's funds}}$$

This ratio shows the extent to which ownership funds are sunk into assets with relatively low turnover. When the amount of proprietor's funds exceed the value of fixed assets, a part of the net working capital is provided by the shareholders, provided there are no other non-current assets, and when proprietor's funds are less than the fixed assets, creditors obligation have been used to finance a part of fixed assets. The yordstick for this measure is 65% for industrial undertakings.

It is a sound principle that proprietors should subscribe sufficient capital to cover fixed aseets, intangible assets, investments in other companies and a reasonable figure for working capital. Some analyst deduct intangible assets from the proprietors funds, but this would depend upon the realisable value of intangibles and the purpose of analysis. Losses should also be deducted and funds payable to others should not be added:

Interpretation:

A ratio of 0.75: 1 (or 75%) is deemed to be a desirable one. A higher ratio, say, 100 per cent means that there are no outside liabilities and all the funds employed are those of shareholders. In such a case the return to shareholders would be a lower rate of dividend and this is also a sign of 'over-capitalisation'.

(5) Current assets to net worth ratio: This is obtained by dividing the value of current assets by the amount of proprietor's funds. The following formula is used:

$$\text{Current assets to net worth ratio} = \frac{\text{Current Assets}}{\text{Proprietor's fund}}$$

The purpose of this ratio is to show the percentage of proprietor's fund investment in current assets. A higher proportion of current assets to proprietor's fund, as compared with the proportion of fixed assets to proprietor's funds is advocated, as it is an indicator of the financial strength of the business. However, different industries have different standards and history of particular concern must be studied before too great a reliance is placed on this ratio. This ratio must be read alongwith the results given by the fixed assets to proprietorship funds ratio:

(6) Current liabilities to net worth ratio: This ratio is expressed as a proportion and is obtained by dividing current liabilities by proprietor's find. The following formula is used:

$$\text{Current liabilities to net worth Ratio} = \frac{\text{Current Liabilities}}{\text{Net Worth}}$$

Interpretation:

This ratio indicates the relative contribution of short-term creditors and owners to the capital of an enterprise. The standard ratio fixed is 1/3. It the ratio is high, it means it is difficult to obtom long-term funds by the business.

(7) Capital gearing ratio: It expresses the relationship between equity capital and fixed Interest bearing securities and fixed Dividend bearing shares. The following formula is used:

$$\text{Capital Gearing Ratio} = \frac{\text{Fixed Interest bearing securities} + \text{Fixed Dividend bearing Shares}}{\text{Equity Shareholders Funds}}$$

Components of fixed interest bearing securities:

1. Debentures
2. Long-term loans
3. Long-term fixed deposits

Components of Equity shareholders funds:

1. Equity share capital
2. Accumulated reserves and profits
3. Deduction of losses and fictitions assets from the total of (1) and (2)

Interpretation:

When fixed Interest-bearing securities and fixed dividend-bearing shares are higher than equity shareholders funds, the company is send to be 'highly geared'. Where the fixed Interest-bearing securities and fixed dividend bearing shares are equal to equity share capital at is said to be 'evenly geared'. Where the fixed interest-bearing securities and fixed dividend bearing shares are lower than equity share capital it is said to be 'low geared'. If capital gearing is high, further raising of long-term loans may be difficult and issue of equity shares may be attractive and *vice-versa.*

(8) Fixed Assets Ratio: It establishes the relation between fixed assets and capital employed. The following formula is used:

$$\text{Fixed Assets Ratio} = \frac{\text{Fixed Assets}}{\text{Capital employed}}$$

Components of capital employed:

1. Owners funds
2. Long-term loans
3. Long-term deposits
4. Debentures

Interpretation:

This ratio enables to know how fixed assets are financed, *i.e.*, by use of long-term funds or by short-term funds. The ideal ratio is 0.67. This ratio should not be more than 1.

(9) Fixed charges cover ratio or debt service ratio: This ratio is determined by dividing net profit by fixed interest charges. The following formula is used:

$$\text{Fixed charges cover ratio} = \frac{\begin{array}{c}\text{Net profit before deduction}\\ \text{of interest and Income tax}\end{array}}{\text{Fixed Interest charges}}$$

Net profit for the purpose of this ratio means net profit before deduction of interest and Income-tax. Fixed charges include interest on long-term loans, deposits and Debentures. This ratio indicates the financial ability of the enterprise to meet interest payment out of current earning.

Interpretation:

The ideal Debt-Service cover is 6 or 7 times. If the ratio is high it means there is higher margin of safety for the long term lenders and as such it is not difficult for the business to obtain further long term funds and *vice-versa.*

(10) Dividend cover ratio: It is the ratio between disposable profit and dividend.

Disposable profit refers to profit left over after paying interest on long-term borrowing and income tax. This ratio is expressed as a rate and is calculated using the following formula.

$$\text{Dividend Cover Ratio} = \frac{\text{Net Profit after interest and Tax}}{\text{Dividend Declared}}$$

Interpretation:

This ratio indicates the ability of the business to maintain the dividend on shares in future. If this ratio is higher is indicates that there is sufficient amount of retained profit. Even if there is slight decreace in profit in the future it will not affect payment of dividend in future.

(III) ACTIVITY RATIOS OR PERFORMANCE RATIOS

Activity ratios indicate the performance of an organisation. This indicate the effective utilisation of the various assets of the organisation. Most of the ratios falling under this category is based on turnover and hence these ratios are called as turnover ratios. The various activity ratios are as follows:

(1) Stock turnover ratio: This ratio establishes the relationship between the cost of goods sold during a given period and the average stock holding during that period. It tells us as to how many times stock has turned (sold) over the period. This ratio indicates the operational and marketing efficiency of the business. It not only helps in determining the liquidity of the firm but also assets in evaluating inventory policy so as to protect the firm from any danger of over-stocking.

Normally, inventory turnover ratio is best expressed through the relationship between cost of goods sold and average inventory at cost, but ratio of sales to inventory may also be used as a substitute for the rate of cost of goods sold to average inventory, in case, cost of goods sold is not available. Besides these methods, some firms like departmental stores, customarily valuing there inventories at selling prices, compute inventory turnover ratio as the ratio between net sales and average inventory at selling prices.

The average inventory for a year is the sum of inventory at the beginning of the year and inventory at the end of the year and the total is divided by 2. The following formula is used to calculate the inventory turnover ratios:

$$\text{Inventory Turnover Ratio} = \frac{\text{Cost of goods sold}}{\text{Average stock}}$$

Interpretation:

The ideal stock turnover ratio is 8 times a year. A low inventory turnover may reflect dull business, over investment in inventory, accumulation of stock at the end of the period in anticipation of higher prices or of greater sales volume, incorrect inventory resulting from the inclusion of obsolute and unsaleable items and excessive quantitites of certain inventory items in relation to immediate requirements.

A high turnover of inventory may not be accompanied by a relatively high net income as, profits may be sacrificed in obtaining a large sale volume with the result that a higher rate of turnover is likely to prove less profitable than a lower turnover unless accompanied by a larger total gross profit. Similarly, a relatively high turnover ratio may not really be an indicator of favourable results as it may indicate serious under-investment in inventories and this may in turn result in loss of customer patronage on account of failure to make prompt deliveries. But, generally, a high stock turnover ratio means that the concern is efficient and hence it sells its goods quickly.

Problem 5: Rate of Gross profit is 25% on cost. Total sales Rs. 5,00,000. Average stock Rs. 80,000. Compute stock turnover ratio. *(Bangalore University, B.Com., November 1994)*

Solution: Gross profit ratio on cost = 25%

or Gross profit ratio on sales = 20%

$$\text{Cross profit} = \frac{20}{100} \times 5,00,000 = 1,00,000$$

Cost of sales = Sales – Gross profit
= 5,00,000 – 1,00,000
= 4,00,000

$$\text{Stock Turnover Ratio} = \frac{\text{Cost of Sales}}{\text{Average stock}}$$

$$= \frac{4,00,000}{80,000} = 5 \text{ times}$$

Problem 6: Calculate the stock turnover ratio

	(Rs.)
Opening stock	45,000
Closing Stock	55,000
Sales	2,50,000
Gross profit	25% on sales

(Osmania University, B.Com., October 1997)

Solution:

Calculation of Gross Profit

$$\frac{20}{100} \times 2,50,000 = 50,000$$

Calculation of Average Stock

$$\text{Average stock} = \frac{\text{Opening stock} + \text{Closing stock}}{2}$$

$$= \frac{45,000 + 55,000}{2} = 50,000$$

Cost of sales or cost of goods sold = Sales – Gross profit
= 2,50,000 – 50,000
= 2,00,000

$$\text{Stock Turnover Ratio} = \frac{\text{Cost of goods sold}}{\text{Average stock}}$$

$$= \frac{2,00,000}{50,000} = 4 \text{ times}$$

(2) Debtors turnover ratio or debtors velocity ratio: This ratio explains the relationship of net (credit) sales of a firm to its book debts indicating the rate at which cash is generated by turnover of receivables or debtors. The following formula is used:

$$\text{Debtors Turnover Ratio} = \frac{\text{Net annual credit Sales}}{\text{Average Debtors}}$$

The term debtors for the purpose of this ratio is used in a comprehansive sense and also includes the amount of bills receivable along with book debts at the end of the accounting period. Moreover debtors which do not arise from regular sales should be excluded, eg., a bill receivable from the buyer of fixed assets. Sometimes, the ratio is computed from the average of debtors at the beginning and at the end of the year. Another important point in connection with the ratio is that reserve for bad and doubtful debts is not deducted from the total amount of trade debtors.

In the absence of the break-up of sales into cash and credit, the analyst has to use total sales for computation of the ratio with the result that, to the extent cash sales are included, the ratio tends to be overstated. So far as the calculation of daily sales are concerned, the denominator is to be the number of working days of the business during the year and while it is customary to use 360 days basis rather than 365 days exact, some writers one of the opinion that the denominator should only be 300 days owing to the remainder days being holidays, when too business is transacted.

The purpose of this ratio is to measure the liquidity of the receivable or to find out the period over which receivables remain uncollected, *i.e.*, ageing of receivables. Since debtors constitute a major element of current assets, the credit and collection policies of the business must be under continuous watch. The amount of trade debtors at the end of the accounting period should not exceed a reasonable proportion of net sales. The larger the amount of trade debtors in relation to net sales, the greater would be the expense in connection with uncontrollable accounts. An over-investment in receivables may be the result of over extension of credit, liberalisation of credit terms, ineffective credit investigation, lack of effective collection policies or the inabitity of the collection department to make collection in periods of depression.

Problem 6: Gross profit ratio 20% on sales. Total gross profit Rs. 1,00,000. Cash sales Rs. 1,20,000. Average debtors Rs. 95,000. Calculate debtors turnover ratio.

(*Bangalore University, B.Com., November 1994*)

Solution:

Gross profit on sales = 20%

Gross profit = Rs. 1,00,000

$$\text{Total sales} = 1{,}00{,}000 \times \frac{100}{20} = 5{,}00{,}000$$

Credit sales = Total sales – Cash sales

= 5,00,000 – 1,20,000

= 3,80,000

$$\text{Debtors turnover ratio} = \frac{\text{Credit Sales}}{\text{Average Debtors}}$$

$$= \frac{3{,}80{,}000}{95{,}000} = 4 \text{ times}$$

(3) Debt collection period ratio: This ratio is helpful in knowing the speed at which debts are collected. It refers to the time involved in collecting the debts by a business enterprise. The following formula is used to calculate debt collection period ratio:

$$\text{Debt Collection Period Ratio} = \frac{\text{No. of days in a year}}{\text{Debtors turnover}}$$

OR

$$= \frac{\text{Debtors}}{\text{Net annual credit Sales}} \times \text{No. of Days in a year}$$

OR

$$= \frac{\text{Net annual credit sales}}{\text{No. of Days in a year}}$$

Problem 7: Find out debtors turnover and average collection period from the following information:

	1994	*1995*
	Rs.	*Rs.*
Annual credit sales	5,00,000	6,00,000
Debtors in the beginning	80,000	90,000
Debtors at the end	1,00,000	1,10,000
No. of days for the year	360 days	360 days

(*University of Madras, B.Com., March 1997*)

Solution:

$$\text{Debtors Turnover Ratio} = \frac{\text{Credit Sales}}{\text{Average Debtors}}$$

$$1994 = \frac{5,00,000}{90,000} = 5.56 \text{ times}$$

$$1995 = \frac{6,00,000}{1,00,000} = 6 \text{ times}$$

Note: Calculation of Average debtors

$$\text{Average Debtors} = \text{Opening Debtors} + \text{Closing Debtors}$$

$$1994 = \frac{80,000 + 1,00,000}{2} = 90,000$$

$$1995 = \frac{90,000 + 1,10,000}{2} = 1,00,000$$

$$\text{Average Collection Period} = \frac{\text{No. of Days}}{\text{Debtors Turnover Ratio}}$$

$$1994 = \frac{360}{5.56} = 65 \text{ days}$$

$$1995 = \frac{360}{6} = 60 \text{ days}$$

(4) Crditor's turnover ratio or creditors velocity: This ratio indicates the number of times the creditors are paid in a year. The following formula is used:

$$\text{Creditors Turnover Ratio} = \frac{\text{Net annual credit purchases}}{\text{Average creditors}}$$

Components:

Credit purchases refers to credit purchase minus purchase returns. Creditors include bills payable. Average creditors is obtained by dividing opening sundry creditors and opening bills payable plus closing sundry creditors and closing bill payable divided by 2. When particulars about opening creditors and opening bills payable are not available, then closing creditors and closing bills payable is taken as denominator.

Problem 8: A company purchases goods both on cash as well as on credit terns. The following particulars are obtained from the books.

	Rs.
Total purchases	3,00,000
Cash purchases	30,000
Purchases returns	51,000
Creditors at the end	1,05,000
Bills payable at the end	60,000
Reserve for discount on creditors	8,000

Calculate average payment period

(*University of Madras, B.Com., March 1994*)

Solution:

Total Purchases	3,00,000
Less cash purchases	30,000
	2,70,000
Less purchase returns	51,000
Net credit purchases	2,19,000

Accounts payable = Creditors + Bills payable

or

Total creditors = 1,05,000 + 60,000

= 1,65,000

$$\text{Creditoros Turnover Ratio} = \frac{\text{Credit purchases}}{\text{Average creditors}}$$

$$= \frac{2,19,000}{1,65,000} = 1.33$$

$$\text{Average Payment Period} = \frac{\text{No. of days}}{\text{Creditors turnover Ratio}}$$

$$= \frac{365}{1.33} = 274.44 \text{ day}$$

(4) Working capital turnover ratio: The term working capital refers to excess of current assets over current liabilities. This ratio establishes a relationship between working capital and sales. The following formula is used:

$$\text{Working Capital Turnover Ratio} = \frac{\text{Net Sales}}{\text{Working Capital}}$$

This ratio enables to know efficient utilisation of working capital of an organisation.

(5) Fixed assets turnover ratio: This ratio establishes a relationship between fixed assets and sales. The following formula is used:

$$\text{Fixed Assets Turnover Ratio} = \frac{\text{Net Sales}}{\text{Fixed Assets}}$$

Interpretation:

The standard fixed turnover ratio is 5 times. A high ratio indicates better utilisation of fixed assets. A low ratio indicates under-utilisation of fixed assets.

(6) Current assets turnover ratio: It establishes a relationship between current assets and sales. The following formula is used:

$$\text{Current Asset Turnover Ratio} = \frac{\text{Net Sales}}{\text{Current Assets}}$$

Just as fixed assets turnover ratio, this ratio indicates the contribution of current assets to sales.

(7) Total assets turnover ratio: This ratio establishes a relationship between total assets and sales. This ratio enables to know the efficient utilisation of total assets of a business. The following formula is used:

$$\text{Total Assets Turnover Ratio} = \frac{\text{Net Sales}}{\text{Total Assets}}$$

Interpretation:

A total asset turnover ratio of 2 times or more indicates that assets are utilised efficiently and a ratio below 2 indicates that the assets are under-utilised.

(8) Sales to net worth: It establishes a relationship between sales and owner's funds. This ratio enables to know the utilisation of owner's finds.

(IV) PROFITABILITY RATIOS

Profitability ratios indicate the profit earning capacity of a business. For the sake of clear understanding profitability ratios are classified into two categories, *viz.*, general profitability ratios and overall profitability ratios.

General Profitability Ratios

They include the following ratios:

1. Gross profit ratio
2. Operating ratio
3. Operating profit ratio
4. Expense ratio
5. Net profit ratio

These ratios are explained below:

(1) Gross Profit Ratio: It expresses the relationship of gross profit to net sales and is expressed in terms of percentage. Sales for this purpose means net sales, *i.e.*, sales after deducting the value of goods returned by the customers. Gross profit results from the difference between net sales and cost of goods sold without taking into account expenses generally charged to profit and loss a/c. Cost of goods sold in the case of a trading concern is the purchase of goods and all expenses directly connected with the purchases of goods, while in the case of manufacturing concern, it consists of the purchase price of raw materials and all manufacturing expenses. The following formula is used to calculate this ratio:

$$\text{Gross Profit Ratio} = \frac{\text{Gross Profit}}{\text{Net Sales}} \times 100$$

This ratio is a measure of general profitability of the business and a tool that indicates the degree to which selling price of goods per unit may decline without resulting in losses on operations for the firm. The gross profit should be adaquate to cover the operating expenses and to provide for fixed charges, dividends and buidling up of reserves.

Interpretation:

A low gross profit ratio may indicate unfavourable purchasing, the instability of management to develop sales volume thereby making it impossible to buy goods in large volume, excessive competition etc.

On the other hand an increase in the gross profit ratio may reflect an increase in the sale price of goods sold without any corresponding increase in costs; a decrease in cost without its impact on the sale price of goods, opening stock valued at a figure lower than it should have been, over valuation of closing stock of the end of accounting period etc. There is no rigid standard to this ratio. Normally 25% to 30% margin is anticipated.

(2) Operating ratio: This ratio establishes a relationship between cost of goods sold plus other operating expenses and net sales. Operating expenses consists of administrative expenses, financial expenses selling and distribution expenses. The following formula is used:

$$\text{Operating Ratio} = \frac{\text{Cost of goods sold + Operating expenses}}{\text{Net Sales}}$$

Interpretation:

This ratio is calculated mainly to ascertain the operational efficiency of the management in their business operations, as it shows the percentage of net sales that is absorbed by the cost of goods sold. Higher the operating ratio, the less favourable it is because it would leave a smaller margin to meet interest, dividend and other corporate needs. In general, for manufacturing concerns, operating retio is expected to touch a percentage of 75% to 85%. This ratio can also be used as a partial index of over-all profitability but cannot be used as a test of financial condition.

(3) Operating Profit Ratio: This ratio establishes the relationship between operating profit and net sales and is calculated as follows:

$$\text{Operating Profit Ratio} = \frac{\text{Operating profit}}{\text{Net Sales}} \times 100$$

For calculating this ratio, non-operating expenses and non-operating incomes are ignored. This ratio indicates the portion remaining out of every rupee worth of sales after all operating costs and expenses have been met.

(4) Expense Ratio: These ratios supplement the information given by the operating ratio. They are calculated by dividing each individual operating expenses (*i.e.*, administrative, selling and general expenses) by the net sales revenue.

i.e. (*a*) Material Consumed Ratio $= \frac{\text{Materials consumed}}{\text{Net Sales}} \times 100$

(*b*) Office and Administration Expenses Ratio

$$= \frac{\text{Office and Adm. expenses}}{\text{Net Sales}} \times 100$$

(*c*) Selling and Distribution Expenses Ratio

$$= \frac{\text{Selling and Distribution Expenses}}{\text{Net Sales}} \times 100$$

(*d*) Financial Expenses Ratio $= \frac{\text{Financial Expenses}}{\text{Net Sales}} \times 100$

(*e*) non-operating Expenditure Ratio

$$= \frac{\text{Non-operating expenditure Ratio}}{\text{Net Sales}} \times 100$$

These ratios which represent a summation of changes in net sales and in the expense items are valuable in comparing similar business or operating data from year to year for the same business.

(5) Net Profit Ratio: It expresses the relationship between net profit after taxes to sales. The following formula is used:

$$\text{Net Profit Ratio} = \frac{\text{Net profit after Tax}}{\text{Net Sales}} \times 100$$

This ratio is widely used as a measure of over-all profitability and is very useful to proprietors, as it gives an idea of the efficiency as well as profitability of the business to a limited extent. It different from the operating ratio in the sense it is calculated after adding non-operating income like interest or dividend on investments etc., to generating profit and deducting non-operating expenses such as loss on sale of old assets, provision for legal damages, etc., from such profit.

Tests of Overall Profitability

The ratios which test the overall profitability are concerned with measuring the overall efficiency of the business relating profit to the investment made in the business. These ratios are as follows:

1. Return on shareholders investment or net worth ratio
2. Return on equity capital
3. Return on capital employed
4. Return on total resourses
5. Dividend yield ratio
6. Preference dividend cover ratio
7. Equity dividend cover ratio
8. Price covering ratio
9. Dividend pay-out ratio
10. Earning per share

The above ratios are explained below:

(1) Return on shareholders investment or net worth ratio: Shareholders investment also called return on proprietor's finds is the ratio of net profit (after tax and interest) to proprietor's finds. It is invariably calculated by the prospective investor in the business to find out whether the investment would be worth-making in terms of return as compared to the risk involved in the business. The following formula is used:

$$\text{Return on Shareholders Investment} = \frac{\text{Net profit (After Tax and interest)}}{\text{Proprietor's fund}}$$

Shareholders investment includes all categories of share capital, capital reserves, contingency reserves, all revenue reserves, undistributed profits. Normally the average of the figures relating to shareholder's investments in the opening and closing balance sheets are considered while computing this ratio. Net profit for the purpose represents the net profit after tax and interest on long-term liabilties.

Returns on capital is one of the effective measures of the profitableness of an enterprise. The realisation of a satisfactory net income is the major objective of a business and this ratio shows the extent to which this objective has been achieved. This ratio is also used in making inter-firm comparison.

(2) Return on equity capital: Thus ratio establishes the relationship between net profit available to equity shareholders and the amount of capital invested by them. The following formula is used:

$$\text{Return on Equity Capital} = \frac{\text{Net Profit} - \text{Dividend due to preference shareholders}}{\text{Equity Share capital (paid - up)}}$$

For the purpose of calculating this return net profits are arrived at after deducting the dividend due to preference shareholders. If participating preference shares are issued, they have a right to participate further in the profits after a certain rate of dividend has been paid to equity shareholders. Such participating dividend would also have to be substracted in order to arrive at profits due to equity shareholders.

This rate of return is designed to show what percentage the earned profit of the period bears to the amount of capital invested by equity shareholders. It is used to compare the performance of company's equity capital with those of other companies, and thus help the investor in choosing a company with higher return on equity capital.

(3) Return on capital employed: This ratio is the most appropriate indicator of the earning power of the capital employed in the business. It also acts as a pointer to the management, showing the progress or deterioration in the earning capacity and efficiency of the business. The following formula is used:

$$\text{Return on Capital Employed} = \frac{\text{Net profit before Taxes and interest on long-term loans, and debentures}}{\text{Capital employed}}$$

The term capital employed refers to the total long-term funds used in a business. It is calculated is shown below:

Net fixed assets	xx
Add: Trade investments, *i.e.*, investments made in associated concern to promote trade	xx
Add: Net working capital, *i.e.*, excess of current assets over current liabilitites capital employed	xx
	xx

Interpretation:

The standard return on capital employed is about 15%. If the actual ratio is equal to or above 15% it indicates higher productivity of the capital employed and *vice-versa.*

(4) Return on total resources: This ratio acts as an yordstick to assess the efficiency of the operations of the business as it indicates the extent to which assets employed in the business are utilised to result in net profit. The following formula is used:

$$\text{Return on Total Resources} = \frac{\text{Net Profit}}{\text{Total Assets}} \times 100$$

(5) Dividend yield ratio: It refers to the percentage or ratio of dividend paid per share to the market price per share. This ratio throws light on the effective rate of return on investment, which potential investors may hope to earn. The following formula is used:

$$\text{Dividend Yield Ratio} = \frac{\text{Dividend paid per equity share}}{\text{Market price per equity share}}$$

(6) Preference dividend cover: It indicates how many times the preference dividend is covered by profits after tax. This ratio measures the margin of safety for preference shareholders. Such investors normally expect their dividend to be coverd about 3 times by profits available for dividend purpose. The following formula is used:

$$\text{Preference Dividend Cover} = \frac{\text{Profit after Tax}}{\text{Annual programme dividend}}$$

(7) Equity Dividend Cover: This ratio indicates the number of times the dividend is covered by the amount of profit available for equity shareholders, *i.e.*, net profit after tax less preference dividend. The following formula is used:

$$\text{Equity Dividend Cover} = \frac{\text{Net profit (after Tax) – preference dividend}}{\text{Dividend paid on equity capital}}$$

or

$$= \frac{\text{Earnings per Equity Share}}{\text{Dividend per Equity Share}}$$

Interpretation:

An ideal equity dividend cover is 2, *i.e.*, out of every Rs. 100 profits available for dividend, Rs. 50 is distributed and Rs. 50 is retained and ploughed back in the business. Higher the dividend cover, the higher is the extent of retained earnings and higher is the degree of certainty that dividend will be repeated in future years also.

(8) Price-earning ratio: It shows how many times the annual earnings the present shareholders are willing to pay to get a share. This ratio helps investors to know the effect of earnings per share on the market price of the share. This ratio when calculated for several years can be used as trend analysis for predicting future price earning ratios and therefore, future stock prices. The following formula is used:

$$\text{Price Earning Ratio} = \frac{\text{Average Market price per share}}{\text{Earning per share}}$$

(9) Dividend pay-out ratio: This ratio indicates the proportion of earnings available which equity share-holders actually receive in the form of dividend. An investor primarily interested should invest in equity shares of a company with high pay-out ratio. A company having low-pay-out ratio need not necessarily be a bad company. A company having income may like to finance expansion out of the income earned and thus have low-pay-out ratio. An investor interested in stock-price appreciation may well invest in such a company even though the pay-out ratio is low. The following formula is used:

$$\text{Pay-out Ratio} = \frac{\text{Dividend paid per share}}{\text{Earning per share}}$$

(10) Earning per share: This ratio indicates the earnings per equity share. It establishes the relationship between net profit avaible for equity shareholders and the number of equity shares. The following formula is used:

$$\text{Earning Per Share} = \frac{\text{Net profit available for equity shareholders}}{\text{Number of equity shares}}$$

Leverage Ratios

Leverage ratios are calculated to test long-term financial position of a firm. Leverage ratios are classified into three types, *viz.*

***(a)* Financial leverage or trading on equity:** Financial leverage refers to use of long-term interest bearing debt and preference share capital along with equity share capital. The following formula is used:

$$\text{Financial Leverage} = \frac{\text{Earnings before Interest and Tax}}{\text{Earnings before Interest and Tax – Interest and preference dividend}}$$

(*b*) Operating leverage: It is obtained by dividing 'contribution' by Earnings before interest and tax. Contribution represents the difference between the sales and variable cost. The following formula is used:

$$\text{Operating Leverage} = \frac{\text{Contribution}}{\text{Earning before interest and Tax}}$$

(*c*) Combined Leverage: This is a product of the above two leverages. The following formula is used:

$$\text{Combined Leverage} = \text{Financial Leverage} \times \text{Operating Leverage}$$

Problem 9: **Rao Insulating Company submitted the following particulars. Calculate (*a*) financial leverage, (*b*) operating leverage under both the situations:**

Sales 50,000 units @	Rs. 15
Variable cost per unit	Rs. 9
Fixed cost	Rs. 20,000
Debenture interest paid	Rs. 40,000
Tax 50%	
Increase in production	10,000 units

Solution: **Statement Showing Profit after Tax**

	50,000 *Units*	60,000 *Units*
Sales		
50,000 × 15		
60,000 × 15	7,50,000	9,00,000
Less variable cost		
50,000 × 9		
60,000 × 9	4,50,000	5,40,000
Contribution	3,00,000	3,60,000
Less Fixed expenses	2,000	20,000
	2,80,000	3,40,000
Less Interest	40,000	40,000
Profit before taxes	2,40,000	3,00,000
Less taxes	1,20,000	1,50,000
Profit after tax	1,20,000	1,50,000

$$\text{Financial Leverage} = \frac{\text{EBIT}}{\text{EBIT} - \text{Interest}}$$

$$\text{For 50,000 units level} = \frac{2,80,000}{2,80,000 - 40,000}$$

$$= \frac{2,80,000}{2,40,000} = 1.167$$

$$\text{For 60,000 units level} = \frac{3,40,000}{3,40,000 - 40,000}$$

$$= \frac{3,40,000}{3,00,000} = 1.13$$

$$\text{Operating Leverage} = \frac{\text{Contribution}}{\text{EBIT}}$$

For 50,000 units level $= \frac{3,00,000}{2,80,000} = 1.07$

For 60,000 units level $= \frac{3,60,000}{3,40,000} = 1.05$

DU-PONT CONTROL CHART

It is a chart designed by an DU-pont company of America. The chart helps management to exercise control by using ratios and their inter-relationship. The actual ratios are compared with standard ratios to judge the performance of the business. The chart is as follows:

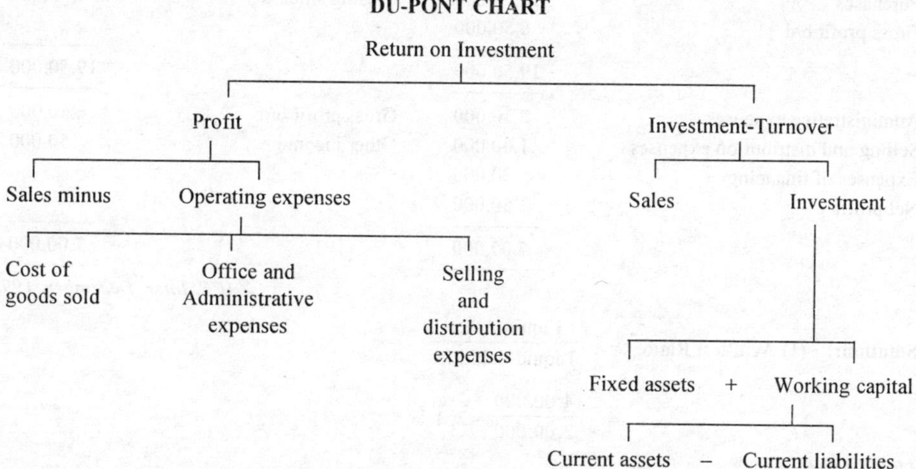

The chart is based on two aspects, *viz.* profit and investment. Profit is the difference between sales and operating expenses. When operating expenses are controlled profit margin will be increased. Earnings is the difference between sales and cost of sales. Cost of sale is the aggregate of cost of goods sold, office and administration expenses and selling and distribution expenses. Investments is the aggregate of fixed assets and working capital. Working capital is the excess of current assets over current liabilities.

The efficiency of a business depends upon the functioning of the business. The return on investment is taken as a basis to measure efficiency. The efficiency is reflected by the profit earned by the business. The efficiency can be increased by minimising costs or effective use of capital or by increasing sales. In case of inefficiency, the management can identify the areas and take remedial steps. Inter-firm comparision is used as a technique to evaluate the performance. The important ratios used in this connection are return on investment, assets turnover ratio and profitability ratios.

Problem 10: From the following final accounts of XYZ Co. Ltd. for the year ended 31st March, 1999, you are required to calculate the following:

1. Acid test ratio
2. Stock turnover ratio
3. Operating ratio
4. Debt collection period and
5. Net profit to capital employed ratio

Balance sheet as on 31st March 1999

Share capital (in shares of Rs. 10 each)	5,00,000	Land and Buildings	5,00,000
General Reserve	4,00,000	Plant and Machinery	2,00,000
Profit and loss a/c	1,50,000	Stock	1,50,000
Sundry creditors	2,00,000	Sundry debtors	2,50,000
		Cash and bank balance	1,50,000
	12,50,000		12,50,000

Profit and loss a/c for the year ended 31st March 1999

Opening stock	2,50,000	Sales	18,00,000
Purchases	10,50,000	Closing stock	1,50,000
Gross profit b/d	6,50,000		
	19,50,000		19,50,000
Administrative expenses	2,30,000	Gross profit b/d	6,50,000
Selling and distribution expenses	1,00,000	Other income	50,000
Expenses of financing	20,000		
Net profit	3,50,000		
	7,00,000		7,00,000

(*CS, Inter, December, 1999*)

Solution: (1) Acid-test Ratio $= \dfrac{\text{Liquid Assets}}{\text{Liquid liabilities}}$

$$= \frac{4,00,000}{2,00,000} = 2:1$$

Liquid Assets

Sundry debtors	=	2,50,000
Cash and Bank balance	=	1,50,000
		4,00,000

(2) Stock Turnover Ratio $= \dfrac{\text{Cost of goods sold}}{\text{Average stock}}$

$$= \frac{11,50,000}{2,00,000} = 5.75 \text{ times}$$

Cost of goods sold

Opening stock	=	2,50,000
Add: Purchases	=	10,50,000
		13,00,000
Less: Closing stock		1,50,000
		11,50,000

Average Stock $= \dfrac{\text{Opening stock + closing stock}}{2}$

$$= \frac{2,50,000 + 1,50,000}{2} = 2,00,000$$

(3) Operating Ratio $= \dfrac{\text{Cost of goods sold + operating expenses}}{\text{Net Sales}} \times 100$

$= \dfrac{11,50,000 + 3,30,000}{18,00,000} \times 100$

$= 82.2\%$

Operating expenses

Administrative expenses + Selling and Distribution expenses

= 2,30,000 + 1,00,000

= 3,30,000

(4) Debt Collection Period $= \dfrac{\text{Total Debtors}}{\text{Sales per day}}$

$= \dfrac{2,50,000}{\dfrac{18,00,00}{365}}$

$= \dfrac{2,50,000 \times 365}{18,00,00} = 50.7 \text{ or } 51 \text{ days}$

(5) Net profit to capital employed $= \dfrac{\text{Net profit}}{\text{Capital employed}} \times 100$

$= \dfrac{3,50,000}{10,50,000} \times 100 = 33.33\%$

Capital employed

Share capital	5,00,000
General reserve	4,00,000
Profit & loss a/c	1,50,000
Shareholders finds	10,50,000

Problem 11: The Balance Sheet of Punjab Auto Ltd. as on 31-12-1991 was as follows:

Liabilities		*Assets*	
Equity share capital	40,000	Plant and machinery	24,000
Capital reserve	8,000	Land and Building	40,000
8% loan on mortagage	32,000	Furniture and	
creditors	16,000	fixture	16,000
Bank overdraft	4,000	Stock	12,000
Taxation:		Debtors	12,000
—current	4,000	Investment	4,000
—Future	4,000	(short term)	
P & C a/c	12,000	Cash in hand	12,000
	1,20,000		1,20,000

From the above compute: (*a*) The Current Ratio, (*b*) Quick Ratio, (*c*) Debt-equity Ratio, (*d*) Proprietory Ratio.

(Bangalore University, B.B.M. April 2000)

Solution: (a) Current ratio $= \dfrac{\text{Current Assets}}{\text{Current Liabilities}}$

$= \dfrac{40,000}{28,000} = 1.42$

Current Assets	
Stock	12,000
Debtors	12,000
Investment (Short-term)	4,000
Cash in hand	12,000
	40,000

Current liabilities	
Creditors	16,000
Bank overdraft	4,000
Taxation	8,000
	28,000

(b) Quick Ratio $= \dfrac{\text{Liquid Assets}}{\text{Liquid liabilities}}$

$= \dfrac{28,000}{24,000} = 1.16$

Liquid Assets	
Debtors	12,000
Investment (Short-term)	4,000
Cash in hand	12,000
	28,000

Liquid liabilities	
Creditors	16,000
Taxation	8,000
	24,000

(c) Debt-equity Ratio $= \dfrac{\text{External Equities}}{\text{Internal Equities}}$

$= \dfrac{52,000}{60,000} = 0.86$

External equities	
8% loan on mortgage	32,000
Creditors	16,000
Bank overdraft	4,000
	52,000

Internal equities	
Equity share capital	40,000
Capital reserve	8,000
P & C a/c	12,000
	60,000

(d) Proprietory Ratio $= \dfrac{\text{Shareholders funds}}{\text{Total Tangible assets}}$

$= \dfrac{60,000}{1,20,000} = 0.50$

Problem 12: Following is the balance sheet of Non-Such Co. Ltd. for the year ending 31st March, 1997. Calculate ratios for (*i*) testing liquidity and (*ii*) testing solvency:

Liabilitites		*Assets*	
Equity share capital	5,00,000	Goodwill	2,50,000
12% preference share capital	2,50,000	Plant and machinery	3,00,000
General reserve	50,000	Land and Building	3,50,000
Profit and loss a/c	2,00,000	Furniture	50,000
Provision for tax	88,000	Stock	3,00,000
Bills payable	62,000	Bills receivable	15,000
Bank overdraft	10,000	Sundry debtors	75,000
Sundry creditors	40,000	Bank	1,00,000
12% debentures	2,50,000	Marketable securities	10,000
	14,50,000		14,50,000

(*Sri Vanhateshwara University, B.Com., April 1999*)

Solution:

Tests of Liquidity

(a) Current ratio $= \dfrac{\text{Current Assets}}{\text{Current Liabilities}}$

$= \dfrac{5,00,000}{2,00,000} = 2.5$

Current Assets	
Stock	3,00,000
Bills receivable	15,000
Sundry debtors	75,000
Bank	1,00,000
Marketable securities	10,000
	5,00,000

Current liabilities	
Provision for tax	88,000
Bills payable	62,000
Bank OD	10,000
Sundry creditors	40,000
	2,00,000

(b) Quick or Liquid Ratio $= \dfrac{\text{Liquid Assets}}{\text{Liquid Liabilities}}$

$= \dfrac{2,00,000}{1,90,000} = 1.05$

Liquid Assets	
Bills Receivable	15,000
Sundry debtors	75,000
Bank	1,00,000
Marketable securities	10,000
	2,00,000

Liquid liabilities = Current liabilities – Bank OD
= 2,00,000 – 10,000
= 1,90,000

(c) Absolute Liquid Ratio $= \dfrac{\text{Absolute Liquid Assets}}{\text{Liquid liabilities}}$

$= \dfrac{1,10,000}{1,90,000} = 0.57$

Absolute liquid assets

Bank	1,00,000
Marketable securities	10,000
	1,10,000

(2) *Solvency Ratios*

(a) Debt-equity Ratio $= \dfrac{\text{Long term liabilities}}{\text{shareholders funds}}$

$= \dfrac{2,50,000}{10,00,000} = 0.25$

Long-term liabilities

12% Debentures = 2,50,000

Shareholders finds

Preference share capital	=	5,00,000
Equity share capital	=	2,50,000
General reserve	=	50,000
P & C a/c	=	2,00,000
		10,00,000

Note: Preference share capital is included in the shareholders funds as it is not redeemable

(b) Proprietory Ratio $= \dfrac{\text{Proprietors funds}}{\text{Total Assets}}$

$= \dfrac{10,00,000}{14,50,000} = 0.69$

(c) Capital Gearing Ratio $= \dfrac{\text{Fixed Interest bearing Securities} + \text{Fixed Dividend bearing Securities}}{\text{Equity Shareholder's funds}}$

$= \dfrac{2,50,000 + 2,50,000}{7,50,000}$

$= \dfrac{5,00,000}{7,50,000} = 0.66$

Fixed Interest Bearing Securities

12% Debentures = 2,50,000

Fixed Dividend bearing securities

12% Preference share capital = 2,50,000

Equity shareholders finds

Equity share capital	=	5,00,000
General reserve	=	50,000
P & C a/c	=	2,00,000
		7,50,000

(*d*) Fixed assets ratio $= \frac{\text{Net Fixed Assets}}{\text{proprietor's funds}}$

$= \frac{9,50,000}{10,00,000} = 0.95$

Net Fixed Assets

Goodwill	=	2,50,000
Plant and machinery	=	3,00,000
Land and building	=	3,50,000
Furniture	=	50,000
		9,50,000

Proprietors Funds

Equity share capital	=	5,00,000
General reserve	=	50,000
P & c a/c	=	2,00,000
12% pref share capital	=	2,50,000
		10,00,000

Problem 13: From the following information calculate current ratio liquid ratio, creditors turnover and average credit sales of Surya Ltd. and Chandra Ltd.

Credit to Debtors	*Surya Ltd.* *3 months* *Rs.*	*Chandra Ltd.* *3 months* *Rs.*
Stock	8,00,000	1,00,000
Debtors	1,70,000	1,40,000
Cash	30,000	60,000
Trade creditors	2,80,000	1,50,000
Bills payable	20,000	10,000
Bank overdraft	4,000	30,000
Creditor for expenses	60,000	10,000
Total purchases	9,30,000	6,60,000
Cash purchases	30,000	20,000

(*University of Bombay, B.Com., October 1999*)

Solution:

Current Ratio $= \frac{\text{Current Assets}}{\text{Current liabilities}}$

Surya Ltd. $= \frac{10,00,000}{4,00,000} = 2.5$ times

Current Assets

Stock	8,00,000
Debtors	1,70,000
Cash	30,000
	10,00,000

Current liabilities

Trade creditors	=	2,80,000
Bills payable	=	20,000
Bank OD	=	40,000
Creditors for expenses	=	60,000
		4,00,000

Chandra Ltd. $= \dfrac{3,00,000}{2,00,000} = 1.5$ times

Current Assets

Stock	=	1,00,000
Debtors	=	1,40,000
Cash	=	60,000
		3,00,000

Current liabilities

Trade creditors	=	1,50,000
Bills payable	=	10,000
Bank overdraft	=	30,000
Creditors for expenses	=	10,000
		2,00,000

(3) Liquid Ratio $= \dfrac{\text{Liquid Assets}}{\text{Liquid Liabilities}}$

or $= \dfrac{\text{Current Assets} - \text{Stock}}{\text{Current Liabilities} - \text{Bank O.D.}}$

Surya Ltd. $= \dfrac{2,00,000}{3,60,000} = 0.56$

Chandra Ltd. $= \dfrac{2,00,000}{1,70,000} = 1.18$

(3) Creditors Turnover Ratio $= \dfrac{\text{Credit purchases}}{\text{Creditors + Bills payable}}$

Surya Ltd. $= \dfrac{9,00,000}{2,80,000 + 20,000}$

$= \dfrac{9,00,000}{3,00,0000} = 3$ times

Chandra Ltd. $= \dfrac{6,40,000}{1,50,000 + 10,000}$

$= \dfrac{6,40,000}{1,60,000} = 4$ times

(4) *Average Credit Sales*

Surya Ltd.:-

for 3 months: Debtors are Rs. = 1,70,000

for 12 months: — ?

$\dfrac{1,70,000 \times 12}{3}$ = Rs. 6,80,000

Chandra Ltd.:-

for 3 months: Debtors are = 1,40,000

for 12 months: — ?

$\dfrac{1,40,000 \times 12}{3}$ = Rs. 5,60,000

Problem 14: From the following balance sheet of Tara Ltd. calculate: (*a*) long-term debt-equity, (*b*) proprietory ratio, (*c*) capital gearing ratio, (*d*) stock-working capital ratios.

Equity share capital	2,00,000	Land and Building	1,40,000
8% pref share capital	60,000	Plant and machinery	80,000
Reserve	30,000	Furniture and fixtures	20,000
P & C a/c	20,000	Debtors	80,000
9% Debentures	40,000	Stock	70,000
Creditors	60,000	Cash in hand	30,000
O/s expenses	5,000	Prepaid expenses	10,000
Provision for taxation	20,000	Preliminary	
Proposed dividend	15,000	expenses	20,000
	4,50,000		4,50,000

(*University of Bombay, B.Com., October 1999*)

Solution:

(1) Long-term debt equity Ratio $= \frac{\text{Long Term Debt}}{\text{Shareholders funds}}$

$= \frac{40,000}{2,90,000} = 0.138$

Long-term Debt

9% Debentures = 40,000

Shareholders finds

Equity share capital	=	2,00,000
Preference share capital	=	60,000
Reserves and surplus	=	30,000
P &C a/c	=	20,000
		3,10,000
Less fictitions assets		20,000
		2,90,000

(2) Proprietory Ratio $= \frac{\text{Proprietor's funds}}{\text{Total Assets}}$

$= \frac{2,90,000}{4,30,000} = 0.67$

Total Assets

Total of all assets			=	4,50,000
Less: Prepaid expenses	=	10,000		
Less: Preliminary expenses	=	20,000		
				30,000
				4,20,000

(3) Capital Bearing Ratio $= \frac{\text{Fixed Interest bearing Securities + Fixed Dividend bearing Securities}}{\text{Equity Shareholders funds}}$

$= \frac{40,000 + 6,00,000}{2,30,000} = 0.43$

Fixed Dividend bearing securities

8% pref shares	=	60,000

Equity shareholders finds

Equity share capital	=	2,00,000
Reserves	=	30,000
P & L a/c	=	20,000
		2,50,000
Less: Preliminary expenses		20,000
		2,30,000

$$\text{(4) Stock-Working Capital Ratio} = \frac{\text{Stock}}{\text{Working Capital}}$$

$$= \frac{70,000}{90,000} = 0.77$$

Working Capital

Current Assets:		
Debtors		80,000
Stock		70,000
Cash in hand		30,000
Prepaid expenses		10,000
		1,90,000
Less: Current liabilities		
Creditors	60,000	
O/s expenses	5,000	
Provision for tax	20,000	
Proposed Dividend	15,000	
	1,00,000	1,00,000
working capital		90,000

Problem 15: The following are the Trading and Profit & loss for the year ended 31st December, 1998 and the balance sheet as on that date of K Ltd.

Trading and P & L A/c

To operning stock	9,950	By Sales	85,000
To purchases	5,4525	By Closing stock	14,900
To wages	1425		
To Gross profit	34,000		
	99,900		99,900
To Administrative expenses	15,000	By Gross profit	34,000
To Selling expenses	3,000	By Interest	300
To Financial expenses	15,000	By Profit on sale of shares	600
To Loss on sale of assets	400		
To Net profit	15,000		
	34,900		34,900

Balance Sheet

Share capital	20,000	Land and Buildings	15,000
Reserves	9,000	Plant and Machinery	8,000
Current liabilities	13,000	Stock	14,900
P & L a/c	6,000	Debtors	7,100
		Cash at bank	3,000
	48,000		48,000

You are required to calculate:

(*a*) Current Ratio
(*b*) Operating Ratio
(*c*) Stock Turnover Ratio
(*d*) Net Profit Ratio
(*e*) Fixed Assets Turnover Ratio

(*Osmania University, B.Com., October 1999*)

Solution:

(*a*) Current Ratio $= \dfrac{\text{Current Assets}}{\text{Current liabilities}}$

$= \dfrac{25{,}000}{13{,}000} = 1.92$

Current Assets

Stock	14,900
Debtors	7,100
Cash at Bank	3,000
	25,000

(*b*) Operating Ratio $= \dfrac{\text{Cost of goods sold + Operating expenses}}{\text{Net Sales}}$

$= \dfrac{51{,}000 + 19{,}500}{85{,}000}$

$= \dfrac{70{,}500}{85{,}000} = 0.829$

Cost of Goods Sold

Opening stock	=	9,950
Purchases	=	54,525
Wages	=	1,425
		65,900
Less: Closing stock		14,900
		51,000

(*c*) Stock Turnover Ratio $= \dfrac{\text{Cost of goods sold}}{\text{Average Stock}}$

$= \dfrac{51{,}000}{12{,}425} = 4.10$ times

Average stock

$= \dfrac{\text{Opening stock + Closing stock}}{2}$

$= \dfrac{9{,}950 + 14{,}900}{2} = 12{,}425$

(*d*) Net Profit Ratio $= \frac{\text{Net profit}}{\text{Net sales}} \times 100$

$= \frac{15{,}000}{85{,}000} \times 100 = 17.64\%$

(*e*) Fixed Assets Turnover Ratio $= \frac{\text{Net Sales}}{\text{Fixed Assets}}$

$= \frac{85{,}000}{23{,}000} = 3.7 \text{ times}$

Problem 16: The profit and loss a/c and balance sheet of XYZ Ltd. are as under:

Profit and loss A/c for the year ended 31st December, 1997

Net sales			3,00,000
Less:	Cost of production		2,58,000
			42,000
Less:	Operating expenses		
	Selling	2,200	
	General administration	4,000	
	Rent of office	2,800	
			9,000
	Gross operating profit		33,000
Less:	Depreciation		10,000
	Net operating profit		23,000
	other income and interest on govt. securities		1,500
	Gross income (before tax)		24,500
Less:	Other expenses:		
	Interest on bank overdraft	300	
	Intrest on debentures	42,000	
			4,500
	Net income (before tax)		20,000
	Tax 50% on net income		10,000
	Net income (after tax)		10,000

Balance sheet as at 31st Dec., 1997

Equity share capital	50,000	Fixed assets	1,80,000	
7% pref share capital	10,000	*Less*: Depreciation	50,000	
Reserves and surplus	40,000			1,30,000
6% Mortgage debentures	70,000	Investment on govt. securities		15,000
Creditors	6,000	Debtors		20,000
Bills payable	10,000	Stock		30,000
O/s expenses	1,000	Cash		5,000
Provision for taxation	13,000			
	2,00,000			2,00,000

You are required to calculate the following ratios:

1. Return on investment
2. Net profit ratio
3. Current ratio
4. Net worth to capital employed
5. Cost of production to capital employed

(CS Intermediate, June, 1999)

Solution:

(1) Return on Investment

$$= \frac{\text{Net Profit (After Tax and Interest)}}{\text{Proprietors funds}}$$

$$= \frac{10{,}000}{1{,}00{,}000} = 0.10$$

Proprietors Funds

Equity share capital	=	50,000
7% pref. share capital	=	10,000
Reserves and surplus	=	40,000
		1,00,000

(2) Net profit ratio $= \frac{\text{Net Profit}}{\text{Net Sales}} \times 100$

$$= \frac{10{,}000}{3{,}00{,}000} \times 100 = 3.33\%$$

(3) Current ratio $= \frac{\text{Current Assets}}{\text{Current Liabilities}}$

$$= \frac{55{,}000}{30{,}000} = 1.88$$

Current Assets

Debtors	20,000
Stock	30,000
Cash	5,000
	55,000

Current liabilities

Creditors	6,000
Bills payable	10,000
O/s expenses	1,000
Provision for taxation	13,000
	30,000

(4) Net worth to capital employed $= \frac{\text{Net Worth}}{\text{Capital employed}}$

$$= \frac{1{,}00{,}000}{1{,}55{,}000} = 0.64$$

Capital employed

Net fixed assets		1,30,000
Add: Current assets:		
Debtors	20,000	
Stock	30,000	
Cash	5,000	
		55,000
		1,85,000
Less: Current liabilities		30,000

Net worth

Equity share capital	=	50,000
7% pref share capital	=	10,000
Reserves and surplus	=	40,000
		1,00,000

(5) Cost of production to capital employed $= \frac{\text{cost of production}}{\text{capital employed}} \times 100$

$$= \frac{2,58,000}{1,55,000} \times 100$$

$$= 166.45\%$$

Problem 17: The actual ratios of a company compared to the industry standard are given below. Comment on each ratio and indicate in one or two sentences the nature of action to be taken by the company:

	Ratio	*Industry standard*	*Actual for The Company*
(i)	Current ratio	2.2	2.7
(ii)	Debtors turnover ratio	6	8
(iii)	Stock turnover ratio	10	3
(iv)	Net profit ratio	5%	2.4%
(v)	Total debt to total assets	7.5%	40%

(*ICWA, Intermediate, December, 1999*)

Solution:

(1) Current Ratio: Normal value is 2. Here the company's position is above the normal value and the industry standard. This may also be due to excessive stock (Also refer to point 3 below).

(2) Debtor's Turnover Ratio: The industry standard indicates an average collection period of two months, while for the company it is only 1½ months. The companys position is better.

(3) Stock Turnover Ratio: The stock is moving very slowly obviously there is excessive stock in the company. Perhaps this has boosted up the current ratio. The sales volume has to be considerably increased and stock level brought down.

(4) Net Profit Ratio: Here the company's performance is very unsatisfactory compared to the overall position in the industry. This calls for steps to get better sales realisation and reduction of the cost of production.

(5) Total Debts to Total Assets: The percentage is disproportionately high in the company indicating a larger proportion of debt in the capital structure. Too high a debt component means too high a risk for equity shareholders.

Problem 18: The Balance Sheets of Katha Ltd., as on 31st December 1996 and 1997 were as follows:

(*Rs. in Thousand*)

Liabilities	*1996*	*1997*	*Assets*	*1996*	*1997*
Equity share capital (Rs. 10 each)	3,000	3,000	Fixed Assets	3,600	4,240
12% preference share	1,000	1,000	Sundry debtors	1,100	1,300
Reserves	1,160	1,770	Bills Receivable	860	1,050
10% Debentures	600	900	Stock	760	920
Creditors	480	640	Prepaird expenses	80	50
Bills payable	100	140	Bank Balance	120	120
Bank overdraft	200	240	Preliminary expenses	20	10
	6,540	7,690		6,540	7,690

During the year 1997, total sales were Rs. 1,80,00,000 and cash sales were 10% of total sales. Stock turnover ratio was 20 times. Net profit before payment of taxes at 40% was Rs. 22,50,000. There were no non-operating expenses and profit on sale of fixed assets Rs. 50,000. Calculate the following ratios for the year 1997.

1. Gross profit ratio
2. Operating ratio
3. Current ratio
4. Debtors turnover ratio and collection period
5. Return on capital employed
6. Earning per share

(University of Bombay, B.Com., October, 1998)

Solution:

(Fig. in Thousand)

(1) Gross Profit Ratio $= \dfrac{\text{Gross profit}}{\text{Net Sales}} \times 100$

$= \dfrac{1,200}{18,000} \times 100 = 6.67\%$

Calculate of Gross Profit

Sales – Cost of goods sold = Gross profit

18,000 – 16,800 = 1,200

Calculation of Cost of Goods Sold

Stock Turnover Ratio $= \dfrac{\text{Cost of goods sold}}{\text{Average stock}}$

$20 = \dfrac{x}{840}$

on cross multiplying x $= 20 \times 840$

$= 16,800$

Calculation of Average Stock

$\dfrac{\text{Opening stock} + \text{Closing stock}}{2}$

$= \dfrac{760+920}{2} = 840$

(2) Operating Ratio $= \dfrac{\text{Operating Cost} + \text{Operating expenses}}{\text{Net Sales}}$

$= \dfrac{16,800+0}{18,000} = 0.93$

(3) Current Ratio $= \dfrac{\text{Current Assets}}{\text{Current Liabilities}}$

$= \dfrac{3,440}{1,020} = 3.37$

Current Assets	
S. Debtors	1,300
Bills Receivable	1,050
Stock	920
Prepaid expenses	50
Bank Balance	120
	3,440

Current Liabilities	
Creditors	640
Bills payable	140
Bank OD	240
	1,020

(4) Debtors Turnover Ratio $= \dfrac{\text{Net Credit Sales}}{\text{Average accounts recoverable}}$

$= \dfrac{16,200}{2,155} = 7.52$ times

Net Credit Sales

Total sales	18,000
Less: Cash sales $\frac{10}{100} \times 18,000$	1,800
	16,200

Average Accounts Receivable

$$= \frac{(\text{Opening Bills Receivable} + \text{Opening Debtors}) + (\text{Closing B.R.} + \text{Closing Debtors})}{2}$$

$$= \frac{(860 + 1,100) + (1,050 + 1,300)}{2}$$

$$= \frac{4,310}{2} = 2,155$$

Debtors Collection Period $= \dfrac{365}{\text{Debtors Turnover Ratio}}$

$= \dfrac{365}{7.52} = 48.53$ or 49 Days

(5) Return on Capital Employed $= \dfrac{\text{Net profit before Tax, Interest}}{\text{Capital employed}}$

$= \dfrac{2,250 + 90}{6,660}$ (Debentures Interest)

$= 0.35$

Capital Employed

Net Fixed Assets			4240
Add: Working Capital:			
Current Assets:			
Debtors		1,300	
B.R.		1,050	
Stock		920	
Prepaid expense		50	
Bank Balance		120	
		3,440	
Less Current liabilities			
Creditors	640		
B.P.	140		
Bank OD	240	1,020	
			2,420
		Capital Employed	6,660

(6) Earning Per Share $= \dfrac{\text{NPAT} - \text{Preference Dividend}}{\text{No. of equity shares}}$

$= \dfrac{1350 - 120}{300} = 4.10$ Rs.

N.P.A.T.	
Net Profit Before Tax	2,250
Less: Tax @ 40%	900
	1,350

Problem 19: The summarised balance sheet of Good Value Traders Ltd. for the year ended 31-3-1998 is given below:

(Rs. in Lakhs)

Equity share capital	140	Fixed Assets	210	
Reserve & surplus	45	*Less:* Depreication	25	
Profit and loss a/c	20	*Current assets:*		185
Provision for taxation	10	Stock	25	
Sundry creditors	40	Debtors	30	
		Cash	15	70
	225			225

The following further particulars one also given for the year

(in Lakh of rupees)

Sales	120
Earning before Interest and Tax (EBIT)	30
Net profit after Tax (PAT)	20

Calculate the following for the company and explain the significance of each in one or two sentences:

1. Current ratio
2. Liquidity ratio
3. Profitability ratio
4. Profitability on funds employed
5. Debtors turnover
6. Stock turnover
7. Average collection period
8. Return on equity

(ICWA, Inter, June 1998)

Solution:

(Figures in Lakh of Rupees)

(1) Current Ratio $= \dfrac{\text{Current Assets}}{\text{Current Liabilities}}$

$= \dfrac{70}{40} = 1.75$

This ratio measures the liquidity of the firm and indicates its ability to meet the liabilities. Normal or ideal ratio is 2: 1.

(2) Liquidity Ratio $= \dfrac{\text{Liquid Assets}}{\text{Liquid liabilities}}$

$= \dfrac{45}{40} = 1.125$

Liquid Assets	
Debtors	30
Cash	15
	45

This is more stringent than current ratio and measures the short term liquidity of the firm. Normal value is 1: 1.

(3) Profitability $= \frac{\text{EBIT}}{\text{Sales}} \times 100$

$= \frac{30}{120} \times 100 = 25\%$

This ratio indicates profit earned on sales

(4) Profitability on funds employed $= \frac{\text{EBIT}}{\text{Share Capital and Long term loans}} = \frac{30}{205}$

Share Capital and Long-term Loans

Equity share capital	140
Reserves and surplus	45
Profit and loss a/c	20
	205

This ratio measures profitability on funds employed

(5) Debtors Turnover Ratio $= \frac{\text{Sales}}{\text{Average Debtors}}$

$= \frac{120}{30} = 4$

This ratio indicates how fast debtors are converted into cash.

(6) Stock Turnover Ratio $= \frac{\text{Cost of goods sold}}{\text{Average stock}}$

$= \frac{90}{25} = 3.6$ times

Cost of Goods Sold

Sales – EBIT

12 – 30 = 90

This ratio indicates the number of times stock is sold during the period.

(7) Average Collection Period $= \frac{\text{Debtors}}{\text{Credit Sales}} \times$ No. of months in a year

$= \frac{30}{120} \times 12 = 3$ months

This ratio indicates the normal credit allowed to customers

(8) Return on Equity $= \frac{\text{PAT}}{\text{Shareholders funds}}$

$= \frac{20}{205} = 9.76$

This ratio indicates the net return earned on shareholders funds.

Problem 20: From the following balance sheet and the sub-joined information of a company, you are required to calculate:

(*a*) Current ratio
(*b*) Quick ratio
(*c*) Inventory turnover
(*d*) Average collection period presuming 360 days in a year
(*e*) Owned finds to liabiltites ratio

Balance Sheet

Share capital	2,00,000	Goodwill	1,20,000
Reserves and surplus	58,000	Plant and machinery	1,50,000
Debentures	1,00,000	Stock	80,000

Creditors	40,000	Debtors	45,000
Bills payable	20,000	Cash	17,000
Other current liabilities	2,000	Miscellaneous current assets	8,000
	4,20,000		4,20,000

Sales (credit) for the year Rs. 4,00,000
Gross pforit Rs. 1,60,000

(CS, Inter, December, 1998)

Solution:

(1) Current Ratio $= \frac{\text{Current Assets}}{\text{Current Liabilities}}$

$= \frac{1,50,000}{62,000} = 2.4$

Current Assets

Stock	80,000
Debtors	45,000
Cash	17,000
Miscellaneous current assets	8,000
	1,50,000

Current liabilities

Creditors	40,000
Bills payable	20,000
Other current liabilities	2,000
	62,000

(2) Quick Ratio $= \frac{\text{Liquid Assets}}{\text{Liquid Liabilities}}$

$= \frac{70,000}{62,000} = 1.1$

(3) Inventory Turnover Ratio $= \frac{\text{Cost of Sales}}{\text{Average stock}}$

$= \frac{4,00,000 - 1,60,00}{80,000}$

= 3 times

Note: **In the absence of information, closing stock has been taken as the average stock.**

(4) Average Collection Period $= \frac{\text{Debtors}}{\text{Net credit Sales per day}}$

$= \frac{45,000}{1.111} = 41$ days

Credit Sales Per Day $= \frac{4,00,000}{360} = 1.11$

(5) Proprietor's Funds to Liabilities Ratio $= \frac{\text{Owners equity}}{\text{Total liabilities}}$

$= \frac{2,58,000}{1,62,000} = 1.6$

Problem 21: The following one the P & C a/c and The Balance Sheet of a company in summarised form

P & C a/c

To Opening stock	76,250	By Sales	5,00,000
To Purchases	3,22,250	By Closing stock	98,500
To Gross profit c/d	2,00,000		
	5,98,500		5,98,500
To Selling and Distribution expenses	22,000	By Gross profit	2,00,000
To Administrative expenses	98,000	By Dividend	9,000
To Loss on sale of assets	2,000	By Profit on sale of share	3,000
To Net profit	90,000		
	2,12,000		2,12,000

Balance Sheet

Share capital (2600 equity) Shares of Rs. 100 each)	2,60,000	Land and Buildings	1,50,000
		Plant and Machinery	80,000
		Stock	98,500
Reserves	70,000	Debtors	61,500
P & L a/c	20,000	Bills Receivable	60,000
Current liabilities	1,30,000	Bank	30,000
	4,80,000		4,80,000

Calculate

1. Gross profit ratio
2. Net profit ratio
3. Operating ratio
4. Operating profit ratio
5. Stock turnover ratio
6. Turnover of fixed assets

(Bangalore University, B.B.M., November, 1998)

Solution:

(1) Gross Profit Ratio $= \frac{\text{Gross Profit}}{\text{Net Sales}} \times 100$

$= \frac{2,00,000}{5,00,000} \times 100 = 40\%$

(2) Net Profit Ratio $= \frac{\text{Net Profit}}{\text{Sales}} \times 100$

$= \frac{90,000}{5,00,000} \times 100 = 18\%$

(3) Operating Ratio $= \frac{\text{Cost of goods sold + Operating expenses}}{\text{Net Sales}} \times 100$

$= \frac{1,01,500 + 1,20,000}{5,00,000} \times 100$

$= \frac{22,15,000}{5,00,000} \times 100 = 44.3\%$

(4) Operating Profit Ratio = 100 – Operating ratio

= 100 – 44.3% = 55.7%

(5) Stock Turnover Ratio $= \dfrac{\text{Cost of goods sold}}{\text{Average Inventory}}$

$= \dfrac{5,98,500 - 2,00,000}{87,375} = 4.56$ times

Average Stock

$= \dfrac{\text{Opening stock + Closing stock}}{2}$

$= \dfrac{76,250 + 98,500}{2} = \dfrac{1,74,750}{2} = 87,375$

(6) Turnover of Fixed Assets $= \dfrac{\text{Net Sales}}{\text{Fixed Assets}}$

$= \dfrac{5,00,000}{2,30,000} = 2.17$

Problem 22: Following are the Trading Account, profit and loss a/c of Sarmer Ltd. for the year ending 31st December, 1996 and Balance Sheet on that date:

P & L A/c

To Operning Stock	1,45,000	By Sales	7,50,000
To Purchases	6,10,000	By Closing stock	1,55,000
To Gross profit c/d	1,50,000		
	9,05,000		9,05,000
To Sundry expenses	80,000	By Gross profit b/d	1,50,000
To Net profit	70,000		
	1,50,000		1,50,000

Balance Sheet

Share capital		7,00,000	Net Block	5,50,000
Reserves and surplus	5,000		Stock	2,55,000
Add: Profit for the year	70,000		Debtors	1,80,000
		1,20,000	Cash	20,000
Bank overdraft		35,000		
Creditors		1,50,000		
		10,50,000		10,50,000

You are required to calculate the following ratios:

1. Current ratio,
2. Quick ratio,
3. Gross profit to sales ratio,
4. Stock turnover ratio,
5. Debtors turnover ratio,
6. Net profit to paid up capital.

(*University of Bombay, B.Com., April, 1998*)

Solution:

(1) Current Ratio $= \dfrac{\text{Current Assets}}{\text{Current Liabilities}}$

$= \dfrac{4,55,000}{1,85,000} = 2.46$

Current Assets

Stock	2,55,000
Debtors	1,80,000
Cash	20,000
	4,55,000

Current Liabilities

Bank OD	35,000
Creditors	1,50,000
	1,85,000

$$\text{(2) Quick Ratio} = \frac{\text{Quick Assets}}{\text{Quick Liabilities}}$$

$$= \frac{2,00,000}{1,50,000} = 1.33$$

Quick Assets

Debtors	1,80,000
Cash	20,000
	2,00,000

Quick liabilities here includes only creditors

$$\text{(3) Gross Profit Ratio} = \frac{\text{Gross profit}}{\text{Net Sales}} \times 100$$

$$= \frac{1,50,000}{7,50,000} \times 100 = 20\%$$

$$\text{(4) Stock Turnover Ratio} = \frac{\text{Cost of goods sold}}{\text{Average stock}}$$

$$= \frac{6,00,000}{1,50,000} = 4 \text{ times}$$

Cost of Goods Sold

Opening stock	1,45,000
Add: Purchases	6,10,000
	7,55,000
Less: Closing stock	1,55,000
	6,00,000

Average Stock

$$= \frac{\text{Opening Stock + Closing stock}}{2}$$

$$= \frac{1,45,000 + 1,55,000}{2} = 1,50,000$$

Alternatively, Average stock may be taken as Rs. 2,00,000 $\left(\textit{i.e.,}\ \frac{1,45,000 + 2,55,000}{2}\right)$ and the stock turnover ratio will be 3 times *i.e.,* $\frac{6,00,000}{2,00,000}$

(5) Debtors Turnover Ratio $= \dfrac{\text{Debtors + Bill Receivable}}{\text{Net credit Sales}} \times 365$

$= \dfrac{1,80,000}{7,50,000} \times 365$

$=$ 88 Days App

(6) Net Profit to Paid up Share Capital $= \dfrac{\text{Net profit after Tax}}{\text{Paid up share capital}} \times 100$

$= \dfrac{70,000}{7,00,000} \times 100 = 10\%$

Problem 23: Following figures have been extracted from the books of Voodoso Ltd.

	Rs.
Land and Building	6,00,000
Plant and Machinery	5,00,000
Equity capital	5,00,000
Preference capital	2,00,000
Stock	2,40,000
Debtors	2,00,000
Cash and Bank	55,000
Miscellaneous current assets	5,000
P & L a/c	2,00,000
General reserve	1,00,000
Sundry creditors	80,000
Bills payable	60,000
Miscellaneous current liabilities	60,000
Debentures	4,00,000

You are required to:

(*a*) Rearrange above figures in the vertical form and

(*b*) Calculate

(*i*) Debt equity ratio,

(*ii*) Proprietory ratio,

(*iii*) Capital gearing ratio.

(*University of Bombay, B.Com., April 1998*)

Solution:

Voodoo Ltd.

Balance Sheet as on

Sources of Fund		
Share capital:		
Preference share capital	2,00,000	
Equity share capital	5,00,000	
		7,00,000
Reserves and surplus:		
Profit and loss a/c	2,00,000	
General Reserve	1,00,000	
		3,00,000
Loan fund:		
Debentures		4,00,000
		14,00,000

Application of Funds

Fixed Assets:			
Land and Building		6,00,000	
Plant and Machinery		5,00,000	
			11,00,000
Working Capital			
Current Assets:			
Stock		2,40,000	
Debtors		2,00,000	
Cash and Bank		55,000	
Miscellaneous current assets		5,000	
		5,00,000	
Less: Current liabilities:			
Creditors	80,000		
Bills payable	60,000		
Miscellaneous current liability	60,000		
		2,00,000	
			3,00,000
Total applications			14,00,000

(1) Debt Equity Ratio $= \dfrac{\text{Long term Debts}}{\text{Shareholders fund}}$

$= \dfrac{4,00,000}{10,00,000} = 0.4$

(2) Proprietory Ratio $= \dfrac{\text{Pr opritors fund}}{\text{Total Assets}}$

$= \dfrac{10,00,000}{16,00,000} = 0.62$

(3) Capital Gearing Ratio $= \dfrac{\text{Fixed Interest bearing Securities} + \text{Fixed Dividend bearing securities}}{\text{Equity Shareholders fund}}$

$= \dfrac{2,00,000 + 4,00,000}{8,00,000} = 0.75$

Equity Shareholders Funds

Equity share capital	5,00,000
Reserves and P & L a/c	3,00,000
	8,00,000

Problem 24: From the following calculate:

(*a*) Gross profit ratio
(*b*) Net profit ratio
(*c*) Operating ratio
(*d*) Current ratio
(*e*) Acid test ratio
(*f*) Stock turnover ratio
(*g*) Debtors turnover ratio
(*h*) Return on investment

Trading and Profit & Loss A/c for the year ended 31st Dec., 1996

To Opening stock	25,000	By Sales	1,80,000
To Purchases	1,05,000	By Closing stock	15,000
To Gross profit	65,000		
	1,95,000		1,95,000
To Administrative expenses	23,000	By Gross profit	65,000
To Selling and distribution expenses	10,000	By Profit on sale of fixed assets	5,000
To Financial expenses	2,000		
To Net profit	35,000		
	70,000		70,000

Balance Sheet as at 31st Dec., 1996

Share capital	50,000	Land and Buildings	50,000
General reserve	40,000	Plant and Machinery	20,000
P & L a/c	15,000	Stock	15,000
Creditors	12,000	Debtors	2,000
Bills payable	8,000	Bills receivable	5,000
		Cash at Bank	15,000
	1,25,000		1,25,000

(*Osmania University, B.Com., March 1999*)

Solution:

(a) Gross Profit Ratio $= \dfrac{\text{Gross profit}}{\text{Net Sales}} \times 100$

$= \dfrac{65,000}{1,80,000} \times 100 = 36.11\%$

(b) Net Profit Ratio $= \dfrac{\text{Net Profit}}{\text{Net Sales}} \times 100$

$= \dfrac{35,000}{1,80,000} \times 100 = 19.44\%$

(c) Operating Ratio $= \dfrac{\text{Cost of goods sold + Operating expenses}}{\text{Net Sales}} \times 100$

$= \dfrac{1,15,000 + 35,000}{1,80,000} \times 100$

$= \dfrac{1,50,000}{1,80,000} \times 100 = 83.33\%$

Cost of Goods Sold

Opening stock	25,000
Add: Purchases	1,05,000
	1,30,000
Less: Closing stock	15,000
	1,15,000

Operating Expenses

Administration expenses	23,000
Selling and distribution expenses	10,000
Financial expenses	2,000
	35,000

(d) Current Ratio $= \dfrac{\text{Current Assets}}{\text{Current Liabilities}}$

$= \dfrac{55,000}{20,000} = 2.75$

Current Assets

Stock	15,000
Debtors	20,000
B.R.	5,000
Cash at Bank	15,000
	55,000

Current liabilities

Creditors	12,000
B.P.	8,000
	20,000

(e) Acid Test Ratio $= \dfrac{\text{Liquid Assets}}{\text{Liquid Liabilities}}$

$= \dfrac{40,000}{20,000} = 2$

Liquid Assets = Current assets – Stock

= 55,000 – 15,000

= 40,000

(f) Stock Turnover Ratio $= \dfrac{\text{Cost of goods sold}}{\text{Average stock}}$

$= \dfrac{1,15,000}{20,000} = 5.75$ times

Average Stock $= \dfrac{\text{Opening stock + Closing stock}}{2}$

$= \dfrac{25,000 + 15,000}{2} = 20,000$

(g) Debtors Turnover Ratio $= \dfrac{\text{Net Sales}}{\text{Debtors + Bills Receivable}}$

$= \dfrac{1,80,000}{20,000 + 5,000}$

$= \dfrac{1,80,000}{25,000} = 7.2$ times

(h) Return on Investment $= \dfrac{\text{Net profit}}{\text{Capital employed}} \times 100$

$= \dfrac{35,000}{1,05,000} \times 100 = 33.33\%$

Capital Employed

= Fixed assets + Current assets – Current liabilities
= 70,000 + 55,000 – 20,000
= 105,000

Problem 25: The comparative statements of income and financial position are given below:

	1990	*1991*
	Rs.	*Rs.*
Net sales	1,00,000	1,50,000
Less: Cost of sales	70,000	1,10,000
Gross profit	30,000	40,000
Less: Operating expesnes	20,000	25,000
Net profit	10,000	15,000
Aseets		
Cash in hand	5,000	8,000
Cash at Bank	4,000	2,000
Debtors	40,000	25,000
Stock at cost	15,000	10,000
Fixed assets (Net)	56,000	65,000
	1,20,000	1,10,000
Liabilities		
Creditors	36,000	12,000
Bills payable	2,000	1,000
Mortgage loan	10,000	20,000
Equity share capital	60,000	70,000
Reserves and surplus	12,000	7,000
	1,20,000	1,10,000

You are required to calculate the following ratios for both the years:

1. Current ratio
2. Acid test ratio
3. Debtors turnover ratio
4. Average collection period
5. Stock turnover ratio
(Assume 360 days in a year)

(Sri Venkateshwara University, B.Com., April 1998)

Solution:

(1) Current Ratio $= \dfrac{\text{Current Assets}}{\text{Current Liabilities}}$

Year 1990	*Year 1991*
$= \dfrac{64,000}{38,000}$	$= \dfrac{45,000}{13,000}$
= 1.68	= 3.46

Current Assets

	1990	*1991*
Cash in hand	5,000	8,000
Cash at Bank	4,000	2,000
Debtors	40,000	25,000
Stock	15,000	10,000
	64,000	45,000

Current Liabilities

Creditors	36,000	12,000
Bills payable	2,000	1,000
	38,000	13,000

(2) Acid Test Ratio $= \dfrac{\text{Liquid Assets}}{\text{Current liabilities}}$

$= \dfrac{49,000}{38,000} \qquad = \dfrac{35,000}{13,000}$

$= 1.29 \qquad = 2.69$

Liquid Assets

	1990	*1991*
Cash in hand	5,000	8,000
Cash at Bank	4,000	2,000
Debtors	40,000	25,000
	49,000	35,000

(3) Debtors Turnover Ratio $= \dfrac{\text{Net Credit Sales}}{\text{Average Trade Debtors}}$

Year 1990   *Year 1991*

$= \dfrac{1,00,000}{40,000} \qquad = \dfrac{1,50,000}{32,500}$

$= 2.5 \qquad = 4.6$

Average Trade Debtors   1990   1991

Rs.   40,000 $\dfrac{40,000 + 25,000}{2}$

$= 32,500$

(4) Average Colletion Period $= \dfrac{\text{Average Trade Debtors}}{\text{Net Credit Sales}} \times \text{No. of working days}$

1990 $= \dfrac{40,000}{1,00,000} \times 360 = 144 \text{ days}$

1991 $= \dfrac{32,500}{1,50,000} \times 360 = 78 \text{ days}$

(5) Stock Turnover Ratio $= \dfrac{\text{Cost of Sales}}{\text{Average Stock}}$

1990 $= \dfrac{70,000}{15,000} = 4.67 \text{ times}$

1991 $= \dfrac{1,10,000}{12,500} = 8.8 \text{ times}$

Average Stock:

1990 = Rs. 15,000

1991 $= \frac{15,000 + 10,000}{2} = 12,500$

Problem 26: From the following Balance Sheet, calculate Current ratio, Acid test ratio, Stock turnover ratio, Debtors turnover ratio and Average collection period:

Share capital	4,00,000	Goodwill	2,50,000
General Reserve	2,88,000	Buildings	4,00,000
8% Debentures	3,00,00	Machinery	3,50,000
Mortgage loan	2,50,000	Closing stock	2,00,000
Creditors	90,000	Debtors	80,000
Bills payable	35,000	Bills receivable	90,000
Bank overdraft	60,000	Cash	65,000
O/s expenses	15,000	Prepaid expenses	3,000
	14,38,000		14,38,000

Additional information opening stocks Rs. 1,50,000: Opening debtors Rs. 1,50,000 and net credit sales Rs. 6,00,000.

(University of Madras, B.Com., May 1997)

Solution:

(1) Current Ratio $= \frac{\text{Current Assets}}{\text{Current liabilities}}$

$= \frac{4,38,000}{2,00,000} = 2.19$

Current Assets

Stock	2,00,000
Debtors	80,000
Bills receivable	90,000
Cash	65,000
Prepaid expenses	3,000
	4,38,000

Current Liabilities

Creditors	90,000
Bills payable	35,000
Bank OD	60,000
O/s expenses	15,000
	2,00,000

(2) Acid Test Ratio $= \frac{\text{Quick Assets}}{\text{Quick liabilities}}$

$= \frac{2,35,000}{1,40,000} = 1.68$

Quick Assets

= Current assets – Stock – Prepaid expenses

= 4,38,000 – 2,00,000 – 3,0000

= 2,35000

Quick Liabilities

= Current liabilities – Bank OD

= 2,00,000 – 60,000 = 1,40,000

(3) Stock Turnover Ratio $= \dfrac{\text{Cost of Sales or Sales}}{\text{Average Stock}} = \dfrac{6,00,000}{1,75,000}$ (Credit Sales)

$= 3.43$ times

Average Stock $= \dfrac{\text{Opening stock + Closing stock}}{2}$

$= \dfrac{1,50,000 + 2,00,000}{2}$

$= \dfrac{3,50,000}{2} = 1,75,000$

(4) Debtors Turnover Ratio $= \dfrac{\text{Credit Sales}}{\text{Average Accounts Receivable}}$

$= \dfrac{6,00,000}{2,05,000} = 2.93$ times

Average Accounts Receivable $= \dfrac{\text{Opening Debtor + Closing Debtor}}{2} + \text{B.R.}$

$= \dfrac{1,05,000 + 80,000}{2} + 90,000$

$= 1,15,000 + 90,000$

$= 2,05,000$

(5) Average Collection Period $= \dfrac{12}{\text{D.T.R.}}$ or $= \dfrac{365}{\text{D.T.R.}}$

$= \dfrac{12}{2.93}$ $= \dfrac{365}{2.43}$

$= 4.09$ months $= 124.57$ days

Problem 27: (*Calculate of Missing Information*)

Calculate:

(*a*) Current assets

(*b*) Inventory, from the following particulars:

Current ratio = 2.6: 1

Current liability = Rs. 40,000

(*Bangalore University. B.Com., April 2,000*)

Solution:

Current Ratio $= \dfrac{\text{Current Assets}}{\text{Current Liabilities}}$

$2.6 = \dfrac{\text{C.A.}}{40,000}$

or CA $= 2.6 \times 40,000$

CA $= 1,04,000$

Inventory is the same as current asset in the absence of liquid assets which is not given in the problem.

Problem 28: Average stock of a firm is Rs. 40,000. Its opening stock is Rs. 5,000 less than the closing stock. Find out opening stock. (*Bangalore University, B.Com., April 2,000*)

Solution:

Average stock = 40,000

Total stock = Average stock × 2

= 40,000 × 2 = 80,000

Add: Opening stock less by 5,000 = 5,000

= 85,000

Hence opening stock $\frac{85,000}{2}$ = 42,500

Problem 29: Gross profit ratio is 20% on sales. Total gross profit Rs. 1,00,000. Cash sales Rs. 1,20,000 Average debtors Rs. 95,000. Calculate debtor's turnover ratio. (*Bangalore University, B.Com., April 2,000*)

Solution:

$$\text{Gross Profit Ratio} = \frac{\text{Gross profit}}{\text{Sales}} \times 100$$

$$\frac{20}{100} = \frac{1,00,000}{\text{Sales}}$$

$$\text{or} \quad \text{Sales} = \frac{1,00,000 \times 100}{20} \text{ (on cross multiplication)}$$

= 5,00,000

Total sales = 5,00,000

Credit sales = Total sales – Cash sales

= 5,00,000 – 1,20,000

= 3,80,000

$$\text{Debtors Turnover Ratio} = \frac{\text{Credit Sales}}{\text{Average Debtors}}$$

$$= \frac{3,80,000}{95,000} = 4$$

Problem 30: Cost of sales of a firm is Rs. 2,50,000 and stock turnover ratio is 5 times. Find out the value of stock:

Solution:

$$\text{Stock Turnover Ratio} = \frac{\text{Cost of Sales}}{\text{Average Stock}}$$

Less: Average stock = x

$$5 = \frac{2,50,000}{x}$$

or $5x$ = 2,50,000

$$x = \frac{2,50,000}{5} = 50,000$$

Problem 31: Gross profit ratio of a firm is 20%. Gross profit is Rs. 30,000. Calculate the sales figure.

Solution:

$$\text{Gross Profit Ratio} = \frac{\text{Gross Profit}}{\text{Sales}} \times 100$$

$$\frac{20}{100} = \frac{30,000}{\text{Sales}}$$

20 sales = 30,000 × 100

$$\text{Sales} = \frac{30,000 \times 100}{200} = 1,50,000$$

Problem 32:

Given:

Gross profit is Rs. 3,00,000

Gross profit ratio at 25% on sales

Compute the cost of sales

Solution:

$$\text{Gross Profit Ratio} = \frac{\text{Gross profit}}{\text{Sales}}$$

$$\frac{25}{100} = \frac{3,00,000}{\text{Sales}}$$

$$\text{or} \quad 25 \text{ sales} = 3,00,000 \times 100$$

$$\text{Sales} = \frac{3,00,000 \times 100}{25}$$

$$= 12,00,000$$

$$\text{Cost of sales} = \text{Sales} - \text{Gross profit}$$

$$= 12,00,000 - 3,00,000$$

$$= 9,00,000$$

Problem 33: Turnover to fixed assets ratio is 1: 1.2 value of goods sold is Rs. 9,00,000. Compute the value of fixed assets.

Solution:

$$\text{Fixed assets to Turnover Ratio} = \frac{\text{Turnover}}{\text{Fixed Assets}}$$

$$1.2 = \frac{9,00,000}{1}$$

$$\text{or} \quad = \frac{9,00,000}{1.2} \text{ (on cross multiplication)}$$

$$= 7,50,000$$

Therefore fixed assets = Rs. 7,50,000.

Problem 34: Given long term debt to equity ratio is 2: 3. Equity amount is Rs. 50,000. Compute the value of long-term debt.

Solution:

$$\text{Long-term Debt to Equity Ratio} = \frac{\text{Long term debt}}{\text{Equity}}$$

$$\frac{2}{3} = \frac{x}{50,000}$$

$$\text{or,} \quad 3x = 2 \times 50,000 \text{ (on cross multiplication)}$$

$$x = \frac{2 \times 50,000}{3} = 33,333$$

Problem 35: Gross profit of a firm is 20% of sales. Cost of goods sold Rs. 1,60,000. Find out the sales.

Solution:

Gross profit on Sales = 20% of sales

Therefore cost of goods sold must be 80 *i.e.*, (100–20)

For cost of goods sold of 80 = 1,60,000

$$\text{For } 100 \rightarrow = \frac{1,60,000 \times 100}{80}$$

$$= 2,00,000$$

$$\text{Sales} = 2,00,000$$

Problem 36: Average stock of a firm is Rs. 40,000. Its opening stock is Rs. 5,000 less than the closing stock. Find out the opening stock.

Solution:

Average stock = 40,000

Total stock = 40,000 × 2 = 80,000

Opening stock is Rs. 5,000 less than the closing stock

= 80,000 – 5,000 = 75,000

$$= \frac{75,000}{2} = 37,500$$

Opening stock = 37,500

Closing stock = 37,500 + 5,000 = 42,500

Problem 37: Gross profit ratio is 20% on sales, stock velocity 5, average stock Rs. 1,10,000. Ascertain the sales.

Solution:

$$\text{Stock Turnover Ratio} = \frac{\text{Cost of goods sold}}{\text{Average stock}}$$

$$5 = \frac{\text{Cost of goods sold}}{1,10,000}$$

or Cost of goods sold = 1,10,000 × 5

= 5,50,000

Sales = Cost of goods sold + Profit

100 = 80 + 20

For 80; cost of goods sold is = 5,50,000

$$\text{For } 100 \rightarrow = \frac{100 \times 5,50,000}{80}$$

= 6,87,500

Problem 38: Closing stock of X Ltd. is Rs. 2,00,000. Total liquid assets are Rs. 10,00,000. Liquid ratio is 2: 1. Find out working capital.

Solution:

Closing stock = 2,00,000

Liquid assets = 10,00,000

$$\text{Liquidity Ratio} = \frac{\text{Liquid Assets}}{\text{Liquid liabilities}} = \frac{2}{1}$$

Current assets = Liquid assets + stock

= 10,00,000 + 2,00,000

= 12,00,000

Working capital = current assets – current liabilities

For liquid assets 2 : The amount is 10,00,000

For liquid asset 1 : →X→

$$= \frac{10,00,000}{2} = 5,00,000$$

Working capital = Current assets – Current liabilities

= 12,00,000 – 5,00,000

= 7,00,000

Problem 39: Total current liabilities are Rs. 80,000 current ratio is 2.5: 1. Acid test ratio 1.5: 1. Total current assets include stock, debtors and cash only. Cash is 2/3 of Debtors. Calculate debtors.

Solution:

$$\text{Current Ratio} = \frac{\text{Current Assets}}{\text{Current Liabilities}} = \frac{2.5}{1}$$

Current liabilities = 1 × 80,000 = 80,000

Therefore current assets = 80,000 × 2.5

= 2,00,000

$$\text{Acid Test Ratio} = \frac{\text{Liquid Assets}}{\text{Liquid Liabilities}} = \frac{1.5}{1}$$

1 = 80,000

Therefore liquid assets = 1.5 × 80,000 = 1,20,000

Stock = Current assets – Liquid assets

= 2,00,000 – 1,20,000

= 80,000

Liquid assets = Cash + Debtors

$1,20,000 = x \times \frac{2}{3} + x$ (Debtors assumed as x)

$x + \frac{2}{3}x = 1,20,000$

or $3x + 2x = 3 \times 1,20,000$

$5x = 3,60,000$

$x = 72,000$

Therefore debtors = Rs. 72,000

$\text{Cash} = \frac{2}{3} \times 720,000 = 48,000$

Verification = Debtors + Cash

= 72,000 + 48,000 = 1,20,000

Problem 40: Current ratio 2.5, Acid test ratio 1.75, stock Rs, 1,50,000. Calculate net working capital

Solution:

$\text{Current Ratio} = \frac{2.5}{1}$

$\text{Liquidity Ratio} = \frac{1.75}{1}$

Current Asset = 2,50

Liquid asset = 1.75

Current asset – Liquid asset = Stock

2.50 – 1.75 = 0.75

$\text{Stock} = 0.75 \text{ or } \frac{3}{4} = 1,50,000$

or $= \frac{4 \times 1,50,000}{3} = 2,00,000$

Current liability = 1 = 2,00,000

Current asset = 2,00,000 × 2.5

= 5,00,000

Net working capital = Current assets – Current liabilities

= 5,00,000 – 2,00,000

= 3,00,000

Problem 41: Current liabilities of a company are Rs. 3,00,000. Its current ratio is 3: 1 and quick ratio is 1: 1. Calculate the value of stock in trade.

Solution:

$$\text{Current Ratio} = \frac{\text{Current Assets}}{\text{Current Liabilities}}$$

$$\frac{3}{1} = \frac{x}{3,00,000}$$

$$x = 3 \times 3,00,000$$

$$= 9,00,000$$

$$\text{Quick Ratio} = \frac{\text{Quick Assets}}{\text{Quick Liabilities}}$$

$$\frac{1}{1} = \frac{x}{3,00,000}$$

$$x = 1 \times 3,00,000$$

$$= 3,00,000$$

Current Assets – Stock = Quick Assets

9,00,000 – x = 3,00,000

x = 6,00,000

Hence stock in Trade = Rs. 6,00,000

Problem 42: Given current ratio is 2.5, working capital is 60,000. Calculate the amount of current assets and current liabilities.

Solution:

Current Assets – Current liabilities = Working capital

2.5 – 1 = 1.5

If working capital is Rs. 1.5, then current asset is 2.5

If working capital is 1, then current asset is $\frac{2.5}{1.5}$

$$\frac{2.5}{1.5} \times 60,000 = 1,00,000$$

Current asset = 1,00,000

1,00,000 – Current liabilities = 60,000

Current liabilities = 40,000

Problem 43: Following information are available from the books of Smart Projects Ltd.

Debtors velocity	3 months
Stock velocity	6 months
Creditors velocity	2 months
Gross profit ratio	20%

Gross profit for the year ended 31st March, 1999 was Rs. 50,00,000, stock on 31st March, 1999 was more than what it was at the beginning of the year. Bills Receivable and bills payable were Rs. 60,000 and Rs. 36,667 respectively.

You are required to calculate the value of (1) Sales, (2) Sundry debtors, (3) Sundry creditors and (4) Closing stock and also prepare a note for the finance director on the overall impact of the results.

(CS, Inter, June, 2,000)

Solution: **(1) Calculation of Sales**

$$\text{Gross Profit Ratio} = \frac{\text{Gross profit}}{\text{Sales}}$$

$$\frac{20}{100} = \frac{5,00,000}{\text{Sales}}$$

$$20 \text{ sales} = 5{,}00{,}000 \times 100$$

$$\text{Sales} = \frac{5{,}00{,}000 \times 100}{20} = \text{Rs. } 25{,}00{,}000$$

(2) Calculation of Sundry Debtors

Sales = 25,00,000

Debtor's velocity = 3 months

Year end sales outstanding

$$25{,}00{,}000 \times \frac{3}{12} = 6{,}25{,}000$$

Less: Bills receivable = 60,000

Sundry Debtors = 5,65,000

(3) Calculation of Creditors

Purchases = Sales – Gross profit + Increase in stock

= 25,00,000 – 5,00,000 + 20,000

Purchases = 20,20,000

Creditor's velocity = 2 months

Year end purchases outstanding

$$20{,}20{,}000 \times \frac{2}{12} = 3{,}36{,}667$$

Less: Bills payable = 36,667

Sundry Creditors = 3,00,000

(4) Calculation of Closing Stock

Cost of goods sold = Sales – Profit

= 25,00,000 – 5,00,000

Cost of goods sold = 20,00,000

Stock velocity = 6 months

$$\text{Average stock} = 20{,}00{,}000 \times \frac{6}{12} = 10{,}00{,}000$$

Let opening stock be = x

Closing stock = $x + 20{,}000$

Twice Average stock = $2x + 20{,}000$

20,00,000 = $2x + 20{,}000$

$2x$ = 19,80,000

x = 9,90,000

Thus opening stock = Rs. 9,90,000

Hence closing stock = 9,90,000 + 20,000

= 10,10,000

Overall Impact of the Results

The debtors velocity and the amount of debtors are more than what the creditors velocity and the amount of creditors. This means that the company is paying liberal credit than what it receives from the creditors. The company is having a low inventory turnover ratio which result in blocking of funds in inventory. The gross profit is merely 20% of the sales which seems to be insufficient to cover up the overheads and maintain a reasonable net profit.

Problem 44: The current ratio of a company is 2: 1 which of the following transactions would:

(*i*) Improve the ratio
(*ii*) Reduce the ratio
(*iii*) Not alter the ratio (give your reasons)

1. Pay a current liability
2. Sell machinery for cash
3. Borrow money us interest repayable at the end of 5 years
4. Purchase stock of goods for cash
5. Accept a bill of exchange drawn by a supplier
6. Issue of bouns shares.

(*University of Bombay, B.Com., October, 1998*)

Solution:

(1) Pay a Current Liability: Paying a current will decrease both in current liability and current asset by the same amount. Therefore current ratio shall improve.

(2) Sell Machinery for Cash: Selling machinery for cash will decrease the fixed assets and increases the current assets therefore current ratio shall be improved.

(3) Borrow Money at Interest Payable at The End of 5 years: This will result in increase in current asset and increase in long-term loans. Therefore current ratio shall be improved.

(4) Purchased Stock of Goods for Cash: This will result in increase in stock and decrease in cash balance. Total current assets and current liabilities remain the same and hence current ratio will not be affected.

(5) Accept a Bill of Exchange Drawn by Supplier: This will increase bills payable and reduce creditors. Total current assets and current liabilities remain the same the hence current ratio will not be affected.

(6) Issue of Bouns Shares: This will increase equity share capital and will reduce the surplus. Both effects are on non-current items, not affecting on current assets and current liabilities. Total current assets and current liabilities remain the same and hence current ratio will not be affected.

Problem 45: From the following information as certain:

(*i*) Long-term loans
(*ii*) Reserves and surplus
(*iii*) Capital employed

Capital gearing ratio	0.75
Debt equity ratio	0.40
(Long-term debts to shareholders funds)	
Equity share capital	Rs. 3,00,000
Preference share capital	Rs. 1,00,000

(*University of Bombay, B.Com., October 1998*)

Solution:

Let long-term loans $= x$
Reserves and surpluses $= y$

$$\text{Capital Gearing Ratio} = \frac{\text{Preference Share Capital + Long Term Debts}}{\text{Equity Share Capital + Reserves and Surpluses}}$$

$$0.75 = \frac{1,00,000 + x}{3,00,000 + y}$$

$$\therefore \quad 0.75\,(3,00,000 + y) = 1,00,000 + x$$

$$\therefore \quad 0.75y + 2,25,000 = 1,00,000 + x$$

$$\therefore \quad x = 0.75y + 1,25,000 \qquad \text{... (1)}$$

$$\text{Debt Equity Ratio} = \frac{\text{Long term debts}}{\text{Shareholders funds}}$$

$$0.40 = \frac{x}{\text{Equity Share capital + Reserves + Preference share capital}}$$

or $$0.40 = \frac{x}{3,00,000 + 1,00,000 + y}$$

$$x = 0.4\,(4,00,000 + y)$$

$$x = 1,60,000 + 0.4y \quad \text{... (2)}$$

or $$0.75y + 1,25,000 = 1,60,000 + 0.4y$$

or $$0.75y - 0.4y = 1,60,000 - 1,25,000$$

or $$0.35y = 35,000$$

or $$y = \frac{35,000}{0.35} = 1,00,000$$

Calculation of Long-term Debts, i.e., *X*

$$\text{Debt Equity Ratio} = \frac{\text{Long term Debt}}{\text{Eqty Shares Capital} + \text{Pref share capital} + \text{Reserves}}$$

$$0.40 = \frac{x}{3,00,000 + 1,00,000 + 1,00,000}$$

$$0.40 = \frac{x}{5,00,000}$$

$$x = 5,00,000 \times 0.40 = 20,00,000$$

Calculation of Capital Employed

Equity share capital	3,00,000
Preference share capital	1,00,000
Reserves and surplus	1,00,000
Long-term loans	2,00,000
Capital employed	7,00,000

Problem 46: From the following details find out (*a*) current assets, (*b*) current liabilities, (*c*) quick asset, (*d*) stock

Current Ratio = 2.5
Quick Ratio = 1.5
Working Capital = Rs. 60,000

(*Osmania University, B.Com., October, 1999*)

Solution:

$$\text{Current Ratio} = \frac{\text{Current Assets}}{\text{Current Liabilities}}$$

$$2.5 = \frac{CA}{CL}$$

or $$CA = 2.5\ CL$$

Let current liabilities be $= x$

∴ Current assets $= 2.5\,x$

Working capital = Current assets – Current liabilities

$= 2.5\,x - x$

$= 1.5x$

But working capital $= 60,000$

$1.5x = 60,000$

$$x = \frac{60,000}{1.5} = 40,000$$

$$\text{Current liabilities} = 40{,}000$$

$$\therefore \quad \text{Current Assets} = 2.5 \times 40{,}000 = 1{,}00{,}000$$

$$\text{Liquidity Ratio} = \frac{\text{Quick Assets}}{\text{Quick Liabilities}}$$

$$1.5 = \frac{\text{Quick Assets}}{\text{Quick Liabilities}}$$

$$\begin{aligned} \text{Q A} &= 1.5 \times \text{Q . L} \\ &= 1.5 \times 40{,}000 \\ &= 60{,}000 \\ \text{Stock} &= \text{Current Assets} - \text{Quick Assets} \\ &= 1{,}00{,}000 - 60{,}000 \\ &= 40{,}000 \end{aligned}$$

Problem 47 (Preparation of Balance Sheet with Ratios): The gross profit of X Ltd. for the year 1998 is Rs. 80,000. This is one-fourth of the year's sales. Out of total sales, three-fourth is on credit. The stock turnover is 10 times and the average collection period is 15 days (assume 360 days). Total assets turnover is 4 times and the long-term debt to equity is 50%. Shareholder's equity is Rs. 40,000. The current ratio is 2: 1.

Find out (1) creditors, (2) long-term debt, (3) cash in hand, (4) debtors, (5) closing stock, (6) fixed assets. And also prepare Balance Sheet of 'X' Ltd. for the year 1998.

(Bangalore University, B.Com., October 2000)

Solution:

(1) Credit Sales

Gross profit = 80,000
Sales, 4 times the gross profit
i.e., 80,000 × 4 = 3,20,000

$$\text{Credit sales } \frac{3}{4} \text{ of } 3{,}20{,}000 = 2{,}40{,}000$$

(2) Inventory or Stock

$$\text{Stock Turnover Ratio} = \frac{\text{Cost of goods sold}}{\text{Average Inventory}}$$

$$10 = \frac{\text{Sales} - \text{Gross profit}}{\text{Inventory}}$$

$$10 = \frac{3{,}20{,}000 - 80{,}000}{\text{Inventory}}$$

$$\text{Inventory} = \frac{2{,}40{,}000}{10} = \text{Rs. } 24{,}000$$

(3) Debtors

$$\text{Average collection period} = 15 \text{ days}$$

$$\text{Debtors Turnover Ratio} = \frac{360}{15} = 24$$

$$24 = \frac{\text{Credit Sales}}{\text{Average Debtors}}$$

$$24 = \frac{2{,}40{,}000}{\text{Average Debtors}}$$

$$\text{Debtors} = \frac{2{,}40{,}000}{24} = 10{,}000$$

(4) Total Assets

$$\text{Assets Turnover Ratio} = \frac{\text{Sales}}{\text{Total Assets}}$$

$$4 = \frac{3,20,000}{\text{Total Assets}}$$

or, $4 \text{ total assets} = 3,20,000$

or $\text{Total assets} = \frac{3,20,000}{4} = 80,000$

(5) Long-term Debt

$$\text{Long-term Debt to Equity} = \frac{\text{Long term debt}}{\text{Equity}}$$

$$\text{50\% of 40,000 long-term debt} = \frac{50}{100} \times 40,000 = 20,000$$

(6) Cash

Current Ratio = 2: 1
Current Assets = Inventory + Debtors + Cash
40,000 = 24,000 + 10,000 + Cash
or Cash = 40,000 – 34,000 = 6,000

(7) Fixed Assets

Total assets – Current Assets
= 80,000 – 40,000 = 40,000

(8) Current Liabilities

Current Liabilities = Total Assets – Shareholders Equity – Long-term Debt
= 80,000 – 40,000 – 20,000
= 20,000

Required Information

(1) Creditors = Rs. 20,000
(2) Long-term debts = Rs. 20,000
(3) Cash in hand = 6,000
(4) Debtors = 10,000
(5) Closing Stock = 24,000
(6) Fixed Assets = 40,000

Balance Sheet

Equity share capital	40,000	Fixed Assets	40,000
Long-term liabilities	20,000	Inventory	24,000
Creditors	20,000	Debtors	10,000
		Cash	6,000
	80,000		80,000

Problem 48: From the following information, make out a statement of proprietor's funds with as many details as possible:

1. Current ratio 2.5
2. Liquid ratio 1.5
3. Proprietory ratio $\left(\frac{\text{Fixed assets}}{\text{Proprietory funds}}\right)$ 0.75
4. Working capital Rs. 60,000
5. Reserves and surplus Rs. 40,000

6. Bank overdraft Rs. 10,000 and
7. There is no long-term loan or fictitions asset (*CS, Inter, December, 1998*)

Solution:

$$\text{Current Ratio} = \frac{\text{Current Assets}}{\text{Current Liabilities}}$$

$$2.5 = \frac{\text{Current Assets}}{\text{Current Liabilities}}$$

or CA = 2.5 CL

Let current liabilities = x

∴ Current assets = 2.5 x

Working capital = Current Assets – Current liabilities

= 2.5x – x

= 1.5x

(1) *Current liabilities*

But working capital is = 60,000

∴ 1.5x = 60,000

$$x = \frac{60,000}{1.5} = 40,000$$

(2) Current Assets = 40,000 × 2.5

= 1,00,000

(3) Creditors = Current liabilities – Bank OD

= 40,000 – 10,000

= 30,000

Note: It is assumed that bank overdraft is included in current liabilities.

(4) Liquid assets = 1.5 × 40,000 = Rs. 60,000

(5) Stock = Current Assets – Liquid Assets

= 1,00,000 – 60,000

= 40,000

(6) Proprietary funds to fixed assets is 1: 0.75. It means 0.25 of the proprietory funds is being used as working capital.

$$\text{Hence proprietory finds} = \frac{60,000}{0.25}$$

= 2,40,000

(7) Since reserves and surplus are Rs. 40,000, paid up capital will be Rs. 2,00,000

(8) Fixed assets will be Re 0.75 of Rs. 2,40,000 = Rs. 1,80,000

Balance Sheet

Equity share capital		2,00,000	Fixed Assets	1,80,000
Reserves and surplus		40,000		
Current Liabilities			*Current Assets*	
Creditors	3,000		Stock	40,000
Bank OD	10,000		Liquid Assets	60,000
		40,000		
		2,80,000		2,80,000

Problem 49: From the following particulars prepare the balance sheet.

$$\frac{\text{Sales}}{\text{Total Assets}} = 3$$

$$\frac{\text{Sales}}{\text{Fixed Assets}} = 5$$

$$\frac{\text{Sales}}{\text{Current Assets}} = 7.5$$

$$\frac{\text{Sales}}{\text{Inventories}} = 20$$

$$\frac{\text{Sales}}{\text{Debtors}} = 15$$

$$\frac{\text{Total Assets}}{\text{Net Worth}} = 2.5$$

$$\text{Current Ratio} = 2$$

$$\frac{\text{Debt}}{\text{Equity}} = 1$$

$$\text{Sales} = 36,00,000$$

(*Osmania University, B.Com., April 1998*)

Solution:

(1) $$\frac{\text{Sales}}{\text{Total Assets}} = 3$$

or $$\text{Total Assets} = \frac{\text{Sales}}{3}$$

$$= \frac{36,00,000}{3} = \text{Rs. } 12,00,000$$

(2) $$\frac{\text{Sales}}{\text{Fixed Assets}} = 5$$

or, $$\text{Fixed Assets} = \frac{\text{Sales}}{5}$$

$$= \frac{36,00,000}{5} = 7,20,000$$

(3) $$\frac{\text{Sales}}{\text{Current Assets}} = 7.5$$

$$\text{Current Assets} = \frac{\text{Sales}}{7.5}$$

$$= \frac{36,00,000}{7.5} = \text{Rs. } 4,80,000$$

(4) $$\frac{\text{Sales}}{\text{Inventories}} = 20$$

$$\text{Inventories} = \frac{\text{Sales}}{20}$$

$$= \frac{36,00,000}{20} = 1,80,000$$

(5) $$\frac{\text{Sales}}{\text{Debtors}} = 15$$

$$\text{Debtors} = \frac{\text{Sales}}{15}$$

$$= \frac{36,00,000}{15} = 2,40,000$$

(6) $$\text{Current Ratio} = 2$$

or, $$\frac{\text{Current assets}}{\text{Current liabilities}} = 2$$

So, Current liabilities $= \frac{\text{Current assets}}{2}$

$= \frac{4,80,000}{2}$

$=$ 2,40,000

(7) $\frac{\text{Total Assets}}{\text{Net worth}} = 2.5$

Net Worth $= \frac{\text{Total Assets}}{2.5}$

$= \frac{12,00,000}{2.5}$ $=$ Rs. 4,80,000

(8) $\frac{\text{Debt}}{\text{Equity}} = 1$

Debt $=$ Equity × 1

$=$ 4,80,000 × 1 $=$ Rs. 4,80,000

(9) Liquid Assets $=$ Current Assets – (Inventories + Debtors)

$=$ 4,80,000 – (1,80,000 + 2,40,000)

$=$ Rs. 60,000

Balance Sheet

Net worth	4,80,000	Fixed Assets	7,20,000
Debt	4,80,000	*Current Assets*	
Current liabilities	2,40,000	Inventories	1,80,000
		Debtors	2,40,000
		liquid assets	60,000
	12,00,000		12,00,000

Problem 50: Using the following ratios, complete the Balance Sheet given below:

$\frac{\text{Total Assets}}{\text{Net Worth}} = 3.5$

$\frac{\text{Sales}}{\text{Fixed Assets}} = 6$

$\frac{\text{Sales}}{\text{Current Assets}} = 8$

$\frac{\text{Sales}}{\text{Inventory}} = 15$

$\frac{\text{Sales}}{\text{Debtors}} = 18$

Current Ratio = 2.5

Annual sales Rs. 25 Lakhs

Balance Sheet

Net worth	....	Fixed assets	....
Long-term debt	....	Inventory	....
Current liabilities	....	Debtors	....
		Liquid assets	....
		Total current assets	....

(*Bangalore University, B.Com., April 2000*)

Solution:

(1) $\frac{\text{Sales}}{\text{Fixed Assets}} = 6$

$$\text{Fixed Assets} = \frac{\text{Sales}}{6}$$

$$= \frac{25{,}00{,}000}{6} = 4{,}16{,}666$$

(2) $\frac{\text{Sales}}{\text{Current Assets}} = 8$

$$\text{Current assets} = \frac{\text{Sales}}{8}$$

$$= \frac{25{,}00{,}000}{8} = 3{,}12{,}500$$

(3) $\frac{\text{Sales}}{\text{Inventories}} = 15$

$$\text{Inventories} = \frac{\text{Sales}}{15}$$

$$= \frac{25{,}00{,}000}{15} = 1{,}66{,}666$$

(4) $\frac{\text{Sales}}{\text{Debtors}} = 18$

$$\text{Debtors} = \frac{\text{Sales}}{18}$$

$$= \frac{25{,}00{,}000}{18} = 1{,}38{,}888$$

(5) $\text{Current Ratio} = \frac{\text{Current Assets}}{\text{Current Liabilities}} = 2.5$

$$\text{Current Liabilities} = \frac{3{,}12{,}500}{25} = 1{,}25{,}000$$

(6) Liquid Assets = Current assets – Inventories – Debtors

= 3,12,500 – 1,66,666 – 1,38,888

= 6946

(7) Total Assets

Fixed assets	=	4,16,666
Current Assets	=	3,12,500
Inventories	=	1,66,666
Debtors	=	1,38,888
Liquid assets	=	6946
		10,41,666

(8) $\frac{\text{Total Assets}}{\text{Net worth}} = 3.5$

$$\text{Net worth} = \frac{\text{Total Assets}}{3.5}$$

$$= \frac{10{,}41{,}666}{3.5} = 2{,}97{,}618$$

Balance Sheet

Net worth	2,97,618	Fixed Assets	4,16,666
Long-term Debt	6,19,048	Current assets	3,12,500
(Balancing figure)		Inventories	1,66,666
Current liabilities	1,25,000	Debtors	1,38,888
		Liquid assets	6,946
	10,41,666		10,41,666

Problem 51: From the following details, prepare the balance sheet of the firm concerned:

Stock velocity	6
Capital turnover ratio	2
Fixed assets turnover ratio	4
Gross profit ratio	20%
Debt collection period	2 months
Creditors payment period	73 days

The gross profit was Rs. 60,000. Closing stock was Rs. 5,000 in excess of the opening stock

(CS, Inter, June 1998)

Solution:

(1) Gross Profit Ratio $= \dfrac{\text{Gross profit}}{\text{Sales}} \times 100$

$$20 = \frac{60{,}000}{\text{Sales}} \times 100$$

$$20 \text{ sales} = 60{,}000 \times 100$$

$$\text{Sales} = \frac{60{,}000 \times 100}{20} = 3{,}00{,}000$$

$$\text{Cost of goods sols} = \text{Sales} - \text{Gross Profit}$$

$$= 3{,}00{,}000 - 60{,}000$$

$$= 2{,}40{,}000$$

(2) Stock Velocity $= \dfrac{\text{Cost of goods sold}}{\text{Average stock}}$

$$6 = \frac{2{,}40{,}000}{\text{Average stock}}$$

$$\text{Average stock} = \frac{2{,}40{,}000}{6} = 40{,}000$$

Total stock = 40,000 × 2 = 80,000

Add: Closing stock amount of Rs. 5,000 more than opening stock = 5,000

= 85,000

Closing Stock $= \dfrac{85{,}000}{2}$ = 42,500

Opening Stock = 42,500 – 5,000

Rs. = 37,500

(3) Capital Turnover Ratio $= \dfrac{\text{Cost of Sales}}{\text{Capital}}$

$$2 = \frac{2{,}40{,}000}{\text{Capital}}$$

$$2 \text{ capital} = 2{,}40{,}000$$

$$\text{Capital} = \frac{2{,}40{,}000}{2} = \text{Rs. } 1{,}20{,}000$$

(4) Fixed Assets Turnover Ratio $= \frac{\text{Cost of Sales}}{\text{Fixed Assets}}$

$4 = \frac{2,40,000}{\text{Fixed Assets}}$

4 FA = 2,40,000

$\text{FA} = \frac{2,40,000}{4} = \text{Rs. } 60,000$

(5) Debt Colletion Period = 2 months

Debtors Turnover Ratio $= \frac{12 \text{ months}}{\text{Debt collection period}}$

$= \frac{12}{2} = 6 \text{ times}$

Also Debtors Turnover Ratio $= \frac{\text{Credit Sales}}{\text{Average Debtors}}$

$6 = \frac{3,00,000}{\text{Debtors}}$

or Debtors $= \frac{3,00,000}{6} = 50,000$

(6) Creditors Payment Period = 73 days

Creditors Turnover Ratio $= \frac{365}{73} = 5 \text{ times}$

Assuming all purchases to be credit purchases the amount of credit puchases is deterimined as follows:

Cost of goods sold = Opening Stock + Purchases – Closing stock

2,40,000 = 37,500 + Purchases – 42,500

Purchases = Rs. 2,45,000

Creditors Turnover Ratio $= \frac{\text{Credit purchases}}{\text{Creditors}}$

$5 = \frac{2,45,000}{\text{Creditors}}$

5 Creditors = 2,45,000

$\text{Creditors} = \frac{2,45,000}{5} = 49,000$

Balance Sheet

Capital	1,20,000	Fixed Assets	60,000
Creditors	49,000	Closing stock	42,500
		Debtors	50,000
		Cash (Balancing figure)	16,500
	1,69,000		1,69,000

Problem 52:

Gross Profit	Rs. 80,000
Gross profit to cost of goods sold ratio	1/3
Stock velocity	6 times
Opening stock	Rs. 36,000
Accounts receivable velocity (year of 360 days)	72 days
Accounts payable velocity	90 days
Current assets	Rs. 1,50,000
Bills receivable	Rs. 20,000
Bills payable	Rs. 5,000
Fixed assets turnover ratio	8 times

From the above, prepare balance sheet with as many details as possible.

(University of Madras, B.Com., September, 1997)

Solution:

Gross Profit = Rs. 80,000

(1) Gross profit to cost of goods sold ratio = $\frac{1}{3}$

$$= \frac{\text{Gross profit}}{\text{Cost of goods sold}} = \frac{1}{3}$$

$$= \frac{80{,}000}{\text{Cost of goods sold}} = \frac{1}{3}$$

= cost of goods sold = 80,000 × 3

= 2,40,000

Sales = Cost of goods sold + Gross profit

= 2,40,000 + 80,000 = 3,20,000

(2) Stock Velocity = 6 times

$$\text{Stock Turnover Ratio} = \frac{\text{Cost of Sales}}{\text{Average stock}}$$

$$\frac{6}{1} = \frac{2{,}40{,}000}{\text{Average stock}}$$

$$\text{Average Stock} = \frac{2{,}40{,}000}{6} = 40{,}000$$

$$\therefore \quad \text{Average Stock} = \frac{\text{Opening stock + closing stock}}{2}$$

40,000 × 2 = 80,000

Less: Opening stock = 36,000

Closing stock = 44,000

(3) Accounts receivable velocity = 72 days

$$\text{Debtors Turnover Ratio} = \frac{360}{72} = 5 \text{ times}$$

$$\text{DTR} = \frac{\text{Sales}}{\text{Average Accounts Receivable}}$$

$$\frac{5}{1} = \frac{3{,}20{,}000}{\text{Average Accounts Receivable}}$$

$$\text{Average Accounts Receivable} = \frac{3{,}20{,}000}{5} = 64{,}000$$

Average Accounts Receivable = Debtors + Bills receivable

or Debtors = Average Accounts receivable – Bills receivable

Debtors = 640,000 – 20,000

= 44,000

(4) Accounts Payable Velocity = 90 days

$$\text{Creditors Turnover Ratio} = \frac{360}{90} = 4 \text{ times}$$

$$\text{Creditors Turnover Ratio} = \frac{\text{Purchases}}{\text{Average Accounts payable}}$$

Purchases = Opening stock + Cost of sales – Closing stock

= 44,000 + 2,40,000 – 36,000

= 2,48,000

$$\text{Creditor Turnover Ratio} = \frac{\text{Purchases}}{\text{Average Accounts payable}}$$

$$\frac{4}{1} = \frac{2{,}48{,}000}{\text{Average Accounts payable}}$$

$$\text{Average Accounts Payable} = \frac{2,48,000}{4} = 62,000$$

Average Account Payable = Creditors + Bills payable

Creditors = Average Accounts payable – Bills payable

= 62,000 – 5,000 = 57,000

(5) Fixed Assets Turnover Ratio = 8 times (assumed on cost of sales)

$$\frac{8}{1} = \frac{\text{Cost of Sales}}{\text{Fixed Assets}}$$

$$\text{Fixed Assets} = \frac{2,40,000}{8} = 30,000$$

Balance Sheet

Capital (Balancing figure)	1,18,000	*Current Assets*:		
		Stock	44,000	
Creditors	57,000	Debtors	44,000	
Bills payable	5,000	B.R.	20,000	
		Cash	42,000	
		(Bal figure)		1,50,000
		Fixed assets		30,000
	1,80,000			1,80,000

Problem 53: From the following details prepare a balance sheet.

Current ratio is 1.75

Liquid ratio is 1.25

Stock turnover ratio (closing stock) is 9 times

Gross profit ratio is 25%

Debt collection period is 1.5 months

Reserves to capital is 0.2

Turnover of fixed assets is 1.2

Capital gearing ratio is 0.6

Fixed assets to net worth is 1.25

Sales for the year is Rs. 12,00,000 *(CS, Inter, December 1997)*

Solution:

Sales	=	12,00,000
Less: Gross profit 25%	=	3,00,000
Cost of goods sold		9,00,000

(1) Stock Turnover Ratio $= \frac{\text{Cost of goods sold}}{\text{Closing stock}}$

$$9 = \frac{9,00,000}{\text{closing stock}}$$

$$\text{Closing Stock} = \frac{9,00,000}{9} = 1,00,000$$

(2) Debt Colletion Period = 1.5 months

$$\text{Debt Collection Ratio} = \frac{\text{Debtors}}{\text{Credit Sales}}$$

$$\frac{1.5}{12} = \frac{\text{Debtors}}{12,00,000}$$

12 Debtors = 12,00,000 × 1.5

$$\text{Debtors} = \frac{12,00,000 \times 1.5}{12} = 1,50,000$$

(3) Turnover to Fixed Assets Ratio $= \dfrac{\text{Cost of goods sold}}{\text{Fixed Assets}}$

$$1.2 = \frac{9{,}00{,}000}{\text{Fixed Assets}}$$

$$\text{F.A} = \frac{9{,}00{,}000}{1.2} = 7{,}50{,}000$$

(4) Fixed Assets to Net Worth Ratio $= \dfrac{\text{Fixed Assets}}{\text{Net worth}}$

$$1.25 = \frac{7{,}50{,}000}{\text{Net worth}}$$

$$\text{Net worth} = \frac{7{,}50{,}000}{1.25} = 6{,}00{,}000$$

Capital	=	1.0	=	5,00,000
Reserve	=	0.2	=	1,00,000
		1.2		6,00,000

(5) Capital Gearing Ratio $= \dfrac{\text{Debt}}{\text{Equity Capital}}$

$$0.6 = \frac{\text{Debt}}{5{,}00{,}000}$$

$$\text{Debt} = 0.6 \times 5{,}00{,}000 = 3{,}00{,}000$$

(6) Current Ratio $= \dfrac{\text{Current Assets}}{\text{Current Liabilities}}$

$$1.75 = \frac{\text{Current Assets}}{\text{Current Liabilities}}$$

or CA = 1.75 CL

(7) Liquid Ratio $= \dfrac{\text{Liquid Assets}}{\text{Current Liabilities}}$

$$1.25 = \frac{\text{Liquid Assets}}{\text{Current Liabilities}}$$

or LA = 1.25 CL

(8) Current Assets = L.A + Stock

$$1.75\text{ CL} = 1.25\text{ CL} + 1{,}00{,}000$$

$$1.75\text{ CL} - 1.25\text{ CL} = 1{,}00{,}000$$

$$0.5\text{ CL} = 1{,}00{,}000$$

$$\text{CL} = \frac{1{,}00{,}000}{0.5} = 2{,}00{,}000$$

$$\text{CA} = 1.75 \times \text{CL} = 1.75 \times 2{,}00{,}000 = 3{,}50{,}000$$

Balance Sheet

Capital	5,00,000	Fixed Assets	7,50,000
Reserve	1,00,000	*Current Assets:*	
Debts	3,00,000	Closing stock	1,00,000
Current liabilities	2,00,000	Debtors	1,50,000
		Cash	1,00,000
	11,00,000		11,00,000

Problem 54 (Preparation of Final Accounts from Ratios): With the following ratios and further information given below, prepare a Trading account, profit and loss account and a balance sheet of Mr. Anand

1. Gross profit ratio	25%
2. $\frac{\text{Net profit}}{\text{Sales}}$	20%
3. Stock Turnoveer Ratio	10
4. $\frac{\text{Net profit}}{\text{capital}}$	$\frac{1}{5}$
5. Capital to total liabilities	$\frac{1}{2}$
6. $\frac{\text{Fixed Assets}}{\text{Capital}}$	$\frac{5}{4}$
7. $\frac{\text{Fixed Assets}}{\text{Total current assets}}$	$\frac{5}{7}$
8. Fixed Assets	Rs. 10,00,000
9. Closing Stock	Rs. 1,00,000

(Bangalore University, B.B.M., November 1999)

Solution:

Trading and Profit and Loss A/c

To Opening stock	20,000	By Sales	8,00,000
To Purchases (Balancing figure)	6,80,000	By Closing stock	1,00,000
To Gross profit	2,00,000		
	9,00,000		9,00,000
To Expenses	40,000	By Gross profit	2,00,000
To Net profit	1,60,000		
	2,00,000		2,00,000

Balance Sheet

Capital			Fixed Assets	10,00,000
Opening balance	6,40,000			
			Closing stock	1,00,000
Add: Net profit	1,60,000		Other current assets	13,00,000
	8,00,000			
		8,00,000		
Liabilities		16,00,000		
		24,00,000		24,00,000

Working Note:

(1) Calculation of Capital

$$\frac{\text{Fixed Assets}}{\text{Capital}} = \frac{5}{4}$$

$$\frac{1,00,000}{\text{Capital}} = \frac{5}{4}$$

or $\quad 5 \text{ capital} = 1,00,000 \times 4$

or $\quad \text{capital} = \frac{1,00,000 \times 4}{5} = 8,00,000$

(2) Calculation of Liabilities

Capital is $\frac{1}{2}$ of total liabilities

Liabilities = 8,00,000 × 2 = Rs. 16,00,000

(3) Calculation of Net Profit

Net profit is $\frac{1}{5}$ of capital

Net profit = 8,00,000 × $\frac{1}{5}$ = 1,60,000

(4) Calculation of Sales

Net Profit is 20% of sales

$$\text{Sales} = 1{,}60{,}000 \times \frac{100}{20} = 8{,}00{,}000$$

(5) Calculation of Gross Profit Ratio

Gross profit ratio is 25% of sales

$$\frac{25}{100} \times 8{,}00{,}000 = 2{,}00{,}000$$

(6) Calculation of Average Inventory

$$\text{Stock Turnover Ratio} = \frac{\text{Cost of Sales}}{\text{Average Inventory}}$$

$$10 = \frac{60{,}00{,}000}{\text{Average Inventory}}$$

$$10 \text{ Average Inventory} = 6{,}00{,}000$$

$$\text{Average Inventory} = \frac{60{,}00{,}000}{10}$$

$$= 60{,}000$$

$$\text{Cost of sales} = \text{Sales} - \text{Gross profit}$$

$$= 8{,}00{,}000 - 2{,}00{,}000$$

$$= 6{,}00{,}000$$

(7) Calculation of Opening Stock

$$\text{Average Inventory} = 60{,}000$$

$$\text{Total Inventory} = 60{,}000 \times 2 = 1{,}20{,}000$$

$$\text{Opening Inventory} = \text{Total Inventory} - \text{Closing Stock}$$

$$= 1{,}20{,}000 - 1{,}00{,}000$$

$$= 20{,}000$$

(8) Calculation of other Current Assets

$$\frac{\text{Fixed Assets}}{\text{Total Current Assets}} = \frac{5}{7}$$

$$\frac{10{,}00{,}000}{\text{Total Current Assets}} = \frac{5}{7}$$

or, $$5 \text{ total current assets} = 10{,}00{,}000 \times 7$$

or, $$\text{Total current assets} = \frac{10{,}00{,}000 \times 7}{5}$$

$$= 14{,}00{,}000$$

$$\text{Other Current Assets} = \text{Total current assets} - \text{Closing stock}$$

$$= 14{,}00{,}000 - 1{,}00{,}000$$

$$= 13{,}00{,}000$$

Problem 55: From the following figures and ratios, draw out balance sheet and trading and profit and loss account:

Share capital	1,80,000
Working capital	63,000
Bank overdraft	10,000

There is no fictitous asset. In current assets there is no asset other than stock, debtors and cash. Closing stock is 20% higher than the opening stock:

Current ratio	2.5
Proprietory ratio	0.7
Stock velocity	4
Net profit ratio	10% (to average capital employed)
Quick ratio	1.5
Gross profit ratio	20% to sales
Debtors velocity	36.5 days

(Sri Venkateshwara University, B.Com., October 1998)

To Opening stock	35,000	By Sales	1,92,500
To Purchases (Balancing figure)	1,61,000	By Closing stock	42,000
To Gross profit	38,500		
	2,34,500		2,34,500
To Expenses (Balancing figure)	20,500	By Gross profit b/d	38,500
To Net profit	18,000		
	38,500		38,500

Balance Sheet

Share capital	1,80,000	Fixed assets	1,47,000
Reserves and surplus		Current Assets	
Reserve	12,000	Stock	42,000
Profit and loss a/c	18,000	Debtors	19,250
Current liabilities			
Creditors	32,000	Cash	43,750
Bank OD	10,000		
	2,52,000		2,52,000

Working Notes:

(1) Calculation of Current Assets and Current Liabilities

Working capital = Current assets – Current liabilities

= 2.5 – 1.0

= 1.5

Since working capital = 63,000

$$\text{Current assets} = 63,000 \times \frac{2.5}{1.5} = 1,05,000$$

$$\text{Current liabilities} = 63,000 \times \frac{1.0}{1.5} = 42,000$$

(2) Calculation of Closing Stock and Opening Stock

Quick ratio = 1.5

∴ Quick assets = 1.5

Quick assets = $63,000 \times \frac{1.5}{1.5} = 63,000$

Stock = Current assets – Quick assets

= 1,05,000 × 63,000 = 42,000 (closing stock)

Opening stock = $42,000 \times \frac{100}{120} = 35,000$

(3) Calculation of Sales

Average stock = $\frac{42,000 + 35,000}{2}$

= $\frac{7,70,000}{2} = 38,500$

Stock velocity = $\frac{\text{Cost of goods sold}}{\text{Average stock}}$

$4 = \frac{\text{Cost of goods sold}}{38,500}$

Cost of goods sold = 38,500 × 4

= 1,54,000

Sales = Cost of goods sold + Gross profit

Cost of goods sold	=	1,54,000
Gross profit $\frac{20}{100} \times 1,54,000$	=	38,500
		1,92,500

(4) Calculation of Debtors

Debtors velocity = 36.5 Days

This means, sales of 36.5 days is equal to debtors

= $1,92,500 \times \frac{36.5}{365} = 19,250$

Debtors = 19,250

(5) Calculation of Cash

Current assets – (Stock + Debtors) = Cash

1,05,000 – (42,000 + 19,250) = 43,750

(6) Calculation of Creditors

Creditors = Current liabilities – Bank OD

= 42,000 – 10,000

= 32,000

(7) Calculation of Net Profit

Net Profit to capital employed = 10%

Capital= 1,80,000

Net Profit = $1,80,000 \times \frac{10}{100} = 18,000$

(8) Calculation of Proprietory Funds

$$\text{Proprietory ratio} = \frac{\text{Fixed Assets}}{\text{Proprietory funds}} = \frac{0.7}{1.0}$$

If proprietory Fund = x, fixed assets = $0.7\,x$

Proprietory Fund + Long-term loan + Current liabiliaites = Fixed assets + Current assets + Fictions assets

$$= x + 0 + 42{,}000 = 0.7x + 1{,}05{,}000 + 0$$

$$x - 0.7x = 1{,}05{,}000 - 42{,}000$$

$$0.3x = 63{,}000$$

$$x = \frac{63{,}000}{0.3} = 2{,}10{,}000$$

Proprietory Funds = 2,10,000

(9) Calculation of Fixed Assets

$$\text{Proprietory Ratio} = \frac{\text{Fixed Assets}}{\text{Proprietory funds}}$$

$$\frac{0.7}{1.0} = \frac{\text{Fixed Assets}}{2{,}10{,}000}$$

$$1 \text{ Fixed Assets} = 2{,}10{,}000 \times 0.7$$

$$\text{Fixed Assets} = \frac{2{,}10{,}000 \times 0.7}{1}$$

$$\text{Fixed Assets} = 1{,}47{,}000$$

(10) Calculation of Reserves

Reserves and surplus = 2,10,000 – 1,80,000
= 30,000

Reserve = 30,000 – 18,000, *i.e.*, Net profit
= 12,000

Problem 56: From the given ratios and other particulars, fill up the trading and profit and loss a/c and balance sheet:

Gross profit ratio	=	25%
Net profit ratio	=	20%
$\frac{\text{Sales}}{\text{Inventory ratio}}$	=	8
$\frac{\text{Fixed Assets}}{\text{Current Assets}}$	=	$\frac{3}{4}$
$\frac{\text{Fixed Assets}}{\text{Total Capital}}$	=	$\frac{3}{2}$
$\frac{\text{Capital}}{\text{Outside liabilities}}$	=	$\frac{2}{5}$
Fixed assets	=	Rs. 15,00,000
Closing stock	=	Rs. 2,00,000

Trading Profit and Loss A/c

To cost of goods sold	....	By sales	....
To gross profit	....		....
To Expenses	....	By gross profit	....
To Net profit			

Balance Sheet

Capital balance	....	Fixed assets	....
Add: Net profit	....	Current assets	....
Other liabilities	....	Stock	....
		Other current assets	....

(Osmania University, B.Com., March 1997)

Solution:

Trading and Profit and Loss A/c

To Cost of goods sold	12,00,000	By Sales	16,00,000
To Gross profit 25%	4,00,000		
Sales	16,00,000		16,00,000
To Expenses (Balancing figure)	80,000	By Gross profit	4,00,000
To Net profit $\left(\frac{20}{100} \times 16,00,000\right)$	3,20,000		
	4,00,000		4,00,000

Balance Sheet

Capital Balance	6,80,000		Fixed assets	15,00,000
Add: Net profit	3,20,000		*Current Assets*	
		10,00,000	Stock	2,00,000
Outside liabilities		25,00,000	Other current assets (20,00,000 – 2,00,000)	18,00,000
		35,00,000		35,00,000

Working Notes:

(1) Calculation of Sales

$$\frac{\text{Sales}}{\text{Stock}} = 8$$

$$= \frac{\text{Sales}}{2,00,000} = 8$$

Sales = 2,00,000 × 8 = 16,00,000

(2) Calculation of Gross Profit

$$\frac{25}{100} \times 16,00,000 = \text{Rs. } 4,00,000$$

(3) Calculation of Cost of Goods Sold

Sales – Gross profit = Cost of goods sold
16,00,000 – 4,00,000 = Rs. 12,00,000

(4) Calculation of Net Profit

$$\frac{20}{100} \times 16,00,000 = \text{Rs. } 3,20,000$$

(5) Calculation of Total Current Assets

$$\frac{\text{Fixed Assets}}{\text{Total current Assets}} = \frac{3}{4}$$

$$\frac{15,00,000}{\text{Total current assets}} = \frac{3}{4}$$

$$3 \text{ Total current assets} = 15,00,000 \times 4$$

$$\text{Total current assets} = 15,00,000 \times \frac{4}{3}$$

$$\text{Rs.} = 20,00,000$$

(6) Calculation of Capital

$$\frac{\text{Fixed Assets}}{\text{Capital}} = \frac{3}{2}$$

$$\frac{15,00,000}{\text{Capital}} = \frac{3}{2}$$

$$3 \text{ Capital} = 15,00,000 \times 2$$

$$\text{Capital} = \frac{15,00,000 \times 2}{3} = \text{Rs. } 10,00,000$$

(7) Calculation of Outside Liabilities

$$\frac{\text{Capital}}{\text{Outside liabilities}} = \frac{2}{5}$$

$$\frac{10,00,000}{\text{Outside liabilities}} = \frac{2}{5}$$

$$2 \text{ Outside liabilities} = 10,00,000 \times 5$$

$$\text{Outside liabilities} = \frac{10,00,000 \times 5}{2}$$

$$= \text{Rs. } 25,00,000$$

QUESTIONS

Simple Questions

1. What do you men by Accounting Ratio?
2. In what ways can ratios be expressed?
3. Define ratio analysis.
4. What are the key steps involved in ratio analysis?
5. Mention the ratios which determine the solvency of a concern.
6. What are liquidity ratios?
7. What are solvency ratios?
8. What is meant by profitability ratios?
9. What are activity ratios?
10. What do you understand by leverage ratios.
11. Explain current ratio.
12. What is 'Window dressing' in current ratio?
13. How is 'Window dressing' done?
14. What is liquid ratio? How is it calculated?
15. What is 'absolute liquidity' ratio?
16. What is a proprietory ratio?
17. What do you mean by debt-equity ratio?

18. What is gross profit ratio?
19. What is net profit ratio?
20. What is operating ratio?
21. What is operating profit ratio?
22. What is an expense ratio?
23. What is mean by 'Return on capital employed'?
24. What is stock turnover ratio?
25. What is meant by 'Debtors Turnover Ratio'?
26. What is meant by 'Creditors Turnover Ratio'?
27. What do you understand by 'Fixed assets turnover ratio'?
28. What is capital gearing?
29. What is meant by dividend coverage ratio?
30. What is interest coverage ratio?
31. How is 'Earnings per share' calculated.
32. What is price earning ratio?
33. What is dividend payout ratio?
34. What is Dupont control chart?
35. Mention any form Balance sheet ratio?
36. What is activity ratio?
37. State the significance of 'Current ratio'.
38. What is acid test ratio?
39. How do you calculate 'average collection period'?
40. What is average collection period ratio?
41. What is average payment period ratio?
42. What is price-earning ratio?
43. What is working capital turnover ratio?
44. What is return on equity capital?
45. What is capital turnover ratio?
46. What is dividend yield ratio?
47. The working capital of a firm is Rs. 80,000 and its current ratio is 5. Calculate the current assets and current liabilities. *(Osmania University, B.Com., March 1999)*

    [*Answer*: Current liabilities = Rs. 20,000
    Current assets = Rs. 1,00,000]

48. Calculation the stock turnover ratio

Opening stock	Rs. 90,000
Closing stock	Rs. 1,10,000
Sales	Rs, 5,00,000
Rate of gross profit	20%

(Osmania University, B.Com., March 1998)

[*Answer:* Stock turnover ratio 4 times]

49. Turnover to fixed assets ratio is 1: 1.5. Value of goods sold is Rs. 5,00,000. Compute the value of fixed assets. *(Bangalore University, B.Com., October 2,000)*

    [*Answer*: Fixed assets Rs. 3,33,333]

50. Current ratio is 2.5, liquid ratio is 1.5. Working capital is Rs. 50,000. Ascertain current assets and Inventory. *(Bangalore University, B.Com., October 2,000)*

    [*Answer*: Current assets = 83,333
    Inventory = 33,333]

51. Current ratio 2.5
    Working capital Rs. 60,000
    Calculate the amount of current assets and current liabilities
    (Sri Venkateshwara University, B.Com., October 1999)

    [*Answer*: Current assets = 1,00,000
    Current liabilities = 40,000]

52. Opening stock Rs. 29,000, Closing stock Rs. 31,000, Sales Rs. 3,20,000, Gross profit ratio 25% on sales. Calculate stock turnover ratio. *(Sri Venkateshwara University, B.Com., October 1999)*

    [*Answer:* Stock Turnover ratio 8 times]

Short Answer Questions

1. Explain the nature of Accounting ratios.
2. Explain different ways of interpreting accounting ratios.
3. Explain the uses of accounting ratios.
4. State the limitations of accounting ratios
5. Explain the various types of Balance Sheet Ratios.
6. Explain the various types of profit and loss account ratios.
7. From the following data, compute current ratio, acid-test ratio, inventory turnover ratio:
   (*a*) Assets
   Stock — Rs. 10,000, Debtors — Rs. 30,000 prepaid expenes — Rs. 2,000,
   cash in hand — Rs. 20,000
   (*b*) Liabilities
   Sundry Creditors — Rs. 25,000, Bank overdraft — Rs. 5,000, Bills payable — Rs. 10,000.
   (*c*) During the year sales amounted to Rs. 3,50,000 (*University of Madras, B.Com. September 19997*)
   [*Answer:* Current Ratio = 1.55; Acid test ratio = 1.43; Inventory turnover ratio = 35 times]
8. The ratios relating to a company are given below:

Gross profit ratio	15%
Stock velocity	6 months
Debtors velocity	3 months
Creditors velocity	3 months

Gross profit for the year ending 31st December, 1995 amounts to Rs. 60,000. Closing stock is equal to opening stock.

Find out (*a*) sales, (*b*) closing stock, (*c*) sundry debtors, (*d*) sundry creditors.

(*University of Madras, B.Com, September 1996*)

[*Answers:* Sales = 4,00,000; Closing Stock = 1,70,000;
Sundry debtors = 1,00,000; Sundry creditors = 85,000]

9. Triveni Ltd. has the following earnings last year:

Particulars	*Rs.*
Profit before tax	26,50,000
Tax rate	40%
Proposed equity dividend	25%
Capital employed	
10% preference share capital	15,00,000
80,000 Equity shares of Rs. 50 each	40,00,000
Current market price per equity	Rs. 125

Calculate (*i*) Earning per share, (*ii*) Price earning ratio, (*iii*) Dividend payout ratio.

(*University of Bombay, B.Com., April 1997*)

Solution: Earning per share = Rs. 18; Price earning ratio = 6.94; Dividend payout ratio = 0.69

Long Answer questions

1. Explain the various types of ratios.
2. Following are the profit and loss a/c and balance sheet of a company. Calculate the following ratios:
   (*a*) Gross profit ratio (*b*) Operating ratio
   (*c*) Current ratio (*d*) Liquid ratio
   (*e*) Stock turnover ratio (*f*) Debt equity ratio

Profit and loss A/c

To Opening stock	1,50,000	By Sales	10,00,000
To Purchases	3,00,000	By Closing stock	2,50,000
To Wages	2,00,000		
To Manufacturing expenses	1,00,000		
To Gross profit	5,00,000		
	12,50,000		12,50,000

To Administration expenses	50,000	By Gross profit	5,00,000
To Selling and distribution expenses	50,000	By Profit on sale of shares	50,000
To Loss on sale of furniture	25,000		
To Interest on debentures	10,000		
To Net profit	4,15,000		
	5,50,000		5,50,000

Balance Sheet

Share capital	2,00,000	Fixed assets	2,50,000
Reserves	1,00,000	Stock	2,50,000
Debentures	2,00,000	Sundry debtors	1,00,000
Sundry debtors	1,00,000	Bank	50,000
Bills payable	50,000		
	6,50,000		6,50,000

(*Osmania University, B.Com., October 1997*)

[*Answer:* Gross profit = 50%; Operating ratio = 61%; Current ratio = 2.66; Liquid ratio = 1; Stock turnover ratio = 2.5; Debt equity ratio = 0.53

3. The balance sheets of Contractors Ltd. as on 31st December 1996 and 1997 were as follows:

	1996	*1997*		*1996*	*1997*
Equity share capital	1,500	1,700	Fixed assets	1,800	2,100
12% preference shares	500	400	Sundry debtors	550	650
Reserve	570	770	B.R.	430	525
10% Debentures	300	450	Stock	380	460
Creditors	240	320	Prepaid expenses	20	30
Bills payable	50	70	Bank	80	65
Bank OD	100	120			
	3,260	3,830		3,260	3,830

During the year 1997, total sales were Rs. 1,20,00,000 and cash sales were 20% of total sales. Stock turnover ratio was 20 times net profit before payment of taxes at 50% was Rs. 18,00,000.

There were no, non-operating expesnes and non-operating incomes. Calculate the following ratios for the year 1997:

1. Gross profit ratio
2. Operating ratio
3. Current ratio
4. Debtor turnover ratio
5. Debt collection period
6. Return on capital employed

(*University of Bombay, B.Com., April 1997*)

Solution: Gross profit ratio = 30%; Operating ratio = 85%;
Current ratio = 3.39; Debtors turnover ratio = 8.91;
Debt collection period = 40.4 days; Return on capital employed = 55.57%.

4. The following figures related to the trading activities of Z Ltd., for the year ended 31st March, 1996.

	Rs.
Sales	10,57,000
Closing stock	4,60,000
Purchases	8,35,000
Loss on sale of assets	45,000
Advertising	32,750
Rent	18,750
Profit on sale of shares	25,000
Provision for taxation	1,00,000
Salaries	35,750
Salesmen's salaries	14,250
Depreciation	36,000

Sales return	57,000
Depreciation on delivery van	8,000
Printing and stationery	17,500
Audit fees	12,000
Opening stock	2,25,000
Dividend received on shares	15,000

You are required to rearrange above income statement in vertical form and compute the following ratios:

(*a*) Gross profit ratio
(*b*) Operating ratio
(*c*) Net operating profit ratio
(*d*) Selling and distribution expenses to sales ratio

(*University of Bombay, B.Com., October 1996*)

Solution: Gross profit ratio = 40%; Operating ratio = 77.50%; Net operating profit ratio = 22.50%; Selling and distribution expenses to sales ratio = 5.50%

5. Re-arrange the following Balance Sheet and profit & loss a/c of Edens Ltd. in a form suitable for analysis and calculate the following ratios:
   1. Current ratio
   2. Stock turnover ratio
   3. Liquidity ratio
   4. Debt equity ratio
   5. Gross profit ratio
   6. Net profit ratio

Balance Sheet as at 31st March 1996

Bills payable	25,000	Fixed assets	1,25,000
Sundry creditors	50,000	Sundry debtors	50,000
Debentures	1,00,000	Bank	25,000
Reserves	50,000	Inventory	1,25,000
Equity share capital	50,000		
Preference share capital	50,000		
	3,25,000		3,25,000

P & C A/c for the year ended 31st March 1996

To Opening inventories	75,000	By Sales	5,00,000
To Purchases	1,50,000	By Closing inventories	1,25,000
To Manufacturing expenses	50,000	By Profit on sale of shares	25,000
To Direct wages	1,00,000		
To Administration expenses	25,000		
To Selling expenses	25,000		
To Loss on sale of assets	27,500		
To Interest on debentures	5,000		
To Net profit	1,92,500		
	6,50,000		6,50,000

(*University of Bombay, B.Com., April 1996*)

[*Answer:* Current ratio = 2.67; Stock turnover ratio = 2.5 times; Liquidity ratio = 1; Debt-equity ratio = 0.4; Gross profit ratio = 50%; Net profit ratio = 39%]

6. Comment on the position of Commentary Ltd., from the following:
Profit and loss accounts and Balance Sheets after calculating stated ratios:

Balance Sheet

	31-3-95	*31-3-94*		*31-3-95*	*31-3-94*
Capital of Rs. 10 each	70,000	70,000	Fixed assets	90,000	92,000
Reserves	80,000	68,000	Current assets	1,10,000	1,12,000
Secured loans	22,000	24,000	Loans and advances	52,000	40,000
Current liabailities	26,000	30,000			
Provision	54,000	52,000			
	2,52,000	2,44,000		2,52,000	2,44,000

P & C A/c for The Year Ended

	31-3-95	31-3-94		31-3-95	31-3-94
To Opening stock	44,000	40,000	By Sales	2,10,000	2,00,000
To Purchases	84,000	72,000	By Closing stock	46,000	44,000
To Wages	40,000	36,000			
To Factory expenses	32,000	28,000			
To Adm. expenses	8,000	6,000			
To Selling expenses	6,000	10,000			
To Managerial remuneration	2,000	2,000			
To Transfer to reserve	2,000	2,000			
To Income-tax	22,000	24,000			
To Proposed dividend	6,000	8,000			
To Balance c/d	10,000	16,000			
	2,56,000	2,44,000		2,56,000	2,44,000

1. Current ratio, 2. Proprietory ratio, 3. Debt equity ratio, 4. Earning per share, 5. Stock working capital ratio, 6. Liquid ratio, 7. Cost of sales to sales ratio, 8. Administrative expenses to sales ratio, 9. Selling expenses to sales ratio. *(University of Bombay, B.Com., October 1995)*

Answer:

	31-3-95	31-3-96
Current ratio	2.025	1.854
Proprietory ratio	0.6	0.57
Debt equity ratio	0.15	0.17
Earning per share	2.571	3.714
Stock working capital ratio	0.56	0.62
Liquid ratio	0.80	0.82
Cost of sales to sales	73.33%	66%
Adm. expenses ratio	4.76%	4.00%
Selling expenses to sales	2.86%	5%

7. The following is the balance sheet of XYX Co. Ltd. as on 31-12-1995:

Equity share capital (Shares of Rs. 100 each)	20,00,000	Plant and equipment	12,50,000
		Land and Building	5,00,000
		Sundry Debtors	4,50,000
Returned earnings	5,00,000	Stock	7,00,000
Sundry creditors	4,00,000	B.R.	1,50,000
Bills payable	1,50,000	Prepared insurance cash	10,000
Other current liabilitites	50,000	Cash	40,000
	31,00,000		31,00,000

Statement of Profit for the year eneded 31-12-95

		Rs.
Sales		50,00,000
Less: Cost of goods sold		38,50,000
	Gross profit	11,50,000
Less: Operating expenses		7,50,000
	Net profit	4,00,000
Less:	Tax at 40%	1,60,000
	Net profit after tax	2,40,000

Sundry debtors and stock at the beginning of the year were Rs. 4,00,000 and Rs, 6,00,000 respectively.

Calculate:

1. Current ratio
2. Acid test ratio
3. Stock turnover ratio
4. Debtors turnover ratio
5. Gross profit ratio
6. Net profit ratio
7. Earning per share
8. Return on equity

(Bangalore University, B.B.M, April 1997)

Answer:	Current ratio	=	2.25
	Acid test ratio	=	1.06
	Stock turnover ratio	=	5.92 times
	Debtors turnover ratio	=	11.76
	Gross profit ratio	=	23%
	Net profit ratio	=	8%
	Earning per share	=	12
	Return on equity	=	12%

8. From the following information make out a balance sheet with as many details as possible:

(*a*)	Gross profit turnover ratio	=	25%
(*b*)	Debtors velocity	=	3 months
(*c*)	Creditors velocity	=	2 months
(*d*)	Stock velocity	=	8 times
(*e*)	Capital turnover ratio	=	2.5 times
(*f*)	Fixed assets-turnover ratio	=	8 times

Gross profit for the year ended 31st December, 1992 was Rs. 80,000. There was no long-term loan or overdraft, Reserves and surplus amounted to Rs. 28,000, Liquid assets were Rs. 97,333.

Closing stock of the year was Rs. 2,000 more than opening stock. Bills receivable and Bills payable were Rs. 5,000 and Rs. 2,000 respectively. *(University of Madras, B.Com., March 1996)*

[*Answer:* Total of Balance Sheet = 1,68,333]

9. From the following information, prepare a balance sheet. Show the workings:

(*a*)	Working capital	=	75,000
(*b*)	Reserves and surplus	=	1,00,000
(*c*)	Bank overdraft	=	60,000
(*d*)	Current ratio	=	1.75
(*e*)	Liquid ratio	=	1.15
(*f*)	Fixed assets to proprietors funds	=	0.75
(*g*)	Long-term liabilities	=	Nil

(University of Madras, B.Com. Correspondence Course, May 1996)

[*Answer:* Balance Sheet Total Rs. 4,00,000]

10. From the following particulars, you are required to prepare the balance sheet of a Zinc Company.

Fixed assets (after writing off 30%)	10,50,000
Fixed assets turnover ratio (on cost of sales)	2
Finished goods turnover ratio (on cost of sales)	6
G P rate on sales	25%
Net profit (before interest) to sales	8%
Fixed charges cover (debenture interest 7%)	8
Debt collection period	1.5 months
Materials consumed to sales	30%
Stock of Raw-materials (in terms of months consumption)	3
Current ratio	2.4
Quick ratio	1.0
Reserve to capital ratio	0.4

(CS, Inter, June 1997)

[*Answer:* Balance Sheet Total 20,10,000]

11. From the following details, prepare a Balance Sheet:
    Current ratio is 1.75
    Liquid ratio is 1.25
    Stock turnover ratio (closing stock) is 9 times
    Gross pforit ratio is 25%
    Debt collection period is 1.5 months
    Reserves to capital is 0.2
    Turnover of fixed assets is 1.2
    Capital gearing ratio is 0.6
    Fixed assets to net worth is 1.25
    Sales for the year is Rs. 12,00,000 (*CS, Inter, December 1997*)

[*Answer:* Balance Sheet Total 11,00,000]

5

FUND FLOW STATEMENT

INTRODUCTION

A fund flow statement is a technical device designed to analyse, the changes in the financial condition of a business enterprise between two dates. It is also called a 'statement of sources and application of funds' as it portrays, the sources and application of working capital and highlights the basic changes in the resources and financial structure of a concern. This statement is intended to supplement and not to supplant, the balance sheet and profit and loss account in whole or in part. The fund flow statement is becoming popular with the management, because it not only helps them in analysing financial operations, providing basis for comparison with budgets, and in serving as a tool of communication, but also explains the financial consequences of such operations such as, the reason why the company is experiencing difficulty in making payments to creditors or why the bank balance is getting thinner.

CONCEPT OF 'FUND' AND 'FLOW OF FUND'

Fund

In its broadest sense, it refers to all financial resources or purchasing power or economic value possessed by a firm at a point of time. According to this concept all assets—both fixed and current would constitute fund. In a popular sense it is used to refer to working capital, *i.e.*, excess of current assets over current liabilities. In a narrow sense it is used to refer to cash and bank balance.

Concept of Flow of Fund

The flow of fund refers to the changes in the existing financial position of a business caused by in-flow and out-flow of resources owing to receipts and payments. It is generally taken to mean a change in working capital of a business. If a transaction results in an increase in fund it is known as source of fund. Where a transaction results in a decrease in the fund, it is known as application of fund. When there is no change in the fund, there is no flow of fund.

Meaning of Fund Flow Statement

It refers to a statement which incorporates working capital that brings about changes in assets, liabilities and capital of owners between two consecutive balance sheets. According to Roy A. Foulke it is a statement of sources and application of fund designed to analyse the change in the financial condition of a business enterprise between two dates.

Objective of Fund Flow Statement

Fund flow statement is a useful tool in the financial manager's analytical kit. The important objectives of this statement are:

1. to indicate the result of current financial management;
2. to lay emphasis on the most singnificant changes that have taken place, during a specific period;
3. to show how general expansion in a business has been financed or to describe the sources from which additional funds were derived;
4. to establish the relationship between profits from operations, distribution of dividend and raising of new capital or contracting of loans;
5. to give recognition to the fact that a business exists on flow of funds and is not a static organisation.

IMPORTANCE OF FUND FLOW STATEMENT

Fund Flow analysis helps in judging the efficiency of financial functions and administration of a business by providing a summary of the sources from which funds have been procured and uses to which such funds have been put to. Such on analysis is particularly useful in long range planning where projections of available liquid resources are vital and are necessarily to be made. Management can come to know about long-term debts or arrange funds for daily needs. Fund flow statement is a parametre for testing the effective use of working capital by the management during a particular period. The adequacy or inadequacy of working capital will reveal to the financial analyst about the possible steps that the management should take for effective use of working capital.

A projected fund flow statement will help the analyst in finding out as to how the management is going to allocate the scarce financial resources for meeting the productive requirements of the business. The use of funds should be phased in such an order that the available resources are put to the best use of the enterprise. Further, fund flow analysis helps in the proper postmortem of the financial policy of the business, thereby providing useful guidance to the management in the matter of debt retirement, expansion or replacement or to the payment of dividends etc. Thus the significance of funds flow statement can be summarised as follows:

(*a*) it suggests the ways of improving working capital position;
(*b*) it helps in planning for retirement of long-term debts;
(*c*) it helps in the formulation of a realistic dividend policy;
(*d*) it helps in deciding about the mode of financing expansion or replacement of facilities;
(*e*) It evaluates the urgency of operational uses;
(*f*) it helps to explain the phenomena of high profitability with low liquidity.

Difference between Statement of Receipts and Payments and Fund Flow Statement

1. The statement of receipts and payments contains a summary of inward and outward movement of cash which is only a part of the working capital, whereas the fund flow statement contains a summary of the inward and outward movement of all items affecting the working capital of a business.
2. The statement of receipts and payments is prepared from cash book, whereas, the fund flow statement is prepared from two balance sheets and other concerned particulars.

Differences between Cash Budget and Fund Flow Statement

1. Cash budget is generally futuristic in approach whereas, fund flow statement is usually based on past data.
2. Cash budget is planning for cash before hand but fund flow is only the postmortem analysis.
3. Cash budget is prepared for a specific period and requires previous data only for the purpose of judicious forecasting whereas fund flow statement is prepared from the accounting data at two specified dates.
4. Cash budget is a tool for management for controlling cash whereas fund flow statement represents the working of the company for previous year and it is for the benefit of external parties too.

DIFFERENCE BETWEEN INCOME STATEMENT AND FUND FLOW STATEMENT

Fund Flow statement	*Profit and Loss A/c*
1. It shows sources and application of funds.	1. It shows profit or loss of the business.
2. Depreication is included in the fund from operation. So fund from operation is greater in volume compared to net profit.	2. Net profit excludes depreciation. So net profit is smaller in volume compared to fund from operation.
3. Fund flow statement explains the way the funds are generated and how it is used in making various payments such as tax, dividend, purchase of fixed assets.	3. The profit and loss account explains how profit or loss has resulted by comparing revenue with expenditure.
4. Fund flow statement does not consider outstanding and prepared expense. It does not consider the problem associated with time.	4. Profit and loss a/c takes into account out standing and prepaid expense. It takes into account problem associated with time.
5. It is meant for management for taking decisions and making policies	5. It is meant for various parties interested in business.

Superiority of fund flow statement over-income statement: Though a fund flow statement and income statement have different functions to perform a fund flow statement is a better substitute for an income statement due to the following reasons:

(*a*) The income statement discloses the operating results while a fund flow statement deals with the financial resources required for running the business. A fund flow statement translates the economic consequences of operations into their financial information as a basis for action.

(*b*) Income statement is prepared at the end of the accounting period, whereas fund flow statement is prepared as and when management wants it.

(*c*) An income statement is static in as much as it gives information on what has happened during the period covered by it. For managerial purposes funds flow statement may be prepared much before business operations and as an instrument of planning and control. It is dynamic and presents financial information in the form of a flow.

(*d*) An income statement is not very reliable as items shown in income statement can be easily maniputated by the management while a funds flow statement is more reliable.

Differences between balance sheet and a fund flow statement

Balance Sheet	*Fund Flow Statement*
1. It reveals the financial position as on a particular date.	1. It reveals the changes in the financial position between two balance sheet period.
2. It portrays all assets and liabilities.	2. It portrays a change in working capital.
3. It is an end product of an accounting system.	3. It is a by-product of balance sheet. It is under taken after the preparation of a balance sheet.
4. It is meant for external parties.	4. It is meant for the use of management.
5. Its preparation is compulsory in higher form of business organisation.	5. It is voluntarily prepared to benefit the management.

Uses and limitations of Fund Flow Analysis

Uses

1. One gets an insight into financial operations of the firm. This will help to analyse the past trends and plan future operation.
2. It is possible to know whether the firm's growth was financed from internal source or from external sources. It will also be clear whether growth was at a rapid pace and financing was strained.
3. It reveals disproportionate growth of inventories and disproportionate increase in creditors in relation to current assets affecting the credit worthiness of the firm.
4. It is possible to detect the imbalance in the use of funds. For example, one can evaluate the ratio of dividends to earnings against the background of the firm's need for funds.
5. In the case of multi-division companies, fund flow statement helps to evaluate the performance of division in the use of funds allotted to them.

Limitations

1. The fund flow statement reveals the overall change in the working capital but not the variation in individual items.
2. Fund flow statement is prepared based on historical information.
3. It is not a substitute to financial statements. Instead it is only supplementary to financial statements.
4. The management may manipulate the working capital by adopting different method of inventory valuation.
5. The concept 'fund' consists of various types of items such as cash, destors, stock, prepaid expesnes etc. Thus fund flow statement lacks homogencity.

Steps Involved in the Preparation of Fund Flow Statement

(1) Preparation of a schedule showing change in working capital: The schedule analysing changes in working capital is prepared with the help of current assets and current liabilities of the two (period) balance sheets one being the previous year, *i.e.*, opening balance sheet and the other being current year, *i.e.*, closing balance sheet. An increase in the amount of any current asset in the current year in comparision to that in the previous year results in an increase in working capital. A decrease in the amount of any current asset in the current year in comparision to that in the previous year results in a decrease in working capital. Similarly current liabilities are also compared, *i.e.*, an increase in any current liability in the current year in comparision to the previous year results in a decrease in the working capital and *vice-versa*. Finally the total increase and total decrease is compared and the difference shows the decrease or increase on the working capital. An increase of working capital is the application of funds and decrease of working capital is the source of funds.

While preparing a schedule of change in working capital, the following points must be borne in mind.

(a) Provision for taxation: Provision for tax may be treated either as a current or non-current liability. When it is treated as a current liability (*i.e.*, as a charge on profit), provision for taxation is considered while preparing statement of working capital and not used for adjusting the profit made during the year for calculating the funds from operation and also tax paid during the year is not treated as an application of fund.

As a non-current liability, the provision for tax is treated as internal appropriation of profit and it is used for adjusting the profit made during the year. In this case it will not appear in the schedule of working capital. A seperate account known as 'Provision for taxation' is prepared. It is credited with the opening balance and credited with tax paid and closing balance. The tax paid during the year is treated as an application of fund in the flow how statement. The balancing figure represents the provision made during the year and is transferred to profit and loss account.

(b) Proposed Dividend· When proposed dividend is treated as a current liability it will be shown in the schedule of working capital as an item decreasing the working capital. Any dividend paid during the current year or an earlier year is not shown as an application of funds because such payment will not change net working capital or fund, *i.e.*, it will affect two current accounts, *viz.*, cash a/c and proposed dividend.

When proposed dividend is treated as a non-current liability, it is taken as an appropriation of profit. So this item will not appear in the schedule of working capital. A separate account is opened entitled 'proposed dividend a/c" to find out proposed dividend made during the year. The adjusted profit and loss a/c is debited with this amount of proposed dividend. The payment of dividend made during the current year in response to the proposed dividend for previous year is shown as an application in the fund flow statement.

(c) Trade investments should be treated as long-term investments and they should not be included in statement of changes in working capital. However, if investments represent surplus fund temporarily invested in marketable securities, they are to be treated as current assets, and as such, are to be considered in determining working capital.

A proforma of a schedule of changes in working capital is shown below:

Schedule of changes in working capital

	Previous year	*Current year*	*Increase*	*Decrease*
Current Assets				
Cash in hand	xx	xx		
Cash at Bank	xx	xx		
Debtors	xx	xx		
Marketable Securities	xx	xx		
Bills receivables	xx	xx		
Stock	xx	xx		

Prepaid expenses	xx	xx
Total (A)		
Current Liabilities		
Creditors	xx	xx
Bills payable	xx	xx
O/s expenses	xx	xx
Total (B)		
Working capital (A–B)	xx	xx
Net increase/ Decrease in working capital		

(d) Preparation of Adjusted Profit and Loss a/c to calculate fund from operation: The current operations of the business is the most important single source of funds and in the long run they constitute the largest source of funds. The repayment of loans, purchase of plant, payment of dividend etc., must ultimately depend upon this source. Funds from operations which are internal in character are arrived after making adjustments in the net profit. These adjustments are necessary because the net profit has been determined after deducting non-cash expenses such as depreciation, depletion charges, amortisation of fictitions and intangible assets like amount written off by way of prelimnary expenses, goodwill, patents, discount on shares or debentures, premium on redemption of preference shares or debentures, deferred charges etc. and loss on sale of fixed assets charged to profit and loss account, which do not result in flow of funds. These transactions, in fact are book adjustments and do not involve use of resources. So the actual fund generated from operations are larger by the amount of such non-cash expenses. Similarly the non-trading or non-operating incomes like dividends and interest received from out side or profit on sale of fixed assets, appreciation in the value of fixed assets will have to be deducted from net profit only if they have been considered already while preparing the profit and loss account. In short, funds from operations may be arrived at by deducting all non-cash credits (incomes) and adding back non-cash debits (expenses) to the net profit. If there has been a net loss as per profit and loss account, non-cash expenses have to be deducted therefrom and non-cash income added thereto.

A proforma of adjusted profit and loss account is given below:

Adjusted Profit & Loss A/c

	Rs.		*Rs.*
To Depreciation and depletion of fictitions and intangible assets such as goodwill, patent, trade marks etc.	xx	By Opening balance of P & L a/c	xx
		By Transfer from excess provision	xx
To Appropriation of Retained earnings such as transfer to general reserve, sinking fund etc.	xx	By Appreciation in the value of fixed assets	xx
		By Dividend received	xx
		By Profit on sale of fixed assets	xx
To Loss on sale of any current or fixed asset	xx	By Funds from operation	xx
To Dividend (in cluding) interim dividend)	xx	(Balancing figure in case debt side exceeds credit side.	

To Proposed dividend (If not taken as a current liability)	xx		
To Provision for taxation (If not taken as a current liability)	xx		
To Closing balance of profit & loss a/c	xx		
To Fund lost on operation (Balancing figure in case credit side exceeds debit side)	xx		
	xx		xx

(3) Reconstruction of all non-fund accounts: The various non-fund accounts which have changed between the two balance sheet period and in respect of which additional information is given is to be reconstructed. Such reconstruction is done by recording opening and closing balances along with additional information given. Any difference in the reconstructed account will represent either a source or application of fund. For example, a debit balance in a fixed asset account represents purchase and it relates to use of funds. If there is a credit balance, it represents sale of asset and it constitutes a source of fund. In case of non-fund liability account, if the balancing figure is on the debit side, is represents repayment and is a use of fund, while it is on the credit side, it will be a source of funds.

(4) Preparation of a statement of sources and application of funds: The final stage will involve the preparation of the statement of sources and uses of funds which portrays the avenues through which funds have been obtained and the uses to which they have been put. This statement contains the balancing figures in various non-fund accounts and the figure of fund from operation. Increase or decrease of working capital is also added as application or sources, as the case may be. The principal sources and application of funds are listed below:

Sources of Funds

1. Funds from operation
2. Issue of share capital
3. Borrowing long-term loans such as debentures, mortgage, long-term deposits, etc.
4. Sale of fixed assets such as land, building, plant, long-term investment, etc.
5. Non-trading receipts such as dividend and interest earnings, damages recovered in legal action etc.
6. Decrease in working capital (as per schedule)

Uses of Funds

1. Funds lost in operation (trading loss)
2. Redemption of preference shares
3. Repayment of long-term loans
4. Purchase of fixed assets
5. Non-trading payments, e.g., loss arising from legal action, loss of cash by embezzlement etc., and payment of taxes and dividends.
6. Increase in working capital (as per schedule)

When we prepare a fund flow statement *i.e.*, sources and application sides, would tally with each other. A specimen form of fund flow statement is shown below:

Specimen of Fund Flow Statement

Sources of Funds	
Fund from operation	xx
Issue of share capital	xx
Raising of long-term loans	xx
Receipts from partly paid shares called up	xx
Sale of fixed assets	xx
Non-trading receipts such as dividend received	xx
Sale of long-term Investments	xx
Decrease in working capital	xx
Total	xx

Application of Funds	
Fund lost in operation	xx
Redemption of preference share capital	xx
Redemption of debentures	xx
Repayment of long-term loans	xx
Purchase of fixed assets	xx
Purchase of long-term Investments	xx
Non-trading payments	xx
Payment of tax	xx
Increase in working capital	xx
Total	xx

Problem 1: (Preparation of schedule of working capital):- From the following Trail balance of 'A' Ltd. You are required to prepare a schedule of changes in working capital.

Trial Balance

	1998		*1999*	
	DR	*CR*	*DR*	*CR*
Capital	—	80,000	—	85,000
Mortage	—	—	—	5,000
Land and Buildings	50,000	—	50,000	—
Plant and Machinery	24,000	—	34,000	—
Stock	9,000	—	7,000	—
Debtors	16,500	—	19,500	—
Cash at Bank	4,000	—	9,000	—
Profit & loss a/c	—	14,500	—	24500
Creditors	—	9,000	—	5,000
	1,03,500	1,03,500	1,19,500	1,19,500

(Bangalore University, B.Com., April 2000)

Solution:

Schedule showing statement of working capital

	1998	*1999*	*Increase*	*Decrease*
Current Assets				
Stock	9,000	7,000	—	2,000
Debtors	16,500	19,500	3,000	—
Cash at Bank	4,000	9,000	5,000	—
Total (A)	29,500	35,500		

Current Liabilities				
Creditors	9,000	5,000	4,000	—
Total (B)	9,000	5,000		
Working Capital (A–B)	20,500	30,500	—	—
Net increase in working capital	10,000	—	—	10,000
	30,500	30,500	12,000	12,000

Problem 2: Prepare a statement showing changes in working capital:

	1990 (Rs.)	*1991 (Rs.)*
Assets:		
Cash	60,000	94,000
Debtors	2,40,000	2,30,000
Stock	1,60,000	1,80,000
Land	1,00,000	1,32,000
	5,60,000	6,36,000
Liabilities:		
Share capital	4,00,000	5,00,000
Creditors	1,40,000	90,000
Retained earnings	20,000	46,000
	5,60,000	6,36,000

(Osmania University, B.Com., March 1997)

Solution: **Schedule showing change in working capital**

	1990	*1991*	*Increase*	*Decrease*
Current Assets				
CAsh	60,000	94,000	34,000	—
Debtors	2,40,000	2,30,000	—	10,000
Stock	1,60,000	1,80,000	20,000	—
Total (A)	'4,60,000	5,04,000		
Current Liabilities:				
Creditors	1,40,000	90,000	50,000	—
Total (B)	1,40,000	90,000		
Working capital (A–B)	3,20,000	4,14,000		
Net increase in working capital	94,000			94,000
	4,14,000	4,14,000	10,4,000	1,04,000

Problem 3 (Problem on calculation of Fund from operation): Calculate funds from operation from the following profit and loss A/c:

P & L A/c

To Rent, salaries paid	75,000	By Gross profit	1,12,500
To Depreciation	17,500	By Grain on sale of land	15,000
To Loss on sale of machinery	1,000		
To Discount on issue of debentures	50		
To Goodwill written off	5,000		
To Net profit	28,950		
	1,27,500		1,27,500

(Osmania University, B.Com., October 1999)

Solution:

Adjusted Profit & Loss A/c

To Depreciation	17,500	By Gain on sale of land	15,000
To Loss on sale of machine	1,000	By Fund from operation	37,500
To Discount	50		
To Goodwill written off	5,000		
To Balance c/d	28,950		
	52,500		52,500

Problem 3 (Effect of Transactions on Working Capital): State with reasons whether the following transactions result in increase or decrease of working capital or do not affect the working capital.

(*a*) preliminary expenses written off Rs. 3,600.

(*b*) Bills receivable Rs. 4,000 was discounted for Rs. 3,850.

(*c*) Advance income tax paid Rs. 5,000.

(*d*) Rs. 50,000, 12% debentures were redeemed by purchase from open market at Rs. 95 for a debenture of Rs. 100.

Solution:

1. This is a non-current item as the amount is treated as deferred revenue expenditure. Hence this may be treated as an outflow of cash and affects the working capital.
2. This is a current liability being paid out and there is an outflow of cash and it decreases working capital.
3. There is an increase in current asset and current liability. This will not affect the working capital.
4. This is a non-current item and hence will not affect working capital.

Problem 4: State with reasons whether the following transactions result in increase or decrease in working capital or do not affect the working capital.

1. Bills accepted and issued to creditors Rs. 8,000.
2. One machine costing Rs. 30,000 (with an accumulated depreciation of Rs. 17,000) was sold for Rs. 15,000.
3. Amount paid for insurance Rs. 2,800 includes Rs. 600 prepaid insurance.
4. Dividend on investment received Rs. 800.

Solution:

1. This represents only an application of funds and it is a current liability. It decreases working capital.
2. There is a decrease in non-current assets and increase in cash. It will increase working capital.
3. There is an increase in current asset and decrease in current asset, *i.e.*, cash. It decreases working capital.
4. It is a non-current asset and does not affect working capital.

Problem 5: The balance sheets of Prasad Ltd. showed a net profit of Rs. 40,000 and Rs. 50,000 for the years 2000 and 2001 respectively. During the year 2001, proposed dividend was Rs. 30,000 and Rs. 20,000 was transferred to general Reserve Depreciation on fixed assets was Rs. 30,000. There was loss on sale of furniture to the extent of Rs. 5,000 and on plant was Rs. 10,000. Investments were sold for Rs. 40,000 and a profit of Rs. 20,000 was made. Preliminary expenses charged to the profit and loss account was Rs. 5,000. Calculate the fund from operation.

Solution:

Adjusted Profit & Loss A/c

To Proposed dividend	30,000	By Balance b/d	40,000
To Transfer to general reserve	20,000	By Profit on sale of investments	20,000
To Depreciation on fixed assets	30,000	By Fund from operation	90,000
To Loss on sale of furniture	5,000		
To Loss on sale of plant	10,000		
To Preliminary expenses	5,000		
To Balance c/d	50,000		
	1,50,000		1,50,000

Problem 6: Tanras Ltd. had the following balance sheet on 31-12-2001

Share capital	1,00,000	Buildings	40,000
Creditors	40,000	Stock	20,000
		Cash	80,000
	1,40,000		1,40,000

Following is the summary of transactions for the year

	Rs.
Purchases:	
Cash	15,000
Credit	35,000
Cash paid to creditors	5,000
Sales:	
Cash	20,000
Credit	80,000
Operating expenses (Cash paid)	20,000
Closing stock	50,000

Show the Net Change in Working Capital

Solution:

Cash A/c

To Balance b/d	80,000	By Cash purchases	15,000
To Cash sales	20,000	By Cash paid to creditors	5,000
		By Operating expenses	20,000
		By Balance c/d (Balancing figure)	60,000
	1,00,000		1,00,000

Creditors A/c

To Cash paid to creditors	5,000	By Balance b/d	40,000
To Balance c/d (Balancing figure)	70,000	By Credit purchases	35,000
	75,000		75,000

Schedule showing change working capital

	2000	*2002*	*Increase*	*Decrease*
Current Assets				
Cash	80,000	60,000	—	20,000
Stock	20,000	50,000	30,000	—
Total (A)	1,00,000	1,10,000		
Current Liabilities				
Creditors	40,000	70,000	—	30,000
Total (B)	40,000	70,000		
Working capital (A–B)	60,000	40,000		
Decrease in working	—	20,000	20,000	—
Capital	60,000	60,000	50,000	50,000

Problem 7: From the following particulars prepare a statement of sources and application of funds for the year ended 31.12.2000 of 'X' Co. Ltd.

(*a*) 'X' Co. Ltd. issued 1,000 shares of Rs. 100 each at a premium of Rs. 20 per share and all the shares are subscribed and fully paid up
(*b*) The company has redeemed preference shares for Rs. 1,00,000 at 10% premium
(*c*) Investments are sold for Rs. 50,000 (resulting in a profit of Rs. 20,000)
(*d*) Sale of machinery during the year Rs. 30,000 (resulting in a loss of Rs. 5,000)
(*e*) Purchase of fixed assets Rs. 1.20,000
(*f*) Dividend paid Rs. 40,000 and income tax paid Rs. 35,000
(*g*) Working capital of the company was Rs. 1,20,000 on 1-1-2000 and Rs. 1,80,000 on 31-12-2000
(*h*) Closing balance in P & L a/c was Rs. 45,000 more than opening balance as per Balance Sheets
(*i*) Depreciation provided for the year was Rs. 50,000 and preliminary expenses written off was Rs. 10,000

Solution:

Adjusted Profit & Loss A/c

To Loss on sale of machinery	5,000	By Profit on sale of investment	20,000
To Dividends	40,000	By Funds from operation	1,65,000
To Income tax	35,000		
To Depreciation	50,000		
To Preliminary expenses written off	10,000		
To Net profit	45,000		
	1,85,000		1,85,000

Fund Flow Statement

Sources		*Applications*	
Sale of machinery	30,000	Purchase of fixed assets	1,20,000
Sale of Investment	50,000	Dividend paid	40,000
Fund from operation	1,65,000	Income tax paid	35,000
Issue of shares	1,20,000	Redemption of preference shares	1,10,000
		Increase in working capital	60,000
	3,65,000		3,65,000

Problem 8: From the following particulars prepare (1) provision for depreciation A/c and (2) machinery A/c

	1.1.2001 Rs.	*31.12.2001* Rs.
Machinery a/c	1,80,000	2,50,000
Provision for depreciation a/c	50,000	60,000

The following information is also obtained:

(*a*) Machinery purchased in 2001 for Rs. 30,000 by issue of debentures
(*b*) One machine costing Rs. 40,000 on 1.1.2001 (with an accumulated depreciation of Rs. 20,000) was sold for Rs. 25,000

Solution:

Machinery A/c

To Balance b/d	1,80,000	By Sales	25,000
To Purchase of machinery by issue of debenture	30,000	By Depreciation	20,000
To Adj. P & L a/c - profit on sale of machinery	5,000	By Balance c/d	2,50,000
To Purchases of machinery for cash (Balancing figure)	80,000		
	2,95,000		2,95,000

Provision for depreciation

To Machinery a/c	20,000	By Balance b/d	50,000
To Balance c/d	60,000	By Adj. P & L a/c (Balancing figure)	30,000
	80,000		80,000

Working Note:

Calculation of profit on sale

Book value of machinery	40,000
Less: Depreciation	20,000
Depreciated value	20,000
Sales value of machinery	25,000
Profit on sale	5,000

Problem 9 (Preparation of Fund Flow Statement): Following are the summari· d balance sheets of Sahana Ltd. as on 31st December, 1998 and 1999

	1998	*1999*		*1998*	*1999*
Share capital	4,50,000	4,50,000	Fixed assets	4,00,000	3,20,000
General reserve	3,00,000	3,10,000	Investments (non-current)	50,000	60,000
P & L a/c	56,000	68,000			
Creditors	1,68,000	1,34,000	Stock	2,40,000	2,10,000
Provision for taxation	75,000	10,000	Debtors	2,10,000	4,55,000
			Bank	1,49,000	1,97,000
Mortgage loan	—	2,70,000			
	10,49,000	12,42,000		10,49,000	12,42,000

Additional Information

(*a*) Investment costing Rs. 8,000 were sold during the year 1999 for Rs. 8,500

(*b*) Provision for taxation made during the year was Rs. 90,000

(*c*) During the year part of the fixed assets costing Rs. 10,000 was sold for Rs. 12,000. The profit was included in the profit and loss account.

(*d*) Dividend paid during the year amounted to Rs. 40,000

Prepare a statement showing the sources and applications of funds for the year ended 31st December 1999. *(Bangalore University, B.Com., April 2000)*

Schedule showing changes in working capital

	1998	*1990*	*Increase*	*Decrease*
Current Assets:				
Stock	2,40,000	2,10,000	—	30,000
Debtors	2,10,000	4,55,000	2,45,000	—
Bank	1,49,000	1,97,000	48,000	—
Total (A)	5,99,000	8,62,000		
Current Liabilities				
Creditors	1,68,000	1,34,000	34,000	—
Total (B)	1,68,000	1,34,000		
Working capital (A–B)	4,31,000	7,28,000		
Increase in working capital	2,97,000	—	—	2,97,000
	7,28,000	7,28,000	3,27,000	3,27,000

Fixed Assets A/c

To Balance b/d	4,00,000	By Cash-sales	12,000
To P & L a/c (Profit on sale)	2,000	By Depreciation (Balancing figure)	70,000
		Balance c/d	3,20,000
	4,02,000		4,02,000

Investments

To Balance b/d	50,000	By Cash-sales	8,500
To P & L a/c - profit	500	By Balance c/d	60,000
To Cash-purchases (Balancing figure)	18,000		
	68,500		68,500

Provision for Taxation A/c

To Cash a/c (Balancing figure)	74,000	By Balance b/d	75,000
		By P & L a/c	9,000
To Balance c/d	10,000		
	84,000		84,000

Adjusted Profit & Loss A/c

To General reserve	10,000	By Balance b/d	56,000
To Dividends	40,000	By Profit on sale of investments	5,000
To Provision for taxation	9,000	By Profit on sale of fixed assets	2,000
To Depreciation on fixed assets	70,000	By Fund from operation	1,38,500
To Balance c/d	68,000		
	1,97,000		1,97,000

Statement of sources and application of funds

Sources		*Applications*	
Funf from operation	1,38,500	Dividend paid	40,000
Sale of fixed assets	12,000	Tax paid	74,000
Sale of Investments	8,500	Purchase of Investments	18,000
Mortgage loan	2,70,000	Increase in working capital	2,97,000
	4,29,000		4,29,000

Problem 10: From the following balance sheets of Joy Ltd. as on 31st December 1998 and 31st December 1999, you are required to prepare a fund flow statement for the year 1999

Liabilities	1998	1999	*Assets*	1998	1999
Share capital	50,000	60,000	Plant and Machinery	30,000	25,000
General reserve	8,000	12,000	Land and Building	20,000	40,000
P & L a/c	6,000	10,000			
Bank loan (Long-term)	10,000	2,000	Stock	26,000	20,000
Sundry creditors	12,000	16,000	Debtors	13,000	20,000
Provision for taxation	4,000	6,000	Cash	5,000	6,000
O/s expenses	4,000	5,000			
	94,000	1,11,000		94,000	1,11,000

Additional Information

1. Interest paid on bank loan amounted to Rs. 1,000
2. Income tax paid for the year 1999 Rs. 4,400
3. Assets of another company were purchased for a consideration of Rs. 10,000 and paid in shares. Assets consisted of land and building Rs. 4,000 and stock Rs. 6,000.
4. A machinery costing Rs. 5,000 (W D V Rs. 3,000) was sold for Rs. 1,000, the loss being written off against general reserve.
5. Closing stock of 1999 was over-valued by Rs. 5,000.
6. O/s expenses paid during the year were Rs. 4,500.

(Bangalore University, B.Com., October, 2000)

Solution: **Schedule showing change in working capital**

	1998	*1999*	*Increase*	*Decrease*
Current Assets				
Stock	26,000	20,000	—	6,000
Sundry debtors	13,000	20,000	7,000	—
Cash	5,000	6,000	1,000	—
Total (A)	44,000	46,000		
Current Liabilities:				
Sundry creditors	12,000	16,000	—	4,000
Total (B)	12,000	16,000		
Working capital (A–B)	32,000	30,000		
Net decrease in working capital	—	2,000	2,000	
	32,000	32,000	10,000	10,000

Outstanding expanses A/c

To Bank - O/s expenses paid	4500	By Balance b/d	4,000
To Balance c/d	5,000	By Adj. P & L a/c	5500
	9,500		9,500

General reserve A/c

To Loss on sale of Machinery (3,000–1,000)	2,000	By Balance b/d	8,000
To Balance c/d	12,000	By Adj. P & L a/c (Balancing figure)	6,000
	14,000		14,000

Provision for taxation

To Bank a/c –Income tax paid	4,400	By Balance b/d	4,000
To Balance c/d	6,000	By Adj. P & L a/c –provision for tax (Balancing figure)	6,400
	10,400		10,400

Machinery A/c

To Balance b/d	30,000	By Depreciation (5,000 – 3,000)	2,000
		By Loss on sale of machinery	2,000
		By Bank a/c—Sale of machinery	1,000
		By Balance c/d	25,000
	30,000		30,000

Land and buildings A/c

To Balance b/d	20,000	By Balance c/d	40,000
To Shares a/c - purchases	4,000		
To Bank a/c cash purchases (Balancing figure)	16,000		
	40,000		40,0,000

Adjusted Profit and Loss A/c

To Transfer to reserve	6,000	By Balance b/d	6,000
To Provision for tax	6400	By Over-valuation of stock	5,000
To Interest on bank loan	1,000	By Fund from operation	19,900
To Outstanding expenses	5,500		
To Depreciation on machinery	2,000		
To Balcne c/d	10,000		
	30,900		30,900

Fund flow statement

Sources		*Applications*	
Funds from operation	19,900	Loan paid	8,000
Sale of machinery	1,000	Income tax paid	4400
Issue of shares	10,000	Outstanding expenses paid	4500
Decrease in working-capital	2,000	Purchase of land & building	16,000
	32,900		32,900

Problem 11: The following is the Balance Sheets of X Ltd. on 31st December, 1992 and 1993

	1992 *(Rs.)*	*1993* *(Rs.)*
Liabilities:		
Equity capital	3,00,000	4,00,000
Cum preference shares	1,50,000	1,00,000
General Reserve	40,000	70,000
P & L a/c	30,000	48,000
Proposed Dividend	42,000	50,000
Sundry creditors	55,000	83,000
Bills payable	20,000	16,000
Provision for taxation	40,000	50,000
	6,77,000	8,17,000

Assets:		
Goodwill	1,15,000	90,000
Buildings	2,00,000	1,70,000
Machinery	80,000	2,00,000
Sundry Debtors	1,60,000	2,00,000
Stock	77,000	1,09,000
Bills receivable	20,000	30,000
Cash in hand and at Bank	25,000	18,000
	6,77,000	8,17,000

Additional Information

(*i*) Depreciation written off on machinery and building in 1993 were Rs. 10,000 and 20,000 respectively.

(*ii*) During the year 1993, dividends of Rs. 20,000 were paid.

(*iii*) The income tax paid during the year was Rs. 35,000.

Prepare Fund Flow Statement. *(Sri Venkateshwara University, B.Com., October 1999)*

Solution:

Schedule of changes in working capital

	1992	*1993*	*Increase*	*Decrease*
Current Assets				
Sundry debtors	1,60,000	2,00,000	40,000	—
Stock	77,000	1,09,000	32,000	—
Bills receivable	20,000	30,000	10,000	—
Cash and Bank	25,000	18,000	—	7,000
Total (A)	2,82,000	3,57,000		
Current Liabilities				
Sundry creditors	55,000	83,000	—	28,000
Bills payable	20,000	16,000	4,000	—
Total (B)	75,000	99,000		
Working capital (A–B)	2,07,000	2,58,000		
Increase in working capital	51,000	—	—	51,000
	2,58,000	2,58,000	86,000	86,000

Equity Share capital

To Balance c/d	4,00,000	By Balance b/d	3,00,000
		By Bank (Balancing figure)	1,00,000
	4,00,000		4,00,000

Cum pref. share capital A/c

To Bank (Balance figure)	50,000	By Balance b/d	1,50,000
To Balance c/d	1,00,000		
	1,50,000		1,50,000

General reserve

	Rs.		Rs.
To Balance c/d	70,000	By Balance b/d	40,000
		By P & L a/c (Balancing figure)	30,000
	70,000		70,000

Proposed dividend A/c

	Rs.		Rs.
To Bank A/c	20,000	By Balance b/d	42,000
To Balance c/d	50,000	By P & L a/c (Balancing figure)	28,000
	70,000		70,000

Provision for taxation A/c

	Rs.		Rs.
To Bank	35,000	By Balance b/d	40,000
To Balance c/d	50,000	By P & L a/c (Balancing figure)	45,000
	85,000		85,000

Goodwill A/c

	Rs.		Rs.
To Balance b/d	1,15,000	By P & L a/c (Balancing figure)	25,000
		By Balance c/d	90,000
	1,15,000		1,15,000

Buildings A/c

	Rs.		Rs.
To Balance b/d	2,00,000	By Depreciation	20,000
		By Bank-sales (Balancing figure)	10,000
		By Balance c/d	1,70,000
	2,00,000		2,00,000

Machinery A/c

	Rs.		Rs.
To Balance b/d	80,000	By Depreciation	10,000
To Bank-purchases (Balancing figure)	1,30,000	By Balance c/d	2,00,000
	2,10,000		2,10,000

Adjusted Profit & Loss A/c

	Rs.		Rs.
To General reserve	30,000	By Balance b/d	30,000
To Proposed dividend	28,000	By Fund from operation	1,76,000
To Provision for taxation	45,000		
To Goodwill written off	25,000		
To Depreciation on:			
Building	20,000		
Machinery	10,000		
To Balance c/d	48,000		
	2,06,000		2,06,000

Fund flow statement

Sources		*Applications*	
Fund from operation	1,76,000	Redemption of cum pref shares	50,000
Issue of equity shares	1,00,000	Dividend paid	20,000
Sale of building	10,000	Income-tax paid	35,000
		Purchase of machinery	1,30,000
		Increase in working capital	51,000
	2,86,000		2,86,000

Problem 12: From the following balance sheet of X Ltd., as on 31st December, 1997 and 31st December 1998, you are required to prepare fund flow statement:

Liabilities	*1997*	*1998*	*Assets*	*1997*	*1998*
Share capital	4,00,000	5,00,000	Land & building	4,00,000	4,80,000
General reserve	80,000	1,40,000			
P & L a/c	64,000	78,000	Machinery	3,60,000	2,60,000
Bank loan	3,20,000	80,000	Stock	2,00,000	2,52,000
(long-term)			Debtors	1,60,000	1,28,000
Creditors	3,00,000	2,60,000	Cash at Bank	1,04,000	18,000
Provision for Taxation	60,000	80,000			
	12,24,000	11,38,000		12,24,000	11,38,000

Additional Information

1. During the year ended 31st December, 1998, dividend of Rs. 84,000 was paid.
2. Assets of another company were purchased for a consideration of Rs. 1,00,000, payable by the issue of shares. The assets included land and building of Rs. 50,000 and stock of Rs. 50,000.
3. Depreciation written off an machinery is Rs. 24,000 and on land & building is Rs. 45,000
4. Income tax paid during the year was Rs. 70,000.
5. Addition to buildings were Rs. 75,000.

(Osmania University, B.Com., October 1999)

Solution:

Schedule showing changes in working capital

	1997	*1998*	*Increase*	*Decrease*
Current Assets:				
Cash at Bank	1,04,000	18,000	—	86,000
Debtors	1,60,000	1,28,000	—	32,000
Stock	2,00,000	2,52,000	52,000	—
Total (A)	4,64,000	3,98,000		
Current liabilities				
Creditors	3,00,000	2,60,000	40,000	—
Total (B)	3,00,000	2,60,000		
Working capital (A–B)	1,64,000	1,38,000		
Decrease in working capital		26,000		
	1,64,000	1,64,000	1,08,000	1,08,000

Provision for taxation A/c

To Cash	70,000	By Balance b/d	60,000
To Balance c/d	80,000	By Adj. P & L a/c	90,000
	1,50,000		1,50,000

Machinery A/c

To Balance b/d	3,60,000	By Adj. P & L a/c depreciation	24,000
		By Sale of machinery	76,000
		By Balance c/d	2,60,000
	3,60,000		3,60,000

Land & buildings A/c

To Balance b/d	4,00,000	By Adj. P & L a/c —Depreciation	45,000
To Share capital	50,000	By Balance c/d	4,80,000
To Cash	75,000		
	5,25,000		5,25,000

General reserve A/c

To Balance c/d	1,40,000	By Balance b/d	80,000
		By Adj P & L a/c	60,000
	1,40,000		1,40,000

Adjusted Profit & Loss A/c

To Machinery a/c	24,000	By Balance b/d	64,000
To Land & Buildings	45,000	By Fund from operation	3,17,000
To Provision for tax	90,000		
To General reserve	60,000		
To Dividend paid	84,000		
To Balance c/d	78,000		
	3,81,000		3,81,000

Fund Flow Statement

Sources		*Application*	
Issue of shares	50,000	Purchase of land & building	75,000
Sale of machinery	76,000	Bank loan paid	2,40,000
Fund from operation	3,17,000	Dividend paid	84,000
Decrease in working capital	26,000	Income tax paid	70,000
	4,69,000		4,69,000

Problem 13: Following are the Balance Sheets of fertilizers India Limited as at 31st December, 1997 and 1998 respectively.

	31.12.97 *Rs.*	*31.12.98* *Rs.*
Liabilities		
Share capital of Rs. 100 each	20,00,000	25,00,000
Reserve and surplus	8,00,000	8,70,000
8% convertible debentures	10,00,000	8,00,000
Public deposits	3,00,000	2,50,000
Current liabilities & provisions	6,20,000	7,10,000
Proposed dividend	2,00,000	2,50,000
	49,20,000	53,80,000

Assets		
Fixed assets at cost	25,00,000	30,00,000
Less: Depreciation till date	6,80,000	8,20,000
	18,20,000	21,80,000
Trade investments	12,50,000	13,50,000
Marketable Investments	60,000	30,000
Inventories	4,10,000	5,20,000
Book Debts	5,30,000	5,05,000
Cash and Bank	1,20,000	1,40,000
Preliminary expenses	1,00,000	50,000
Capital work-in-progress	6,30,000	6,05,000
	49,20,000	53,80,000

You are informed that during 1998:

1. Debentures of Rs. 2,00,000 were converted into shares at par.
2. Shares of Rs. 2,00,000 were issued as fully paid bouns shares out of reserves.
3. Shares worth Rs. 1,00,000 at par were issued to a vendor in part payment of a machine costing Rs. 1,.20,000 supplied by him.
4. A machine costing Rs. 50,000 (Book value Rs. 30,000 as on 31st December 1997) was disposed off for Rs. 20,000.
5. Trade Investments costing Rs. 30,000 were disposed off for Rs. 36,000.

Prepare fund flow statement along with detailed schedule of changes in working capital for the year 1998.

(University of Bombay, B.Com., October 1999)

Solution:

Schedule showing change in working capital

	1997	*1998*	*Increase*	*Decrease*
Current Assets				
Inventories	4,10,000	5,20,000	1,10,000	—
Book debts	5,30,000	5,05,000	—	25,000
Cash & Bank	1,20,000	1,40,000	20,000	—
Capital work-in-progress	6,30,000	6,05,000	—	25,000
Marketable Investment	60,000	30,000	—	30,000
Total (A)	17,50,000	18,00,000		
Current Liabilities				
Current liabilties & provisions	6,20,000	7,10,000	—	90,000
Total (B)	6,20,000	7,10,000		
Net Working Capital	11,30,000	10,90,000	—	—
Decrease in Working Capital		40,000	40,000	—
	11,30,000	11,30,000	1,70,000	1,70,000

Proposed dividend A/c

To Bank	2,00,000	By Balance b/d	2,00,000
To Balance c/d	2,50,000	By P & L a/c	2,50,000
	4,50,000		4,50,000

Fixed Assets A/c

To Balance b/d	25,00,000	By Machine sold	50,000
To Equity share capital	1,00,000	By Balance c/d	30,00,000
To Cash a/c	20,000		
To Cash-purchases (Balancing figure)	4,30,000		
	30,50,000		30,50,000

Provision for Depreciation A/c

To Depreciation on machine sold	20,000	By Balance b/d	6,80,000
To Balance c/d	8,20,000	By Depreciation a/c	1,60,000
	8,40,000		8,40,000

Trade Investment

To Balance b/d	12,50,000	By Bank a/c	36,000
To Reserves	6,000	By Balance c/d	13,50,000
To Bank a/c	1,30,000		
	13,86,000		13,86,000

Calculation of Loss on Sale of Machine

Cost price	50,000
Less: Depreciation	20,000
Written down value	30,000
Sold	20,000
Loss on sale	10,000

Adjusted Profit & Loss A/c

To Preliminary expenses	50,000	By Balance b/d	8,00,000
To Equity share capital (Bonus)	2,00,000	By Profit on sale	6,000
To Proposed Dividend	2,50,000	By Fund from operation	7,34,000
To Loss on sale of machine	10,000		
To Depreciation	1,60,000		
To Balance c/d	8,70,000		
	15,40,000		15,40,000

Fund Flow Statement

Sources		*Application*	
Sale of machine	20,000	Dividend for last year paid	2,00,000
Sale of investment	36,000	Public deposit repaid	50,000
Decrease in working capital	40,000	Purchase of machine	4,50,000
Fund from operation on	7,34,000	Purchase of trade investment	1,30,000
	8,30,000		8,30,000

Problem 14: Prepare (*i*) statement of changes in working capital and (*ii*) fund flow statement for the year ended 31st December, 1998 from the following balance sheets of Shivani Ltd.

Liabilities	*1997*	*1998*	*Assets*	*1997*	*1998*
Equity share capital (Shares of Rs. 10 each Rs. 8 paid up)	1,20,000		Fixed assets	2,10,000	2,30,000
			Investments	40,000	52,000
			Stock	1,10,000	1,36,000
Equity share capital (shares of Rs. 10 each fully paid)		1,80,000	Debtors	90,000	88,000
			Cash & Bank	14,000	33,000
12% Preference share capital	1,00,000	70,000	Preliminary expenses	2,000	1,000
Share premium	5,000	3,500			
General reserve	80,000	40,000			
Profit & loss A/c	26,600	45,000			
15% Debentures	20,000	60,000			
Creditors	80,000	95,000			
Proposed equity dividend	14,400	22,500			
Provision for taxation	20,000	24,000			
	4,66,000	5,40,000		4,66,000	5,40,000

Additional information is as follows:

1. During the year (*i.e.*, 1998) the company has paid a bouns of Rs. 2 per share to make the partly paid shares fully paid up and for this purpose general reserve was utilised.
2. During the year, the company then issued equity shares as rights, shares in the ratio of one for every five held.
3. Prepference shares were redeemed at 5% premium on 31st December, 1998.
4. During the year, a machine costing Rs. 12,000 on which depreciation written off to data was Rs. 3,000 was sold for Rs. 9,500 and current years depreciation provided on fixed assets was Rs. 15,000
5. Paid proposed equity dividend of last year and also paid in term dividend of Rs. 9,000.
6. The preference share dividend was paid on 31st December each year.
7. Income-tax of Rs. 24,000 was paid during the year. (*University of Bombay, B.Com., April 1999*)

Solution: **Schedule showing change in working capital**

	1997	*1998*	*Increase*	*Decrease*
Current Assets				
Stock	1,10,000	1,36,000	26,000	—
Debtors	90,000	88,000	—	20,000
Cash & Bank	14,000	33,000	19,000	—
Total (A)	2,14,000	2,57,000		
Current Liabilities				
Sundry creditors	80,000	95,000		
Total (B)	80,000	95,000		
Working capital (A–B)	1,34,000	1,62,000		
Increase in working capital	28,000	—	—	—
	1,62,000	1,62,000	45,000	45,000

Working Notes:

(1) Calculation of amount utilised from general reserve for issue of bouns

No. of shares $\frac{1,20,000}{8}$ = 15,000 shares

15,000 shares @ Rs. 2 per share = 30,000

(2) Issue of right shares

No. of shares already issued = 15,000
For 5 shares 1 New shares

For 15,000 shares = $\frac{15,000 \times 1}{5}$ = 3,000 shares

3,000 shares of Rs. 10 each = 30,000
Total share capital on 31.12.1998
15,000 + 3,000 = 18,000 shares of Rs. 10 each, *i.e.*, 1,80,000

Fixed Assets A/c

To Balance b/d	2,10,000	By Bank-sale	9,500
To P & L a/c profit sale	500	By Depreciation	15,000
To Cash-purchases (Balancing figure)	44,000	By Balance c/d	2,30,000
	2,54,500		2,54,500

Calculation of Profit on sale of Machine

Cost price	12,000
Less: Depreciation	3,000
Written down value	9,000
Sold for	9500
Profit on sale	500

Equity Share Capital A/c

To Balance c/d	1,80,000	By Balance b/d	1,20,000
		By General Reserve	30,000
		By Cash (Balancing figure)	30,000
	1,80,000		1,80,000

General Reserve A/c

To Equity capital	30,000	By Balance b/d	80,000
To P & C a/c	10,000		
To Balance c/d	40,000		
	80,000		80,000

Proposed Equity Dividend A/c

To Bank	14,400	By Balance b/d	14,400
To Balance c/d	22,500	By P & L a/c	22,500
	36,900		36,900

Provision for taxation

To Cash	24,000	By Balance b/d	20,000
To Balance c/d	24,000	By P & L a/c	28,000
	48,000		48,000

Adjusted Profit & Loss A/c

To Preliminary expenses	1,000	By Balance b/d	26,600
To Depreciation	15,000	By Profit on sale of machinery	500
To Interim Dividend	9,000	To Transfer from general reserve	10,000
To Pref dividend	12,000		
To Provision for tax	28,000	By Fund from operation	95,400
To Proposed dividend	22,500		
To Balance c/d	45,000		
	1,32,500		1,32,500

Fund Flow Statement

Sources		*Application*		
Issue of Debentures	40,000	Investment purchased		12,000
Issue of Right shares	30,000	Redemption of pref shares	30,000	
Sale of machinery	9,500	*Add:* Premium	1500	
Fund from operation	95,400			31,500
		Increase in working capital		28,000
		Equity dividend paid		14,400
		Interim dividend paid		9,000
		Preference dividend		12,000
		Income tax paid		24,000
		Fixed assets purchased		44,000
	1,74,900			1,74,900

Problem 15: From the following Balance Sheets of ABC Ltd. on 31st December, 1996 and 1997, you are required to prepare (*i*) A schedule of changes in working capital, (*ii*) A fund flow statement:

	1996	*1997*		*1996*	*1997*
Share capital	2,00,000	2,00,000	Goodwill	24,000	24,000
Gen. reserve	28,000	36,000	Building	80,000	72,000
P & L a/c	32,000	26,000	Plant	74,000	72,000
Creditors	16,000	10,800	Investments	20,000	22,000
Bills payable	2,400	1,600	stock	60,000	46,800
Provision for taxation	32,000	36,000	B.R.	4,000	6,400
Provision for doubtful debts	800	1200	Debtors	36,000	38,000
			Cash	13,200	30,400
	3,11,200	2,11,600		3,11,200	3,11,600

Additional Information

(*a*) Depreciation provided on plant was Rs. 8,000 and on Buildings Rs. 8,000.
(*b*) Provision for taxation made during the year Rs. 38,000.
(*c*) Interim dividend paid during the year Rs. 16,000 (*Osmania University, B.Com., March 1999*)

Solution:

Schedule showing change in working capital

	1996	*1997*	*Increase*	*Decrease*
Current Assets				
Cash	13,200	30,400	17,200	—
Debtors	36,000	38,000	2,000	—
B.R.	4,000	6,400	2400	—
Stock	60,000	46,800	—	13,200
Total (A)	1,13,200	1,21,600		

Current Liabilities				
Provision for doubtful debts	800	1,200	—	400
Bills payable	2,400	1,600	800	—
Creditors	16,000	10,800		
Total (B)	19,200	13,600		
Working capital (A–B)	94,000	1,08,000		
Increase in working capital	14,000	—	—	14,000
	1,08,000	1,08,000	27,600	27,600

Provision for taxation A/c

To Bank-tax paid	34,000	By Balance b/d	32,000
To Balance c/d	36,000	By P & L a/c	38,000
	70,000		70,000

Plant A/c

To Balance b/d	74,000	By Depreciation	8,000
To Bank-purchase	6,000	By Balance c/d	72,000
	80,000		80,000

Buildings A/c

To Balance b/d	80,000	By Depreciation	8,000
		By Balance c/d	72,000
	80,000		80,000

Investment A/c

To Balance b/d	20,000	By Balance c/d	22,000
To Bank-purchases	2,000		
	22,000		22,000

Adjusted Profit & Loss A/c

To Transfer to general reserve	8,000	By Balance b/d	32,000
To Provision for tax	38,000	By Fund from operation	72,000
To Depreciation on:			
–plant	8,000		
–Building	8,000		
To Interim dividend	16,000		
To Balance c/d	26,000		
	1,04,000		1,04,000

General Reserve A/c

To Balance c/d	36,000	By Balance b/d	28,000
		By P & L A/c	8,000

Fund Flow Statement

Sources		*Applications*	
Funds from operation	72,000	Purchase of plant	6,000
		Tax paid	34,000
		Purchase of investment	2,000
		Interim dividend paid	16,000
		Increase in working capital	14,000
	72,000		72,000

Problem 16: Following are the summarised balance sheets of the Gamges Ltd. as on 31st December, 1996 and 1997

	1996	*1997* (Rs. '000)		*1996*	*1997* (Rs. '000)
Share capital	200	250	Land & building	200	190
General Reserve	50	60	Plant & machinery	150	169
P & C a/c	30.5	30.6	Stock	100	74
Bank loan	70	—	Sundry debtors	80	64.2
Sundry creditors	150	135.2	Cash balance	0.5	0.6
Provision for taxation	30	35	Bank balance	—	8
			Goodwill	—	5
	530.5	510.8		530.5	510.8

The following additional information is available:

(*a*) During the year ended 31st December, 1997:

(*i*) Dividend of Rs. 23,000 was paid

(*ii*) Assets of another company were purchased for Rs. 50,000 payable in shares, assets purchased were: stock Rs. 20,000 and machinery Rs. 25,000

(*iii*) Machinery of Rs. 8,000 was purchased in addition to that of (*ii*) above.

(*b*) Depreciation written off during the year 1997:
Building Rs. 10,000 and machinery Rs. 14,000.

(*c*) The net profit for the year 1997 was Rs. 66,100.

(*d*) Income-tax paid during the year 1997 was Rs. 28,000 and provision of Rs. 33,000 was made to profit & loss a/c.

Preare a statement of sources and applications of funds for the year ended 31st December, 1997 and a schedule setting out the changes in working capital. (*CS, Inter, December 1998*)

Solution:

Schedule showing change in working capital

	1996	*1997*	*Increase*	*Decrease*
Current Assets				
Stock	1,00,000	74,000	—	26,000
Sundry Debtors	80,000	64,200		15,800
Cash	500	600	100	—
Bank	—	8,000	8,000	—
Total (A)	1,80,500	1,46,800		
Current Liabilities				
Sundry creditors	1,50,000	1,35,200	14,800	—
Total (B)	1,50,000	1,35,200		
Working capital	30,500	11,600		
Decrease in working capital	—	18,900	18,900	—
	30,500	30,500	41,800	41,800

Machinery A/c

	Rs.		Rs.
To Balance b/d	1,50,000	By Depreiciation	14,000
To Vendor	25,000	By Balance c/d	1,69,000
To Cash-purchases	8,000		
	1,83,000		1,83,000

Provision for income tax

	Rs.		Rs.
To Cash	28,000	By Balance b/d	30,000
To Balance c/d	35,000	By P & L A/c	33,000
	63,000		63,000

Share Capital A/c

	Rs.		Rs.
To Balance c/d	2,50,000	By Balance b/d	2,00,000
		By Vendor's A/c	50,000
	2,50,000		2,50,000

Goodwill A/c

	Rs.		Rs.
To Vendor	5,000	By Balance c/d	5,000

Adjusted Profit & Loss A/c

	Rs.		Rs.
To Dividend	23,000	By Balance b/d	30,500
To Depreciation (10,000+14,000)	24,000	By Fund from operation	90,100
To Provision for taxation	33,000		
To General reserve	10,000		
To Balance c/d	30,600		
	1,20,600		1,20,600

Fund Flow Statement

Sources		*Applications*	
Issue of shares (for stock)	20,000	Dividend paid machinery	23,000
Fund from operation	90,100	Purchased	8,000
Decrease in working capital	18,900	Income tax paid	28,000
		Bank loan paid	70,000
	1,29,000		1,29,000

Problem 17: From the following information of XYZ Ltd. prepare a statement showing changes in working capital position along with funds flow statement:

	31st December Previous year *Rs.*	*31st December current year* *Rs.*
Current assets	1,35,000	1,27,200
Investments	15,000	21,400
Land	9,000	9,000
Plant and machinery	81,100	1,05,000
(Accumulated depreciation)	(24,000)	(26,000)
Patents	16,200	12,600
Total assets	2,32,200	2,32,200
Current liabilities	24,600	34,800
12% debentures	43,400	—
14% debentures	—	39,000

Equity share capital	90,000	1,00,000
Reserve for future losses on investments	6,000	36,000
Retained earnings	68,200	71,800
Total liabilities and capital	2,32,200	2,32,200

Additional Information

(*i*) a reconciliation of the balances in retained earnings is as follows:

	Rs.
Beginning balance	68,200
Net income for current year	3,000
Award received from settlement of patent, infringement case	15,600
Dividends	(15,000)
Ending Balance	71,800

(*ii*) Net income of the current year includes a loss of Rs. 48,000 on the sale of a part of plant. The plant was for Rs. 19,000 at the beginning of the year, accumulated depreciation being Rs. 6,000.

(*iii*) Investments of Rs. 15,000 were sold during the year at a loss. The loss was charged to the reserve for future losses on investments and did not appear on the income statement.

(*iv*) During the current year the 12% debentures were called for redemption. Most of them were refunded through the issuanee of new 14% debentures, and the rest were retired for cash.

(v) The equity shares were issued in exchange of machinery. The rest of the plant and machinery were purchased for cash. *(CS, Intermediate, June, 1998)*

Solution:

Schedule showing change in Working Capital

	Previous year	*Current year*	*Increase*	*Decrease*
Current assets	1,35,000	1,27,200	—	78,00
Less: Current liabilities	24,600	34,800	—	10,200
Working capital	1,10,400	92,400		
Decrease in working capital	—	18,000	18,000	—
	1,10,400	1,10,400	18,000	18,000

Accumulated Depreciation

To Plant & machinery A/c	6,000	By Balance b/d	24,000
To Balance c/d	26,000	By P & L a/c - (Balancing figure)	8,000
	32,000		32,000

Calculation fo sale of machinery

Book value	19,000
Less: Depreciation	6,000
Written down value	13,000
Less: Loss on sale	4,800
Sale of machinery	8,200

Plant & Machinery A/c

To Balance b/d	81,000	By Cash-sales	8,200
To Share capital (1,00,000–90,000)	10,000	By Accumulated depreciation a/c	6,000
To Bank-purchases (Balancing figure)	33,000	By Loss on sale machinery	4,800
		By Balance c/d	1,05,000
	1,24,000		1,24,000

Calculation of sale of Investments

Book value	15,000
Less: Loss (6,000–3600)	2400
Sale of investments	12,600

Investments A/c

To Balance b/d	15,000	By Cash-sales	12,600
To Bank-purchases (Balancing figure)	21,400	By Reserve for future loss	2,400
		By Balance c/d	21,400
	36,400		36,400

Adjusted Profit & Loss A/c

To Patent written off	3600	By Balance b/d	68,200
To Depreciation on plant & machinery	8,000	By Award received	15,600
To Loss on sale of plant	4,800	By Fund from operation	19,400
To Dividend	15,000		
To Balance c/d	71,800		
	1,03,200		1,03,200

Fund Flow Statement

Sources		*Applications*	
Issue of 14% debentures	39,000	Purchase of plant	33,000
Sale of Investments	12,600	Redemption of 12% debentures	43,400
Award received	15,600	Purchase of investments	21,400
Sale of plant	8,200	Dividend paid	15,000
Fund from operation	19,400		
Decrease in working capital	18,000		
	1,12,800		1,12,800

Problem 18: Timbaktu Limited furnishes the following details with the direction to prepare fund flow statement for the year 1997:

Balance Sheet

	1997	*1996*		*1997*	*1996*
Share capital	90,000	80,000	Working capital:		
Profit & loss a/c	46,000	30,000	Current assets	1,20,000	96,000
			Less: current liabilities	42,000	30,000
				78,000	66,000
			Fixed assets	56,000	40,000
			Share Issue expenses	2,000	4,000
	1,30,000	1,10,000		1,36,000	1,10,000

Other Information

1. An old machine costing Rs. 8,000 (W D V Rs. 6,000) was sold during the year for Rs. 7,000.
2. Depreciation for the year was Rs. 2,000.
3. Interim devidend of Rs. 4,000 was paid during the year. Final dividend was not declared.
4. The company made the bonus issue of shares during the year at one equity share for 8 equity shares held by the existing shareholders by utilising the profits.

(*University of Bombay, B.Com., October 1998*)

Solution:

Statement showing change in Working Capital

	1996	1997	Increase	Decrease
Current assets	96,000	1,20,000	24,000	—
Less: Current liabilities	30,000	42,000	—	12,000
Working capital	66,000	78,000		
Increase in working capital	12,000	—	—	12,000
	78,000	78,000	24,000	24,000

Working Notes:

(1) Calculation of profit on sale of machinery

Machinery at cost	8,000
Less: Accumulated depreciation	2,000
Written down value	6,000
Sold for	700
Profit on sale	1,000

(2) Calculation of Bonus issue of shares

For 8 equity shares — 1 Bonus share

For 80,000 → $\frac{80,000 \times 1}{8}$ = Rs. 10,000

Fixed Assets A/c

To Balance b/d	40,000	By Sale of machine	7,000
To Profit on sale	1,000	By Depreciation	2,000
To Bank-purchases (Balancing figure)	24,000	By Balance c/d	56,000
	65,000		65,000

Adjusted Profit & Loss A/c

To Depreciation on fixed assets	2,000	By Balance b/d	30,000
To Interim dividend	4,000	By Profit on sale of machinery	1,000
To Bonus to share-holders	10,000	By Fund from operation	33,000
To Share issue expenses	2,000		
To Balance c/d	46,000		
	64,000		64,000

Fund Flow Statement

Sources		*Applications*	
Sale of machinery	7,000	Purchase of fixed assets	24,000
Fund from operation	33,000	Interim dividend paid	4,000
		Increase in working capital	12,000
	40,000		40,000

Problem 19: From the following Balance Sheets of X, Y and Z Ltd. as on 31.12.1996 and 31.12.1997 you are required to prepare:

(*a*) Schedule of changes in working capital.

(*b*) Fund flow statement.

	1996	1997		1996	1997
Share capital	1,00,000	1,00,000	Goodwill	12,000	12,000
General reserve	14,000	18,000	Building	40,000	36,000
P & L a/c	16,000	13,000	Plant	37,000	36,000
Sundry creditors	8,000	5,400	Investment	10,000	11,000
Bills payable	1,200	800	Stock	30,000	23,400
Provision for taxation	16,000	18,000	B.R.	2,000	3,200
Provision for doubtful debts	400	600	Debtors	18,000	19,000
			Bank	6,600	15,200
	1,55,600	1,55,800		1,55,600	1,55,800

Further Information

1. Depreciation charged on plant was Rs. 4,000 and on building Rs. 4,000.
2. Provision for taxation Rs. 19,000 was made during the year 1997.
3. Interim dividend of Rs. 8,000 was paid during 1997.

(Bangalore University, B.B.M., November 1998)

Solution:

Schedule of changes in Working Capital

	1996	*1997*	*Increase*	*Decrease*
Current Assets				
Cash at Bank	6,600	15,200	8,600	—
Debtors	18,000	19,000	1,000	—
B.R.	2,000	3,200	1,200	
Stock	30,000	23,400	—	6,600
Total (A)	56,600	60,800		
Current Liabilities				
Provision for doubtful debts	400	600	—	200
Bills payable	1,200	800	400	—
Sundry	8,000	5,400	2,600	—
Total (B)	9,600	6,800		
Working capital (A–B)	47,000	54,000		
Increase in working capital	7,000	—	—	7,000
	54,000	54,000	13,800	13,800

Plant A/c

To Balance b/d	37,000	By Depreication	4,000
To Bank-purchases (Balancing figure)	3,000	By Balance c/d	36,000
	40,000		40,000

Provision for Tax A/c

To Bank-tax paid (Balancing figure)	17,000	By Balance b/d	16,000
		By P & L a/c	19,000
To Balance c/d	18,000		
	35,000		35,000

Adjusted Profit & Loss A/c

To Transfer to general reserve	4,000	By Balance b/d	16,000
To Provision for tax	19,000	By Fund from operation	36,000
To Depreciation on plant	4,000		
To Depreciation on building	4,000		
To Interim dividend paid	8,000		
To Balance c/d	13,000		
	52,000		52,000

Fund Flow Statement

Sources		*Applications*	
Fund from operation	36,000	Purchase of plant	3,000
		Tax paid	17,000
		Investments purchased	1,000
		Interim dividend paid	8,000
		Increase in working capital	7,000
	36,000		36,000

Problem 20: Following are the summarised balance sheets of 'X' Ltd. as 31st December, 1996 and 1997. You are required to prepare a funds flow statement for the year ended 31st December, 1997:

	1996	*1997*		*1996*	*1997*
Share capital	1,00,000	1,25,000	Goodwill	—	2,500
General reserve	25,000	30,000	Buildings	1,00,000	95,000
P & L A/c	15,250	15,300	Plant	75,000	84,500
Bank loan	35,000	67,600	Stock	50,000	37,000
(long-term)			Debtors	40,000	32,100
Creditors	75,000	—	Bank	—	4,000
Provision for tax	15,000	17,500	Cash	250	300
	2,65,250	2,55,400		2,65,250	2,55,400

Additional Information

1. Dividend of Rs. 11,500 was paid.
2. Depreciation written off on plant Rs. 7,000 and on building Rs. 5,000.
3. Provision for tax was made during the year Rs. 16,500.(*Osmania University, B.Com., October 1998*)

Solution: **Schedule of changes in working capital**

	1996	*1997*	*Increase*	*Decrease*
Current Assets				
Cash	250	300	50	—
Bank	—	4,000	4,000	
Debtors	40,000	32,100	—	7900
Stock	50,000	37,000	—	13,000
Total (A)	90,250	73,400		
Current Liabilities				
Creditors	75,000	—	75,000	—
Total (B)	75,000	—		
Working capital (A–B)	15,250	73,400		
Increase in working capital	58,150	—	—	58,150
	73,400	73,400	79,050	79,050

Share Capital A/c

To Balance c/d	1,25,000	By Balance b/d	1,00,000
		By Bank a/c	25,000
	1,25,000		1,25,000

General Reserve A/c

To Balance c/d	30,000	By Balance b/d	25,000
		By P & L a/c	5,000
	30,000		30,000

Provision for Taxation A/c

To Bank A/c	14,000	By Balance b/d	15,000
To Balance c/d	17,500	By P & L A/c	16,500
	31,500		31,500

Bank Loan A/c

To Balance c/d	67,600	By Balance b/d	35,000
		By Bank a/c	32,600
	67,600		67,600

Land & Building A/c

To Balance b/d	1,00,000	By Depreciation a/c	5,000
		By (P & L a/c)	
		By Balance c/d	95,000
	1,00,000		1,00,000

Plant A/c

To Balance b/d	75,000	By Depreciation	7,000
To Bank a/c	16,500	(P & L a/c)	
		By Balance c/d	84,500
	91,500		91,500

Goodwill A/c

To Bank a/c	2,500	By Balance c/d	2,500

Adjusted Profit & Loss A/c

To General reserve a/c	5,000	By Balance b/d	15,250
To Provision for tax a/c	16,500	By Fund from operation	45,050
To Dividend paid	11,500		
To Depreciation on:			
—Building	5,000		
—Plant	7,000		
To Balance c/d	15,300		

Fund Flow Statement

Sources		*Applications*	
Fund from operation	45,050	Purchase of plant	16,500
Issue of shares	25,000	Income tax paid	14,000
Bank loan	32,600	Dividend paid	11,500
		Goodwill paid	2,500
		Net increase in working capital	58,150
	1,02,650		1,02,650

Problem 21: The Balance Sheets of XYZ Co. Ltd. as on 31st December 1992 and 1993 are given below:

Liabilities & Capital	*1992*	*1993*
Share capital	1,00,000	1,50,000
Share premium	—	5,000
General reserve	50,000	60,000
Profit & loss a/c	10,000	17,000
6% Debentures	70,000	50,000
Provision for depreciation:		
on plant	50,000	56,000
on furniture	5,000	6,000
Provision for taxation	20,000	30,000
Sundry creditors	86,000	95,000
	3,91,000	4,69,000
Assets		
Freehold land	1,00,000	1,00,000
Plant at cost	1,04,000	1,00,000
Furniture at cost	7,000	9,000
Investment at cost	60,000	80,000
Debtors	30,000	70,000
Stock	60,000	65,000
Cash	30,000	45,000
	3,91,000	4,69,000

A plant purchased for Rs. 4,000 (Depreciation Rs. 2,000) was sold for cash Rs. 800 on 30th September 1993. On 30th June 1993 an item of furniture was purchased for Rs. 2,000. These were the only transactions concerning fixed assets during 1993.

Depreciation was provided on plant at 8% on cost (the sold out item is not taken into consideration) and on furniture at 12½% on average cost. A dividend of 22½% on original shares are paid.

(*Sri Venkateshwara University, B.Com., October 1998*)

Solution:

Schedule showing changes in Working Capital

	1992	*1993*	*Increase*	*Decrease*
Current Assets				
Debtors	30,000	70,000	40,000	—
Stock	60,000	65,000	5,000	—
Cash	30,000	45,000	15,000	—
Total (A)	1,20,000	180,000		
Current Liabilities				
Creditors	86,000	95,000	—	9,000
Total (B)	86,000	95,000		

Working capital (A–B)	34,000	85,000		
Increase in working capital	51,000	—	—	51,000
	85,000	85,000	60,000	60,000

Plant & Machinery A/c

To Balance b/d	1,04,000	By Cash a/c	800
		By Provision for depreciation	2,000
		By P & L a/c – loss on sale (Balancing figure)	1,200
		By Balance c/d	1,00,000
	1,04,000		1,04,000

Provision for Depreciation on Plant A/c

To Plant & machinery A/c	2,000	By Balance b/d	50,000
To Balance c/d	56,000	By P & L a/c $\left(\frac{8}{100} \times 1,00,000\right)$	8,000
	58,000		58,000

Furniture A/c

To Balance b/d	7,000	By Balance c/d	9,000
To Cash-purchases	2,000		
	9,000		9,000

Provision for Depreciation on Furniture A/c

To Balance c/d	6,000	By Balance b/d	5,000
		By P & L a/c $\left(\frac{12.5}{100} \times 8,000\right)$	1,000
	6,000		6,000

Investment A/c

To Balance b/d	60,000	By Balance c/d	80,000
To Cash-purchases	20,000		
	80,000		80,000

Share Capital A/c

To Balance c/d	1,50,000	By Balance b/d	1,00,000
		By Cash-Issue	50,000
	1,50,000		1,50,000

Share Premium A/c

To Balance c/d	5,000	By Cash	5,000

General Reserve

To Balance c/d	60,000	By Balance b/d	50,000
		By P & L a/c (Balancing figure)	10,000
	60,000		60,000

6% Debentures A/c

To Cash (Balancing figure)	20,000	By Balance b/d	70,000
To Balance c/d	50,000		
	70,000		70,000

Provision for Taxation a/c

To Balance c/d	30,000	By Balance b/d	20,000
		By P & L a/c (Balancing figure)	10,000
	30,000		30,000

Adjusted Profit & Loss A/c

To Loss on sale of plant	1,200	By Balance b/d	10,000
To Depreciation on plant & machinery	800	By Fund from operation	59,700
To Depreciation on furniture	1,000		
To General reserve	10,000		
To Dividend $\left(\frac{22.5}{100} \times 1,00,000\right)$	22,500		
To Provision for taxation	10,000		
To Balance c/d	17,000		
	69,700		69,700

Fund Flow Statement

Sources		*Applications*	
Fund from operation	59,700	Increase in working capital	51,000
Sale of plant	800	Purchase of Furniture	2,000
Issue of shares	50,000	Purchase of investment	20,000
Share premium	5,000	Redemption of debentures	20,000
		Payment of dividend	22,500
	1,15,000		1,15,000

Problem 22: The balance sheets of Parasman Ltd. are given below:

	31.12.96	*31.12.97*		*31.12.96*	*31.12.97*
Share capital	3,00,000	4,00,000	Fixed assets	5,70,000	6,60,000
Capital reserve	—	10,000	Trade investment	1,00,000	80,000
General reserve	1,70,000	2,00,000	Current assets	2,80,000	3,30,000
Profit & loss A/c	60,000	75,000	Preliminary expenses	20,000	10,000
Debentures (of Rs. 100)	2,00,000	1,40,000			
Current liabilities	1,20,000	1,30,000			
Provision on tax	90,000	85,000			
Proposed dividend	30,000	36,000			
Unpaid dividend	—	4,000			
	9,70,000	10,80,000		9,70,000	10,80,000

For 1997 the following information is given:

1. Sold one machine for Rs. 25,000, the cost of which was Rs. 50,000 and the depreciation provided on it was Rs. 21,000.
2. The provision for depreciation (accumulated) was Rs. 2,90,000 on 31-12-97 which was Rs. 60,000 more than that on 31.12.96.
3. Some debentures were redeemed @ Rs. 103.
4. Fixed assets costing Rs. 14,000 which were fully depreciation were written off.
5. Some trade investments were sold at some profit which was adjusted in capital reserve.
6. Decided to value stock at cost on 31.12.97 whereas previously it was valued at cost less 10% on 31.12.96 which was Rs. 54,000.

You are required to prepare statement of sources and application of funds during 1997, showing the detailed changes in working capital and provision for taxation, proposed dividend account.

(University of Bombay, B.Com., April 1998)

Solution:

Schedule of changes in Working Capital

	31.12.96	*31.12.97*	*Increase*	*Decrease*
Current assets	2,80,000	3,30,000		
Add: Increase in stock value	6,000			
Total (A)	2,86,000	3,30,000	44,000	—
Current Liabilities	1,20,000	1,30,000	—	10,000
Total (B)	1,20,000	1,30,000		
Working capital (A–B)	1,66,000	2,00,000		
Increase in working capital	34,000	—	—	34,000
	2,00,000	2,00,000	44,000	44,000

Working Notes:

(1) Calculation of Loss on sale of Machine

Cost	50,000
Less: Accumulated depreciation	21,000
	29,000
Sold for	25,000
Loss on sale	4,000

(2) Calculation of Premium on Debenture Redemption

Face value of 100 Redeemed at Rs. 103

For face value of 60,000 → ?

$$\frac{103 \times 60,000}{100} = 61,800$$

So premium on Redemption = 61,800 – 60,000 = 1,800.

This is shown as a loss on the debit side of adjusted profit & loss account and also shown as application of fund.

(3) Fixed assets fully depreciated means accumulated depreciation is equal to cost of fixed assets. The accumulated depreciation is debited to provision for depreciation a/c and credited to fixed assets account.

(4) Calculation of undervalued opening stock

For 90 → 54,000
For 10 → ?

$$54.000 \times \frac{10}{90} = \text{Rs. } 6,000$$

Proposed Divident A/c

To Cash	26,000	By Balance b/d	30,000
To Unpaid dividend a/c	4,000	By P & L a/c	36,000
To Balance c/d	36,000	(Balancing figure)	
	66,000		66,000

Provision for Taxation

To Cash	90,000	By Balance b/d	90,000
To Balance c/d	85,000	By P & L a/c	85,000
	1,75,000		1,75,000

Fixed Assets A/c

To Balance b/d	8,00,000	By Cash	
To Profit on sale of machine	25,000	Sale of machine	25,000
To Cash purchases	2,14,000	By Provision for	
(Balancing figure)		depreciation a/c	14,000
		By balance	9,50,000
	10,14,000		10,14,000

Note:

1. Opening Balance of fixed assets — 5,70,000
   Add: Provision for depreciation on fixed assets (2,90,000 – 60,000) — 2,30,000
   8,00,000

2. Closing Balance of fixed assets — 6,60,000
   Add: Provision for depreciation on fixed assets — 2,90,000
   9,50,000

Provision for Depreciation A/c

To Depreciation on machinery sold	21,000	By Balance b/d (2,90,000 – 60,000)	2,30,000
To Machinery written off	14,000	By P & L a/c	95,000
To Balance c/d	2,90,000	(Balancing figure)	
	3,25,000		3,25,000

Trade Investment A/c

To Balance b/d	1,00,000	By Cash-sales	30,000
To Capital Reserve	10,000	(Balancing figure)	
–profit on sale		By Balance c/d	80,000
	1,10,000		1,10,000

Adjusted P & L a/c

	Rs.		Rs.
To Loss on sale of machinery	4,000	By Balance b/d	60,000
To Proposed dividend	36,000	By Opening stock	6,000
To Provision for taxation	85,000	By Fund from operation	2,70,800
To Premium on redemption of debentures	1,800		
To Transfer to general reserve	30,000		
To Preliminary expenses written off	10,000		
To Provision for depreciation on fixed assets	95,000		
To Balance c/d	75,000		
	3,36,800		3,36,800

Fund Flow Statement

Sources		*Applications*	
Issue of share capital	1,00,000	Proposed dividend of 1996 paid	26,000
Sale of machinery	25,000	Income tax paid	90,000
Sale of Investment	30,000	Debentures redeemed	61,800
Fund from operation	2,70,800	Purchase of fixed assets	2,14,000
		Increase in working capital	34,000
	4,25,800		4,25,800

Problem 23: Following are the summaries of balance sheets of a Limited Company as on 31st December 1997 and 1998

	1997 *Rs.*	*1998* *Rs.*
Paid up share capital	1,00,000	1,00,000
General reserve	21,400	26,000
Profit & loss a/c	17,000	16,000
Creditors	9,750	6,380
Provision for taxation (non-current)	19,000	21,000
Provision for doubtful debts	1,000	1200
	1,68,150	1,70,580
Buildings	46,800	45,000
Machinery	38,280	42,030
Goodwill	13,000	13,000
Investments	10,000	11,250
Stock	30,000	28,000
Debtors	22,000	22,000
Prepaid expenses	70	300
Cash balance	8,000	9,000
	1,68,150	1,70,580

Additional Information

1. The profit for the year 1998 was Rs. 8,600 which has been arrived at after charging Rs. 3,050 by way of depreciation and increase in provision for doubtful debts Rs. 200.
2. An interim dividend of Rs. 5,000 was paid in October 1998.
3. Additional machinery was purchased in May 1998 for Rs. 5,000.
4. Investments (cost Rs. 5,000) were sold in November 1998 for Rs. 4,800 and on 1st December, 1998 another investment was made for Rs. 6,250.
5. Income tax Rs. 18,000 was paid during the year and charged against the provision.

(Sri Venkateshwara University, B.Com., April 1998)

Solution:

Schedule of changes in Working Capital

	1997	*1998*	*Increase*	*Decrease*
Current Assets				
Stock	30,000	28,000	—	2,000
Debtors	22,000	22,000	—	—
Prepaid expenses	70	300	230	
Cash	8,000	9,000	1,000	
Total (A)	60,070	59,300		
Current Liabilities				
Creditors	9,750	6,380	3,370	—
Provision for doubtful debts	1,000	1,200	—	200
Total (B)	10,750	7,580		
Working Capital (A–B)	49,320	51,720		
Increase in working capital	2,400	—		2,400
	51,720	51,720	4,600	4,600

General Reserve A/c

To Balance c/d	26,000	By Balance b/d	21,400
		By P & L a/c	4,600
	26,000		26,000

Provision for Taxation

To Income tax paid	18,000	By Balance b/d	19,000
To Balance c/d	21,000	By P & L a/c (Balancing figure)	20,000
	39,000		39,000

Buildings A/c

To Balance b/d	46,800	By P & L a/c (Balancing figure)	1800
		By Balance c/d	45,000
	46,800		46,800

Machinery A/c

To Balance b/d	38,280	By P & L a/c (Balancing figure)	1,250
To Cash	5,000	By Balance c/d	42,030
	43,280		43,280

Investments A/c

To Balance b/d	10,000	By Cash-sale of investment	4,800
To Cash	6,250	By Loss on sale of investment	200
		By Balance c/d	11,250
	16,250		16,250

Adjusted Profit & Loss A/c

To Depreciation on:		By Balance b/d	17,000
Building	1,800	By Fund from operation	31,850
Machinery	1,250		
To Interim dividend	5,000		
To Loss on sale of investment	200		
To Provision for taxation	20,000		
To Transferred to general reserve	4,600		
To Balance c/d	16,000		
	48,850		48,850

Fund Flow Statement

Sources		*Applications*	
Fund from operation	31,850	Increase in working capital	2,400
Sale of investment	4,800	Machinery purchased	5,000
		Investment purchased	6,250
		Interim dividend paid	5,000
		Income tax paid	18,000
	36,650		36,650

Problem 24: From the following balance sheets of Bharat Ltd. prepare (*a*) statement of changes in working capital and (*b*) funds flow statement.

Balance Sheet as on

	1995	*1996*		*1995*	*1996*
Equity share capital	30,000	40,000	Goodwill	10,000	8,000
8% Redeemable preference shares	15,000	10,000	Land & Building	20,000	17,000
Capital Reserve	—	2,000	Plant	8,000	2,000
General reserve	4,000	5,000	Investment	2,000	3,000
P & L a/c	3,000	48,000	Debtors	14,000	17,000
Proposed dividend	4,200	5,000	Stock	7,700	10,900
Sundry Creditors	2,500	4,700	Bills receivable	2,000	3,000
Bills payable	2,000	1,600	Cash in hand	1,500	1,000
Liability for expenses	3,000	3,600	Cash at Bank	1,000	800
Provision for taxation	4,000	5,000	Preliminary expenses	1,500	1,000
	67,700	81,700		67,700	81,700

Additonal Information

1. A piece of land has been sold out in 1996 and the profit on sale has been credited to capital reserve.
2. A machine has been sold for Rs. 1,000. The written down value of the machine was Rs. 1200. Depreciation of Rs. 1,000 is charged on plant account in 1996.
3. The investments are trade investment. Rs. 300 by way of dividend is received including Rs. 100 from pre-acquisition profit which has been credited to investment account.
4. An interim dividend of Rs. 2,000 has been paid on 1996.

(*Sri Sathya Sai University, B.Com., March 1997*)

Solution:

Schedule of change in Working Capital

	1995	1996	Increase	Decrease
Current Assets:				
Sundry debtors	14,000	17,000	3,000	—
Stock	7,700	10,900	3,200	—
Bills receivable	2,000	3,000	1,000	—
Cash in hand	1,500	1,000	—	500
Cash at Bank	1,000	800	—	200
Total (A)	26,200	32,700		
Current Liabilities				
Sundry creditors	2,500	4,700	—	2,200
Bills payable	2,000	1,600	400	—
Liability for expenses	3,000	3,600	—	600
Provision for taxation	4,000	5,000	—	1,000
Total (B)	11,500	14,900		
Working capital (A–B)	14,700	17,800		
Increase in working capital	3,100	—	—	3,100
	17,800	17,800	7,600	7,600

Land A/c

To Balance b/d	20,000	By Cash-sale (Balancing figure)	5,000
To Profit on sale-capital reserve	2,000	By Balance c/d	17,000
	22,000		22,000

Adjusted Profit & Loss A/c

To Depreciation	1,000	By Balance b/d	3,000
To General reserve	1,000	By Dividend received out of post acquisition profit (300–100)	200
To Proposed dividend	5,000	By Fund from operation	13,300
To Interim dividend	2,000		
To Good will written off	2,000		
To Loss on sale of machinery (1,200–1,000)	200		
To Preliminary expenses written off	500		
To Balance c/d	4,800		
	16,500		16,500

Fund Flow Statement

Sources		*Applications*	
Issue of share capital	10,000	Redemption of preference shares	5,000
Sale of land	5,000	Purchase of plant	14,200
Sale of machinery	10,000	Purchase of investment (1,000+100)	1,100
Dividend received	300		
Fund from operation	13,300		

		Dividend paid:	
		Interim	2,000
		for 1995	4,200
			6,200
		Increase in working capital	3,100
	29,600		29,600

Problem 25: Prepare fund flow statement from the following data:

	31-12-96	*31-12-97*
Assets:		
Cash	2,000	2,500
Accounts receivable	2,400	2,700
Inventories	3,100	3,200
Other assets	800	700
Fixed assets	5,000	5,800
	13,300	14,900
Liabilities		
Accumulated depreciation	2,100	2,500
Accounts payable	2,000	2,100
Long-term debt	1,400	1,300
Equity capital	5,000	5,300
Retained earnings	2,800	3,700
	13,300	14,900

Note:

1. Fixed assets costing Rs. 1,200 were purchased for cash.
2. Fixed assets (original cost Rs. 400, accumulated depreciation Rs. 150) were sold for Rs. 200.
3. Depreciation for the year 1997 amounted to Rs. 550 and duly debited to profit & loss account.
4. Dividend paid amounted to Rs. 300 in 1997.
5. Reported income for 1997 was Rs. 1,200.

(Bangalore University, B.B.M., April 1998)

Solution:

Schedule of changes in working capital

	1996	*1997*	*Increase*	*Decrease*
Current Assets:				
Cash	2,000	2,500	500	—
Accounts receivable	2,400	2,700	300	—
Inventories	3,100	3,200	100	—
Other assets	800	700	—	100
Total (A)	8,300	9,100		
Current Liabilities				
Accounts payable	2,000	2,100	—	100
Total (B)	2,000	2,100		
Working capital (A–B)	6,300	7,000		
Increase in working capital	700	—	—	700
	7,000	7,000	900	900

Fixed Assets A/c

To Balance b/d	5,000	By Bank a/c	200
To Bank-purchases	1,200	By Loss on sale	50
		By Accumulated depreciation	150
		By Balance c/d	5,800
	6,200		6,200

Accumulated Depreciation A/c

To Fixed assets	150	By Balance b/d	2,100
To Balance c/d	2,500	By P & L a/c	550
	2,650		2,650

Adjusted P & L A/c

To Accumulated depreciation a/c	550	By Balance b/d	2,800
To Loss on sale	50	By Income	1,200
To Dividend paid	300	By Fund from operation	600
To Balance c/d	3,700		
	4,600		4,600

Fund Flow Statement

Sources		*Applications*	
Fund from operation	600	Payment of long-term debt	100
Issue of equity capital	300	Dividend paid	300
Sale of fixed assets	200	Fixed assets purchased	1,200
Income received	1,200	Increase in working capital	700
	2,300		2,300

Problem 26: The comparative balance sheets of star Ltd. are given below:

	1995	*1996*		*1995*	*1996*
12% preference share capital	2,00,000	1,00,000	Goodwill	85,000	80,000
Equity share capital	6,00,000	8,00,000	Land & Building	2,02,000	2,16,000
Share premium	10,000	30,000	Investments	1,00,000	75,000
Reserves	52,000	70,000	Patents	30,000	24,000
Profit & loss a/c	1,75,000	1,50,000	Plant	4,20,000	5,10,000
6% debentures	1,25,000	1,00,000	Stock	2,85,000	3,37,000
Sundry creditors	1,02,000	1,33,000	Sundry debtors	1,30,800	1,46,400
Interim dividend payable	—	2,000	Prepaid expenses	3,200	4,600
Provision fo taxation	38,000	48,000	Advance income tax	40,000	35,000
			Discount on issue of debentures	6,000	5,000
	13,02,000	14,33,000		13,02,000	14,33,000

Additional Information

1. Preference share redemption was carried out on 31st December, 1996.
2. Dividend 12% p.a was paid on preference shares and Interim dividend on equity shares Rs. 43,000 was paid in the year 1996.
3. Depreciation of Rs. 26,000 and Rs. 79,000 has been provided on land and buidlings and plant respectively in the year 1996.

4. Plant costing Rs. 60,000 purchased on 1st Januarey, 1994, depreciated by 20% (on W.D.V.) was sold on 1st January 1996 for Rs. 30,000.
5. Investment having book value Rs. 57,000 sold for Rs. 49,000.
6. Income tax assessment for the year ended 31st December, 1995 was completed on 1st April, 1996 for a gross demand of Rs. 45,000. The Balance amount of demand after adjusting advance-tax (1995) was paid on 10th April, 1996.

You are required to prepare:

1. Statement of funds flow during the year 1996.
2. Schedule of changes in working capital showing individual item wise figures therein.
3. Provision for taxation account and advance tax account.

(University of Bombay, B.Com., October 1997)

Solution:

Schedule of changes in Working Capital

	1995	*1996*	*Increase*	*Decrease*
Current Assets:				
Stock	2,85,000	3,37,000	52,000	—
Sundry debtors	1,30,800	1,46,400	15,600	—
Prepaid expenses	3,200	4,600	1,400	—
	4,19,000	4,88,000		
Current Liabilities				
Sundry creditors	1,02,000	1,33,000	—	31,000
Working capital	3,17,000	3,55,000		
Increase in working capital	38,000	—	—	38,000
	3,55,000	3,55,000	69,000	69,000

Working Notes

(1) Calculation of loss on sale of plant

Cost	60,000
20% Depreciation for 1994	12,000
	48,000
20% Depreciation for 1995	9600
W.D.V.	38,400
Sold for	30,000
Loss on sale	8,400

(2) Loss on sale of Investment

Cost	57,000
Sold at	49,000
Loss on sale	8,000

Plant A/c

To Balance b/d	4,20,000	By Depreciation	79,000
To Bank-plant purchased (Balancing figure)	2,07,400	By Plant sold -Bank	38,400
		By Balance c/d	5,10,000
	6,27,400		6,27,400

Land & Building

Particulars	Amount	Particulars	Amount
To Balance b/d	2,02,000	By Depreciation	26,000
To Bank-land purchased	40,000	By Balance c/d	2,16,000
	2,42,000		2,42,000

Investment A/c

Particulars	Amount	Particulars	Amount
To Balance b/d	1,00,000	By Bank-sale of investment	57,000
To Bank-Investment purchased	32,000	By Balance c/d	75,000
	1,32,000		1,32,000

Provision for Tax A/c

Particulars	Amount	Particulars	Amount
To Advance tax a/c	45,000	By Balance b/d	38,000
To Balance c/d	48,000	By P & L a/c (Balancing figure)	55,000
	93,000		93,000

Advance Tax A/c

Particulars	Amount	Particulars	Amount
To Balance b/d	40,000	By Provision for tax	45,000
To Bank a/c	5,000		
To Bank a/c	35,000	By Balance c/d	35,000
	80,000		80,000

Interim Dividend Payable A/c

Particulars	Amount	Particulars	Amount
To Bank a/c	43,000	By Balance b/d	—
To Balance c/d	2,000	By P & L a/c (Balancing fig.)	45,000
	45,000		45,000

Adjusted Profit & Loss A/c

Particulars	Amount	Particulars	Amount
To Depreciation on:		By Balance b/d	1,75,000
Land & building	26,000	By Fund from operation	2,50,400
Plant	79,000		
To Loss on sale of:			
Plant	8,400		
Investment	800		
To Provision for tax	55,000		
To Dividend on preference shares	24,000		
To Interim dividend	45,000		
To Transfer to reserve	18,000		
To Goodwill written off	5,000		
To Patent written off	6,000		
To Discount on debentures	1,000		
To Balance c/d	1,50,000		
	4,25,400		4,25,000

Fund Flow Statement

Sources		*Applications*	
Plant sold	30,000	Increase in working capital	38,000
Investment sold	49,000	Plant purchased	2,07,400
Issue of shares	2,00,000	Land & Building purchased	40,000
Share premium	20,000	Investment purchased	32,000
Fund from operation	2,50,400	Tax paid (35,000+5,000)	40,000
		Redemption of pref. shares	1,00,000
		Dividend on pref. shares	24,000
		Interim dividend paid	43,000
		Redemption of debentures	25,000
	5,49,400		5,49,400

QUESTIONS

Simple Questions

1. What is a fund?
2. What is meant by flow of funds?
3. Define a funds flow statement.
4. State the need for fund flow statement?
5. State two uses of funds flow statement to management.
6. Mention any two limitations of fund flow statement analysis.
7. What are the major sources of funds for a business?
8. State two points of differences between funds flow statement and an income statement.
9. State two points of differences between funds flow statement and position statement.
10. State the common 'inflows' to working capital.
11. State the common 'outflows' from working capital.
12. What is 'positive' and 'negative' changes in working capital?
13. Mention the important steps involved in the preparation of funds flow statement.
14. Give the meaning of working capital.
15. How do you treat provision for taxation while preparing a funds flow statement.
16. State the rules to ascertain which transaction give rise to a source or use of working capital.
17. What is 'Fund from operation'?
18. State the significance of preparing a funds flow statement.
19. How do you treat 'proposed dividend'? While preparing a funds flow statement?

Short Answer Questions

1. Analyse the managerial uses of funds flow analysis.
2. A fund flow statement is a better substitute for an income statement comment.
3. State the reasons whether the following transactions result in increase or decrease of working capital or do not effect the working capital.
   (*a*) A company issued 10,000 shares of Rs. 10 each at par fully paid up.
   (*b*) Debentures for Rs. 1,00,000 are commented into equity shares.
   (*c*) Investments were sold for Rs. 50,000
   (*d*) Building was purchased for Rs. 1,50,000
   (*e*) Bills payable accepted and issued to creditors Rs. 40,000
   (*f*) Bills receivable Rs. 10,000 discounted for 9,500.
   (*g*) Fixed assets purchased by issue of shares for Rs. 1,00,000
   (*h*) Cash paid to creditors Rs. 30,000
   (*i*) Preliminary expenses written off Rs. 5,000.
   (*j*) Advance income tax paid Rs. 50,000. (*Bangalore University, B.Com., April 1994*)

Exercise 1: From the following information, calculate fund from operation:

Profit & Loss A/c

To Expenses:		By Gross profit	2,00,000
Operation	1,00,000	By Gain on sale of building	20,000
Depreciation	40,000		
To Loss on sale of machinery	10,000	By Other incomes	2,000
To Advertisement suspense a/c	5,000		
To Discount on debtors	500		
To Discount on issue of shares	500		
To Goodwill	12,000		
To Preliminary expenses	2,000		
To Net profit	52,000		
	2,22,000		2,22,000

(*University of Madras, B.Com., May 1997*)
[*Answer:* Rs. 1,01,500]

Exercise 2: Calculate fund from operation from the following profit & loss a/c.

Profit & Loss A/c

To Rent	10,000	By Gross profit	9,86,000
To Salary	25,000		
To Depreciation on furniture	3,000		
To Discount on issue of shares	10,000		
To Goodwill written off	5,000		
To Preliminary expenses	6,000		
To New profit	9,27,000		
	9,86,000		9,86,000

(*University of Madras, B.Com., March, 1996*)
[*Answer*: Rs.9,51,000]

Exercise 3: Prepare an adjusted profit & loss account to determine the funds from operations from the following information extracted from Crown Ltd. for the year 2000:

Profit & loss a/c balance on 1.1.2000	Rs. 2,00,000
Profit & loss a/c balance on 31.12.2000	Rs. 6,40,000
Profit earned during the year was	Rs. 6,40,000

After the following adjustments were made:

Depreciation on assets	2,80,000
Preliminary expenses written off	20,000
Patents written off	30,000
Provision for tax	3,20,000
Proposed dividend	1,20,000
Provision for doubtful debts	40,000
Profit on sale of fixed assets	10,000
Loss on sale of investments	5,000

In addition the profit was overstated by Rs. 20,000 due to change in the method of revaluation of closing stock. There was also a transfer of Rs. 2,00,000 to reserves (out of Rs. 6,40,000)

Prepare a profit & loss (adjusted) account for arriving at your answer.

[*Answer*: Rs. 12,85,000]

Exercise 4: Following information is extracted from the books of Omega Ltd. for the year 2000:

Opening balance of P & L a/c	25,000
Closing balance of P & L a/c	60,000
Salaries paid	5,000
Rent paid	3,000
Refund of tax paid	3,000

Profit on sale of building	5,000
Depreciation on plant	5,000
Provision for tax	4,000
Loss on sale of plant	2,000
Discount on issue of debentures	2,000
Provision for bad debts	1,000
Transfer to general reserve	1,000
Preliminary expenses written off	3,000
Goodwill written off	2,000
Proposed dividend	6,000
Dividend received	5,000

Prepare a statement showing funds from operations through an adjusted profit & loss account.

[*Answer:* Rs. 48,000]

Exercise 5: Prepare a statment showing changes in working capital from the following balance sheets of excel for the years 1999-2000

	1990	*2000*		*1999*	*2000*
Equity share capital	15,00,000	6,00,000	Fixed assets	10,00,000	11,20,000
			Less: Dep.	3,70,000	4,60,000
Reserves	1,50,000	1,80,000		6,30,000	6,60,000
P & L a/c	40,000	65,000	Stock	2,40,000	3,70,000
7% Debentures	3,00,000	2,50,000	A/c Receivable	2,50,000	2,30,000
A/c payable	1,70,000	1,60,000	Cash at bank	80,000	60,000
Provision for income tax	60,000	80,000	Preliminary expenses	20,000	15,000
	12,20,000	13,35,000		12,20,000	13,35,000

[*Answer:* Increase in working capital Rs. 10,00,000]

Exercise 6: From the following information prepare a funds flow statement including a schedule of changes in working capital for the year ended 31.12.96:

Balance Sheet

	31.12.95	*31.12.96*		*31.12.95*	*31.12.96*
Share capital	1,40,000	1,48,000	Cash	18,000	15,600
Debentures	24,000	12,000	Debtors	29,800	35,400
Reserve for doubtful debts	14,000	1,600	Stock	98,400	85,400
Creditors	20,720	23,680	Land	40,000	60,000
P & L a/c	20,080	21,120	Goodwill	20,000	10,000
	2,06,200	2,06,400		2,06,200	2,06,400

Additional Information

(*a*) Dividends paid Rs. 7,000

(*b*) During the year 1996 land purchased for Rs. 20,000. (*Osmania University, B.Com., March 1998*)

[*Answer*: Total of fund flow statement Rs. 39,000

Exercise 7: From the following Balance sheets of Nav Bharat Ltd. as on 31st December, 1995 and 1996 you are required to prepare a fund flow statement.

	1995	*1996*		*1995*	*1996*
Share capital	2,00,000	2,50,000	Land & building	2,00,000	1,90,000
General reserve	50,000	60,000	Plant	1,50,000	1,69,000
P & L a/c	30,500	30,600	Stock	90,000	74,000
Bank loan (short-term)	70,000	—	Debtors	80,000	64,200
Creditors	1,50,000	1,35,200	Cash	2,500	8,600
Provision for tax	30,000	35,000	Goodwill	8,000	5,000
	5,30,500	5,10,800		5,30,500	5,10,800

Additional Information

1. Dividends paid during the year 1996 Rs. 23,000.
2. Depreciation written off on plant Rs. 14,000 and on building Rs. 10,000.
3. Income tax provision made during the year 1996 Rs. 33,000.

(*Osmania University, B.Com., October 1997*)

[*Answer*: Total by Fund Flow Statement Rs. 1,43,100]

Exercise 8: The comparative balance-sheets of Star Ltd. are given below:

Liabilities	*1995*	*1996*
12% pref share capital	2,00,000	1,00,000
Equity share capital	6,00,000	8,00,000
Share premium	10,000	30,000
Reserves	52,000	70,000
P & L a/c	1,75,000	1,50,000
6% Debentures	1,25,000	1,00,000
Sundry creditors	1,02,000	1,33,000
Interim dividend payablae	—	2,000
Provision for taxation	38,000	48,000
	13,02,000	14,33,000
Assets		
Goodwill	85,000	80,000
Land & Building	2,02,000	2,16,000
Investments	1,00,000	75,000
Patents	30,000	24,000
Plant	4,20,000	5,10,000
Stock	2,85,000	3,37,000
Sundry debtors	1,30,800	1,46,400
Prepaid expenses	3,200	4,600
Advance income tax	40,000	35,000
Discount on issue of debentures	6,000	5,000
	13,02,000	14,33,000

Additional Information

1. Preference share redemption was carried out on 31st December, 1996.
2. Dividend 12% p.a was paid on preference share and interim dividend on equity shares Rs. 43,000 was paid in the year 1996.
3. Depreciation of Rs. 26,000 and Rs. 79,000 has been provided on land and buidling and plant respectively in the year 1996.
4. Plant costing Rs. 60,000 purchased on 1st January 1994, depreciated by 20% (on WDV) was sold on 1st January 1996 for Rs. 30,000
5. Investments having book value Rs. 57,000 sold for Rs. 49,000.
6. Income tax assessment for the year ended 31st December 1995 was completed on 1st April 1996 for a gross demand of Rs. 45,000. The balance amount of demend often adjusting advance-tax (1995) was paid on 10th April, 1996.

You are required to prepare

1. Statement of funds flow during the year 1996.
2. Schedule of changes in working capital showing separate item wise figures therein.
3. Provision for taxation a/c and advance-tax a/c.

(*University of Bombay, B.Com., October 1997*)

[*Answer:* Fund from operation Rs. 2,50,400
Total of fund flow statement Rs. 5,49,400]

Exercist 9: From the following balance sheets of Ananth Co. Ltd., prepare a statement of changes in the working capital and the fund flow statement for the year ended 31st March 1996.

	1995	1996		1995	1996
Share capital	3,00,000	3,50,000	Goodwill	1,00,000	80,000
Debentures	1,50,000	2,50,000	Machinery	4,10,000	5,40,000
P & L a/c	60,000	70,000	Investments	30,000	80,000
General reserve	1,00,000	1,50,000	Discount on issue of debentures	5,000	—
Provision for Depreciation on Machinery	90,000	1,30,000	Cash at Bank	1,20,000	1,30,000
Sundry creditors	75,000	1,10,000	Sundry debtors	80,000	1,90,000
Bills payable	10,000	15,000	Stock in trade	40,000	55,000
	7,85,000	10,75,000		7,85,000	10,75,000

During the year investments costing Rs. 30,000 were sold for Rs. 28,000. A new machine was purchased for Rs. 45,000 and payment was made in fully paid shares. *(Bangalore University, B.B.M., November 1997)*

[*Answer:* Total of FFS Rs. 3.50,000]

Exercise 10: From the following balance sheets of XYZ Co. Ltd., prepare funds flow statement:

	(Rs. 000) 1995	1996		(Rs. 000) 1995	1996
Equity share capital	600	800	Goodwill	230	180
Preference share capital	300	200	Land & buildings	400	340
General reserve	80	140	Plant & machinery	160	400
P & L a/c	60	96	Debtors	320	400
Proposed dividend	84	100	Stock	154	218
Creditors	110	166	Bills receivable	40	60
Bills payable	40	32	CAsh	30	20
Tax provision	80	100	Bank	20	16
	1,354	1,634		1,354	1,634

Additional Information

1. Proposed dividend made during 1995 has been paid during 1996.
2. Depreciation: (*a*) Rs. 20,000 on plant & machinery
   (*b*) Rs. 4,000 on land & buildings.
3. Interim dividend has been paid Rs. 40,000 in 1996.
4. Income-tax Rs. 70,000 has been paid during 1996. *(CS, Inter, December 1997)*

[*Answer:* Fund from operation Rs. 4,36,000
Total of fund flow statement Rs. 6,56,000]

Exercise 11: Prepare a funds flow statement and a statement of changes in working capital from the following particulars furnished by X Company Ltd.

Owner's Equity & Liabilities	*End of 1995*	*(Rs. in Lakhs)* *End of 1996*
Share capital	50	50
Reserves & surpluses	60	70
Long-term debt	95	80
Short-term bank borrowings	70	80
Trade creditors	50	60
Provisions	20	15
	345	355
Assets:		
Fixed assets (net)	180	190
Inventories	70	60
Debtors	60	70
Cash	20	15
Other assets	15	20
	345	355

The income statement of X Company Ltd. for the year 1996 is given below:

	(Rs. in Lakhs)		(Rs. in Lakhs)
To Cost of goods sold	520	By Sales	800
To Operational expenses	150		
To Non-operational expenses	50		
To Interest	30		
To Tax	20		
To Dividend	20		
To Balance c/d	10		
	800		800

(*CS, Inter, June 1997*)
[*Answer:* Fund from operation Rs. 35 (lakhs)
Total of fund flow statement Rs. 95 (in lakhs)]

Exercise 12: From the following balance sheets of X Ltd. prepare a schedule of changes in working capital and fund flow statement:

	31.12.90	*31.12.91*		*31.12.90*	*31.12.91*
Share capital	6,00,000	8,00,000	Machinery (cost)	4,00,000	6,45,000
Debentures	2,00,000	3,00,000	Buildings (cost)	3,00,000	4,00,000
P & L a/c	1,25,000	2,50,000	Stock	20,000	40,000
Creditors	1,15,000	90,000	Preliminary expenses	7,000	6,000
Provision for bad debts	6,000	3,000	Debtors	69,000	61,000
Provision for depreciation:					
on building	20,000	24,000			
on machinery	30,000	35,000			
	10,96,000	15,02,000		10,96,000	15,02,000

Additional Information

(*a*). During the year a part of the machinery costing Rs. 70,000 (accumulated depreciation thereon Rs. 2,000) was sold for Rs. 6,000.

(*b*) Dividend of Rs. 50,000 were paid during the year 1991.(*University of Madras, B.Com., September 1997*)

[*Answer*: Fund from operation Rs. 2,49,000
Total of fund flow statement Rs. 5,55,000.]

Exercise 13: The following are the summarised balance sheets of Archana Polygraph Limited as on 31st March, 1995 and 1996.

	31.12.95	*31.12.96*		*31.12.95*	*31.12.96*
Share capital	4,60,000	4,60,000	Land & building	3,00,000	3,00,000
P & L A/c	32,000	46,000	Machinery	1,04,000	1,40,000
Reserve for contingency	1,20,000	1,20,000	Investments	2,20,000	1,48,000
8% Debentures	1,80,000	1,40,000	Stock	1,64,000	2,12,000
Depreciation fund	80,000	88,000	Debtors	1,34,000	86,000
Creditors	2,06,000	1,92,000	Cash	1,80,000	1,80,000
O/s liability for expenses	26,000	24,000	Prepaid expenses	2,000	4,000
	11,04,000	10,70,000		11,04,000	10,70,000

Additional Informations

1. 10% Dividend was paid during the year 1996.
2. Machinery for Rs. 6,000 was purchased and old machinery costing Rs. 24,000 (accumulated depreciation Rs. 12,000) was sold for Rs. 8,000.
3. Rs. 40,000, 8% debentures were redeemed by purchase from open market at Rs. 96 for a debenture of Rs. 100.
4. Investments worth Rs. 72,000 were sold at book value.

You are required to prepare a schedule of changes in working capital and a statement showing sources and application of funds.

(*University of Bombay, B.Com., April 1997*)

[*Answer*: Fund from operation Rs. 28,400
Total of fund flow statement Rs. 1,08,400]

Exercise 14: From the following balance sheets of 'A' Ltd. for the year ending 31st December, 1994 and 1995 draw out a fund flow statement and a statement of changes in working capital:

	1994	*1995*		*1994*	*1995*
Equity share capital	3,00,000	4,00,000	Goodwill	60,000	55,000
9% Redeemable pref share capital	80,000	50,000	Land & building	1,25,000	85,000
			Plant & machinery	1,20,000	2,25,000
Capital revenue	—	20,000	Furniture	15,000	12,000
General reserve	30,000	40,000	Investment	12,000	48,000
P & L A/c	26,000	35,000	Sundry debtors	65,000	1,05,000
Sundry creditors	30,000	58,000	Stock	90,000	84,000
Bills payable	12,000	8,000	Bills receivable	16,000	30,000
O/s expenses	6,000	5,000	Cash in hand	13,000	20,000
Proposed dividend	30,000	42,000	Cash at bank	15,000	20,000
Provision for Taxation	32,000	36,000	Preliminary expenses	15,000	10,000
	5,46,000	6,94,000		5,46,000	6,94,000

Additional Information

(*a*) A piece of land has been sold out in 1995 and the balance has been revalued. Profits on sale and revaluation being transferred to capital reserve a/c.

(*b*) Depreciation on plant & machinery has been written off Rs. 24,000 in 1995 and no depreciation has been charged on land and buildings.

(*c*) A machinery was sold for Rs. 16,000 (written down value being Rs. 20,000) and no furniture has been sold during the year.

(*d*) An interim dividend of Rs. 20,000 has been paid in 1995.

(*e*) Rs. 3,000 has been received as dividend on investment.

(*Sri Sathya Sai University, B.Com. (Hons), March 1996*)

[*Answer:* Fund from operation Rs. 77,000
Total of fund flow statement Rs. 2,56,000]

Exercise 15: Balance sheet of Govind as on 31.12.1989.

Capital	50,000	Machinery	60,000
P & L A/c	20,000	Furniture	5,000
Long-term loan	30,000	Investments	25,000
Creditors	40,000	Debtors	25,000
General reserve	10,000	Cash	5,000
		Stock	30,000
	1,50,000		1,50,000

The following transactions took place in the year 1990:

1. Machinery (Book value Rs. 20,000 on 1.1.1990) was sold on 1.4.1990 for Rs. 18,000.
2. Investments were sold for Rs. 30,000.
3. Depreciation was provided at 10% p.a on machinery and 20% p.a on furniture.
4. New machinery was purchased on 1.7.1990.
5. Total depreciation provided on machinery was Rs. 6,500 for the year 1990.
6. Drowings of Mr. Govind was Rs. 15,000 in the year 1990 and additional capital was Rs. 25,000.
7. Loan Rs. 10,000 was paid.
8. Transfer to general reserve was Rs. 10,000.
9. On 31.12.1990 it was found that there was increase in creditors by Rs. 20,000, stock by Rs. 20,000; debtors by Rs. 35,000 and total increase in working capital was Rs. 52,000.

(*Bangalore University, B.Com., April 1996*)

[*Answer:* Closing balance of P & L a/c on preparing a balance sheet is Rs. 50,000.
Fund from operation Rs. 49,000
Total of fund flow statement Rs. 1,17,000]

Exercise 16: From the figures given below, prepare a statement showing the application and sources of funds during the year 1995:

Assets	*31.3.1994*	*31.12.1995*
Fixed assets (net)	5,10,000	6,20,000
Investments	30,000	80,000
Current assets	2,40,000	3,75,000
Discount on debentures	10,000	5,000
	7,90,000	10,80,000
Liabilities:		
Share capital (equity)	3,00,000	3,50,000
Share capital (preference)	2,00,000	1,00,000
Debentures	1,00,000	2,00,000
Reserves	1,10,000	2,70,000
Provision for doubtful debts	10,000	15,000
Current liabilities	70,000	1,45,000
	7,90,000	10,80,000

You are informed that during the year:

(*i*) A machine costing Rs. 70,000 (book value Rs. 40,000) was disposed off for Rs. 25,000.

(*ii*) Preference share redemption was carried out at a premium of 5%.

(*iii*) Divdend at 15% was paid on equity shares for the year 1994.

Further:

(*a*) The provision for depreciation stood at Rs. 1,50,000 on 31.3.1994 and at Rs. 1,90,000 on 31.3.1995.

(*b*) Stock which was valued at Rs. 90,000 as on 31.3.1994 was written up to its cost Rs. 1,00,000 for preparing the profit and loss account for 1995. (*CS, Inter, June 1996*)

[*Answer:* Fund from operation Rs. 2,90,000; Total of fund flow statement Rs. 4,65,000]

6

CASH FLOW STATEMENT

INTRODUCTION

Cash flow statement is one of the analytical tool used by the management Accountant to interpret the financial soundness of the business. It shows the changes in the cash position between two dates of balance sheet. This change in cash position is known by considering the inflow and outflow of cash. This statement indicates the sources from where cash is obtained and the uses to which cash is utilised. The term 'cash' used in 'cash flow' includes cash as well as bank balance. Cash flow refers to the movement of cash in and out of business. Sometimes the inflow of cash is referred to as positive flow and the outflow as negative flow. The difference between them is net cash flow. Inflow of cash takes place when a transaction increases the cash position. Examples of transactions which increases cash position are sale of assets, issue of shares and debentures etc., outflow of cash takes place when a transaction decreases the cash position. Examples of transactions which decreases cash position are purchase of assets, redemption of debentures.

Cash flow are of two types, *viz.*, (*a*) actual cash flow and (*b*) notional cash flow. Actual cash flow implies direct flow of cash into or out of the business. For example, when shares are issued, there is direct inflow of cash. Notional cash flow refers to indirect flow of cash into or out of business. This takes place when there is increase or decrease in current assets such as bills receivable, debtors, stock etc.

Cash Flow Statement

It is a statement designed to high light upon the causes which brings changes in cash position between two balance sheet dates. This statement depicts the various sources of cash and the uses to which it is put. Cash flow results on account of three activities, viz., (*a*) operating, (*b*) investing and (*c*) financing activities.

(*a*) Cash flow from operating activities : These are the transactions which determine the net profit or loss of the business. The business operations result in cash receipts and cash payments. Cash receipts arise from sale of goods. Operating expenses and cost of goods sold result in cash payment. Cash receipts arising from operating activities are listed below :

(*i*) Cash receipts from sale of goods.
(*ii*) Cash receipts from royalities, commission.
(*iii*) Collection from sundry debtors.
(*iv*) Dividend and interest received on investment.
(*v*) Cash sale of fixed assets and current investment.
(*vi*) Refund of tax.

Cash payments arising from operating activities are listed below :

(*i*) Cash payment to suppliers for having suplied raw-materials.
(*ii*) Cash payment to employees.
(*iii*) Cash payment to creditors and bills payable.
(*iv*) Cash payment of interest and dividend.

(*v*) Cash payment as fines and penalty.

(*vi*) Cash payment of Income-tax.

(*b*) Cash flow from investing activities : Investing activities are those activities relating to acquisition and disposal of fixed assets and long-term investment. Cash receipts arising from investing activities are listed below :

(*i*) Cash receipt from sale of fixed and intangible assets.

(*ii*) Cash receipt from the disposal of shares, warrants or debt instrument of other companies.

The cash payment arising from investing activities are listed below :

(*i*) Cash payment to acquire fixed assets.

(*ii*) Cash payment to acquire shares, warrants or debt instrument of other enterprises.

(*iii*) Cash advances and loans made to third parties.

(*c*) Cash flow from financing activities : Whenever there is change in capital (both equity and preference) and borrowings by a business, it is referred to as financing activities. The cash receipts arising from financing activities are listed below :

(*i*) Cash received on issue of shares.

(*ii*) Cash received on issue of debentures.

The cash payments arising from financing activities are listed below :

(*i*) Redemption of redeemable preference shares.

(*ii*) Redemption of debentures.

(*iii*) Payment of dividend.

Importance or Utility of Cash Flow Statement

A cash flow statement is an important tool in the hands of management to evaluate financial policies and current cash position. A business needs sufficient cash to meet its various obligations in near future. Cash flow statement helps the management to know the sources and applications of cash and in turn enables the management to plan for investment of cash. The utility of cash flow can be stated as under :

(1) Helps in efficient management of cash : No business operation can be carried out without cash. It is therefore necessary to know the requirements of cash, the internal and external sources of cash, and proper use of cash. The projected cash flow statement enables the management to plan and coordinate the financial operations properly. It helps in evaluating financial policies and current cash position. The management knows how much finds are needed, how much can be generated internally, and how much should be obtained externally.

(2) It helps in internal financial management : Cash flow statement reveals the cash from trading operations, *i.e.*, internal source of cash. The replacement of assets, repayment of long term debts, dividend policies and such other programme can be chalked out on this basis.

(3) Discloses movement of Cash: It throws light on the factors causing low cash balance when the operating profit are high or for heavy cash balance when the operating profits are low. Inflows of cash and outflows of cash indicate the movement of cash, which otherwise would not have been known.

(4) Discloses success or failure of cash planning : Comparision of projected cash flow statement with the actual cash flow statement reveals the variation in actual cash flow statement. This interim throws light on financial planning and enables the management to take remedial measures.

(5) Helps to control cash expenditure : Cash budget can be prepared with the help of cash flow statement. A comparision of the cash flow statement and the budgeted forecast of cash is helpful in comparing and controlling cash expenditure.

(6) It provides a better measure for inter-period and inter-firm comparision.

Limitation of Cash Flow Statement

1. It reveals only the movement of cash but fails to show liquidity position of the business.
2. It shows cash income of the business, but to determine the income of the business, non-cash income should also be considered.
3. In cash flow statement, the term 'fund' is used in a narrow sense, *i.e.*, cash only. This will not therefore give a complete picture of financial position of the business.
4. It connot replace income statement and find flow statement as they have specific purpose of there own.

Types of Cash Flow Statement

Cash Flow Statement may relate to past or future. In the former case it is referred to as historical cash flow statement and projected cash flow or cash budget in the case of latter. Historical cash flow statement is prepared at the end of accounting year to know sources and uses of cash. In fact the cash flow statement which is normally prepared relates to historical cash flow statement.

Difference between Cash Flow Statement and Cash Budget

Cash budget is different from cash flow statement. Cash budget reveals the probable cash position as a result of planned operation and thus the excess or shortage of cash is known. This helps in arranging short-term borrowings in advance to meet the situations of shortage of cash or making investment in times of cash in excess. Cash can be coordinated in relation to total working capital, sales, investment and debt. On the other hand, a statement of cash flow provides detailed information about how particular assets, liabilities and owners equity elements changed as a result of cash receipts and cash payment from business's operating, investing and financiang activities.

Differences between cash flow statement and fund flow statement

Fund flow statement	*Cash flow statement*
1. It is based on the concept of working capital.	1. It is based on the concept of cash.
2. It reveals changes in working capital position between two balance sheet dates.	2. It reveals change in cash position between two balance sheet dates.
3. It is of primary importance.	3. It is of secondary importance.
4. Classification of assets and liabilities into current and non-current category is essential.	4. No such classification is necessary.
5. This statement match sources and application of fund.	5. It commences with opening cash balance and ends with closing cash balance.
6. An improvement in cash position results. in improvement in working capital.	6. An increase in cash on hand does not result in increase in working capital.
7. It is long-term tool of financial analysis.	7. It is a short-term tool of financial analysis.

Procedure Involved in Preparing Cash Flow Statement

The following steps are involved in the prepareation of cash flow statement :

(1) Calculation of cash flow from operation : Ascertainment of cash flow from operation involves the following two steps :

(*a*) *Ascertainment of operating profit or operating cash profit* : Operating profit is to be ascertained because net profit shownn in the income statement contain non-cash and non-operating expenses and non-operating incomes. Hence specifically operating cash profit has to be calculated. The operating cash profit can be ascertained by preparing an adjusted profit and loss account which resembles to the one prepared under fund flow statement. A proforma of adjusted profit and loss account is shown below :

Adjusted Profit & Loss A/c

To Non-cash and non-operating expesnes :			By Balance b/d	xx
– Depreciation on fixed assets	xx		By Non-operating and non-cash incomes :	
– Preliminary expenses	xx		– Interest received	xx
– Discount on issue of shares & debentures	xx		– Dividend received	xx
– Underwriting commission wirtten off			– Compensation received	xx
– Reserve for bad debts	xx		– Donation received	xx
– Reserve for discount on debtors	xx		– Profit on sale of investment	xx
– Provision for taxtaion	xx		– Profit on sale of fixed assets	xx
– Donation given	xx		By Operating cash profit (Balancing figure)	xx
– Compensation paid	xx			
– Fines & penalties	xx			
		xx		
To Appropriation of profit :				
– Transfer to reserve		xx		
– Dividend declared		xx		
To Balance c/d		xx		
		xx		xx

Problem 1 (Ascertainment of cash from operation) : From the following profit & loss account, you are required to compute cash from operation :

Profit & Loss A/c for the year ended 31.12.98

To Salaries	5,000	By Gross profit	25,000
To Rent	1,000	By Profit on sale of land	5,000
To Depreciation	2,000	By Income on investment	3,000
To Loss on sale of plant	1,000		
To Goodwill written off	4,000		
To Proposed dividend	5,000		
To Provision for taxation	5,000		
To Net profit	10,000		
	33,000		33,000

(*Bangalore University, B.B.M., April 2002*), (*CS, Inter December, 1997*)

Solution :

Adjusted Profit & Loss A/c

	Rs.		Rs.
To Depreciation	2,000	By Balance b/d	Nil
To Loss on sale of plant	1,000	By Profit on sale of land	5,000
To Goodwill written off	4,000	By Income on investment	3,000
To Proposed dividend	5,000	By Opering cash	8,000
To Provision for taxation	5,000	By Profit (Balancing figure)	19,000
To Balance c/d	10,000		
	27,000		27,000

(*b*) **Ascertainment of Cash Flow from Operation :** Cash flow from operation consists of both operating cash profit and changes in current assets and changes in current liabilities. The total cash flow from operation can be shown under the following proforma :

Proforma showing the Cash Flow from the Operation

Operating cash profit (as ascertained by preparing adjusted P & L a/c)		xx
Add : Decrease in current assets	xx	
Add : Increase in current liabilities	xx	
		xx
		xx
Less : Increase in current assets	xx	
Less : Decrease in current liabilities	xx	
		xx
Cash Flow from Operation		xx

Problem 2 (Ascertainment of Cash flow from operation) : From the following information, you are required to ascertain cash flow from operation :

	31-12-96 (*Rs.*)	*31-12-97* (*Rs.*)
Net profit	–	70,000
Debtors	42,000	40,000
Bills receivable	8,000	13,000
Creditors	47,000	50,000
Bills payable	15,000	10,000
Stock	58,000	65,000

(*Osmania University, B.Com., March 1999*)

Solution :

Calculation of Cash from Operation

Profit made during the year		70,000
Add : Decrease in debtors	2,000	
Add : Increase in creditors	3,000	5,000
		75,000
Less : Increase in bills receivable	5,000	
Less : Increase in stock	7,000	
Less : Decrease in bills payable	5,000	
		17,000
Cash from Operation		58,000

Problem 3 : From the following balances you are required to calculate cash from operation :

	31.12.1989	*31.12.1990*
Debtors	50,000	47,000
Bills receivable	10,000	12,500
Creditors	20,000	25,000
Bills payable	8,000	6,000
O/s expenses	1,000	1,200
Prepaid expenses	800	700
Accrued income	600	750
Income received from advance	300	250
Profit made during the year	–	1,30,000

(Bangalore University, B.B.M., November 1999)

Solution :

Cash from Operation

Profit made during the year		1,30,000
Add : Decrease in debtors	3,000	
Decrease in prepaid expenses	100	
Increase in creditors	5,000	
Increase in O/s expenses	200	
		8,300
		1,38,300
Less : Increase in Bills receivable	2,500	
Increase in Accrued Income	150	
Decrease in Bills payable	2,000	
Decrease in Income received in advance	50	
		4,700
Cash from operation		1,33,600

Problem 4 : From the following information, calculation cash from operation :

	1996 *Rs.*	*1997* *Rs.*
P & L a/c (Credit)	40,000	50,000
Debtors	20,000	26,000
Bills receivable	20,000	12,000
Prepaid rent	2,000	3,000
Prepaid insurance	1,000	800
Goodwill	20,000	14,000
Depreciation	32,000	40,000
Creditors	20,000	30,000

(Osmania University, B.Com., October 1999)

Solution :

Adjusted P & L A/c

To Goodwill written off	6,000	By Balance b/d	40,000
To Depreciation	8,000	By Operating cash profit	24,000
To Balance c/d	50,000		
	64,000		64,000

Cash from Operation

Operating cash profit			24,000
Add :	Decrease in bills receivable	8,000	
	Decrease in prepaid insurance	200	
	Increase in creditors	10,000	
			18,200
			42,200
Less :	Increase in debtors	6,000	
	Increase in prepaid rent	1,000	
			7,000
	Cash from operation		35,200

Problem 5 (Preparation of cash flow statement):
Balance sheets of A and B on 1.1.1990 and 31.12.1990 were as follows :

	1.1.1990 *Rs.*	*31.12.1990* *Rs.*		*1.1.90* *Rs.*	*31.12.90* *Rs.*
Creditors	40,000	44,000	Cash	10,000	7,000
Mrs A's loan	25,000	-	Debtors	30,000	50,000
Loan from bank	40,000	50,000	Stock	35,000	25,000
Capital	1,25,000	1,53,000	Machinery	80,000	55,000
			Land	40,000	50,000
			Building	35,000	60,000
	2,30,000	2,47,000		2,30,000	2,47,000

During the year, a machine costing Rs. 10,000 (accumulated depreciation Rs. 3,000) was sold for Rs. 5,000. The provisions for depreciation against machinery as on 1.1.1990 was Rs. 25,000 and on 31.12.1990 Rs. 40,000. Net profit for the year 1990 amounted to Rs. 45,000. You are required to prepare a cash flow statement. *(Bangalore University, B.B.M., April 1999)*

Solution :

Adjusted P & L A/c

To Depreciation on machinery	18,000	By Balance b/d	Nil
To Loss on sale of machinery	2,000	By Operating profit	65,000
To Balance c/d	45,000		
	65,000		65,000

Statement showing Cash from Operation

Operating profit			65,000
Add :	Decrease in stock	10,000	
	Increase in creditors	4,000	14,000
			79,000
Less :	Increase in debtors		20,000
	Cash from operation		59,000

Machinery A/c

To Balance b/d	1,05,000	By Bank	5,000
		By Loss on sale of machinery	2,000
		By Provision for depreciation	3,000
		By Balance c/d	95,000
	1,05,000		1,05,000

Provision for Depreciation

To Machinery a/c	3,000	By Balance b/d	25,000
To Balance c/d	40,000	By P & L a/c (Balancing figure)	18,000
	43,000		43,000

Cash Flow Statement

Sources		*Uses*	
Cash balance (1.1.1990)	10,000	Purchase of land	10,000
Cash from operation	59,000	Purchase of building	25,000
Loan from bank	10,000	Mrs A's loan paid	25,000
Sale of machinery	5,000	Drawings	17,000
		Cash balance (31-12-1990)	7,000
	84,000		84,000

Problem 6 : Balance sheets of Aneeta Ltd. as on 31.12.1997 and 31.12.1998

	1997	*1998*		*1997*	*1998*
Share capital	2,00,000	3,00,000	Plant & machinery	2,00,000	3,00,000
Share premium	–	10,000	Land & buildings	50,000	1,10,000
8% Debentures	1,00,000	50,000	Investments	10,000	50,000
General reserve	50,000	80,000	Stock	80,000	60,000
P & L a/c	50,000	70,000	Debtors	90,000	80,000
Provision for taxation	30,000	40,000	Cash and bank	70,000	50,000
Proposed dividend	20,000	30,000			
Sundry creditors	50,000	70,000			
	5,00,000	6,50,000		5,00,000	6,50,000

Additional Information

1. Investment costing Rs. 8,000 was sold for Rs. 15,000, the profit being credited to P & L a/c.
2. An interim dividend of Rs. 20,000 was paid during the year.
3. Accumulated depreciation on :

	1997 *Rs.*	*1998* *Rs.*
Land & building	30,000	40,000
Plant & machinery	40,000	60,000

4. Depreciation charged during the year :

Land & building	10,000
Plant & machinery	20,000

5. Debentures were redeemed at par
6. Profit and loss a/c (balance) 1997

Profit and loss a/c (balance) 1997	Rs, 50,000
Add : Profit for 1998	40,000
	90,000
Less : Interim dividend	20,000
	70,000

Prepare a cash flow statement. *(Bangalore University, B.Com., October 2000)*

Solution :

Plant & Machinery A/c

To Balance b/d	2,00,000	By Balance c/d	3,00,000
To Accumulated depreciation	40,000	By Accumulated depreciation	60,000
	2,40,000		

To Bank-purchases (Balancing figure)	1,20,000		
	3,60,000		3,60,000

Provision for Depreciation in Plant

To Balance c/d	60,000	By Balance b/d	40,000
		By P & L a/c - Dep. on machinery (Balancing figure)	20,000
	60,000		60,000

Land & Building A/c

To Balance b/d	50,000	By Balance c/d	1,10,000
To Accumulated depreciation	30,000	By Accumulated depreciation	40,000
To Bank-purchases (Balancing figure)	70,000		
	1,50,000		1,50,000

Provision for Depreciation on Land & Building

To Balance c/d	40,000	By Balance b/d	30,000
		By P & L a/c - depreciation	10,000
	40,000		40,000

Investment A/c

To Balance b/d	10,000	By Bank-sale	15,000
To P & L a/c - profit	7,000	By Balance c/d	50,000
To Bank-purchases (Balancing figure)	48,000		
	65,000		65,000

Adjusted P & L A/c

To Provision for depreciation on plant & machinery	20,000	By Balance b/d	50,000
To Provision for depreciation on land & building	10,000	By Profit on sale of investment	7,000
To Interim dividend	20,000	By Operating profit	93,000
To General reserve	30,000		
To Balance c/d	70,000		
	1,50,000		1,50,000

Cash from Operation

Operating Profit		93,000
Add: Decrease in debtors	10,000	
Decrease in stock	20,000	
Increase in creditors	20,000	
Increase in proposed dividend	10,000	
Increase in provision for tax	10,000	
		70,000
Cash from operation		1,63,000

Cash Flow Statement

Cash Balance (1.1.97)	70,000	Purchase of plant & machinery	1,20,000
Cash from operation	1,63,000	Purchase of land & building	70,000
Sale of investment	15,000	Purchase of investment	48,000
Issue of share with premium	1,10,000	Payment of interim dividend	20,000
		Redemption of debentures	50,000
		Closing cash balance	50,000
	3,58,000		3,58,000

Problem 7 : From the following Balance Sheets of Mr. 'X' prepare a cash flow statement for the year 1999 indicating therein separately the cash from operations :

Balance Sheet

	1999	*1998*		*1999*	*1998*
Capital	4,00,000	3,00,000	Fixed assets	4,90,000	5,44,000
Loans	1,20,000	2,60,000	Stock	44,000	30,000
Creditors	30,800	51,200	Debtors	90,000	60,000
Provision for taxation	8,000	20,000	Cash	11,200	15,000
			Bank	40,000	30,000
Bills payable	1,17,200	57,400	Deferred-Revenue expenses	2,800	9,600
Unpaid income tax	2,000	—			
	6,78,000	6,88,600		6,78,000	6,88,600

Other Particulars

1. An item of fixed assets having book value of Rs. 5,000 was sold for Rs. 6,000 during the year 1999.
2. Capital st the end of 1999 was arrived after making adjustment of the newly introduced capital of Rs. 20,000 and drawings of Rs. 50,000.
3. Income-tax assessment for the year 1998 was completed resulting in a gross demand of Rs. 22,000 out of which Rs. 20,000 being undisputed demand was paid.(*University of Mumbai, B.Com., October 1999*)

Solution :

X's Capital A/c

To Drawings	50,000	By Balance b/d	3,00,000
To Balance c/d	4,00,000	By Cash	20,000
		By P & L a/c -profit for the year (Balancing figure)	1,30,000
	4,50,000		4,50,000

Fixed Assets a/c

To Balance b/d	5,44,000	By Depreciation -P & L a/c	49,000
		By Bank-sale of fixed assets	5,000
		By Balance c/d	4,90,000
	5,44,000		5,44,000

Provision for Tax

To Cash	20,000	By Balance b/d	20,000
To Unpaid income tax	2,000	By P & L a/c (Balancing figure)	10,000
To Balance c/d	8,000		
	30,000		30,000

Adjusted P & L A/c

	Rs.		Rs.
To Provision for tax	10,000	By Profit on sale of fixed assets	1,000
To Deferred revenue expenses written off	6,800	By Operating profit	1,94,800
To Depreciation on fixed assets	49,000		
To Net profit transfered to capital a/c	1,30,000		
	1,95,800		1,95,800

Statement of Cash from Operation

Operating profit		1,94,800
Add : Increase in Bills payable		59,800
		2,54,600
Less : Increase in stock	14,000	
Increase in debtors	30,000	
Decrease in creditors	29,400	
		64,400
Cash from operation		1,90,200

Cash Flow Statement

Opening balance of			Loans repaid		1,40,000
Cash	15,000		Tax amount of 1998 paid		20,000
Bank	30,000				
		45,000	X's Drawings		50,000
Capital Introduced		20,000	Closing balance		
Sale of fixed assets		6,000	Cash	11,200	
Cash from operation		1,90,200	Bank	40,000	
					51,200
		2,61,200			2,61,200

Problem 8 : Balance sheets of MN Rao as on 1-1-1993 and 31-12-1993 was as follows ;

	1-1-1993 (Rs.)	*31-12-1993 (Rs.)*
Liabilities		
Capital	1,25,000	1,53,000
Creditors	1,40,000	1,44,000
Bank loan	65,000	50,000
Bills payable	20,000	30,000
	3,50,000	3,77,000
Assets		
Cash	20,000	17,000
Debtors	30,000	80,000
Stock	45,000	35,000
Machinery	80,000	65,000
Land	90,000	80,000
Buildings	65,000	70,000
Goodwill	20,000	30,000
	3,50,000	3,77,000

During the year, a machine costing Rs. 12,000 (accumulated depreciation Ps. 4,000) was sold for Rs. 7,000. Balance of provision for depreciation against machinery as on 1.1.93 was Rs. 35,000 and on 31.12.93 Rs. 50,000.

Prepare cash flow statement. Net profit for the year 1993 Rs. 55,000.

(Sri Venkateshwara University, B.Com., October 1999)

Solution :

Capital A/c

To Drawings (Balancing figure)	27,000	By Balance b/d	1,25,000
To Balance c/d	1,53,000	By P & L a/c –Net profit	55,000
	1,80,000		1,80,000

Bank Loan

To Bank (Balancing figure)	15,000	By Balance b/d	65,000
To Balance c/d	50,000		
	65,000		65,000

Machinery A/c

To Balance b/d (80,000+35,000)	1,15,000	By Provision for depreciation	4,000
To Bank (Balancing figure)	12,000	By Bank-sale	7,000
		By P & L a/c - loss on sale	1,000
		By Balance c/d (65,000+50,000)	1,15,000
	1,27,000		1,27,000

Provision for Depreciation on Machinery A/c

To Machinery a/c	4,000	By Balance b/d	35,000
To Balance c/d	50,000	By P & L A/c (Balancing figure)	19,000
	54,000		54,000

Land A/c

To Balance b/d	90,000	By Bank (Balancing figure)	10,000
		By Balance c/d	80,000
	90,000		90,000

Buildings A/c

To Balance b/d	65,000	By Balance c/d	70,000
To Bank (Balancing figure)	5,000		
	70,000		70,000

Goodwill A/c

To Balance b/d	20,000	By Balance c/d	30,000
To P & L a/c (Balancing figure)	10,000		
	30,000		30,000

Adj. P & L A/c

To Loss on sale of machinery	1,000	By Balance b/d	Nil
To Depreciation on machinery	19,000	By Appreciation in goodwill	10,000
To Balance c/d	55,000	By Operating profit	65,000
	75,000		75,000

Statement showing Cash from Operation

Operating profit		65,000
Add : Increase in creditors	4,000	
Increase in bills payable	10,000	
Decrease in stock	1,000	
		24,000
		89,000
Less : Increase in debtors		50,000
Cash from operation		39,000

Cash flow Statement

Balance of cash on 1.1.93	20,000	Drawings	27,000
Sale of land	10,000	Bank loan repaid	15,000
Sale of machinery	7,000	Building purchased	5,000
Cash from operation	39,000	Machinery purchased	12,000
		Balance of cash on 31.3.93	17,000
	76,000		76,000

Problem 9 : Umesh Ltd. has provided the following Balance sheets and requests you to prepare cash flow statement :

	1997	*1998*
Liabilities :		
Share capital	3,00,000	3,75,000
Reserve fund	75,000	90,000
Profit & loss a/c	45,000	46,000
Mortgage loan	1,00,000	–
Creditors	2,25,000	2,10,000
Provision for taxation	45,000	52,500
	7,90,000	7,73,500
Assets		
Land and building	3,00,000	2,85,000
Plant & machinery	2,25,000	2,53,500
Stock	1,50,000	1,20,000
Debtors	1,14,000	96,000
Cash	1,000	1,500
Bank	–	10,000
Goodwill	–	7,500
	7,90,000	7,73,500

Additional Information

1. Dividend paid Rs. 32,000.
2. Assets of another company were purchased for a consideration of Rs. 75,000 payable in shares. The following assets were purchased, stock, Rs. 30,000, machinery Rs. 37,500.

3. Machinery was further purchased for Rs. 12,000.
4. Loss on sale of machinery Rs. 300 was written off to reserve fund.
5. Income tax provided during the year Rs. 50,000. (*Bangalore University, B.Com., April 2001*)

Solution :

Machinery A/c

To Balance b/d	2,25,000	By General reserve	300
To Share capital	37,500	By Bank-sales (Balancing figure)	20,700
To Bank-purchases	12,000	By Balance c/d	2,53,500
	2,74,500		2,74,500

General Reserve

To Machinery	300	By Balance b/d	75,000
To Balance c/d	90,000	By P & L a/c - transfer	15,300
	90,300		90,300

Provision for Tax

To Bank-Tax paid (Balancing figure)	42,500	By Balance b/d	45,000
To Balance c/d	52,500	By P & L a/c	50,000
	95,000		95,000

Share Capital A/c

To Balance c/d	3,75,000	To Balance b/d	3,00,000
		To Machinery –Shares issued	37,500
		By Stock –shares issued	30,000
		By Goodwill	7,500
	3,75,000		3,75,000

Adj. P & L A/c

To Dividend	32,000	By Balance b/d	45,000
To Depreciation on building	15,000	By Operating profit	1,13,300
To Provision for tax	50,000		
To General reserve Transfer	15,300		
To Balance c/d	46,000		
	1,58,300		1,58,300

Statement showing Cash from Operation

Operating profit	1,13,300
Add : Decrease in stock (1,50,000+30,000–1,20,000)	60,000
Add : Decrease in debtors	18,000
	1,91,300
Less : Decrease in creditors	15,000
Cash from operation	1,76,300

Cash Flow Statement

Opening balance of cash	1,000	Payment of mortgage loan		1,00,000
Sale of machinery	20,700	Purchase of machinery		12,000
Cash from operation	1,76,300			
		Payment of tax		42,500
		Payment of dividend		32,000
		Closing Balance :		
		Cash	1500	
		Bank	10,000	
				11,500
	1,98,000			1,98,000

Problem 10 : The financial position of Anu and Parmanu as on 1st July, 1997 and 30th June, 1998 was as follows :

	1.7.1997	*30.6.1998*
Assets :		
Cash	4,000	3,600
Debtors	35,000	38,400
Stock	25,000	22,000
Land	20,000	30,000
Building	50,000	55,000
Machinery	80,000	86,000
	2,14,000	2,35,000
Liabilities		
Mrs Anu's loan	–	20,000
Bank loan	30,000	25,000
Current liabilities	36,000	41,000
Capital accounts	1,48,000	1,49,000
	2,14,000	2,35,000

Other Information

1. Drawings during the year Rs. 26,000.
2. Provision for depreciation :

	1.7.1997	*30.6.1998*
Machinery	27,000	36,000
Building	8,000	10,000

Prepare cash flow statement showing cash from operations separately for the year ended 30th June, 1998.

(*University of Mumbai, B.Com., April 1999*)

Solution :

Machinery A/c (At Cost)

To Balance b/d (80,000+27,000)	1,07,000	By Balance c/d (86,000+36,000)	1,22,000
To Cash (Balancing figure)	15,000		
	1,22,000		1,22,000

Building A/c (At Cost)

To Balance b/d (50,000+8,000)	58,000	By Balance c/d (55,000+10,000)	65,000
To Cash (Balancing figure)	7,000		
	65,000		65,000

Provision for Taxation

To Drawings	26,000	By Balance b/d	1,48,000
To Balance c/d	1,49,000	By P & L a/c (Balancing figure)	27,000
	1,75,000		1,75,000

Capital A/c

To Drawings	26,000	By Balance b/d	1,48,000
To Balance c/d	1,49,000	By P & L a/c (Balancing figure)	27,000
	1,75,000		1,75,000

Adj. P & L A/c

To Depreciation :- Machinary	9,000	By Balance b/d	Nil
Building	2,000	By Operating profit	38,000
To Balance c/d	27,000		
	38,000		38,000

Statement showing Cash from Operation

Operating profit		38,000
Add : Increase in current liability	5,000	
Decrease in stock	3,000	
		8,000
		46,000
Less : Increase in debtors		3,400
Cash from operation		42,600

Cash Flow Statement

Opening Balance of cash	4,000	Repayment of bank loan	5,000
Loan from Mrs. Anu	20,000	Purchase of land	10,000
Cash from operation	42,600	Purchase of building	7,000
		Purchase of machinery	15,000
		Drawings	26,000
		Closing balance of cash	3,600
	66,600		66,600

Problem 11 : B Ltd., supplies you the following balance sheets as on December:

	1988	*1989*
Liabilities		
Share capital	70,000	74,000
Bonds	12,000	6,000
Sundry creditors	10,360	11,840
Provision for doubtful debts	700	800
Reserves and surplus	10,040	10,560
	1,03,100	1,03,200

Assets :		
Bank balance	9,000	7,800
Debtors	14,900	17,700
Inventories	49,200	42,700
Land	20,000	30,000
Goodwill	10,000	5,000
	1,03,100	1,03,200

Following additional information is also supplied to you :

(*a*) Dividend amounted to Rs. 3,500 were paid during the year.

(*b*) Land was purchased for Rs. 10,000.

(*c*) Rs. 5,000 were written off on goodwill during the year.

(*d*) Bonds of Rs. 6,000 were paid during the course of the year.

You are required to prepare a cash flow statement. (*Sri Venkateshwara University, B.Com., April 1999*)

Solution :

Land A/c

To Balance b/d	20,000	By Balance c/d	30,000
To Cash	10,000		
	30,000		30,000

Goodwill A/c

To Balance b/d	10,000	By P & L A/c	5,000
		By Balance c/d	5,000
	10,000		10,000

Share Capital A/c

To Balance c/d	74,000	By Balance b/d	70,000
		By Cash	4,000
	74,000		74,000

Bonds A/c

To Cash	6,000	By Balance b/d	12,000
To Balance c/d	6,000		
	12,000		12,000

Adjusted P & L A/c

To Dividend	3,500	By Reserve & surplus —Opening Balance	10,040
To Goodwill written off	5,000		
To Provision for D.D.	100	By Operating profit	9,120
To Reserves & surplus —Closing balance	10,560		
	19,160		19,160

Statement of Cash from Operation

Operating profit		9,120
Add : Decrease in stock	6,500	
Increase in creditors	1,480	7,980
		17,100
Less : Increase in debtors		2,800
Cash from operation		14,300

Cash Flow Statement

Opening Bank balance	9,000	Purchase of land	10,000
Issue of shares	4,000	Payment of Bonds	6,000
Cash from operation	14,300	Dividend paid	3,500
		Closing bank balance	7,800
	27,300		27,300

Problem 12 : From the following Balance Sheet of 'X' Company Ltd. for the year ending 31st December 1997 and 31st December, 1998, prepare cash flow statment for 1998.

	1997	*1998*		*1997*	*1998*
Equity share capital	2,00,000	2,50,000	Goodwill	50,000	45,000
9% Preference share capital	60,000	40,000	Land & building	80,000	55,000
			Plant & machinery	90,000	1,60,000
Capital reserve	–	10,000	Furniture	12,000	10,000
General reserve	15,000	20,000	Trade Investment	10,000	45,000
P & L a/c	25,000	40,000	Sundry debtors	32,000	25,000
Sundry creditors	28,000	52,000	Stock	64,000	45,000
Bills payable	8,000	10,000	Bills Receivable	10,000	35,000
O/s expenses	4,000	3,000	Cash in hand	10,000	25,000
Proposed dividend	18,000	25,000	Cash at Bank	15,000	26,000
Provision for taxation	20,000	24,000	Preliminary expenses	5,000	3,000
	3,78,000	4,74,000		3,78,000	4,74,000

Additional Information

1. An interim dividend of Rs. 10,000 has been paid in 1998.
2. Rs. 2,000 has been received as dividend on trade investment.
3. A piece of land has been sold out in 1998 and the remaining has been revalued. Profit on sale and revaluation being transferred to capital reserve.
4. Depreciation on plant and machinery has been written off Rs. 15,000 in 1998 and no depreciation has been charged on land and building.
5. A machinery was sold for Rs. 18,000 (W.D.V. being Rs. 20,000) and no furniture has been sold during the year. *(Bangalore University, B.Com., April 2000)*

Solution :

Land & Building A/c

To Balance b/d	80,000	By Bank-sales (Balancing figure)	35,000
To Capital reserve (profit on sale)	10,000	By Balance c/d	55,000
	90,000		90,000

Plant A/c.

To Balance b/d	90,000	By P & L a/c —Depreciation	15,000
To Bank-purchases (Balancing figure)	1,05,00	By P & L a/c —Loss on sale	2,000
		By Bank a/c sales	18,000
		By Balance c/d	1,60,000
	1,95,000		1,95,000

Investments

To Balance b/d	10,000	By Balance c/d	47,000
To Dividend	2,000		
To Bank-purchases (Balancing figure)	35,000		
	47,000		47,000

Adjusted P & L A/c

To Plant-Depreciation	15,000	By Balance b/d	25,000
To General reserve (20,000–15,000)	5,000	By Dividend received	2,000
To Goodwill written off	5,000	By Operating	86,000
To Preliminary expenses written off	2,000		
To Interim dividend	10,000		
To Provision for tax	4,000		
To O/s expenses	3,000		
To Depreciation on furniture	2,000		
To Loss on sale of plant	2,000		
To Proposed dividend	25,000		
To Balance c/d	40,000		
	1,13,000		1,13,000

Statement of Cash from Operation

Operating profit		86,000
Add : Decrease in debtors	7,000	
Decrease in stock	19,000	
Increase in creditors	24,000	
Increase in B.P	2,000	
		52,000
		1,38,000
Less : Increase in B.R		25,000
Cash from operation		1,13,000

Cash Flow Statement

Opening cash and Bank Balance (10,000+15,000)	25,000	Purchase of plant	1,05,000
Issue of shares	50,000	Purchase of Investment	35,000
Sale of land	35,000	Redemption of pref shares	20,000
Sale of Plant	18,000	Interim dividend	10,000
Dividend received	2,000	Proposed dividend	18,000
Cash from operation	1,13,000	Payment of liability for expenses	4,000
		Closing cash and bank balance (25,000+26,000)	51,000
	2,43,000		2,43,000

Problem 13 : Following are the balance sheets of Young India Ltd.:

	1998	*1997*		*1998*	*1997*
Share capital	7,00,000	6,00,000	Fixed assets	6,50,000	4,00,000
General reserve	2,00,000	1,50,000	Debtors	3,50,000	2,00,000

P & L A/c	2,00,000	1,00,000	Stock	2,50,000	1,50,000
14% Debentures issued for purchase of fixed assets	2,00,000	Nil	Cash	1,30,000	1,00,000
Proposed dividend	80,000	70,000	Underwriting Commission	Nil	70,000
	13,80,000	9,20,000		13,80,000	9,20,000

Assuming the depreciation for the year to be Rs. 50,000 and interim dividend paid during the year to be 5% on opening capital. Prepare cash flow statement indicating therein separately cash from operations.

(University of Mumbai, B.Com., October 1998)

Solution :

Fixed Assets A/c

To Balance b/d	4,00,000	By Depreciation	50,000
To 14% Debentures	2,00,000	By Balance c/d	6,50,000
To Cash (Balancing figure)	1,00,000		
	7,00,000		7,00,000

Adjusted P & L A/c

To Interim dividend	30,000	By Balance b/d	1,00,000
To Proposed dividend	80,000	By Operating profit	3,80,000
To Depreciation on fixed assets	50,000		
To Transfer to general reserve	50,000		
To Underwriting commission	70,000		
To Balance c/d	2,00,000		
	4,80,000		4,80,000

Statement of Cash from Operation

Operating profit		3,80,000
Less : Increase in debtors	1,50,000	
Increase in stock	1,00,000	
		2,50,000
Cash from operation		1,30,000

Cash Flow Statement

Opening cash balance	1,00,000	Interim dividend	30,000
Issue of equity shares	1,00,000	Dividend paid	70,000
Cash from operation	1,30,000	Fixed assets purchased	1,00,000
		Closing cash Balance	1,30,000
	3,30,000		3,30,000

Problem 14 : Ayodhya Limited has provided the following balance sheets as on 31.3.95 and 31.3.96:

	1995	*1996*		*1995*	*1996*
Share capital	17,00,000	18,35,000	Building	8,00,000	10,00,000
Reserves	40,000	83,700	Furniture	5,000	6,000
P & L a/c	1,00,000	1,30,000	Machinery	2,50,000	3,70,000
Creditors	1,00,000	95,000	Book debts	1,00,000	45,000
Provision for dividend	70,000	50,000	B.R.	8,000	9,000
Bank OD	8,000	18,000	Inventories	4,00,000	3,43,700
Bills payable	14,000	13,000	Investments	1,64,000	1,70,000

Long-term loan	10,000	70,000	Patents	3,00,000	3,43,700
			Cash	2,000	2,200
			Preliminary expenses	10,000	2,000
			Prepaid insurance	3,000	3,100
	20,42,000	22,94,700		20,42,000	22,94,700

Additional Information

(*a*) Depreciation charged on building at 3% of cost of 9,00,000; on machinery 8% of cost of Rs. 4,00,000; on furniture at 5% of cost of Rs. 8,000.

(*b*) Investments were purchased and interest of Rs. 3,000 was received which was used in writing down the book value of investments.

(*c*) The declared dividend for 1995 was paid and interim dividend for Rs. 20,000 paid out of P & L A/c.

(*Bangalore University, B.Com., April 1999*)

Solution :

(1) Calculation of Depreciation

(*a*) on Buildings $= 9{,}00{,}000 \times \frac{3}{100} = 27{,}000$

(*b*) on Machinery $= 4{,}00{,}000 \times \frac{8}{100} = 32{,}000$

(*c*) on Furniture $= 8{,}000 \times \frac{5}{100} = 400$

(2) Share Capital A/c

To Closing balance	18,35,000	By Balance b/d	17,00,000
		By Bank-issue of shares	1,35,000
	18,35,000		18,35,000

(3) Reserve A/c

To Balance c/d	83,700	By Balance b/d	40,000
		By P & L a/c transfer	43,700
	83,700		83,700

(4) Provision for dividends

(*a*) Balance of 1995 : It is paid in 1996, so it is an item of cash outflow.

(*b*) Balance of 1996 : Opening balance is completely utilised to pay dividend. So the closing balance of Rs. 50,000 is an item of appropriation.

(*c*) Interim dividend paid for 1996 :- It is an item of appropriation and also cash flow.

Loan A/c

To Balance c/d	70,000	By Balance b/d	10,000
		By Bank-loan raised	60,000
	70,000		70,000

Building A/c

To Balance b/d	8,00,000	By Depreciation	27,000
To Bank-purchases (Balancing figure)	2,27,000	By Balance c/d	10,00,000
	10,27,000		10,27,000

Machinery A/c

To Balance b/d	2,50,000	By Depreciation	32,000
To Bank-purchases	1,52,000	By Balance c/d	3,70,000
	4,02,000		4,02,000

Furniture A/c

To Balance b/d	5,000	By Depreciation	400
To Bank-purchases	1,400	By Balance c/d	6,000
	6,400		6,400

Investment A/c

To Balance b/d	1,64,000	By Bank-Interest received credited	3,000
To Bank-purchases	9,000	By Balance c/d	1,70,000
	1,73,000		1,73,000

Patents A/c

To Balance b/d	3,00,000	By Balance c/d	3,43,700
To Bank-purchases	43,700		
	3,43,700		3,43,700

Preliminary Expenses

To Balance b/d	10,000	By P & L a/c wirtten off	8,000
		By Balance c/d	2,000
	10,000		10,000

Adjusted P & L A/c

To Depreciation on building	27,000	By Balance b/d	1,00,000
To Depreciation on machinery	32,000	By Operating profit	2,14,100
To Depreciation on fixtures	400		
To Preliminary expenses written off	8,000		
To Transfer to reserve	43,700		
To Provision for dividends	50,000		
To Interim dividend	20,000		
To Prepaid expenses at the beginning of the year	3,000		
To Balance c/d	1,30,000		
	3,14,100		3,14,100

Statement of cash from Operation

Operating profit		2,14,100
Add : Decrease in debtors	55,000	
Decrease in stock	56,300	
		1,11,300
		3,25,400

Less : Increase in bills receivables	1,000	
Decrease in creditors	5,000	
Decrease in bills payable	1,000	
		7,000
Cash from operation		3,18,400

Cash Flow Statement

Opening balance :		Dividend paid for 1995	70,000
Cash	2,000	Interim dividend paid	20,000
Bank overdraft	(–) 8,000	Purchase of buildings	2,27,000
Issue of shares	1,35,000	Purchase of machinery	1,52,000
Long-term loan	60,000	Puchase of furniture	1,400
Cash from operation	3,18,400	Purchase of investment	9,000
Interest on Investment	3,000	Purchase of patent	43,700
		Prepaid expenses (Paid in the current year)	3,100
		Closing Balance:	
		Cash	2,200
		Bank overdraft (–)	18,000
	5,10,400		5,10,400

Problem 15 : The following are the summarised balance sheets of a company as on 31st December, 1997 and 1998

Liabilities	*1997*	*1998*
Share capital	2,00,000	2,50,000
General reserve	50,000	60,000
Profit & loss A/c	30,500	30,600
Bank loan (long-term)	70,000	–
Sundry creditors	1,50,000	1,35,200
Provision for taxation	30,000	35,000
	5,30,500	5,10,800
Assets :		
Land and Buildings	2,00,000	1,90,000
Machinery	1,50,000	1,69,000
Stock	1,00,000	74,000
Sundry debtors	80,000	64,200
Cash	500	600
Bank	–	8,000
Goodwill	–	5,000
	5,30,500	5,10,800

Additional Information

1. During the year ended 31st December, 1998 dividend of Rs. 23,000 was paid.
2. Assets of another company were purchased for a consideration of Rs. 50,000 payable in shares. The following assets were purchased stock Rs. 20,000, machinery Rs. 25,000.
3. Machinery was further purchased for Rs. 8,000.
4. Depreciation written off on machinery Rs. 12,000.
5. Income tax provided during the year Rs. 33,000.
6. Loss on sale of machinery Rs. 200 was written off to general reserve.

You are required to prepare cash flow statement. (*Sri Venkateshwara University, B.Com., April 1998*)

Solution :

Machinery A/c

To Balance b/d	1,50,000	By Depreciation	12,000
To Cash	8,000	By Sale of machinery	
To Vendor company	25,000	–Cash	1,800
		(Balancing figure)	
		By Loss on sale of machinery	200
		By Balance c/d	1,69,000
	1,83,000		1,83,000

Provision for Taxation

To Cash	28,000	By Balance b/d	30,000
(Balancing figure)		By P & L a/c	33,000
To Balance c/d	35,000		
	63,000		63,000

Purchase of Assets from another company

Purchase consideration payable in shares		50,000
Less : Assets purchased		
Stock	20,000	
Machinery	25,000	
		45,000
Goodwill (Balancing figure)		5,000

Adjusted P & L A/c

To Transfer to general reserve	10,000	By Balance b/d	30,500
To Provision for taxation	33,000	By Operating profit	88,300
To Dividend	23,000		
To Depreciation on machinery	12,000		
To Depreciation on land & building	10,000		
To Loss on sale of machinery	200		
To Balance c/d	30,600		
	1,18,800		1,18,800

Cash from Operation

Operating profit		88,300
Add : Decrease in debtors	15,800	
Decrease in stock	46,000	
		61,800
		1,05,100
Less : Decrease in creditors	14,800	14,800
Cash from operation		1,35,300

Cash Flow Statement

Balance on 1.1.98		Bank loan paid	70,000
Cash	500	Income tax paid	28,000
Cash from operation	1,35,300	Dividend paid	23,000
Sale of machinery	1,800	Machinery purchased	8,000
		closing balance on 31.12.98	
		Cash	600
		Bank	8,000
	1,37,600		1,37,600

Problem 16 : Following are the comparative Balance Sheet of Company of two different dates :

Balance Sheet

	1995	*1996*		*1995*	*1996*
Share capital	30,000	40,000	Plant & machinery	40,000	45,000
Share premium	–	1,000	*Less* : Depreciation	14,000	15,000
P & L a/c	10,000	10,000	Net	26,000	30,000
Profit for the year	–	20,000	Property	20,000	25,000
Debentures	15,000	10,000	Shares in subsidiary co.	–	1,500
Profit on Redemption of debentures	–	200	Stock	14,000	15,000
			Debtors	10,000	15,000
Creditors	14,000	11,000	Bank balance	3,500	15,700
Provision for taxation	5,000	10,000			
Proposed dividend	1,500	2,000			
	75,500	1,04,200		75,500	1,04,200

Additional Information

1. Plant costing Rs. 5,000, accumulated depreciation thereon being Rs. 3,000 was sold for Rs. 1,000. The loss on sale has been charged to P & L a/c.
2. Taxation paid for the year amounts to Rs. 6,000.
3. An interim dividend of Rs. 1,000 has been paid during the year 1996. You are required to prepare a cash flow statement from the above information. Also ascertain cash from operation.

(*University of Mumbai, B.Com., April 1998*)

Solution :

Plant & Machinery A/c

To Balance b/d	40,000	By Plant sold	5,000
To Cash	10,000	–Cash	
		By Balance c/d	45,000
	50,000		50,000

Provision for depreciation A/c

To P & L a/c	3,000	By Balance b/d	14,000
To Balance c/d	15,000	By P & L a/c	4,000
	18,000		18,000

Provision for Tax A/c

To Cash	6,000	By Balance b/d	5,000
To Balance c/d	10,000	By P & L a/c	11,000
	16,000		16,000

Proposed Dividend A/c

To Cash	1,500	By Balance b/d	1,500
To Balance c/d	2,000	By P & L a/c	2,000
	3,500		3,500

Adjusted P & L A/c

To Loss on sale of plant & machinery		1,000	By Balance b/d	10,000
To Depreciation on		4,000	By Operating profit	39,000
To Proposed dividend		2,000		
To Provision for tax		11,000		
To Interim dividend paid		1,000		
To Profit for the year	20,000			
To Balance c/d	10,000			
		30,000		
		49,000		49,000

Statement of Cash from Operation

Operating profit		30,000
Less : Increase in loan to subsidiary Company	1,500	
Increase in stock	1,000	
Increase in debtors	5,000	
Decrease in creditors	3,000	
		10,500
Cash from operation		28,500

Cash Flow Statement

Opening Balance of cash	3,500	Purchase of property	5,000
Cash from operation	28,500	Tax paid for 1995	6,000
Sale of plant & machinery	1,000	Interim dividend paid	1,000
Issue of shares at premium	11,000	Plant & machinery purchased	10,000
		Proposed dividend paid	1,500
		Debentures redeemed	4,800
		Closing Balance of bank	15,700
	44,000		44,000

Problem 17 : From the following balance sheets of Exe. Ltd. make out the statement of sources and uses of cash :

Liabilities	1996	1997
Equity share capital	3,00,000	4,00,000
8% Redeemable preference Share capital	1,50,000	1,00,000
General reserve	40,000	70,000
Profit & loss a/c	30,000	48,000
Proposed dividend	42,000	50,000
Creditors	55,000	83,000
Bills payable	20,000	16,000
Provision for taxation	40,000	50,000
	6,77,000	8,17,000

Assets		
Goodwill	1,15,000	90,000
Land & buildings	2,00,000	1,70,000
Plant	80,000	2,00,000
Debtors	1,60,000	2,00,000
Stock	77,000	1,09,000
Bills receivable	20,000	30,000
Cash at Bank	10,000	8,000
Cash in hand	15,000	10,000
	6,77,000	8,17,000

Additional Information

(*a*) Depreciation of Rs. 10,000 and Rs, 20,000 have been charged on plant and land and buildings respectively in 1997.

(*b*) An interim dividend of Rs. 20,000 has been paid in 1997.

(*c*) Rs. 35,000 Income-tax was paid during the year 1997.

(*Sri Venkateshwara University, B.Com., October 1998*)

Solution :

Equity Share Capital A/

To Balance c/d	4,00,000	By Balance b/d	3,00,000
		By Cash (Balancing figure)	1,00,000
	4,00,000		4,00,000

8% Redeemable Pref Share Capital

To Cash (Balancing figure)	50,000	By Balance b/d	1,50,000
To Balance c/d	1,00,000		
	1,50,000		1,50,000

General Reserve A/c

To Balance c/d	70,000	By Balance b/d	40,000
		By P & L a/c (Balancing figure)	30,000
	70,000		70,000

Provision for Taxation A/c

To Cash	35,000	By Balance b/d	40,000
To Balance c/d	50,000	By P & L a/c (Balancing figure)	45,000
	85,000		85,000

Goodwill A/c

To Balance b/d	1,15,000	By P & L a/c (Balancing figure)	25,000
		By Balance c/d	90,000
	1,15,000		1,15,000

Land & Building A/c

To Balance b/d	2,00,000	By P & L a/c –Depreciation	20,000
		By Cash-sales (Balancing figure)	10,000
		By Balance c/d	1,70,000
	2,00,000		2,00,000

Plant & Machinery A/c

To Balance b/d	80,000	By P & L a/c –Depreciation	10,000
To Cash (Balancing figure)	1,30,000	By Balance c/d	2,00,000
	2,10,000		2,10,000

Adjusted P & L A/c

To General reserve	30,000	By Balance b/d	30,000
To Proposed dividend	50,000	By Operating profit	2,18,000
To Interim dividend	20,000		
To Provision for tax	45,000		
To Depreciation on plant & building	30,000		
To Goodwill written off	25,000		
To Balance c/d	48,000		
	2,48,000		2,48,000

Statement of Cash from Operation

Operating profit			2,18,000
Add :	Increase in creditors		28,000
			2,46,000
Less :	Increase in debtors	40,000	
	Increase in stock	32,000	
	Increase in B.R.	10,000	
	Decrease in B.P	4,000	
	Cash from operation		86,000
			1,60,000

Cash Flow Statement

Cash & Bank balance (31.12.96)	25,000	Redemption of 8% pref shares	50,000
Issue of equity shares	1,00,000	Proposed dividend of 1986 paid	42,000
Sale of building	10,000	Income tax paid	35,000
Cash from operation	1,60,000	Plant purchased	1,30,000
		Interim dividend paid	20,000
		Closing cash & bank balance	18,000
	2,95,000		2,95,000

Problem 18 : Following are balance sheets of X Co. for 1996 and 1997 :

Liabilities	*1996*	*1997*
Shareholders fund	60,000	70,000
Long-term loan	–	15,000
Outstanding salaries	2,000	2,000
Provision for tax	3,000	5,000
Creditors	5,000	8,000
Bills payable	20,000	–
	90,000	1,00,000
Assets		
Buildings	50,000	55,000
Other fixed assets	8,000	5,000
Investments	5,000	7,000
Stock	12,000	15,000
Debtors	10,000	15,000
Cash	5,000	3,000
	90,000	1,00,000

Profit & loss a/c for the year ending 31.12.97

Net Sales		50,000
Expenses :		
Cost of goods sold	25,000	
Administration and selling expenses	5,000	
Depreciation on building	5,000	
Interest	1,000	
		36,000
		14,000
Provision for tax (50%)		7,000
		7,000
Profit & loss a/c on 1.1.97		40,000
		47,000
Dividend paid		3,000
Profit & loss a/c on 31.12.97		44,000

Prepare Cash Flow Statement

(*Bangalore University, B.Com., April 1998*)

Solution :

Buildings A/c

To Balance b/d	50,000	By P & L a/c depreciation	5,000
To Cash-purchases	10,000	By Balance c/d	55,000
	60,000		60,000

Provision for tax

To Cash-tax paid	5,000	By Balance b/d	3,000
To Balance c/d	5,000	By P & L a/c	7,000
	10,000		10,000

Adjusted P & L A/c

To Depreciation on building	5,000	By Balance b/d	40,000
To Provision for tax	7,000	By Operating profit	18,000
To O/s expenses	2,000		
To Balance c/d	44,000		
	58,000		58,000

Cash from Operation

Operating profit		18,000
Add : Increase in creditors		3,000
		21,000
Less : Increase in Debtors	5,000	
Increase in stock	3,000	
Decrease in B.P	20,000	
		28,000
Cash lost in operation		7,000

Cash Flow Statement

Opening cash balance	5,000	Tax paid	5,000
Issue of share capital	10,000	Purchase of building	10,000
Long-term loan	15,000	Interest paid	1,000
Sale of fixed assets	3,000	Dividend paid	3,000
		O/s expenses paid	2,000
		Purchase of investment	2,000
		Cash lost in operation	7,000
		Closing cash balance	3,000
	33,000		33,000

QUESTIONS

Simple questions

1. What is cash flow?
2. Distinguish between 'Fund' and 'Cash'.
3. State the objectives of cash flow analysis.
4. State limitations of cash flow analysis.
5. How are cash flows classified?
6. What are cash flows from operating activities?
7. What are cash flows from investing activities?
8. What are the cash flows from financing activities?
9. What is meant by historical cash flow statement?
10. What is meant by projected cash flow statement?
11. What do you mean by actual cash flow.
12. What is meant by notional cash flow?
13. What is cash flow statement?

Short Answer Question

1. Explain the utility of cash flos statement.
2. Distinguish between fund flow statement and cash flow statement.
3. State the various sources and uses of cash flow.

Exercise 1 (Cash from Operation) : From the following information, you are required to calculate cash from operations :

	31.12.96	*31.12.97*
Net profit for the year	—	35,000
Debtors	21,000	20,000
Bills receivable	4,000	6,500
Creditors	23,500	25,000
Bills payable	7,500	5,000
Stock	29,000	32,500

(*Osmania University, B.Com., October 1998*)

(*Answer* : Cash from operation Rs. 29,000)

Exercise 2 : Following information is available from the books of Standard Company Ltd. :

	1994-95	*1993-94*
Profit made during the year	2,50,000	—
Income received in advance	500	600
Prepaid expenses	1,600	1,400
Debtors	80,000	95,000
Bills receivable	25,000	20,000
Creditors	45,000	40,000
Bills payable	13,000	15,000
Outstanding expenses	2,500	2,000
Accrued income	1,500	1,200

Calculate cash flow from operation (*CS, Inter, December 1996*)

[*Answer* : Cash from operation Rs. 2.62,900]

Exercise 3 : The current assets and current liabilities of the business for the years ending 31st December 1992 and 1993 are as follows :

Compute cash from operation, given profit for the year 1993 is Rs. 10,000 after providing depreciation of Rs. 2,000.

	31.12.92	*31.12.93*
Sundry debtors	10,000	12,000
Provision for bad debts	1,000	1,200
Bills receivable	4,000	30,000
Bills payable	5,000	6,000
Sundry creditors	8,000	9,000
Inventories	5,000	8,000
Short-term investments	10,000	12,000
O/s expenses	1,000	1,500
Prepaid expenses	2,000	1,000
Accrued income	3,000	4,000
Income received in advance	2,000	1,000

(*University of Madras, B.Com., September 1994*)

[*Answer* : Cash from operation Rs. 7,700]

Exercise 4 (Cash Flow Statement): The following are the Balance Sheets of X Ltd. on 1.1.1996 and 31.12.1996:

	1.1.96	*31.12.96*		*1.1.96*	*31.12.96*
Capital	1,25,000	1,53,000	Cash	10,000	47,000
Bank loan	40,000	50,000	Sundry debtors	30,000	50,000
Loan from Financial Co.	25,000	—	Stock	35,000	25,000
			Machinery	80,000	55,000
Sundry creditors	40,000	44,000	Land	40,000	50,000
P & L a/c	1,00,000	1,20,000	Buildings	35,000	60,000
			Goodwill	1,00,000	80,000
	3,30,000	3,67,000		3,30,000	3,67,000

Additional Information

1. Dividend paid during the year amounted to Rs. 15,000.
2. Rs. 20,000 worth of machinery was sold prepare the cash flow statement from the above particulars.

(Osmania University, B.Com., March 1997)

[*Asnwer* : Total of cash flow statement Rs. 1,42,000]

Exercise 5 : The following are the balance sheets of Mrs. Sridhar:

	1.1.96	*31.12.96*		*1.1.96*	*31.12.96*
Capital	2,96,000	3,08,000	Cash	8,000	7,200
Hire-purchase	—	40,000	Debtors	70,000	75,800
Vendor			Stock	50,000	44,000
Loan from bank	60,000	50,000	Land	40,000	60,000
Current liabilities	72,000	82,000	Buildings	1,00,000	1,10,000
Mrs. Sridhar's loan	—	40,000	Machinery less dep.	1,60,000	1,72,000
			Delivery van		50,000
	4,28,000	5,20,000		4,28,000	5,20,000

The delivery van was purchased on hire-purchase basis in December 1996, a payment of Rs. 10,000 was made at the time of agreement and the balance amount is to be paid in 20 monthly instalments of Rs. 2,000 each together with interest @ 12% p.a. During the year the proprietor with draw Rs. 52,000 for household expenses. The provision for depreciation on machinery as on 1.1.96 was Rs. 54,000 and on 31.12.96 was Rs. 72,000. You are required to prepare a cash flow statement.

(Sri Sathya Sai University, B.Com. (Hons) March 1997)

[*Answer* : Total of Cash Flow Statement Rs. 1,39,200]

Exercise 6 : Following are the summarised balance sheets of Mayur Industries Private Ltd. as on 31st March 1995 and 31st March, 1996.

Balance Sheet

	1996	*1995*
Assets		
Premises	4,75,000	5,00,000
Machinery	4,22,500	3,75,000
Equipments	40,500	45,000
Stock	74,000	1,00,000
Sundry debtors	1,60,000	2,00,000
Cash	7,000	3,000
Bank	10,000	—
Goodwill	—	12,500
	11,89,000	12,35,500
Liabilities		
Share capital	5,00,000	5,00,000
General reserve	1,50,000	1,25,000
Profit & loss a/c	76,500	76,250
Term loan from ICICI	1,55,000	1,75,000
Sundry creditors	2,31,250	2,75,000
Provision for taxation	76,250	84,250
	11,89,000	12,35,000

Other Information

(*i*) Interim dividend of Rs. 25,000 was paid during the year.
(*ii*) Depreciation on Premises is provided at 5%
(*iii*) Machinery of Rs. 75,000 was a acquired during the year.
(*iv*) Income tax provision for the year was Rs. 75,000.

Prepare (*a*) cash flow statement, (*b*) statement showing cash from operation.

(*University of Mumbai, B.Com., October 1997*)

[*Answer* : Total of cash flow statement Rs. 2.20,000; Cash from operation Rs. 2,17,000]

Exercise 7 : The balance sheet of Yash Ltd. as on 31st December, 1995, 1996 are as under :

(*Figures in thousand*)

	31.12.95	*31.12.96*		*31.12.95*	*31.12.96*
Equity share capital	350	400	Fixed assets	210	320
General reserve	20	—	Stock	90	140
P & L a/c	40	—	Sundry debtors	60	55
Secured loan	—	180	Bills receivable	50	75
Sundry creditors	30	45	Investments	70	40
Bills payable	50	25	Cash	30	20
O/s expenses	10	30	P & L a/c	—	30
Unpaid dividend	10	—			
	510	680		510	680

Accumulated Depreciation was Rs. 60,000 on 31st December, 1995 and on 31st December, 1996. It was Rs. 57,000. Machinery having written down value Rs. 90,000 was sold for Rs. 15,000 on 1.7.1996, plant costing Rs. 2,30,000 purchased on 1st July, 1996, prepare :

(*i*) Statement showing cash from operation.

(*ii*) Statement of cash flow for the year ended 31st December, 1996.

(*University of Mumbai, B.Com., April 1997*)

[*Answer* : (1) Total of cash flow statement Rs. 305 (000)

(2) Cash lost in operation (–) 45 (000)]

Exercise 8 : The financial position of M/s A and B on 1st July, 1994 and 30th June, 1995 was as follows :

	1.7.1994	*30.6.1995*
Cash	4,000	3,600
Debtors	35,000	38,400
Stock	25,000	22,000
Land	20,000	30,000
Buildings	50,000	55,000
Machinery	80,000	86,000
	2,14,000	2,35,000
Current liabilities	36,000	41,000
Mrs A's loan	—	20,000
Loan from bank	30,000	25,000
Capital	1,48,000	1,49,000
	2,14,000	2,35,000

During the year, the partners withdraw Rs. 26,000 for domestic expenditure. The provision for depreciation against machinery as on 1.7.1994 was Rs. 27,000 and on 30.6.1995 was Rs. 36,000.

You are required to prepare a cash flow statement. (*Sri Sathya Sai University, B.Com. (Hons), March 1996*)

[*Answer* : Total of cash flow statement Rs. 68,000]

Exercise 9 : From the following particulars prepare a cash flow statement of AB Traders :

	1.1.95	*31.12.95*
Cash	7,500	6,000
Debtors	60,000	67,500
Stock	45,000	37,500
Land	45,000	60,000
Building	75,000	82,500
Machinery	1,05,000	1,20,000
	3,37,500	3,73,500

Current liability	52,500	60,000
Loan from Mr. K	—	37,500
Bank loan	60,000	45,000
Capital	2,25,000	2,31,000
	3,27,500	3,73,500

During the year the firm brought in additional capital of Rs. 15,000 and the drawings during the year was Rs. 46,500.

Provision for depreciation on machinery; opening balance Rs. 45,000, closing balance Rs. 60,000. No depreciation need be provided on other assets. *(Bangalore University, B.B.M., November 1996)*

[*Answer* : Total of cash flow statement Rs. 1.20,000]

Exercise 10 : The following details are available from a Company:

	31.12.85	*31.12.86*		*31.12.85*	*31.12.86*
Share capital	70,000	74,000	Cash	9,000	7,800
Debentures	12,000	6,000	Debtors	14,900	17,700
Reserve for D.D	700	800	Stock	49,200	42,700
Trade creditors	10,360	11,840	Land	20,000	30,000
P & L a/c	10,040	10,560	Goodwill	10,000	5,000
	1,03,100	1,03,200		1,03,100	1,03,200

(*a*) Dividend paid Rs. 3,500.
(*b*) Land was purchased for Rs. 10,000.
(*c*) Amount provided for amortisation of goodwill Rs. 5,000.
(*d*) Debentures paid off Rs. 6,000.

Prepare cash flow statement. *(University of Madras, B.Com., September 1996)*

[*Answer :* Cash flow from operation Rs. 14,300
Total of cash flow statement Rs. 27,300]

Exercise 11 : The following are the Summarised balance sheets of M/s Rahul Brothers Private Limited as on March 31, 1992 and 1993 :

	1992	*1993*		*1992*	*1993*
7% Redeemable preferecen shares	—	1,000	Fixed assets	4,100	4,000
Equity shares	4,000	4,000	*Less* : Depreciation	1,100	1,500
General reserve	200	200		3,000	2,500
P & L a/c	100	120	Debtors	2,000	2,400
Debentures	600	700	Stock	3,000	3,500
Creditors	1,200	1,100	Prepaid expenses	30	50
Provision for taxation	300	420	Cash	120	350
Proposed dividend	500	580			
Bank overdraft	1,250	680			
	8,150	8,800		8,150	8,800

(University of Madras, B.Com., May 1996)

[*Answer :* Cash from operation 400
Total of cash flow statement Rs. 470]

7

MARGINAL COSTING

ABSORPTION COSTING

Absorption costing is a conventional technique of ascertaining the cost of production. It is, therefore, sometimes referred to as 'orthodox costing'. It is a technique of ascertaining cost of goods or services manufactured under which both variable and fixed cost are taken into cosideration. As under this technique all costs—fixed and variable—are taken into account, it is also known as 'full costing' technique. The total or 'full' cost is classified on the functional basis into production cost, administration cost, selling and distribution cost. Under this technique, the total cost per unit remains constant only when the level of output remains same from time to time. But in today's dynamic world the level of activity differs from time to time and so does the cost. The cost of production may be Rs. 18 today and Rs. 20 next week. This change in the cost of production is on account of change in the volume of output and the way in which fixed cost tend to behave. The differences in the cost of production from time to time often poses a problem to the management in decision-making process. Hence, the marginal costing technique is used to enable management in carrying out its day-to-day functions of planning, decision-making and controlling. However, the proponents of absorption costing technique argue that both fixed and variable costs must be charged to the cost of production in order to meet the requirements of generally accepted accounting principles and income tax reporting.

The total cost under this technique is classified into two types, *viz.*, (*i*) production cost and (*ii*) period cost. These costs are further classified into various types of costs. These costs are shown in the following chart :

COST CLASSIFICATION UNDER ABSORPTION COSTING

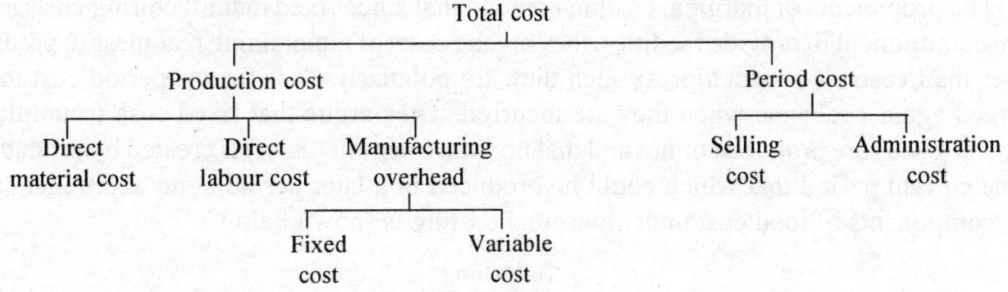

Fig. 7.1 : Chart showing total components of total cost under absorption costing.

MARGINAL COSTING

Before dealing with the marginal costing technique, it would be appropriate at this stage to know the meaning and definition of 'marginal cost'.

Marginal Cost

From the Economist's point of view, the cost incurred in producing an additional unit of product is known as marginal cost. However, from the cost accounting point of view marginal cost applies to the total cost obtained by adding prime cost and variable cost. In other words all costs other than fixed costs are the marginal cost.

The ICMA Terminology defines marginal cost as 'the amount at any given volume of output by which aggregate costs are changed if the volume of output is increased or decreased by one unit. In practice, this is measured by the total variable costs attributable to one unit. In this context a unit may be a single article, a batch of articles, an order, a stage of production capacity, a man hour, a process or a department. It relates to change in output in the particular circumstance under consideration.

Marginal Costing

This is one of the technique of ascertaining cost of production of goods or services manufactured. It is not a method of costing but it could be used in conjunction with any method of costing such as job or process costing. This technique can also be used along with other techniques of costing such as standard costing and budgetary control. This technique is also known by other names such as direct costing, variable costing, attributable costing, out-of-pocket costing and so on. Whereas in USA it is termed as 'direct costing', in UK it is referred to as 'marginal costing'.

Definition of marginal costing : According to NAA Bulletin on Direct Costing Research Series 23, "direct costing should be defined as seggregation of manufacturing cost between those which are fixed and those which vary directly with volume. Only the prime cost plus variable factory overheads are used to value inventory and cost of sales. The remaining factory expenses are charged off currently to profit and loss account".

In simple words, marginal costing may be defined as "the ascertainment of marginal costs and the effect on profit of changes in volume by differentiating between fixed cost and variable cost".

It is a technique whereby marginal costs of cost units are ascertained. Only variable costs are charged to cost units. The fixed costs attributable to a relevant period being written off in full against the contribution for that period.

The term contribution represents excess of sales over total variable costs. Contribution is also sometimes called as marginal income.

The proponents of marginal costing contend that since fixed manufacturing costs arise from commitment to provide facilities, they are the costs of maintaining readiness to produce rather than costs of producing. As such they are popularly classified as period cost to be charged against revenue when they are incurred. They argue that fixed cost accumulates whether goods are produced or not and that no future benefit (asset) is created by producing in the current period that which could be produced in a later period at no additional cost. The components of total cost under marginal costing is shown below :

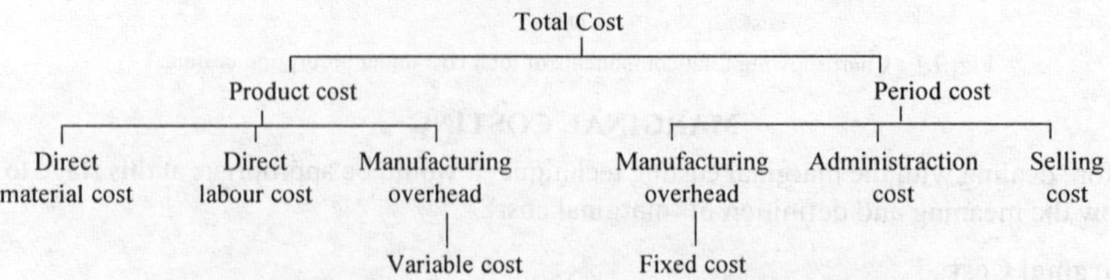

Fig. 7.2 : Chart showing components of total cost under marginal costing.

Theory of marginal costing : The theory of marginal costing is very clearly laid down by the ICMA, London, in the booklet on *A Report on Marginal Costing*. It can be stated thus; in relation to a given volume of output, additional output can normally be obtained at less than proportionate cost because within limits the aggregate of certain items of cost will tend to remain fixed and only the aggregate of the remainder will tend to rise proportionately with the increase in output. Coversely, a decrease in the volume of output will normally be accompanied by a less than proportionate fall in the aggregate cost. In simple words, when the volume of output increases the cost per unit will decrease. Similarly, if the volume of output is reduced, the cost per unit will increase. For example, if a company produces 100 units at a cost of Rs. 200, and by increasing the output by 2 units, the cost goes up to Rs. 204. The marginal cost of the increased output is Rs. 4.

Features of marginal costing : The features of marginal costing may be summarised under the following points :

(*a*) It is a technique of costing used to ascertain the marginal cost and to know impact of variable cost on the volume of output.

(*b*) All costs are classified on the basis of variability into fixed and variable cost. Semi-variable costs are segregated into fixed and variable costs.

(*c*) Variable costs alone are charged to production. Fixed costs are recovered from contribution.

(*d*) Stock of work-in-progress and finished goods are valued on the basis of marginal cost.

(*e*) Selling price is based on marginal cost plus the contribution.

(*f*) Profit is calculated not in the usual manner. When marginal cost is deducted from sales it gives rise to contribution. When fixed cost is deducted from conbtribution it results in profit.

(*g*) Break-even analysis and cost-volume-profit analysis (discussed in the next chapter) are integral part of this technique.

(*h*) The profitability of product or department is based on contribution made availabe by each department or product.

SIMILARITIES AND DISSIMILARITIES BETWEEN ABSORPTION AND MARGINAL COSTING

Similarities

1. Both the techniques agree that fixed and variable administration and selling expenses are period cost.
2. Both agree that the variable manufacturing costs are product cost.
3. Both agree that marginal costing presents the data for internal use.

Dissimilarities

Absorption Costing	*Marginal Costing*
1. All costs are charged to the cost of production.	1. Only variable cost is charged to cost of production. Fixed costs are recovered from contribution.
2. Stock of work-in-progress and finished goods are valued at full or	2. Stock of work-in-progress and finished goods are valued at marginal

Absorption Costing	Marginal Costing
total cost. Fixed costs are carried over from one period to another period which distort cost comparison.	cost. This facilitates cost comparison.
3. The differences between sales and total cost constitute profit.	3. The excess of sales revenue over variable cost is known as contribution. When fixed cost is deducted from contribution, it results in profit.
4. The apportionment of fixed costs on an arbitrary basis gives rise to under or over absorption of overheads.	4. As only variable costs are charged to products, it does not give rise to over or under absorption of overheads.
5. Costs are classified according to functional basis such as production cost, administration cost, selling and distribution cost.	5. Costs are classified according to variability.

Cost Presentation under Absorption and Marginal Costing

The difference between absorption and marginal costing in respect of cost ascertainment and cost presentation can be better understood by considering the following problems :

Problem 1 (Without stock balance) : Given the following data :

	Rs.
Direct material cost per unit	5.00
Direct labour cost per unit	9.00
Variable manufacturing overhead per unit	0.60
Total fixed manufacturing overhead per year	92,000
Number of units produced per year	10,000

Calculate the cost of production per unit under (*1*) absorption costing and (*2*) marginal costing.

Solution : **Statement of cost under absorption and marginal costing**

	Absorption costing	*Marginal costing*
Direct material cost	5.00	5.00
Direct labour cost	9.00	9.00
Variable manufacturing cost	0.60	0.60
Fixed mfg. cost $\frac{92,000}{10,000}$	9.20	—
Cost of production per unit	23.80	14.60

Note : Under marginal costing fixed manufacturing cost of Rs. 92,000 is treated as period cost.

Problem 2 (When closing stock balance is given) : Considering the data given in the above problem and the following additional information. Calculate the profit under (*i*) absorption costing and (*ii*) marginal costing.

Opening stock of finished goods	*NIL*
Units produced	10,000
Units sold	8,000
Sale price per unit	Rs. 35
Variable selling and administration expenses	Rs. 1.20 per unit sold
Fixed administration and selling expenses	Rs. 58,000

Solution : **Statement of profit under absorption and marginal costing**

Absorption costing

Sales 8,000 × 35			2,80,000
Opening stock		NIL	
Add : Cost of goods produced 10,000 × 23.80		2,38,000	
(as per the Ist problem)			
		2,38,000	
Less : Closing Stock 2,000 × 23.80		47,600	1,90,400
			89,600
Less : Selling and distribution expenses			
Fixed	58,000		
Variable 8,000 × 1.20	9,600		67,600
Profit			22,000

Marginal costing

Sales 8,000 ×35			2,80,000
Opening Stock		NIL	
Add : Cost of goods produced (10,000 × 14.60)		1,46,000	
		1,46,000	
Less : Closing Stock 2,000 × 14.60		29,2000	1,16,800
			1,63,200
Less : Variable selling and administration expenses			
contribution			9,600
			1,53,600
Less : Fixed cost :			
Mfg. Overhead	92,000		
Fixed selling & Admn. exp.	58,000		1,50,000
Profit			3,600

The difference in the profit of Rs. 18,400 (22,000 – 3,600) is because of the different accounting treatment of fixed manufacturing costs under marginal costing and absorption costing. Under the marginal costing, the fixed manufacturing costs are accounted for as a period cost and the entire fixed manufacturing cost of Rs. 92,000 is deducted in calculating profit. Under absorption costing, the fixed manufacturing costs are treated as a product cost and charged to 10,000 units produced during the year. This means the closing stock of finished goods of 2,000 units will 'absorb' a part of the fixed manufacturing cost. The valuation of closing stock of finished goods under absorption costing is shown below :

Variable manufacturing cost	2,000 × 14.60	= 29,200
Fixed manufacturing cost	2,000 × 9.20	= 18,400
Total manufacturing cost	2,000 units @ 23.80	= 47,600

The fixed manufacturing cost of Rs. 18,400 assigned to closing finished goods is carried forward in the balance sheet until these, 2,000 units are sold in the next accounting year. In fact the difference in the profit under the two methods shown earlier is this amount of Rs. 18,400. When this 2,000 units are sold, the fixed cost of Rs. 18,400 is deducted in the profit statement. In other words, under absorption costing, the total fixed manufacturing cost of Rs. 92,000 is divided between the unsold finished goods (18,400) and finished goods that are sold (73,600).

Thus, in calculating net profit under absorption costing only Rs. 73,600 of fixed manufacturing costs are included in cost of goods sold, whereas, under marginal costing the entire fixed manufacturing cost of Rs. 92,000 is included as part of the fixed cost in the profit statement.

COST BEHAVIOUR AND ITS IMPACT OVER MARGINAL COSTING

The concept of marginal costing is based on the behaviour of the costs with volume of output. The assumption is that some components of costs change directly in proportion to the change in volume of activity and some remain unchanged with the change in the activity level. The pattern of cost behaviour is the result of an interplay of many forces which cause some costs to fluctuate and others to remain constant. The most important of these forces are the following :

(a) Volume
(b) Inherent nature of the cost
(c) Capacity
(d) Managerial policies
(e) Effective control
(f) Prices of input factors
(g) Strikes and lockouts
(h) Weather and economic conditions

Accordingly, the costs can be classified on the basis of their behaviour into three types. They are as follows :

1. Fixed Cost

A fixed cost is defined as "a cost which accrues in relation to the passage of time and which within certain output and turnover limits tend to be unaffected by fluctuations in the level of activity, *i.e.*, output or turnover.

The key points in this definition are :

(1) Fixed costs are time related.
(2) It remains fixed within the limits of output or turnover.
(3) It is unaffected by changes in the level of activity.
(4) Though it is called fixed cost in the short run, in the long it may vary as for example when the policy of management is to expand after 10 years, fixed cost will increase no matter what volume of output is produced. Therefore, fixed cost is sometimes called as 'policy cost'.

Fixed costs are of two types. They are as follows :

(a) **Committed cost :** These costs are related to the provision of a capacity to do business. The amount of committed costs is fixed by decisions which were made in the past and is not subject to management control in the present on a short run basis. Since there is no direct relationship between committed costs and either the planned or actual utilisation of existing facilities, the amount will remain constant over the whole range of operating activity.

(b) **Programmed or managed cost :** These costs are related to the utilisation of the capacity provided :

Fixed cost can be shown graphically as under :

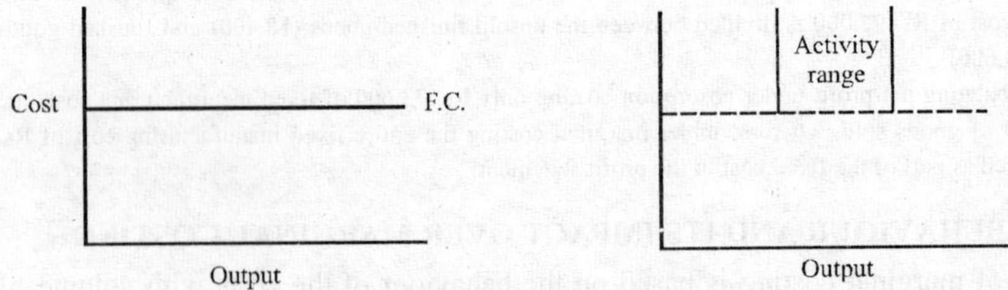

Fig. 7.3 : Graphic presentation of fixed cost.

Fixed cost can be expressed algebraically thus :

Cost = a

where 'a' is contant, 'v' the volume of output does not appear in this equation to indicate the change in activity is deemed not to affect the fixed cost.

2. Variable Cost

It is defined as a cost which, in the aggregate, tends to vary in direct proportion to changes in the volume of output or turnover.

Variable costs are of two types. They are as follows :

(*A*) Linear variable cost or engineered cost : When the relationship between variable cost and output can be shown as a straight line on a graph, they are termed as linear variable cost. This is shown graphically below :

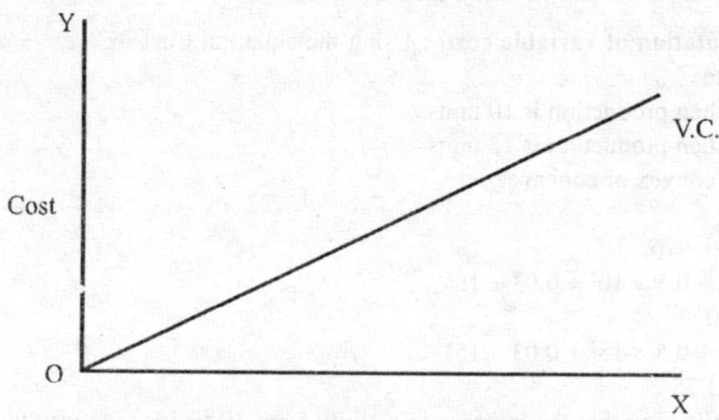

Fig. 7.4 : Graph showing linear variable cost.

A variable cost is called as engineered cost because an optimum relationship can be carefully determined by work measurement technique between input and output. Direct material cost and direct labour cost are good examples of engineered cost.

For calculation and analysis it is more convenient to express the linear relationship algebraically, thus

Cost = bx

where x is the volume of output in units, b is a constant representing the variable cost per unit.

(B) Non-linear or curvilinear variable cost : When the relationship between variable cost and output can be shown as a curved line on a graph, it is said to be curvilinear. This is shown graphically below :

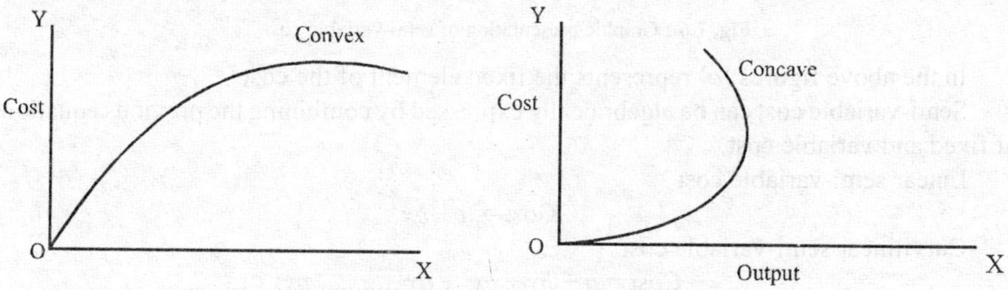

Fig. 7.5 : Graphic presentation on non-linear variable cost

The non-linear variable cost may be of two types. They are as follows :

(*a*) *Convex-linear variable cost :* It is a cost where each extra unit of output causes a less than proportionate increase in cost.

(*b*) *Concave-linear variable cost* : It is a cost where each extra unit of output causes a more than proportionate increase in cost. Differential piece rate system of wage payment is a good example for this type of cost.

Curvilinear variable cost—the parabola : When the slope of the cost function changes uniformly with changes in output, the curve is known as a parabola and is algebraically expressed thus :

Cost : $bx + cx^2 + dx^3$ ....px^4

where x is as defined previously and $b, c, d,$ .... p are constant.

Problem 3 (Calculation of variable cost) : Using the equation Cost $bx + cx^2 + dx^3$, where $b = 8$, c = 0.5 and $d = 0.03$, calculate

(*i*) variable cost when production is 10 units.

(*ii*) variable cost when production is 15 units.

Is the function convex or concave?

Solution :

Cost = $bx + cx^2 + dx^3$

$8 \times 10 + 0.5 \times 10^2 + 0.03 + 10^3$

Rs. 160

= $8 \times 15 + 0.5 \times 15^2 + 0.03 \times 15^3$

= Rs. 333.75

From the above it is seen that the increase in activity from 10 to 15 units results in more than a doubling of variable cost. This shows that there is a more than proportionate increase in the unit cost of extra production. Hence the function is concave.

3. Semi-variable Cost

It is defined as a cost containing both fixed and variable elements, which is, therefore partly affected by fluctuation in the volume of output or turnover. It is also sometimes called as a stepped cost or hybrid cost.

Semi-variable cost can be shown graphically thus :

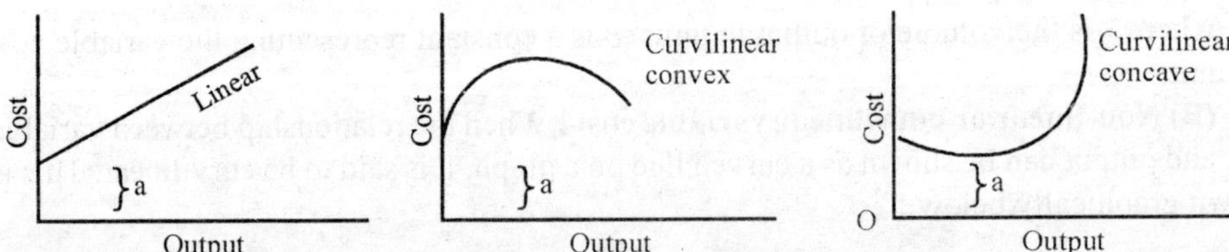

Fig. 7.6 : Graphic presentation of semi-variable cost.

In the above figures '*a*' represents the fixed element of the cost.

Semi-variable cost can be algebraically expressed by combining the previous equations of fixed and variable cost.

Linear semi-variable cost

$$\text{Cost} = a + bx$$

Curvilinear semi-variable cost

$$\text{Cost} = a + bx + cx^2 + dx^3 \text{ .... } px^4$$

Problem 4 (Calculation of total cost) : The analysis of repairs department of Jain & Co. shows that there is a fixed cost of Rs. 500 per month and a variable cost related to machine hours amounting to Rs. 2.25 per machine hour.

What is the expected cost for a month when the budgeted activity level is (*i*) 1,500 machine hours and (*ii*) 1,800 machine hours.

Solution :

Total cost	=	$a + bx$
(*i*)		500 × 2.25 (1,500)
	=	Rs. 3,875
(*ii*)		500 × 2.25 (1,800)
	=	Rs. 4,550

As, under marginal costing technique, only variable cost alone is charged to the product, it becomes necessary to segregate semi-variable cost into fixed and variable cost. Besides this, the segregation of semi-variable cost into fixed and variable has the following uses :

1. It facilitates budgeting the expenses for various levels of production.
2. It helps in exercising control over variable cost once semi-variable cost is segregated into fixed and variable.
3. It helps in fixing prices especially during the period of depression.
4. It helps in making useful decisions.

Methods of Segregating Semi-variable Cost

1. High-low method : This method is based on the analysis of past records of expenses.

This method takes into account only the highest and lowest values contained in the data in order to determine the rate of cost change and thereafter variable cost. The variable cost is then deducted from total cost to get fixed cost.

Limitations : (*i*) It is not based on all the items of the given data.

(*ii*) It assumes that the variable portion of semi-variable cost has linear relationship. In other words, the variable portion of cost per unit is constant which is not always true.

Steps involved : 1. Take the difference between high and low costs.

2. Take the difference between level of activity corresponding these costs.
3. Divide the difference in cost by the difference in level of activity. We get variable cost per unit.
4. Find out the variable cost by multiplying the rate so obtained under step 3 by the number of units.
5. Deduct this variable cost from semi-variable cost to get fixed cost.

Problem 5 (Segregation of semi-variable cost under high-low method) : From the following data segregate the semi-variable cost into fixed and variable cost under High-Low method.

Level of activity (Units)	*Cost (Rs.)*	*Level of activity (Units)*	*Cost (Rs.)*
36	800	72	950
48	700	75	1,170
49	970	76	1,020
55	790	82	1,200
57	1,050	86	1,060
59	900	92	1,100
65	880	94	1,310
66	1,020	97	1,250
67	1,180		

Solution :

High point	94 units at a cost of Rs.	1,310
Low point	48 units at a cost of Rs.	700
Difference	46	610

$$\text{Variable cost per unit} = \frac{610}{46} = 13.26 \text{ per unit.}$$

Semi-variable cost at 48 units = Rs. 700

Less : Variable cost 48 × 13.26	=	Rs.	636
Fixed cost	=	Rs.	64

In this process for each level of activity, fixed cost and variable cost can be found out.

2. Scatter graph technique : This is a graphic method of segregating semi-variable cost into fixed and variable cost. This method is also known as regression line method. This method is also based on past data, but it takes into account all the data when compared to the high-low method. The following steps are involved under this method :

(1) On the *X*-axis is taken to represent the output sales.

(2) On the *Y*-axis the cost is represented.

(3) Plot the points on the graph.

(4) Draw a line through the points plotted, with the same number of points on each side of the line. In the process of drawing the line ignore any abnormal cost if there is any. The line so drawn is known as the line of best fit.

(5) Extend the line so drawn above the *Y*-axis. The point where the line of best fit intersects the Y-axis is taken to be the amount of fixed cost.

One main limitation of this method is that there will be a change in fixed cost even if there is a slight bias in drawing the straight line.

Problem 6 (Scatter graph method of segregating semi-variable cost into fixed and variable cost) : From the following data extracted from the books of Arun Food Products Ltd. Calculate the fixed cost using scatter graph method :

Output (units)	*Semi-variable cost (Rs.)*	*Output (units)*	*Semi-variable cost (Rs.)*
500	2,500	900	3,700
600	2,800	840	3,520
700	3,100	800	3,400
940	3,820	860	3,580
740	3,220	760	3,280
880	3,640	540	2,620

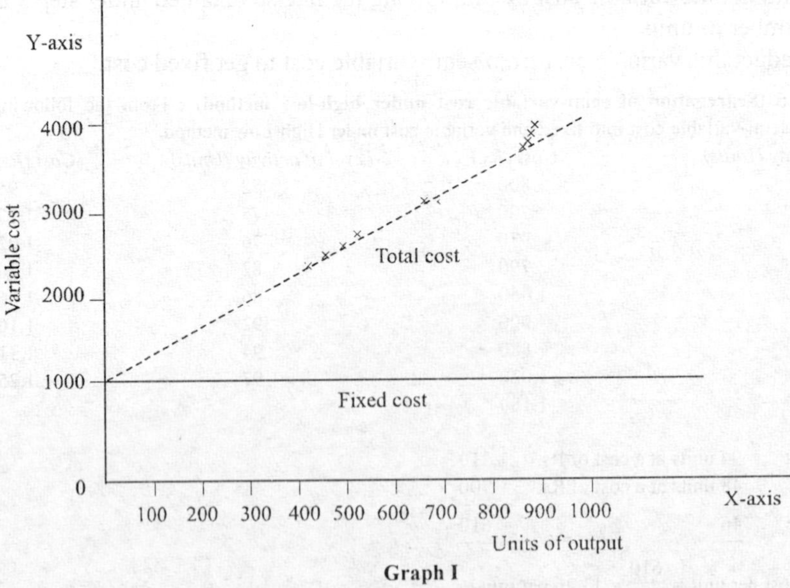

Y-axis

4000

3000

Variable cost

Total cost

2000

1000

Fixed cost

0

100 200 300 400 500 600 700 800 900 1000

X-axis

Units of output

Graph I

Solution : From the graph it is clear that fixed cost is Rs. 1,000.

(3) Method of least squares : This is a statistical method used for establishing a line of best fit to data. The linear cost function can be represented by the following equation :

$$y = a + bx$$

where y = cost. Other symbols are as defined previously.

To find out the values of '*a*' and '*b*' which are constants, we have to solve two simultaneous equations

$$\Sigma y = an + b\,\Sigma x$$

$$\Sigma xy = a\Sigma x + b\Sigma x^2$$

Where n = number of pairs of cost and activity figures.

Problem 7 (Simultaneous equation method of segregating semi-variable cost) : From the following data obtain an equation to indicate the linear cost function under the method of least squares :

Unit x	*Cost y*
4	56
5	62
7	80
7	72
9	88
10	94

Solution :

x	y	xy	x^2
4	56	224	16
5	62	310	25
7	80	560	49
7	72	504	49
9	88	792	81
10	94	940	100
$\Sigma x = 42$	$\Sigma y = 452$	$\Sigma xy = 3{,}330$	$\Sigma x^2 = 320$

Σy	=	$ax + b\Sigma x^2$
Σxy	=	$a\Sigma x + b\Sigma x^2$
452	=	$6a + 42b \times 7$
3,330	=	$42a + 320b$
3,164	=	$42a + 294b$
3,330	=	$42a + 320b$

Subtracting

$$166 = 26b$$

$$b = 6{,}385$$

Substituting the value of b in equation 1

$6a + 42b$	=	452
$6a$	=	$-42 \times 6.385 + 452$
$6a$	=	$-268 + 452$
a	=	30.6

∴ The linear cost function is $y = 30.6 + 6.385x$

When the given problems has many digits of variables and costs, it becomes difficult to adopt the above method. An alternate method which could be termed as short-cut method or indirect method can be followed in such situations. The steps involved under this method are as follows :

(*a*) Calculate the average of '*x*' series. This is found out by the formula $x = \frac{\Sigma x}{N}$.

(*b*) Calculate the average of '*y*' series. This is found out the formula $y = \frac{\Sigma y}{N}$

(c) Take the deviations from the average of 'x' series for each and every item of 'x' series.
(d) Take the deviations from the average of 'y' series for each and every item of 'y' series.
(e) Square the deviations of 'x' series to get x^2.
(f) Obtain the products of the deviations of 'x' and 'y' series. This is denoted under the column 'xy'.
(g) Add up the products so obtained under step (f) and denote it with Σxy.
(h) Apply the following formula $b = \frac{\Sigma xy}{\Sigma x^2}$

Problem 8 (Short-cut or indirect method of segregating semi-variable cost) : The following semi-variable costs are taken from Ajanta Metal Works for the period January to June, 1993 :

Month	*Machine hours*	*Semi-variable cost*
Jan.	2,000	300
Feb.	2,200	320
Mar.	1,700	270
Apr.	2,400	340
May	1,800	280
June	1,900	290

Find out the amount of variable and fixed cost.

Solution :

Month	*Machine hours (x)*	*Semi-variable Cost (y)*	*Deviations from x (2,000)*	*Deviations from y (300)*	x^2	xy
Jan.	2,000	300	0	0	0	0
Feb.	2,200	320	+200	+20	40,000	+4,000
Mar.	1,700	270	−300	−30	90,000	+9,000
Apr.	2,400	240	+400	+40	1,60,000	+16,000
May	1,800	280	−200	−20	40,000	+4,000
June	1,900	290	−100	−10	10,000	+1,000
	Σx = 12,000	Σxy = 1,800			Σxy = 3,40,000	Σxy = 34,000

$$x = \frac{\text{Total machine hrs}}{\text{No. of months}} = \frac{12,000}{6} = 2,000$$

$$y = \frac{\text{Total semi-variable cost}}{\text{No. of months}} = \frac{1,800}{6} = 300$$

$$b = \frac{\Sigma xy}{\Sigma x^2} = \frac{34,000}{3,40,000} = 0.10$$

The variable element of the semi-variable cost is 0.10 per unit.

The fixed cost can be calculated thus :

	y	=	$a + bx$
Jan.	300	=	$a + 2,000 \times 0.10$
	300	=	$a + 200$
	a	=	100
Feb.	320	=	$a + 2,200\ (0.10)$
	320	=	$a + 220$
	a	=	100

Fixed cost of Rs. 100 is thus same whatever may be the level of activity.

ARGUMENTS IN FAVOUR OF MARGINAL COSTING

The exclusion of fixed costs in the ascertainment of cost of production (marginal costing) is justified on the following grounds :

1. Fixed costs relate to a particular period of time and therefore, it should be charged for that period. Thus, it is treated as a period cost not as a product cost.

2. There is no accurate basis to apportion fixed cost. So it is charged to profit and loss account instead of charging to cost of production.
3. Since fixed cost remain constant irrespective of change in the level of activity, it does not affect production capacity. It is only variable cost that affects various levels of productive activity. Hence fixed cost is excluded from cost of production.
4. To facilitate cost comparison and to maintain accuracy of trading results, fixed costs are excluded from cost of production.
5. Fixed costs under absorption costing is carried over from one period to another as part of inventory value. Such carrying forward is not justified as it does not facilitate matching of cost with revenue.
6. For the current operation of any level of activity only variable cost alone is relevant but not the fixed cost. Hence it is excluded from cost of production.

MARGINAL COST EQUATION

The marginal cost equation is stated below :

Sales – Variable Cost = Contribution

or $S - V = C$

Contribution = Fixed cost + Profit

or $C = F.C. + P$

or $S - V = F.C. + P$

If there is loss

$S - V = FC - L$

At the point of no-profit-no-loss (break-even point)

$S - V = F + \text{Zero}$

The usefulness of marginal cost equation is, given any of the three pariticulars, we can find out the fourth unknown particular. From the above equation it is clear that contribution is used to meet fixed cost and any balance left out is equal to profit.

Problem 9 : From the following particulars extracted from the books of Sunshine Enterprises for the period ending 31st Dec., 1992. Find out the amount of profit.

Number of units produced	=	500 units
Variable cost for the period	=	Rs. 2 per unit
Fixed cost for the period	=	Rs. 800
Selling price per unit	=	Rs. 4

Solution :

Sales – Variable cost = Fixed cost + Profit

or Sales – Variable cost – Fixed cost = Profit

$500\,(4-2) - 800 = P$

$1{,}000 - 800 = P$

$P = \text{Rs. } 200$

MARGINAL COSTING AND VALUATION OF FINISHED STOCK

Under marginal costing technique closing stock is valued at marginal cost. However, under absorption costing, fixed cost is included in the value of closing stock. Because of this treatment the amount of fixed overhead charged under absorption costing for the current year will differ from the actual fixed overhead pertaining to that year. The reason is the amount of fixed cost carried down from the previous year, will differ from the amount of fixed cost carried forward to the next year. This can better be understood by the following examples :

> *Example :* On 1.1.92, Opening stock of finished goods of 2,000 units is valued at Rs. 4 of which fixed cost is Rs. 1.
>
> On 31.12.1992, closing stock of finished goods of 1,600 units valued at Rs. 5 per unit of which fixed cost is Rs. 1.50.

Value of fixed cost brought in is 2,000 (2,000 × Re. 1). Whereas the value of fixed cost carried forward is Rs. 2.400 (1.600 × 1.50).

If the actual fixed cost for the year 1992 is Rs. 50,000, then the fixed cost charged for the year will be Rs. 49,600 (50,000 + 2,000 – 2,400).

When compared to absorption costing, considering the output, sales and closing stock the following conclusions are arrived at :

1. When production volume is equal to sales volume, net profit is same under both marginal costing and absorption costing.
2. When sales are less than production, profit under marginal costing are less than that of absorption costing.
3. When sales exceed production, profit under marginal costing are more than that of absorption costing.

UTILITY, ADVANTAGES AND LIMITATIONS OF MARGINAL COSTING

Utility of Marginal Costing

1. It is used as one of the techniques of costing, *i.e.*, to ascertain the cost of production.
2. It aids management for making useful decision by providing useful information.
3. It serves as a tool of cost control.

Advantages

1. It avoids the complications of over or under absorption of fixed cost by excluding it from cost of production.
2. The technique provides useful data for managerial decision-making.
3. By not carrying forward fixed cost from period to period, it facilitates cost comparison.
4. The impact of profit on sales fluctuations are clearly shown under marginal costing.
5. The technique is flexible in the sense it can be used along with other techniques such as budgetary control and standard costing.
6. It establishes a clear relationships between cost, sales and volume of output and break-even analysis which shows the effect of increasing and decreasing production acitivity on the profitability of the company.
7. It provides useful data for the management in determination of policies regarding future production and sales.
8. Stock of work-in-progress and finished goods are valued at marginal cost, which is uniform.

Limitations

1. The segregation of semi-variable costs often poses a problem.
2. Closing stock of work-in-progress and finished goods are understated which is not acceptable to tax authorities.

3. With the change of technology and owing to automation of industries, it results in more fixed cost. Marginal costing fails to reflect the exact change because of adoption of new technology.
4. It does not provide any yardstick to exercise control. So an effective means of control cannot be exercised.
5. The technique is not suitable under cost plus contract because the technique ignores fixed cost in calculating total cost.
6. Variable cost per unit remains constant only in the short run but not in the long run.
7. Cost comparison of two jobs will be difficult. Though marginal costing may be same for both the jobs, yet a job which takes more time to complete involves more of overhead.
8. When sales are based on marginal cost or marginal cost with some contribution, it may result in losses or low profit.

PRECAUTIONS TO BE TAKEN WHILE ADOPTING MARGINAL COSTING

1. As fixed cost is not included in the cost of production, care must be taken to see that while fixing the selling price, profit is realised after full recovery of fixed cost.
2. It is necessary to check composition of marginal cost from time to time. There can be a change of variable cost into fixed and *vice versa* when production method is changed.
3. Based on contribution margin, orders are accepted with a view to increase profits. This may lead to uneconomic expansion in the business involving more capital. However, during the period of falling business this proves to be burden.

APPLICATIONS OF MARGINAL COSTING

The technique of marginal costing is largely used in the managerial decision-making process. The application of marginal costing in the day-to-day decision-making process are as follows :

1. Make or Buy Decision

Very often management is confronted with the problem of deciding whether to buy a component or product from an outside source or to manufacture the same if it is economical as compared to the price quoted by a supplier. In deciding this absorption costing (total cost analysis) would mislead. If the decision is to buy from an external source the price quoted by the supplier should be less than marginal cost. If the decision is to make within the organisation, the cost of production should include all additional cost such as depreciation on new plant interest on capital, etc. If this cost of production is less than the quotation price, it should be decided in making the product rather than procure it from an external source.

Problem 10 (Make or buy decision) : Expansion Ltd. manufactures automobiles accessories and parts. The following are the total costs of processing 1,00,000 units :

Direct materials cost	Rs. 5 lakhs
Direct labour cost	Rs. 8 lakhs
Variable factory overhead	Rs. 6 lakhs
Fixed factory overhead	Rs. 5 lakhs

The purchase price of the component is Rs. 22. The fixed overhead would continue to be incurred even when the component is bought from outside, although there would have been reduction to the extent of Rs. 2,00,000.

Required :

(*a*) Should the part be made or bought considering that the present facility when released following a buying decision would remain idle?

(*b*) In case the released capacity can be rented out to another manufacturer for Rs. 1,50,000 having good demand. What should be the decision? (*C.S., Inter, June 1990*)

Solution :

Cost Analysis

Particulars	*(1) Whether to make*	*(2) Whether to buy at Rs. 22 each present facility remaining idle*	*(3) Whether to buy at Rs. 22 each when released capacity is rented out*
1. Variable cost of production	19	–	–
2. Cost of buying from outside	–	22	22
3. Saving in fixed cost when bought	–	(2)	(2)
4. Rent receipt when idle capacity is rented out	–	–	(1.5)
	19	20	18.5

Recommendations :

1. For decision to situation (*a*)—make the component.
2. For decision to situation (*b*)—buy the component.

Problem 11 (Make or buy decision) : Stoner Company uses three different components (materials) in manufacturing its primary product. Stoner manufactures two of the components and purchases one (designated as component 1) from outside suppliers. The company is currently developing the annual profit plan. Sales are highly seasonal. Component 2 cannot be acquired from outsiders. However, component 3 can be purchased. The three components have critical specifications. The annual profit plan provided data for the following computations :

	Components 3 (Unit cost at 12,000 units)
Material (direct)	Rs. 1.40
Labour (direct)	Rs. 2.20
Factory overhead (apportioned)	Re. 0.40
Annual machine rental (special machine used only for component 3)	Rs. 0.50
Variable factory overhead	Rs. 1.00
Average storage cost per year (fixed)	Rs. 0.40
Total	Rs. 5.90
Average inventory level	500 units

The purchase manager investigated outside suppliers and found one that would sign a one year contract to deliver "12,000 top quality units as needed during the year at Rs. 5.20 per unit". Serious consideration is being given to this alternative. Should Stoner make or buy component 3? Explain the relevant factors influencing your decision. (*ICWA, Inter, Dec., 1988*)

Solution :

Total cost of component 3 can be bifurcated into fixed and variable portion as follows :

Variable cost :

Material (direct)	Rs. 1.40
Labour (direct)	Rs. 2.20
Annual machine rental (special machine used only for component 3)	Re. 0.50
Variable factory overhead	Re. 1.00
	Rs. 5.10

Fixed cost :		
Fixed overhead apportioned		Re. 0.40
Average storage cost per year		Re. 0.40
		Re. 0.80
	Total	Rs. 5.90

On comparison of the price offered by outside supplier with the variable cost, if made inhouse, it is observed that variable cost of inhouse production is lower (fixed cost remains same whether made in-house or purchased). This is also on the assumption that labour (direct) is variable if it is possible to get rid of the workers when required. Hence, labour cost is treated as fixed. If labour is treated as fixed, variable cost of inhouse production is Rs. 2.90 (5.10–5.20) per unit which is per unit less than the purchase price per unit (5.20 – 2.90 = 2.30).

Hence it is advisable to make component no. 3.

2. Comparing mannual with machine labour : Whenever a new product is launched management may have to decide whether the new product is to be manufacutured mannually or mechanically. Some of the factors which are to be considered in this regard are the (*i*) savings arising in the labour cost, (*ii*) additional investment on machinery, (*iii*) additional capacity of machine, (*iv*) the possible displacement of employees and (*v*) the danger of obsolescence of the machine. However, cost of production is the significant factor which determines the method of production. Under marginal costing that method which gives the largest contribution, *i.e.*, lowest marginal cost would be preferred. Under absorption costing that method of manufacture which gives lowest cost will be selected.

Problem 12 (Manual vs. machanical production) : The Navabharath Enterprise has a plan to introduce a new product A numbering 10,000 units for the year 1993. The following details are available :

	Machine (Rs.)	*Mannual labour (Rs.)*
Purchase price of machine	20,000	–
Direct material	5,000 PA	5,000 PA
Direct labout	500 PA	3,000 PA
Variable overheads	2,000 PA	1,000 PA
Fixed overheads (not including depreciation)	1,500 PA	1,00 PA

The selling price of the products has been fixed at Rs. 3 each. If the machines is purchased it will have an estimated life of 10 years with little or no residual; value.

You are required to show the decision to be taken regarding the method of production under (*i*) marginal costing and (*ii*) absoption costing including interest @ 5%.

Solution :

Statement of marginal cost

			Machine (Rs.)	*Mannual labour (Rs.)*
Sales			30,000	30,000
Less : Variable cost :				
Direct material	5,000	5,000		
Direct labour	500	3,000		
Variable overheads	2,000	1,000	7,500	9,000
Contribution			22,500	2,000

On this basis (the lower marginal cost and large contribution) the machine is preferable.

Statement of total cost

	Machine (Rs.)	Mannual labour (Rs.)
Direct material	5,000	5,000
Direct labour	500	3,000
Overheads : Variable	2,000	1,000
Fixed	1,500	1,000
Depreciation $\frac{1}{10} \times 20,000$	2,000	–
	11,000	10,000
Interest @ 5%	550	500
	11,550	10,500

From the above statement, mannual method of production is cheaper. This problem illustrates a weakness of the marginal costing. Obviously, fixed costs have to be covered as they are incurred on the specific products.

3. Replacing existing machinery with new machinery : Sometimes with a view to derive maximum efficiency an existing plant may have to be replaced by a new one. Again the guiding factors mentioned earlier will help in such decision-making process.

Problem 13 : A factory engaged in the manufacture of electronic goods has a ten-year old equipment depreciated on straight-line basis. The useful life of the equipment was estimated to be 20 years with a residual value of Rs. 3 lakhs (original cost of the equipment being Rs. 23 lakhs). The output of the equipment is 1,200 units per hour.

The management now proposes to install a new equipment worth Rs. 50 lakhs which has an estimated life of 15 years and a residual value of Rs. 5 lakhs. The payment terms for the new equipment include a part exchange provision of Rs. 6 lakhs in respect of the existing equipment. The output of the new equipment is 3,000 units per hour.

Other comparative annual cost data relating to the two equipments are as under :

	Existing equipment (Rs.)	New equipment (Rs.)
Wages	1,00,000	1,20,000
Repairs and maintenance	20,000	52,000
Consumables	3,20,000	4,80,000
Power	1,20,000	1,50,000
Allocation of fixed cost	60,000	80,000
Total hours run per year	2,400	2,400

You are required to prepare a comparative schedule showing total conversion cost as well as cost per 1,000 units after considering interest @ 10% on net cash out flow for procuring the new equipment and also for providing for the yearly recovery of the loss suffered in the transaction. *(ICWA, Inter, Dec. 1991)*

Solution :

Comparative statement of cost of equipment

	Existing equipment (Rs.)	New equipment (Rs.)
Capital cost of equipment including cost of installation	23,00,000	50,00,000
Less : Residual value	3,00,000	5,00,000
	20,00,000	45,00,000
Less : Depreciation written off	10,00,000	
	10,00,000	45,00,000

Comparative statement of operation cost of equipment

Annual depreciation	—New	–	3,00,000
(*See Note 1*)	—Old	1,00,000	70,000
Interest on capital (new cash outflow) (*See Note 2*)		–	4,40,000
Wages		1,00,000	1,20,000
Repairs and maintenance		20,000	52,000
Consumables		3,20,000	4,80,000
Power		1,20,000	1,50,000
Allocation of fixed expense		60,000	80,000
		7,20,000	16,92,000
Total hours run per annum		2,400	2,400
Operating cost per hour		Rs. 300	Rs. 705
Output per hour (units)		1,200	3,000
Operating cost per 1,000 unit		Rs. 250	Rs. 235

Therefore, there is a net saving in cost of Rs. 15 per, 1,000 units.

Working Note 1 : Depreciation on new equipment

$$= \frac{\text{Original cost} - \text{Residual value}}{\text{Estimated life}}$$

$$= \frac{45,00,000}{15} = 3,00,000$$

Depreciation (yearly recovery) on loss on sale of existing equipment

$$= \frac{\text{Book value of existing equipment} - \text{Part exchange value}}{\text{Residual life of existing equipment}}$$

$$= \frac{13,00,000 - 6,00,000}{10 \text{ years}} = \text{Rs. } 70,000$$

Working note 2 : Interest is calculated on net cash outflow in procuring the new equipment is Rs. 44,00,000 (Cost of old equipment Rs. 50 lakhs less part exchange value Rs. 6 lakhs).

4. Alternative use of plant or productive facility : To take advantage of alternative use of production facility or alternative use of plant it is necessary to know the contribution margin. That alternative which yields highest contribution margin shall be selected.

Problem 14 : The management of Alpha Co. Ltd. are considering the following two alternative proposals :

(*a*) A semi-automatic lathe costing Rs. 58,000. The annual cost for its operation being estimated at Rs. 42,000 and

(*b*) A fully automatic lathe costing Rs. 95,000 the annual costs for its operation being estimated at Rs. 38,000.

The life of each is estimated as 12 years with zero salvage value. The capacity of the automatic plant is assessed as 30% more than that of semi-automatic plant, but this extra capacity is likely to remain unutilised for two years. Using straight line depreciation with an interest charge of 6% on the capital investment. Make your recommendations as to which alternative is preferable.

Solution :

	Semi-automatic lathe	*Fully automatic lathe*
Purchase cost (Rs.)	58,000	95,000
Expenses on machines :		
Operating expenses	42,000	38,000
Depreciating $\frac{1}{12}$ of cost	4,833	7,917
Interest 6%	3,480	5,700
	50,313	51,617
Percentage increase		2.5%

In the first two years the semi-automatic lathe is more profitable because extra 30% capacity of fully automatic lathe is not utilised. But in the remaining 10 years the fully automatic lathe will be much more profitable because the extra cost incurred by that plant is only about 2.5%, whereas the extra output capacity is 30%. So the fully automatic lathe is preferable. However, it is assumed that (*i*) additional 30% output will have ready market and (*ii*) revenue from the same is more than the additional expenses imparted above.

Problem 15 : Given below are the details of cost of production of two products *X* and *Y* manufactured by Adam's Co. Pvt. Ltd. Both the products use the same raw materials.

	X	*Y*
% of total capacity utilised	60%	40%
Units produced	1,200	2,000
Selling price per unit	Rs. 2,000	Rs. 1,200
Cost per unit :		
Raw materials	Rs. 1,400	700
Direct labour	Rs. 200	150
Variable expense	Rs. 180	230
Contribution per unit	Rs. 220	10
Fixed overhead	Rs. 3,00,000	

Would you recommend increasing the capacity utilised on product *X*.

Solution :

	1		2		3	
	X	Y	X	Y	X	Y
Percentage of capacities	60%	40%	50%	50%	70%	30%
Units produced	1,200	2,000	1,000	2,500	1,400	1,500
Contribution per unit	220	120	220	120	220	120
Contribution	2,64,000	2,40,000	2,20,000	3,00,000	3,08,000	1,80,000
Total contribution	5,04,000		5,20,000		4,88,000	
Fixed overhead	3,00,000		3,00,000		3,00,000	
Net profit	2,04,000		2,20,000		1,88,000	

Thus by increasing capacity usage on product *Y* profit is increased whereas by increasing capacity usage on product *X*, profit is reduced.

This is so because contribution per unit percentage of capacity for product *X* is $\frac{2,64,000}{60\%}$ = Rs. 4,400 and for product *Y* is $\frac{2,400,000}{40\%}$ = Rs. 6,000. Hence it is better to increase 40% of the capacity utilised on product *Y* and not on product *X*.

5. Product-mix, profit planning and profit maximisation : Companies manufacturing varieties of products often have to decide which product-mix is more profitable. That product-mix which gives maximum contribution is to be considered as best product-mix. Similarly, profit planning is often considered so as to earn reasonable profit if not maximum profit. The profit planning is affected by factors such as (*i*) volume of output, (*ii*) product mix, (*iii*) costs to be incurred, (*iv*) prices to be charged and so on. Marginal costing techniques guides the management in this regard.

Problem 16 : The directors of *A* Ltd. are considering the sales budget for the budget period 1993. You are required to present to the board a statement showing the marginal cost of each product and to recommend which of the following product-mix should be adopted :

(*a*) 450 units of *A* and 300 units of *B*
(*b*) 900 unit of *A* only
(*c*) 600 units of *B* only
(*d*) 600 units of *A* and 200 units of *B*

The following additional information is furnished :

	Product A	Product B
Fixed overhead Rs. 10,000 p.a.		
Direct labour @ Re. 1 per hour	10 hrs.	15 hrs.
Variable overheads—100 % of labour		
Direct material	Rs. 20	Rs. 25
Selling price	Rs. 60	Rs. 100

Solution :

Marginal cost statement

	Product A	Product B
Direct materials	20	25
Direct labour	10	15
Variable overhead	10	15
Marginal cost	40	55
Contribution	20	45
Sales	60	100

Product-mix

(*i*) 450 units of *A* and 300 units of *B*

	A	*B*		*Total*
Contribution	9,000	13,500		22,500
Less : Fixed overheads				10,000
			Profit	12,500

(*ii*) 900 units of A

Contribution	18,000			18,000
Less : Fixed overheads				10,000
			Profit	8,000

(*iii*) 600 units of *B*

Contribution		17,000		27,000
Less : Fixed overhead				10,000
			Profit	17,000

(*iv*) 600 units of *A* and 200 units of *B*

Contribution	12,000	9,000		21,000
Less : Fixed overhead				10,000
			Profit	11,000

Thus alternative (*iii*) is the one recommended.

Problem 17 : From the following particulars find the most profitable product-mix and prepare a statement of profitability of that product-mix.

	Product A	*Product B*	*Product C*
Units budgeted to be produced and sold	1,800	3,000	1,200
Selling price per unit (Rs.)	60	55	50
Requirement per unit :			
Direct materials	5 kg.	3 kg.	4 kg.
Direct labour	4 hrs.	3 hrs.	2 hrs.
Variable overhead	Rs. 7	Rs. 13	Rs. 8
Fixed overhead	Rs. 10	Rs. 10	Rs. 10
Cost of direct material per kg.	Rs. 4	Rs. 4	Rs. 4
Direct labour hour rate	Rs. 2	Rs. 2	Rs. 2
Maximum possible units of sale	4,000	5,000	1,500

All the three products are produced from the same direct material using the same type of machines and labour, direct labour which is the key factor, is limited to 18,600 hours. *(C.A., Inter, May 1990)*

Solution : **Statement showing most profitable product-mix**

				A	*B*	*C*
Selling price per unit				60	55	50
Less : variable cost :						
Direct material	20	12	16			
Direct labour	8	6	4			
Variable overhead	7	13	8	35	31	28
Contribution				25	24	22
Contribution per hour = $\frac{\text{Contribution per unit}}{\text{Direct labour hour per unit}}$				$\frac{25}{4}$	$\frac{24}{3}$	$\frac{22}{2}$
				= 6.25	= 8	= 11
Ranking of most profitable product-mix				III	II	I

Statement of profitability of the most profitable product-mix.

	A	*B*	*C*	*Total*
Total contribution on unit sold	3,750	1,20,000	33,000	1,56,750
Less : Fixed cost	18,000	30,000	12,000	60,000
			Profit	96,750

Note : Here direct labour hour is the key factor and only 18,600 hours are avaiable to produce the three products. The available 18,600 hours are utilised in the order of the ranking assigned, i.e. product *C*, *B* an *A*.

The number of units of each product to be produced will depend upon the maximum possible sale of each product. The details of the products to be produced keeping in view of available hours and their ranking are as below :

		Total hrs. utilised
Product *C*	1,500 × 2 Hrs.	3,000
Product *B*	5,000 × 3 Hrs.	15,000
Product *A*	150 × 4 Hrs.	600
		18,600

Problem 18 : A farmer wants your recommendations for optimal mix of production for the coming year. The current data is given below :

	Items produced			
	A	*B*	*C*	*D*
Area occupied (acres)	25	20	30	25
Yield per acre (tonnes)	10	8	9	12
Sale price per tonne (Rs.)	1,000	1,250	1,500	1,350
Variable cost per acre :				
Material (Rs.)	700	600	950	900
Labour (Rs.)	2,000	2,500	3,000	3,700
Variable overhead (Rs.)	2,000	2,000	2,000	2,000
Fixed overhead	*(Rs.)*			
Cultivation and growing	1,00,000			
Harvesting and transport	2,40,000			
Land revenue	90,000			
Administration	1,10,000			
	5,40,000			

The land which is being used for producing items A and B can be used for either items but not items C and D. The land which is being used for producing items C and D can be used for either items but not for items A and B.

In order to provide adequate market service, the farmer must produce each year at least 40 tonnes each of A and B and 36 tons each of C and D.

You are requried to calculate the following :

(*a*) The profit for the current year and

(*b*) The profit for the production-mix which you would recommend. (*C.S., Inter, Dec., 1989*)

Solution : **Statement showing profit for the current year**

	Products			
	A	*B*	*C*	*D*
Sale value (per acre)	10,000	10,000	13,500	16,200
Variable cost (per acre)	4,700	5,100	5,950	6,600
Contribution per acre	5,300	4,900	7,550	9,600
Total acres	25	20	30	25
Total contribution	1,32,500	98,000	2,26,500	2,40,000
Total contribution ($A + B + C + D$)		6,97,000		
Less : Fixed cost		5,40,000		
Profit		1,57,000		

Statement of profit for the profitable product-mix

	A	*B*	*C*	*D*
Minimum required production (tonnes)	40	40	36	36
Yield per acre (tonnes)	10	8	9	12
Acre required for minimum production	4	5	4	3
Surplus area allocated to profitable production (*i.e.* A and B)	36	–	–	48
Total acres	40	5	4	51
Contribution per acre	5,300	4,900	7,550	9,600
Total contribution	2,12,000	24,500	30,200	4,89,600
Total contribution ($A + B + C + D$)	= 7,56,300			
Less : Fixed overhead	5,40,000			
Profit	2,16,300			

Note : The distribution of area to different products has been made in the manner given because the area is not interchangeable between all products but only partly interchangebale, *i.e.*, between A and B and C and D only. Therefore, the total area denoted to A and B is 45 acres (25 + 20) so that, on the basis of the per acre contribution, maximum possible land to the production of product A and similarly to product D.

6. Profitability of the department or products : The preparation of a departmental profit and loss account under marginal costing is useful in determining which department is making profit and which department is incurring a loss. This enables the management to decide whether a particular department must continue operation or it should be eliminated. The decision is taken by referring to the contribution made or loss incurred by the department or product.

Problem19 : A company produces three products. The cost data are as under :

		A	*B*	*C*
Direct materials		Rs. 64	152	117
Direct labour :				
Department	Rate per hour *(Rs.)*	Hrs.	Hrs.	Hrs.
1	5	18	10	20
2	6	5	4	7
3	4	10	5	20
Variable overhead		Rs. 16	9	21

Fixed overheads Rs. 4,00,000 per annum

The budget was prepared at a time, when the market was sluggish. The budgeted quantities and selling prices are as under :

Product	*Budgeted qty.*	*Selling price (Rs.)/unit*
A	9,750	270
B	7,800	280
C	7,800	400

Later the market improved and the sales quantities could be increased by 20 for product '*A*' and 25% for product '*B*' and '*C*'. The sales manager confirmed that the increased quantities could be achieved at the prices originally budgeted. The production manager stated that the output cannot be increased beyond the budgeted level due to limitation of direct labour hours in department Z.

Required :

(*i*) Present a statement of budeted profitability.

(*ii*) Statement of optimal product mix and calculate the optimal profits.

(*C.A., Inter, May 1998*)

Solution :

Statement of budgeted profitability

	A	*B*	*C*	*Total*
Selling price (p.u.)	270	280	400	
Variable cost (p.u.) :				
Direct materials	64	152	117	
Direct labour	160	94	222	
Variable overheads	16	9	21	
Total variable cost	240	255	360	
Contribution per unit	30	25	40	
Budgeted qty. (units)	9,750	7,800	7,800	
Total contribution	2,92,500	1,95,000	3,12,000	7,99,500
Less fixed cost				4,00,000
			Profit	3,99,500

Statement of optimal product mix and profit

	A	*B*	*C*	*Total*
Contribution (*A*)	30	25	40	
Direct labour hors. in dept. 2 (*B*)	5	4	7	
Contribution per hr.	6	6.25	5.71	

$\frac{A}{B}$

Ranking	II	I	III	
Optimal product-mix				
Units (*C*) (*See Notes*)	11,700	9,750	5,292	
Total contribution	3,51,000	2,43,750	2,11,680	8,06,430
(*A* × *C*)				
Less : Fixed cost				4,00,000
			Optimal profit	4,06,430

Working note :

Total hours aviable in dept. 2

Products	*Units*	*Hours per unit*	*Total hours*
A	9750	5	48,750
B	7800	4	31,200
C	7800	7	54,600
			1,34,550

Maximum sales quantities of products (under improved market conditions)

Products	*Units*	*Increase in percentae*	*Total number of units*
A	9750	20	11700
B	7800	25	9750
C	7800	25	9750

Problem 20 : A Ltd. Co. has three departments. The following data relates to the period ending 31st Dec., 1992 :

	Department		
	A	*B*	*C*
Sales (Rs.)	80,000	40,000	60,000
Marginal cost :			
Direct material	10,000	5,000	10,000
Direct labour	4,000	5,000	16,000
Variable overhead	10,000	5,000	20,000
Fixed overheads	20,000	10,000	20,000
Total cost	44,000	25,000	66,000

The manager in charge of department is disappointed with the results because of higher marginal cost and there is no hope of being reduced further. You are required to present the information in the most suitable manner indicating whether or not department *C* should be closed down.

Solution :

Marginal profit and loss 'A' Ltd. Co.

Dept.	*Sales Value (Rs.)*	*Marginal Cost (Rs.)*	*Contribution (Rs.)*
A	80,000	24,000	56,000
B	40,000	15,000	25,000
C	60,000	46,000	14,000
	1,80,000	85,000	95,000
Less : Fixed cost			50,000
Net profit			45,000

Department *C* makes a contribution of Rs. 14,000 towards fixed cost. If this department is eliminated altogether, the following would be the position :

Dept.	Sale value	Marginal cost	Contribution
A	80,000	24,000	56,000
B	40,000	15,000	25,000
	1,20,000	39,000	81,000
Less : Fixed cost			50,000
Net profit			31,000

From the above is clear that the net profit has fallen down to Rs. 31,000 from 45,000, if Department *C* is eliminated.

Problem 21 : *XYZ* Ltd. is selling three brands of its products in the brand names *X*, *Y* and *Z*. The details regarding unit costs and selling prices are as under :

	X (Rs.)	*Y (Rs.)*	*Z (Rs.)*
Direct materials	6	12	16
Direct labour	8	8	20
Variable overheads	6	20	14
Selling price	36	50	96

The monthly fixed expenditure is Rs. 5,40,000.

Sales volume for the months of July and August of 1989 are as follows :

	X	Y	Z
July	20,000	20,000	20,000
August	40,000	26,000	10,000

Find out the monthly profits and if your computations brings out that higher profit was earned in the month having lower sales volume, kindly justify the finding with reasons. (*ICWA, Inter, Dec. 1989*)

Solution :

Statement of cost per unit

	X (Rs.)	*Y (Rs.)*	*Z (Rs.)*
Direct material	6	12	16
Direct labour	8	8	20
Variable overhead	6	20	14
Marginal cost	20	40	50
Selling price	36	50	96
Contribution	16	10	46

For July	X	Y	Z	*Total*
Sales (units)	20,000	20,000	20,00	60,000
Contribution per unit	16	10	46	
Total contribution	3,20,000	2,00,000	9,20,000	1,44,000
Less : Fixed cost				5,40,000
			Profit	Rs. 9,00,000

For August				
Sales (units)	40,000	26,000	10,000	76,000
Contribution per unit	16	10	46	
Total contribution	6,40,000	2,60,000	4,60,000	13,60,000
Less : Fixed cost				5,40,000
			Profit	Rs. 8,20,000

Here it can be seen that although the sale quantity has been more in August at 76,000 than 60,000 in July, both contribution and profit were lower in August. The reason for this apparent mismatch is a drop in sales of product *Z* having the highest contribution of Rs. 46 per unit when compared to figure of Rs. 16 and 10 for products X and Y respectively. This means one unit of Z earns Rs. 20 more compared to one unit of X and Y taken together. Thus the increase in sales of X and Y though significant in quantitative measurement could not compensate the loss in contribution due to reduction of sales of Z in the month of August.

7. Selling at or below marginal cost : Some time it may become necessary to sell the goods at a price below the marginal cost. Some such situations are as follows :

(*a*) Where mateials are of perishable nature.

(*b*) Where large quantities of stock is accumulated and whose market prices have fallen. This will save the carrying cost of stocks.

(*c*) In order to popularise a new product.

(*d*) In order to increase sales of those products which have higher margin of profit.

If the selling price is below the total cost but above the marginal cost, the contribution will leave an under-recovering of fixed cost. If the selling price fixed is equal to marginal cost, there will be a loss which is equal to fixed cost. However, where the selling price fixed is lesser than the marginal cost, the loss will be greater then fixed cost.

Problem 22 : Garden Product Limited manufactures the 'Rainpour' garden spray. The accounts of the company for the year 1981 are expected to reveal profit of Rs. 14,00,000 from the manufacturer of 'Rainpour' after charging fixed costs of Rs. 1,00,000. The rainpour is sold for Rs. 50 per unit and has a variable unit cost of Rs. 20.

Market sensitivity tests suggest the following response to price changes L

Alternatives	*Selling price reduced by*	*Quantity sold increased by*
A	5%	10%
B	7%	20%
C	10%	25%

Evaluate these alternatives and state which, on profitability consideration, should be adopted for the forthcoming year,assuming cost structure unchanged from 1981. (*University of Delhi, B.Com. (Hons.) 1988*)

Solution :

	Present	*Proposed*		
		A	*B*	*C*
Selling price	50	47.50	46.50	45
Less : Variable cost	20	20	20	20
Contribution	30	27.50	26.50	25
Quantity (units)	80,000	88,000	96,000	1,00,000
Total contribution	24,00,000	24,20,000	25,44,000	25,00,000
Less : Fixed cost	10,00,000	10,00,000	10,00,000	10,00,000
	14,00,000	14,20,000	15,44,000	15,00,000

Contribution and profit of proposal *B* is the largest and should, therefore, be adopted.

Note : Units produced and sold is calculated by employing the formula of = $\frac{\text{Total contribution}}{\text{Contribution per unit}}$

8. Determination of selling price and volume of output : The determination of selling price and volume of output is based on 'differential costing'. The difference in total cost due to difference in sales volume is known as differential costing. The increase in sales value due to increase in sales volume is known as 'incremental revenue'. The analysis of differential cost and incremental revenue helps in determining selling price which will yield the optimum profit. So long as incremental reneue is more than the differential cost it is advantageous to increase the output. But as soon as incremental revenue equals the differential cost further increase in output is not advantageous. Differential cost analysis thus helps to determine the selling price and the level of activity which are expected to yield the highest profit.

Problem 23 : *X* Ltd. manufactures a standard product, the marginal costs (per unit) of which are as follows :

Direct materials	Rs. 160.00
Direct wages	120.00
Variable overheads	20.00
Total	300.00

Its annual budget includes the following :

Output : 40,000 units

Fixed overheads :

Production	Rs. 80,00,000
Administration	Rs. 48,00,000
Marketing	Rs. 40,00,000
Total	Rs. 1,68,00,000
Contribution	Rs. 2,00,00,000

Recently, the top management of the organisation has started thinking in terms of revising its budget and some alternative in the form of proposals (stated below) were discussed in its last board meeting.

Proposal 1

The organisation expects a profit of Rs. 48,00,000 and wants to know the selling price to be quoted for that purpose. It is estimated that (*a*) an increase in advertising expenditure of Rs. 9,44,0000 would result in a 10% increase in sales and (*b*) fixed production overheads and marketing overheads would increase by Rs. 2,00,000 and Rs. 1,36,000 respectively.

Proposal 2

The organisation expects that with an additional advertising expenditure, sales would go up by 20% and a profit margin of 15% would be obtained. Under the circumstances, fixed production overheads and marketing overheads are expected to increase by Rs. 3,20,000 and Rs. 2,00,000 respectively. The organisation wants to know the additional expenditure on advertisement required with a view to achieving the result.

You are required to draw up forecast statements for each of these alternatives and determine the selling price per unit to be quoted (proposal 1) and the additional expenditure on advertisement required (proposal 2).

(*ICWA, Inter, June 1992*)

Solution :

Forecast statement

	Present position	*Proposal 1*	*Proposal 2*
Sales (units)	40,000	44,000	48,000
Sales value (Rs.)	3,20,00,000	3,60,80,000	3,84,00,000
Less : Variable cost	1,20,00,000	1,32,00,000	1,44,00,000
Contribution	2,00,00,000	2,28,80,000	2,40,00,000
Less : Fixed cost	1,68,00,000	1,80,00,000	1,82,40,000
Profit	32,00,000	48,00,000	5,76,00,000

Selling price required per unit (proposal 1) = Rs. 820.

Additional expenditure on advertisement required (proposal 2) = Rs. 9,20,000

Problem 24 : Gemini Steel Ltd. manufactures a single product for which market demand exists for additional quantity. Present sales of Rs. 6,000 per month utilises only 60% capacity of the plant. Marketing Manager assures that with the reduction of 10% in price he would be in a position to increase the sale by about 25% to 30%. The following data are available :

(i) The operating profits at 60%, 70% and 80% levels at current selling price and
(ii) The operating profit at proposed selling price at the above levels.

(*University of Delhi, B.Com. (Hons.) 1991*)

Solution : **Statement of profit at current price and reduced price**

	60% capacity 6,000 units	*70% capacity 7,000 units*	*80% 8,000 units*
Fixed cost	20,000	20,000	24,000
Semi-variable cost	6,000	6,000	6,000
(6,000 + 50 paise per unit)	3,000	3,500	4,000
Variable cost (Rs. 3 per unit)	18,000	21,000	24,000
Total costs	47,000	50,500	58,000
Sales			
(1) At current selling price Rs. 10 per unit	60,000	70,000	80,000
(2) At reduced price	54,000	63,000	72,000
Profit at (1)	13,000	19,500	22,000
Profit at (2)	7,000	12,500	14,000

Note : Present sales of Rs. 60,000 at selling price of Rs. 10 per units is equal to sales of 6,000 units.

Problem 25 : The following data are extracted from the Venus Co. Pvt. Ltd. for the year 1981 :

Production	50,000 units
Selling price per unit Rs. 12	Rs.
Materials consumed	75,000
Direct wages	50,000
Variable production expenses	1,00,000
Variable selling expenses	2,00,000
Fixed expenses	75,000
	5,00,000

It is expected that in 1982 :

(a) The company will produce 1,00,000 units.

(b) Prices of materials will go up by $33\frac{1}{3}$%.

(c) There will be increase of 25% in variable selling expenses rate due to increase in the rate of commission to salesmen and extensive advertisements.

(d) Fixed expenses will go up by Rs. 25,000.

What will be the cost per unit in 1982, based on a production of 1,00,000 units?

If it is desired to maintain the same rate of profit on sales as in 1981, what should be the selling price in 1982?

Solution :

	1981		*1982*	
	Total 50,000	*Per unit*	*Total 1,00,000*	*Per unit*
Materials	75,000	1.50	2,00,000	2.00
Direct wages	50,000	1.00	1,00,000	1.00
Variable production expenses	1,00,000	2.00	2,00,000	2.00
Total variable product cost	2,25,000	4.50	5,00,000	5.00
Variable selling expenses	2,00,000	4.00	5,00,000	5.00
Total variable cost of sales	4,25,000	8.50	10,00,000	10.00
Fixed cost	75,000	1.50	1,00,000	1.00
Cost of sales	5,00,000	10.00	11,00,000	11.00
Gross profit	1,00,000	2.00	2,20,000	2.20
Sales	6,00,000	12.00	13,20,000	13.20

Problem 26 : The following particulars are extracted from the books Swarna Enterprises for the year 1981 :

Annual volume of sales (units)		*5,000*
Fixed cost		Rs. 5,10,000
Current selling price per unit		800
Variable cost per unit :		
Direct materials		300
Direct labour		120
Factory overhead		60
	Total variable cost per unit	480

A 10% increase in wages of the employees (direct and indirect) at the factory is anticipated. The incidence of this increase in fixed overhead will amount to Rs. 20,000 only. Semi-variable costs have been segregated into their fixed and variable segments in computing the data provided above.

The following proposals are now under study for the purpose of formulating a reasonable product strategy :

(*a*) Increase the selling price suitably to cover the increase in costs and maintain the level of overall profit.

(*b*) Increase the sale suitably (in number of units) so that, without any increase in selling price per unit, the net profit at the level of 1981 can be maintained.

(*c*) An additional investment of Rs. 19,00,000 in machinery (to be depreciated at 10% annually) will increase the present capacity (6,000 units) by 40% cost of capital will be at 10% p.a.

You are required to :

(1) Ascertain the increase in selling price per unit needed to implement plan (*a*).

(2) Determine the extra units to be sold if plant (*b*) is to be implemented, and

(3) Estimate the net profit for a complete year if the entire increased ouput, if plan (c) is implemented, can be sold at the present price per unit.

Solution : **Statement of profit under marginal costing**

	Before increase in cost		*After increase in cost*	
Sale (per unit)		800		800
Loss : Variable cost per unit				
Direct materials	300		300	
Direct labour	120		132	
Factory overhead	60	480	60	480
Contribution per unit		320		308
Contribution for 5,000 units		16,00,000		15,40,000
Loss : Fixed costs		5,10,000		5,30,000
Profit		10,90,000		10,10,000

P/V Ration $100 \times \frac{320}{800} = 40\%$ $\qquad 100 \times \frac{320}{800} = 38.5\%$

(*i*) Implementation of plan (*a*)

Profit decreased by Rs. 80,000 for increase in costs

Units sold = 5,000 units

Thus, unit selling price should be increased by Rs. 16 (80,000 ÷ 5,000)

Selling price per unit will be Rs. 816.

(*ii*) Implementation of plan (*b*)

To maintain the same level of profit as earned in 1981, additional sales will be

$$\frac{\text{Additional profit}}{\text{P / V Ratio}} = \frac{80,000}{38.5\%} = \text{Rs. } 2,07,792$$

Thus additional units will be Rs. $\frac{2,07,792}{800}$ = 260 units

(*iii*) Additional investment in machinery of Rs. 19,00,000
Additional cost will be

Depreciation @ 10% p.a.	Rs. 1,90,000
Interest @ 10% p.a.	Rs. 1,90,000
	3,80,000

Capacity will be increased to 8,400 units (6,000 × 140%)

Estimate of net profit if plan (*c*) is implemented

Sales	(8,400 × Rs. 800)		67,20,000
Less :	*Variable costs :*		
	Direct materials (8,400 × Rs. 300)	25,20,000	
	Direct labour (8,400 × Rs. 132)	11,08,000	
	Factory overhead (8,400 × Rs. 60)	5,04,000	41,32,800
	Contribution		25,87,200
Less :	Fixed cost	5,30,000	
	Additional cost	3,80,000	9,10,000
	Net profit		16,77,200

9. Determination of sales volume for a desired profit : Sometimes one of the decisions that is to be taken by the management is to determine the volume of sales in order to earn a desired profit. The cost-volume-profit analysis which is again based on marginal costing helps management in taking such decisions.

Problem 27 : Frazer Ltd. manufactures and sells a product the selling price and raw material cost which have remained unchanged during the past two years. The following are the relevant data :

	Year 1	*Year 2*
Quantity sold (kgs.)	100	150
	Rs.	*Rs.*
Sales value	20,000	?
Raw materials	10,000	?
Direct wages	3,000	?
Factory overheads	5,000	5,700
Profit	2,000	2,550

During year 2 direct wages rates increased by 50% but there was a saving of Rs. 300 in fixed factory overhead.

Required : What quantity (in kgs) the company should have produced and sold in year 2 in order to maintain the same amount of net profit per kg. as it earned during the year. (*C.A., Inter, Nov., 1988*)

Solution : **Statement of quantity to be produced and sold during year 2**

			Rs.
	Selling price per kg. (*See Working Note 1*)		200
	Variable costs per kg :		
	Raw material	100	
	Direct wages (*See Working Note 2*)	45	
	Variable factory overhead (*See Working Note 3*)	20	165
			35
Less :	Profit required per Kg. (at 100 kgs. of sales)		20
	Balance contribution per kg. for meeting fixed cost		15
	Total fixed cost (*See Working Note 4*)		2700

Quantity of kgs. produced sold $\frac{2,700}{15}$ = 180 kgs.

Working notes:

(1) Selling price per kg. = $\frac{\text{Rs. } 20{,}000}{100 \text{ kg}}$ = Rs. 200 per kg.

(2) Direct wages = Rs. $\frac{\text{Rs. } 3{,}000}{100 \text{ kg}}$ = Rs. 150% = Rs. 45

(3) Variable factory overhead per kg. :

	Rs.
Total factory overhead in year 2	5,700
Add : Savings in fixed factory overhead	300
	6,000
Less : Total factory overhead in year 1	5,000
Increase in factory overhead	1,000

Increase in quantity (150 kg. – 100 kg.) = 50 kg.

∴ Variable factory overhead per kg. $\frac{\text{Rs. } 1{,}000}{50 \text{ kg}}$ = Rs. 20

(4) Fixed factory overhead

	Year 1	*Year 2*
Total factory overhead	5,000	5,700
Less : Variable factory overhead	2,000	3,000
	3,000	2,700

Problem 28 : X Ltd. manufactures and markets a single product. The following information is available :

	Rs. per unit
Materials	8.00
Conversion costs (variable)	6.00
Dealers margin	2.00
Selling price	20.00

Fixed cost Rs. 2,50,000
Present sales 80,000 units
Capacity utilisation 60 per cent

There is accute competition. Extra efforts are necessary to sell. Suggestions have been made for increasing sales :

(1) By reducing sales price by 5%
(2) By increasing dealers margin by 25% over the existing rate.

Which of the two suggestions you would recommend if the company desires to maintain the profit? Give reasons :

Solution :

Present Marginal cost per unit

Materials	8.00
Conversion costs	6.00
Dealer's margin	2.00
Total	16.00

Contribution per unit = Selling price – Marginal cost
= 20 – 16 = 4

Total contribution= 90,000 × 4 = 3,60,000

Profit = Contribution – Fixed cost
= 3,60,000 – 2,50,000 = 1,10,000

Since in both suggestions, fixed costs remain unchanged, the present profit can be maintained by keeping the total contribution at the present level, *i.e.*, Rs. 3,60,000

(1) **Reducing sales price by 5%**

New sales price = (20 – 1) = 19
New dealers margin = 10% of Rs. 19
= 1.90

∴ Variable cost = 8 + 6 + 1.90 = Rs. 15.90

Contribution per unit = 19 – 15.90 = Rs. 3.10

Sales (units) required to maintain the present level of profit =

$$= \frac{\text{Total contribution}}{\text{Contribution per unit}} = \frac{3.60,000}{3.10}$$

= 1,16,111 units

(2) **Increasing dealers margin by 25%**

New dealer's margin = Rs. 2 + 25% = 2.50

New variable cost = 8 + 6 + 2.50 = 16.50

Contribution = 20 – 16.50 = Rs. 3.50

$$\text{Sales (units)} = \frac{3,60,000}{3.50} = 1.02$$

The second proposal is recommended because the contribution per unit is higher and the sales (in units) are lower. Lower sales efforts and less finance would be required in implementing the proposal (*ii*)

10. Acceptance or rejection of a special order within the country : Sometimes a decision regarding acceptance of a special order is to be made. This, however, depends on the availability of spare capacity. The contribution available from such an order helps in making such decision.

Problem 29 : *Z* Ltd. manufactures and sells a soft drink at 0.20 paise per cup. Current output is 4,00,000 cups per month which represents 80% of capacity. They have the opportunity to utilise their surplus capacity by selling their product at 0.13 paise per cup to a supermarket chain who will sell it as 'own lable' product.

Total costs for the previous month were Rs. 56,000 out of which Rs. 16,000 were fixed costs. This represented a total cost of 14 paise per cup.

Based on the above data should Z accept the super market order. What other factors should be considered.

Solution : **Statement showing the present situation**

Sales 4,00,000 @ 0.20 p		80,000
Less :	Marginal cost 0.10 per cup	40,000
	Contribution	40,000
Less :	Fixed cost	16,000
	Net profit	24,000

On the assumption that fixed costs are unchanged, the special order will produce the following contribution :

Sales 1,00,000 × 0.13		13,000
Less :	Marginal cost 1,00,000 × 0.10)	10,000
	Contribution	3,000

However, there are several other factors which would need to be considered before a final decision is taken :

(*a*) Will the acceptance of one order at a lower price lead other customers to demand lower prices as well?

(*b*) Is this special order the most profitable way of using the spare capacity?

(*c*) Will the special order lock up capacity which could be used for future full price business?

Problem 30 : A mechanical toy factory presents the following information for the year 1990 :

Material cost (Rs.)	1,20,000
Labour cost (Rs.)	2,40,000
Fixed overhead (Rs.)	1,20,000
Variable overhead (Rs.)	60,000
Units produced	12,000
Selling price per unit (Rs.)	50

The available capacity is a production of 20,000 units per year. The firm has an offer for the purchase of

5,000 additional units at a price of Rs. 40 per unit. It is expected that by accepting this offer there will be saving of rupee one per unit in the material cost on all units manufactured, the fixed overhead will increase by Rs. 35,000 and the overall efficiency will drop by 2% on all production.

State whether offer is aceptable or not? *(C.S., Inter, June 1993)*

Solution :

Available capacity — 20,000 units : 100%
Capacity utilised — 12,000 units : 60%

Statement of production and sales of 12,000 units

		Total	*Per unit*
(A)	Sales	6,00,000	50.00
	Variable cost of sales :		
	(a) Materials	1,20,000	10.00
	(b) Labour cost	2,40,000	20.00
	(c) Variable overheads	60,000	5.00
(B)	Total variable cost of sales	4,20,000	35.00
(C)	Contribution *(A – B)*	1,80,000	15.00
(D)	Fixed overheads	1,20,000	10.00
(E)	Profit	60,000	5.00

Profit prospect of the offer for 5,000 units is accepted.		
Existing sales revenue	6,00,000	
Additional sales revenue (5,000 × Rs. 40)	2,00,000	
		8,00,000
Less : Variable cost of sales :		
Materials 17,000 units × Rs. 9	= 1,53,000	
Labour 17,000 units ×Rs. 20.40	= 3,46,800	
Variable overhead 17,000 units × Rs. 5	= 85,000	
		5,84,800
Total contribution from sales		2,15,200
Less : Original fixed overhead	1,20,000	
Additional fixed overhead	35,000	1,55,000
	Total profit	60,200
Total profit		60,200
Original profit before acceptance of offer		60,000
Additional profit		200

The offer is not acceptable in view of insignificant incremental profit. However, if the offer is likely to result in a wider market for the future.

Working note :

New marginal cost Rs. 10 – 10% of 10 = Rs. 9
New labour cost Rs. 20 + 2% of 20 = Rs. 22
Note : Efficiency is related to labour cost.

Problem 31 : *PQR* Ltd. manufactures medals for winners of athletic events and other contests. Its manufacturing plant has the capacity to produce 10,000 medals each month. The company has current production and sales level of 7,500 medals per month. The current domestic market price of the medal is Rs. 150.

The cost data for the month of October 1999 is as under :

Variable costs : (That vary with units produced)

Direct materials	Rs. 2,62,500
Direct labour cost	3,00,000

Variable costs (That vary with number of batches)		
Set ups : Materials handling :		
Quality control		
150 batches × Rs. 500 per batch		75,000
Fixed manufacturing costs		2,75,000
Fixed marketing costs		1,75,000
		10,87,500

PQR Ltd. has received a special one-time-only order for 2,500 medals at Rs. 100 per medal.

PQR Ltd. makes medals for its existing customers in batch sizes of 50 medals (150 batches × 50 medals per batch = 7,500 medals).

The special order for 2,500 medals required *PQR* Ltd. to manufacture the medals in 25 batches of 100 each :

Required :

(*i*) Should *PQR* Ltd. accept the special order? Why? Explain briefly.

(*ii*) Suppose the plant capacity was 9,000 medals instead of 10,000 medals each month. The special order must be taken either in full or rejected totally. Should *PQR* Ltd. accept the special order? Why?

(C.A., Inter, November 1999)

Solution : Statement of contribution margin on accepting the special order of 2,500 medals

Sales revenue (2,500 medals × Rs. 100 per medal)		2,50,000
Less : Variable costs :		
Direct materials (2,500 × 35)	87,500	
Direct wages (2,500 × 40)	1,00,000	
Setups, materials handling, quality control (25 batches × 500)	12,500	
		2,00,000
	Contribution	50,000

Decision :

PQR Ltd. should accept the special order, because its acceptance would increase the operating profit of the concern by Rs. 50,000.

Statement showing present contribution on 7,500 medals

Sales revenue (7,500 × 150)		11,25,000
Less : Variable costs :		
Direct materials (7,500 × 35)	2,62,500	
Direct wages (7,500 × 40)	3,00,000	
Setups, material handling and quality control (150 × 500)	75,000	
		6,37,500
	Contribution	4,87,500

Statement showing contribution margin on 6,500 medals

Sales revenue (6,500 × 150)		9,75,000
Less : Variable cost :		
Direct materials (6,500 × 35)	2,27,500	

Direct labour cost	2,06,000	
(6,500 × 40)		
Setups, material handling and quantity control	65,000	
		5,52,000
	Contribution	4,22,500

Statement showing acceptance of special order when the plant capacity was 9,000 medals

Gain in contribution because of	
Special order of 2,500 medals	50,000
Contribution on reduction of 1,000 medal sales in the internal market (4,87,500 – 4,22,500)	(–65,000)
Loss of contribution	(–15,000)

Decision :

The special order of 25,000 medals (when the plant capacity was reduced to 9,000 medals) should not be accepted, as its acceptance will result in a loss of margin by Rs. 15,000.

11. Acceptance or rejection of an offer from foreign market : The acceptance or rejection of an offer from a foreign market depends upon the incremental cost and incremental revenue.

Problem 32 : A manufacturer has planned his level of operation at 50% of his plant capacity of 30,000 units. His expenses are estimated as follows, if 50% of the plant capacity is utilised :

(*i*) Direct materials	Rs. 8,280
(*ii*) Direct wages	Rs. 11,160
(*iii*) Variable and other manufacturing expenses	Rs. 3,960
(*iv*) Total expenses irrespective of capacity utilisation	Rs. 6,000

The expected selling price in the domestic market is Rs. 2 per unit. Recently, the manufacturer has received a trade enquiry from an overseas organisation interested in purchasing 6,000 units at a price of Rs. 1.45 per unit.

As a professional management what would be your suggestion regarding acceptance or rejection of the offer? Support your suggestion with suitable quantitative information. (*ICWA, Inter, Dec. 1991*)

Solution :

Statement of costs and profits

Particulars	*15,000 units (Expected output for domestic market)*		*6,000 units (Additional output for the foreign market)*		*Total*
	Amount	*Unit*	*Amount*	*Unit*	
Direct materials	8,280	0.552	3,312	0.552	11,592
Direct wages	11,160	0.744	4,464	0.744	15,624
Variable and other mfg. expenses	3,960	0.264	1,584	0.264	5,544
Variable cost	23,400	1.560	9,360	1.560	32,760
Sales	30,000	2.000	8,700	1.450	38,700
Contribution	6,600	0.440	(660)	0.11	5,940
Less : Fixed cost	6,000				6,000
Profit (Loss)	600		(660)		(60)

The price that can be obtained from the foreign market is Rs. 1.45 per unit of additional product which is less than the estimated variable cost of production, *i.e.*, Rs. 1.56 per unit. This will result in an estimated negative contribution of Re. 0.11 per unit and thereby will generate an expected loss of Rs. 660 on 6,000 additional costs.

Therefore, if the offer from the overseas organisation is accepted, the profit of Rs. 6,000 on 15,000 units (based on the 50% plant capacity utilisation) will be wiped out and expected net loss of Rs. 60 will arise. Therefore, it is suggested not to accept the offer.

Problem 33 : *A* company manufacturing electric motors at a price of Rs. 6,900 each made up as under :

	Rs.
Direct material	Rs. 3,200
Direct labour	400
Variable overheads	1,000
Fixed overheads	200
Depreciation	200
Variable selling overheads	100
Royalty	200
Profit	1,000
	6,300
Central excise duty	600
	6,900

(1) A foreign buyer has offered to by 200 such motors at Rs. 5,000 each. As a cost accountant of the company, would you advise acceptance of the offer?

(2) What should the company quote for a motor to be purchased by a company under the same management if it should be at cost. *(CS, Inter, June 1990)*

Solution :

Statement showing contribution

	Price offered		5,000
Less :	Variable cost		
(i)	Direct material	3,200	
(ii)	Direct labour	400	
(iii)	Variable overhead	1,000	
(iv)	Variable selling overheads	100	
(v)	Royalty (presumed to be production based)	200	4,900
	Contribution		100

From the above it appears that is would be worthwhile to accept the offer since the price offered covers marginal cost in full and gives Rs. 100 contribution towards the recovery of fixed cost. Secondly there will not be the incidence of central excise duty because this is an export order. Further there will also be government incentive for export order. This will help the company to recover further the fixed cost and balance if any the depreciation.

Problem 34 : New product company is contemplating to launch a new product in the market. The estimated cost details are as follows :

(i) Materials cost per unit = Rs. 40

(ii) Labour cost per unit = Rs. 36

(iii) Production overheads are to be calculated from the following data :

Production departments	*Hourly overhead rate (Rs.)*	*Normal monthly hours for over head rate*	*Fixed overhead included n overhead (Rs.)*	*Time to be taken by new product (Hour)*
A	3.60	30,000	36,000	5
B	4.80	20,000	12,000	2.5
C	6.00	40,000	60,000	4

(iv) Annual administration and selling expenses — Rs. 2,50,000 (Applicable to new product).

(v) Estimated sales quantity — 50,000 per annum.

Based on the above information prepare a cost-sheet and find out the unit selling price with a profit margin of 40% on total cost.

A foreign buyer offers to by additional 10,000 units of the new product at Rs. 125 per unit. Advise management whether this offer is acceptable? *(ICWA, Inter, Dec. 1992)*

Solution : **Cost-sheet of new product company**

Direct material			40.00
Direct labour			36.00
Prime cost			76.00
Variable overheads :			
Dept. *A*	Rs. 2.40 × 5 hrs.	= 12.00	
Dept. *B*	Rs. 4.20 × 2.5 hrs.	= 10.50	
Dept. *C*	Rs. 4.50 × 4 hrs.	= 18.00	40.50
		Variable cost of production	116.50
Fixed overhead :			
Dept. *A*	Rs. 1.20 × 5 hrs.	= 6.00	
Dept. *B*	Rs. 0.60 × 2.5 hrs.	= 1.50	
Dept. *C*	Rs. 1.50 × 4 hrs.	= 6.00	13.50
		Total cost of production	130.00
Administration and selling overheads :			
$\frac{\text{Rs. 2,50,000}}{\text{50,000 pieces}} = 5$			5.00
Cost of sales			135.00
Profit 40% of cost of sales			54.00
Selling price			189.00

The price of Rs. 125 per piece offered by the foreign buyer leaves a gross contribution of Rs. 8.50 per piece calculated as under:

Selling price per piece	Rs. 125.00
Variable cost of production	116.50
Gross contribution	8.50

While the selling price of Rs. 125 is far below the cost of sales at Rs. 135 per price in the domestic market, assuming that the entire fixed expenses are recovered in the domestic market itself, the gross contribution of Rs. 8.50 earned per unit in the following market would add to the overall profitability by Rs. 8.50 × 10,000 units = Rs. 85,000. Hence this offer should be accepted.

Working note :

Calculation of variable and fixed rates

	A	*B*	*C*
Total monthly overheads (Full oh. rate × Normal hrs.)	1,08,000	96,000	2,40,000
Fixed overhead	36,000	12,000	60,000
Variable overhead	72,000	84,000	1,80,000
Rate per hour —Variable	2,40	4.20	4.50
— Fixed overhead	1.20	0.60	1.50

Problem 35 : *ABC* Ltd. has been operating at 70% capacity and the following particulars relate to the present level of activity :

Units	3,500
Direct materials	Rs. 10,500
Direct labour	Rs. 5250
Variable overhead (200% of direct labour)	
Fixed overhed	14,000
Sales	47,250

ABC Ltd. receivied an export order for 1,000 units of its product @ Rs. 10 per unit. The export order will entail on extra expenditure in the form of special packing at Re 0.50 per unit.

Is the export order worth trying. *(University of Madras, B.Com., March 95)*

Solution :

Statement showing profit

	Present 70% capacity 3,500 units @ Rs. 13.50		Extra order 1,000 units @ Rs. 10		Total	
Sales :						
Less : Variable cost :		47,270		1,000		57,250
Direct materials @ Rs. 3	10,500		3,000		13,500	
Direct labour @ Rs. 1.50	5,250		1,500		6,750	
Variable cost @ Rs. 3	10,500		3,000		13,500	
Packing @ Rs. 0.50	-		500		500	
		26,250		8,000		34,250
Contribution		21,000		2,000		23,000
Less : Fixed overhead		14,000		–		14,000
Profit		7,000		2,000		9,000

Comments :

The extra order is worth and it will earn extra profit of Rs. 2,000 subjected to reduction of selling price for Rs. 13.50 to Rs. 10 in export will not affect the local market. Therefore the export order may be worth trying.

12. Differential pricing in the different markets/pricing in depression or recession : Under normal circumstances, the selling price is fixed by adding a margin of profit to the total cost. However, selling price is not always determined by the total cost of production. The market conditions play an important factor and hence, selling price is sometimes fixed considering market condition. In the long run they tend to equal the cost of production of marginal firm. Occasionally, a factory may have to sell below the total cost. Such pricing has the following advantages :

(*a*) The services of talented employees can be utilised without discharging them.

(*b*) The idle capacity of plant may be prevented.

(*c*) The factory will be in a position to take the benefit arising out of a favourable condition at a later stage.

(*d*) The business can complete successfully.

Problem 36 : A Company is at present working at 90% of its capacity and producing 13,500 units per annum. It operates a flexible budgetary control system. The following figures (excluding material and labour cost) are obtained from its budget.

		90%	*100%*
(*a*)	Sales	Rs.15,00,000	16,00,000
(*b*)	Fixed expenses	Rs. 3,00,500	3,00,500
(*c*)	Semi-fixed expenses	Rs. 97,500	1,00,500
(*d*)	Variable expenses	Rs. 1,42,000	1,49,500

Material and labour cost per unit are constant under present conditions. Profit margin is 10% at 90% capacity.

(*a*) You are required to determine the cost of producing an additional 1,500 units.

(*b*) What would you recommend for an export price for these 1,500 units taking into account that overseas are much lower than indigenous prices. (*ICWA, Inter, June 1990*)

Solution :

(*i*) Calculation of material and labour cost for 13,500 units :

	Amount (Rs.)	*Per Unit (Rs.)*
Sale of 13,500 units	15,00,000	111.11
Less : 10% profit	1,50,000	11.11
	13,50,000	100.00

Less : Overhead —Fixed, semi-fixed and variable	5,40,000	40.00
Material & labour cost	8,10,000	60.00

Statement of cost of producting 1,500 units

	Total	*Per unit*
Material & Labour cost	90,000	60.00
Semi-fixed expenses (Differential cost 1,00,500 – 97,500)	3,000	2.00
Variable expenses (Differential cost 1,49,500 – 142,000)	7,500	5.00
Marginal cost	1,00,500	67.00

(*ii*) Indegenous price is Rs. 111.11. Though overseas prices are much lower than indigenous prices, an export price of Rs. 67 per unit plus any direct costs incurred for export is recommended in view of the foreign exchange earnings.

Problem 37 : Banu Co. Ltd. produces three products *A*, *B* and *C* through two departments, *viz.*, machining department and finishing department. The production costs are as follows :

	A (Rs.)	*B (Rs.)*	*C (Rs.)*
Material cost per unit	46	70	100
Labour Hours :			
Machine Dept. at Rs. 5 per hr.	3	4	2
Finishing Dept. at Rs. 10 per hr.	2	2	6
Selling price per unit	140	160	275

Overhead rates based on normal production budget are :

Machine Dept. Rs. 15 per hour (40% variable)

Finishing Dept. 8 per hour (50% variable)

Present information to the management to enable relative profitability of the three products to be assessed in :

(*a*) a time of depression

(*b*) normal times

(*c*) when there is a shortage of labour in finishing department.

Solution :

		A	*B*	*C*
Selling price per unit		140	160	274
Less : Material		46	70	100
Added value		94	90	175
Variable cost :				
Machine dept. :	Labour	15	20	10
	Overhead	18	24	12
Finishing dept. :	Labour	20	20	60
	Overhead	8	8	24
	Total variable cost	61	72	106
Contribution		33	18	69
Fixed cost :	Machinery	27	36	18
	Finishing	8	8	24
	Total fixed cost	35	39	42
Profit/Loss		–2	–26	27

(*a*) During depression all the products are to be manufactured.

(*b*) During normal times, *Z* is the only profitable product to be manufactured.

(*c*)

	A	*B*	*C*
Finishing hours per unit	2	2	6
Contribution per hour	Rs. 16.5	Rs. 9	Rs. 11.5
Profitability ranking	*A*	*C*	*B*

13. Decision-making and profit miximisation based on key factor : It is a situation under which a company has a choice between various types of product which it can manufacture but subjected to a limiting factor. A limiting factor or a key factor is a factor involved in the productive activity of a company, which at a point of time will limit the production capacity. It is also, therefore, termed as scarce factor, principal budget factor and so on. The limiting factor is affected by both internal and external environment. The contribution per unit of key factor is ascertained and it can be maximised according to the priority needs. Some of the examples of key factors are scarce raw materials, shortage of labour, plant capacity, inefficient, management, shortage of capital and shortage of demand.

Probleme 38 : You are given the following information in respect of products *X* and *Y* of *AB* Co. Ltd.

	Product X	*Product Y*
Selling price	Rs. 42	Rs. 33
Direct materials	Rs. 15	Rs. 15
Labour hours	18 hrs.	9 hrs.
(50 paise per hour)		

Variable overheads 50% of direct wages Rs. 6,750

Show which product is more profitable during labour shortage :

Solution : **Statement showing contribution**

	Product *X*	Product *Y*
Selling price	42	33
Less : Variable cost	28.50	21.75
Contribution	13.50	11.25

$$\text{Profitability} = \frac{\text{Contribution}}{\text{Key Factor}}$$

$$\text{Product X} = \frac{13.5}{18} = 0.75$$

$$\text{Product Y} = \frac{11.25}{9} = 1.25$$

Thus, product *Y* is more profitable then *X* during labour shortage.

Problem 39 : In its budget period for the period ahead *X* Ltd. is considering two possible sales forecasts for its three products as follows :

Forecast		*Products* A	B	C
I	Sales (units)	22,000	40,000	6,000
	Selling price per unit	Rs. 10	Rs. 6	Rs. 7.50
II	Sales (units)	30,000	50,000	7,000
	Selling price per unit	Rs. 9	Rs. 5.50	Rs. 7.50

Variable costs per unit are expected to be the same at the different levels of possible sales. The variable costs per unit are as follows :

	Products A (Rs.)	B (Rs.)	C (Rs.)
Direct material	3	2	4
Direct labour	2	1.50	1
Variable overhead	1	0.50	1

Fixed overheads are expected to total Rs. 1,00,000. These are expected to be unaffected by the possible changes in activity which are being considered. Due to recent high labour turnover problems, direct labour will be restricted to a maximum of Rs. 1,30,000 in the period. It can be assumed that all labour is of the same grade and is freely transferable between products. Other resources are expected to be generally available.

Your are required to :

Taking each of the possible sales forecasts in turn :

(*i*) Say what the principal budget factor is for each of the forecast.

(*ii*) For each forecast calculate the sales budget that you would recommend to maximum profit.

(*iii*) What profit would you expect from each sales budget?

Solution :

(*i*) Forecast I

	Products			Total
	A	*B*	*C*	
Sales quantity (units)	22,000	40,000	6,000	
Labour cost per unit	Rs. 2	1.50	1	
Total labour cost	Rs. 44,000	6,000	6,000	1,10,000
Labour cost available				1,30,000

Principal budget factor for Forecast I is sales.

Forecast II

Sales quantity (units)	30,000	50,000	7,000	
Labour cost per unit (Rs.)	2	1.50	1	
Total labour cost (Rs.)	60,000	75,000	7,000	1,42,000
Labour cost available (Rs.)				1,30,000

Principal budget factor for Forecast II is labour.

(*ii*) Sales budget

	Forecast I (Sales being the principal budget factor)			Forecast II (Labour being the principal budget factor)		
Product	*Units to be sold*	*Selling price*	*Amount*	*Units to be sold*	*Selling price*	*Amount*
A	2,20,000	10	2,20,000	30,000	9	2,70,000
B	40,000	6	2,40,000	42,000	5.50	2,31,000
C	6,000	7.50	45,000	7,000	7.50	52,500
			5,05,000			5,53,500

(*iii*) Expected profit from each sales budge

Forecast I

	Products			Total
	A	*B*	*C*	
Selling price P.V.	Rs. 10	6	7.50	
Variable cost P.U.	Rs. 6	4	6.00	
Contribution on P.V. (*A*)	4	2	1.50	
Sales (units)	22,000	40,000	6,000	
Contribution Rs. *A* × *B*	88,000	80,000	9,000	1,77,000
Less : Fixed cost				1,00,000
			Profit (Rs.)	77,000

Forecast II

	Products			Total
	A	*B*	*C*	
(*a*) Selling price P.U. (Rs.)	9	5.50	7.50	
(*b*) Variable price P.U. (Rs.)	6	4	6	
(*c*) Contribution P.U. (Rs.)	3	1.50	1.50	

(*d*) Sales (units)	30,000	42,000	7,000	
$c \times d$ contribution	90,000	63,000	10,500	1,63,500
Less : Fixed cost				1,00,000
			Profit	63,500

Working note :

(*i*) Ranking the products when labour is a limiting factor.

		A	*B*	*C*
A	Selling price per unit (Rs.)	9	5.50	7.50
	Direct material per unit (Rs.)	3	2	4
	Direct labour per unit (Rs.)	2	1.50	1
	Variable oh. per unit (Rs.)	1	0.50	1
B	Total variable cost per unit	6	4	6
(*A* – *B*)	Contribution per unit	3	1.50	1.50
	Contribution per rupee (6 : 4 : 6)	1.50	1	1.5
	Ranking	1	2	1

From the above ranking it is apparent that product *B* is least profitable. Therefore 30,000 units of product *A* and 7,000 units of product *C* (as per forecast II) would be manufactured by utilising labour cost worth Rs. 67,000 (30,000 × Rs. 2 + 7,000 × Re. 1). As the total available labour cost is for Rs. 1,30,000 threrefore, the remaining labour cost of Rs. 63,000 (Rs. 1,30,000 ÷ 67,000) will be utilised for manufacturing 42,000 units (Rs. 63,000 – 1.50) of product *B*.

Problem 40 : The profit and loss of '*A*' Co. Ltd. is given below :

Sales		Rs. 15,00,000
Direct materials	4,50,000	
Direct wages	3,00,000	
Variable overheads	1,20,000	
Fixed overheads	4,30,000	Rs. 1,30,000
	Profit	2,00,000

The budget capacity of the company is Rs. 2,00,000 but the key factor is sales demand. The sales manager is proposing that in order to utilise the exising capacity, the selling price of the only product manufactured by the company should be reduced by 50.

You are required to prepare a statement of forecast which should show the effect of the proposed reduction in selling price and to include and changes in costs expected during the coming year. The following additional information is also available.

(*a*) Sales forecast : Rs. 19,00,000.

(*b*) Direct materials prices are expected to increase by 2%.

(*c*) Direct wage rates are expected to increase by 5% per unit.

(*d*) Variable overhead costs are expected to increase by 5% per unit.

(*e*) Fixed overheads will increase by Rs. 20,000.

Solution : **Statement showing the effect of change in selling price**

Sales		19,00,000
Direct materials	6,12,000	
Direct wages	4,20,000	
Variable overheads	1,68,000	12,00,000
Contribution		7,00,000
Less : Fixed overheads		4,50,000
	Profit	2,50,000

The above statement clearly shows that even though costs have increased owing to price increased and wages etc., the forecast for the coming year is still in excess of that achieved last year. The increased volume of sales at the reduced sales price will result in increased contribution more than sufficient to cover the increased fixed overheads.

Working Note :

(1) Sales volume has increased by $33\frac{1}{3}$%. Rs. 19,00,000 represents sales at the reduced selling price 5% reduction or 1/20 of the old selling price represents 1/19 of the new selling price. Therefore, sales volume would have been Rs. 19,00,000 + 1/19 at the old selling price. This figure of Rs. 20,00,000 compared with last year's sales volume of 15,00,000 represents an increase in volume of $33\frac{1}{3}$%. It is essential to compare sales volume based on the same selling price in order to calculate the change in volume.

(2) Direct material cost will rise by $33\frac{1}{3}$% owing to the increase in production volume required. To this figure must be added the 2% price change, *i.e.*

Last year's cost	4,50,000
Add : $33\frac{1}{3}$% of volume change	1,50,000
	6,00,000
Add : 2% increase	12,000
	6,12,000

(3) Direct wages

Last year's cost	3,00,000
Add : $33\frac{1}{3}$% of volume change	1,00,000
	4,00,000
Add : 5% increase	20,000
	4,20,000

(4) Variable overheads are calculated similar to direct wages.

14. Dropping out a product : When a company produces several range of products, a decision that is to be often taken is whether all the products are to be produced in spite of the fact that one or two products are responsible for incurring losses. Marginal costing helps in taking decision of such nature by calculating the margin of contribution.

Problem 41 : Synthetic Rubber Co. Ltd. manufactures and sell three varieties of shoes. The income statement for the year ending 31.12.1992 is as follows :

		Varieties of shoes (Rs. in lakh)		
		A	*B*	*C*
Sales		1.00	4.00	2.00
Works cost	Variable	50	1.80	70
	Fixed	30	1.00	40
Selling cost	Variable	12	50	20
	Fixed	10	40	20
Profit/Loss		(2)	30	50

The income statement reveals loss in the product *A*, previous years also. The management is considering a proposal to discontinue product *A* and intensify production of *C*. It is anticipated that an advertisement of Rs. 20,000 annually would yield an increase of 30% in its sales volume and this would exactly fit in the plant facilities released by discontinuance of the product *A*.

The variable overheads both works and selling, etc. are directly proportional to sales. The total fixed overheads will remain the same irrespective of the change in production policy. The present allocations are based on capacity utilisation on works side and sales effort on selling side.

The management desires to know comparative positions whether (*a*) the present production/sales policy should be continued, (*b*) the product *A* to be discontinued without any further change or (*c*) the proposal of increasing the product *C* in lieu of the product *A* should be accepted. Present the information assuming sales and costs will remain the same as in last year.

Solution :

(*a*) Present policy

				Products (Rs. in lakh)			
				A	*B*	*C*	*Total*
Sales				1.00	4.00	2.00	7.00
Variable cost :				0.62	2.30	0.90	3.82
Works	0.50	1.80	0.70				
Selling	0.12	0.50	0.20				
	0.62	2.30	0.90				
Contribution				0.38	1.70	1.10	3.18
Fixed Cost :							
Works	0.30	1.00	0.40				
Selling	0.10	0.40	0.20	0.40	1.40	0.60	2.40
	0.40	1.40	0.60				
		Profit or loss		0.02	0.30	0.50	0.78

(*b*) If 'A' is discontinued

	Products		
	B	*C*	*Total*
Sales	4.00	2.00	6.00
Variable cost	2.30	0.90	3.20
Contribution	1.70	1.10	2.80
Less : Fixed cost			2.40
Profit			0.40

(*c*) If C is expanded

	Products		
	B	*C*	*Total*
Sales	4.00	2.60	6.60
Variable cost	2.30	1.17	3.47
Contribution	1.70	1.43	3.13
Fixed cost & Advt.			2.60
Profit			0.53

From the above statement it is clear that the profit is highest under the present policy. Hence, the present policy should continue.

Problem 42 : Alpha Ltd. has prepared the following budget estimates for the year 1991-92 :

	Product A	*Product B*
Sales (in units)	*6,000*	*16,000*
	Rs. per unit	*Rs. per unit*
Selling price	40	64
Direct materials	12	22
Direct wages @ Re. 1 per hour	8	12
Variable overheads	4	6
Fixed overheads	8	12
Total cost	32	52
Profit	8	12

After finalisation of the above budget estimates, it is observed that $\frac{1}{3}$ of the production capacity is still idle. In order to improve the performance, the following proposals are under consideration :

(*i*) Product *A* will be discontinued and the capacity so released will be used for product *B*. The selling price of product *B* will, however, have to be reduced by Rs. 2 per unit in order to increase the volume of sales.

(*ii*) Product *B* will be discontinued and the capacity so released will be diverted to the production of product *C*. The particulars relating to per unit of product *C* are as under :

Selling price	Rs. 52
Direct materials	Rs. 15
Direct labour	Rs. 10
Variable overheads	Rs. 5

(*iii*) The idle capacity will be utilised for meeting an export demand for product *D*. The particulars relating to per unit of product *D* are as under :

Selling price	Rs. 72
Direct materials	Rs. 40
Direct labour	Rs. 20
Variable overheads	Rs. 10

(*iv*) The idle capacity will be hired out by fixing a price in such a way that the same rate of profit per direct labour hour as obtained in the budget estimates is achieved.

Prepare a statement showing the profitability of the products *A* and *B* as envisaged in the budget estimates. Also evaluate each of the above four proposals separately and preapre statements showing the profitability under each proposal. (*ICWA, Inter, June 1991*)

Solution :

	Product A	*Product B*
Direct labour hour per unit	8	12
No. of units	6,000	16,000
Direct labour hours utilised	48,000	1,92,000

Total direct labour hours utilised = 48,000 + 92,000 = 2,40,000 hours

Idle capacity $= 2{,}40{,}000 \times \frac{3}{2} \times \frac{1}{2} = 1{,}20{,}000$ hrs.

Total fixed cost $= 6{,}000 \times 8 + 16{,}000 \times 12$

$= 48{,}000 + 1{,}92{,}000 = 2{,}40{,}000$

(*a*) Profitability statement (based on budget estimates)

	Product A	*Product B*
Units	6,000	16,000
Selling price per unit (Rs.) :	40.00	64.00
Less : Variable cost per unit (Rs.) :		
Direct material cost	12	22
Direct wages	8	12
Variable overhead	4	6
	16	24
Contribution		

Total contribution = 6,000 × 16 + 16,000 × 24 = 96,000 + 3,84,000 =	4,80,000
Less : Fixed cost	2,40,000
Profit	2,40,000

(*b*) Proposal I

Capacity released by discontinuing product *A* = 48,000 hrs.

The capacity released will produce product $B = \frac{48{,}000}{12} = 4{,}000$ units.

Therefore, production will be product *A* – nil, and product *B* – 2,000 units.

Profitability statement

	Product B
Units	20,000
Sale price per unit (Rs.)	62.00
Less : Variable cost per unit	
Direct material	22.00
Direct wages	12.00
Variable overhead	6.00
Contribution per unit	22.00
Total contribution (Rs.) = 20,000 × 22	Rs. 4,40,000
Less : Fixed cost (Rs.)	Rs. 2,40,000
Profit	Rs. 2,00,000

Proposal II

Capacity released by discontinuing product *B* = 16,000 × 2 = 1,92,000 hrs.

The capacity released will produce product C $= \frac{1,92,000}{10}$ = 1,92,000 units

Profitability statement

	Product A	Product C
Units	6,000	19,200
Selling price per unit (Rs.)	40	52
Less : Variable cost per unit		
Direct materials	12	15
Direct labour	8	10
Variable overhead	4	5
Contribution per unit	16	22

Total contribution
= 6,000 × 16 + 19,200 × 22
= 96,000 + 4,22,400 = Rs. 5,18,400
Less : Fixed cost = Rs. 2,40,000
Profit Rs. 2,78,400

Proposal III

	Product A	Product B	Product D
Units	6,000	16,000	6,000
Selling price per unit (Rs.)	40	64	72
Less : Variable cost per unit			
Direct materials	12	22	40
Direct labour	8	12	20
Variable overhead	4	6	10
Contribution per unit	16	24	2

Total contribution = 6,000 × 16 + 16,000 × 24 + 6,000 × 2
= 96,000 + 3,84,000 + 12,000 = Rs. 4,92,000
Less : Fixed cost = Rs. 2,40,000
Rs. 2,52,000

Proposal IV

Hiring out the idle capacity

Profit as per the budget estimates	Rs. 2,40,000
Direct labour hours as per the budget estimaes	2,40,000 hrs.
∴ Profit for direct labour hour	Re. 1
Idle capacity (direct labour hrs.)	1,20,000 hrs.
Additional profit by hiring out the idle capacity	Rs. 1,20,000
Profit as per estimates	Rs. 2,40,000
Total profit after hiring out the idle capacity	Rs. 3,60,000

Proposal IV is recommended.

QUESTIONS

I. Choose the correct answer

1. Production cost under marginal costing include:
   (*a*) Prime cost only
   (*b*) Prime cost and variable overhead
   (*c*) Prime cost and fixed overhead
   (*d*) Price cost, variable overhead and fixed overhead [ ]
2. One of the primary difference between marginal costing and absorption costing is regarding the treatment of :
   (*a*) Direct material (*c*) Fixed overhead
   (*b*) Variable overhead (*d*) Prime cost [ ]
3. Period costs are :
   (*a*) Variable costs (*c*) Prime cost
   (*b*) Fixed cost (*d*) Overhead costs [ ]
4. Absorption costing offeres from marginal costing in the
   (*a*) fact that standard costs can be used with absorption costing but not with marginal costing
   (*b*) amount of fixed costs that will be incurred
   (*c*) kind of activities for which each can be use
   (*d*) amount of costs assigned to individual units of products [ ]
5. Chosse the true statement from the following :
   (*a*) Variable costing is a method of costing in which only direct materials and direct labour are charged to work-in-process.
   (*b*) Under variable costing, all costs which vary with sales volume are changed to work-in-progress.
   (*c*) Because certain manufacturing costs are treated as period costs, net earnings will always be lower under variable costing than under full costing.
   (*d*) Variable costing clearly points out the fact that if additional units of product can be sold for more than the variable costs of producing and selling them, net earnings will increase. [ ]

[*Answers :* 1. (b), 2. (*c*), 3. (*c*), 4. (*d*), 5. (*d*)]

(B) Mark true or false

1. In marginal costing, fixed costs are excluded in the valuation of work-in-progress and finished goods stocks. *T/F*
2. Marginal costing may be used in conjunction with standard costing or budgetary control. *T/F*
3. In marginals costing, fixed costs are apportioned on some arbitrary basis. *T/F*
4. In absorption costing, the valuation of stock in higher than in marginal costing. *T/F*
5. In marginal costing, managerial decisions are guided by contribution margin than by profit. *T/F*
6. Absorption costing is generally accepted approach to product cost determination. *T/F*
7. Under marginal costing, variable overhead is treated as part of the cost of an assets, the goods produced, while fixed overhead is viewed as an expense. *T/F*
8. Marginal costing is sometimes referred to as variable costing. *T/F*

9. Under marginal costing, variable overhead is a period costs. *T/F*
10. Under variable costing only the costs of materials and labour are reviewed as product cost. *T/F*
11. Fixed factory overhead is not treated as a product cost under variable costing while it so treated under full costing. *T/F*
12. Variable selling expenses are deducted from revenue under the variable costing technique in arriving at net earnings. *T/F*
13. In general, if production volume exceeds sales volume, net earnings under full costing will be greated than under marginal costing. *T/F*
14. In the earning statement under marginal costing, marginal earnings are directly related to the volume of units sold. *T/F*
15. An unresolved issue in the variable full costing controversy is whether fixed overhead costs are period cost or product costs. *T/F*
16. The effect upon net earnings of the sale of some additional units of product is readily determinable under full costing. *T/F*

[***Answer :*** *True* : 1, 2, 4, 5, 6, 7, 8, 11, 13, 14, 15, *False* : 3, 9, 10, 12, 16]

II. Short answer questions

(1) What is 'analysis of margin of contribution'? Discuss the need for it.

(Calicut University, M.Com., April 1992)

(2) Define marginal costing. What are the features of marginal costing?

(Bangalore University, B.Com., April, 1992)

EXERCISE

Exercise 1 (High/Low method of segregating semi-variable cost) : From the following data segregate semi-cariable cost into fixed and variable cost :

Month	*Units*	*Semi-variable cost*
Jan.	15,000	12,000
Feb.	12,000	11,400
Mar.	14,000	11,800
Apr.	16,000	12,200
May	18,000	12,600
June	17,000	12,400
	92,000	72,400

[***Answer :*** For the month of Jan. variable cost is Rs. 3,000 and fixed cost is Rs. 9,000. For the month of Feb. the variable cost is Rs. 2,400 and fixed cost is Rs. 9,000 and so on]

Exercise 2 (High/Low method and method of least square) : From the following semi-variable cost calculate the fixed and variable cost under (*i*) High and low method, (*ii*) Method of least squares :

Month	*Units*	*Semi-variable cost*
Jan.	500	2,500
Feb.	600	2,800
Mar.	700	3,100
Apr.	940	3,820
May	740	3,220
June	880	3,640
July	900	3,700
Aug.	840	3,520
Sept.	800	3,400
Oct.	860	3,580
Nov.	760	3,280
Dec.	540	2,620

[***Answer :*** For the month of Dec. the fixed cost under High-low method is Rs. 1,000 and variable cost is Rs. 2,820. Under method of least squares the fixed cost is Rs. 1,000 and variable cost per unit is Rs. 3]

Exercise 3 : The following figures have been extracted from the books of a manufacturing company for the first half year ending 30th June, 1979 :

Month	*Volume (Units)*	*Semi-variable cost overhead cost (Rs.)*
Jan.	150	2,700
Feb.	300	3,900
Mar.	450	5,100
Apr.	750	7,500
May	1,050	9,900
June	1,350	12,300

Find out the fixed and variable cost. *(University of Kerala, B.Com., May 1989)*

[*Answer :* Adoting indirect method the variable cost per unit is Rs. 8. The fixed cost is Rs. 1,500]

Exercise 4 (Make or buy decision) : *X* Ltd. manufactures component *A*-100 and the costs for the year 1992 when 50,000 units are produced is as follows :

Materials	Rs. 2.50
Labour	Rs. 1.25
Variable overheads	Rs. 1.75
Fixed overhead	Rs. 3.50
Total cost	Rs. 9.00

Component *A*-100 could be bought in for Rs. 7.75 and if so the production capacity at utilised in 1992 would be unused. Assuming that there is no technical cnsideration. Should component *A* be bought in or manufactured.

[*Answer :* The component should be manufactured and not bought because marginal cost of manufacture is Rs. 5.50 and the buying price is Rs. 7.75. The reason for this is that the fixed cost of Rs. 17,500 (50,000 units × Rs. 3.50) would continue and as the capacity is not used, the fixed overhead would not be absorbed into production. If component *A*-100 is bought, overall profit will fall by Rs. 1,12,500 being the difference between buying price and marginal cost of manufacture *i.e.* (7.75 – 5.50 × 50,000)]

Exercise 5 (Make or buy decision based on cost savings) : A firm is considering whether to manufacture or purchase a particular component. This would be in batches of 10,000 and the buying price is Rs. 6.50. The marginal cost of manufacturing this component is Rs. 4.75 per unit and the component will have to be made on a machine which was currently working at full capacity. If the component is manufactured, it is estimated that the sales of the finished product would be reduced by 1,000 units. The finished product has a marginal cost of Rs. 60 per unit and is sold at Rs. 80 per unit.

Should the firm manufacture or purchase the component.

[*Answer :* Marginal cost of manufacture is Rs. 47,500.
Add iost contribution of the finished product 100 × Rs. 20 = 20,000/67,500. Buying price is Rs. 65,000 (10,000 × Rs. 6.50). Thus there is a saving of Rs. 1.500 per 10,000 batch by buying rather than manufacture.]

Exercise 6 : A radio manufacture company finds that while it costs Rs. 6.75 each to make component of 376 R, the same is available in the market at Rs. 5.75 each with the assurance of continued supply. The breakdown of cost is as follows :

Materials	Rs. 2.75 each
Labour	Rs. 1.75 each
Other variable	Re. 0.50 each
Fixed cost	Rs. 1.25 each
	Rs. 6.25

(*a*) Should you make or buy.
(*b*) What would be your decision if the supplier offered the component at Rs. 4.55 each.

(Bangalore University, M.Com., May 1990)

[*Answer :* The marginal cost of production is Rs. 5 whereas market price is Rs. 5.75. Since market price is more, the component is to be manufactured. If the offer is 4.85, the proposal to buy may be examined in relation to other factors, *viz.*, more profitable use of available resources, the fixed cost to be borne by other products, the ability to sell at the same rate in the long run by the supplier etc.]

Exercise 7 (Product mix) : Tourus Ltd. produces three products : *A*, *B* and *C* from the same manufacturing facilitites. The cost and other details of the three products are as follows :

	A	*B*	*C*
Selling price per unit (Rs.)	200	160	100
Variable cost per unit (Rs.)	120	120	40
Fixed expenses per unit (Rs.)			2,76,000
Maximum production per month (units)	5,000	8,000	6,000
Total hours available for the month			
Maximum demand per month (unit)	2,000	4,000	2,400

The processing hours cannot be increased beyond 200 hours per month.

You are required to compute the most profitable product mix. (*CA, Inter, May 1988*)

[*Answer :* Contribution of A = 1,60,000, B = 64,000, C = 1,44,000. Total contribution is 3,68,000 and profit is Rs. 92,000]

Exercise 8 (Product mix) : A company engaged in plantation activities has 200 hectares of virgin land which can be used for growing jointly or individually tea, coffee and cardamom. The yield per hectare of the difference crops and their selling prices per kg. are as under :

	Yield kg.	*Selling price Rs. per kg.*
Tea	2,000	20
Coffee	500	40
Cardamom	100	25

The relevant cost data are given below :

(*a*) Variable cost per kg.

	Tea (Rs.)	*Coffee (Rs.)*	*Cardamom (Rs.)*
Labour charges	8	10	120
Packing materials	2	2	10
Other costs	4	1	20
Total cost	14	13	150

(*b*) Fixed cost per annum

Cultivation and growing cost	10,00,000
Administrative cost	2,00,000
Land revenue	50,000
Repairs and maintenance	2,50,000
Other costs	3,00,000
Total cost	18,00,000

The policy of the company is to produce and sell all the three kinds of products and maximum and minimum area to be cultivated per products is as follows :

	Maximum Area (Hectares)	*Minimum Area (Hectares)*
Tea	160	120
Coffee	50	30
Cardamom	30	10

Calculate the priority of production, the most profitable product mix and the maximum profit which can be achieved. (*CS, Inter, June 1988*)

[*Answer :* Contribution per heactare for tea is Rs. 12,000, for coffee Rs. 13,500 and for cardamom Rs. 10,000. Profits is Rs. 6,55,000]

Exercise 9 (Acceptance or rejection of an offer) : A factory produces 5,000 articles for home consumption at the following costs :

Materials		Rs. 50,000
Wages		Rs. 30,000
Factory overheads		
Fixed	30,000	
Variable	10,000	40,000
Adm. overheads (fixed)		28,000
Selling and distribution overheads		
Fixed	15,000	
Variable	10,000	25,000
Total		1,73,000

The home market can consume only 5,000 articles at a price of Rs. 40 each and no more. The foreign market for this product can, however, consume 3,000 additional pieces at a price of Rs. 22 each C.I.F. If this export order is extended, the following additional costs will be incurred :

(1) Special packing, forwarding charges etc. Rs. 1.00 per unit.
(2) Freight, insurance etc. Rs. 2.00 per unit.

The following 'export benefits' should also be considered :

(1) Duty drawback on direct materials cost at 10%.
(2) Cash subsidy at 10% on F.O.B. value if foreign market worth trying?

(Bangalore University, M.Com., May 1990)

[*Answer :* The acceptance of foreign market results in an additional profit of Rs. 5,000. Hence the foreign market is worth trying]

8

COST-VOLUME-PROFIT ANALYSIS

INTRODUCTION

Earning of maximum profit is the ultimate objective of all business establishments. The profit in its turn is determined by a number of factors, both internal and external. One such factor is the sales revenue of the business. Increase in the sales revenue will lead to increase in the profits. But the sales itself is based on other factors such as demand for the product, the competition, the selling price fixed, marketing strategies adopted by the management. The other important factor that determines the amount of profit is the cost of production. A reduced cost of production will result in an increased profit, keeping the selling price constant. But cost of production itself is affected by many factors such as volume of production, product mix, capacity utilisation, efficiency in production and so on. Though all these factors affect the profit earning capacity of a business, a speical mention about the volume of output deserves to be mentioned in this regard. This is because volume of output changes more frequently and rapidly, and are not susceptible to management control. More than this the profit is more closely related to volume rather than cost. This is because costs seldom vary in direct proportion to volume. Hence, small change in the volume has a significant effect on profit. Whereas a change in other factors such as an order size or lot size will have insignificant effect on profit. However, it is the duty of management to consider the cost and volume while planning the profit earning capacity of the business. One such technique which is used by the management is known as cost-volume-profit analysis. As the name suggests, cost-volume-profit analysis examines the relationship of costs and profit to the volume of business with a view to maximise profit.

Kohler in his *Dictionary for Accountants* defines cost-volume-profit relationship as "the area of interest within an organisation, of management and accountants in observing and controlling the relations between prospective and actual manufacturing costs—both fixed and variable—rates of production and gross profit.

OBJECTIVES OF COST-VOLUME-PROFIT ANALYSIS

According to *NAA Research Bulletin*, Vol. 31, "the cost-volume-profit analysis appears to be useful principally as a technique for the study of problems encountered in business planning. As such it is a tool used largely by those executives responsible for strategic planning and policy-making". More specifically the objectives of cost-volume-profit analysis are as follows :

(*a*) To forecast the profit accurately.

(*b*) To facilitate in the preparation of flexible budgets.

(*c*) To evaluate the performance of the business. For evaluating the profit earned and cost increased, it is necessary to know the impact of cost on the changed volume of output.

(*d*) To enable management in determining the pricing policies.

(e) To enable the charging of overheads to cost of production at different levels of operation.

ASSUMPTIONS OF COST-VOLUME-PROFIT ANALYSIS

1. The analysis is valid for a limited range of values, *i.e.*, 'the relevant ranges' and for a limited period of time.
2. Costs can be classified as fixed and variable. The latter type of cost changes proportionately with the volume within the relevant volume range. Fixed costs are constant within the relevant volume of range.
3. Revenues change proportionately with volumes.
4. There exists a constant product mix.
5. There is no significant change in the inventories in terms of physical units. In other words, the units produced are assumed to be sold.
6. Changes in volume alone are responsible for changes in costs and revenues.
7. The analysis is deterministic in nature. It ignores uncertainty and probabilistic approach.

LIMITATIONS OF COST-VOLUME-PROFIT ANALYSIS

1. It is presumed that the anticipated capacity of production remains same. But it may be increased depending upon the need.
2. The analysis of cost-volume-profit gives satisfactory result only if elements of costs remain stable. But in actual practice it varies.
3. It is again presumed that plant capacity remains same. However, the cost-volume-profit relationship does not hold good if mannual labour is replaced by machines or high cost of materials are substituted by low cost materials.
4. In a business with many varieties of products, it becomes difficult to forecast the profits more accurately.

PRESENTATION OF COST-VOLUME-PROFIT ANALYSIS

One method of presenting cost-volume-profit analysis is by the method of break-even-analysis. It is a technique which is designed to help management in planning and decision-making functions involving the effect of change in volume on the profitability. This method helps management by establishing relationship between cost, volume and profit at different levels of activity. The management of every business desires to know the impact of changes in sales volume on profit. It is interesting in knowing the level at which the cost of production is equal to the sales value. This point where no-profit or no-loss is incurred is known as break-even point. Below this point any production will result only loss and beyond this point it brings profit to the business. Hence, break-even anlalysis and its study beyond the break-even point only relates to cost-volume-profit analysis.

There are two methods of presenting break-even analysis. They are (*i*) Algebraic method and (*ii*) Graphic method. The method to be used depends upon the choice of management and the data available.

ALGEBRAIC METHOD OF PRESENTING CVP ANALYSIS

This method of analysing cost-volume-profit relationship is based on the fundamental equation of marginal costing, *i.e.*, Sales – Variable cost = Fixed cost + Profit. Given any of the three variables, it is possible to find out the fourth unknown variable. This formula can be modified in different ways according to the need. For example, at the break-even point, the profit is nil. So the equation can be written as $S - V = F + 0$ (zero). Similarly, in order to calculate the sales, at the break-even point, it is possible to arrive at the following formula by multiplying it with sales :

$$S(S - V) = F \times S$$

$$\text{or } S \text{ (Sales at break-even point)} = \frac{F \times S}{S - V}$$

Because sale minus variable cost constitute contribution, the above formula may also be written as follows :

$$S = \frac{F \times S}{C}$$

Alternative, fixed cost and profit must be equal to contribution. So the formula can be written as follows :

$$S = \frac{F \times S}{F + P}$$

In the same way for determining different requirements different formula are available. They are indicated below :

1. To determine the break-even sales in terms of units, the formula is

$$\text{BEP (units of Sales)} = \frac{\text{Fixed cost}}{\text{Contribution per unit}}$$

$$\text{or} = \frac{\text{Fixed cost}}{\text{Unit selling price} - \text{Unit variable cost}}$$

2. To determine break-even Sales in terms of rupees

$$\text{BEP (Sales in Rs.)} = \frac{\text{Fixed cost} \times \text{Selling price}}{\text{Contribution per unit}}$$

$$\text{or BEP (Sales in Rs.)} = \frac{\text{Fixed cost} \times \text{Sales}}{\text{Fixed cost} + \text{Profit}}$$

$$\text{or BEP (Sales in Rs.)} = \frac{\text{Fixed cost}}{1 \frac{\text{Variable cost}}{\text{Sales}}}$$

3. Level of sales in units to earn a desired amount of profit

$$\text{BEP (Sales in units)} = \frac{\text{Fixed cost} + \text{Desired profit}}{\text{Contribution per unit}} \times \text{SP}$$

4. To determine the value of sales to earn a desired profit before tax

$$\text{BEP (Sales in Rs.)} = \frac{\text{Fixed cost} + \text{Desired profit}}{1 - \frac{\text{Variable cost}}{\text{Sales}}}$$

5. To determine the level of sales (in units) to result a desired prodit after tax.

$$\text{BEP (Sales in units)} = \frac{\text{Fixed cost} + \frac{\text{After tax profit}}{1 - \text{Tax rate}}}{\text{Contribution rate per unit}}$$

6. To determine BEP after additional fixed cost owing to plant expansion.

$$\text{BEP} = \frac{\text{Present fixed cost} + \text{Additional fixed cost}}{1 - \frac{\text{Variable cost}}{\text{Sales}}}$$

7. **To determine sales volume required to earn existing profit**

$$\textbf{BEP (Sales in units)} = \frac{\text{Present fixed cost + Additional fixed cost + Existing profit}}{1-\dfrac{\text{Variable cost}}{\text{Sales}}}$$

8. **To determine shut down point**

$$= \frac{\text{Fixed cost} - \text{Shut down cost}}{1-\dfrac{\text{Variable cost}}{\text{Sales}}}$$

Problem 1 : From the following particulars find out break-even point :

Variable cost per unit	Rs.	10
Selling price per unit	Rs.	15
Fixed expenses	Rs.	40,000

What will be the selling price per unit if break-even point is brought down to 5,000 units.

(SV University, B.Com., October 1999)

Solution :

$$\text{BEP} = \frac{\text{Fixed cost}}{\text{Sales} - \text{Variable cost}}$$

$$= \frac{40,000}{15-10} = \frac{40,000}{5} = 8,000 \text{ units}$$

Selling price per unit if BEP is brought down to 5,000 units :

Variable cost 5,000 × 10		= 50,000
Fixed cost		= 40,000
	Total cost	90,000
	Profit/loss	NIL
	Sales value	90,000

$$\text{Selling price per unit} = \frac{90,000}{5,000} = 18$$

Note : There is no profit or loss as is clear from the following :

Sales (8,000 × 15)		1,20,000
Less : Variable cost	8,000 × 10	80,000
	Contribution	40,000
	Less : Fixed cost	40,000
	Profit	–

Problem 2 : You are given the following particulars

Selling price	Rs.	200 per unit
Variable cost	Rs.	100 per unit
Total fixed cost	Rs.	96,000

Calculate :

(1) Break-even units and value

(2) Sales to earn a profit of Rs. 20 per unit. *(University of Delhi, B.Com. (Pass), April 1993)*

Solution:

Contribution = Sales – Variable cost
= 200 – 100 = 100 per unit

$$(i)\quad \text{BEP} = \frac{\text{Fixed cost}}{\text{Contribution per unit}}$$

$$\frac{96,000}{100} = 960 \text{ units}$$

BEP in value = 960 × 200 = Rs. 1,92,000

(*ii*) Sales to earn a profit of Rs. 20 per unit

Let Sales = x units

Then total sales = $200x$

Sales = Fixed cost + Variable cost + Profit

$$200x = 96,000 + 100x + 20x$$
$$200x - 120x = 96,000$$
$$80x = 96,000$$
$$x = \frac{96,000}{80} = 1,200 \text{ units}$$

Problem 3 : From the following data calculate :

(*i*) Break-even point expressed in amount of sales in rupees

(*ii*) How many units must be sold to earn a net profit of 10% of sales?

Selling price	Rs. 20 per unit
Variable cost	Rs. 12 per unit
Fixed cost	Rs. 2,40,000

(*University of Delhi, B.Com. (Pass), April 1991*)

Solution :

$$BEP = \frac{\text{Fixed cost}}{\text{Contribution per unit}}$$
$$= \frac{2,40,000}{20-12} = \frac{2,40,000}{8}$$
$$= 30,000 \text{ units}$$

(1) BEP in rupees = 30,000 units × 20

= Rs. 6,00,000

Units to be sold to earn a net profit of 10 % on sales

Let Sales units = x

Selling price = Rs. 20

Total sales = $20x$

$$\text{Profit 10\% of sales} = \frac{10}{100} \times 20x = 2x$$

Sales value = Fixed cost + Variable cost + Profit

$$20x = 2,40,000 + 12x + 2x$$
$$20x - 12x - 2x = 2,40,000$$
$$6x = 2,40,000$$
$$x = \frac{2,40,000}{6} = 40,000 \text{ units}$$

Problem 4 : Gifts Land Ltd. is considering hiring a machine at an annual charge of Rs. 12,000 to increase the output of a product from its present level of 6,000 units. It is anticipated that with the introduction of the machine, the variable cost per unit will be reduced by Re. 1 due to saving in labour cost. The new machine will not affect fixed cost in total apart from the hiring charges. The selling price of the product is Rs. 12 per unit. The present cost structure of the products is variable cost Rs. 9 per unit and fixed cost per unit Re. 1 per unit.

(*University of Madras, B.Com., September 1995*)

Solution :

$$\text{Break-even point for new machine} = \frac{\text{Revised total fixed cost}}{\text{Revised contribution per unit}}$$

Calculation of revised contribution per unit :

Selling price per unit		12
Less : Revised variable cost :		
Variable cost	9	
Less : Saveing in labour cost	1	8
Revised contribution per unit		4

Calculation of revised total fixed cost :

Present fixed cost 6,000 × 1	=	6,000
Add : Additional Hire charges	=	12,000
Revised total fixed cost		18,000

$$\text{New BEP} = \frac{18,000}{4} = 4,500 \text{ units}$$

$$\text{Existing BEP} = \frac{\text{Total Fixed cost}}{\text{Contribution per unit}}$$

Exiting fixed cost = 6,000 × 1 = 6,000

Contribution per unit = $S - V$

= 12 – 9 = 3

$$\text{Exiting BEP} = \frac{6,000}{3} = 2,000 \text{ units}$$

∴ Extra units produced in justifying Hiring machine is (4,500 units – 2,000 units) = 2,500 units for break even.

Problem 5 : Indian Plastics make plastic buckets. An analysis of their accounting reveal

Variable cost per bucket	Rs. 20
Fixex cost	Rs. 50,000 for the year
Capacity	2,000 buckets per year
Selling price per bucket	Rs. 70

Required :

(*i*) Find the break-even point.

(*ii*) Find the number of buckets to be sold to get a profit of Rs. 30,000.

(*iii*) If the company can manufacture 600 buckets more per year with an additional fixed cost of Rs. 2,000 what should be the selling price to maintain the profit per bucket as at (*ii*) above?

(University of Delhi, B.Com. (Hons.), April 1991)

Solution :

$$(i)\ \text{BEP} = \frac{\text{Fixed cost}}{SP - VC \text{ per unit}}$$

$$= \frac{50,000}{70-20} = \frac{50,000}{50} = 1,000 \text{ units}$$

Verification :

Total cost (at 1,000 units) = $FC + VC$

= 50,000 + 20,000

Rs. = 70,000

Sales = 1,000 buckets @ Rs. 70 = Rs. 70,000

Total cost of Rs. 70,000 is equal to total sales of Rs. 70,000, *i.e.*, no-profit-no-loss or BEP.

(*ii*) Number of buckets to be sold to earn profit of Rs. 30,000

$$\frac{\text{Fixed cost + Desired profit}}{\text{Contribution}}$$

$$= \frac{50,000+30,000}{50} \text{ or } \frac{80,000}{50} = 1,600 \text{ buckets}$$

Varification :

Total cost (at 1,600 buckets) $= FC + VC$

$= 50{,}000 + 32{,}000 = 82{,}000$

Sales = 1,600 buckets @ Rs. 70= Rs. 1,12,000

Profit = Sales – Total cost

= 1,12,000 – 82,000 = Rs. 30,000

(*iii*) Selling price to maintain the profit per bucket as at (*ii*) :

Further profit per bucket under (*ii*) will be

$$\frac{\text{Rs. } 30{,}000}{1{,}600 \text{ buckets}} = \text{Rs. } 18.75 \text{ per bucket}$$

And fixed cost will be Rs. 52,00 (50,000 + 2,000)

$$\text{Desired sales (units)} = \frac{FC + \text{Desired profit}}{\text{Contribution}}$$

$$2{,}600 = \frac{52{,}000 + (2{,}600 \times 18.75)}{SP - VC}$$

$$2{,}600 = \frac{52{,}000 + 48{,}750}{SP - 20}$$

$$2{,}600\,(SP - 20) = 1{,}00{,}750$$

$$SP - 20 = \frac{1{,}00{,}750}{2{,}600}$$

$$SP - 20 = 38.75$$

$$SP = 38.75 + 20 = \text{Rs. } 58.75$$

Verification :

At 2,600 buckets, capacity utilisation :

Fixed cost = Rs. 52,000

Variable cost = 20 × 2,600 = 52,000

Total cost = 52,000 + 52,000 = 1,04,000

Sales = 2,600 buckets @ Rs. 58.75 = Rs. 1,52,750

Profit = Sales – Total cost

= 1,52,750 – 1,04,000 = Rs. 48,750

Problem 6 : Quickwell Ltd. manufactures pressure cookers, the selling price of which is Rs. 300 per unit. Currently, the capacity utilisation is 60% with a sales turnover of Rs. 18 lakhs. The company proposes to reduce the selling price by 20% but desires to maintain the same profit position by increasing the output. Assuming that the increased output could be made and sold, determine the level at which the company should operate to achieve the desired objective.

The following further data are available :

(*i*) Variable cost per unit = Rs. 60.

(*ii*) Semi-variable cost (including a variable element of Rs. per unit) = Rs. 1,80,000

(*iii*) Fixed cost Rs. 3,00,000 will remain constant up to 80% level. Beyond this an additional amount of Rs. 60,000 will be incurred. (*ICWA, Inter December 1998*)

Solution : **Statement of present profitability at 60% capacity**

		Amount	*Per Unit*
(*a*)	Sales	18,00,000	300
	Variable cost	3,60,000	60
	Variable portion of semi-variable cost	60,000	10
(*b*)	Total variable cost	4,20,000	70
(*c*)	Contribution (*a* – *b*)	13,80,000	230

(*d*)	Fixed cost	3,00,000	50
	Fixed portion of semi-variable cost	1,20,000	20
(*e*)	Total fixed cost	4,20,000	70
	Profit ($c - e$)	9,60,000	160
	Revised selling price per unit Rs. 300 – 20% of Rs. 300		240
	Total variable cost per unit		70
	Revised contribution per unit		170

$$\text{BEP (Sales in units)} = \frac{FC + \text{Profit}}{\text{Contribution per unit}}$$

$$= \frac{4,20,000 + 9,60,000}{170}$$

$$= \frac{13,80,000}{170} = 8,118 \text{ units } i.e., 81.18\% \text{ of capacity.}$$

But if the level of capacity is beyond 80%, an additional amount of Rs. 60,000 will be increased towards fixed cost. Then in such the position will be as follows :

$$\text{Sales in unit} = \frac{(4,20,000 + 60,000) + 9,60,000}{170}$$

$$= \frac{14,40,000}{170} = 8,470.58$$

8,471 units are to be sold to maintain the same profit. Therefore, the company should operate at 84.71% level of capacity.

Problem 7 : You are given the following data :

Sales price	Rs. 350 per unit
Variable cost	Rs. 200 per unit
Fixed expenses	Rs. 16,50,000

Ascertain :

(*a*) Break-even point.

(*b*) Sales per unit, if break-even point is brought up to 15,000 units.

(*c*) Sales per unit if break-even point is brought down to 10,000 units.

(Bangalore University, B.Com., April 1992)

Solution :

Contribution = Sales price – Variable cost

= 350 – 200 = Rs. 150

(*a*) $\text{BEP } \frac{\text{Fixed expenses}}{\text{Contribution}} = \frac{16,50,000}{150} = 11,000 \text{ units}$

(*b*) Selling price if BEP is brought up to 15,000 units.

Variable cost 15,000 × 200	30,00,000
Add : Fixed cost	16,50,000
Total cost	46,50,000

$$\text{Selling price} = \frac{46,50,000}{15,000} = \text{Rs. } 310$$

(*c*) Selling price if break-even point is brought down to 10,000 units

Variable cost 10,000 × 200	20,00,000
Add : Fixed cost	16,50,000
Total cost	36,50,000

$$\text{Selling price} = \frac{35,50,000}{10,000} = \text{Rs. } 365$$

Problem 8 : A manufacturer provides you the following data regarding his operations for the year 1991 :

	Rs.
Break-even sales	6,66,667
Direct materials	2,20,000
Gross profit	2,50,000
Contribution margin	3,00,000
Direct labour	3,00,000
Sales	10,00,000
Variable manufacturing overhead	5,000

Calculate the following using the above data :

(*a*) Fixed manufacturing overhead.

(*b*) Variable selling and administrative overhead.

(*c*) Fixed selling and administrative overhead.

(*Calicut University, M.Com., April 1992*)

Solution :

Cost of goods sold = Sales – Gross profit

= 10,00,000 – 2,50,000 = 7,50,000

(*a*) Fixed factory overhead

Let fixed factory overhead = x

Then cost of goods sold will be equal to

$2,20,000 + 3,00,000 + 5,000 + x = 750,000$

$5,25,000 + x = 7,50,000$

$x = 2,25,000$

(*b*) Calculation of fixed selling and administrative overhead

Sales at BEP	6,66,667
Less : Contribution	3,00,000
Total fixed cost	3,66,667
Less : Fixed factory overhead	2,25,000
Fixed selling and administrative overhead	1,41,667

(*c*) Calculation of variable selling and administrative overhead

Sales – Variable cost = Contribution

$10,00,000 - (2,20,000 + 3,00,000 + 5,000 + x) = 3,00,000$

$10,00,000 - 5,25,000 + x = 3,00,000$

$4,75,000 + x = 3,00,000$

$x = - 4,75,000 + 3,00,000$

$x = 1,75,000$

Problem 9 : Sharada Painters Ltd., manufactures and sells four types of points under the brand names of P, Q, R and S. The sales mix in value comprises of $33\frac{1}{3}$%, $41\frac{2}{3}$%, $16\frac{2}{3}$% and $8\frac{1}{3}$ respectively.

The total budgeted sales are Rs. 60,000 per month. Operating costs are :

Variable cost of P	60% of selling price
Variable cost of Q	68% of selling price
Variable cost of R	80% of selling price
Variable cost of S	40% of selling price

Fixed cost amount to Rs. 14,700 per month. Calculate BEP for all paints on an overall basis.

(*Bangalore University, M.Com., May 1989*)

Solution :

	Products				Total
	P	*Q*	*R*	*S*	
Sales mix	$33\frac{1}{3}\%$	$41\frac{2}{3}\%$	$16\frac{2}{3}\%$	$8\frac{1}{3}\%$	100%
Sales (Rs.)	20,000	25,000	10,000	5,000	60,000
Variable cost	12,000	17,000	8,000	2,000	39,000
Contribution					21,000
Less : Fixed cost					14,700
				Profit	6,300

$$\text{BEP} = \frac{\text{Fixed cost}}{\text{Contribution}} \times \text{Sales}$$

$$= \frac{14,700}{21,000} \times 60,000 = \text{Rs. } 42,000$$

PROFIT-VOLUME RATIO OR CONTRIBUTION—SALES PERCENTAGE

The profit volume (P/V) ratio establishes the relation between contribution to sales. The ratio is expressed as a percentage and it furnishes the details of profitability of various products, processes or departments. A high P/V ratio shows that even a slight rise in the volume without a corresponding increase in fixed cost would result in high profit. Therefore, it is advisable for management to increase sales by taking suitable measures such as advertising and other sales promotional measures. The P/V ratio can be increased by maximising contribution, which is possible by increasing the selling price, reducing the variable cost and by improving the product mix. The formula to calculate P/V ratio is as follows :

$$\text{P/V Ratio} = \frac{\text{Contribution}}{\text{Sales}} \times 100$$

Uses of P/V Ratio

1. It helps in the determination of BEP. The formula is

$$\text{BEP} = \frac{\text{FC}}{\text{P / V Ratio}}$$

2. It helps in the determination of profit at any volume of sales. The formula is

$$\text{Volume} \times \text{P/V Ratio} = \text{Contribution} - \text{FC} = \text{Profit}$$

3. It helps in the determination of sales to earn a desired amount of profit. The formula is

$$\text{Sales} = \frac{\text{F+P}}{\text{P / V Ratio}}$$

4. It helps in determining the required selling price per unit. The formula is

$$\text{Selling price} = \frac{\text{Variable cost}}{(100 - \text{P / V Ratio})}$$

5. It helps in ascertaining the variable cost for any volume of sales by reverse method, *i.e.*, by deducting P/V ratio from sales considering it as 100%.

Margin of Safety

The excess of actual sales oveer the break-even sales is known as margin of safety. The formula is as follows :

MS = Sales Volume – Break-even sales volume

The soundness of the business can be known by looking into the margin of safety. If the distance between sales revenue and break-even point on the graph is long, it shows the soundness, of the business. On the other hand a small margin of safety involving a fall in sales revenue results in a loss. The margin of safety can be improved by taking the following measures :

(*a*) Increasing the selling price.
(*b*) Increasing the sales volume by increasing the capacity.
(*c*) By improving the contribution margin through reducing the variable cost.
(*d*) By lowering BEP through reduction of fixed cost.
(*e*) By adopting a better profitable product mix.

Margin of safety can be calculated by using the following formula :

$$\text{MS (in rupees)} = \frac{\text{Profit}}{\text{P / V Ratio}} \text{ or Profit} \times \frac{\text{Contribution}}{\text{Sales}}$$

$$\text{MS (in units)} = \frac{\text{Profit}}{\text{Contribution per unit}}$$

It can also be expressed as a percentage using the following formula :

$$\text{MS Ratio} = \frac{\text{MS}}{\text{Sales}} \times 100$$

$$\text{MS Ratio} = \frac{\text{Actual Sales} - \text{BEP Sales}}{\text{Sales}} \times 100$$

The other formulae used to calculate P/V ratio are as follows :

$$\text{P/V Ratio} = \frac{\text{Contribution}}{\text{Sales}}$$

$$\text{P/V Ratio} = \frac{\text{FC + Profit}}{\text{Sales}}$$

$$\text{P/V Ratio} = \frac{\text{FC + Loss}}{\text{Sales}}$$

$$\text{P/V Ratio} = \frac{\text{Change in contribution}}{\text{Change in sales}}$$

$$\text{P/V Ratio} = \frac{\text{Change in profit (or loss)}}{\text{Change in sales}}$$

Angle of Incidence

The angle at which sales line cuts the total cost line is known as angle of incidence. In other words it represents the angle between sales line and total cost line. The angle of incidence shows the profit earning capacity of the business. Hence, higher the angle of incidence, higher the profit and *vice versa*. A high margin of safety with a broader angle of incidence reveals a highly favourable position of the business.

Problem 10 : Given the following information :

Fixed cost	= Rs. 4,000
Break even sales	= Rs. 20,000
Profit	= Rs. 1,000

Selling price per unit = Rs. 20

You are required to calculate :

(*i*) Sales and marginal cost of sales and

(*ii*) New break-even point if selling price is reduced by 10%

(University of Delhi, B.Com. (Pass), April 1999)

Solution :

Contribution at BEP = Fixed cost is 4,000

$$\text{P/V ratio} = \frac{\text{Contribution}}{\text{Sales}} \times 100$$

$$= \frac{4,000}{20,000} \times 100 = 20\%$$

(*i*) Sales of earn a profit of Rs. 1,000

$$= \frac{\text{Fixed cost + Profit}}{\text{P / V Ratio}}$$

$$= \frac{4,000+1,000}{20\%} = \frac{5,000}{20\%} = 25,000$$

Marginal cost at sales of Rs. 25,000 is found as follows :

Contribution = Sales × P/V ratio

$$= 25,000 \times \frac{20}{100} = 5,000$$

Marginal cost = Sales – Contribution

= 25,000 – 5,000 = Rs. 20,000

(*ii*) New BEP if selling price is reduced by 10%

New sales = 25,000 – 10%

= 22,500

New contribution = 22,500 – 20,000 = Rs. 2,500

$$\text{New P/V Ratio} = \frac{\text{New Contribution}}{\text{New Sales}}$$

$$= \frac{2,500}{22,500} = \frac{1}{9}$$

$$\text{New BEP} = \frac{\text{Fixed cost}}{\text{P / V Ratio}}$$

$$= \frac{4,000}{\frac{1}{9}} \text{ or } = 36,000$$

Problem 11 : Ascertain profit when

Sales	= Rs. 2,00,000
Fixed cost	= Rs. 40,000
BEP	= Rs. 1,60,000

(CA, Inter, May 1999)

Solution :

$$\text{P/V Ratio} = \frac{\text{Fixed cost}}{\text{BEP}} \times 100$$

$$= \frac{40,000}{1,60,000} \times 100 = 25\%$$

Contribution = Sales × P/V Ratio = FC + Profit

= 2,00,000 × 25% = FC + Profit

50,000 = 40,000 – Profit

or Profit = 10,000

Problem 12 : Ascertain sales, when

Fixed cost	= Rs. 20,000
Profit	= Rs. 10,000
BEP	= Rs. 40,000

(CA, Inter, May 1999)

Solution :

Contribution = Fixed cost + Profit
= 20,000 + 10,000
= 30,000

$$\text{P/V Ratio} = \frac{\text{Fixed cost}}{\text{BEP}} \times 100$$

$$= \frac{20{,}000}{40{,}000} \times 100 = 50\%$$

$$\text{Also P/V Ratio} = \frac{\text{Contribution}}{\text{Sales}} \times 100$$

$$\text{or Sales} = \frac{\text{Contribution}}{\text{PV Ratio}} \times 100$$

$$= \frac{30{,}000}{50\%}$$

$$= \frac{30{,}000 \times 100}{50} = 60{,}000$$

Problem 13 : Raj Ltd. manufactures three products *X*, *Y* and *Z*. The unit selling prices of these products are Rs. 100, Rs. 160 and Rs. 75 respectively. The corresponding unit variable costs are Rs. 50, Rs. 80 and Rs. 30. The proportions (quantity wise) in which these products are manufactured and sold are 20%, 30% and 50% respectively. The total fixed costs are Rs. 14,80,000.

Calculate break-even quantity and the productwise break up of such quantity. *(CA, Inter, May 1999)*

Solution :

Overall Break-even Quantity

Products	*X*	*Y*	*Z*
Selling price per unit	100	160	75
Less : Variable cost per unit	50	80	30
Contribution per unit	50	80	45
Contribution at break-even point	$0.20x \times 50$	$0.30x \times 80$	$0.50x \times 45$
(see working note)	$10x$	$24x$	$22.5x$

At break-even point, contribution = Fixed cost

Hence $10x + 24x + 22.5x$ = Rs. 14,80,000

$$\text{or} \quad x = \frac{14{,}80{,}000}{56.5} = 26{,}195 \text{ units}$$

Productwise break-up of overall break-even quantity

Product *X* = 26,195 units × 0.20 = 5,239 units
Product *Y* = 26,195 units × 0.30 = 7,858 units
Product *Z* = 26,195 units × 0.50 = 13,098 units

Working note :

Let *x* be the overall break-even quantity of three products *X*, *Y* and *Z*. At break-even *X* has 20%, 30% and 50% units of *X*, *Y* and *Z*. The productwise production and sale of three given products in terms of overall break-even quantity are $0.20x$, $0.30x$ and $0.50x$ units respectively.

Problem 14 : When volume is 3,000 units, average cost in Rs. 4 per unit. When volume is 4,000 units, average cost is Rs. 3.50. The break-even point is 5,000 units. Find the P/V ratio. *(ICWA, Inter, Dec. 1999)*

Solution :

	Output	*Average Cost*	*Total Cost*
	3,000	4	12,000
	4,000	3.50	14,000
change	1,000		2,000

$$\text{Variable cost per unit} = \frac{2,000}{1,000} = \text{Rs. } 2$$

$$\begin{aligned}\text{Total fixed cost} &= \text{Total cost} - \text{Variable cost}\\ &= 12,000 - 3,000 \text{ units} \times \text{Rs. } 2\\ &= 12,000 - 6,000\\ &= 6,000\\ \text{or} \quad &= 14,000 - 4,000 \text{ units} \times \text{Rs. } 2\\ &= 14,000 - 8,000\\ &= 6,000\end{aligned}$$

$$\begin{aligned}\text{At BEP,} \quad \text{BEP sales} &= \text{Variable cost} + \text{Fixed cost}\\ 5,000 \text{ units} &= 5,000 \times 2 + 6,000\\ &= 10,000 + 6,000\\ &= 16,000\end{aligned}$$

$$\text{BEP} = \frac{\text{Fixed Cost}}{\text{P/V Ratio}}$$

$$\text{or P/V Ratio} = \frac{\text{Fixed cost}}{\text{BEP}}$$

$$= \frac{6,000}{16,000} = \frac{3}{8} \text{ or } 37.5\%$$

Problem 15 : ABC Ltd. fixed costs of Rs. 2,00,000. It has two products, that it can sell; *A* and *B*. The company sells these products at a rate of 2 units of *A* to 1 unit of *B*. The unit contribution is Re. 1 per unit for A and 2 per unit for B. How many units of A and B would be sold at the break-even point.

(ICWA, Inter, Dec. 1999)

Solution :

Products	*A*	*B*	*Total*
Sales unit be (in the ratio of 2 : 1)	2	1	3 units
Contribution per unit	Re. 1	Rs. 2	
Total contribution	Rs. 2	2	Rs. 4

$$\text{Hence, contribution per unit (composite)} = \frac{4}{3}$$

$$\text{Total fixed cost} = \text{Rs. } 2,00,000$$

$$\text{BEP (composite)} = \frac{\text{Fixed cost}}{\text{Contribution per unit}}$$

$$= \frac{2,00,000}{\frac{4}{3}}$$

$$\text{or BEP in units} = \frac{2,00,000 \times 3}{4}$$

$$= 1,50,000 \text{ units}$$

$$\frac{2}{3} A = 1,00,000 \text{ units}$$

$$\frac{1}{3} B = 50,000 \text{ units}$$

Problem 16 : A company had incurred fixed expenses of Rs. 2,25,000 with sales of Rs. 7,50,000 and earned a profit of Rs. 1,50,000 during the first half year. In the second half year, it suffered a loss of Rs. 75,000 calculate :

(*i*) The P/V ratio, break-even point and margin of safety

(*ii*) Expected sales-volume for the second half year assuming that selling price and fixed expenses remained unchanged during second helf year. *(CS, Inter, June 1998)*

Solution : **Calculations for the first half-year**

$$\text{P/V Ratio} = \frac{\text{Fixed cost + Profit}}{\text{Sales}}$$

$$= \frac{2,25,000 + 1,50,000}{7,50,000} = 50\%$$

$$\text{BEP} = \frac{\text{Fixed Cost}}{\text{P / V Ratio}} =$$

$$= \frac{2,25,000}{50\%} = 4,50,000$$

Margin of safety = Actual sales – Sales at BEP

= 7,50,000 – 4,50,000 = Rs. 3,00,000

(*ii*) Expected sales volume for second half year

$$= \frac{\text{Fixed Cost} - \text{Loss}}{\text{P / V Ratio}}$$

$$= \frac{2,25,000 - 75,000}{50\%}$$

$$= \frac{1,50,000}{50} \times 100 \quad = 3,00,000$$

Problem 17 : The profit volume ratio of X Ltd. is 50% and the margin of safety is 40%. You are required to calculate the net profit if the sales value is Rs. 1,00,000. *(CA, Inter, November 1998)*

$$\text{Margin of safety ratio} = \frac{\text{Margin of safety in absolute terms}}{\text{Actual sales}} \times 100$$

$$40 = \frac{\text{Margin of safety in absolute terms}}{1,00,000} \times 100$$

or $$\text{Margin of safety in absolute terms} = \frac{1,00,000 \times 40}{100}$$

$$= 40,000$$

Also $$\text{Margin of safety in absolute terms} = \frac{\text{Profit}}{\text{P / V Ratio}}$$

or $$40,000 \times \frac{\text{Profit}}{50\%}$$

or $$\text{Profit} = 40,000 \times \frac{50}{100} = \text{Rs. } 20,000$$

Problem 18 : A Single product company sells its products at Rs. 60 per unit. In 1996, the company operated at a margin of safety of 40%. The fixed costs amounted to Rs. 3,60,000 and the variable cost ratio to sales was 80%.

In 1997, it is estimated that the variable costs will go up by 10% and the fixed costs will increase by 5%. Find the selling price required to be fixed in 1997 to earn. The same P/V ratio as in 1996.

Assuming the same selling price of Rs. 60 per unit in 1997, find the number of units required to be produced and sold to earn the same profit as in 1996. *(CA, Inter, May 1998)*

Solution : **Calculation of P/V ratio (in 1996)**

$$\text{P/V ratio} = \frac{\text{Selling price} - \text{Variable Cost per unit}}{\text{Selling price}} \times 100$$

$$= \frac{60-48}{60} \times 100$$

$$= \frac{12}{60} \times 100 = 20\%$$

Calculation of units sold (in 1996)

$$\text{BEP} = \frac{\text{Fixed cost}}{\text{Contribution per unit}}$$

$$= \frac{3,60,000}{12} = 30,000 \text{ units}$$

Since, Margin of safety is 40%, therefore BEP is 60% of units sold

$$\text{or, No. of units sold} = \frac{\text{BEP}}{60\%}$$

$$= \frac{30,000 \text{ units}}{60\%} = 50,000$$

Calculation of profit earned in 1996

Profit = Total contribution – Fixed cost
= 50,000 units × Rs. 12 per unit – 3,60,000
= 6,00,000 – 3,60,000 = 2,40,000

Selling price to be fixed in 1997

Variable cost per unit in 1997 =
Rs. 52.80 (Rs. 48 + 4.80)
Fixed cost in 1997 :
Rs. 3,78,000 (3,60,000 + 18,000)
P/V ratio in 1996 = 20%
Since P/V ratio is 20% variable cost is 80%

$$\text{Hence, the required SP} = \frac{52.80}{80\%}$$

$$\text{or} \quad \frac{52.80}{80} \times 100$$

= Rs. 66

Number of units to be produced and sold in 1997 to earn the same profit as in 1996

Profit in 1996 = Rs. 2,40,000
Fixed cost in 1997 = Rs. 3,78,000
Desired contribution in 1997
(2,40,000 + 3,78,000) = Rs. 6,18,000
Contribution per unit in 1997 = SP – Variable cost per unit
= 60 – 52.80
= 7.20

$$\text{No. of units to be produced and sold in 1997} = \frac{\text{Fixed cost in 1997}}{\text{Contribution per unit in 1997}}$$

$$= \frac{3,78,000}{7.20}$$

= 52,500 units

Problem 19 : A Ltd. maintains, a margin of safety of 37.5% with an overall contribution to sales ratio of 40%. Its fixed costs amount to Rs. 5 lakhs.

Calculate the following :

(*i*) Break-even sales

(*ii*) Total sales

(*iii*) Total variable costs

(*iv*) Current profit

(*v*) New margin of safety if the sales value is increased by $7\frac{1}{2}$%.

(ICWA, Inter, December 1998)

Solution :

(1) Break-even sales $= \frac{\text{Fixed Cost}}{\text{Contribution / Sales}}$

$= \frac{\text{5 lakhs}}{40\%} = 12.50$ lakhs

(2) Total sales = Break-even sales + Margin of safety

$= \text{Break-even sales} + \frac{37.5}{100} \times \text{Sales}$ [Given MS = 37.5% of sales]

or, Break-even sales $= \text{Sales} - \frac{37.5}{100}\text{ sales}$

or, 12.50 lakhs $= \frac{62.5}{100}\text{ sales}$

or, Sales $= \frac{12.50 \text{ lakhs} \times 100}{62.5} = 20$ lakhs

(3) Total variable cost = 60% of Rs. 20 lakhs

= 12 lakhs

Because, Sales – Variable cost = Contribution

(4) Current profit = Sales – (Variable cost + Fixed cost)

= 20 lakhs – (12 lakhs + 5 lakhs)

= 20 lakhs – 17 lakhs

= 3 lakhs

(5) **New margin of safety if sales value is increased by $7\frac{1}{2}$%**

New sales value = Rs. 20 lakhs + $7\frac{1}{2}$%

= 21.50 lakhs

Hence, new margin of safety = New sales – Break-even sales

= 21.50 lakhs – 12.50 lakhs

= Rs. 9 lakhs

Problem 20 :

(*i*) Find out BEP sales if budgeted output is 80,000 units, Fixed cost is Rs. 4,00,000, Selling price per unit is Rs. 20 and variable cost per unit is Rs. 10.

(*ii*) Calculate selling price, if marginal cost as Rs. 2,400 and P/V Ratio is 20%.

(*iii*) Find out margin of safety if profit is Rs. 20,000 and P/V Ratio is 40%.

(University of Delhi, B.Com. (Pass), April 1997)

Solution :

(*i*) BEP $= \frac{\text{Fixed Cost}}{\text{Contribution}}$

$= \frac{4,00,000}{20-10} = \frac{4,00,000}{10} = 40,000$ units

BEP Sales = 40,000 units × Rs. 20

= Rs. 8,00,000

(*ii*) When P/V Ratio is 20%, then variable cost is 80% of sales

$$\text{Thus, Selling price} = 2{,}400 \times \frac{100}{80} = \text{Rs. } 3{,}000$$

$$(iii)\ \text{Margin of safety} = \frac{\text{Profit}}{\text{P / V Ratio}}$$

$$= \frac{20{,}000}{40\%} = \text{Rs. } 50{,}000$$

Problem 21 : From the following data, you are required to calculate : (*a*) P/V Ratio, (*b*) Break-even sales, (*c*) Sales required to earn a profit of Rs. 4,50,000.

Fixed expenses	Rs. 90,000
Variable cost per unit :	
Direct material	Rs. 5
Direct labour	Rs. 2
Direct expenses	Rs. 2
Selling price per unit	Rs. 12

(*University of Madras, B.Com., Sept. 1997*)

Solution :

$$(a)\ \text{P/V Ratio} = \frac{\text{Sales} - \text{Variable Cost}}{\text{Sales}} \times 100$$

$$= \frac{12-9}{12} \times 100$$

$$= \frac{3}{12} \times 100 = 25\%$$

$$(b)\ \text{BEP Sales} = \frac{\text{Fixed Cost}}{\text{P / V Ratio}}$$

$$= \frac{90{,}000}{25\%} \text{ or } \frac{90{,}000 \times 100}{25} = 3{,}60{,}000$$

(*c*) Sales required to earn profit of Rs. 4,50,000

$$= \frac{\text{Total Fixed Cost + Profit required}}{\text{P / V Ratio}}$$

$$= \frac{90{,}000 + 4{,}50{,}000}{25\%}$$

$$= \frac{90{,}000 + 4{,}50{,}000}{25} \times 100$$

$$= \text{Rs. } 21{,}60{,}000$$

Problem 22 : The Sales Turnover and Profit during two years were as follows :

Year	*Sales* Rs.	*Profit* Rs.
1991	1,40,000	15,000
1992	1,60,000	20,000

Calculate :

(*a*) P/V Ratio

(*b*) BEP

(*c*) Sales required to earn a profit of Rs. 40,000

(*d*) Fixed expenses

(*University of Madras, B.Com., March 1997*)

Solution :

Year	*Sales*	*Profit*
1991	1,40,000	15,000
1992	1,60,000	20,000
Difference	20,000	5,000

(*i*) P/V Ratio $= \frac{\text{Difference in profit}}{\text{Difference in Sales}} \times 100$

$= \frac{5,000}{20,000} \times 100 \quad = 25\%$

Total fixed cost :

Contribution = Sales × P/V Ratio

$= 1,40,000 \times \frac{25}{100} \quad = 35,000$

Less : Profit $= 15,000$

Total fixed cost $20,000$

(*ii*) BEP $= \frac{\text{Total Fixed Cost}}{\text{P / V Ratio}}$

$\frac{20,000}{25} \times 100 = 80,000$

(*iii*) *Sales to earn a profit of Rs. 40,000*

$\frac{\text{Total Fixed Cost + Profit}}{\text{P / V Ratio}}$

$= \frac{20,000 + 40,000}{25\%} = 2,40,000$

(*iv*) Fixed cost as calculated above is Rs. 20,000.

Problem 23 : Given the following, find the margin of safety :

(1) Profit earned Rs. 24,000

(2) Selling price per unit Rs. 10

(3) Marginal cost per unit Rs. 7

(*CS, Inter, June 1997*)

Solution :

Contribution per unit $= 10 - 7 = \text{Rs. } 3$

Margin of safety sales (units) $= \frac{\text{Profit earned}}{\text{contribution per unit}}$

$= \frac{24,000}{3} = 8,000$ units

Margin of safety sales (value) $= 8,000 \times \text{Rs. } 10 = \text{Rs. } 80,000$

Problem 24 : Given the following, calculate P/V ratio and profit when sales are Rs. 20,000, fixed cost Rs. 4,000 and Break-even point Rs. 10,000. (*CS, Inter, June 1997*)

Solution :

Variable cost = Break-even point – Fixed cost

$= 10,000 - 4,000$

$= 6,000$

P/V Ratio $= \frac{\text{Contribution}}{\text{Sales}} \times 100$

$= \frac{10,000 - 6,000}{10,000} \times 100$

$= \frac{4,000}{10,000} \times 100 \quad = 40\%$

Profit when sales are Rs. 20,000

$$S \times P/V = F + P$$

$$20{,}000 \times \frac{40}{100} = 4{,}000 + P$$

$$8{,}000 = 4{,}000 + P$$

$$P = 4{,}000$$

Problem 24 : The ratio of variable cost to sales is 70%. The break-even point occurs at 60% of the capacity sales. Find the capacity sales when fixed costs are Rs. 90,000. Also compute profit at 75% of the capacity sales. *(CA, Inter, November 1997)*

Solution :

Basic Data Given

Since $\frac{\text{Variable Cost}}{\text{Sales}} = 70\%$

Therefore, $\frac{\text{Contribution}}{\text{Sales}} = 30\%$ which is also P/V ratio

Capacity sales

$$BEP = \frac{\text{Fixed Cost}}{P/V \text{ Ratio}}$$

$$= \frac{90{,}000}{30\%} \text{ or } \frac{90{,}000 \times 100}{30}$$

$$= 3{,}00{,}000$$

BEP (as given) = 60% of capacity sales

Hence capacity sales $= \frac{3{,}00{,}000}{60\%} = 5{,}00{,}000$

Calculation of profit at 75% of the capacity sales

75% of capacity sales (75% of Rs. 5,00,000)	3,75,000
Less : Variable cost	2,62,500
Contribution	1,12,500
Less : Fixed cost	90,000
Profit	22,500

Problem 26 : If margin of safety is Rs. 2,40,000 (40% of sales) and P/V Ratio is 30% of AB Ltd., calculate its (*i*) Break-even sales, (*ii*) Amount of profit on sales of Rs. 9,00,000. *(CA, Inter, May 1997)*

Solution :

Calculation of Margin of Safety

$$M\,S = \frac{\text{Profit}}{P/V \text{ Ratio}}$$

or Profit = M S × P/V Ratio

$$= 2{,}40{,}000 \times \frac{30}{100} = \text{Rs. } 72{,}000$$

Calculation of Total sales

$$\frac{\text{Margin of Safety}}{40\%}$$

$$\text{or } \frac{2{,}40{,}000 \times 100}{40} = \text{Rs. } 6{,}00{,}000$$

Calculation of contribution

Contribution = Sales × P/V Ratio

$= 6,00,000 \times \frac{30}{100} = 1,80,000$

Calculation of fixed cost

Fixed cost = Contribution – profit
= 1,80,000 – 72,000
= Rs. 1,08,000

(*i*) Break-even sales $= \frac{\text{Fixed Cost}}{\text{P / V Ratio}}$

$= \frac{1,08,000}{30\%} = \text{Rs. } 3,60,000$

(*ii*) *Amount of profit on sales of Rs. 9,00,000*

$S \times P/V = F + P$

$9,00,000 \times \frac{30}{100} = 1,08,000 + P$

$2,70,000 = 1,08,000 + P$

$P = 2,70,000 \times 1,08,000$

$P = \text{Rs. } 1,62,000$

Problem 27 : X Ltd. has earned contribution of Rs. 2,00,000 and net profit of Rs. 1,50,000 on sales of Rs. 8,00,000. What is its margin of safety. (*CA, Inter, May 1997*)

Solution :

P/V Ratio $= \frac{\text{Contribution}}{\text{Sales}} \times 100$

$= \frac{2,00,000}{8,00,000} \times 100 = 25\%$

Margin of safety $= \frac{\text{Profit}}{\text{P / V Ratio}}$

$= \frac{1,50,000}{25\%} = \text{Rs. } 6,00,000$

Problem 28 : From the following data, calculate :

(1) Break-even point expressed in amount of sales in rupees

(2) Number of units that must be sold to earn a profit of Rs. 1,60,000 per year

Selling price	Rs. 20	per unit
Variable manufacturing cost	Rs. 11	per unit
Variable selling cost	Rs. 3	per unit
Fixed factory overheads	Rs. 5,40,000	P.A
Fixed selling cost	Rs. 2,52,000	P.A.

(*University of Delhi, B.Com. (Pass), April 1996*)

Solution :

Given Data

Variable cost per unit = Rs. 11 + 3 = Rs. 14
Total fixed cost = 5,40,000 + 2,52,000
= 7,92,000

Contribution = SP – VC
= 20 – 14 = Rs. 6

P/V Ratio $= \frac{\text{contribution}}{\text{sales}} \times 100$

$= \frac{6}{20} \times 100 = 30\%$

(1) BEP $= \dfrac{\text{Total Fixed Cost}}{\text{P / V Ratio}}$

$= \dfrac{7,92,000}{30\%} = \text{Rs. } 26,40,000$

(2) *Sales to earn a profit of Rs. 1,60,000*

$= \dfrac{\text{Fixed Cost + Profit}}{\text{Contribution per unit}}$

$= \dfrac{7,92,000 + 1,60,000}{6} = 1,58,667 \text{ units}$

Problem 29 : The records of a company show the following :

Period	*Sales*	*Profit*
	Rs.	*Rs.*
I	1,20,000	9,000
II	1,40,000	13,000

Find out : (*a*) P/V ratio, (*b*) Break-even point, (*c*) Fixed cost, (*d*) Profit when sales are Rs. 10,00,000, (*e*) Sales required to earn a profit of Rs. 20,000, (*f*) Margin of safety and, (*g*) Variable cost for period *II*.

(*University of Madras, B.Com., Sept. 1996*)

Solution :

(*a*) P/V Ratio $= \dfrac{\text{Difference in Profit}}{\text{Difference in Sales}} \times 100$

$= \dfrac{4,000}{12,000} \times 100 = 20\%$

(*b*) BEP $= \dfrac{\text{Total Fixed Cost}}{\text{P / V Ratio}}$

$= \dfrac{15,000}{20\%} = 75,000$

(*c*) Total fixed cost :

Taking sales of period *III*	=	1,20,000
Contribution = $1,20,000 \times \dfrac{20}{100}$	=	24,000
Less : Profit		9,000
Fixed cost		15,000

(*d*) *Profit when sales is Rs. 1,00,000*

$$S \times P/V = F + P$$

$$1,00,000 \times \frac{20}{100} = 15,000 + P$$

$$20,000 = 15,000 + P$$

$$P = 5,000$$

(*e*) *Sales when profit is Rs. 20,000*

$$S \times P/V = F + P$$

$$S \times \frac{20}{100} = 15,000 + 2,000$$

$$S \times \frac{1}{5} = 35,000$$

$$S = 35,000 \times 5$$

$$S = 1,75,000$$

(*f*) *Margin of safety for period II*

Margin of safety = Actual sales – Break-even sales

= 1,40,000 – 75,000

= 65,000

(*g*) *Variable cost for period II*

Sales for period *II*	1,40,000
Less : Contribution $\left(1,40,000 \times \frac{20}{100}\right)$	28,000
Variable cost	1,12,000

Problem 30 : R.S. Manufacturing Ltd., budgets production of 3,00,000 units at a variable cost of Rs. 10 each. The fixed cost are Rs. 20,00,000. The selling price is fixed to yield 20% profit on cost.

You are required to calculate :

(*i*) P/V Ratio

(*ii*) Break-even production units

(*University of Delhi, B.Com. (Pass), April 1995*)

Solution :

Variable cost = 3,00,000 × 10	=	30,00,000
Fixed cost	=	20,00,000
Total cost		50,00,000
Profit		10,00,000
Sales		60,00,000

$$\text{P/V Ratio} = \frac{S-V}{S} \times 100$$

$$= \frac{60,00,000-30,00,000}{60,00,000} \times 100$$

$$= \frac{30,00,000}{60,00,000} \times 100 = 50\%$$

$$\text{Selling price per unit} = \frac{60,00,000}{3,00,000} = \text{Rs. } 20$$

Variable cost = Rs. 10 per unit

Contribution = S – V

= 20 – 10 = 10

$$\text{BEP} = \frac{\text{Fixed cost}}{\text{Contribution per unit}}$$

$$= \frac{20,00,000}{10} = 2,00,000 \text{ units}$$

Problem 31 : Firm '*X*' manufactures Surgical goods. Its normal production is 2,600 units per month at a total cost of Rs. 32,000. At full capacity it can manufacture 3,400 units per month at a total cost of Rs. 38,000 calculate :

(1) Average cost per instrument under normal operating condition.

(2) Average variable cost per instrument.

(3) Total fixed cost.

(4) Average fixed cost under normal operating condition. (*University of Madras, B.Com., March 95*)

Solution :

Note : Since the selling price is not given in problem, it is assumed as Rs. 15 per unit.

	Sales	Total cost	Profit
Normal production (2,600 units × 15)	39,000	32,000	7,000
Full capacity (3,400 units × 15)	51,000	38,000	13,000
	12,000		6,000

$$\text{P/V Ratio} = \frac{\text{Difference in profit}}{\text{Difference in Sales}} \times 100$$

$$= \frac{6,000}{12,000} \times 100 = 50\%$$

(*a*) *Average cost per instrument under normal operating condition :*

$$\frac{\text{Total cost}}{\text{Normal production}} = \frac{32,000}{2,600 \text{ units}} = 12.31$$

(*b*) *Average variable cost per instrument*

P/V Ratio = 50%

Variable cost = 50% (balance %)

Normal production sales = 39,000

Variable cost $39,000 \times \frac{50}{100}$ = 19,500

Variable cost per unit = $\frac{19,500}{2,600}$ units = Rs. 7.50

(*c*) *Total fixed cost* :

Taking normal production total cost	= 32,000
Less : Variable cost 2,600 × 7.50	19,500
Total fixed cost	12,500

(*d*) Average fixed cost under normal operating

Total fixed cost = 12,500

Normal production = 2,600 units

Average fixed cost = $\frac{12,500}{2,600}$ = Rs. 4.81

Problem 32 :

	Sales Rs.	Profit Rs.
Period 1	10,000	2,000
Period 2	15,000	4,000

You are required to calculate :

(*i*) P/V Ratio

(*ii*) Fixed cost

(*iii*) Break-even sales volume

(*iv*) Sales to earn a profit of Rs. 3,000 and

(*v*) Profit when sales are Rs. 8,000

(*CS, Inter, June 1995*)

Solution :

(*a*) $$\text{P/V Ratio} = \frac{\text{Change in profit}}{\text{Change in sales}} \times 100$$

$$= \frac{2,000}{5,000} \times 100 = 40\%$$

(*b*) $\dfrac{\text{Fixed Cost}}{S \times P/V = F+P}$

$$= 10{,}000 \times \frac{40}{100} = F + 2{,}000$$

$$= 4{,}000 = F + 2{,}000$$

$$F = \text{Rs. } 2{,}000$$

(*c*) Break-even sales value $= \dfrac{\text{Fixed Cost}}{P/V \text{ Ratio}}$

$$= \frac{2{,}000}{40\%} = \text{Rs. } 5{,}000$$

(*d*) Sale value to earn a profit of Rs. 3,000

$$= \frac{\text{Fixed Cost + Desired Profit}}{P/V \text{ Ratio}}$$

$$= \frac{2{,}000 + 3{,}000}{40\%} = \frac{5{,}000}{40\%} = \text{Rs. } 12{,}500$$

(*e*) Profit when sales are Rs. 8,000

$$S \times P/V = F + P$$

$$8{,}000 \times \frac{40}{100} = 2{,}000 + P$$

$$3{,}200 = 2{,}000 + P$$

$$P = 1{,}200$$

Problem 33 : A Company had incurred fixed expenses of 4,50,000 with sales of Rs. 15,50,000 and earned a profit of Rs. 3,00,000 during the first half year. In the second half, it suffered a loss of Rs. 1,50,000. Calculate :

(*i*) The profit valume ratio, Break-even point and margin of safety for the first half year

(*ii*) Expected sales-volume for the second half year assuming that selling price and fixed expenses remained unchaged during the second half year

(*iii*) The break-even point and margin of safety for the whole year.

(*CA, Inter, May 1996*)

Solution :

(*i*) *Calculation of P/V Ratio BEP and M.S*

$$\text{P/V Ratio} = \frac{\text{Contribution}}{\text{Sales}} \times 100$$

$$\text{or,} \quad = \frac{(\text{Fixed expenses + Profit})}{\text{Sales}} \times 100$$

$$= \frac{4{,}50{,}000 + 3{,}00{,}000}{15{,}00{,}000} \times 100$$

$$= \frac{7{,}50{,}000}{15{,}00{,}000} \times 100 = 50\%$$

$$\text{BEP} = \frac{\text{Fixed Cost}}{P/V \text{ Ratio}}$$

$$= \frac{4{,}50{,}000}{50\%} = 9{,}00{,}000$$

Margin of safety = Actual sales – Break-even sales
= 15,00,000 – 9,00,000
= 6,00,000

(*ii*) Expected sales value for the second half year :

$$\text{Expected sales value} = \frac{\text{Fixed cost} - \text{loss}}{\text{P / V Ratio}}$$

$$= \frac{4,50,000 - 1,50,000}{50\%}$$

$$= \frac{3,00,00}{50\%} = 6,00,000$$

(*iii*) *BEP and MS for the whole year*

$$\text{BEP} = \frac{\text{Fixed cost for the whole year}}{\text{P / V Ratio}}$$

$$= \frac{9,00,000}{50\%} = \text{Rs. } 18,00,000$$

$$\text{MS} = \frac{\text{Profit for the year}}{\text{P / V Ratio}}$$

$$= \frac{3,00,000 - 1,50,000}{50} = \text{Rs. } 3,00,000$$

or M S = Sales above BEP
= Actual sales – Break even sales
= (15,00,000 + 6,00,000) – 18,00,000
Rs. 3,00,000

Problem 34 : A company sells its product at Rs. 15 per unit. In a period, if it produces and sells 8,000 units, it incurrs a loss of Rs. 5 per unit. If the volume is raised to 20,000 units, it earns a profit of Rs. 4 per unit. Calculate BEP both in terms of rupees as well as in units. (*CA, Inter, November 1996*)

Solution :

Average Cost at 8,000 units

= Selling price per unit + Less Component per unit
= 15 + 5 = Rs. 20

Average cost at 20,000 units

Selling price per unit – profit component per unit
= 15 – 4 = Rs. 11

Total cost at 8,000 units = 8,000 × 20 = 1,60,000
Total cost at 2,000 units = 20,000 × 11 = 2,20,000

$$\text{Variable cost per unit} = \frac{\text{Change in the total cost}}{\text{Change in the volume of production}}$$

$$= \frac{2,20,000 - 1,60,000}{20,000 - 8,000 \text{ units}}$$

$$= \frac{60,000}{12,000} = \text{Rs. } 5$$

Fixed cost = Total cost – Variable cost
= 1,60,000 – 40,000
= 1,20,000

$$\text{P/V Ratio} = \frac{S - V}{S} \times 100$$

$$= \frac{15 - 5}{15} \times 100 = 66\frac{2}{3}\%$$

$$\text{BEP (in Rs.)} = \frac{\text{FC}}{\text{P / V Ratio}}$$

$$= \frac{1{,}20{,}000}{66\frac{2}{3}\%} = \text{Rs. } 1{,}80{,}000$$

$$\text{BEP (in units)} = \frac{\text{FC}}{\text{Contribution per unit}}$$

$$= \frac{1{,}20{,}000}{15-5}$$

$$= \frac{1{,}20{,}000}{10} = 12{,}000 \text{ units}$$

Problem 35 : Two firms A & Co. and B & Co. sell the same type of product in the same market. Their budgeted profit & loss a/c for the year ending 31.3.1966 are as follows :

	A & Co			*B & Co.*
Sales		5,00,000		6,00,000
Variable cost	4,00,000		4,00,000	
Fixed cost	30,000	4,30,000	70,000	4,70,000
	Net profit	70,000		1,30,000

Required :

(1) Calculate at which sales value both the firms will earn equal profit.

(2) State which firm is likely to earn greater profits in condition of

(*i*) heavy demand for the product

(*ii*) Low demand for the product give reasons. (*CA, Inter, November 1995*)

Solution :

	A & Co.	*B & Co.*
(1) Sales	5,00,000	6,00,000
Less : Variable cost	4,00,000	4,00,000
Contribution	1,00,000	2,00,000
P/V Ratio = $\frac{C}{S} \times 100$	20%	$33\frac{1}{3}\%$

$$\text{Sales volume for both the firm to earn equal profits} = \frac{\text{Difference in FC}}{\text{Difference in P / V Ratio}}$$

$$= \frac{40{,}000}{13.33\%} = \text{Rs. } 3{,}00{,}000$$

(2) The P/V Ratio of B & Co. at $33\frac{1}{3}\%$ is higher than that of A & Co. at 20% and therefore B & Co., will earn higher profit if the sales volume exceeds Rs. 3,00,000 level.

In fact, for each additional unit of products sales above Rs. 3,00,000; the profit of B & Co. will rise by Rs. $33\frac{1}{3}$ which exceeds by Rs. $13\frac{1}{3}\%$. The profit of A & Co. under similar conditions. However, below that level profit for A & Co. will be greater. We can therefore, generally conclude that B & Co. is likely to earn higher profit under conditions of heavy demand for the product above Rs. 3,00,000. On the other hand, A & Co. is likely to earn higher profits under conditions of low demand for the product (below Rs. 3,00,000)

Problem 36 : A company earned a profit of Rs. 30,000 during the year 1994-95. If the marginal cost and the selling price of a product are Rs. 8 and Rs. 10 per unit respectively, find out the amount of margin of safety. (*CA, Inter, May 1995*)

Solution :

$$\text{P/V Ratio} = \frac{\text{Contribution}}{\text{Sales}} \times 100$$

$$= \frac{2}{10} \times 100 = 20\%$$

$$\text{Margin of safety} = \frac{\text{Profit}}{\text{P / V Ratio}}$$

$$= \frac{30,000}{20\%} = \text{Rs. } 1,50,000$$

Problem 37 : From the following data, compute break-even sales and margin of safety :

Sales	10,00,000
Fixed cost	3,00,000
Profit	2,00,000

(CS, Inter, December 1994)

Solution :

$$S - V = F + P$$

$$10,00,000 - V = 3,00,000 + 2,00,000$$

$$V = -10,00,000 + 3,00,000 + 2,00,000$$

$$V = \text{Rs. } 5,00,000$$

$$\text{P/V Ratio} = \frac{S - V}{S} \times 100$$

$$= \frac{10,00,000 - 5,00,000}{10,00,000} \times 100$$

$$= \frac{5,00,000}{10,00,000} \times 100 = 50\%$$

$$\text{BEP (Sales)} = \frac{\text{Fixed Cost}}{\text{P / V Ratio}}$$

$$= \frac{300,000}{50\%} = \text{Rs. } 6,00,000$$

Margin of safety = Sales – Break-even sales
= 10,00,000 – 6,00,000
= Rs. 4,00,000

Problem 38 : From the following data find out (*i*) Sales and (*ii*) New break-even sales, if selling price is reduced by 10%

	Rs.
Fixed cost	4,000
Break-even sales	20,000
Profit	1,000
Selling price per unit	20

(CS, Inter, December 1994)

Solution :

$$\text{P/V Ratio} = \frac{\text{Contribution}}{\text{Sales}} \times 100$$

Fixed cost = 4,000 *i.e.*, contribution at BEP sales

$$\text{P/V Ratio} = \frac{4,000}{20,000} \times 100 = 20\%$$

(*i*) Sales $= \dfrac{FC + P}{P / V \text{ Ratio}}$

$= \dfrac{4,000 + 1,000}{20\%} = \text{Rs. } 25,000$

(*ii*) New selling price = 20 – 10% = Rs. 18 per unit

Variable cost = 80% of Rs. 20 = 16 per unit

New contribution Rs. 2 per unit

New P/V Ratio $= \dfrac{2}{18} \times 100 = 11\dfrac{1}{9}\%$

New break-even sales $= \dfrac{\text{Fixed Cost}}{P / V \text{ Ratio}}$

$= \dfrac{4,000}{11\frac{1}{9}\%} = \text{Rs. } 36,000$

Problem 39 : From the following data, calculate BEP

Selling price per unit	20
Variable cost per unit	15
Fixed overheads	20,000

If sales are 20% above BEP, determine the net profit. (*CS, Inter, Dec. 1994*)

Solution :

Contribution per unit = 20 – 15 = Rs. 5

P/V Ratio $= \dfrac{\text{Contribution}}{\text{Sales}} \times 100$

$= \dfrac{5}{20} \times 100 = 25\%$

BEP $= \dfrac{\text{Fixed Cost}}{P / V \text{ Ratio}} = \dfrac{20,000}{25\%} = \text{Rs. } 80,000$

If sales are 20% above BEP :

Sales = 80,000 + 20% = Rs. 96,000

= S × P/V Ratio = F + P

$96,000 \times \dfrac{25}{100} = 20,000 + P$

$24,000 = 20,000 + P$

P = Rs. 4,000

Problem 40 : The following figures are extracted from books of a manufacturing concern for the year 1990-91 :

Direct material	2,05,000
Direct labour	75,000
Fixed overhead	60,000
Variable overhead	1,00,000
Sales	5,00,000

Calculate the break-even point. What will be the effect on BEP on an increase of 10% in (*i*) Fixed expenses and (*ii*) Variable expenses. (*CS, Inter, June 1992*)

Solution :

P/V Ratio $= \dfrac{\text{Contribution}}{\text{Sales}} \times 100$

$= \dfrac{1,20,000}{5,00,000} \times 100 = 24\%$

$$\text{BEP} = \frac{\text{Fixed Cost}}{\text{P / V Ratio}} = \frac{60{,}000}{24\%} = \text{Rs. } 2{,}50{,}000$$

(*i*) If fixed cost increases by 10%.
Revised fixed cost = 60,000 + 10% = Rs. 66,000

$$\text{BEP} = \frac{\text{FC}}{\text{P / V Ratio}} = \frac{66{,}000}{24\%} = \text{Rs. } 2{,}75{,}000$$

(*ii*) If variable cost increases by 10% :
Variable cost :

Direct material	2,05,000
Direct labour	75,000
Variable overhead	1,00,000
	3,80,000
Add : 10 % Increase	38,000
Revised variable cost	4,18,000

$$\text{P/V Ratio} = \frac{\text{Contribution}}{\text{Sales}} \times 100$$

$$= \frac{82{,}000}{5{,}00{,}000} \times 100 = 16.4\%$$

$$\text{BEP} = \frac{60{,}000}{16.4\%} = \text{Rs. } 3{,}65{,}854$$

Problem 41 : The profit ratio of BB & Co. dealing in precision instrument is 50% and the margin of safety is 40%.

You are required to work out the break-even point and the net profit if the sale volume is Rs. 50 lakhs.

(CS, (Inter), June 1991)

Solution :

(1) Sales of break-even point

Sales	50,00,000
Less : Margin of safety 40%	20,00,000
Sales at break-even point	30,00,000

(2) Contribution at break even point = Sales at BEP × P/V Ratio
= Rs. 3,00,000 × 50% = Rs. 15,00,000

(3) Calculation of fixed cost

Sales at BEP	3,00,000
Less : Contribution at BEP	15,00,000
Fixed cost	15,00,000

(4) Calculation of net profit for total sales :

Contribution on total sales = Sales × P/V Ratio	
= 50,00,000 × 50% =	25,00,000
Less : Fixed cost	15,00,000
Net profit	10,00,000

Problem 42 : *XY* Ltd. has been offered a choice to buy machine *A* or machine *B*. From the following data, you are required to compute :

(*a*) Break-even point for each of the machines.
(*b*) The level of sales at which both machines earn equal profits.
(*c*) The range of sales at which one is more profitable than the other.

	Machine A	Machine B
Annual output (in units)	10,000	10,000
Fixed cost (Rs.)	30,000	16,000
Profit at given level of production (Rs.)	30,000	24,000

The market price of the product is expected to be Rs. 10 per unit. *(CS, Inter, Dec., 1990)*

Solution : **Calculation of break-even point**

	Machine A	Machine B
Sales 10,000 @ Rs. 10	1,00,000	1,00,000
Less : Variable cost (balancing figure)	40,000	60,000
Contribution	60,000	40,000
Less : Fixed cost	30,000	16,000
Profit	30,000	24,000

P/V Ratio $= \frac{\text{Contribution}}{\text{Sales}} \times 100 = \frac{60,000}{1,00,000} \times 100 = 60\%$ $\quad \frac{40,000}{1,00,000} \times 100 = 40\%$

(*a*) BEP $= \frac{\text{Fixed Cost}}{\text{P / V Ratio}}$ $\quad \frac{30,000}{60} \times 100$ $\quad \frac{16,000}{40} \times 100$

$= \text{Rs. } 50,000$ $\quad = \text{Rs. } 40,000$

BEP in units $= \frac{50,000}{10}$ $\quad \frac{40,000}{10}$

$= 5,000$ units $\quad = 4,000$ units

(*b*) Since the selling price of the products produced by *A* and *B* are equal the machines will earn equal profit. When the total cost of operation of both the machines are the same.

So, if '*x*' be the output where the total cost of operation on each machine is as below :

For *A* $= 4x + 30,000$

For *B* $= 6x + 16,000$

$$4x + 30,000 = 6x + 16,000$$
$$2x = 14,000$$
$$x = 7,000$$

At a production of level of 7,000 units the profits made by the machine *A* and *B* are equal.

(*c*) The breakdown points *A* is at 5,000 units compared to that of 4,000 units in case of *B* and at a production level of 7,000 units they earn equal profit. Therefore, it is quite clear that the profit earning for machine *B* is more in the range of 4,000 to 6,999 units.

Problem 43 : A Japanese soft drink company is planning to establish a subsidiary company in India to produce mineral water.

Based on the estimated annual sales of 40,000 bottles of the mineral water cost studies produced the following estimates for the Indian subsidiary :

	Total annual Cost (Rs.)	*Per cent of total annual cost which is variable*
Material	2,10,000	100%
Labour	1,50,000	80%
Factory overhead	92,000	60%
Administration overhead	40,000	35%

The Indian production will be sold by manufacturer's representatives who will receive a commission of 8% of the sale price. No portion of the Japanese office expenses is to be allocated to the Indian subsidiary. Required to :

(*a*) Compute the sale price per bottle to enable the management to realise an estimated 10% profit on sale proceeds in India.

(*b*) Calculate break-even point in Rupee Sales as also in number of bottles for the Indian subsidiary on the assumption that the sale price is Rs. 14 per bottle. (*CS, Inter, June, 1992*)

Solution : **Calculation of sales value**

Commission is 8% of sales revenue

Profit is 10% of sales revenue

Hence cost of sales is 82% of sales value

For a cost of sales of Rs. 82, the sales value is 100

For a cost of sales of Rs. 4,92,000, the sales value is $\frac{4,92,000 \times 100}{82}$ = Rs. 6,00,000

Calculation showing selling price per bottle = $\frac{\text{Sales Value}}{\text{No. of bottles sold}} = \frac{6,00,000}{40,000}$ = Rs. 15

Calculation of variable cost

	Total	*Per unit*
No. of bottles	40,000	1.00
Materials	2,10,000	5.25
Labour (80% of 1,50,000)	1,20,000	3.00
Factory overhead (60% of 92,000)	55,200	1.38
Administration expenses (35% of 40,000)	14,000	0.35
Commission (14 × 40,000 × 8%)	44,800	1.12
	4,44,000	11.10

Calculation of fixed cost

Fixed labour cost + Fixed factory overhead + Fixed Adm. overhead

(1,50,000 × 20% + 92,000 × 40%) + (40,000 × 65%)

= 30,000 + 36,800 + 26,000

= Rs. 92,800

$$\text{P/V Ratio} = \frac{\text{Sales} - \text{Variable Cost}}{\text{Sales}} \times 100$$

$$= \frac{14 - 11.10}{14} \times 100$$

Contribution per bottle = Sales – Variable cost

= 14 – 11.10 = 2.90

$$\text{BEP (in rupee sales)} = \frac{\text{Fixed Cost}}{\text{P/V ratio}}$$

$$= \frac{92,800}{20.7142\%} = 4,48,000$$

$$\text{BEP (in number of bottles)} = \frac{\text{FC}}{\text{Contribution per bottle}}$$

$$= \frac{92,800}{2.90} = 32,000 \text{ bottles}$$

Problem 44 : The cost accountant of *X* Co. Ltd. furnishes you the following informations :

Fixed cost for the year	Rs. 40,000
Net profit for the year	Rs. 50,000
P/V Ratio	30%

What is the amount of sales made during the year?

What will be the selling price per unit when variable cost per unit is Rs. 8.40 and P/V ratio is 40%?

(University of Delhi, B.Com. (Pass), April 1990)

Solution :

$$\text{Sales} = \frac{\text{Fixed cost + Profit}}{\text{P / V ratio}}$$

$$= \frac{40,000 + 50,000}{30\%} = \text{Rs. } 3,00,000$$

Variable cost = Rs. 8.40% per unit

P/V Ratio = 40%

Variable cost ratio = 100 – 40 = 60%

If 60% = 8.40,

$$\text{then } 100\% = 8.40 \times \frac{100}{60} = \text{Rs. } 14$$

Selling price is Rs. 14

Problem 45 : The projected output of a plant, when sold, would earn Rs. 70,000 in sales income to Mixers Ltd. The variable costs for this production volume would be Rs. 30,000. The fixed cost are Rs. 20,000. Determine the following :

(*a*) The break-even point of the company.

(*b*) The profit or loss to the company on sales of Rs. 49,000 and Rs. 28,000.

(*c*) The amount of sales that will enable the company to earn a net profit of Rs. 28,000.

(University of Delhi, B.Com., (Hons.), April 1990)

Solution :

At projected capacity of 100%

$$\text{P/V Ratio} = \frac{\text{Contribution}}{\text{Sales}} \times 100$$

$$= \frac{40,000}{70,000} \times 100 = 57.14\%$$

$$(i) \text{ BEP} = \frac{\text{FC}}{\text{P / V ratio}} = \frac{20,000}{57.14\%} = \text{Rs. } 35,000$$

Verification :

Sales at BEP = Rs. 35,000

$$\text{VC at BEP} = \frac{1}{2} \text{ of } 30,000 = 15,000$$

FC = 20,000

Hence no profit and no loss.

(*ii*) **Profit or loss on sale of Rs. 49,000 and Rs. 28,000**

	Rs. 49,000 *i.e.*, 70% capacity	Rs. 28,000 40% capacity
Variable cost	21,000	12,000
Fixed cost	20,000	20,000
Total cost	41,000	32,000
Profit or loss	+8,000	– 4,000
Sales	49,000	28,000

(*iii*) **Sales to earn profit of Rs. 28,000**

$$\text{Sales} = \frac{\text{FC + Desired profit}}{\text{P / V ratio}} = \frac{20,000 + 28,000}{57.14\%} = \text{Rs. } 84,000$$

At 100% capacity company is making profit of Rs. 20,000. So company will have to run over and above its capacity. Assuming fixed costs will remain same even at this exceeded capacity, sales to earn profit of Rs. 28,000 should be Rs. 84,000.

Verifications :

For a sale of Rs. 70,000, VC is Rs. 30,000

For a sale of Rs. 84,000, VC is

$$VC = \frac{30,000 \times 84,000}{70,000} = \qquad 36,000$$

Fixed cost	20,000
Total cost	56,000
Profit	28,000
Sales	84,000

Problem 46 : From the following particulars calculate break-even point :

Sales	Rs. 2,00,000
Variable cost	Rs. 1,20,000
Fixed overhead	Rs, 30,000

Also calculate

(*a*) New BEP if selling price is reduced by 10%

(*b*) New BEP, if variable cost increased by 10%

(*c*) New BEP, if fixed cost increases by 10%. *(Madurai Kamaraj University, B.Com., April 1992)*

Solution :

$$P/V \text{ ratio} = \frac{\text{Contribution}}{\text{Sales}} \times 100$$

$$= \frac{80,000}{2,00,000} \times 100 = 40\%$$

$$BEP = \frac{FC}{P/V \text{ ratio}} = \frac{30,000}{40\%} = 75,000$$

(*a*) New BEP if selling price is reduced by 10%

Original sales	2,00,000
Less : 10%	20,000
Revised sales	1,80,000

$$P/V \text{ ratio} = \frac{\text{Contribution}}{\text{Sales}} \times 100$$

$$= \frac{60,000}{1,80,000} = 33\frac{1}{3}\%$$

$$BEP = \frac{FC}{P/V \text{ ratio}}$$

$$= \frac{30,000}{33\frac{1}{3}} = 90,000$$

(*b*) New BEP, if variable cost increases by 10%

Present variable cost	1,20,000
Add : 10%	12,000
Revised variable cost	1,32,000

$$P/V \text{ ratio} = \frac{68,000}{2,00,000} \times 100 = 34\%$$

BEP $= \frac{FC}{P/V}$

$= \frac{30,000}{34\%} = 88,325$

(c) Now BEP if fixed cost increases by 10%

Original fixed cost	30,000
Add : 10%	3,000
Revised fixed cost	33,000

BEP $= \frac{\text{Fixed Cost}}{\text{P / V ratio}}$

$= \frac{33,000}{40\%} = 82,500$

Problem 47 : From the following data find out :

(a) P/V Ratio
(b) Sales required to break-even and
(c) Sales required to earn a profit of Rs. 1,60,000

Selling price per unit	Rs.40
Variable costs per unit :	
Direct materials	Rs. 10
Direct labour	Rs. 7
Variable overheads—100% direct labour cost	
Fixed expenses	Rs. 64,000

(*Kakatiya University, M. Com., Aug. 1991*)

Solution :

Selling price		Rs. 40
Less : Variable cost		
Direct materials	10	
Direct labour	7	
Variable overhead	7	Rs. 24
Contribution		16

(a) P/V ratio $= \frac{\text{Contribution}}{\text{Sales}} \times 100$

$= \frac{16}{40} \times 100 = 40\%$

(b) BEP (sales volume) $= \frac{\text{Fixed cost}}{\text{Contribution per unit}}$

$= \frac{64,000}{16} = 4,000$

Sales value $= 4,000 \times 40 = 1,60,000$

(c) Sales required to earn a profit of Rs. 1,60,000

Sales $= \frac{\text{Fixed cost + Desired profit}}{\text{Contribution per unit}}$

$= \frac{64,000 + 1,60,000}{16}$

$= \frac{2,24,000}{16} = 14,000 \text{ units}$

Problem 48 : The P/V ratio of a firm dealing with electrical goods is 50% and the margin of safety is 40%. You are required to workout the break-even point and the net profit if the sales volume is Rs. 5,00,000.

(Kakatiya University, M. Com., Aug. 1991)

Solution :

$$\text{M.S. Ratio} = \frac{\text{Margin of safety}}{\text{Sales}} \times 100$$

$$40 = \frac{\text{Margin of safety}}{50,00,000} \times 100$$

$$100 \text{ M.S.} = 20,00,00,000$$

$$\text{M.S.} = 20,00,000$$

$$\text{Margin of safety} = \frac{\text{Profit}}{\text{P / V ratio}}$$

$$20,00,000 = \frac{\text{Profit}}{40\%}$$

$$20,00,000 \times 40 = \text{Profit} \times 100$$

$$100 \text{ profit} = 80,00,00,000$$

$$\text{Profit} = 8,00,000$$

Problem 49 : From the following information pertaining to a company find out *(a)* P/V ratio, *(b)* BEP, *(c)* Profit when sales amounted to Rs. 12,00,000 and *(d)* Sales required to earn a profit of Rs. 2,00,000.

Variable cost	Rs. 6,00,000
Fixed cost	Rs. 3,00,000
Net profit	Rs. 1,00,000
Sales	Rs. 10,00,000

(Gulbarga University, B. Com., November 1991)

Solution :

(a) P/V ratio

$$= \frac{\text{Contribution}}{\text{Sales}} \times 100$$

$$= \frac{4,00,000}{10,00,000} \times 100 = 40\%$$

(b) BEP

$$= \frac{\text{Fixed cost}}{\text{P / V ratio}}$$

$$= \frac{3,00,000}{40\%} = \text{Rs. } 7,50,000$$

(c) Profit when sales amounted to Rs. 12,00,000

$$\text{S (P/V)} = \text{F} + \text{P}$$

$$12,00,000 \times \frac{40}{100} = 3,00,000 + \text{P}$$

$$4,80,000 = 3,00,000 + \text{P}$$

$$\text{P} = 1,80,000$$

(d) Sales required to earn a profit of Rs. 2,00,000

$$\text{S (P/V)} = 3,00,000 + 2,00,000$$

$$\text{S} \times \frac{40}{100} = 5,00,000 = 1,25,000$$

Problem 50 : Two businesses *Y* Ltd. and *Z* Ltd. sell, the same type of product in the same type of market. Their budgeted profit and loss accounts for the coming year are as follows :

		Y Ltd.		*Z Ltd.*
Sales		1,50,000		1,50,000
Less : Variable cost	1,20,000		1,00,000	
Fixed cost	15,000	1,35,000	35,000	1,35,000
Budgeted net profit		15,000		15,000

You are required to :

(*a*) Calculate the break-even point of each business.

(*b*) Calculate the sales volume at which each of business will earn Rs. 5,000 profit.

(*c*) State which business is likely to earn greater profit in conditions of (*i*) Heavy demand for the product, (*ii*) Low demand for the product and briefly give your reasons.

(*University of Madras, B. Com., March 1991*)

Solution :

Y Ltd. :

$$\text{BEP} = \frac{\text{Fixed cost}}{1-\dfrac{\text{Variable cost}}{\text{Sales}}}$$

$$= \frac{15{,}000}{1-\dfrac{1{,}20{,}000}{1{,}50{,}000}} = \frac{1{,}50{,}000}{2} = \text{Rs. } 75{,}000$$

$$\text{P/V ratio} = \frac{\text{Contribution}}{\text{Sales}} \times 100$$

$$= \frac{30{,}000}{1{,}50{,}000} \times 100 = 20\%$$

Margin of safety = 1,50,000 – 75,000 = Rs. 75,000

M/S ratio = 50%

Z Ltd.

$$\text{BEP} = \frac{\text{Fixed cost}}{1-\dfrac{\text{Variable cost}}{\text{Sales}}}$$

$$= \frac{35{,}000}{1-\dfrac{1{,}00{,}000}{1{,}50{,}000}} = \frac{35{,}000}{0.333} = \text{Rs. } 1{,}05{,}000$$

$$\text{P/V ratio} = \frac{\text{Marginal contribution}}{\text{Sales}} \times 100$$

$$= \frac{50{,}000}{1{,}50{,}000} \times 100 = 33\frac{1}{3}\%$$

$$\text{M/S Ratio} = \frac{45{,}000}{1{,}50{,}000} \times 100 = 30\%$$

(*b*) (*i*) From the above calculation it is clear that P/V ratio is higher in case of *Z* Ltd. therefore, in case of heavy demand *Z* Ltd. will earn higher profits.

(*ii*) In case of low demand *Y* will be an advantageous position as fixed costs and break-even point are low and consequently margin of safety is higher. Assuming sales at Rs. 1,00,000. *Y* Ltd. will still earn profit while *Z* Ltd. will incur a loss.

GRAPHIC METHOD OF PRESENTING CVP ANALYSIS

This method is preferred under two conditions *viz.* (*a*) where a simple overview is sufficient and (*b*) to avoid detailed calculations involved under equation method. The following procedure is involved under the graphic method :

(*a*) **Vertical line :** Draw a vertical line on the left side of the graph paper to show cost and sales revenue.

(*b*) **Horizontal line :** Draw a horizontal line to show the number of units in such a way it should intersect the vertical line at the point of zero.

(*c*) **Fixed cost line :** A line parallel to X-axis (horizontal line) is to be drawn to represent the fixed cost considering the units manufactured and fixed cost incurred.

(*d*) **Total sales revenue line :** This line is drawn starting at the zero point on the left hand corner and ending on the right hand side considering the sales revenue.

(*e*) **Total cost line :** This is the total of fixed and variable cost. This line is drawn starting at the Y-axis fixed cost point and moving to the right considering the total cost.

(*f*) **BEP :** This is the point where total cost line intersects the sales line.

A typical graph depicting the BEP is shown in the Fig. 8.1.

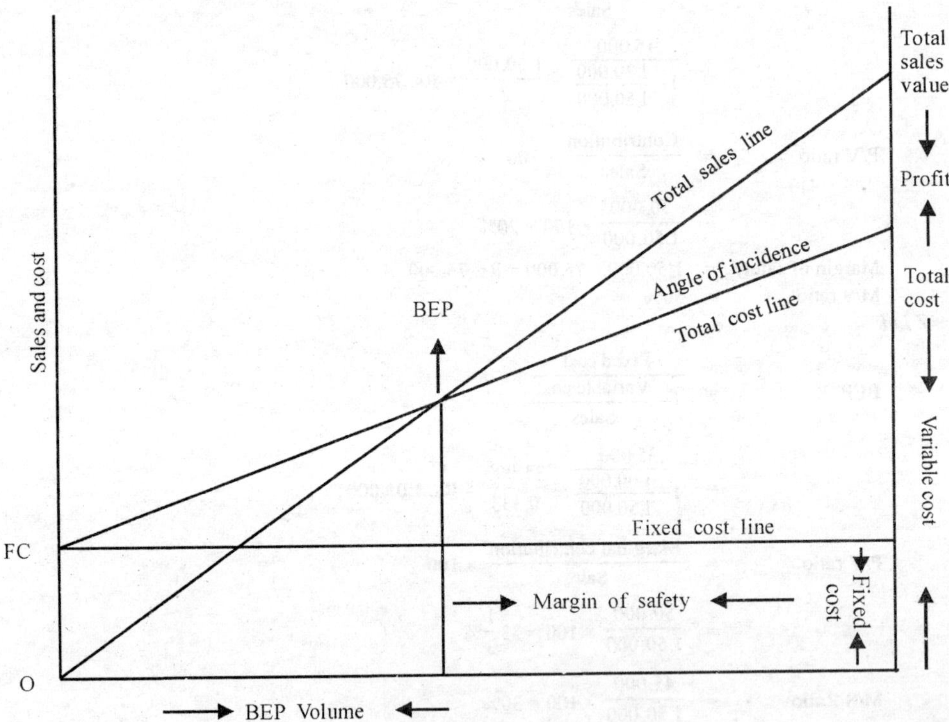

Fig. 8.1 Break-even chart.

Problem 45 : From the following data, draw a single break-even chart :

Selling price per unit	Rs. 10.00
Trade discount	5%
Direct material cost per unit	Rs. 3.00
Direct labour cost per unit	Rs. 2.00
Fixed overhead	Rs. 10.000

Variable overhead 100% of direct labour cost. If sales are 10% and 15% above the break even-volume, determine the net profit. *(Bangalore University, M. Com., April 1992)*

Solution :

Contribution = Selling price – Variable cost

Sales		Rs. 10
Less : 5% trade discount		9.50
Less : Variable costs :		
Direct materials	3.00	
Direct labour	2.00	
Variable overhead :		
100% of labour cost	2.00	7.00
Contribution		Rs. 2.50

$$\text{BEP} = \frac{\text{Fixed cost}}{\text{Contribution per unit}} = \frac{10,000}{2.50} = 4,000 \text{ units}$$

Profit if sale is 10% above BEP	
Sales = 4,000 × Rs. 9.50 + 10%	41,800
Less : Variable cost 4,400 × 7	30,800
	11,000
Less : Fixed cost	10,000
Profit	1,000
Profit is sales are above 15%	
4,000 × Rs. 9.50 + 15%	43,700
Less : Variable cost = 4,600 × 7	32,200
	11,500
Less : Fixed cost	10,000
Profit	1,500

For break-even chart see fig. 8.2.

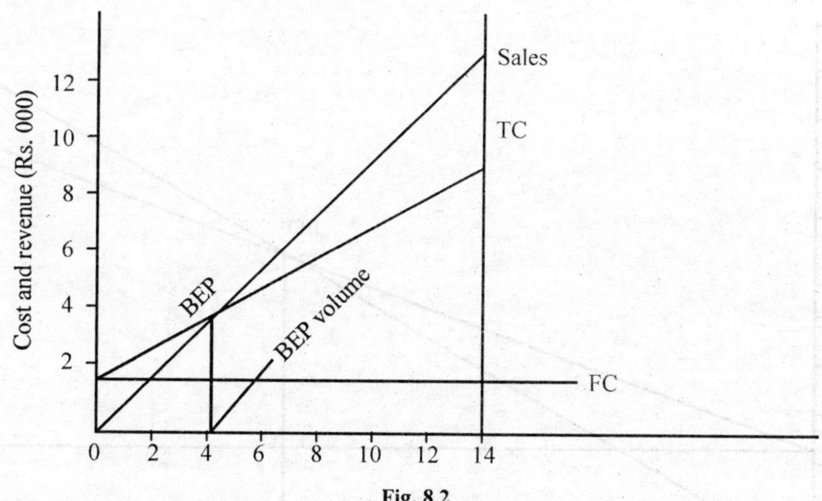

Fig. 8.2

Problem 52 : You are given the following data for a costing year for a factory :

Budgeted output	1,00,000 units
Fixed expenses	Rs. 5,00,000
Variable expense per unit	Rs. 10
Selling price per unit	Rs. 20

Draw a break-even chart showing the break-even point, if the selling price is reduced to Rs. 18 per unit. What will be the new break-even point? (*Bangalore University, M. Com., April 1991*)

Solution : *See* Figs. 8.3 and 8.4.

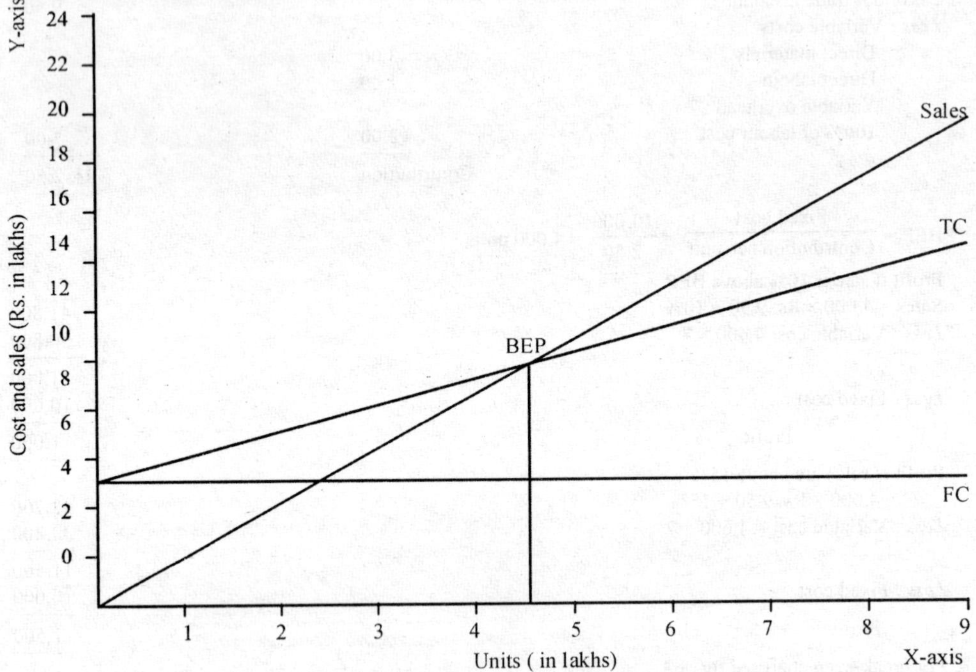

Fig. 8.3 BEP if selling price is Rs. 20.

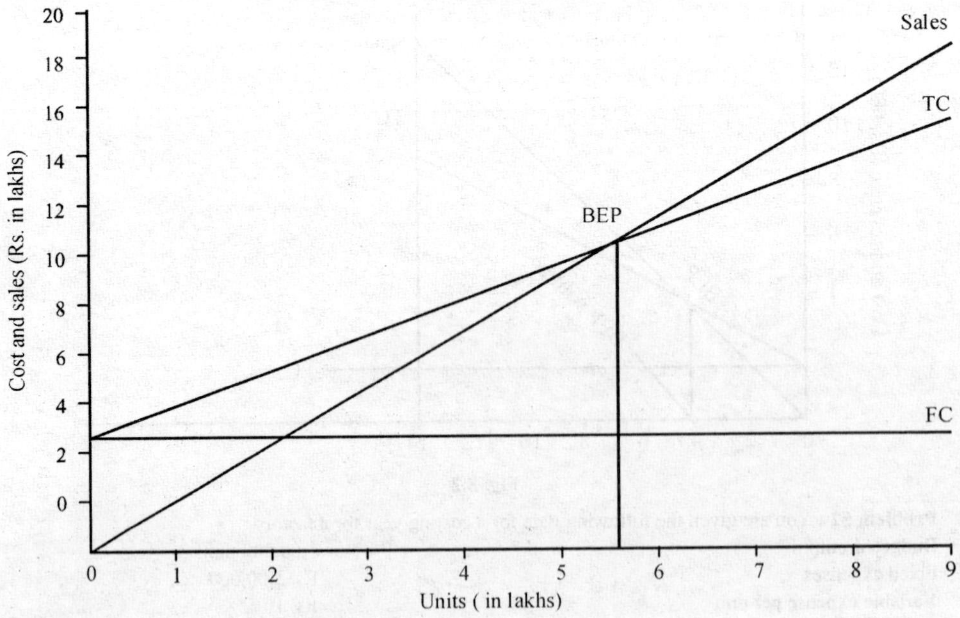

Fig. 8.4 BEP if selling price is reduced to Rs. 18.

TYPES OF BREAK-EVEN CHARTS

1. Break-even chart showing profit appropriation : This is one of the orthodox type of break-even chart which shows additional information as to how the profit is distributed. This is illustrated below :

Problem 53 : From the following information draw up a break-even chart showing the distribution of profit :

Fixed cost	Rs. 20,000
Variable cost	Rs. 2 per unit
Debenture interest not included in the fixed cost	Rs. 10,000
Preference shares dividends	Rs. 10,000
Equity shares dividends	Rs. 20,000
Sales	10,000 units at Rs. 10 each.

Solution : *See* Fig. 8.5.

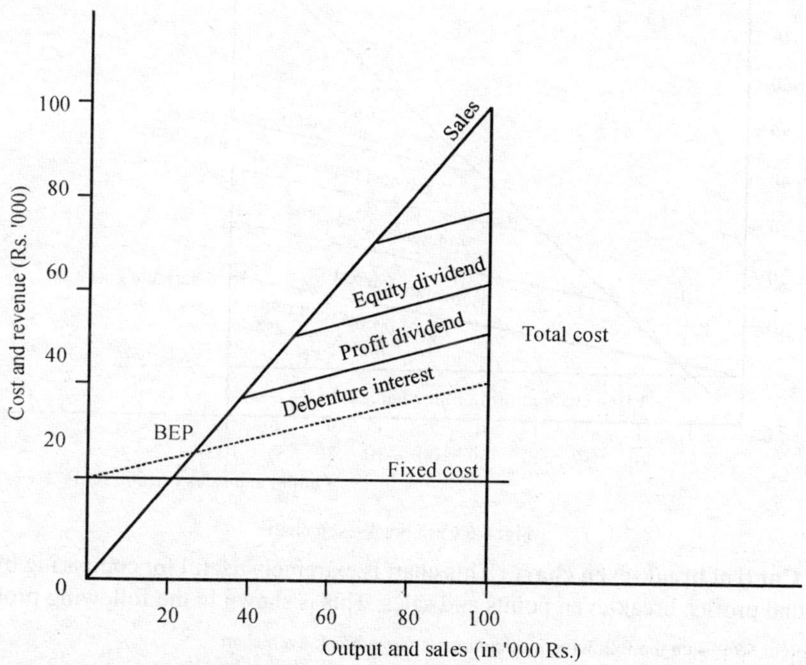

Fig. 8.5 BEP showing profit appropriation.

2. Cash break chart : Under this type the fixed costs are classified into two types *viz.* (*i*) fixed cost requiring immediate cash. Some examples of this type of cost are rent and rates, wages and salaries, insurance, etc. The term "immediate" here refers to the period covered by the chart and (*ii*) fixed cost not requiring immediate cash. Some examples of such costs are depreciation, advertising, research and development cost. The presentation of these two types of fixed cost in the chart deserve special mention. The fixed cost requiring immediate cash is shown at the base line (horizontal line) of the chart. Whereas the fixed cost not requiring immediate cash is shown last. The variable cost is assumed to be payable in cash. Where credit transactions are involved their impact on cash available is measured and cash payments are adjusted. This is shown in the following problem :

Problem 54 : From the following particulars prepare a cash break-even chart :

Fixed cost	Cash Rs. 1,00,000
Already paid	Rs. 10,000
Variable cost	Rs. 2 per unit
Preference dividend and debenture interest	Rs. 10,000 each
Sales	10,000 units of Rs. 10 each

Solution : *See* Fig. 8.6.

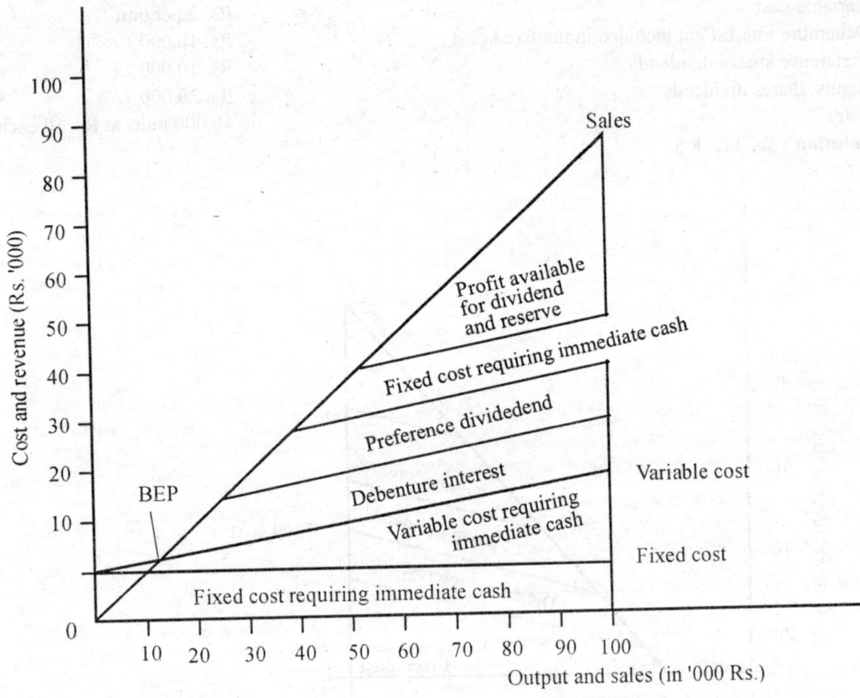

Fig. 8.6 Cash break-even chart.

3. Control break-even chart : This chart is extremely useful for comparing budgeted and actual profits, break-even points and sales. This is shown in the following problem :

Problem 55 : From the following particulars prepare a break-even chart :

Budgeted fixed costs	Rs. 15.000
Budgeted variable costs	Rs. 12.000 for budgeted sales
Budgeted sales	Rs. 40.000
Actual fixed costs	Rs. 15.000
Actual variable costs	Rs. 16.200
Actual sales	Rs. 45.000

Solution : *See* Fig. 8.7 on next page.

Notes :		
Profit for budgeted sales	=	Rs. 13,000
Profit for actual sales :		*Rs.*
Budgeted profit—Actual profit		16,500
		13,800
Profit variance		2,700

Note : The budgeted total cost line and actual cost line have been drawn on the variable costs for sales amount of Rs. 50,000. For 40,000 amount of sales, the variable costs are Rs. 12,000. Therefore, for Rs.

50,000, amount of sales, the variable cost should be Rs. 15,000, *i.e.*, at the rate of Rs. 3,000 for every Rs. 10,000 amount of sales. Hence, the total budgeted costs for Rs. 50,000 amount of sales should be Rs. 15,000 variable + Rs. 15,000 fixed costs, *i.e.*, total Rs. 30,000 as shown by budgeted total cost line. For actual sales amount of Rs. 45,000, variable costs are Rs. 16,200 considering Rs. 50,000 amount of sales, the actual respective costs will be Rs. 18,000 and the actual total cost will be Rs. 18,000 + 15,000 (fixed cost), *i.e.*, Rs. 33,000 which is represented by budgeted actual cost.

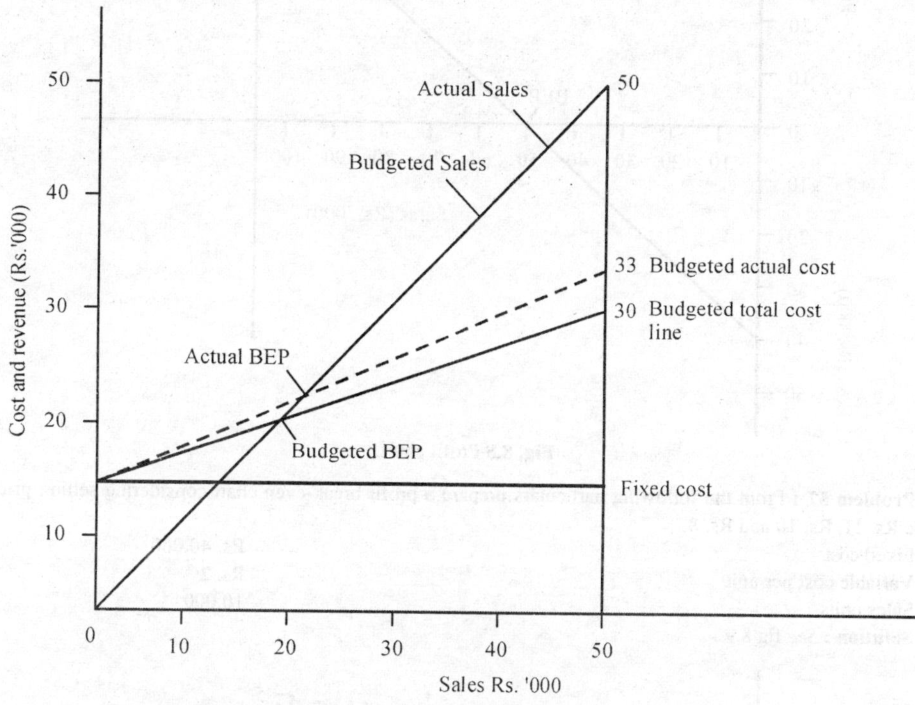

Fig. 8.7 Control break-even chart.

4. Profit chart : It is a variety of break-even chart. It shows the profit or loss at different levels of sales. As usual, volume of sales is shown under horizontal line. The vertical lines show the profit or loss position. The line shown above the horizontal line shows profit, whereas the line below shows loss.

Problem 56 : From the following particulars prepare a profit chart :

Fixed cost	Rs. 40,000
Variable cost	Rs. 2 per unit
Sales	10,000 units @ Rs. 10 per unit

Solution :

$$\text{BEP} = \frac{\text{Fixed cost}}{\text{Contribution per unit}}$$

$$= \frac{40,000}{8} = \text{Rs. } 5,000$$

For chart *see* Fig. 8.8 on next page.

5. Profit chart for different prices : This chart shows the effect on profit of charging different prices.

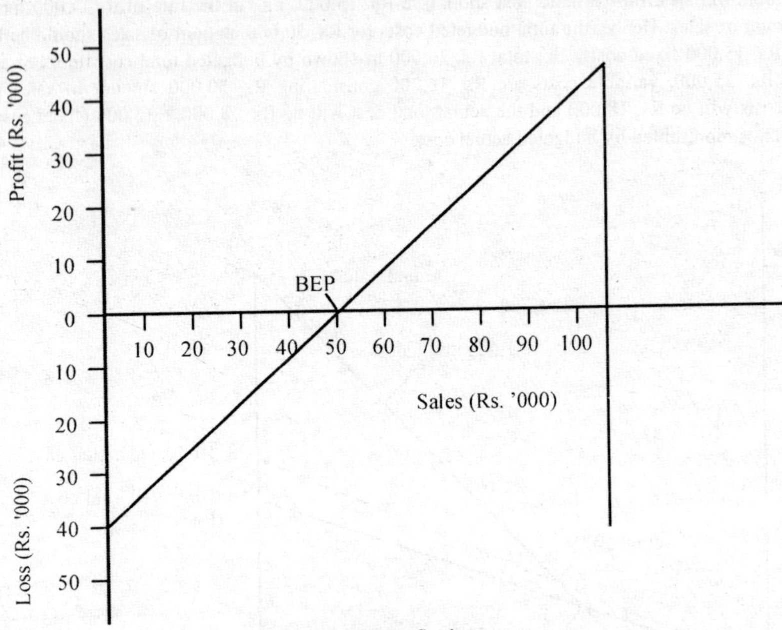

Fig. 8.8 Profit chart.

Problem 57 : From the following particulars prepare a profit break-even chart considering selling prices to be Rs. 11, Rs. 10 and Rs. 8.

Fixed cost	Rs. 40,000
Variable cost per unit	Rs. 2
Sales units	10,000

Solution : *See* fig 8.9..

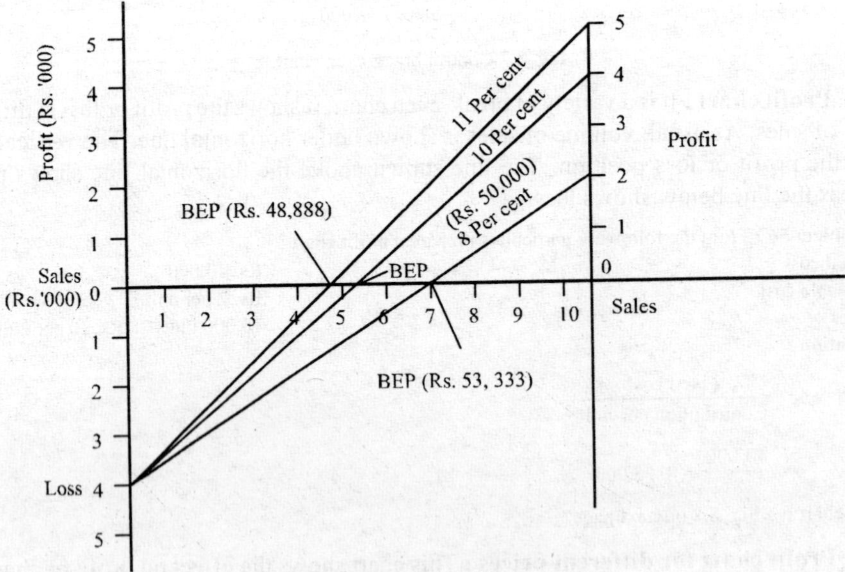

Fig. 8.9 Profit chart for different prices.

6. Analysis break-even chart : This chart portrays the components of variable cost such as direct material, direct labour and variable factory, administrative and selling and distribution overheads. The appropriation of profit such as taxation, preference dividend, equity dividends and creation of various reserves.

Problem 58 : From the following particulars prepare an analysis break-even chart :

Fixed cost	Rs. 10,000
Variable cost Rs. 30,000 divided into	
Direct labour	Rs. 5,000
Direct materials	Rs. 4,000
Factory overheads	Rs. 6,000
Administration overheads	Rs. 5,000
Selling overheads	Rs. 5,000
Distribution overheads	Rs. 5,000
Taxation Rs. 2,000 at maximum output decreasing in direct proportion to reduction in profit	
Preference dividend	Rs. 4,000
Equity dividend	Rs. 5,000

Solution : *See* Fig. 8.10.

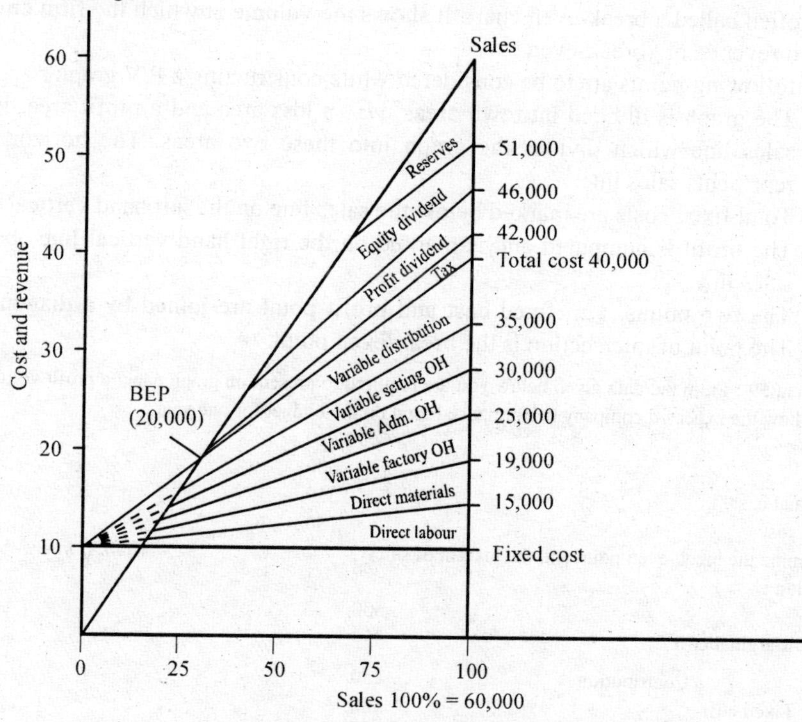

Fig. 8.10 Analysis break-even chart.

LIMITATIONS OF BREAK-EVEN CHARTS

1. The preparation of BEP involves separation of semi-variable cost into fixed and variable, which cannot be carried out accurately.
2. It is presumed that the revenue and cost can be represented by straight lines which may not always be true.
3. It assumes that a selling price is constant at different levels of sales which may

not be true. Selling price either increases or decreases due to decrease or increase in sales units.

4. Apportionment of fixed cost over a variety of products poses a problem.
5. It assumes that the business conditions may not change which is not true.
6. Under a break-even chart only one product is studied. It fails to provide the effects of various product mixes on profit.
7. Capital employed which is one of the important guiding factors determining profitability is ignored by the break-even chart.

PROFIT-VOLUME CHART OR P/V CHART

Vance in his *Theory and Techniques of Cost Accounting* defines a profit graph as a graph showing the amounts of fixed and variable costs and sales revenue at different volumes of operation. The name P/V chart has arisen from the fact that the difference between the total of fixed on variable costs and the sales revenue at any volume gives the profit at that volume. Because of the importance of the point at which the total costs and revenue are equal the graph is often called a break-even chart. It shows the volume at which the firm covers all costs with revenue or "break-even".

The following points are to be considered while constructing a P/V graph :

(*a*) The graph is divided into two areas, *viz.*, a loss area and a profit area. It is the sales line which divides the graph into these two areas. The horizontal line represents sales line.

(*b*) Total fixed costs are marked below the sales line on the left hand vertical line.

(*c*) The profit is computed and is marked on the right hand vertical line above the sales line.

(*d*) The two points, *viz.*, fixed cost and profit point are joined by a diagonal line. The point of intersection is the break-even point.

Problem 59 : From the data given below you are required to present on graph paper a profit volume (P/V) graph to show the expected company performance based on the budget for one year :

	('000 Rs.)
Sales	600
Marginal cost	350
Fixed cost	150

Determine the break-even point and the margin of safety. *(ICWA, Inter., June 1990)*

Solution :

Sales	600
Less : Marginal cost	350
Contribution	250
Less : Fixed cost	150
Profit	100

Calculation of BEP (for verification)

$$\text{C/S Ratio} = \frac{\text{Contribution}}{\text{Sales}} = \frac{250}{600} = 41.66\%$$

$$\text{BEP} = \frac{\text{Fixed cost}}{\text{C/S ratio}} = \frac{1,50,000}{41.66} \times 100$$

$$= 3,60,000$$

Margin of safety = Sales – BES
6,00,000 – 3,60,000 = Rs. 2,40,000

For P/V graph *see* Fig. 8.11.

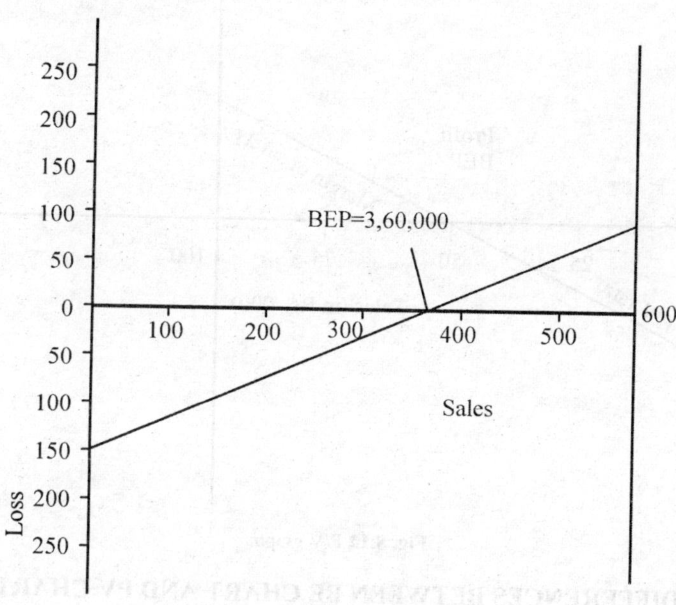

Fig. 8.11 P/V graph.

Problem 60 : From the particulars given below relating to Avinash (Pvt.) Co. Ltd. find out (*a*) P/V ratio, (*b*) BEP, (*c*) Margin of safety and (*d*) Plot P/V graph :

Sales	Rs. 1,00,000
Total cost	80,000
Fixed cost	20,000
Net profit	20,000

Solution :

$$\text{P/V Ratio} = \frac{\text{Sales} - \text{Variable expenses}}{\text{Sales}} \times 100$$

$$= \frac{1,00,000 - 60,000}{1,00,000} \times 100 = 40\%$$

$$\text{BEP} = \frac{\text{Fixed cost}}{\text{P / V ratio}}$$

$$= \frac{20,000}{40\%} = \text{Rs. } 50,000$$

$$\text{Margin of safety} = \frac{\text{Profit}}{\text{P / V ratio}}$$

$$= \frac{20,000}{40\%} = \text{Rs. } 50,000$$

For P/V graph *see* Fig. 8.12.

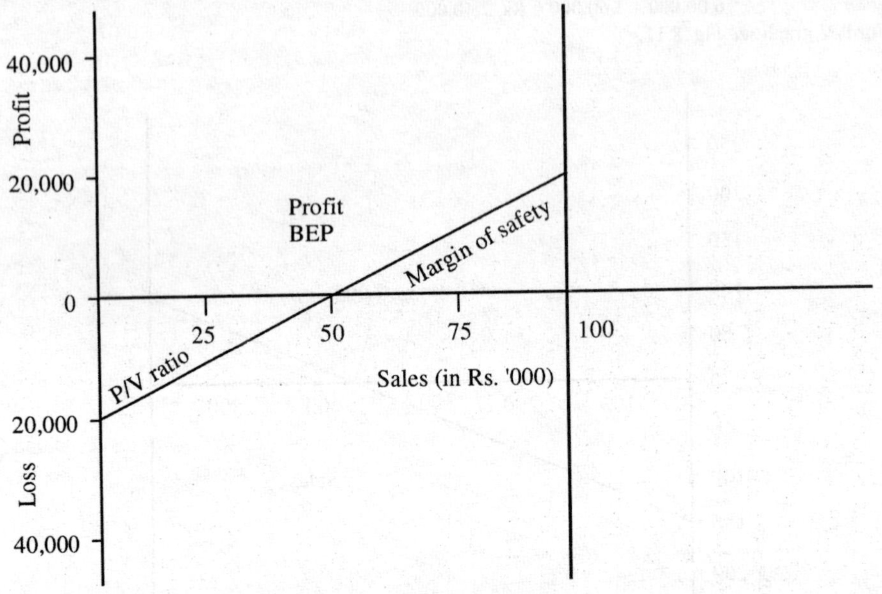

Fig. 8.12 P/V graph.

DIFFERENCES BETWEEN BE CHART AND PV CHART

P/V Chart	*BE Chart*
1. Only one line, *viz.*, profit line is shown.	1. Profit line is not shown instead sales and cost lines are shown.
2. Profit line starts below the horizontal line. Fixed cost incurred at zero point of production indicates loss. This loss is indicated below the horizontal line.	2. All lines are drawn above the horizontal line. The area up to the point of break-even shows loss and the area beyond the point shows profit.
3. The break-even point is found on the horizontal axis.	3. The break-even point is at the intersection of cost and sales lines.
4. Fixed cost is always considered as fixed and the ratio of sales and variable cost is again assumed as constant at different levels of sales.	4. The break-even chart can even measure break-even point when sales line is a curve because of price changes at different volumes of sales.
5. It is possible to measure the impact of individual products in a sales mix.	5. This chart can show the effect of a sales mix only in aggregate. For different items of sales, separate charts are to be prepared.
6. The chart shows profit and loss at different sales.	6. It can be drawn even to show the various elements of cost and profit appropriation.

QUESTIONS

I. Choose the correct answer from the following

1. **An accountant would typically have the following in mind when referring to the "margin of safety" :**
   (*a*) The excess of actual sales over the variable expenses and the fixed cost at break-even.
   (*b*) The excess of actual sales revenue over the fixed expense.
   (*c*) The excess of actual sales over budgeted sales.
   (*d*) The excess of sales revenue over the variable cost. [ ]
2. **Which of the following alternatives would generally decrease contribution margin per unit the most?**
   (*a*) A 15% decrease in selling price.
   (*b*) A 15% increase in variable cost.
   (*c*) A 15% increase in selling price.
   (*d*) A 15% decrease in variable cost. [ ]
3. **If fixed cost decrease while variable cost per unit remains constant, the new contribution margin in relation to the old will be**
   (*a*) unchanged
   (*b*) higher
   (*c*) higher
   (*d*) intermediate [ ]
4. **If a firm has a negative contribution margin, to reach break-even :**
   (*a*) Sales volume must be increased.
   (*b*) Sales volume must be decreased.
   (*c*) Fixed cost must be decreased.
   (*d*) Fixed cost must be increased. [ ]
5. **If total contribution margin is decreased by a given amount, operating profit would**
   (*a*) Decrease by the same amount.
   (*b*) Decrease by more than the given amount.
   (*c*) Increase by the same amount.
   (*d*) Remain unchanged. [ ]
6. **The break-even point would be increased by**
   (*a*) a decrease in fixed cost.
   (*b*) an increase in contribution margin ratio.
   (*c*) an increase in variable cost.
   (*d*) a decrease in variable cost. [ ]
7. **Given the following formula, which one represents the break-even sales level in units. P = Selling price per unit, F = Fixed cost, V = Variable cost per unit.**
   (*a*) $\frac{F}{P-V}$
   (*b*) $\frac{P}{F \div V}$
   (*c*) $\frac{F}{V \div P}$
   (*d*) $\frac{F}{SP-V}$ [ ]
8. **Which one of the following assumptions is not made in break-even analysis?**
   (*a*) Volume is the only factor affecting cost.
   (*b*) No change between beginning and closing stock.
   (*c*) The sales mix is maintained as volume changes.
   (*d*) All of the above are assumptions sometimes required in break-even analysis. [ ]
9. **The cost-volume-profit analysis underlying the conventional break-even chart does not assume that**
   (*a*) prices will remain fixed.
   (*b*) production will equal sales.
   (*c*) some costs vary inversely with volume.
   (*d*) costs are linear and continuous over the relevant range. [ ]
10. **The most useful information derived from a break-even chart is the**
    (*a*) amount of sales revenue needed to cover enterprise variable cost.
    (*b*) amount of sales revenue needed to cover enterprise fixed costs.
    (*c*) relationship among revenues, variable cost and fixed costs at various levels of activity.
    (*d*) volume or output level at which the enterprise break-even. [ ]

11. The major assumption as to cost and revenue behaviour underlying conventional cost-volume-profit calculation is the
    (*a*) Constancy of fixed cost. (*c*) Curvilinearity of relationships.
    (*b*) Variability of unit prices and efficiency. (*d*) Linearity of relationships. [ ]
12. Given the following notations, what is the break-even sales level in units? SP = Selling price, FC = Fixed cost, VC = Variable cost per unit :
    (*a*) $\frac{SP}{FC \div VC}$ (*c*) $\frac{FC}{VC \div SP}$
    (*b*) $\frac{VC}{SP - FC}$ (*d*) $\frac{FC}{SP - FC}$ [ ]
13. P/V ratio is an indicator of :
    (*a*) the volume of sales. (*c*) the rate at which goods are sold.
    (*b*) the volume of profit. (*d*) all of the above. [ ]
14. When P/V ratio is 40% and sales value Rs. 10,000, the variable cost will be
    (*a*) Rs. 4,000
    (*b*) Rs. 6,000
    (*c*) Rs. 10,000
    (*d*) Variable cost cannot be calculated from the data given. [ ]
15. Cost-volume-profit analysis is most important for the determination of the
    (*a*) volume of operations necessary to break-even.
    (*b*) variable revenues necessary to equal fixed cost.
    (*c*) relationship between revenues and costs at various levels of operations.
    (*d*) sales revenue necessary to equal fixed cost. [ ]

II. Mark True or False in the space provided

1. At break-even point, contribution is equal to fixed cost. T/F
2. Margin of safety shows the excess of actual sales over budgeted sales. T/F
3. When P/V ratio is 50% and margin of safety is 40%, the net profit is 20% of sales. T/F
4. Margin of safety may come before or after the break-even point. T/F
5. Marginal costing and cost-volume-profit analysis is useful in profit planning. T/F
6. If the selling price per unit is assumed to be constant, total revenue will be proportionate to number of units sold. T/F
7. Decreasing the selling price decreases the break-even point. T/F
8. The contribution margin perunit is proportional to volume. T/F
9. It is impossible to obtain a break-even point with a negative contribution margin. T/F
10. To obtain the break-even point in units, the total fixed costs should be divided by the contribution margin ratio. T/F
11. The margin of safety is found by subtracting fixed cost from sales. T/F
12. If the variable cost per unit increase, the contribution margin ratio will increase. T/F
13. As production volume increases, the contribution margin rate increases. T/F
14. Accountants usually assume that variable costs are linear. T/F

III. Simple Questions

1. Define cost-volume-profit analysis.
2. State any four objectives of cost-volume-profit analysis.
3. State any four assumptions of cost-volume-profit analysis.
4. State any four limitations of cost-volume-profit analysis.
5. Define break-even analysis.
6. Mention any four assumptions underlying break-even analysis.
7. What do you mean by margin of safety? What purpose does it?
8. What do you mean by angle of incidence?
9. Define profit-volume ratio.
10. State any usefulness of profit-volume ratio.
11. Distinguish between break-even chart and profit-volume chart.

IV. Short Answer Questions

1. What do you mean by break-even point? Discuss in detail. *(ICWA, Inter., Dec. 1990)*
2. What is meant by cost-volume-profit analysis? What are its limitations? Discuss the utility of determining cost-volume-profit relationship? *(Kakatiya University, M. Com., Aug. 1991)*
3. What do you understand by the term break-even analysis? Enumerate its assumptions and uses. *(Calicut University, B. Com., Oct. 1989)*
4. What is break-even point and state its usefulness to management? *(University of Kerala, B. Com., April 1990)*
5. What are the uses of cost-volume-profit analysis? Discuss the various ways of presenting the CVP relationship? *(Bangalore University, M. Com., May 1990)*

EXERCISES

Exercise 1 : A company budgets a production of 10,000 units. The variable cost is estimated at Rs. 12 per unit. The fixed costs are estimated Rs. 40,000. The selling price is fixed to earn a profit of 25% on cost. You are required to

(*i*) Compute break-even point in terms of units and sales.
(*ii*) Compute how many units must be produced and sold to earn a profit of Rs. 60,000.

(University of Delhi, B. Com.,(Pass), April 1986)

[*Answer :* (*i*) BEP 5,000 units, (*ii*) Sales in units to earn a profit of Rs. 60,000 *vs* 125,000 units.]

Exercise 2 : From the following data calculate :

(*i*) Break-even point expressed in amount of sales in rupees.
(*ii*) Number of units that must be sold to earn a profit of Rs. 60,000 per year.
(*iii*) How many units are to be sold to earn a net income of 10% of sales.

	Rs.
Sale price	20 per unit
Variable manufacturing costs	11 per unit
Variable selling costs	3 per unit
Fixed factory overheads	5,40,000 per year
Fixed selling costs	2,52,000 per year

(University of Delhi, B. Com.(Hons.), April 1987)

[*Answer :* (*i*) BEP Rs. 26,40,000, (*ii*) No. of units to be sold to earn a profit of Rs. 60,000 is 1,42,000 units, (*iii*) No. of units to be sold to earn a net income of 10% on sales is 1,98,000 units.]

Exercise 3 : *XY* Ltd. has been offered a choice to buy machine *A* or machine *B*. From the following data, you are required to compute :

(*a*) Break-even point for each of the machines.
(*b*) The level of sales at which both machines earn equal profits.
(*c*) The range of sales at which one is more profitable than the other.

	Machine	
	A	*B*
Annual output (in units)	10,000	10,000
Fixed cost (Rs.)	30,000	16,000
Profit at given level of production (Rs.)	30,000	24,000

The market price of the product is expected to be Rs. 10 per unit. *(CS, Inter., June 989)*

[*Answer :* P/V Ratio is 60% and 40%, BEP is Rs. 50,000 and Rs. 40,000.]

Exercise 4 : The following figures are available from the records of Venus Enterprises as at 31st March :

	1988	*1989*
	Rs. Lakhs	*Rs. Lakhs*
Sales	150	200
Profit	30	50

Calculate

(1) The P/V ratio and total fixed expenses.

(3) Sales required to earn a profit of Rs. 90 lakhs.

(4) Profit or loss that would arise if the sales were Rs. 280 lakhs. (*CA, Inter., May 1989*)

[***Answer :*** (*a*) P/V ratio 40%, (*b*) BEP = 75 lakhs, (*c*) Profit Rs. 82 lakhs.]

Exercise 5 : The following figures relate to a factory manufacturing a varied range of products :

Period 1	Sales Rs. 15,00,000	Profit Rs. 40,000
Period 2	Sales Rs. 19,00,000	Profit Rs. 1,15,000

Calculate

(*a*) The P/V ratio.

(*b*) The profit when sales are 12,00,000.

(*c*) The sales required to earn a profit of Rs. 2,00,000.

(*d*) How the P/V ratio be improved apart from increasing selling prices or reducing cost.

(*University of Madras, M. Com., April 1991*)

[***Answer :*** (*a*) P/V ratio = 18.75%, (*b*) Rs. 16,250, (*c*) Rs. 23,53,333.]

Exercise 6 : The trading results of a company for two periods are as under :

Period	*Sales (Rs.)*	*Profit (Rs.)*
1	1,30,000	6,000
2	1,50,000	10,000

Calculate

(*a*) P/V ratio.

(*b*) Sales required to earn a profit of Rs. 15,000.

(*c*) Profit when sales are Rs. 1,10,000 and

(*d*) Break-even sales. (*University of Kerala, B. Com., Apart, 1990*)

[***Answer :*** (*a*) P/V ratio = 50%, (*b*) Rs. 1,48,000, (*c*) Rs. 4,000, (*d*) Rs. 1,18,000.]

Exercise 7 : Find out the break-even point from the following information :

(*a*) Fixed cost Rs. 20,000, variable cost Rs. 2 per unit. Sales price Rs. 4 per unit.

(*b*) Sales Rs. 6,000, Variable cost Rs. 3,600, fixed cost Rs. 2,000.

(*c*) Sales Rs. 4,000, variable cost Rs. 2,400, profit Rs. 400. (*Calicut University, B. Com., April 1988*)

[***Answer :*** (*a*) BEP = 10,000 units, (*b*) Rs. 5,000, (*c*) Rs. 3,000.]

Exercise 8 : The following data of a company for the year 1987 are given :

Variable cost (Rs.)	60,000
Fixed cost	30,000
Net profit	10,000
Sales	1,00,000

Find out break-even sales and margin of safety. (*Madurai University, B. Com., Nov. 1988*)

Exercise 9 : An analysis of *S* Ltd., cost records gives the following information :

	Variable cost *(% of sales)*	Fixed cost *(Rs.)*
Direct material	32.8	
Direct labour	28.4	
Factory overhead	12.6	1,89,000
Distribution overhead	4.1	58,400
General administration overhead	1.1	66,700

Budgeted sales for the next year Rs. 18,50,000. You are required to determine

(*a*) Break-even sales value.

(*b*) Profit at the budgeted sales valume.

(*c*) Profit if the actual sales (*i*) drop by 10%, (*ii*) decrease by 5% from the sale.

(*Bharathidasan University, M. Com., April 1988*)

Exercise 10 (Preparation of break-even chart) : Prepare a break-even chart from the following information :

Total costs	(Rs.) 60,000
Fixed costs	30,000
Sales	1,00,000

Also calculate margin of safety. (*University of Delhi, B. Com.(Pass), April 1988*)

[***Answer :*** P/U ratio = 70%, BEP = Rs. 42,859, Margin of Safety = Rs. 57,143.]

Exercise 11 (Preparation of profit chart) : Following cost data for products *X*, *Y* and *Z* are given :

Products	*Sales (Rs.)*	*Variable cost*	*Fixed cost*
X (Rs.)	15,000	3,000	–
Y (Rs.)	15,000	10,500	–
Z (Rs.)	7,500	9,000	–
Total (Rs.)	37,500	22,500	10,000

Prepare a profit graph for products *X*, *Y* and *Z*. (*Bangalore University, M. Com., May 1992*)

Exercise 12 (P/V Graph) : From the following details prepare a profit-volume graph showing break-even point at different price levels :

Sales levels	80,000 and 60,000 units
Fixed expenses	Rs. 4,00,000
Variable expenses	Rs. 10 per unit
Selling price	Rs. 20 per unit

Assume that the price is changed to Rs. 18 and Rs. 22. (*Bangalore University, M. Com., May 1991*)

9

DIFFERENTIAL COSTING

INTRODUCTION

Differential costing is a broader and more fundamental concept than marginal costing and hence has a much wider application. It helps in making appropriate decision by examining all the revenues and cost differences between alternatives. While marginal costing analyses the changes in only the variable costs, differential costing examines the differences in both variable and fixed costs. Hence this technique is more useful for those situations where fixed costs also differ and thus more appropriate for both short run and long run decisions.

Differential costs are costs that change in respect of an alternate course of action. The A.A.A. Committee on cost concepts and standards (*Accounting Review*, Vol. 27) defines it as "the increase or decrease in total cost or the change in specific elements of cost that result from any variation in operation". The alternative actions may be owing to change in sales, volume, price, product mix, or methods of production or change in decision. When two levels of activity are under review, differential cost is obtained by deducting the cost at one level from another level.

The technique used for analysing differential costs is known as differential costing. The ICMA terminology defines differential costing as "a technique used in the preparation of *ad hoc* information in which only cost and income differences between alternative courses of action are taken into consideration."

It is the process of determining how costs in particular and profit in general will be affected if one alternative is chosen over another.

The term "incremental cost" is used to denote differential cost when the increase in cost in due to increase in the level of production. Similarly the term "decremental cost" is used when the difference in cost is due to decrease in the level of production.

FEATURES AND IMPLICATIONS OF DIFFERENTIAL COSTING

The features of differential costing can be enumerated under the following points :

(*a*) It is expressed in total but not cost per unit.

(*b*) The data considered for such analysis are (*i*) cost, (*ii*) revenue, (*iii*) investment which are relevant to the problem under consideration.

(*c*) It is not a part of accounting though it is a form of budgeting. It is used only by the management to make decisions.

(*d*) The constant cost at different levels are ignored and only the differentials are considered. Absolute cost is not much importance in this analysis.

(*e*) Differentials are measured from a common position or level of activity.

(*f*) Where the difference between revenue and cost is highest, that course of action is adopted.

The differential costing is based on the implication that only the relevant cost, which will change as a result of the decision is useful for decision-making. Any costs which are not expected to alter, then they are irrelevant for decision-making. The following are the examples of cost that are irrelevant :

(*a*) Sunk cost, *i.e.*, those costs which have already been incurred are irrelevant.
(*b*) Book values of assets.
(*c*) Cost of fully utilised resources, *i.e.*, where a limiting factor exists it will be used to the full extent and will, therefore, cost the same whatever alternative is considered.
(*d*) *Fixed cost* : Any item which remains constant whichever alternative is chosen is not a differential cost and can be ignored in choosing alternatives.

MARGINAL VS. DIFFERENTIAL COSTING

The differential costing is similar to marginal costing under the following respects :

(*a*) Both the techniques are based on cost analysis for presenting the information to management.
(*b*) Costs are analysed on the basis of their behaviour under both the techniques.
(*c*) Both the techniques serve the same purpose of planning and decision-making by the management.
(*d*) Both the techniques will be same if the fixed costs remain same for alternative proposals.
(*e*) Differential cost resembles to economist's concept of marginal cost.

However, differential costing differs from marginal costing in the following respects :

(*a*) The scope of marginal costing is narrow, while that of differential costing is broader and hence it has wider applications.
(*b*) Marginal costing technique is useful in making decisions in the short run, whereas differential costing is useful in taking both short run and long run decisions where fixed costs do alter.
(*c*) Marginal cost is defined as the sum of all variable costs. Such a concrete definition is not possible under differential cost. It can at best be defined as an increase or decrease of total cost owing to rise or fall in production.
(*d*) Marginal costing presents cost information under contribution margin approach. Whereas differential costing can be presented both under absorption costing and marginal costing techniques.
(*e*) Under marginal costing technique the performance is judged by the "contribution" and P/V ratio. Whereas under differential costing, the performance is evaluated by comparing differential cost with incremental revenue.
(*f*) Marginal costing is a part of accounting system whereas differential cost analysis is not a part of accounting system. It may be a part of budgeting.
(*g*) Marginal cost is expressed in terms of cost per unit whereas differential cost is expressed in total.

APPLICATIONS OF DIFFERENTIAL COSTING

Differential costing techniques is used to solve the problems relating to the following :

(*a*) Make or buy decisions.
(*b*) Expanding the marketability of the products.

(c) Changing the product mix.
(d) Further processing of products.
(e) Changing the method of production.
(f) Introducing a new product line.
(g) Replacing mannual labour with mechanical labour.
(h) Fixation of selling price below the competitive price.
(i) Accepting or rejecting a new order.
(j) Dealing about the most profitable level of production.
(k) Shut down or continue operation.

Problem 1 (Determination of level of production) : A company's flexible budget reveals the following market conditions and costs :

Output in units	*Selling price per unit (Rs.)*	*total semi-fixed cost (Rs.)*	*Total variable cost (Rs.)*	*Total fixed cost (Rs.)*
60,000	12	1,50,000	4,18,000	1,42,000
1,20,000	11	1,50,000	8,18,000	1,42,000
1,80,000	10	1,70,000	12,78,000	1,42,000
2,40,000	9	1,70,000	15,78,000	1,42,000
3,00,000	8	2,00,000	17,78,000	1,42,000
3,60,000	7	2,00,000	19,02,000	1,42,000

(a) Prepare a schedule showing the total differential costs and incremental revenue.
(b) At what level should the company set its level of production?
(c) What selling price should be established in order to obtain the most profitable operations for the year?

Solution :

(a) Statement showing projected cost and revenue

	Output (Units)					
	60,000	*1,20,000*	*1,80,000*	*2,40,000*	*3,00,000*	*3,60,000*
Fixed cost	1,42,000	1,42,000	1,42,000	1,42,000	1,42,000	1,42,000
Semi-fixed cost	1,50,000	1,50,000	1,70,000	1,70,000	2,00,000	2,00,000
Variable cost	4,18,000	8,18,000	12,78,000	15,78,000	17,78,000	19,02,000
Total cost	7,10,000	11,10,000	15,90,000	18,90,000	21,20,000	22,44,000
Differential cost		40,00,000 (Col 2 – Col 1)	4,80,000 (Col 3 – Col 2)	3,00,000 (Col 4 – Col 3)	2,30,000 (Col 5 – Col 4)	1,24,000 (Col 6 – Col 5)
Sales value	7,20,000	13,20,000	18,00,000	21,60,000	24,00,000	25,20,000
Marginal revenue	–	6,00,000	4,80,000	3,60,000	2,40,000	1,20,000

(b) As long as the increment in total revenue exceeds the differential costs, it pays to increase output, but as soon as the incremental revenue equals differential costs, it is no longer profitable to read the volume of production. In the above case the incremental revenue is about equal to differential costs at 3,00,000 output level and beyond that it is decreasing so the production should be fixed at this level (correctly between 3,00,000 and 3,60,000 levels).

(c) The sale price at this level is Rs. 8 per unit which should be adopted for the year, which would bring in maximum profit.

Problem 2 (Acceptance or rejection of an offer) : The following particulars are extracted from the books of Adarsh Co. Ltd. for the period ending 31st Dec., 1992 :

Capacity	*Unit cost (Rs.)*	*Unit selling price (Rs.)*
6,000	80	100
7,000	75	97
8,000	74	95
9,000	72	
10,000	71	

The firm is operating at 8,000 units capacity and has received an order for 2,000 units from an export market at a price of Rs. 70 per unit. Advise the company as to whether the export order should be accepted or not?

Solution : **Statement showing incremental cost and revenue**

Capacity	*Unit cost*	*Total cost*	*Incremental cost*	*Unit price*	*Total sales*	*Incremental revenue*
6,000	80	4,80,000		100	6,00,000	
7,000	75	5,25,000	45,000	97	6,79,000	79,000
8,000	74	5,92,000	67,000	95	7,60,000	8,000
9,000	72	6,48,000	56,000			
10,000	71	7,10,000	62,000			

At 8,000 level of output, the total sales revenue is Rs. 7,60,000 and the total cost is Rs. 5,92,000 leaving a profit of Rs. 1,68,000. The fact that this level of output leaves a profit means that the fixed costs have been recovered already. Hence we have to take only the incremental cost for further level of output. For an additional sales of 2,000 units the incremental cost is Rs. 7,10,000 – Rs. 5,92,000 = Rs. 1,18,000. The cost per unit, therefore, is $\frac{1,18,000}{2,000}$ = Rs. 59 for which the price quoted is Rs. 70 per unit. Hence the offer is to be accepted.

Problem 3 (Increasing production capacity) : A company is at present working at 90% of its capacity and producing 13,500 units per annum. It operates at flexible budgetary control system. The following figures are obtained from its budget :

	Capacity 90% (Rs.)	*Utilisation 100% (Rs.)*
Sales	15,00,000	16,00,000
Fixed	3,00,500	3,00,600
Semi-fixed expenses	97,500	1,00,500
Variable expenses	1,45,000	1,49,500
Units manufactured	13,500	15,000

Labour and material costs per unit are constant under the present conditions. Profit margin is 10%.

(*a*) You are required to determine the differential cost of producing 1,500 units by increasing capacity utilisation to 100 per cent.

(*b*) What would you recommend as an export price for these 1,500 units after considering that overseas prices are much lower than in land prices? (*ICWA, Inter., June 1992*)

Solution :

Sales at 90% capacity utilisation	15,00,000
Less : Profit (10%)	1,50,000
Cost of goods sold	13,50,000
Less : Expenses (fixed, semi-fixed and variable)	5,43,000
Cost of materials and labour	8,07,000

∴ Cost of materials and labour at 100% capacity utilisation

$$8,07,000 \times \frac{100}{90} = \text{Rs. } 8,96,667$$

Differential cost analysis will be as follows :

	90% Capacity *utilisation*	100% Capacity *utilisation*
Production (Units)	13,500	15,000
Materials and Labour (Rs.)	8,07,000	8,96,667
Variable expenses (Rs.)	1,45,000	1,49,500
Semi-fixed expenses (Rs.)	97,500	1,00,500
Fixed expenses (Rs.)	3,00,500	3,00,600
	13,50,000	14,47,267

(*a*) Differential cost = 14,47,267 – 13,50,000
= Rs. 97,267

(*b*) Minimum price per export = $\frac{97,267}{1,500}$ = Rs. 64.84 per unit.

At this price, there is no addition to revenue. Any price above Rs. 64.84 per unit may be accepted. A price below this may be considered, if other benefits, *i.e.*, other than mere sales and revenue are likely to accrue. It is assumed that no capital investment is necessary and no export changes have to be incurred and that the export price will have no effect on the home market where the product will continue to be sold at the old price.

Problem 4 (Equipment replacement) : A factory engaged in the manufacture of electronic goods has a ten-year old equipment depreciated on straight-line basis. The useful life of the equipment was estimated to be 20 years with a residual value of Rs. 3 lakhs (original cost of the equipment being Rs. 23 lakhs). The output of the equipment is 1,200 units per hour.

The management now proposes to instal a new equipment worth Rs. 50 lakhs which has an estimated life of 15 years and a residual value of Rs. 5 lakhs. The payment terms for the new equipment include a part exchange provision of Rs. 6 lakhs in respect of the existing equipment. The output of the new equipment is 3,000 units per hour.

Other comparative annual cost data relating to the two equipments are as under :

	Existing equipment (Rs.)	*New equipment (Rs.)*
Wages	1,00,000	1,20,000
Repairs and maintenance	20,000	52,000
Consumables	3,20,000	4,80,000
Power	1,20,000	1,50,000
Allocation of fixed cost	60,000	80,000
Total hours run per year	2,400	2,400

You are required to prepare a comparative schedule showing total conversion cost as well as cost per 1,000 units after considering interest @ 10% on net cash outflow for procuring the new equipment and also for providing for the yearly recovery of the loss suffered in the transaction. (*ICWA, Inter., Dec. 1991*)

Solution : **Comparative statement of cost of equipment**

	Existing equipment	*New equipment*
Capital cost of equipment including cost of installation	23,00,000	50,00,000
Less : Residual value	3,00,000	5,00,000
	20,00,000	45,00,000
Less : Depreciation written off	10,00,000	–
	10,00,000	45,00,000

Comparative statement of operation cost of equipment

Annual depreciation		
New equipment	–	3,00,000
Old equipment	1,00,000	70,000

Interest on capital (net cash outflow)	–	4,40,000
Wages	1,00,000	1,20,000
Repairs and maintenance	20,000	52,000
Consumables	3,20,000	4,80,000
Power	1,20,000	1,50,000
Allocation of fixed expenses	60,000	80,000
	7,20,000	16,92,000
Total hours run per annum	2,400	2,400
Operating cost per hour (Rs.)	300	705
Output per hour (Units)	1,200	3,000
Operating cost per 1,000 unit (Rs.)	250	235

Therefore, there is a net saving in cost of Rs. 15 per 1,000 units.

Working Note 1 : Depreciation on new equipment

$$\text{Depreciation} = \frac{\text{Original cost} - \text{Residual value}}{\text{Estimated life}}$$

$$= \frac{45,00,000}{15} = 3,00,000$$

Working Note 2 : Depreciation (yearly recovery) on loss on sale of existing equipment

$$= \frac{\text{Book value of existing equipment} - \text{Part exchange value}}{\text{Residual life of existing equipment}}$$

$$= \frac{\text{Rs. } 13,00,000 - \text{Rs. } 6,00,000}{10 \text{ years}} = \text{Rs. } 70,000$$

Working Note 3 : Interest is calculated on net cash outflow in procuring the new equipment is Rs. 44,00,000 (cost of old equipment Rs. 50 lakhs less part exchange value of Rs. 6 lakhs).

Problem 5 (Evaluating profitability of different products) : *G* Ltd. is a process industry which manufactures three joint products, *viz., A, B* and *C*. The joint costs of production are Rs. 4,80,000 and sales are :

A = 30,000 units @ Rs. 6 per unit
B = 10,000 units @ Rs. 20 per unit
C = 20,000 units @ Rs. 12 per unit

It is possible to adopt two alternative production programmes after completion of the joint products. First, product *C* can further processed, which will create a new product *D*. This additional processing will cost Rs. 1,60,000 p.a., but the 20,000 units of product *D* can be sold for Rs. 24 per unit. Secondly, processing of product *C* need not be continued further, but the resources which could have been used in converting product *C* to product *D* can be used to produce an additional product *E*. The cost of this programme would be Rs. 60,000 per annum, but sales of *E* would be obtained of 5,000 units at Rs. 16 per unit. Evaluate the two alternative production programmes.

Solution :

Statement showing incremental cost

Details	*Proposal I*	*Total*	*Proposal II*	*Total*	*Incremental cost*
Sales					
A	1,80,000		1,80,000		
B	2,00,000		2,00,000		
C	–		2,40,000		
D	4,80,000		–		
E	–	8,60,000	80,000	7,00,000	1,60,000
Costs					
A, *B*, C	4,80,000		4,80,000		

D	1,60,000		–		1,00,000
E	–	6,40,000	60,000	5,40,000	60,000
Profit		2,20,000		1,60,000	

Statement of profit for the opportunity foregone

Sales of *D*			4,80,000
Less : Costs of *D*			1,60,000
			3,20,000
Sales foregone if *D* produced	*C* =	2,40,000	
	E =	80,000	
		3,20,000	
Costs foregone if *D* produced	*E* =	60,000	2,60,000
		Profit	60,000

Problem 6 (Dropping or continuing an area for effecting sales) : *X* Co. Ltd. produces and sells three products : *A*, *B* and *C*. These products are sold in a local market and in a regional market. At the end of the first quarter of the year 1993, the following income statement has been prepared :

	Total	*Local*	*Regional*
Sales Revenue	13,00,000	10,00,000	3,00,000
Cost of goods sold	10,10,000	7,75,000	2,35,000
Gross margin	2,90,000	2,25,000	65,000
Marketing cost	1,05,000	60,000	45,000
Administrative cost	52,000	40,000	12,000
Cost production and sales	1,57,000	1,00,000	57,000
Operating profit	1,33,000	1,25,000	8,000

The management has expressed special concern with the regional market because of the extremely poor return on sales. This market was entered a year ago because of excess capacity. It was originally believed that the return on sales would improve with time, but after a year, no noticeable improvement can be seen from the results as reported in the above quarterly statement.

In attempting to decide whether to eliminate the regional market, the following information has been gathered :

	Product A	*Product B*	*Product C*
Sales revenue (Rs.)	5,00,000	4,00,000	4,00,000
Variable cost as a percentage to sales	60%	70%	60%
Variable marketing cost as a percentage to sales	3%	2%	2%

Sales by market

	Local	*Regional*
A	Rs. 4,00,000	Rs. 1,00,000
B	Rs. 3,00,000	Rs. 1,00,000
C	Rs. 3,00,000	Rs. 1,00,000

All administrative cost and fixed manufacturing costs are common to the three products and the two markets and are fixed for the period. Remaining marketing costs are fixed for the period and separable by market. All fixed costs are based upon a prorated yearly amount.

Required :

(*a*) Assuming there are no alternative used for the *X* Co. Ltd.'s present capacity, would you recommend dropping the regional market.

(*b*) Prepare the quarterly income statement showing contribution margin by products.

(*c*) It is believed that a new product can be ready for sale next year. The new product can be produced by simply converting equipment presently used in producing product *C*. This conversion will increase fixed cost by Rs. 10,000 per quarter. What must be the minimum contribution margin per quarter for the new product to make the changeover financially feasible.

Solution :

(*a*) The regional market should not be dropped as this market not only covers all the variable costs and separable fixed costs but also gives net market contribution of Rs. 65,000 towards the common fixed cost

Sales = Rs. 3,00,000

Variable manufacturing cost = (6 × 1,00,000) + (7 × 1,00,000) + (6 × 1,00,000)
= 1,90,000

Marketing costs = Rs. 45,000

(*b*) **Statement showing quarterly income statement**

In thousands

		A	*B*	C	*Total*
Sales (Rs.)		500	400	400	1,300
Less :	Variable cost				
	Manufacturing	300	280	240	820
	Marketing	15	8	8	31
	Total variable cost	315	288	248	851
	Contribution margin	185	112	152	449
Less :	Fixed costs :				
	Manufacturing				190
	Marketing				74
	Administrative				52
	Total fixed cost				316
	Operating profit				133

(*c*) The new product must contribute at least Rs. 1,62,000 (Rs. 1,52,000 + Rs. 10,000) per quarter so as not to leave the company worse off when product *C* is replaced.

Problem 7 (Acceptance of rejection of an export order) : *MX* Ltd. having an installed capacity of 1,00,000 units of a product is currently operating at 70% utilisation. At current levels of input prices the FOB unit cost (after credit for applicable export incentives) works out as follows :

Capacity utilisation%	*FOB unit cost (Rs.)*
70	97
80	92
90	87
100	82

The company has received three foreign offers from different sources as under :

Source *A* 5,000 units @ Rs. 54 per unit FOB

Source *B* 10,000 units @ Rs. 52 per unit FOB

Source *C* 10,000 units @ Rs. 51 per unit FOB

Advise the company as to whether any or all the export orders should be accepted or not.

Solution :

Statement showing differential cost

Capacity	*Production (Units)*	*FOB unit cost (Rs.)*	*Installed total cost*	*Differential cost*	*Per unit differential cost*
70	70,000	97	67,90,000	–	–
80	80,000	92	73,60,000	5,70,000	57
90	90,000	87	78,30,000	4,70,000	47
100	1,00,000	82	82,00,000	3,70,000	37

Statement showing gain or loss on accepting various export orders

Source of export order	*Export order in units*	*Capacity utilisation*	*Differential cost per unit*	*Differential cost Total*	*FOB price per unit*	*Sales revenue from the export*	*Gain or loss*
A	5,000	75	57	2,85,000	55	2,75,000	(10,000)
B	10,000	85	5,000 @ 57 5,000 @ 47	5,20,000	52	5,20,000	NIL
C	10,000	95	5,000 @ 47 5,000 @ 37	4,20,000	51	5,10,000	90,000
	25,000	95%		12,25,000		13,05,000	80,000

From the above analysis it can be said that when all the three export orders are accepted, the company will make a profit of Rs. 80,000. But accepting only source *A* and *B* orders will give a loss of Rs. 10,000.

Problem 8 (Accepting an order at a lower selling price) : The overhead expenses of a factory, producing a single article at different operating levels are as follows :

Operating level capacity	*Works overhead (Rs.)*
80%	36,000
100%	40,000
120%	50,000
60%	33,000

The factory is currently working at 60% operating level and its annual sales amount is Rs. 1,44,000.

Selling prices have been based on 100% capacity and have the following relationship with costs at this level :

Factory cost	66.67% of sales value
Price cost	75% of factory cost
Adm. and selling expenses (of which 75% is variable)	20% of sales value.

The management receives an offer for carrying out some work for another company valued at Rs. 33,000 per annum which will take up 40% of capacity. The price cost for the work is estimated at Rs. 20,000. There will be an addition to administration expenses of Rs. 1,500 per annum.

The sales manager estimates that the sales of the company's own product will increase to 80% capacity by the time new order materialises.

Calculate the profit on current production. Give your views, supported by figure, on the advisability of taking on the new work. (*Sri Venkateshwara University, M. Com., Sept. 1988*)

Solution : **Statement showing profitability**

				100%	*60%*
Sales				2,40,000	1,44,000
Less :	Cost sales :				
	Prime cost	1,20,000	72,000		
	Works overhead	40,000	33,000		
	Factory cost	1,60,000	1,05,600		
Adm. and selling		48,000	33,600	2,08,000	1,38,600
			Profit	32,000	5,400

At 100% capacity :

Factory cost 66.67% of sales value or $\frac{2}{3}$ of sales

$$\frac{2}{3} \times 2,40,000 = \text{Rs. } 1,60,000$$

Prime cost = –75% of factory cost

$$\frac{75}{100} \times 1{,}60{,}000 = \text{Rs. } 1{,}20{,}000$$

Factory overhead at 100% level given in the problem is 40,000

Administration and selling overhead

$$\frac{20}{100} \times 2{,}40{,}000 = \text{Rs. } 48{,}000$$

of 48,000, 75% is variable, *i.e.*, Rs. 36,000 and Rs. 12,000 is fixed.

At 60% capacity :

Prime cost is 60% of Rs. 1,20,000 = Rs. 72,000

Works overhead is Rs. 33,000 as is given

Administration and selling overhead

Variable 75% and fixed Rs. 12,000

Statement showing profitability for new work

	80%	*40% Additional*	*Total 100%*
Capacity			
Sales	1,92,000	33,000	2,25,000
Less : Cost of sales			
Prime cost	96,000	20,000	1,16,000
Works overhead	36,000	14,000	50,000
Factory overhead	1,32,000	34,000	1,66,000
Adm. and selling	40,800	6,450	47,250
	1,72,800	40,450	2,13,250
Profit or loss	19,200	7,450	11,750

As profit is reduced by Rs. 7,450 additional order is not profitable.

Problem 9 (Expanding the marketability of the product) :

The following extracts are taken from sales budget of a company for the current year

		(Rs. '000)
Sales : 40,000 units @ Rs. 25 per unit		1,000
Selling costs :		
Advertising	100	
Salesmen salaries	80	
Travelling expenses	50	
Rent of sales office	10	
Others	10	
		250

The management is considering a proposal to establish a new market in the eastern region in the next year. It is proposed to increase the advertising expenditure by 25% and appoint an additional sales supervisor at a salary of Rs. 30,000 per year to establish a market. This will involve additional travelling, and the travelling expenses shall increase by 10%.

Target annual sales volume at the existing selling price for the new market is 10,000 units. The estimated variable cost of production is Rs. 12 per unit. Should the company try to establish the new market?

(C.S., Inter., Dec. 1997)

Solution :

Statement showing profit

	Current cost and Revenue	*Budget cost and Revenue*	*Incremental cost and Revenue*
Sales (units)	40,000	50,000	10,000
		(Rs. in '000)	
Sales value	1,000	1,250	250
Less : Advertising	100	125	25

Sales salaries	80		110		30
Travelling expenses	50		55		5
Rent	10		10		–
Others	10		10		–
	250		310		60
Variable cost of	480		600		120
Production		730		910	180
Profit		270		340	70

On the incremental sale, return is 28% of additional sales value and is higher than the current return. Hence the proposal is acceptable.

QUESTIONS

Simple Questions

1. Define "differential cost".
2. Define differential costing.
3. State any four characteristics of differential costing.
4. State any four implications of differential costing.
5. State any four similarities between marginal costing and differential costing.
6. State any four dissimilarities between marginal costing and differential costing.
7. Mention any eight uses of differential costing technique to management of an industry.

EXERCISES

Exercise 1 (Acceptance or rejection of an offer) : A company currently operating at full capacity, manufactures and sells, saucepans at Rs. 2 each current volume is 1,00,000 pans per annum with the following cost structure.

Operating statement for the year 1992

Sales 1,00,000 @ Rs. 2		Rs. 2,00,000
Less : Materials cost	50,000	
Labour cost	80,000	Rs. 1,30,000
	Contribution	70,000
Less : Fixed cost		30,000
	Profit	Rs. 40,000

An opportunity has arisen to supply 30,000 pans per annum at Rs. 1.80.

Acceptance of this order would incur extra materials cost of Rs. 15,000 per annum and fixed cost of Rs. 8,000 per annum for the hire for additional machinery and the payment of an overtime premium of 20% for the extra direct labour required.

Should this order be accepted?

[*Answer :* The incremental revenue generated by accepting order is Rs. 2,200. So the order is to be accepted.]

Exercise 2 (Equipment replacement) : *P* Ltd. is considering the replacement of machine *A* by a new machine *B*. Comparative data are as follows :

	Existing machine A	*Proposed machine B*
Purchase price	Rs. 2,000	6,000
Disposal value now	600	
Disposal value in one year's time	450	
Rate of depreciation	10%	10%
Estimated scrap value (Rs.)		500

Indirect labour and materials	1,000	1,000
Scrap losses	200	100
Direct wages	2,000	1,000

[*Answer :* Saving is Rs. 700 per annum. So new machine is to bought.]

Exercise 3 (Acceptance or rejection of order) : A company has a capacity of producing 1,00,000 units of a certain product in a month. The sales department reports that the following schedule of sale prices is possible :

Volume of production	*Selling price per unit (Re.)*
60%	0.90
70%	0.80
80%	0.75
90%	0.67
100%	0.61

The variable cost of manufacture between these levels is Re. 0.15 per unit and fixed cost Rs. 40,000.

(*a*) Prepare a statement showing incremental revenue and differential cost of each stage. At which volume of production will the profit be maximum?

(*b*) If there is a bulk offer at Re. 0.50 per unit of the balance capacity over the maximum profit volume for export and the price quoted will not affect the internal sale, will you advise this bid?

[*Answer :* As the incremental revenue is higher than differential cost up to the level of 80%, the level of production should be set out 80%.

The bulk offer for export for the balance capacity of 2,000 units (over and above 80%) at 50 paise per unit will add Rs. 7,000 to profit. Hence the offer for export is to be accepted.]

10

BUDGETARY CONTROL

INTRODUCTION

A budget is a quantitative expression of a plan of action prepared in advance for the period to which it relates. It may be prepared for the entire organisation or for various departments or for various functions involved in that organisation. Budget is a means of translating the overall objectives of the business into detailed feasible plan of action.

The concept of "budget" is being made use of by every individual who undertake a work involving expenditure. While some express it orally others put it in written form. For example, a person who wants to go on a holiday tour will prepare a budget involving expenditure on fares, boarding, lodging, purchasing, etc. After returning, he will compare the actual expenses incurred with budgeted expenses to know whether he spent more or less as compared to budgets and if so what factors were responsible for it. This enables him to increase or decrease his budget for the next year.

In the same way, every business undertakes to budget its expenditure for utilising the available funds more judiciously. Similarly, to ensure proper utilisation of scarce raw materials and other factors of production, the management of every business will prepare a budget relating to material, labour, production and various expenditure. This enables in proper planning of all activities, their co-ordination and finally controlling such activities. In this process it enables the management to know the performance of business for a given period of time.

BUDGET AND BUDGETARY CONTROL

Definition of a Budget

The ICMA terminology defines a budget as "a plan quantified in monetary items, prepared and approved prior to a defined period of time, usually showing planned income to be generated and/or expenditure to be incurred during that period and the capital to be employed to attain a given objective".

George R. Terry defines budget as "an estimate of future needs arranged according to an orderly basis, covering some or all the activities of an enterprise for a definite period of time".

Definition of Budgetary Control

According to F.H. Rowland and W.H. Barr, budgetary control is a "Tool of management used to plan, carryout and control the operations of the business".

In the words of C.L. Van Sickle, "a budgetary control system is a carefully worked out financial plan, including the procedure involved in its operations for conducting the various divisions of a business for the ultimate purpose of earning a profit".

The ICMA terminology defines budgetary control as, "the establishment of budgets relating the responsibilities of executives to the requirements of a policy and the continuous comparison of actual with budgeted result either to secure by individual action the objective of that policy or to provide a basis for its revision".

An analysis of this definition reveal the following important points:

(*a*) **Executive responsibility :** It means that every manager has to do his job directed towards the overall objects of the business, *i.e.*, the policy. In other words, every manager is responsible for attaining the task delegated to him and thereby the ultimate object of the business.

(*b*) **The requirements of a policy :** The budget is a statement of policy relating to the position of business and plans to attain it. The business has to establish certain goals and necessary actions must be taken to achieve those aims. This is essential for proper growth and development of the business and for efficient utilisation of labour force and other assets.

(*c*) **Comparison of actual with budgeted results :** This facilitates control over the planned activities. The actual result is measured and compared with budgets. When there exists any unfavourable difference, management can take remedial steps.

(*d*) **The revision of policy :** The policy may have to be revised in order to make the best use of prevailing situation after considering unfavourable factors.

The budgetary control is exercised by applying the following steps :

1. **Preparation of the budget :** The process of preparing the budget will be explained under the heading "budget organisation".

2. **Publishing the budget :** This implies informing each executive what is expected of him. The publishing of the budget is most important, as no system is able to work unless the people concerned with it understand and are prepared to make it work.

3. **Measuring the results :** This implies the measurement of actual results achieved in order to know whether they are as per plan or otherwise.

4. **Comparing the results with the budget :** The comparison of actual results with the budget enables to know the efficiency or otherwise of the activity.

5. **Reporting the results of the above activity :** This is done by means of budgetary control statements, which enable the budget officer to know whether the objectives set out in the budget are being fulfilled and if not, in which areas attention should be concentrated.

6. **Correcting the unfavourable variances :** Necessary steps are then taken to avoid the occurrence of unfavourable variances. This is the function of the departmental manager or the supervisor. The budgetary control statements will assist as tools to the manager in correcting the unfavourable differences.

OBJECTIVES OF BUDGETARY CONTROL

1. Planning and Co-ordination

Budgeting involves preparation of a detailed operational plans to achieve the objectives of a business. The success of every business depends upon the planning of activities and budgeting forces planning to become more effective. As budgets are prepared covering all the activities and departments of a business, it also serves as a means of co-ordinating the efforts of all concerned in such a way that every department contributes towards the overall plan. The summary of all such plan is known as master plan. The budget forces every departmental manager to establish relationship with other departments and contribute to the achievement of objectives.

2. Clarification of Authority and Responsibility

Budgeting enables the superior to delegate the authority to his subordinates. This also clarifies the responsibility of each manager who can be held accountable if the targets are not reached. Thus budgeting facilitates management by exception.

3. Communication

Since all levels of management are involved in the preparation of budget, it facilitates communication process to become more effective. The objectives of the business, problems involved in achieving them, and finalisation of budgets are all promptly communicated. It also co-ordinates the various functions such as sales, purchases and production more efficiently.

4. Motivation

The preparation of budgets by middle and lower management against which performance can be judged serves as a good motivation for them.

5. Control

The control over various activities is achieved by comparing the achievements with the targets. If there are any deviations, the causes for the same is investigated and remedial action taken.

ESSENTIAL REQUIREMENTS OF BUDGETARY CONTROL

The essential requirements of a budgetary control system as quoted by Robert I Dickey are as follows :

1. Budget must have the complete cooperation of the chief executive.
2. The ultimate realisation of the maximum amount of profit should always be kept uppermost.
3. Responsibility for the preparation of the estimate should rest on those individuals responsible for performance.
4. The budget must be realistic and the goals attainable.
5. A budget committee should be established consisting of the budget director, the chief executive officer, and the executives of the various divisions of the organisation.
6. The budget should cover all phases of operations.
7. Budgeting should be continuous.
8. Periodic reports should be prepared promptly, comparing budget and actual results.
9. The accounting system must be adequate.
10. A good organisation must be developed.

ADVANTAGES AND LIMITATIONS OF BUDGETARY CONTROL

Advantages

The important advantages of budgetary control are as follows :

1. It helps the process of planning by reducing it to concrete numerical goals. Through the budgets, the executives know what they are to produce or sell, how

much they can spend, how much income to expect and so on.

2. It provides an effective means by which top management can delegate authority and responsibility without sacrificing its overall control. Limits for each department or division are laid down in the budget.
3. It keeps expenditure under check and constantly reminds employees and management of the targets and goals to be achieved. It helps in the cautious utilisation of resources and promotion of efficiency.
4. As a control devise, it supplies the means of checking results and comparing performance, of revealing weaknesses and making corrections.
5. The budget is not merely an instrument of planning but also a tool of co-ordination. It brings together the activities of various sections, departments and divisions in an overall perspective.
6. It helps in determining the policies of the factory.
7. It gives complete information in advance regarding the amount of capital needed for the budget period.
8. It gives the idea of where executive action is required.
9. It aids in measuring performance of each department of the factory.
10. It promotes cooperation among the different executives for determining future plans.
11. It acts as a control tool for administration.
12. It centralises management control.

Limitations of Budgetary Control

1. The budget is always based on estimates. The success or failure of a budget, to a large extent, depends upon the accuracy of estimates. The estimates cannot be accurately made in this dynamic world, although many statistical techniques are available.
2. To evolve a budgetary control system, normally, it takes several years as it has to be tried, improved, and discarded, depending upon the changing circumstances.
3. The success of budgetary control depends upon the enthusiastic participation of all levels of management. But it is difficult to secure the wholehearted cooperation of all in a factory.
4. Budgeting is only a tool of management but it cannot replace management.
5. It may be difficult to instal a system of budgetary control in small factories owing to expenditure involved.

ORGANISATION FOR BUDGETARY CONTROL

A sound organisation is essential for an effective budgeting programme. It ensures cooperation from all levels of management. The organisation should facilitate control of all elements of cost. The essential ingredients of a sound organisation are as follows :

1. Organisation Chart

An organisation chart depicts the functional responsibilities of every manager. It shows the relative position of every manager and his relationship with others. A typical organisation chart is shown below :

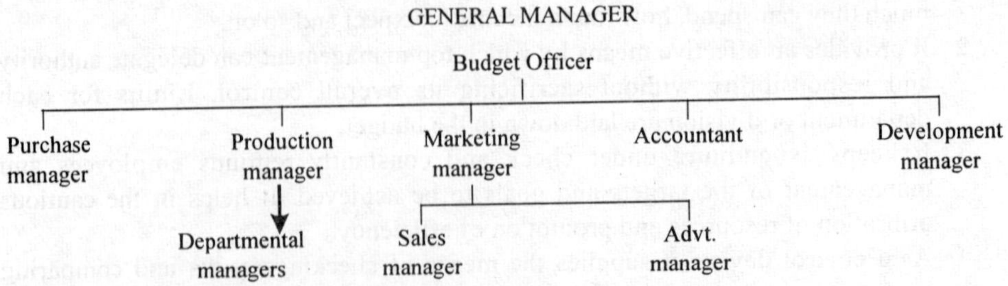

GENERAL MANAGER

Budget Officer

Purchase manager | Production manager | Marketing manager | Accountant | Development manager

Departmental managers | Sales manager | Advt. manager

Fig. 10.1. Budgetary control organisation chart.

From the chart it is clear that, the entire responsibility of budgetary control process lies with general manager. He entrusts the authority to implement the budget programme to the budget officer. He shall co-ordinate the budgets prepared by all the departmental managers.

2. Budget Officer

A budget officer is a person who is nominated by the general manager to look after the functions of budgeting. He is responsible to general manager for completing the budgeting process. He acts as co-ordinator and adviser integrating the budgets prepared by the departmental managers so as to get a master budget. His functions are as follows :

(*a*) Issuing instructions to departments regarding requirements, dates of submission of data, etc.

(*b*) Providing historical information to departmental managers to help them in their forecasting.

(*c*) Receiving and checking budget estimates.

(*d*) Suggesting possible revisions.

(*e*) Discussing difficulties with managers.

(*f*) Ensuring that budgets are received in agreed time.

(*g*) Preparing budget summaries.

(*h*) Charting the departmental estimates on a master plan.

(*i*) Submitting budgets to the committee and furnishing explanations on particular points.

(*j*) Informing the departmental managers of any revisions made in their budgets by the committee.

(*k*) Preparing the final master plan approved by the committee.

(*l*) Co-ordinating all budget work.

3. Budget Committee

It serves as a co-ordinating authority of the budgeting process. It is concerned with resolving difficulties or disputes which may arise among functional heads and to take decisions so as to alter production, price, etc. The budget officer will submit the draft master budget to the committee for consideration after which it is finally approved by board of directors. The budget committee will functions in an advisory capacity and it performs the following functions :

(*a*) To receive and review individual budget estimates.

(*b*) To suggest revisions.

(*c*) To decide on general policies affecting more than one primary department.

(*d*) To revise and approve the budgets.

(*e*) To receive and consider budget reports showing actual results compared with the budget.

(*f*) To recommend actions where necessary.

4. Budget Centre

A budget centre is a section of an organisation defined for the sake of budgetary control. It is established for the sake of fixation of responsibilities on the executives.

5. Budget Mannual

The ICMA terminology defines a budget mannual as "a document which sets out standing instructions governing the responsibilities of persons and the procedures, forms and records relating to the preparation and use of budgets". It serves as a basis of guidance and information about budgeting process. It is more like an instructional mannual about the way budget operates. Lucey, in his book *Costing* sets out the contents of a budget mannual as under :

Foreword :

Preferably by managing director

Objectives/explanation of the budgetary process.

- Explanation of budgetary control.
- Objectives of each stage of the budgetary process.
- Relationship to long term planning.

Organisation structure and responsibilities :

- Structure of the organisation showing titles, responsibilities and relationships.
- Titles and names of current budget holders.

Main budgets and relationship :

- Outline of all main budgets and their accounting relationships.
- Explanation of key budgets (master budget, cash budget)

Budget development :

- Budget committee, membership and terms of reference.
- Sequence of budget preparation.
- Time-table for budget preparation and publication.

Accounting procedure :

- Name and terms of reference of the budget officer.
- Coding lists.
- Sample forms.
- Time-table for accounting procedures, production of reports, closing date.

6. Chart of Accounts

It refers to maintaining a systematic set of accounting books which should be able to record and analyse the information required. A chart of accounts may be maintained separately for every budget centre. In simple words, a chart of accounts denotes accounting structure useful for budgetary control.

7. Budget Period

It is a period relating to which a budget is prepared. A budget period may relate to a short term period or a long term period. Some time these period may relate even to a month for monitoring and control of budgets. It is always desirable to have a short-term budget period excepting those functions which may prolong for a longer period as for example, research and development. The duration of the budget period depends upon type of business, the length of manufacturing cycle, the ease or difficulty of forecasting future market conditions and so on. The budget period may be accordingly short-term budget period or long-term budget period.

The short-term budget period may cover a period of 3 months to 1 year. According to Matz-Curry and Frank (*Cost Accounting*) the following factors should be considered in determining the length of budget period :

(*a*) The budget period should be long enough to complete production of the various products.

(*b*) For a business of a seasonal nature, the budget period should cover at least one entire seasonal cycle.

(*c*) The budget period should be long enough to allow for the financing of production well in advance of actual needs.

(*d*) Major operations and drastic changes in plant layout or manufacturing methods must be planned far in advance to determine financial requirements.

(*e*) The budget period should coincide with the financial accounting period to compare actual results with budget estimates.

A long-term budget may be taken to mean a budget prepared for a period of more than a year. Such a budget is best suited for research and development activities, long-term capital investment, financial and profit planning. It is mostly based on probability of events. It is very much affected by risk factor.

8. Key Factor

The factor which governs the quantity which is manufactured or sold is known as key factor. The ICMA terminology defines a key factor as "a factor which at any time or over a period may limit the activity of an entity often one where there is a shortage or difficulty of supply". This will have an adverse effect over the achievement of budget. Therefore it must be identified and its effect on each of the budget is to be carefully considered during the preparation of budget. Key factor can be changed by the management action. For example, when production process is hampered by plant capacity, the purchase of additional plant will allow increase in production. The following are considered as key factors :

(*a*) *Materials* : (*i*) Availability of supply.
(*ii*) Restrictions imposed by licences, quotas, etc.

(*b*) *Labour* : (*i*) General shortage.
(*ii*) Shortage in certain key processes.

(*c*) *Plant* : (*i*) Insufficient capacity due to lack of capital.
(*ii*) Insufficient or lack of space.
(*iii*) Insufficient or lack of market.
(*iv*) Bottlenecks in certain key processes.

(*d*) *Sales* : (*i*) Low market demand.
(*ii*) Shortage of experienced salesmen.
(*iii*) Inadequate advertisement for want of money.

(*e*) *Management* : (*i*) Lack of "know-how".
(*ii*) Inefficient executives.
(*iii*) Insufficient research into product design and methods.
(*iv*) Lack of capital thereby restricting policy.

ROLLING BUDGET

The concept of rolling budget or continuous budgeting is an attempt to update budgets. The ICMA terminology defines it as "the continuous updating of a short term budget by adding, say, a further month or quarter and deducting the earliest month or quarter, so that the budget can reflect current condition". Rolling budget is used to indicate continuity in the budgeting process. Suppose a budget is prepared for a period of 1 year, then at the end of each month, the results of the previous month's operations together with any new information or changes in business conditions are used to revise the budget for the next 11 months and to prepare a budget for one additional month beyond so that the budget always covers the next 12 months. Each month the budget "rolls" forward one month by adding one month to replace the month just past. The advantage of the rolling budget is that it makes planning a continuous activity.

TYPES OF BUDGET

The various types of budgets are shown in the following chart :

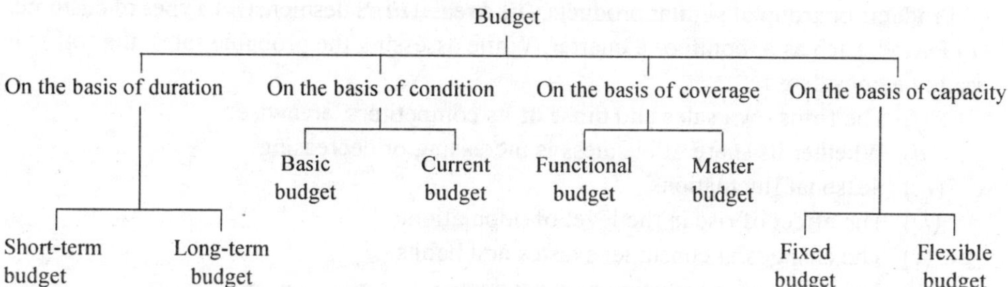

Fig. 10.2. Chart showing types of budgets.

1. On the Basis of Duration

On the basis of duration, budget can be classified into two types, *viz.*, (*a*) short-term budget and (*b*) long-term budget.

(*a*) **Short-term budget :** A short-term budget is prepared to cover a duration of less than 1 year. Sometimes they are prepard for a month also. Cash budget is an example of short-term budget. Short-term budget is followed in many cases as it difficult to forecast events on a long-term basis.

(*b*) **Long-term budget :** A budget which is prepared to cover a period of more than a year is known as long-term budget. The examples of a long-term budget are research and development budget, capital expenditure budget.

2. On the Basis of Condition

On the basis of conditions prevailing, a budget can be classified into two types : (*a*) basic budget and (*b*) current budget.

(*a*) **Basic budget :** The ICMA terminology defines a basic budget as "a budget which is established for use unaltered over a long period of time". The budget does not take into account changes occurring from external environment which are beyond the control of management. This budget is more useful to top level management for formulating policies.

(*b*) **Current budget :** The ICMA terminology defines a current budget as "a budget which is established for use over a short period and is related to the current conditions". The budget under review will be adjusted to the current conditions prevailing in the business. This budget motivates the people preparing the budgets as they are sure of attaining the budget.

3. On the Basis of Coverage

On the basis of coverage of information and activities of a business, budget can be classified into two types, *viz.*, (*a*) Functional budget and (*b*) Master budget.

(*a*) **Functional budget :** As the name suggests functional budgets are prepared in respect of various functions performed in a business. Accordingly we have the following functional budgets.

1. ***Sales budget :*** A sales budget is a statement of planned sales in terms of quantity and value and analysed by products. It is the most important budget as it is most difficult to forecast and attain. It is prepared by the sales manager based on sales forecast. The factors to be considered in forecasting sales are (*a*) Past years sales, (*b*) Forecast of business conditions, (*c*) Market analysis and (*d*) Assessment by the sales department on the basis of (*i*) Products or group of similar products, (*ii*) Areas, (*iii*) Salesmen, (*iv*) Types of customers, (*v*) Period, such as a month or a quarter. While assessing the probable sales, the following are to be considered :

(*i*) The firms own sales and those of its competitors, areawise.
(*ii*) Whether its share of business is increasing or decreasing.
(*iii*) Seasonal fluctuations.
(*iv*) The effect of rise in the level of population.
(*v*) The changes in consumer's tastes and habits.
(*vi*) The effect of introducing new products.
(*vii*) Advertising.
(*viii*) The effect of sales promotion.
(*ix*) The possibility of extending the market.

Problem 1 : Dutta Enterprises sells two products, *A* and *B*. During the year 1993, it plans to sell the following quantities of each product.

Sales budget (in units)

	Total	*I Quarter*	*II Quarter*	*III Quarter*	*IV Quarter*
A	7,00,000	90,000	2,30,000	3,00,000	80,000
B	3,00,000	85,000	75,000	55,000	85,000

Each of these two products is sold on a seasonal basis. Product *A* tends to sell better in summer months, while product *B* sells better during the winter. Dutta Enterprises plan to sell product *A* throughout the year at a price of Rs. 10 a unit and product *B* at a price of Rs. 20 a unit.

A study of the past experience reveals that Dutta Enterprises has lost about 3% of its invoice each year because of returns (constituting 2% of loss of revenue) allowances and bad debts (1% of loss).

Prepare a sales budget incorporating the above information.

Solution :

Sales budget

	I Quarter	*II Quarter*	*III Quarter*	*IV Quarter*	*Total*
Product *A*	9,00,000	23,00,000	30,00,000	8,00,000	70,00,000
Product *B*	17,00,000	15,00,000	11,00,000	17,00,000	60,00,000
(*A*) Total sales	26,00,000	38,00,000	41,00,000	25,00,000	1,30,00,000

Loss for returns @ 2% on total sales	52,000	76,000	82,000	50,000	2,60,000
Loss for bad debts and allowance @ 1% of total sales	26,000	38,000	41,000	25,000	1,30,000
(*B*) Total deductions	78,000	1,14,000	1,23,000	75,000	3,90,000
Net sales (*A* – *B*)	25,22,000	36,86,000	39,77,000	24,25,000	1,26,10,000

Problem 2 : Ambitions company Ltd. has three sales divisions at Mumbai, Chennai and Kolkata. It sells two products – product *X* and product *Y*. The budgeted sales for the year ending 31st December, 2000 at each place are given below :

Mumbai :	Product X	1,00,000 units @ Rs. 8 each
	Product Y	70,000 units @ Rs. 5 each
Chennai :	Product Y	1,10,000 units @ Rs. 5 each
Kolkata :	Product X	1,50,000 units @ Rs. 8 each

The actual sales during the same period were as follows :

Mumbai :	Product X	1,25,000 units @ Rs. 8 each
	Product Y	75,000 units @ Rs. 5 each
Chennai :	Product Y	1,25,000 units @ Rs. 5 each
Kolkata :	Product X	1,55,000 units @ Rs. 8 each

From the reports of the sales personal, it was considered that the sales budget for the year ending 31st December, 2001 would be higher than 2,000 budget in the following aspects

Mumbai :	Product X	8,000 units
	Product Y	5,000 units
Chennai :	Product Y	13,000 units
Kolkata :	Product X	10,000 units

Intensive sales compaign in Chennai and Kolkata is expected to result in additional sales of 25,000 units in product X in Chennai and 18,000 units of product Y in Kolkata.

You are required to prepare a sales budget for the period ending 31st December, 2001.

Solution : **Ascertainment of quantity of Budgeted sales for the year 2001**

Mumbai Division

Product X :–

		Units
	Budgeted sales for the year 2,000	1,00,000
Add :	Expected increase in the sales for the year 2001	8,000
	Budgeted sales for 2001	1,08,000

Product Y

	Budgeted sales for the year 2,000	70,000
Add :	Expected increase in the sales for the year 2001	5,000
	Budgeted sales for 2001	75,000

Chennai Division

Product X :–

		Units
	Budgeted sales for the year 2,000	NIL
Add :	Expected sales for the year 2001	25,000
	Budgeted sales for the year 2001	25,000

Product Y :–

	Budgeted sales for the year 2,000	1,10,000
Add :	Expected increase in the sales for the year 2001	13,000
	Budgeted sales for the year 2001	1,23,000

KolKata Division :–

Product 'X'

	Budgeted sales for the year 2000	1,50,000
Add :	Expected increase in the sales for the year 2001	10,000
		1,60,000

Product Y

	Budgeted sales for the year 2000	NIL
Add :	Expected sales for the year 2001	18,000
	Budgeted sales for the year 2001	18,000

Sales Budget

Sales Division	*Pro-duct*	*Budget for the year 2,000*			*Actuals for the year 2,000*			*Budget for the year 2001*		
		Qty.	*Rate*	*Amt.*	*Qty.*	*Rate*	*Amt.*	*Qty.*	*Rate*	*Amt.*
Mumbai	X	1,00,000	8	8,00,000	1,25,000	8	10,00,000	1,08,000	8	864,000
	Y	70,000	5	3,50,000	75,000	5	3,75,000	75,000	5	3,75,000
		1,70,000		11,50,000	200,000		13,75,000	1,83,000		1239000
Chennai	X	–	–	–	–	–	–	25,000	8	2,00,000
	Y	1,10,000	5	5,50,000	1,25,000	5	6,25,000	1,23,000	5	6,15,000
		1,10,000		5,50,000	1,25,000		6,25,000	1,48,000		815,000
Kolkota	X	1,50,000	8	12,00,000	1,55,000	8	12,40,000	1,60,000	8	12,80,000
	Y	–	–	–	–	–	–	18000	5	90,000
		1,50,000		12,00,000	1,55,000		12,40,000	1,78,000		13,70,000

Problem 3 : Adventurous Co. Ltd. manufactures two products *X* and *Y* and sells them through two divisions Bangalore and Cochin. For the purpose of submission of sales budget to the budget committee, the following information has been made available.

Budgeted sales for the current year were :

Product	*Bangalore*	*Cochin*
X	2,000 units @ Rs. 9	3,000 units @ Rs. 9
Y	1,500 units @ Rs. 21	2,500 units @ Rs. 21

Actual sales for the current year were :

Product	*Bangalore*	*Cochin*
X	2,500 units @ Rs. 9	3,500 units @ Rs. 9
Y	1,000 units @ Rs. 21	2,000 units @ Rs. 21

Market survey reveal that product 'Y' is popular but under-priced. It is observed that if the price of product '*X*' is increased by Re. 1, it will still find a ready market. On the other hand, product *Y* is over-priced to the customers and the market could absorb more if the sales price of product *Y* is reduced by Re. 1. The management has agreed to give effect to the above price changes.

From the information relating to these price changes and reports from salesmen, the following estimates have been prepared by divisional managers.

Percentage increase in sales over current budget is

Product	*Bangalore*	*Cochin*
X	+ 10%	+ 5%
Y	+ 20%	+ 10%

With the help of an intensive advertisement campaign, the following additional sales above the estimated sales of divisional managers are possible

Product	*Bangalore*	*Cochin*
X	300 units	350 units
Y	200 units	250 units

You are required to prepare a budget for sales incorporating the above estimates and also show the budgeted and actual sales of the current year.

Solution :

Working notes :

Ascertainment of Quantity of budgeted sales for future period

Bangalore Division :

Product X		*Units*
	Budgeted sales for the current year	2,000
Add :	Expected increase in sales 10/100 × 2,000	200
Add :	Further increase in sales with intensive advertising	300
	Budgeted sales for future period	2,500

Product Y		
	Budgeted sales for the current year	1,500
Add :	Expected increase in sales $\frac{20}{100} \times 1{,}500$	300
Add :	Further increase in sales with intensive advertising	200
	Budgeted sales for future period	2,000

Cochin Division

Product X		
	Budgeted sales for the current year	3,000
Add :	Expected increase in sales–5%	150
Add :	Further expected increase	350
	Budgeted sales for future period	3,500

Product Y		
	Budgeted sales for the current year	2,500
Add :	Expected increase in sales–10%	250
Add :	Further expected sales	250
		3,000

Sales Budget

Sales Division	*Product*	*Budget for the current year*			*Actuals for the current year*			*Budget for the future period*		
		Qty.	*Rate*	*Amt.*	*Qty.*	*Rate*	*Amt.*	*Qty.*	*Rate*	*Amt.*
Bangalore	X	2,000	9	18,000	2,500	9	22,500	2,500	10	25,000
	Y	1,500	21	31,500	1,000	21	21,000	2,000	20	40,000
		3,500		49,500	3,500		43,500	4,500		65,000
Cochin	X	3,000	9	27,000	3,500	9	31,500	3,500	10	35,000
	Y	2,500	21	52,500	2,000	21	42,000	3,000	20	60,000
		5,500		79,500	5,500		73,500	6,500		95,000

2. *Selling and distribution cost budget :* The success of sales depends upon selling and distribution expenses incurred. Selling expenses are incurred to increase the sales volume. While preparing a selling budget, a classification is made according to the variability of cost. This budget is prepared by the sales managers. Common examples of selling expenses included in a selling cost budget are salesmen's salaries, commissions, and travelling expenses. Sometimes a separate distribution cost budget is prepared apart from selling cost budget. The purpose is to know the expenditure involved in making available finished goods safely to customers. Two important costs go to make up distribution cost budget *viz.*, (*a*) storage and warehousing cost and (*b*) transportation cost. As in the case of selling cost budget, distribution costs are also classified into fixed and variable cost. A specimen of selling and distribution cost budget is shown below :

SELLING & DISTRIBUTION COST BUDGET
(For the period ending 31st Dec. 1993)

	Previous year's budget	*Previous year's actual*	*Current budget*
A. Personnel cost :			
Salaries			
Commission			
Travelling			
B. Sale's office cost			
Office supplies			
Salaries			
Postage			
Telephone			
Rent & rates			
C. Publicity :			
Salaries			
Press			
Journals			
Television			
Samples			
D. Warehousing packing & despatch			
Salaries			
Packing wages			
Driver's wages			
Sundries			
	———	———	———
	———	———	———

Fig. 10.3. Specimen of selling and distribution cost budget.

Problem 4 : Prepare a sales overhead budget for the months of January, February and March from the estimates given below :

	Rs.
Advertisement	2,500
Salaries of sales department	5,000
Expenses of the sales department	1,500
Counter salesman's salaries & D.A.	6,000

Commission to counter salesmen at 1% of their sales

Travelling salesmen's commission at 10% on their sales and expenses at 5% on their sales.

The sales during the period were estimated as follows :

Month	*Counter sales (Rs.)*	*Travelling salesmen's sales (Rs.)*
January	80,000	10,000
February	1,20,000	15,000
March	1,40,000	20,000

(University of Delhi, B. Com.,(Hons.) April 1989)

Solution : **Sales overhead budget**

	Jan.	*Feb.*	*March*
Estimated sales	90,000	1,35,000	1,60,000
Fixed overhead :			
Advertisement	2,500	2,500	2,500
Salaries of sales dept.	5,000	5,000	5,000
Expenses of sales dept.	1,500	1,500	1,500
Salaries of counter salesmen & their DA	6,000	6,000	6,000
	15,000	15,000	15,000
Variable overheads :			
Commission of counter salesmen—10% of counter sales	800	1,200	1,400
Commission of travelling salesmen—10% of their sales	1,000	1,500	2,000
Expenses of travelling salesmen (5% of their sales)	500	750	1,000
	2,300	3,450	4,400
Total sales overhead	17,300	18,450	19,400
Total sales	90,000	1,35,000	1,60,000
% of sales overhead to sales	19.22%	13.67%	12.13%

3. ***Advertising budget :*** In large factories, to undertake an intensive sales programme, a separate advertising department is established. It will be looked after by an advertising manager. The advertising manager will have to deal with the following while budgeting advertising cost :

(*i*) Determine the best method or methods of advertising for the business concerned.

(*ii*) Fix the total amount to be spent on advertising in the budget period. This amount is known as the advertising appropriation.

(*iii*) Co-ordinate the sales function and advertising.

(*iv*) Control the expenditure within the limits laid down and also attempt to measure the effectiveness of advertising.

The best method of advertisement to be selected depends upon reference to the product, channel of distribution, method of selling, types of consumers served. Care must be taken to see that the advertisement cost does not increase cost of production drastically. In other words, advertising cost should be incurred as long as there is an increase in sales and net profit. The matching of advertising cost and benefits derived therefrom is a vital part of advertising budget.

A specimen of advertising budget is shown below :

Advertising budget for the year ended.......

Expenses	*Media of Advertisement*						
	Total (Rs.)	*News-paper*	*Magazines & journals*	*T.V.*	*Cinema*	*Catalogue*	*Samples*
Salaries							
Rent							
Travelling expenses							
Heating & lighting							
Payment to agencies							
Total							

Fig. 10.4. Specimen of advertising cost budget.

4. ***Production budget :*** This budget is prepared by production manager based upon (*a*) sales budget, (*b*) the production capacity and (*c*) the budgeted finished goods stock requirements. According to Blocker and Weltmer, a production budget deals with :

(*i*) The determination of the total estimated volume of production.
(*ii*) The division of the estimated output into different types of products.
(*iii*) The scheduling of operations by days, weeks and months.
(*iv*) The establishment of finished goods inventory requirements.
(*v*) The storage of finished products until delivery can be made in accordance with sales orders.

Advantages : The preparation of a production budget has the following advantages :

(*i*) Plans can be made to keep inventories at reasonable levels consistent with production and sales requirements.
(*ii*) The requirements of raw materials and the sources of their supply can be selected for deriving best terms of purchases along with quality.
(*iii*) By maintaining production schedule, the promised delivery dates can be maintained. This increases reputation of the business.

Procedure : According to Heckert and Wilson (*Business Budgeting and Control*) the preparation of a production budget involves the following steps :

(*i*) Determine the period of time to be used as a basis for the production budget.
(*ii*) Ascertain what physical quantities should be produced to meet the sales budget and to provide properly balanced inventories.
(*iii*) Determine when the goods should be produced.
(*iv*) Determine where the goods should be produced.
(*v*) Determine the manufacturing operations required by the production.
(*vi*) Establish standards of production performance for use in measuring production efficiency.
(*vii*) Develop a programme of materials, labour and equipment requirements.
(*viii*) Use the production budget for purpose of cost control.
(*ix*) Make necessary revisions of the production budget.

5. ***Production cost budget :*** This budget shows the cost of production taking into account the elements of costs *viz.*, direct materials cost, direct labour cost and production overheads.

Problem 5 (Production budget and production cost budget) : *X* Co. Ltd. manufactures two products *A* and *B*. Forecast of the number of units to be sold in the first seven months of the year is given below :

	Product A	*Product B*
Jan.	1,000	2,800
Feb.	1,200	2,800
Mar.	1,600	2,400
Apr.	2,000	2,000
May	2,400	1,600
June	2,400	1,600
July	2,000	1,800

It is anticipated that:

(*i*) There will be no work-in-progress at the end of every month.
(*ii*) Finished units equal to half of the sales for the next month will be in stock at the end of each month (including previous December).

Budgeted production and costs for the whole year are as follows :

	Product A	Product B
Products (units)	22,000	24,000
Direct materials cost per unit	12.50	19
Direct labour cost per unit	4.50	7
Total factory overhead apportioned	66,000	96,000

Prepare for the six months period ending 30th June, 1993 (*a*) production budget for each month and (*b*) summarised production cost budget.

Solution :

Production budget (in units)

Product A

	Jan.	Feb.	Mar.	April	May	June	July	Total
Sales of current month	1,000	1,200	1,600	2,000	2,400	2,400	2,000	
Add : Closing stock	600	800	1,000	1,200	1,200	1,000		
	1,600	2,000	2,600	3,200	3,600	3,400		
Less : Opening balance	500	600	800	1,000	1,200	1,200		
	1,100	1,400	1,800	2,200	2,400	2,200		11,100

Product B

	Jan.	Feb.	Mar.	April	May	June	July	Total
Sales of current month	2,800	2,800	2,400	2,000	1,600	1,600	1,800	
Add : Closing stock	1,400	1,200	1,000	800	800	900		
	4,200	4,000	3,400	2,800	2,400	2,500		
Less : Opening balance	1,400	1,400	1,200	1,000	800	800		
Total units to be produced	2,800	2,600	2,200	1,800	1,600	1,700		12,700

Production cost budget

	Product A	Product B
Direct material cost per unit	12.50	19.00
Direct labour cost per unit	4.50	7.00
Factory overhead	3.00	4.00
	20.00	30.00
Total budget cost	11,100 × Rs. 20 = Rs. 2,20,000	12,700 × Rs. 30 = Rs. 3,81,000

Problem 6 (Production cost budget) : The production cost of Modern Machine Co. Ltd. for the year 1992 are as under :

Direct material cost		Rs. 1,20,000
Direct wages		75,000
Overheads : Variable	70,000	
Fixed	45,000	1,15,000

The following changes are anticipated in 1993 :

(*a*) The purchase price per unit of direct materials, and of other materials included in overheads will remain unchanged.

(*b*) The average rate for direct labour will fall from Rs. 4 per hour to Rs. 3 per hour, and direct labour hours will increase by 10%.

(*c*) Production efficiency will decrease by 4%.

The overheads are absorbed on a direct wages basis. Draw up a production cost budget for 1993.

Solution :

Production cost budget for 1993

	Original budget in 1992	Budget for 1993
Direct materials cost	1,20,000	1,32,000
Direct labour cost	75,000	64,350
Prime cost	1,95,000	1,96,350

Overheads —Fixed	45,000	45,000
—Variable	70,000	77,000
Total cost	3,10,000	3,18,350

Notes :

1. Labour hours will increase by 10%. Therefore it is presumed that production will increase by 10% and hence 10% increase in the cost of materials.

2. Direct labour is affected by production efficiency of 4% and increase in labour hours of 10%.

$$\text{Labour hours} = \frac{\text{Rs. } 75{,}000}{\text{Rs. 4 per hour}} = 18{,}750 \text{ hrs.}$$

Add : 10% increase in labour hrs. = 1,875 hrs.

= 20,625 hrs.

Add : 4% decrease in production efficiency

$$\frac{4}{100} \times 20{,}625 = 825 \text{ hrs.}$$

= 21,450 hrs.

Total labour cost = 21,450 × Rs. 3 = 64,350

3. Variable overheads are related to production, 10% rise in production will result 10% rise in variable overhead.

6. ***Plant utilisation budget :*** This budget indicates the plant capacity required to meet the production budget. While preparing this budget allowance must be made for the time lost in repairs and maintenance, setting up time, etc. For a smooth flow of production the capacity of plant must be balanced. For this purpose it is necessary to decide whether to (*a*) reduce the production volume, (*b*) purchase new machinery, (*c*) work extra shift, (*d*) use of subcontractors and so on. A specimen of plant utilisation budget is shown below :

Plant utilisation budget for the period.......

Department	*Machines*	*Number of hours available during the period (2,000)*	*Normal lost time (200)*	*Standard capacity in hrs. (1,800)*	*Output per std. hr. (5)*	*Std. qty. (units) (9,000)*
A	1					
	2					
	3					
B	4					
	5					
	6					
	Total					

Fig. 10.5. Specimen showing plant utilisation budget.

7. ***Material purchase budget :*** This budget is prepared by the purchase manager for the purchase of raw materials and component parts. While preparing this budget priority must be given for the purchase of materials which are in short supply. This budget is prepared considering both quantities and value of materials. The following factors are to be considered before materials purchase budget is prepared :

(*a*) Planned increase or decrease in the stock of raw materials during the budget period.

(*b*) The date on which materials are required.
(*c*) The fluctuation in the prices of material.
(*d*) The duration of credit allowed.

Problem 7 : The following are the estimated sales of a company for eight months ending 30.11.98.

Months	*Estimated sales (units)*
Apr. 1998	12,000
May 1998	13,000
June 1998	9,000
July 1998	8,000
Aug. 1998	10,000
Sept. 1998	12,000
Oct. 1998	14,000
Nov. 1998	12,000

As a matter of policy, the company maintains the closing balance of finished goods and raw materials as follows :

Stock Item	*Closing balance of a month*
Finished goods	50% of the estimated sales for the next month
Raw materials	Estimated consumption for the next month

Every unit of production requires 2 kg of raw material costing Rs. 5 per kg

Prepare production Budget (in units) and raw materials purchase budget (in units and cost) of the company for the half year ending 30th Sept. 1998. (*ICWA, Inter., June 1999*)

Solution :

Production Budget

Month	*Sales*		*Closing Balance 50% of the estimated sales for next month*		*Operating Balance*	*Production*
1998						
Apr.	12,000	+	6,500	–	6,000	12,500
May	13,000	+	4,500	–	6,500	11,000
June	9,000	+	4,000	–	4,500	8500
July	8,000	+	5,000	–	4,000	9000
Aug.	10,000	+	6,000	–	5,000	11,000
Sept.	12,000	+	7000	–	6,000	13,000
	64,000					65,000

Purchase Budget

Consumption 2 kg per unit	*Closing Balance*	*Opening Balance*	*Purchase in kg*	*Rate*	*Amt.*
25,000	22,000	25,000	22,000	5	1,10,000
22,000	17,000	22,000	17,000	5	85,000
17,000	18,000	17,000	18,000	5	90,000
18,000	22,000	18,000	22,000	5	1,10,000
22,000	26,000	22,000	26,000	5	1,30,000
26,000	26,000	26,000	26,000	5	1,30,000
1,30,000					6,55,000

Problem 8 : A company is drawing its production plan for the year 1997-98 in respect of two of its products "Gamma" and "Delta". The company's policy is not to carry any closing work-in-progress at the end of any month. However, its policy is to hold a closing stock of finished goods at 50% of the anticipated quantity of sales of the succeeding month. For the year 1997-98 the company's budgeted production is 20,000 units of "Gamma" and 25,000 units of "Delta". The following is the estimated cost data.

	Gamma	Delta
	Rs.	Rs.
Direct material per unit	50	80
Direct labour cost per unit	20	30
Other manufacturing expenses apportionable to each type of product based on production	2,00,000	3,75,000

The estimated units to be sold in the first 7 months of the year 1997-98 are as under :

	Apr.	*May*	*June*	*July*	*Aug.*	*Sept.*	*Oct.*
Gamma	900	1,100	1,400	1,800	2,200	2,200	1,800
Delta	2,900	2,900	2,500	2,100	1,700	1,700	1,900

You are required to :

(*a*) Prepare a production budget showing month-wise number of units to be manufactured

(*b*) Present a summarised production cost budget for the half year ending 30-9-97.

(*ICWA, Inter., Dec. 1996*)

Solution :

Production budget for half year ending 30th Sept. 97

	Apr.	*May*	*June*	*July*	*Aug.*	*Sept.*	*Total*
Product – Gama							
Budgeted sales	900	1,100	1,400	1,800	2,200	2,200	9,600
Add : Closing stock to be built up (*See note* 1)	550	700	900	1,100	1,100	900	900
	1,450	1,800	2,300	2,900	3,300	3,100	10,500
Less : Carry-over stock -opening (*See note* 2)	450	550	700	900	1,100	1,100	450
Budgeted production	1,000	1,250	1,600	2,000	2,200	2,000	10,050
Product – Delta							
Budgeted sales	2,900	2,900	2,500	2,100	1,700	1,700	13,800
Add : Closing stock to be built up	1,450	1,250	1,050	850	850	950	950
	4,350	4,150	3,550	2,950	2,550	2,650	14,750
Less : Carry-over stock -opening (*See note* 2)	1,450	1,450	1,250	1,050	850	850	1450
Budgeted production	2,900	2,700	2,300	1,900	1,700	1,800	13,300

Note-1 :

Closing stock of finished goods at the end of each month is to be ascertained as per company's policy, *i.e.*, 50% of the anticipated quantity of sales of the succeeding month. Closing stock under total column is 50% of October month, *i.e.*, $\frac{50}{100} \times 1{,}800 = 900$

Note-2 :

Opening stock of each month is the closing stock of preceeding month. The opening stock under total column is 50% of Sept. closing stock, *i.e.*, $\frac{50}{100} \times 900 = 450$

Summarised production cost Budget for the half-year ending 30th Sept. 1997

	Gama		*Delta*	
Production (units)	10,050		13,300	
	Cost		Cost	
	Per unit	Amount	Per unit	Amt.
Direct Materials	50	5,02,500	80	10,64,000
Direct labour	20	2,01,000	30	3,99,000
Other manufacturing expenses	10	1,00,500	15	1,99,500
	80	8,04,000	125	16,62,500

Note-3 :

Other manufacturing expenses are apportioned on the following basis :

$$\frac{\text{Other Manufacturing expenses}}{\text{No. of units to be produced in 1997–98}}$$

$$\frac{2,00,000}{20,000} = 10 \qquad \frac{3,75,000}{25,000} = 15$$

Problem 9 (Materials purchase budget) : Draw a material procurement budget (quantitative) from the following information :

Estimated sales of a product 40,000 units. Each unit of the product requires 3 units of material *A* and 5 units of material *B*.

Estimated opening stock at the commencement of the next year :

Finished product	5,000 units
Material *A*	12,000 units
Material *B*	20,000 units
Materials on order :	
Material *A*	7,000 units
Material *B*	11,000 units

The desirable closing stock at the end of the next year :

Finished product	7,000 units
Material *A*	15,000 units
Material *B*	25,000 units
Material on order :	
Material *A*	8,000 units
Material *B*	10,000 units

Solution :

Production budget

Estimated sales	40,000 units
Add : Closing stock	7,000 units
	47,000 units
Less : Opening stock	5,000 units
Production during the year	42,000 units

Materials procurement budget

		A (units)		*B (units)*
Materials required 3 units of *A* and 5 units of *B* for 42,000 units		1,26,000		2,10,000
Add : Closing stock required	15,000		25,000	
Material on order	8,000	23,000	10,000	35,000
		1,49,000		2,45,000
Less : Opening stock	12,000		20,000	
Material on order	7,000	19,000	11,000	31,000
Unit to be procured		1,30,000		2,14,000

Problem 10 : The *XY* Company expects the following sales by month in units for the first six months of next year :

January	–	5,400	April	–	5,700
February	–	5,700	May	–	6,000
March	–	7,500	June	–	4,500

The company has a policy of maintaining an inventory equal to budgeted sales for the following two months. The beginning inventory reflects this policy. Each unit cost Rs. 10.

You are required to prepare purchase budget for as many months as you can both in units and rupees. Explain also why you had to stop where you did. *(University of Kerala, M. Com., May 1992)*

Solution :

Production budget for 3 months

	Jan.	Feb.	March
Sales	5,400	5,700	7,500
Add : Closing stock	5,700	6,000	4,500
	11,100	11,700	12,000
Less : Opening stock	7,500	5,700	6,000
Units to be produced	3,600	6,000	6,000

Purchase budget in quantity

	Jan.	Feb.	March
Units of materials required (*see note 1*)	3,600	6,000	6,000
Add : Desired stock at the end of the year	5,700	6,000	4,500
	9,300	12,000	10,500
Less : Expected stock at the beginning	7,500	5,700	6,000
Quantity of materials to be purchased	1,800	6,300	4,500

Note : In the problem the policy of opening stock is expected to be the sale units equal to the following two months. As the opening stock of every month is the closing stock of the previous month, it has been treated for every month in the same manner. The budget could be prepared only for three months because of the policy of the management in considering opening stock.

Regarding the purchase budget as separate unit of materials required for production, it is presumed that for every unit of finished goods to be produced, one unit of raw materials is required.

Purchase cost budget

Month	Qty.	Rate	Amount
Jan.	1,800	10	18,000
Feb.	6,300	10	63,000
March	4,500	10	45,000
		Total	Rs. 1,26,000

8. ***Labour cost budget :*** This budget represents the direct labour required to meet the production demand of the factory during the budget period. The labour hours required for budgeted production will be determined on the basis of output which must conform standard. It shows the information relating to the number of employees along with the grade required to achieve the output and the probable labour cost for budget period. The advantages of preparing a labour cost budget are as follows :

(*a*) It determines the labour force required.

(*b*) It facilitates the personnel department to plan ahead in recruitment and training of labourer.

(*c*) It helps in the preparation of production cost budget and cash budget. A specimen of labour cost budget is shown below :

Labour cost budget for the period......

Grade	Number of employees	Hours employed	Rate per hour	Amount
(1) Skilled				
(2) Semi-skilled				
(3) Unskilled				
			Total	

Fig. 10.6. Specimen showing labour cost budget.

Problem 11 : The sales director of a manufacturing company reports that next year he expects to sell 40,000 units of a particular product. The production department gives the following particulars :

Two kinds of raw materials *A* and *B* are required for manufacturing the product. Each product requires 3 units of material *A* and 2 units of material *B*. The estimated opening balance of the next year will be :

Finished product	–	10,000 units
Materials *A*	–	12,000 units
Materials *B*	–	15,000 units

The desired closing balances at the end of the year are :

Finished product	–	16,000 units
Material *A*	–	14,000 units
Material *B*	–	15,000 units

Draw up a materials purchase budget (*University of Madras, B. Com., September 1994*)

Solution :

Production Budget

Sales units	40,000
Less : Opening finished goods	10,000
	30,000
Add : Closing finished goods	16,000
Production units	46,000

Purchase Budget

	A	*B*
Raw materials consumed		
A 46,000 × 3	1,38,000	92,000
B 46,000 × 2		
Less : Opening raw materials	12,000	15,000
	1,26,000	77,000
Add : Closing raw materials	14,000	15,000
Purchase of Raw Materials required	1,40,000	92,000

Problem 12 (Labour cost budget) : The direct labour hour requirements of three of the products manufactured in a factory each involving more than one labour operation are estimated as follows :

Direct labour hours per unit (in minutes)

	Products		
	1	*2*	*3*
Operation : 1	18	42	30
2	–	12	24
3	9	6	–

The factory works 8 hours per day, 6 days in a week. The budget quarter is taken as 13 weeks and during a quarter, lost hours due to leave and holidays and other causes are estimated to be 124 hours.

The budgeted sales of the products during the quarter are :

Product 1	9,000 units
2	15,000 units
3	12,000 units

There is a opening balance of 5,000 units of product 2 and 4,000 units of product 3 and it is proposed to build up a stock at the end of the budget quarter as follows :

Product 1	1,000 units
3	2,000 units

Prepare a manpower budget for the quarter showing for each operation (*i*) Direct labour hours, (*ii*) Direct labour cost and (*iii*) The number of workers.

Solution : **Production budget**

	Products		
	1 (units)	*2 (units)*	*3 (units)*
Sales	9,000	15,000	12,000
Add : Closing stock	1,000	–	2,000
	10,000	15,000	14,000
Less : Opening stock	–	5,000	4,000
	10,000	10,000	10,000

Total available hours in a quarter per man

Total hrs. = 8 × 6 × 13	=	624 hrs.
Less : Hours lost	=	124 hrs.
Total available hours per man		500 hrs.

Total time duration and manpower requirement

Products →	1		2		3		Total
Units →	10,000		10,000		10,000		hrs.
Operations	Time in min.	Time in hrs.	Time in min.	Time in hrs.	Time in min.	Time in hrs.	
1	1,80,000	3,000	4,20,000	7,000	3,00,000	5,000	15,000
2	–	–	1,20,000	2,000	2,40,000	4,000	6,000
3	90,000	1,500	60,000	1,000	–	–	2,500

Number of workers required for each operation

Operation	*Total hours*	*No. of workers requied*
1	15,000	30
2	6,000	12
3	2,500	5

Quarterly manpower budget

Opera-tion	*Hourly rate* (Rs.)	*Product1* *Direct* labour *hours*	*Cost* (Rs.)	*Product 2* *Direct* labour *hours*	*Cost* (Rs.)	*Product 3* *Direct* labour *hours*	*Cost* (Rs.)	*Total* *Direct* labour *hours*	*Cost* (Rs.)	*No. of workers*
1	2.00	3,000	6,000	7,000	14,000	5,000	10,000	15,000	30,000	30
2	2.50	–	–	2,000	5,000	4,000	10,000	6,000	15,000	12
3	3.00	1,500	4,500	1,000	3,000	–	–	2,500	7,500	5
		4,500	10,500	10,000	22,000	9,000	20,000	23,500	52,000	47

9. ***Factory overhead budget :*** This budget is prepared by production manager or persons in charge of various production departments. To facilitate control it is necessary to classify the overheads into fixed and variable and controllable and uncontrollable overhead. The budget officer may assist the production manager in supplying the past year's data to prepare this budget more comprehensively.

Problem 13 (Factory overhead budget) : The following particulars are extracted from the books of Jai Engineering Co. The production overhead apportionment has been prepared to show overheads for each of the production and service departments. Service departments overheads are apportioned as shown below :

Service department	*Production departments*		
	A	*B*	*C*
1	30%	20%	50%
2	25%	30%	45%

Overhead	*Basis of apportionment*	*Total*	*A*	*B*	*C*	*1*	*2*
Salaries	Actual	14,700	4,000	3,000	5,000	1,500	1,200
Indirect wages	Actual	31,600	9,000	7,000	10,000	3,000	2,600
Consumable stores	No. of employees	1,650	400	350	500	300	100
Depreciation	Value of asset	22,200	6,000	5,000	10,000	700	500
Insurance	Value of asset	2,480	750	650	900	100	80
Rent	Area occupied	3,790	1,200	1,000	1,500	50	40
Power	Meter	2,170	600	700	800	40	30
Light	Area occupied	395	100	110	140	20	25
Maintenance	Value of asset	2,525	800	700	1,000	15	10
Employee's insurance	No. of workers	3,150	900	800	1,000	250	200
Scrap	Actual	775	225	205	345	–	–
Sundries	Actual	1,105	375	235	455	25	15
	Total	86,540	24,350	19,750	31,640	6,000	4,800
Service dept. 1		–	1,800	1,200	3,000		
Service dept. 2		–	1,200	1,440	2,160		
		86,540	27,350	22,390	36,800		

Solution :

Factory overhead budget for the period

Overhead	*Total*	*A*	*B*	*C*
Variable :				
Consumable stores	1,250	400	350	500
Scrap	775	225	205	345
Fixed :				
Salaries	12,000	4,000	3,000	5,000
Depreciation	21,000	6,000	5,000	10,000
Insurance	2,300	750	650	900
Rent	3,700	1,200	1,000	1,500
Sundries	1,065	375	235	455
Service dept. 1	6,000	1,800	1,200	3,000
Service dept. 2	4,800	1,200	1,440	2,160
Semi-variable :				
Indirect wages	26,000	9,000	7,000	10,000
Power	2,100	600	700	800
Light	350	100	110	140
Maintenance	2,500	800	700	1,000
Insurance	2,700	900	800	1,000
	86,540	27,350	22,390	36,800

10. ***Administration cost budget :*** This budget is prepared by chief accountant and approved by the managing director. This budget is likely to pose some problems since most of the administration cost is fixed in nature. The main budget is divided into separate budget covering separate administrative activity such as accounting, secretarial work and so on. The factors to be considered in preparing this budget are (*a*) the existing number of staff, (*b*) their rates of pay, (*c*) change in volume of work and (*d*) legal and other administrative overheads. A specimen of administrative cost budget is shown below :

Specimen of administration cost budget

For the period——————

Items of expenses	*Previous year's budget*	*Previous year's actual*	*Current budget*
Materials :			
Stationery			
Supplies			
Salaries & wages :			
Manager's salary			
Director's salary			
Clerical salary			
Expenses :			
Rent & rates			
Telephone			
Postage			
Travelling			
Insurance			
Bank charges			
Audit fee			
Subscriptions			
Total			

11. ***Research and development budget :*** The preparation of this budget is governed by the policy of the Board of Directors and head of production departments. This budget may be prepared by elements of cost or by specific project. Similarly this budget can be prepared from the point of view of short-range or long-rang activities. While long-range research programme is carried out in tune with future market trends and demands, short-range programme are carried out to achieve a satisfactory margin of profit. The research and development budget may relate to (*a*) Basic research, (*b*) New product development, (*c*) Product improvement, (*d*) Cost and capacity improvement and (*e*) Safety, health and welfare. A specimen of research and development budget is shown below :

Research and development budget for the period ....

	Projects				
	1	*2*	*3*	*4*	*Total*
Project costs :					
Materials :					
Raw materials					
Small tools					
Oil & lubricants					
Sundries					
Wages & salaries :					
Chemists					
Technicians					
Others					
Expenses :					
Professional fees					
Total					

General costs :

Supervisory salary
Laboratory cost
Technical publications
Office costs
Subscriptions

Total

12. ***Capital expenditure budget :*** This budget shows the estimated expenditure on fixed assets during the period concerned. This budget is subject to strict management control as it involves heavy amount of investment requiring the approval of top management. This budget is prepared based on the requirements of various assets for the following departments :

(*i*) Production department—For the purchase of machineries and plant either for replacing the existing machinery or new machinery for producing new products.
(*ii*) Transport department—For the purchase of new vehicles.
(*iii*) Office department—For the purchase of new office equipments.
(*iv*) Service departments—For purchasing equipments peculiar to such departments.
(*v*) Equipments to control pollution such as liquid, gaseous and noise pollution.

The capital expenditure budget offers the following advantages :

(*i*) It estimates the capital expenditure requirements and accordingly provides or arranges for it.
(i) The priority of procuring assets can be determined. Those assets which are very important and unavoidable is given first preference and others are postponed to a later period.
(*iii*) It serves as a tool of controlling capital expenditure.

13. ***Cash budget :*** This budget ir preapared to know the estimated cash balance each month along with the estimated receipts and payments during the month. It performs two important functions, *viz.*, (*i*) to ensure sufficient availability of cash and (*ii*) to take necessary action when there is shortage of cash. If there is any surplus, which is not immediately required, the same may be invested for a short period. According to Matz-Curry-Frank, a cash budget serves the following purposes :

(*i*) It indicates the effect on the cash position of seasonal requirements, large inventories, unusual receipts and slowness in collecting bills receiveable.
(*ii*) It indicates cash requirements for a plant or equipments expansion programme.
(*iii*) It points to the need for additional funds from external sources such as bank loans, issue of securities.
(*iv*) It indicates the availability of cash for taking advantage of discounts offered.
(*v*) It helps in planning redemption of preference shares or redeemable debentures, payments of pension, etc.
(*vi*) It shows the availability of excess funds for short or long term investments.

A cash budget can be prepared under any of the following three methods.

(*i*) *The receipts and payments method :* Under this method all the cash receipts and payments expected during the budget period is considered. However care must be taken to ensure that cash adjustments and accruals are not shown in the cash budget. The cash transactions for preparing this budget is obtained from various functional budgets discussed above. For example, materials cost from material budget, labour cost from labour budget, overheads from overhead budget, sales revenue from sales budget and so on.

Problem 14 (Cash budget under receipts and payments method) : The following particulars are extracted from the books of Ajanta Co. Ltd. for the quarter ending 31.3.1993 :

Opening cash balance as on 1.1.93 Rs. 30,000

Sales budget were as follows :

	Rs.
November 1992	80,000
December 1992	90,000
January 1993	75,000
February 1993	75,000
March 1993	80,000

Analysis of records shows that debtors settle according to the following pattern :

60% within the month of sale.

25% the month following.

15% the month following.

Extracts from the purchase budget were as follows :

	Rs.
December 1992	60,000
January 1993	55,000
February 1993	45,000
March 1993	55,000

All purchase are on credit and past experience show that 90% are settled in the month of purchase and the balance settled the month after.

Wages are Rs. 15,000 per month and overheads Rs. 20,000 per month (including Rs, 5,000 depreciation) are settled monthly.

Taxation of Rs. 8,000 has to be settled in February and the company will received settlement of an insurance claim of Rs. 25,000 in March.

Prepare a cash budget for January, February and March 1993.

Solution : **Calculation of sales revenue**

	January Rs.
November 1992 (15% of 80,000)	12,000
December 1992 (25% of 90,000)	22,500
January 1993 (60% of 75,000)	45,000
	79,500

	February Rs.
December 1992 (15% of 90,000)	13,500
January 1993 (25% of 75,000)	18,750
February 1993 (60% of 75,000)	45,000
	77,250

	March Rs.
January 1993 (15% of 75,000)	11,250
February 1993 (25% of 75,000)	18,750
March 1993 (60% of 80,000)	48,000
	78,000

Payments for purchases

	January
	Rs.
December 1992 (10% of 60,000)	6,000
January 1993 (90% of 55,000)	49,500
	55,000

	February
	Rs.
January 1993 (10% of 55,000)	5,500
February 1993 (90% of 45,000)	40,500
	46,000

	March
	Rs.
February 1993 (10% of 45,000)	4,500
March 1993 (10% of 55,000	49,500
	54,000

Cash budget for the quarter ending March 1993

	Jan.	*Feb.*	*March*
Opening balance	30,000	24,000	17,250
Receipts from sales	79,500	77,250	78,000
Insurance claim			25,000
Total cash available	1,09,500	1,01,250	1,20,250
Purchases	55,500	46,000	54,000
Wages	15,000	15,000	15,000
Overhead (less depreciation)	15,000	15,000	15,000
Taxation		8,000	
Total payment	85,500	84,000	84,000
Closing balance c/o	24,000	17,250	36,250

Problem 15 (Cash budget) : The Swadeshi Manufacturing Co. has a cash balance of Rs. 27,000 at the beginning of March 1993. you are required to prepare a cash budget for March, April and May 1993 having regard to the following information :

Creditors give 1 month credit.

Salaries are paid in the current month.

Fixed costs are paid one month in arrears and include a charge for depreciation of Rs. 5,000 per month.

Credit sales are settled as follows :

40% in month of sale, 45% in next month and 12% in the following month. The balance represents bad debts.

Month	*Cash sales*	*Credit sales*	*Purchases*	*Salaries*	*Fixed overhead*
	(Rs.)	*(Rs.)*	*(Rs.)*	*(Rs.)*	*(Rs.)*
Jan.	–	74,000	55,200	9,000	30,000
Feb.	–	82,000	61,200	9,000	30,000
March	20,000	80,000	60,000	9,500	30,000
April	22,000	90,000	69,000	9,500	32,000
May	25,000	1,00,000	75,000	10,000	32,000

Solution :

Statement showing receipts from debtors

	March		April		May
40% of March sales	32,000	40% of April sales	36.000	40% of May sales	40,000
45% of Feb. sales	36,900	45% of March sales	36,000	45% of April sales	40,500
12% of Jan. sales	8,880	12% of Feb. sales	9,840	12% of March sales	9,600
	77,780		81,840		90,100

Cash budget for the months of March, April & May 1993

	March	April	May
Opening balance	27,000	29,080	38,420
Receipts from debtors	77,780	81,840	90,100
Cash sales	20,000	22,000	25,000
Total cash available	1,24,780	1,32,920	1,53,520
Salaries	9,500	9,500	10,000
Fixed overheads	25,000	25,000	27,000
Purchases	61,200	60,000	69,000
Total disbursement	95,700	94,500	1,06,000
Closing balance c/o	29,080	38,420	47,520

Problem 16 (Cash budget) : From the following budgeted figures prepare a cash budget in respect of the three months to June 30, 1993 :

Month	Sales	Materials	Wages	Overhead
Jan.	30,000	20,000	5,500	3,100
Feb.	28,000	24,000	5,800	3,300
March	32,000	25,000	6,000	3,400
April	40,000	28,000	6,200	3,600
May	42,000	31,000	6,500	4,300
June	38,000	25,000	7,000	4,000

Estimated cash balance on April Ist 1993 Rs. 10,000.

Materials and overheads are paid during the month following the month of supply. Wages are paid during the month in which they are earned.

Credit items of sale are payment by the end of the month following the month of sale. It is estimated that one-half of sales are paid when due, the other half being paid during the next month.

A sales commission of 5% on sales is to be paid within the month following actual sales.

Preference share dividend of 10% on capital of Rs. 3,00,000 is to be paid on May 1, 1993.

Plant and machinery to be installed in May at a cost of Rs. 10,000 will be payable on Ist June, 1993.

10% calls on equity shares capital of Rs. 2,50,000 are due on April Ist and June Ist 1993.

Solution :

Statement showing sales

	April		May		June
½ of March	16,000	½ of April	20,000	½ of May	21,000
½ of Feb.	14,000	½ of March	16,000	½ of April	20,000
	30,000		36,000		41,000

Cash budget for period ending 30th June, 1993

	April	May	June
Opening balance	10,000	28,800	(5,300)
Sales	30,000	36,000	41,000
Capital	25,000	–	25,000
Total receipts	65,000	64,800	60,700

Materials	25,000	28,000	31,000
Wages	6,200	6,500	7,000
Overheads	3,400	3,600	4,300
Sales commission	1,600	2,000	2,100
Pref. share dividend	–	30,000	–
Plant & machinery	–	–	10,000
Total payment	Rs. 36,200	70,100	54,400
Balance c/o	Rs. 28,800	Rs. (5,300)	Rs. 6,300

Problem 17 : From the following data prepare a cash budget for the 3 months commercing 1st June, 1996, when the bank balance was Rs. 1,00,000.

Month	*Sales*	*Purchases*	*Wages*	*Production expenses*	*Adm. expenses*
	(Rs.)	*(Rs.)*	*(Rs.)*	*(Rs.)*	*(Rs.)*
April	80,000	41,000	5,600	3,900	10,000
May	76,500	40,500	5,400	4,200	14,000
June	78,500	38,500	5,400	5,100	15,000
July	90,000	37,000	4,800	5,100	17,000
August	95,000	35,000	4,700	6,000	13,000

There is two month credit period allowed to customers and received from suppliers. Wages, production expenses and administration expenses are payable in the following month.

(*University of Madras, B.Com., Sept 1997*)

Solution :

Cash budget from June to August 1996

	June	*July*	*August*
Opening balance	1,00,000	1,15,400	1,25,900
Add : Receipts :			
Collection from debtors	80,000	76,500	78,500
	1,80,000	1,91,900	204,400
Less : Payment			
paid to creditors	41,000	40,500	38,500
wages	5,400	5,400	4,800
Production expenses	4,200	5,100	5,100
Administration expenses	14,000	15,000	17,000
	64,600	66,000	65,400
Closing balance	1,15,400	1,25,900	1,39,000

Note 1 :

Delay in payment allowed to customers from suppliers is 2 montsh *i.e.*, April payment paid in June.

Note 2 :

Delay in payment allowed to wages, production expenses, administration expenses are one month *i.e.*, May payment paid in June.

Problem 18 : Infotech Ltd., commences business on 1st April, 2000 and deposits Rs. 1,00,000 in the Global Trust Bank. The sum deposited would not be sufficient to finance its operations over a period of four months. As a company secretary, you are asked to prepare a cash budget from 1st April, 2000 to 31st July, 2000 to ascertain the monthly overhead limits to seek from the company's bankers.

Requisite data is as under :

(*i*) Sales are made to one distributor only on 30 days terms 2% discount and cheques are received on the first date of the following due date.

(*ii*) Furniture purchases for Rs. 10,000 preferred to be made in April, 2000 (*iii*) Budget figures are :

	April	*May*	*June*	*July*
Purchases	50,000	40,000	30,000	40,000
Wages	40,000	50,000	40,000	40,000
Cash expenses	4,000	5,000	4,000	4,000
Sales	60,000	70,000	80,000	80,000

All purchases are made on net 30 days terms and cheques are posted to creditors on the last day of the month due. (*CS, Inter, June 2000*)

Solution : **Cash budget for April to July**

	Apr.	*May*	*June*	*July*
(*A*) Cash receipts :				
Cash receipts from distributor (Sales – 2% discount with one month time lag.)	–	58,800	68,600	78,400
(*B*) Cash payments :				
Payment to Creditors (one month time lag)	–	50,000	40,000	30,000
Wages	40,000	50,000	40,000	40,000
Cash expenses	4,000	5,000	4,000	4,000
Furniture purchases	10,000	–	–	–
Total cash payments	54,000	1,05,000	84,000	74,000
(*C*) Net cash receipts/ Deficit (A – B)	(54,000)	(46,200)	(15,400)	4,400
Balance (overdraft) at the start of the month (crummilative)	1,00,000	46,000	(200)	(15,600)
(Overdraft) required monthwise	–	(200)	(15,400)	–

Problem 19 : Prepare a cash budget for the three months ended 30th September 1998 based on the following information :

	Rs.
Cash at bank on 1st July 1998	25,000
Monthly salaries and wages (estimated)	10,000
Interest payable in August 1998	5,000

Estimated	*June* Rs.	*July* Rs.	*August* Rs.	*September* Rs.
Cash sales (actual)	1,20,000	1,40,000	1,52,000	1,21,000
Credit sales	1,00,000	80,000	1,40,000	1,20,000
Purchases	1,60,000	1,70,000	2,40,000	1,80,000
Other expenses	18,000	20,000	22,000	21,000

Credit sales are collected 50% in the month of sale and 50% in the month following. Collections from credit sales are subject to 10% discount if received in the month of sale and to 5% if received in the month following :

10% of the purchases are in cash and balance is paid in next month. (*CS, Inter, June 1999*)

Solution : **Calculation of collection from Debtors (Credit sales)**

		July	*Aug.*	*Sept.*
July	50% of 1,00,000	50,000		
	50% of 80,000	40,000		
Aug.	50% of 80,000		40,000	
	50% of 1,40,000		70,000	

Sept. 50% of 1,40,000			70,000
50% of 1,20,000			60,000
Total collections	90,000	1,10,000	1,30,000
Less : Discount allowed			
(*a*) 5% on 50,000 + 10% on 40,000	6,500		
(*b*) 5% on 40,000 + 10% on 70,000		9,000	
(*c*) 5% on 70,000 + 5% on 60,000			9,500
Net collections after discount	83,500	1,01,000	1,20,500

Calculation of payments to creditors

(*a*) 90% of 1,60,000 + 10% of 1,70,000	1,61,000		
(*b*) 90% of 1,70,000 + 10% of 2,40,000		1,77,000	
(*c*) 90% of 2,40,000 + 10% of 1,80,000			2,34,000
	1,61,000	1,77,000	2,34,000

Cash budget for three months July to Sept.

	July	*Aug.*	*Sept.*
Opening balance	25,000	57,500	96,500
Add : Receipts :			
Sales cash	1,40,000	1,52,000	1,21,000
Credit	83,500	101,000	1,20500
Total cash	2,48,500	3,10,500	3,38,000
Payments :			
Purchases	1,61,000	1,77,000	2,34,000
Other expenses	20,000	22,000	21,000
Interest	-	5,000	-
Salaries & wages	10,000	10,000	10,000
Total payment	1,91,000	2,14,000	2,65,000
Closing cash balance	57,500	96,500	73,000

Problem 20 : On 30th September, 1996, The balance sheet of M Ltd. (retailer) was as under :

Equity shares of Rs. 10 each fully paid	20,000	Equipment	20,000	
		Less : Dep.	5,000	15,000
Reserves	10,000			
Trade creditors	40,000	Stock		20,000
Proposed dividend	15,000	Trade debtors		15,000
		Bank		35,000
	85,000			85,000

The company is developing a system of forward planning and on 1st October 1996 it supplies the following information :

	Sales		*Purchases*
	Credit	*Cash*	*Credit*
	Rs.	*Rs.*	*Rs.*
September 1996 (actual)	15,000	14,000	40,000
October 1996 (budget)	18,000	5,000	23,000
November 1996 (budget)	20,000	6,000	27000
December 1996 (budget)	25,000	8000	26,000

All trade debtors are allowed one months credit and are expected to settle promptly. All trade creditors are paid in the month following delivery :

On 1st October, 1996, all equipment were replaced at a cost of Rs. 30,000 Rs. 14,000 was allowed in exchange for the old equipment and a net payment of Rs. 16,000 was made.

The proposed dividend will be paid in December 1996.
The following expenses will be paid :
Wages Rs. 3,000 per month.
Administration Rs. 1,500 per month.
Rent Rs. 3,600 for the year upto 30th Sept., 1997 (to be paid in October 1996).
You are required to prepare a cash budget for the months of October, November and December 1996.

(CS, Inter, June 1997)

Solution : **Cash budget for 3 months ending 1996**

	October	*November*	*December*
Opening balance of bank/Bank overdraft	35,000	(9,100)	(12,600)
Add : Cash inflows :			
Sales : cash sales of current month	5,000	6,000	8000
Credit sales of previous month	15,000	18000	2,000
Total receipts	55,000	14,900	15,400
Less : Cash inflow :			
Credit purchases of previous month	40,000	23,000	27,000
Equipment	16,000	-	-
Wages	3,000	3,000	3,000
Administration	1,500	11,500	1,500
Rent	3,600	-	-
Dividend	-	-	15,000
Total payment	64,100	27,500	46,500
Closing balance/overdraft (A – B)	(9,100)	(12,600)	(31,100)

Problem 21 : Prepare cash budget of fashion fabrics for the months April 1999 to July 1999 (four months) from the details given below :

(*i*) Estimated sales :

	Rs.
February 1999	12,00,000
March 1999	12,00,000
April 1999	16,00,000
May 1999	20,00,000
June 1999	18,00,000
July 1999	16,00,000
August 1999	14,00,000

(*ii*) On an average 20% of sales are cash sales. The credit sales are realised in the third month (January sales in March)

(*iii*) Purchases amount to 60% of sales. Purchases made in a month are generally sold in the third month and payment for purchases is also made in the third month.

(*iv*) Variable expenses (other then sales commission) constitute 10% of sales and there is a time lag of half a month in these payment.

(*v*) Commission on sales is paid at 5% of sales value and payment is made in the third month.

(*vi*) Fixed expenses per month amount to Rs. 75,000 approximately.

(*vii*) Other items anticipated :

			Due
Interest payable on deposits	Rs.	1,60,000	(April 99)
Sales of old asserts	Rs.	1,25,000	(May 99)
Payment of Tax	Rs.	80,000	(June 99)
Purchase of fixed assets	Rs.	6,50,000	
(*viii*) Opening cash balance	Rs.	1,50,000	

(ICWA, Inter, December 1999)

Solution :

Cash budget for April to July 1999

	April	*May*	*June*	*July*
Opening balance	1,50,000	35,000	5,000	1,40,000
Add : Receipts :				
Cash sales	3,20,000	4,00,000	3,60,000	3,20,000
Collection from Debtors	9,60,000	9,60,000	12,80,000	16,00,000
Sales of old assets	–	1,25,000	–	–
Total	14,30,000	15,20,000	16,40,000	19,20,000
Payments :				
Payments for purchases	9,60,000	12,00,000	10,80,000	9,60,000
Variable expenses	1,40,000	1,80,000	1,90,000	1,70,000
Commission on sales	60,000	60,000	80,000	1,00,000
Fixed expenses	75,000	75,000	75,000	75,000
Interest on Deposits	1,60,000	–	–	–
Tax	–	–	80,000	–
Purchase of fixed asset	–	–	–	6,50,000
Total	13,95,000	15,15,000	15,05,000	19,55,000
Closing balance	35,000	5,000	1,40,000	1,05,000

Working Note :

(1) *Calculation of sales*

April

Cash sales 20% of April sales

$$\frac{20}{100} \times 16,00,000 = 3,20,000$$

Credit sales 80% of February sales

$$\frac{80}{100} \times 12,00,000 = 9,60,000$$

May

Cash sales 20% of May sales

$$\frac{20}{100} \times 20,00,000 = 4,00,000$$

Credit sales $\frac{80}{100}$ of March sales

$$\frac{80}{100} \times 12,00,000 = 9,60,000$$

June

Cash sales 20% of June sales

$$\frac{20}{100} \times 18,00,000 = 3,60,000$$

Credit sales 80% of April sales

$$\frac{80}{100} \times 16,00,000 = 12,80,000$$

July

Cash sales 20% of July sales

$\frac{20}{100} \times 16,00,000 = 3,20,000$

Credit sales 80% of May sales

$\frac{80}{100} \times 20,00,000 = 16,00,000$

(2) *Calculation of Purchases*

April $16,00,000 \times \frac{60}{100} = 9,60,000$

May $20,00,000 \times \frac{60}{100} = 12,00,000$

June $18,00,000 \times \frac{60}{100} = 10,80,000$

July $16,00,000 \times \frac{60}{100} = 9,60,000$

(3) *Calculation of variable expenses*

April

March time lag

$\frac{10}{100} \times 12,00,000 \times \frac{1}{2} = 60,000$

April sales $\frac{10}{100} \times 16,00,000 \times \frac{1}{2} = 80,000$

1,40,000

May

April sales $\frac{10}{100} \times 16,00,000 \times \frac{1}{2} = 80,000$

May sales $\frac{10}{100} \times 20,00,000 \times \frac{1}{2} = 1,00,000$

1,80,000

June

May sales $\frac{10}{100} \times 20,00,000 \times \frac{1}{2} = 1,00,000$

June sales $\frac{10}{100} \times 18,00,000 \times \frac{1}{2} = 90,000$

1,90,000

July

June sales $\frac{10}{100} \times 18,00,000 \times \frac{1}{2} = 90,000$

July sales $\frac{10}{100} \times 16,00,000 \times \frac{1}{2} = 80,000$

1,70,000

(4) *Calculation of commission on sales*

April,	Feb. sales 12,00,000 × $\frac{5}{100}$	=	60,000
May,	Mar. sales 12,00,000 × $\frac{5}{100}$	=	60,000
June,	Apr. sales 16,00,000 × $\frac{5}{100}$	=	80,000
July,	May sales 20,00,000 × $\frac{5}{100}$	=	1,00,000

(*ii*) *Adjusted profit and loss method:* This method presents the cash budget in the form of cash flow statement. When compared to receipts and payments method, this method is less detailed but more useful for long-term budgeting. In preparing a long-term budget management is concerned with overall position of cash rather than cash receipts and payments. The preparation of a cash flow statement involves the use of the following information :

(a) Cash balance in the begining.
(b) Net profit forecast for the period (before charging depreciation and other provisions)
(c) Changes in working capital.
(d) Capital expenditure and sale of plant and machinery.
(e) Capital receipts
(f) Dividents.

This method differs from the previous method in one respect, *i.e.*, it considers particularly non-cash transactions. That is to say, this method is based on the assumption that profit = cash. In other words, if there were no credit transactions, capital transactions, accrual, provisions, or appropriation of profit, the amount of profit shown in the profit and loss account will be equal to the balance of cash shown by the cash book. But in practice such a situation rarely arises and hence requires adjustments. Hence the name adjusted profit and loss method.

(*iii*) *Balance sheet method :* This method resembles the adjusted profit and loss method explained above. In addition to a cash flow statement a budgeted balance sheet is prepared for the next period under this method. In preparing the balance sheet all assets and liabilities are taken into account except cash. The two sides of balance sheet is then balanced and the balancing figure represents cash. When the asset side is heavier than liablilities side, it denotes bank overdraft and if the liability side is heavier than asset side it denotes cash on hand or at bank.

Problem 22 (Preparation of different budgets) : Ratna Enterprises manufactures three products *A*, *B* and *C*. You are required to prepare (*a*) Sales budget, (*b*) Production budget, (*c*) Material budget for the month of January 1993.

Sales of products	*Quantity*	*Rate*
A	1,000	100
B	2,000	120
C	1,500	140

Materials used in the company's products are :

Material	M_1	M_2	M_3
Rate	Rs. 4	Rs. 6	Rs. 9

	Units	Units	Units
Quantities used in			
A	4	2	–
B	3	3	2
C	2	1	1
Finished stock as on :	*A (units)*	*B (units)*	*C (units)*
1.1.93	1,000	1,500	500
31.1.93	1,100	1,650	550
Material stocks :	M_1	M_2	M_3
1.1.93	(units) 26,000	20,000	12,000
31.1.93	(units) 31,200	24,000	14,400

Solution :

Sales budget

	A	*B*	*C*
Sales quantities	1,000	2,000	1,500
Selling price (per unit)	Rs. 100	120	140
Sales	Rs. 1,00,000	2,40,000	2,10,000

Statement showing production budget

	A	*B*	*C*
Sales units	1,000	2,000	1,500
Add : Closing stock	1,100	1,650	550
	2,100	3,650	2,050
Less : Opening stock	1,000	1,500	500
Production	1,100	2,150	1,550

Statement showing material usage budget

Production Budget	M_1 *Unit per product*	M_1 *Total*	M_2 *Unit per product*	M_2 *Total*	M_3 *Unit per product*	M_3 *Total*
A—1,100	4	4,400	2	2,200	–	–
B—2,150	3	6,450	3	6450	2	4,300
C—1,550	2	3,100	1	1,550	1	1,550
Material usage		13,950		10,200		5,850

Material purchase budge (Qty, and value)

		M_1	M_2	M_3
Material usage	(units)	13,950	10,200	5,850
Add : Closing stock	(units)	31,200	24,000	14,400
		45,150	34,200	20,250
Less : Opening stock		26,000	20,000	12,000
Required purchases	(units)	19,150	14,200	8,250
Unit rate		Rs. 4	6	9
Value of materials		76,600	85,200	74,250

(*b*) **Master budget :** It is a summary of all the functional budgets dicussed above. According to the ICMA terminology, "A master budet is the summary budget incorporating its component functional budgets and which is finally approved, adopted and employed. A master budget shows the operating profit of the business for the budget period and budgeted balance sheet at its close.

Problem 23 (Master budget) : A glass manufacturing company requires you to calculate and present the budget for the year from the following information :

Toughened glass	–	Rs. 3,60,000
Bent toughened glass	–	Rs. 5,40,000
Direct material cost	–	60% of sales
Direct wages of 20 workers at the rate of	–	Rs. 200 per month
Factory overheads :		
Works manager	–	Rs. 600 per month
Foreman	–	Rs. 500 per month
Stores and spares	–	2½% on sales
Depreciation on machinery	–	Rs. 12,500
Light and power	–	Rs. 5,000
Repairs and maintenance	–	Rs. 8,000
Other sundries	–	10% on direct wages
Administration, selling and distribution expenses	–	Rs. 16,000 per year.

(*University of Kerala, M.Com., May 1992*)

Solution : **Master budget for the period ending**

Sales budget		
Toughened glass		3,60,000
Bent toughened glass		5,40,000
		9,00,000
Less : Administration and selling and distribution overheads		16,000
Net sales revenue		8,84,000
Production cost budget :		
Direct materials—60% of sales		5,30,400
Direct wages—20 × 200 × 12		48,000
Prime cost		5,78,400
Variable factory overheads :		
Stores and spares 2½% on sales	22,500	
Light	5,000	
Repairs	5,000	37,500
Fixed factory overhead :		
Works manager's salary	7,200	
Foreman's salary	6,000	
Depreciation	12,500	
Sundries 10% of wages	4,800	30,500
Works cost		6,46,400

Expected profit = Sales – Works cost
= 8,84,000 – 6,46,400 = 2,37,600

4. On the Basis of Capacity

On the basis of capacity operated budgets are classified into two types. They are as follows :

(*a*) **Fixed budget :** The ICMA terminology defines fixed budget as "a budget which is designed to remain unchanged irrespective of the volume of output or turnover attained. All the budgets explained above are fixed budgets, *i.e.*, they are based on a fixed level of operation. In other words, it is assumed that the various departments of a factory work at a stated level of activity and that a specified production level is going to be achieved and that sales budget will be attained. A fixed budget does not help as a controlling tool. Hence flexible budgets are made use of.

(*b*) **Flexible budget or variable budget :** It is defined by the ICMA terminology as "a budget which by recognising the difference in behaviour between fixed and variable costs in relation to fluctuations in output, turnover or other variable factors such as number of employees, is designed to change appropriately with such fluctuation". A flexible budget is not rigid as in the case of fixed budget. Instead it adapts itself to any level of activity. The budget varies according to a change in the level of output. Hence it is also known as variable budget. It serves as a useful tool of controlling cost.

Problem 24 (Flexible budge) : Prepare a flexible budget from the following data :

Capacity	50%
Volume	10,000 units
Selling price per unit	Rs. 200
Material	Rs. 100
Labour	Rs. 30
Factory overhead	Rs. 30 (Rs. 12 fixed)
Administration overhead	Rs. 20 (Rs. 10 fixed)

At 60% working, material cost per unit increased by 2% and selling price per unit falls by 2%.

At 80% working, material cost per unit increases by 5% and selling price per unit falls by 5%. Estimate the profit at 60% and 80% working. *(Nagarjuna University, M.Com., March 1992)*

Solution : **Flexible budget**

	Level of activity					
	50%		*60%*		*80%*	
	Per unit	*Amount*	*Per unit*	*Amount*	*Per unit*	*Amount*
Units	10,000		12,000		16,000	
Raw materials	100	10,00,000	102	12,24,000	105	16,80,000
Labour	30	3,00,000	30	3,60,000	30	4,80,000
Factory overhead – Fixed	12	1,20,000	10	1,20,000	7.5	1,20,000
– Variable	18	1,80,000	18	2,16,000	18.0	2,88,000
Administration overhead						
– Fixed	10	1,00,000	8.33	1,00,000	6.25	1,00,000
– Variable	10	1,00,000	10	1,20,000	10	1,60,000
Total cost	180	18,00,000	178.33	2,14,000	176.75	28,28,000
Profit	20	2,00,000	17.67	2,12,000	13.25	2,12,000
Sales	200	20,00,000	196.00	23,52,000	190	30,40,000

Problem 25 : Draw up a flexible budget for overhead expenses on the basis of the following data and determine the overhead rates at 70%, 80% and 90% plant capacity.

	Capacity level		
Variable overheads :	70%	80%	90%
Indirect labour	–	12,000	–
Indirect materials	–	4,000	–
Semi–variable overheads :			
Power (30% fixed)	–	20,000	–
Repairs and maintenance 60% fixed	–	2,000	–
Fixed overhead :			
Depreciation	–	11,000	–
Insurance	–	3,000	–
Salaries	–	10,000	–
Total overheads	–	62,000	–
Estimated direct labour hours	–	1,20,000	–

(Madurai Kamaraj University, B.Com., April 1992)

Solution : **Flexible budget**

	Level of activity		
	70%	*80%*	*90%*
Variable overheads			
Indirect labour	10,500	12,000	13,500
Stores	3,500	4,000	4,500
Semi-variable overhead			
Power — Fixed	6,000	6,000	6,000
— Variable	12,250	14,000	15,750
Repairs — Fixed	1,200	1,200	1,200
— Variable	700	800	900
Fixed overhead			
Depreciation	11,000	11,000	11,000
Insurance	3,000	3,000	3,000
Salaries	10,000	10,000	10,000
Total overheads	58,150	62,000	65,850
Estimated labour hours	1,08,500	1,24,000	1,39,500
Overhead rate	0.53	0.50	0.47

Problem 26 : For production of 10,000 articles the following are budgeted expenses per unit :

	Rs.
Direct materials	60.00
Direct labour	30.00
Variable overhead	20.00
Fixed overhead (Rs. 1,60,000)	16.00
Variable expenses (direct)	5.00
Selling expenses (20% fixed)	15.00
Administration expenses (Rs. 50,000 fixed for all level of production)	5.00
Distribution expenses (20% fixed)	5.00
	156.00

Prepare a flexible budget for production of 6,000, 7,000 and 8,000 units of articles, showing clearly variable cost, fixed cost and total cost. *(University of Madras, B.Com., March 1997)*

Solution : **Flexible budget**

	6,000 units		7,000 units		8,000 units		10,000 units	
	Per unit	*Amount*	*Per unit*	*Amount*	*Per unit*	*Amount*	*Per unit*	*Amount*
Material	60	3,60,000	60	4,20,000	60	4,80,000	60	6,00,000
Labour	30	1,80,000	30	2,10,000	30	2,40,000	30	3,00,000
Variable overhead	20	1,20,000	20	1,40,000	20	1,60,000	20	2,00,000
Fixed overhead	26.66	1,60,000	22.85	1,60,000	20	1,60,000	16	1,60,000
Variable expense	5	30,000	5	35,000	5	40,000	5	50,000
Selling expense :								
—Fixed	5	30,000	4.28	30,000	3.75	30,000	3	30,000
—Variable	12	72,000	12	84,000	12.00	96,000	12	1,20,000
Administration expense	8.34	50,000	7.14	50,000	6.25	50,000	5	50,000
Distribution expense								
—Fixed	1.66	10,000	1.42	10,000	1.25	10,000	1	10,000
—Variable	4.00	24,000	4.00	28,000	4.00	32,000	4	40,000
Total cost	172.66	10,36,000	166.69	11,67,000	162.25	12,98,000	156	15,60,000

Problem 27 : The following figures are available from sales and costs forecast of M/s. Asiad and Company for the year ended 31st December, 1984 at 50% (5,000 units) capacity utilisation :

(i) Fixed expenses remain constant for all levels of production and sales.
(ii) Selling price between 50% and 75% capacity is Rs. 25 per unit.
(iii) Semi-variable expenses will remain unchanged at 50% to 65% capacity but will increase by 10% between 65% and 80% capacity and 30% between 80% and 100% capacity.
(iv) At 90% level, material cost increases by 5% and selling price is reduced by 5%.
(v) At 100% level both material and labour costs increase by 10% and selling price is reduced by 8%.
(vi) Semi-variable expenses are Rs. 50,000.
(vii) Fixed expenses are Rs. 58,000.
(viii) Variable expenses are, material Rs. 5 per unit, labour Rs. 2 per unit and direct expenses, Re. 1 per unit.

Prepare a profit forecast statement throught flexible budget at 60%, 75%, 90% and 100% capacity.

(Bangalore University, M.Com., May 1989)

Solution :

Flexible budget

	60% (6,000 units)	*75% (7,500 units)*	*90% (9,000 units)*	*100% (10,000 units)*
Materials	30,000	37,500	47,250	55,000
Labour	12,000	15,000	18,000	22,000
Expenses	6,000	7,500	9,000	10,000
Semi-variable cost	50,000	55,000	65,000	65,000
Fixed cost	58,000	58,000	58,000	58,000
Total	1,56,000	1,73,000	1,97,250	2,10,000
Profit/Loss	(6,000)	14,500	16,500	20,000
Sales	1,50,000	1,87,500	2,13,750	2,30,000

Working Note : Sales value for 9,000 units and 10,000 units

9,000 × 25 = 2,25,000		10,000 × 25 = 2,50,000	
Less : 5%	11,250	Less : 8%	20,000
	2,13,750		2,30,000

Problem 28 : The following data are available for a manufacturing company for a yearly period :

	Rs. (in lakhs)
Fixed expenses :	
Wages and salaries	9.5
Rent, rates and taxes	6.6
Depreciation	7.4
Sundry administration expenses	6.5
Semi-variable expenses (at 50% capacity)	
Maintenance and repairs	3.5
Indirect labour	7.9
Sales department salaries	3.8
Sundry administrative expenses	2,8
Variable expenses (at 50% capacity)	
Materials	21.7
Labour	20.4
Other expenses	7.9
Total cost	98.0

Assume that the fixed expenses remain constant at all levels of production, semi-variable expenses remain constant between 45% and 65% capacity increasing by 10% between 65% and 80% capacity and by 20% between 80% and 100% capacity.

Sales at various levels are :

	Rs. (in lakhs)
50% Capacity	100
60% Capacity	120
75% Capacity	150
90% Capacity	180
100% Capacity	200

Prepare a flexible budget for the year at 60% and 90% capacities and estimate the profit at these levels of buget. *(C.S., Inter, Dec. 1991)*

Solution : **Flexible budget**

	Rs. (in lakhs)	
	60%	*90%*
Variable cost :		
Materials	26.04	39.06
Labour	24.48	36.72
Other expenses	9.48	14.22
Semi-variable cost :		
Maintenance	3.5	4.20
Indirect labour	7.9	9.48
Sales department salaries	3.8	4.56
Sundry administration expenses	2.8	3.36
Fixed cost :		
Wages and salaries	9.50	9.50
Rent, rates and taxes	6.60	6.60
Depreciation	7.40	7.40
Sundry administration expenses	6.50	6.50
Total cost	108	141.60
Profit	12	38.40
Sales	120	180

Problem 29 : The monthly budgets for manufacturing overhead of a concern for two levels of activity were as follows :

Capacity	*60%*	*100%*
Budgeted production (units)	600	1,000
	Rs.	*Rs.*
Wages	1,200	2,000
Consumable stores	900	1,500
Maintenance	1,100	1,500
Power and fuel	1,600	2,000
Depreciation	4,000	4,000
Insurance	1,000	1,000
	9,600	12,000

You are required to :

(*i*) Indicate which of the items are fixed, variable and semi-variable,

(*ii*) Prepare a budget for 80% capacity and

(*iii*) Find the total cost both fixed and variable per unit of output at 60%, 80% and 100% capacity.

(C.S., Inter, December 1990)

Solution : Fixed costs are : (*i*) Depreciation
(*ii*) Insurance

Variable costs are : (*i*) Wages at Rs. 2 per unit
(*i*) Consumable stores at 1.50 p.u.

Semi-variable cost :

$$\text{Maintenance} = \left(\frac{1{,}500-1{,}100}{1{,}000-600}\right) = \frac{400}{400} = \text{Re. 1 p.u. variable}$$

Rs. 1,100 – 600 × Re. 1 = 500 fixed

$$\text{Power and fuel} = \left(\frac{2{,}000-1{,}600}{1{,}000-600}\right) = \frac{400}{400} = \text{Re. 1 p.u. variable}$$

Rs. 1,600 – 600 × Re. 1 = 1,000 fixed

Budget for 80% capacity

	Output 800 units
Wages @ Rs. 2 per unit	1,600
Consumable stores @ Rs. 1.50 per unit	1,200
Maintenance Rs. 500 + Re. 1.00 per unit	1,300
Power and fuel Rs. 1,000 + Re. 1.00 per unit	1,800
Depreciation	4,000
Insurance	1,000
Total cost	10,900

Statement showing total cost

Capacity	*60%*	*80%*	*100%*
Units	600	800	1,000
	Rs.	*Rs.*	*Rs.*
Fixed cost :			
Depreciation	4,000	4,000	4,000
Insurance	1,000	1,000	1,000
Maintenance	500	500	500
Power and fuel	1,000	1,000	1,000
Total fixed cost	6,500	6,500	6,500
Variable cost :			
Wages @ Rs. 2 per unit	1,200	1,600	2,000
Consumable stores @ Rs. 1.50 p.u.	900	1,200	1,500
Maintenance cost @ Re. 1 p.u.	600	800	1,000
Power and fuel at Re. 1 p.u.	600	800	1,000
Total variable cost	3,300	4,400	5,500
Fixed cost per unit	10.83	8.125	6.50
Variable cost per unit	5.50	5.50	5.50
Total cost per unit	16.33	13.625	12.000

ZERO BASED BUDGETING (ZBB)

Zero based budgeting is a new technique of budgeting introduced first in USA in the year 1969. This system of budgeting was developed by Peter Pyhrr of Texas Instruments of USA. This technique of budgeting is more useful in government budgeting but can also be used in factories for non-manufacturing activitites. Such as administration and selling activitites.

The ICMA terminology defines ZBB as "a method of budgeting whereby all activities are re-evaluated each time a budget is formulated. Each functional budget starts with the assumption that the function does not exist and is a zero cost. Increments of cost are compared with increments of benefits culminating in the planned maximum benefits for a given budgeted cost."

The technique of budgeting is considered to be an improvement over traditional method of budgeting, which is also known as 'incremental budgeting'. Under incremental budgeting every departmental manager would prepare a budget for his department based upon the previous experience and allow for a certain increase in amount in the budget for meeting contingency. However, in spite of a best forecast, sometimes the targets may not be achieved owing to inefficiency. Thus whenever previous budget is taken as a basis to prepare a current budget, the current budget involves an element of inefficiency that is carried forward from the previous year. Hence under ZBB, the budget is prepared by considering the base for the current year as zero and this eliminates the accrual of inefficiency for preparing future years budget.

The basic steps in implementing ZBB are as follows :

(*i*) Identify each function and activity of the organisation—this is referred to as a 'decision packing'.

(*ii*) Evaluate each decision package so as to ensure that is cost effective.

(*iii*) Compare each activity with possible alternatives.

(*iv*) Rank each activity—in some cases decision packages can be evaluated in terms of profitability or in any subjective terms using cost-benefit analysis.

(*v*) Allocate resources in accordance with the ranking of activitites and with resources available to the organisation.

BUDGET REPORT

The work of a budget officer does not end with the preparation and approval of budgets. The has to prepare reports on a continuous basis so as to facilitate comparison of actuals with budgets. The budgets reports are sent to various departmental managers showing favourable or adverse variance from the budget. Based on this the departmental managers will prepare a report to be submitted to the managing director pointing out the reasons for the variances. This enable remedial actions to be taken to set right unfavourable variance. The reports so furnished will also help as a guide for future planning.

According to W.W. Bigg, while preparing reports on budgets it is necessary to follow the undermentioned principles so as to make reports more effective :

1. The report should be clearly headed and the period covered shown. The unit, *viz.*, cash, tonnes, litre, etc., should be indicated.
2. Like must be compared with like and there must be no ambiguity of description. For example, it must be clear whether a sales report refers to 'deliveries made and invoiced' or to 'orders received'.
3. Information not relevant to the purpose for which the report is prepared should be omitted so that conclusions from the report can be drawn quickly and with certainty.
4. The report should not attempt to portray so much information that clarity is lost. If the information to be conveyed is complicated, more than one statement may be desirable. For example, to show actual sales compared with budget, analysed over both 'areas' and 'commodities', a separate statement for each analysis would improve clarity.
5. The information included should be limited to the sphere of the person to whom it is furnished. The data to be given to a foreman would normally be confined to that affecting his particular shop, but the factory manager would require broader information covering all departments for which he is responsible.
6. Promptness is to be prepferred to absolute accuracy, the purpose is not merely to

convey information but to convey it promptly and to the person who has the authority to take action.

7. All reports should be reviewed periodically to ensure that they are still useful and to ascertain whether they should be expanded contracted or discontinued.

QUESTIONS

I. Choose the correct answer from the following :

1. A budget that gives a summary of all the functional budgets and projected profit and loss account is known as
   (*a*) Capital budget (*c*) Master budget
   (*b*) Flexible budget (*d*) Discretionary budget [ ]
2. The fixed-variable cost classification has a speical significance in the preparation of
   (*a*) Flexible budget (*c*) Cash budget
   (*b*) Master budget (*d*) Capital budget [ ]
3. The basis difference a fixed budget and a flexible budget is that a fixed budget
   (*a*) includes only fixed costs and a flexible budget only variable cost.
   (*b*) is a budget for a single level of some measures of activity, what a flexible budget consists of several budgets based on different activity levels.
   (*c*) is concerned with future acquisition of fixed assets, while a flexible budget is concerned with expenses that vary with sales.
   (*d*) cannot be changed after a fiscal period begins, while a flexible budget can be changed after a fiscal period begins. [ ]
4. Which of the following is usually a long-term budget?
   (*a*) Sales budget (*c*) Capital expenditure budget
   (*b*) Cash budget (*d*) Fixed budget [ ]
5. Under flxeible budgeting
   (*a*) statements included in the budget report vary from period to period.
   (*b*) budget standards may be adjusted at will.
   (*c*) reporting dates vary according to the activity level reported upon.
   (*d*) planned activity level is adjusted to the actual activity level before the budget comparison report is prepared. [ ]

[***Answer :*** 1. (*c*), 2. (*a*), 3. (*b*), 4. (*c*), 5. (*d*)]

II. Mark 'T' or 'F' in the space provided

1. A budget is nothing but an estimate. *T/F*
2. Budgets are drawn up by the chief accountant. *T/F*
3. Budgets are blue prints for action. *T/F*
4. On the basis of budgets, next year's balance sheet and P & L a/c can be drawn up. *T/F*
5. Raw material supply is always the key factor. *T/F*
6. Diverse production is reduced to common basis on the basis of standard hours involved. *T/F*
7. Standing costing can operate without budgetary control. *T/F*
8. A system of budgetary control cannot be operated when standard costing system is in use. *T/F*
9. All functional budgets should be co-ordinated with sales budget which is always prepared first. *T/F*
10. A budget mannual is a summary of all the functional budget. *T/F*
11. Budgetary control system does not suit small business concern. *T/F*
12. Purchase budget and material budget is the same thing. *T/F*
13. A flexible budget is one which changes from year to year. *T/F*
14. A flexible budget system will recast quickly for changes in the volume of activity. *T/F*
15. A flexible budget carefully differentiates between fixed and variable cost. *T/F*

[***Answer :*** True—3, 4, 5, 6, 7, 14. Rest are all false]

III. Short and long answer questions

1. Define budgetary control and state its advantages. (*Kakatiya University, B.Com., Oct. 1989*)
2. Write notes on : (*a*) Limiting factor, (*b*) Budget mannual. (*Calicut University, M.Com., April 1992*)

3. What are 'budget' and 'budgetary control'? Discuss various advantages and essentials for success of budgetary control. *(Kakatiya University, M.Com., August 1991)*
4. What is budgetary control and how it is exercised? Discuss various advantages and essentials for the success of budgetary control. *(Mangalore University, B.Com., Oct. 1991)*
5. Briefly explain the steps in the installation of a system of budgetary control. *(University of Kerala, B.Com., April 1989)*
6. What is meant by 'budgetary control'? State the essentials of good budgetary control system". What are the advantages and limitations of a budgetary control system? *(Calicut University, B.Com., Oct. 1989)*
7. What is a flexible budget? How does it differ from a fixed budget? *(University of Kerala, B.Com., March 1990)*
8. What are the facts to be considered in setting up an annual sales budget? *(ICWA, Inter, Dec. 1989)*
9. What is zero base budgeting? What are the advantages of zero based approach over the traditional approach? *(ICWA, Inter, Dec. 1989)*
10. (*a*) Define the terms 'budget' and 'budgetary control'.
    (*b*) List down any five objectives of a budgetary control system. *(CA, Inter, Nov. 1990)*

EXERCISES

Exercise 1 (Sales budget) : The Sunshine Co. Ltd. has four sales divisions each consisting of four regions; North, South, East and West. The company sells two products *X* and *Y*. Budgeted sales for the six months ended 30th June, 1993, in each area of divison 1 were as follows :

North — X	10,000	units @ Rs. 10 each
— *Y*	6,000	units @ Rs. 5 each
South — *Y*	12,000	units @ Rs. 5 each
East — *X*	15,000	units @ Rs. 10 each
West — *X*	8,000	units @ Rs. 10 each
— *Y*	5,000	units @ Rs. 5 each

Actual sales for the same period in division 1 were as follows :

North — *X*	11,500	units @ Rs. 10 each
— *Y*	7,000	units @ Rs. 5 each
South — *Y*	12,500	units @ Rs. 5 each
East — *X*	16,500	units @ Rs. 10 each
West — *X*	9,500	units @ Rs. 10 each
— *Y*	5,250	units @ Rs. 5 each

From the salesmen's report, it is thought that sales could be budgeted for the six months ended June 30, 1994 as follows :

North — *X*	Budgeted increase of	2,000	units on 30.6.93
— *Y*	Budgeted increase of	500	units on 30.6.93
South — *Y*	Budgeted increase of	1,000	units on 30.6.93
East — *X*	Budgeted increase of	2,000	units on 30.6.93
West — *X*	Budgeted increase of	1,000	units on 30.6.93
— *Y*	Budgeted increase of	500	units on 30.6.93

At a meeting of area sales manager with the divisional sales manager it is decided that sales campaign will be undertaken in areas South and East. It is anticipated that these campaigns will result in additional sales of 3,000 units of *X* in the South area and 5,000 units of *Y* in the East area.

Prepare a sales budget for the period ending 30th June, 1994. Showing also the budgeted and actual sales for June 30th, 1993.

[***Answer :*** Total sales for all areas and for products *X* and *Y* for the budgeted period 30.6.94 is Rs. 5,60,000 for the budgeted period 30.6.93 is Rs. 4,45,000 and actual total sales for 30.6.93 is Rs. 4,98,750]

Exercise 2 (Selling and distribution cost budget) : Hardcore Ltd. incurred the following selling costs in its last budget year.

	Sales area			Head office	Total
	A	*B*	*C*		
Personnel cost :					
Salesmen's salary	27,000	33,000	5,000	—	65,000
Commission	5,000	7,000	500	—	12,500
Travelling expenses	8,000	11,000	3,000	—	22,000
Sales management :					
Salaries	—	—	—	11,000	11,000
Building services	—	—	—	7,000	7,000
Other costs	—	—	—	1,500	1,500
Publicity :					
	30,000	45,000	8,000	—	83,000
	70,000	96,000	16,500	19,500	2,02,000

From the above particulars and the following additional information prepare a selling cost budget for the year 1993 :

(1) A new sales area *D* is to be formed to cover what is mostly virgin territory, but to take in certain areas previously covered by *B* sales are. Salemen's salaries of the new area are estimated to be Rs. 8,000, which includes Rs. 2,000 to bd paid to *B* salesmen transferred to the *D* area. Travelling expenses of *B* representative in the *D* area last year was Rs. 900. For the whole *D* area they are expected to be Rs. 2,400 next year.

(2) An additional clerk will be needed in the sales manager's office at a salary of Rs. 900 per annum and the building service budget shows an increase of 5%.

(3) The publicity budget allows for expenditure of *A*—Rs. 25,000, *B*—Rs. 40,000, *C*—Rs. 10,000, *D*—Rs. 25,000. Rs. 15,000 is budgeted as the cost of an international exhibition.

(4) Commission is paid at the rate of ½% of all sales. The sales budget specifies sales of *A*—Rs. 12,00,000, *B*—Rs. 15,00,000, *C*—Rs. 5,00,000, *D*—Rs. 4,00,000.

[***Answer :*** Selling budget cost for *A*—Rs. 66,000, *B*—Rs. 88,600, *C*—Rs. 20,500, *D*—Rs. 37,400, H.O. Rs. 35,750, Total Rs. 2,48,250]

Exercise 3 (Production budget and production cost budget) : Gaira Engineering Co. Ltd. manufactures two products *X* and *Y*. An estimate of number of units expected to be sold in the first seven months of 1985 is given below :

	Product X	*Product Y*
Jan.	500	1,400
Feb.	600	1,400
Mar.	800	1,200
Apr.	1,000	1,000
May	1,200	800
June	1,200	800
July	1,000	900

It is anticipated that :

(*a*) There will be no work-in-progress at the end of any month.

(*b*) Finished units equal to half the anticipated sales for the next month will be in stock at the end of each month (including December 1984). The budgeted production and production costs for the year ending 31st Dec., 1985 are as follows :

	Product X	*Product Y*
Production units	11,000	12,000
Direct material cost per unit	Rs. 12	Rs. 19
Direct wages per unit	5	7
Other manufacturing charges apportioned	33,000	48,000

You are required to prepare :

(*a*) Production budget showing the number of units to be manufactured for each month.

(*b*) A summarised production cost budget for the 6 month period Jan. to June 1985.

[*Answer :* Production of *X*—5,550 units and that of *Y*—6,350 units. Total cost of *X* Rs. 1,11,000 and *Y* Rs. 1,90,500]

Exercise 4 (Purchase budget) : The sales director of manufacturing company reports that next year he expects to sell 50,000 units of a certain product.

The production manager consults the storekeeper and casts his figure as follows: Two kinds of raw materials *A* and *B* are required for manufacturing the product. Each unit of the product requires 2 units of *A* and 3 units of *B*. The estimated opening balances at the commencement of the next year are—finished product 10,000 units; *A* : 12,000 units; *B* : 15,000 units. The desirable closing balances at the end of the next year are—finished product, 14,000 units; *A* : 13,000 units, *B* : 16,000 units.

Draw up a quantitative chart showing the materials purchases budget for the next year.

[*Answer :* Budgeted purchase of *A* material is 1,09,000 units and *B* material is 1,63,000 units]

Exercise 5 (Cash budget under receipts & payments method) : From the following information with regard to the budget of the Ray Engineering Co. Ltd., you are required to prepare a cash budget for the six months ending 31st Dec. 1992, on the assumption that the balance in hand on 1st July 1992 will be Rs. 96,000.

Month	*Sales (Rs.)*	*Selling cost (Rs.)*	*Raw materials (Rs.)*	*Wages (Rs.)*	*Production overhead (Rs.)*	*Administration overhead (Rs.)*
May	95,000	3,600	35,000	9,000	6,000	2,500
June	84,000	3,400	36,000	9,200	6,100	2,400
July	88,000	3,500	40,000	9,800	6,300	2,400
Aug.	84,000	3,200	45,000	10,500	7,000	2,300
Sept.	95,000	14,000	55,000	13,000	8,600	2,400
Oct.	1,20,000	15,000	40,000	10,400	8,100	3,000
Nov.	1,25,000	16,000	30,000	9,000	5,900	2,600
Dec.	1,18,000	7,000	28,000	7,000	4,900	2,500

In addition, it is necessary to provide for the payment of 10,800 in July 1992 and 86,600 in December 1992 in respect of capital expenditure detailed in that budget.

It is anticipated that a dividend of Rs. 23,000 will be paid in August 1992.

Rs. 10,000, 5% debentures are to be redeemed at 104 on 1st July 1992.

Debtors are allowed two month's credit (Thus, May sales are paid for in July)

Creditors (for goods or overhead) grant one month's credit.

The slight time lag in payment of wages is to be disregarded and payments in advance and accruals are to be ignored for the sake of simplicity.

[*Answer :* Closing cash balance for July Rs. 12,100, Aug. 1,10,400, Sept. 1,27,900, Oct. 1,12,500, Nov. Rs. 1,13,300, Dec. 1,13,300]

Exercise 6 (Master budget) : A glass manufacturing company requires you to calculate and present the buget for the next year from the following information :

Sales :	
Toughened glass	Rs. 3,00,000
Bent toughened glass	Rs. 5,00,000
Direct material cost	60% of sales
Direct wages	20 workers @ 1.50 p.m.
Factory overheads :	
Indirect labour — Works manager	Rs. 500 p.m.
— Foreman	Rs. 400 p.m.
Stores and spares	2½% on sales
Depreciation on machinery	Rs. 12,600
Light and power	Rs. 5,000
Repairs, etc.	Rs. 8,000
Sundries	10% on wages

Administration, selling and distribution expenses Rs. 14,000 p.m.

(*Bharathidasan University, B.Sc., Apr. 1988*)

[*Answer :* Expected profit Rs. 2,10,000]

Exercise 7 (Flexible budget) : A manufacturing company produces 8,000 units per month. Split up cost and sales value of which is given below :

	Rs.
Direct material per unit	Rs. 30
Direct labour	20
Fixed overhead (Rs. 2,00,000)	25
Variable overhead	40
	115
Selling and distribution expenses	
Fixed (Rs. 80,000)	10
Variable	15
General administration, etc.	
Fixed (Rs. 2,40,00)	30
Margin of profit (subject to taxtation)	5
Selling price	175

Due to increase in demand and consequent extention of delivery dates and disatisfaction to customers, the management decided to provide for an output of 12,000 units per month in the next year which would involve a capital outlay of Rs. 6,00,000 on which interest and finance charge would amount to 10% per annum. Prepare a comparative consolidated cost statement showing anticipated margin of profit for the present output (8,000 units) and the proposed output (12,000 units).

Assume that in the coming year there will be an allround increase of 5% in the different item of expenses except fixed expense.

Due-to the proposed increase in output there will be in an increase of 25% in fixed overhead, 20% in fixed selling and distribution expenses and 10% in general administration, etc., apart from the interest and finance charges.

If it is decided to maintain the present level of sales an increase of 2% on sales price is possible and this figure should be taken for the level of production at 8,000 units per month.

Draw a flexible budget for 8,000 units and 12,000 units.

[*Answer :* Sales for 8,000 units Rs. 14,28,000 and for 12,000 units Rs. 21,00,000 and profit for 8,000 units Rs. 26,000 and for 12,000 units Rs. 1,62,000]

Exercise 8 (Flexible budget) : From the following information prepare a flexible budget to show levels of activity of 80%, 90% and 100%.

(1) Sales based on normal level of activity of 80% are 80,000 units at Rs. 20 per unit. If output is increased to 90% it is thought that the selling price should be reduced by 2½% and if output reaches 100% it would be necessary to reduce the original selling price by a further 2½% in order to reach a wider market.

(2) Prime costs are :

	Per unit (Rs.)
Direct material	2.00
Direct labour	2.00
Direct expenses	1.00
	5.00

If output reaches a 90% level of activity as above, the quantity discount will be received and this will lead to reduction of purchase price of raw materials by 5%.

(3) Variable overheads : Salemen's commission is 5% on sales value.

(4) Semi-variable overheads at normal level of activity are :

Supervision	80,000
Power	70,000
Heat and light	40,000
Maintenance	50,000

Indirect labour	1,00,000
Salesmen's expense	60,000
Transport	2,00,000
	6,00,000

Semi-variable overheads are expected to increase by 5% if output reaches a level of activity of 90% and by a further 5% if it reaches the 100% level.

(5) Fixed overheads are :

Rent and rates	10,000
Depreciation	40,000
Administration	75,000
Sales department	20,000
Advertising	50,000
General	5,000

[*Answer :* Sales for 80% level of activity is Rs. 16,00,000 for 90% level of activity Rs. 17,55,000 and 100% level of activity Rs. 19,00,000. Profit for 80% level of activity is Rs. 3,20,000, for 90% level of activity is 17,55,000 and for 100% level of activity is 19,00,000]

11

STANDARD COSTING

HISTORICAL COSTING

Historical costing is one of the techniques of ascertaining cost of production. It is based on accumulation of actual or historical cost. The National Association of Accountants has defined historical cost as "the cost which is accumulated during the process of production by the usual historical costing technique as opposed to the cost which has been determined in advance of the production process. The term 'actual' is not intended to convey any implication as to the accuracy with which costs are measured." Historical costing is not a very popular technique as it suffers from the following limitations :

(*a*) It provides cost information only after the completion of production. So cost of production cannot be ascertained until production is completed. The fixation of selling price becomes difficult under such situation.

(*b*) It is not possible to exercise control over the costs which are actually incurred.

(*c*) It becomes difficult to take decisions based on actual costs.

(*d*) Actual costs may vary from period to period and fixation of selling price on the basis of actual cost will lead to differences in selling price which may not be accepted by customers.

(*e*) It is an expensive and time consuming technique. For example, in a larger sized business, to ascertain the cost of production of say 1 lakh units involving different materials and various expenses will involve more time and clerical work.

In order to overcome the above limitations, standard costing was developed.

STANDARD COST AND STANDARD COSTING

A standard cost has been defined by Lucey (*Costing*) as "a predetermined calculation of how much costs should be under specified working conditions".

Brown and Howard in their book *Principles and Practice of Management Accountancy* define a standard cost as a predetermined cost which determines what each product or service should cost under given circumstances.

The ICMA terminology defines a standard cost as "a predetermined cost calculated in relation to a prescribed set of working conditions, correlating technical specifications and scientific measurements of materials and labour to the prices and wage rates expected to apply during the period to which the standard cost is intended to relate, with an addition of an appropriate share of budgeted overhead".

The objects of standard costs are as follows :

1. Promoting and measuring efficiencies.
2. Controlling and reducing costs.
3. Simplifying costing procedure.
4. Valuing inventories.
5. Fixing selling price.

Standard costing has been defined by Brown and Howard as "a technique of cost accounting which compares the 'standard cost' of each product or service with the actual cost to determine the efficiency of the operation, so that any remedial action may be taken immediately".

The ICMA terminology defines standard costing as "the preparation and use of standard costs, their comparison with actual cost and the analysis of variances to their causes and points of incidence".

According to the above two definitions, standard costing involves the following steps :

(*a*) Setting of standards.
(*b*) Measurement of results.
(*c*) Comparison of actuals with standards to determine the variance.
(*d*) Investigation of variance.
(*e*) Taking remedial action to set right adverse variance.

DIFFERENCES BETWEEN A BUDGET AND STANDARD

1. A standard is a unit concept, *i.e.*, the apply to a particular product, process or operation, whereas budgets are concerned with totals, *i.e.*, for the firms as a whole.
2. Standards are revised only when they are inapproporiate for current operating conditions, whereas budgets are revised on a periodic basis generally once a year.
3. Standards and the resulting variances are part of the double entry system of accounting, whereas budgets are memorandum figures and do not form part of double entry system of accounting.

DIFFERENCES BETWEEN A BUDGETARY CONTROL AND STANDARD COSTING

Budgetary control	*Standard costing*
1. It is prepared to cover various functions of a business such as purchases, sales, production, finance, etc. In other words it has a macro-approach.	1. It is prepared in respect of a cost unit. In other words it has a micro-approach.
2. It is more extensive as it covers all the operations of the business.	2. It is more intensive technique of controlling costs.
3. It is a projection of financial accounts.	3. It is a projection of cost accounts.
4. It can be implemented even in parts, *i.e.*, to cover one or more than one area of business.	4. It covers all items of expenses without leaving any item. So it cannot be operated in part.
5. It can be operated without standards.	5. It cannot exist without budget.
6. It is more management oriented.	6. It is more engineering oriented.
7. It can be implemented in all industries.	7. It is not possible in certain industries.
8. It does not involve any accounting after computing variances.	8. Variances are accounted for under standard costing.
9. Its objects are formulation of policy, co-ordination of activities, and delegation of authority.	9. Its aim is to enable management in making decisions, in price-flxing and valuation of closing stock.

STANDARD COSTING AND STANDARDISED COSTING

Standard costing should not be confused with standardised costing as both are completely different. Standard costing is a tool of cost control whereas standardised costing refers to a uniform application of costing and cost accounting principles and procedures to a firm having number of plants. The object of standardised costing is to facilitate inter-firm comparison of results.

Secondly, standard costing technique makes use of only standard cost. Whereas standardised costing can be operated with the help of historical cost also.

Thirdly standard costing is operated on the principles of exception, whereas, standardised costing in based on the principle of example.

Lastly, the objective of standard costing is to set and maintain the standard. Whereas, the objective of standardised costing is to improve upon the standard in addition to maintaining the standard.

ADVANTAGES AND LIMITATIONS OF STANDARD COSTING

The advantages of standard costing are as follows :

1. It provides a yardstick against which actuals are measured.
2. Standard costing helps in standardising the various activities of a business. Thus it enables use of standard materials and better method of production.
3. It increases the cost consciousness among all concerned by fixing targets and to achieve them.
4. This technique follow the principles of management by exception.
5. It simplifies the accounting procedure which involves less clerical work and time.
6. It helps in valuing the closing stock.
7. It pinpoints the responsibility of everybody concerned in the organisation.
8. It facilitates cost control by analysing the causes of inefficiency and by taking remedial measures. This will result in reduced cost of production.
9. It enables in periodic preparation of profit and loss account which helps management in knowing the trends of the business.
10. It helps in introducing incentives to employees and provides a basis for motivating them.
11. It helps in fixing selling price in advance of production. Thus quotations can be sent and orders secured.

The limitations of standard costing are as follows :

1. It is difficult to establish standards in practice.
2. Standards established may have to be revised owing to changing conditions. But frequent revision of standards is costly and may create problems.
3. Standards which are inaccurate, unreliable and outdated may do more harm than good.
4. If the standards set are not attained it will lead to psychological effects resulting in frustration.
5. It may not be suitable for small concerns.
6. It cannot be applied to non-standardised industries and in industries where goods are to be manufactured according to specification of customers.

PRELIMINARIES IN ESTABLISHING A SYSTEM OF STANDARD COSTING

Before establishing a system of standard costing the following preliminary factors are to be considered.

1. Establishment of Cost Centre

In order to identify the areas of efficiency or otherwise of it and to fix responsibilities for the persons who are concerned with attaining the standards, it is necessary to establish cost centre. A main cost centre can again be sub-divided into sub-cost centre for exercising better control. Having established cost centres, the next requirement is to fix up responsibility on the persons who are incharge of such cost centres.

2. Classification of Accounts

It refers to classifying the costs under a suitable accounting heading. This facilitates quick identification and collection of expenses, their analysis and in prompt reporting. As was explained under chapter 2, costs can be classified on the basis of number of characteristics. Having classified, it is desireable to give a code number for each heading of cost. For example, raw materials may be given a code number from 0 to 10, direct labour cost 11 to 20 factory overheads 21 to 30 and so on. This results in convenience in dealing with costs and ensures secrecy.

3. Determination of Duration

This refers to the period for which standard are used. It may be a short or long duration.

4. Determine the Capacity

It refers to fixation of standard output for the sake of fixing fixed and variable overheads.

5. Types of Standard

It refers to the level of attainment accepted by management as the basis on which standard costs are determined. The following are the important types of standards.

(*a*) **Basic or fixed or static standard :** It is defined by the ICMA terminology as "a standard established for use over a long period from which a current standard can be developed. These standards remain constant for a long period of time and hence they are also termed as long-term standards. They show the trend over a period of time relating to material prices, labour rates, effects of changing methods. They serve at the most as the statistical data and is not used to evaluate current efficiency or inefficiency.

(*b*) **Ideal standard :** It is defined by the ICMA terminology as "a standard which can be attained under the most favourable conditions". Such standards are based on the best possible operating conditions. In other words the productive activity is carried out assuming that there are no breakdown in machineries, no wastage in materials, no idle time. This standard, while using is revised periodically to reflect improvement in methods, materials and technology. It is difficult to attain ideal standard in practice and hence rarely used. Therefore, such standards are used for the purpose of investigation and development but not for controlling day-to-day activities.

(*c*) **Attainable or expected or practical standard :** It is defined by the ICMA termonolgy as "a standard which can be attained if a standard unit of work is carried out efficiently, a machine properly operated or materials properly used. This is most widely used in practice. This standard is based on efficient operating condition though not a perfect condition. This standards covers allowances for normal material wastages, for fatigue, machine breakdown, etc. This standard is more realistic in nature and hence used for cost control, valuing stock and a basis for budgeting.

(*d*) **Current standard :** It is defined by the ICMA terminology as "a standard established for use over a short period of time related to current conditions". This standard is used to reflect the current condition. It can be equated to attainable standard during the period of stable prices and normal conditions.

(*e*) **Normal standard :** It is defined by the ICMA terminology as "the average standard which it is anticipated can be attained over a future period of time, preferably, long enough to cover one trade cycle". Accordingly, this standard may be prepared once in 10 years.

STANDARD HOUR

It is a measure used in standard costing by means of which products in different forms such as solid, liquid and gases are measured. The standard hour is the quantity of output or amount of work which should be produced in one hour. In other words, a standard hour is the expression of the actual output in terms of standard time instead of units. The ICMA terminology defines it as "a hypothetical unit pre-established to represent the amount of work which should be performed in one hour under standard performance". The concept of standard hour has a practical advantage in the measurement of efficiency ratio, activity ratio of an organisation.

Problem 1 : A factory produces three products *X, Y* and *Z*. The standard time allowed are 10 hours, 15 hours and 12 hours respectively. The actual production in January 1993 and February 1993 are as under :

		Jan. 1993 (units)	*Feb. 1993 (units)*
Product	*X*	20,000	12,000
	Y	10,000	12,000
	Z	15,000	18,000

By what percentage has production changed in February over January. If the actual hours paid for each in January and February were 6,00,000 what is the rate of labour efficiency?

Solution :

Statement showing production in Jan. & Feb.

	January		*February*	
	Units	*Std. hrs.*	*Units*	*Std. hrs.*
X	20,000	2,00,000	12,000	1,20,000
Y	10,000	1,50,000	12,000	1,80,000
Z	15,000	1,80,000	18,000	2,16,000
Total	45,000	5,30,000	42,000	5,16,000

Output in February has declined by 14,000 hrs. (5,30,000 – 5,16,000), *i.e.*, by 2.6% over January.

Labour efficiency in :

January $\frac{5,30,000}{6,00,000} \times 100 = 88.33\%$

February $\frac{5,16,000}{6,00,000} \times 100 = 86\%$

STANDARD COST CARD

A standard cost card is used for recording the standard cost. It is prepared for each product or service. It contains particulars relating to quantity and price of materials consumed, time and rate of labour required, overheads and the total cost. A specimen of standard cost card is shown below :

Standard Cost Card

Part No.________ Description________ Batch Qty.________

Elements of cost	Standard rate	Dept. 1	Dept. 2	Dept. 3	Total
Direct material					
Direct labour					
Production overhead					
Administration overhead					
Selling and distribution		____	____	____	____
		____	____	____	____

Fig. 11.1. Specimen showing standard cost card.

PROCEDURE FOR INTRODUCING STANDARD COSTING

Introduction of standard costing system involves a number of steps. Setting up of standard cost for each element of cost—direct material, direct labour and overheads is a complex task. Standards must be setup carefully since a low standard which everyone can achieve does not bring out the best performance. Too high a standard on the other hand, is being impossible to achive, is treated with disdain and indifference. Setting up of standards is not merely an accounting job, it involes the cooperation of various functional departments. The following steps are to be followed while introducing a standard costing in a factory.

1. To study the technical aspects of the factory. This involves a study of the various methods of manufacture and the process involved. The input-output relationship of each process is to be worked out. For this purpose, the total production process has to be sub-divided into various sub-process of manufacture. The pattern of losses—normal and abnormal—in each sub-process over a considerable period of time should be examined. By going through the previous production records, the number of defectives and their cost of rectification should also be looked into. Previous records should be studied in order to work out the normal efficiency of labour in each production process. This study of the technical aspect of the factory is essential since a system of standard cost must be based on the actual situation in the factory.

2. The existing cost system should be reviewed with special reference to the existing records and forms. This is important since the standard costing system has to be established as an extension to the existing system of maintaining cost.

3. The organisation chart showing the various lines of authority and responsibilities should be studied so that the responsibility of supplying basic data regarding the various operations of the undertaking can be established.

4. One of the important steps involved in the implementation of standard costing is to secure the cooperation of all executive in the factory in order to fix the quality and efficient standard. The standard costing will be successful only if it receives full-fledged support from various line managers. If line managers view it merely as an imposition by the accounting department they will never cooperate with it. It is essential to classify that the system is for the benefit and would be run only if they find it useful. A standard cost committee may be formed comprising important line managers to discuss the various problems regarding standard costing system.

5. The existing cost policies specially with regard to the methods of allocation and apportionment of overheads should be studied so that what should constitutes as the standard cost can be clearly defined.

6. The budgetary control and internal control procedures should also be reviewed since the standard costing system is to be built up on the existing system of control and budgeting.

7. A detailed manual should be prepared for the guidance of the staff. This manual should briefly describe the system about to be enforced and should list benefits arising there from. It should then clearly demarcate responsibilities of generating the activity and cost data. The various definitions must be clearly defined and the following procedure of the system outlined :

(*a*) Establishment of standard cost.
(*b*) Target dates for fixing the standards.
(*c*) Target dates for fixing standard cost.
(*d*) Various reports of actual performances to be sent to accounts department for ascertaining the variances.
(*e*) Variance analysis reports to be sent by the accounts department.
(*f*) Any other relevant information.

8. The office-staff required to work the system should be properly trained. When the system goes into force, a number of alterations would be required in the scheme of making entries and in document flow.

9. To fix up the material quantity standard. The following is the procedure involved in setting material quantity standards.

(*a*) *Standardisation of products* : This involves drawing detailed specifications, blue prints, norms for normal wastage.
(*b*) *Classification of products* : This involves preparation of details lists of products to be manufactured.
(*c*) *Standardisation of materials* : This involves determination of quality, specifications, etc. to be used in the standard products.
(*d*) *Bill of materials* : This involves preparation of a bill of materials for each product showing the quantity of materials needed.
(*e*) *Test runs* : This helps in setting standards when production is to be undertaken under regulated conditions.

The material price standards are then fixed based on the following factors :

(*a*) Stock of materials on hand and its value.
(*b*) The prices at which orders for future deliveries of materials have been placed.
(*c*) Possible price fluctuations.

10. To fix up labour quantity standards by applying the following steps :

(*a*) Standardisation and classification of products.
(*b*) Training facilities required.
(*c*) Time and motion studies.
(*d*) Production planning techniques.
(*e*) Selection of right machines, deciding the method of operation.

The labour cost standard can be set up by studying data regarding the wage rates paid.

11. Determination of standard overhead rate : This involes the following steps :

(*a*) Determination of standard overhead cost.
(*b*) Estimation of the level of activity.

By dividing standard overhead for the budget period by the estimated level of activity, the standard overhead rate can be compiled.

12. Determination of standard administration cost : The purpose of setting standard administration cost is to secure maximum service at minimum cost. This objective can be achieved by a study conducted by organisation and method department. Setting up of standards also depends upon standardisation and simplification of office procedure. The standard quantity of work to be performed can be set on the following basis :

(*a*) Past performance.

(*b*) On the advise of O & M studies.

(*c*) Time and motion studies.

13. Determination of standard selling and distribution cost : Selling and distribution expenses bears a close relationship with sales volume. Hence a sales forecast is necessary before setting standard cost for selling and distribution. The classification into fixed and variable will help in setting standard cost.

VARIANCE ANALYSIS

The ICMA terminology defines a variance as "the difference between a standard cost and the comparable actual cost incurred during a given period. The purpose of knowing the variance is to enable the management to exercise control over cost. It enables to know whether the standards set is achieved or not.

Variance analysis has been defined by the terminology as "the process of computing the amount of and isolating the cause of variances between actual costs and standard cost". Thus variance analysis involves : (*a*) computation of individual variances and, (*b*) determination of the cause of each variance. The purpose of variance analysis is to enable management to improve operations, increase efficiency, utilise resources more effectively and reduce cost. To serve these purposes variance analysis must be easy to understand, they must be calculated immediately and the causes must be immediately enquired and remedial measures quickly taken.

A variance is said to be favourable when the actual results are better than the standards and an adverse or unfavourable variance when actuals are not up to the standard. Similarly, a variance is said to be controllable when it is amenable to control by an executive action and an uncontrollable variance when it is not amenable to control by executive action. An unfavourable variance is caused by external environment such as market conditions, fluctuations in demand, supply etc. In other words, no individual in the organisation can be held responsible for it.

Before calculating various cost variances it would be appropriate to know the meaning of the following concepts :

(*a*) *Actual production :* It means actual quantity produced during the actual hours worked.

(*b*) *Budgeted production :* It means the budgeted quantity to be produced during the budgeted hours to be worked.

(*c*) *Standard production :* It means the quantity which should have been produced during the actual hours worked.

(*d*) *Actual cost :* It means the actual quantity produced at the actual cost per unit.

(*e*) *Budgeted cost :* It means the budgeted quantity to be produced at the standard cost per unit.

(*f*) *Standard cost :* It means the actual quantity produced at the standard cost per unit. The various cost variances are as follows :

1. Material Variance

The various material cost variances can be shown under the following chart :

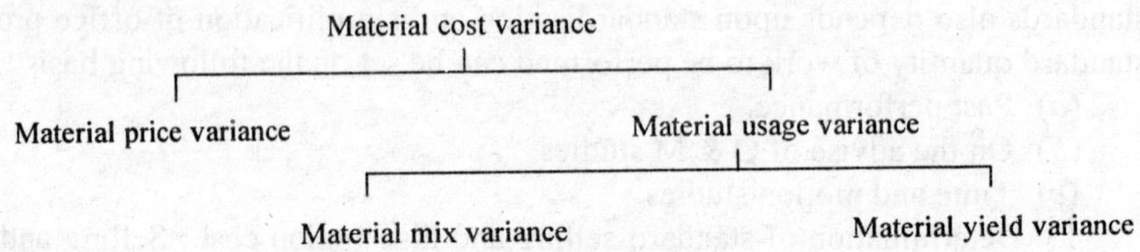

Fig. 26.2. Chart showing material cost variance.

(*a*) **Material cost variance :** It refers to the difference between the standard cost of materials specified and the actual cost of materials used. It arises owing to variation in the price of the material or in its usage. The ICMA terminology defines it as, "the difference between the standard direct material cost of the actual production volume and the actual cost of direct material." The following formula is used to calculate this variance.

Material cost variance = (Standard units × Standard price) – (Actual units × Actual price)

Material cost variance is the aggregate of material price and usage variance.

(*b*) **Material price variance :** It refers to that portion of material cost variance which is due to the difference between the standard price and the actual price paid. The ICMA terminology defines it as, "that portion of the direct material cost variance which is the difference between the standard price specified and the actual price paid for the direct material used". This variance arises on account of extra price paid on the units purchased. It can be calculated at the time of purchase or at the time of usage. Generally the former is preferable. The formula to calculate material price variance is as follows :

Direct material price variance = (Standard price – Actual price) × Actual quantity

The direct material price variance arises on account of the following causes :

(*a*) Higher or lower prices paid than planned.
(*b*) Discounts received or foregone depending upon quantity bought.
(*c*) Purchase of superior or inferior quality of materials than planned.
(*d*) Buying substitute materials.
(*e*) Increase in charges such as transport cost, etc.

(*c*) **Material usage variances :** It refers to that portion of material cost variance owing to the difference between the standard quantity of materials specified and the actual quantity used. The ICMA terminology defines it as "the difference between the standard quantity specified for the actual production and the actual quantity used at standard purchase price". The following formula is used to calculate this variance :

Material usage variance = (Standard quantity – Actual quantity) × Std. price

The following causes give rise to material usgage variance :

(*a*) Low or high yield from material than expected.
(*b*) Gain or loss arising out of substitue materials.
(*c*) Difference in the quality of materials than planned.
(*d*) Increased or decreased quantity of scrap than expected.
(*e*) Use of sub-standard or defective materials.

(*f*) Carelessness in the use of materials.

(*g*) Pilferage.

(*h*) Defective method of production.

(*i*) Wrong mixture of raw materials.

The material usage variance can be sub-divided into material mix and material yield variance.

(*d*) **Material mix variance :** The calculation of this variance arises in those industries where different types of raw materials are mixed to obtain required output. Examples of such industries are fertilisers, chemical, cement, food processing industries and so on. One distinct feature of such industries is, it involves losses by way of evaporation, breakage, shrinkage, etc. and are responsible for difference in the output. The ICMA terminology defines it as "the difference between total quantity in standard proportion, priced at the standard price and the actual quantity of materials used priced the standard price. In simple words it is that portion of material usage variance which is due to the difference between the standard and the actual composition of mixture.

Material mix variance may arise under the following two situations :

1. Where the ratio of standard mix differ from the ratio of actual mix, but the total quantity of both the actual mix and standard mix remaining the same.

The following formula is used in this situation.

$$\text{Material mix variance} = (\text{Revised std. qty.} - \text{Actual qty.}) \times \text{Std. price}$$

In this case the revised standard quantity is the same as the standard quantity.

2. Where both the ratio as well as total quantity differ between the standard and the actual mix.

The above formula is applicable in this situation also with a difference in calculating the revised standard quantity. The following formula is used to calculates the revised standard quantity.

$$\text{Revised std. qty.} = \frac{\text{Total weight of actual mix}}{\text{Total weight of std. mix}} \times \text{Std. qty. of material in question}$$

This is because, the standard quantity of each material will be revised, when the total weight of actual mix varies from the total weight of standard mix.

(*e*) **Material yield variance :** It is the difference between the standard yield specified and the actual yield obtained. The ICMA terminology defines it as "the difference between the standard yield of the actual material input and the actual yield both valued at the standard material cost.

There are two situations under which material yield variance can arise, *viz.*, (*i*) where actual mix does not differ from standard mix. In this situation the following formula is used

$$\text{Material yield variance} = (\text{Total actual yield} - \text{Total std. yield}) \times \text{Std. yield rate}$$

$$\textit{where}, \text{ Std. yield rate} = \frac{\text{Standard cost of std. mix}}{\text{Net standard output}}$$

(*ii*) Where actual mix differ from standard mix. The following formula is used in this situation.

$$\text{Material yield variance} = (\text{Actual yield} - \text{Revised std. yield}) \times \text{Std. yield rate}$$

$$\textit{where}, \text{ Std. yield rate} = \frac{\text{Std. cost of revised std. mix}}{\text{Net std. output}}$$

Material yield variance will arise owing to the following causes :

(*a*) Use of sub-standard quality of materials.

(*b*) Losses arising out of chemical reaction.

(c) Defective method of production.

(*d*) Inadequete supervison.

Problem 2 : Bello Chemical Industries provide the following information from their records :

For making 10 kgs. of OMO, the standard material requirement is :

Material	*Qty. (kg.)*	*Rate per kg.*
X	8	6
Y	4	4

During December 1990, 100 kgs. of OMO were produced. The actual consumption of material is as under :

Material	*Qty. (kg.)*	*Rate per kg.*
X	75	7
Y	50	5

Calculate (*i*) Material cost variance.

(*ii*) Material price variance.

(*iii*) Material usage variance. (*University of Delhi, B.Com. (Hons.), 1991*)

Solution :

For 100 kgs. of OMO

Material	*Standard*		*Actuals*	
	Qty.	*Rate*	*Qty.*	*Rate*
X	80*[1]	6	75	7
Y	40*[2]	4	50	5

(*i*) Material cost variance = (Std. units × Std. price) – (Actual units × Actual price)

X = (80 × 6) – (75 × 7)

= 480 – 525 = – 45 (*A*)

Y = (40 × 4) – (50 × 5)

= 160 – 250 = – 90 (*A*)

Total (–) 135 (*A*)

(*ii*) Material price variance = (Std. price – Actual price) × Actual qty.

X = (6 – 7) × 75 = 75 (*A*)

Y = (4 – 5) × 50 = 50 (*A*)

Total 125 (*A*)

(*iii*) Material usage variance = (Std. qty. – Actual qty.) × Std. price

X = (80 – 75) × 6 = 30 *F*

Y = (40 – 50) × 4 = 40 *A*

Total 10 A

Varification :

Material cost variance = Material price variance + Material usage variance

135 (*A*) = 125 *A* + 10*A*

*[1] For 10 kgs. → 8kg in requried

For 100 kgs. → $\frac{8}{10} \times 100 = 80$

*[2] For 10 kgs. → 4 kg. is required

For 100 kgs. → ? $\frac{4}{10} \times 100 = 40$

Problem 3 : From the given data, calculate :

(*a*) Material price variance.

(*b*) Material usage variance.

(*c*) Material cost variance.

Standard :

(1) 250 kg. of raw materials is required for producing 175 kgs. of finished products.

(2) Price of material per kgs. Rs. 4

Actuals :

(1) Production 52,500 kg.

(2) Materials consumed 70,000 kgs.

(3) Cost of materials Rs. 2,73,000

(*SV, University, B.Com., April 1999*)

Solution :

$$\text{Calculation of Actual price} = \frac{\text{Actual Material Cost}}{\text{Actual Materials Consumed}}$$

$$= \frac{2,73,000}{70,000 \text{ kg}} = \text{Rs. } 3.90 \text{ per kg.}$$

(1) Material price variance = (Std. Price – Actual Price) × Actual usage
= (4.00 – 3.90) × 70,000
= 0.10 × 70,000 = 7,000 *F*

Calculation of Standard usage

For 175 kgs. of production, 250 kgs. of raw materials

For 52,500 kgs. → ?

$$\frac{52,500}{175} \times 250 = 75,000 \text{ kgs.}$$

(2) Material usage variance = Std. qty. – Actual qty.) × Std. price
= (75,000 – 70,000) × 4
= 5,000 × 4 = 20,000 *F*

(3) Material cost variance = (Std. qty. × Std. price) – (Actual qty. – Actual price)
= (75,000 × 4) – (70,000 × 3.90)
= 3,00,000 – 2,73,000
= 27,000 *F*

Varification :

Material cost variance = Material price variance + Material usage variance

27,000 *F* = 7,000 *F* + 20,000 *F*

27,000 *F* = 27,000 *F*

Problem 4 : From the given data below, calculate (*i*) the material price variance, (*ii*) Material usage variance, (*iii*) Material cost variance

Quantity of materials purchased	3,000 units
Value of materials purchased	Rs. 9,000
Standard quantity of materials required per tonne of output	30 units
Standard rate of materials	Rs. 2.50 per unit
Opening stock of materials	NIL
Closing stock of materials	500 units
Output during the period	80 tonnes

Solution :

Calculation of quantity of materials used

Qty. of opening stock of materials	Nil
Add : Qty. of materials purchased	3,000
	3,000
Less : Qty. of closing stock of materials	500
	2,500

Calculation of actual price of materials purchased

$$= \frac{\text{Value of materials purchased}}{\text{Qty. of materials purchased}}$$

$$= \frac{9,000}{3,000} = 3$$

Calculation of standard qty. of materials for actual output

= Std. qty. of materials required per tonne of output × Actual output during the year
= 30 × 80 = 2,400 units

(1) Material price variance = (Std. price – Actual price) × Actual qty.
= (2.50 – 3.00) × 2,500
= 0.50 × 2,500 = 1,250 *A*

(2) Material usage variance = (Std. qty. – Actual qty.) × Std. price
= (2,400 – 2,500) × 2.50
= 100 × 2.50 = 250

(3) Material cost variance = (Std. qty. × Std. rate) – (Actual qty. × Actual rate)
= 2,400 × 2.50) – (2,500 × 3)
= 6,000 – 7,500 = Rs. 1,500 *(A)*.

Problem 4 : From the following data extracted from the books Arvind Parimal Works, calculate the material mix variance :

	Standard	*Actual*
Material *A*	70 units @ Rs. 6 per unit	60 units @ Rs. 10 per unit
Material *B*	30 units @ Rs. 4 per unit	40 units @ Rs. 2 per unit
Output	100 units	100 units

Solution : In this problem the total weight of the standard mix (70 + 30) = 100 units and the total weight of the actual mix (60 + 40) = 100 units are the same. So the revised standard quantity of each material will be the same as its standrad quantity.

Materials mix variance = Revised Std. qty. – Actual qty.) × Std. price
A = (70 – 60) × 6
= 10 × 6 = 60 *F*
B = (30 – 40) × 4
= 10 × 4 = 40 *A*

Total material mix variance :

Material *A*	= 60	F
Material *B*	= 40	A
	20	F

Problem 5 : Calculate the material mix variance from the following data :

	Standard			*Actual*		
	Qty. kg.	*Rate Rs.*	*Amt. Rs.*	*Qty. kg.*	*Rate Rs.*	*Amt. Rs.*
Material *X*	6	1.50	9	5	2.40	12
Material *Y*	2	3.50	7	1	6.00	6
	8	2.00	16	6	3.60	18

Solution : In this problem, the total standard mix is different from the total actual mix. So, we have to calculate the revised standard quantity in respect of each materials.

$$\frac{\text{Total weight of actual mix}}{\text{Total weight of standard mix}} \times \text{Std. Qty. of the material in the mix}$$

Material A $= \frac{6}{8} \times 6 = 4.5$ kgs.

Material B $= \frac{6}{8} \times 2 = 1.5$ kgs.

Materials mix variance = Revised Std. Qty. – Actual Qty.) × Std. price

A = (4.5 – 5) × 1.50
= 0.5 × 1.50 = 0.75 (A)

B = (1.5 – 1) × 3.50
= 0.50 × 3.50 = 1.75 (F)

Net material mix variance :

Material A = 0.75 (A)
Material B = 1.75 (F)

1.00 (F)

Problem 6 : From the given data below, calculate the material price variance, the material usage variance, material cost variance and material mix variance.

Consumption per 100 units of product

Raw material	*Standard*	*Actual*
A	40 units @ Rs. 50 per unit	50 units @ Rs. 50 per unit
B	60 units @ Rs. 40 per unit	60 units @ Rs. 45 per unit

(*S.V. University, B.Com., October 1999*)

Solution :

Calculation of actual quantity used

A = 100 units @ 50 units per unit = 5,000 units
B = 100 units @ 60 units per unit = 6,000 units

(1) Material price variance = (Std. price – Actual price) × Actual Qty.

A = (50 – 50) × 5,000
= 0 × 5,000 = Nil

B = (40 – 45) × 6,000
= 5 – 6,000 = 30,000 A

Calculation of Standard quantity

A = 100 × 40 = 4,000 units
B = 100 × 60 = 6,000 units

(2) Materials usage variance = (Std. Qty. – Actual Qty.) × Std. price

A = (4,000 – 5,000) × 50
= 1,000 × 50= 50,000 A

B = (6,000 – 6,000) × 40
= 0 × 40 = NIL

(3) Material cost variance = (Std. Qty. × Std. price) – (Actual Qty. × Actual price)

A = (4,000 × 50) – (5,000 × 50)
= 2,00,000 – 2,50,000 = 50,000 (A)

B = (6,000 × 40) – (6,000 × 45)
= 2,40,000 – 2,70,000 = 30,000 (A)

Verification :

	Material cost variance	=	Material price variance + Material usage variance
A	50,000 A	=	NIL + 50,000 A
B	30,000 A	=	30,000 A + NIL

(4) Calculation of Revised Std. Qty.

$$\text{Revised Std. Qty.} = \frac{\text{Total weight of Actual mix}}{\text{Total weight of Std. mix}} \times \text{Std. Qty. of material in question}$$

$$A = \frac{11,000}{10,000} \times 4,000 = 4,400$$

$$B = \frac{11,000}{10,000} \times 6,000 = 6,600$$

Material mix variance = (Revised Std. Qty. – Actual Qty.) × Std. price

A = (4,400 – 5,000) × 50
= 600 × 50 = 30,000 *A*

B = (6,600 – 6,000) × 40
= 600 × 40 = 24,000 *F*

Problem 7 : Mixers Ltd. is engaged in producing a standard mix by using 60 kgs. of Chemical *X* and 40 kgs. of Chemical *Y*. The standard loss of production is 30%. The standard price of *X* is Rs. 5 per kg. and *Y* is Rs. 10 per kgs.

The actual mix and yield were as follows :

X — 80 kgs. @ Rs. 4.5 per kg.
Y — 70 kgs. @ Rs. 8 per kg.

Actual yield is 115 kgs.

Calculate material variances. *(CS, Inter, December 1998)*

Solution :

	Standard cost			Actual cost			Standard cost for actual input qty.		
	Qty.	Rate	Amt.	Qty.	Rate	Amt.	Qty.	Rate	Amt.
$X = \frac{60}{70} \times 115$	= 98.571	5	493	80	4.50	360	80	5	400
$Y = \frac{40}{70} \times 115$	= 65.714	10	657	70	8.00	560	70	10	700
	164.3		1,150	150		920	150		1,100
Less : 30%	49.3		–	35		–			
	115		1,150	115		920			

(1) Material cost variance = (SQ × SR) – (AQ × AR)

X = (98.571 × 5) – (80 × 4.50)
= 492.86 – 360 = 132.86 *F*

Y = (65.714 × 10) – (70 × 8)
= 657.14 – 560 = 97.14 *F*

230 *F*

(2) Material usage variance = (SQ – AQ) × SP

X = (98.571 – 80) × 5 = 92.86 *F*

Y = (65.714 – 70) × 10 = 42.86 *A*

50.00 *F*

(3) Material price variance = (SP – AP) × SQ

X = (5 – 4.50) × 80 = 40 *F*

Y = (10 – 8) × 70 = 140 *F*

180 *F*

(4) *Calculation of Revised Std. Qty.*

$$\frac{\text{Total weight of Actual Mix}}{\text{Total weight of std. mix}} \times \text{Std. Qty. of material in question}$$

$$X = \frac{150}{164.3} \times 98.6 = 90$$

$$Y = \frac{150}{164.3} \times 65.7 = 60$$

Material mix variance = (Revised Std. Qty. – Actual Qty.) × Std. price

X = (90 – 80) × 5 = 50 F

Y = (60 – 70) × 10 = 100 A

50 A

(5) *Calculation of standard yield*

$$\frac{115}{164.3} \times 150 = 105 \text{ kgs.}$$

Material yield variance = (Actual yield – Std. yield) × Std. price

= (115 – 105) × 10 = 100 F

Problem 8 : The standard cost of a certain chemical mixture was :

40% Materials A at Rs. 200 per ton

60% Material B at Rs. 300 per ton

A standard loss of 10% is expected in production. During the period the following materials were used :

90 tons. Material A at the cost of Rs. 180 per ton.

110 tons. Material B at the cost of Rs. 340 per ton.

The weight produced was 182 tons of good production.

Calculate :

(*i*) Material price variance

(*ii*) Material usage variance

(*iii*) Material mix variance

(*iv*) Material yield variance

(*CS, Inter, Dec. 1997*)

Solution :

Calculation of variances

		Standard			*Actual*		
		Qty.	*Rate*	*Amount*	*Qty.*	*Rate*	*Amt.*
A	40%	80	200	16,000	90	180	16,200
B	60%	120	300	36,000	110	340	37,400
		200		52,000	200		53,600
Less :	Normal Loss	20			18		
		180			182		

(*i*) Material price variance = (SP – AP) × AQ

A = (200 – 180) × 90

= 20 × 90 = 1800 F

B = (300 – 340) × 110

= 40 × 110 = 4400 A

2600 A

(*ii*) *Material usage variance :*

Calculation of Std. Qty. for actual output

$$\frac{\text{Std. Qty.}}{\text{Std. output}} \times \text{Actual output}$$

$$A = \frac{80}{100} \times 182 = 80$$

$$B = \frac{120}{180} \times 182 = 121$$

Material usage variance = (Std. Qty. for actual output – Actual Qty) × Std. price

A = (80 – 90) × 200 = 2,000 *A*

B = (121 – 110) × 300 = 330 *F*

1,670 *A*

(iii) Material mix variance :

As the Std. mix (200) is equal to actual mix (200), Revised Std. Qty. for both *A* & *B* is the same as std. qty.

Material mix variance = (Revised Std. Qty. – Actual Qty.) × Std. price

A = (80 – 90) × 200

= 10 × 200 = 2,000 *A*

B = (120 – 110) × 300

= 10 × 300 = 3,000 *F*

= 1,000 *F*

Calculation of std. cost per unit

$$= \frac{\text{Total cost of Std. Mix}}{\text{Std. Output}}$$

$$= \frac{52{,}000}{180} = \text{Rs. } 288.88$$

(*iv*) Material yield variance = (Std. output for actual mix – Actual output) × Std. yield price

= (180 – 182) × 288.88

= 2 × 288.88 = 577

Problem 9 : The following information has been extracted from the records of a chemical company :

Standard price — Raw material *A* — Rs. 2 per kg.

— Raw material *B* — Rs. 10 per kg.

Standard usage — '*A*' 75% — 2,250 kgs.

— 'B' 25% — 750 kgs.

Standard yield — 90%

In a period, the actual costs, usages and output were as follows :

Used : 2,200 kgs. of '*A*' costing Rs. 4,650

800 kgs. of '*B*' costing Rs. 7,850

Output : 2,850 kgs. of products

Calculate material cost variance. *(CS, Inter, June 1994)*

Solution :

Calculation of variances

		Standard			Actual		
		Qty.	*Rate*	*Amt.*	*Qty.*	*Rate*	*Amt.*
A	75%	2,250	2	4,500	2,200	2.11	4,650
B	25%	750	10	7,500	800	9.81	7,850
		3,000			3,000		
Less :	10% loss	300			150		
		2,700			2,850		

Material cost variance = (SQ × SP) – (AQ × AP)

A = (2,250 × 2) – (2,200 × 2.11)

= 4,500 – 4,650 = 150 *A*

B = (750 × 10) – (800 × 9.81)

= 7,500 – 7,850 = 350 *A*

500 *A*

Material price variance = (AP – SP) × AQ

A = (2.11 – 2) × 2,200

= 11 × 2,200 = 242 *A*

B	= (9.81 – 10) × 800		
	= 0.19 × 800		= 152 *F*
			90 *A*

Calculation of Std. Qty for actual output :

$$= \frac{\text{Std. Qty.}}{\text{Std. output}} \times \text{Actual output}$$

$$A = \frac{2,250}{2,700} \times 2,850 = 2,375$$

$$B = \frac{750}{2,700} \times 2,850 = 792$$

Material usage variance	= (Std. Qty. for actual output – Actual Qty.) × Std. price		
A	= (2,375 – 2,200) × 2		
	= 175 × 2	=	350 *F*
B	= (792 – 800) × 10		
	8 × 10	=	80 *A*
			270 *F*
Material mix variance	= (Revised Std. Qty. – Actual Qty.) × Std. price		
A	= (2,250 – 2,200) × 2		
	= 50 × 2	=	100 *F*
B	= (750 – 800) × 10		
	= 50 × 10	=	500 *A*
			400 *A*

Calculation of Std. yield price :

$$\frac{\text{Std. cost of std. mix}}{\text{Net std. output}}$$

$$= \frac{12,000}{2,700} = 4.44$$

Material yeild variance = (Total actual yield – Total Std. yield) × Std. yield price
= (2,850 – 2,700) × 4.44
= 150 × 4.44 = 666 *F*

Problem 10 : Product '*A*' is manufactured by mixing three basic raw materials *X*, *Y* and *Z* in the standard proportion of 5 : 3 : 2 and processing the mixture. Production is carried out in batches to give a standard output of 100 kg. from an input of 120 kg. per batch. The company operates standard costing system for cost control.

In the month of December 1998, due to non-availability of raw material, the company had to change the standard propartion. Further details regarding the standards and actual consumption during December 1998 are given below :

Materials	*Standard for 1998-99*		*Actuals for December 1998*	
	Proportion	*Price per kg. (Rs.)*	*Proportion*	*Price per kg. (Rs.)*
X	50	20	60	19
Y	30	10	20	11
Z	20	5	20	6
	100		100	

In December 1998, 50 batches were processed to produce 4,800 kg. of A.
Calculate material price usage, mix and yield variance. (*ICWA, Inter, June 1999*)

Solution :

Material	Std. Qty of materials required per batch and standard cost				Actual cost incurred during December 1998			
	Qty.		*Rate*	*Amt.*	*Qty*	*Total Qty. for 50 batches*	*Rate*	*Amt.*
X	$\frac{5}{10} \times 120 =$	60	20	1,200	$\frac{60}{100} \times 120 =$ 72	3,600 kg.	19	68,400
Y	$\frac{3}{10} \times 120 =$	36	10	360	$\frac{20}{100} \times 120 =$ 24	1,200 kg.	11	13,200
Z	$\frac{2}{10} \times 120 =$	24	5	120	$\frac{20}{100} \times 120 =$ 24	1,200 kg.	6	7,200
		120		1,680	120	6,000		88,800
Less : Loss		20			20			
		100			100			

(1) Material price variance = (Std. price – Actual price) × Actual Qty.

X = (20 – 19) × 3,600 = 3,600 *F*

Y = (10 – 11) × 1,200 = 1,200 *A*

Z = (5 – 6) × 1,200 = 1,200 *A*

1,200 *A*

(2) Material usage variance = (Std. usage – Actual usage) × Std. price

X $= (4{,}800 \times \frac{60}{100} - 3{,}600) \times 20$

= (2,880 – 3600) × 20 = 14,400 *A*

Y $= (4{,}800 \times \frac{36}{100} - 1{,}200) \times 10$

= 1,728 – 1,200) × 10 = 5,280 *F*

Z $= (4{,}800 \times \frac{24}{100} - 1{,}200) \times 5$

= (1,152 – 1,200) × 5 = 240 *A*

9,360 *A*

(3) Material mix variance = (Std. mix for actual qty. of 50 batches – Actual mix of actual qty.) × Std. price

X = (50 × 60 kg. – 3,600) × 20

= (3,000 – 3,600) × 20 = 12,000 (*A*)

Y = (50 × 36 kg. – 1,200) × 10 = 6,000 (*F*)

Z = (50 – 24 kg. – 1,200) × 5 = Nil

6,000 *A*

(4) Material yield variance = (Std. yield from 50 batches – Actual yield) × Std. cost of output

= (50 × 100 kgs. – 4,800) × 16.80

= 200 × 16.80 = 3,360 *A*

Working Note :

$$\text{Std. cost of output} = \frac{\text{Std. cost}}{\text{Std. output}} = \frac{1{,}680}{100} = 16.80$$

Problem 11 : S.V. Ltd. manufactures a simple product, the standard mix of which is

Material *A* 60% at Rs. 20 per kg.

Material *B* 40% at Rs. 10 per kg

Normal loss in production is 20% of input. Due to shortage of material *A*, the standard mix was changed. Actual result for March 1989 were :

Material *A* 105 kg. at Rs. 20 per kg.
Material *B* 95 kg. at Rs. 9 per kg.
Input 200 kg.
Loss 35 kg.
Output 165 kg.

Calculate : (*i*) Material price variance, (*ii*) Material usage variance, (*iii*) Material mix variance, (*iv*) Material yield variance. (*University of Delhi, B.Com., (Hons.) 1990*)

Solution :

Calculation of variance

	Standard			*Actual*		
	Qty.	*Rate*	*Amout*	*Qty.*	*Rate*	*Amount*
A 60%	120	20	2,400	105	20	2,100
B 40%	80	10	800	95	9	855
	200		3,200	200		2,955
Normal loss 20%	40			35		
Output	160			165		

(1) Material price variance = (Standard price – Actual price) × Actual Quantity

A = (20 – 20) × 105= 0

B = (10 – 9) × 95 = 95 *F*

Total material price variance = 0 + 95 = 95 *F*

(2) Material usage variance = (Standard quantity for actul output *[1] – Actual quantity for actual output) × Std. price

*[1]Standard quantity for actual output = $\frac{\text{Standard quantity}}{\text{Standard output}}$ × Actual output

$$A = \frac{120}{160} \times 165$$

$$B = \frac{80}{160} \times 165$$

$$\text{MUV for } A = \left(\frac{120}{160} \times 165 - 105\right) \times 20$$

$= (123.75 – 105) \times 20$

= Rs. 2,475 (*F*)

$$\text{MUV for B} = \left(\frac{80}{100} \times 165 - 95\right) \times 10$$

$= (82.5 – 95) \times 10$

= Rs. 125 (*A*)

Total MUV = 2,475 – 125 = Rs. 2,350 (*F*)

(3) Material mix variance= (Revised standard quantity – Actual mix of actual quantity) × Std. price

Revised standard quantity = $\frac{\text{Std. Qty. for each material}}{\text{Std. qty. total}}$ × Actual qty. total

$$A = \frac{120}{200} \times 200 = 120$$

$$B = \frac{80}{200} \times 200 = 80$$

As Std. mix (200) = Actual mix (200)

∴ Revised standard quantity for both *A* and *B* is the same as standard quantity

$$\text{MMV for } A = (120 - 105) \times 20$$
$$= 15 \times 20 = 300\ F$$
$$\text{MMB for } B = (80 - 95) \times 10$$
$$= -15 \times 10 = 150\ A$$
$$\text{Total MMV} = 300 - 150 = \text{Rs. } 150\ F$$

(4) Material yield variance = (Standard output for actual mix – Actual output) × Std. yield price

$$\text{Standard output for actual mix} = \frac{\text{Standard output}}{\text{Standard mix}} \times \text{Actual mix}$$
$$= \frac{160}{200} \times 200 = 160$$
$$\text{Standard cost per unit} = \frac{\text{Total cost of Std. mix}}{\text{Std. output}}$$
$$= \frac{3,200}{160} = \text{Rs. } 20 \text{ per unit}$$
$$\text{MYV} = (160 - 165) \times 20$$
$$= -5 \times 20 = 100\ (A)$$

Problem 12 : *ABC* Ltd. produces an article by blending two basic raw materials. It operates a standard costing system and the following standards have been set for raw materials.

Material	*Standard mix*	*Standard price (Rs. per kg.)*
A	40%	4
B	60%	3

The standard loss in processing is 15%. During April 1990, the company produced 1,700 kgs. of finished output.

The position of stock and purchases for the month of April 1990 are as under :

Material	*Stock on 1.4.90*	*Stock on 30.4.90*	*Purchased during April 1990*	
	(kgs.)	*(kgs.)*	*Cost*	*(Rs.)*
A	35	5	800	3,400
B	40	50	1,200	3,000

Calculate the following variances :

(*i*) Material price variance.
(*ii*) Material usage variance.
(*iii*) Material yield variance.
(*iv*) Material mix variance and
(*v*) Total material cost variance. (*C.S., Inter, Dec. 1991; CA, Inter, Nov. 1991*)

Solution :

Type of material	*Standard*			*Actual*		
	Qty. kg.	*Rate Rs.*	*Amt.*	*Qty. kg.*	*Rate Rs.*	*Amt.*
A	800	4	3,200	35	4	140
				795	4.25	3378.75
B	1,200	3	3,600	40	3	120
				1,150	2.50	2,875
	2,000		6,800	2,020		6,513.75

(*i*) Material price variance = (Std. rate – Actual rate) × Actual qty.

Material A : Since the actual price and standard price in respect of 35 kg. of raw materials *S* are the same, there will be no price variance in respect of this quantity. Price variance will be in respect of only 795 kg. as shown below :

$$(4 - 4.25) \times 795 = \text{Rs. } 198.75\ (A)$$

Material B : In respect of material *B* also, price variance will be in respect of 1,150 kg. only as shown below :

$$(\text{Rs. } 3 - 2.50) \times 1{,}150 = \text{Rs. } 575\ (F)$$

$$\text{Total} = \text{Rs. } 198.75\ (A) + 575\ (F) = \text{Rs. } 376.25\ (F)$$

(*ii*) Material usage variance = Std. quantity for actual output – Actual qty.) × Std. rate

A	=	(800 – 830) × 4	=	120 (*A*)
B	=	(1,200 – 1,190) × 3	=	30 (*F*)
				Rs. 90 (*A*)

(*iii*) Material yield variance = (Std. output for actual mix – Actual output) × Std. cost per unit

$$= \left(\frac{1{,}700}{2{,}000} \times 2{,}020 - 1{,}700\right) \times 4$$

$$= (1{,}717 - 1{,}700) \times 4 = \text{Rs. } 68\ (A)$$

(*iv*) Material mix variance = (Revised std. quantity – Actual qty.) × Std. rate

Revised std. qty. *A* $= \dfrac{2{,}020}{2{,}000} \times 800 = 808$ kg.

Revised std. qty *B* $= \dfrac{2{,}020}{2{,}000} \times 1{,}200 = 12.12$ kg.

Material *A* = (808 – 830) × 4 = 88 (*A*)

Material *B* = (1,212 – 1,190) × 3 = 66 (*F*)

Rs. 22 (*A*)

(*v*) Total material cost variance = Std. cost for actual output – Actual cost

6,800 – 6,513.75 = 286.25 (*F*)

Verification :

Material cost variance = Material price variance + Material usage variance

= 376.25 (*F*) + 90 (*A*) = 286.25 (F)

Material usage variance = Material mix variance + Material yield variance

= 22 (*A*) + 68 (*A*) = 90 (*A*)

Working Notes :

(1) The standard loss being 15%. It means to produce, 1,700 kg. of the article, standard quantity of material required is :

$$\frac{100}{85} \times 1{,}700 \text{ kgs.} = 2{,}000 \text{ kgs.}$$

Out of 2,000 kg. of material used 40% is of type *A* and 60% is of type *B*, *i.e.*,
Standard use for actual output

Material *A* $= 2{,}000 \times \dfrac{40}{100} = 800$ kg.

Material *B* $= 2{,}000 \times \dfrac{60}{100} = 1{,}200$ kgs.

Actaul usage of material = Opening stock + Purchases – Closing stock

A = 35 + 800 – 5 = 830 kgs.

B = 40 + 1,200 – 50 = 1,190 kgs.

(2) Standard cost per unit $= \dfrac{\text{Total standard cost}}{\text{Total standard output of std. mix}}$

$$= \frac{\text{Rs. } 6{,}800}{1{,}700} = \text{Rs. } 4 \text{ per kg.}$$

Problem 13 : One kilogram of product *K* requires two chemicals *A* and *B*. The following were the details of product *K* for the month of June 87 :

(*a*) Standard mix chemical *A* 50% and chemical *B* 50%.
(*b*) Standard price kilogram of chemical *A* Rs. 12 and chemical *B* Rs. 15.
(*c*) Actual input of chemical *B* 70 kilograms.
(*d*) Actual price per kilogram of chemical *A* Rs. 15.
(*e*) Standard normal loss 10% of total input.
(*f*) Materials cost variance total Rs. 650 adverse.
(*g*) Material yield variance total Rs. 135 adverse. (*CA, Inter, November 1987*)

Solution : In this problem actual output is not given. So let actual output be = 96 kg.

(*i*) Calculation of standard mix of input

	Qty. (Kg.)	*Price (Rs.)*	*Amount (Rs.)*
Chemical *A*	50	12	600
Chemical *B*	50	15	750
	100	13.50	1,350
Standard loss	10		
	90		1,350

(*ii*) Calculation standard rate of output

$$\frac{\text{Rs. } 1350}{90} = \text{Rs. } 15 \text{ per kg.}$$

(*iii*) Calculation of standard yield for actual output

Yield variance = (Std. yield for actual input – Actual yield) × Std. rate of output

135 (*A*) = (Std. yield for actual input – 90 kg.) × 15

Std. yield for actual input = 99 kgs.

***(iv)* Calculation of actual output**

For 99 kg. of input, the output is 100 kg.

For 90 kgs. of input, output is $\frac{100}{90} \times 99 = 110$ kgs.

(*v*) Calculation of actual input of chemical A

= 110 kg. – Actual input of chemical B

= 110 kgs. – 70 kg. = 40 kg.

(*vi*) Material cost variance is given 650 (*A*). hence the actual cost of actual mix of chemical *A* and *B* will be Rs. 1,350 + 650 = 2,000

(*vii*) The actual cost of 40 kg. of chemical *A* @ Rs. 15 per kg. is Rs. 600. Thus the cost of one kg. of chemical *B* used is Rs. $\frac{2{,}000 - 600}{70}$ = Rs. 20 per kg.

(*viii*) Standard cost of actual mix

= Rs. 12 × 40 kg. + Rs. 15 × 70 kg. = Rs. 1,530

(1) Material mix variance = (per kg. std. cost of std. mix – Per kg, std. cost of actual mix) – Actual qty.

$$= \left(\frac{1{,}350}{100} - \frac{1{,}530}{110}\right) \times 110 \text{ kg.}$$

= Rs. 45 (*A*)

(2) Material usage variance = (Std. qty. – Actual qty.) × Std. price

A = (50 – 40) × 12 = 120 *F*

B = (50 – 70) × 15 = 300 *A*

180 *A*

(3) Material price variance = (Std. price – Actual price) × Actual qty.

A = (12 – 15) × 40 = 120 A

B = (15 – 20) × 70 = 350 A

470 A

(4) Actual loss of actual input :

Actual total input	=	110 kg.
Less : Actual output	=	90 kg.
Actual loss		20 kg.

(5) Actual input of chemical A = 40 kg. refer working note v.

(6) Actual price per kg. of chemical B = Rs. 20 (refer to working note vii.)

Problem 14 : *XYZ* Company manufactures a product *ABC* by mixing three raw materials. For every 100 kg. of *ABC*, 125 kg. of raw materials are used. In April 1990, there was an output of 5,600 kg. of *ABC*. The standard actual particulars of April 1990 are as follows :

Raw material	*Standard*		*Actual*	
	Mix %	*Price per kg.* *Rs.*	*Mix* %	*Price per kg.* *Rs.*
Raw material *I*	50	40	60	42
Raw material *II*	30	20	20	16
Raw material *III*	20	10	20	12

Calculate all variances (*ICWA, Inter, June 1990*)

Solution : Actual material used = $\frac{125 \text{ kg}}{100} \times 5{,}600 = 7{,}000$

(*A*) Actual cost of actual material used

I	60% of 7,000	=	4,200 kg. × 42	=	1,76,400
II	20% of 7,000	=	1,400 kg. × 16	=	22,400
III	20% of 7,000	=	1,400 kg. × 12	=	16,800
					2,15,600

(*B*) Standard cost of material used

I	4,200 × 40	=	1,68,000
II	1,400 × 20	=	28,000
III	1,400 × 10	=	14,000

(*C*) Standard cost of materials if it had been used in standard production

I	3,500 × 40	=	1,40,000
II	2,100 × 20	=	42,000
III	1,400 × 10	=	14,000
			1,96,000

(*D*) Standard cost of production (for 100 kg.)

I	62.50 kg. × 40	=	2,500
II	37.50 kg. × 20	=	750
III	25 kg. × 10	=	250

Standard cost for output of 5,600 kg. $= \frac{3{,}500}{100} \times 5{,}600$

Rs. = 1,96,000

Material price variance	=	*A*	–	*B*			
	=	2,15,600	–	10,000	=	5,600	(*A*)
Material mix variance	=	*B*	–	*C*			
	=	2,10,000	–	1,96,000	=	14,000	(*A*)
Material yield variance	=	*C*	–	*D*			
	=	1,96,000	–	1,96,000	=	NIL	

Material usage variance	=	B – D	
	=	2,10,000 – 1,96,000 = 14,0,000 (*A*)	
Material cost variance	=	Material price variance +	Materials usage variance
19,600 (*A*)	=	5,600 (*A*) +	14,000 (*A*)

or $D - A$ = 1,96,000 – 2,15,600 = 19,600 (*A*)

2. Labour Cost Variance

The various labour cost variances can be shown under the following chart :

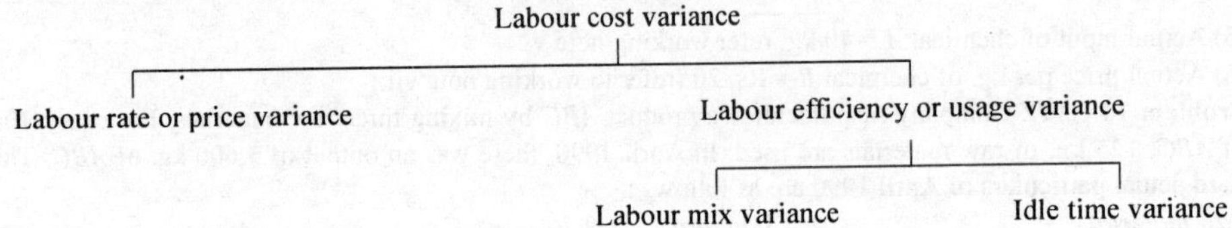

Fig. 26.3. Chart showing labour cost variance.

(A) Labour cost variance

This is also known as direct wages variance and represents the difference between standard direct wages specified for the actual production and the actual direct wages paid. The formula to calculate labour cost variance is as follows :

Labour cost variance = (Actual hours × Actual rate) – (Std. hours × Std. rate)

Labour cost variance is analysed into the following two variances.

(*a*) Labour rate or price variance : The ICMA terminology defines labour rate variance as "the difference between the standard and actual direct labour hour rate per hour for the total hours worked". In other words it is that portion of labour cost variance owing to difference between the actual rate and standard rate of pay specified. The following formula is used for calculating this variance.

Labour rate variance = (Standard rate – Actual rate) × Actual hour

The following factors are responsible for direct labour rate variance :

(*i*) Payment of high wage rate than estimated.
(*ii*) Use of more skilled or unskilled labourers than planned.
(*iii*) Payment of excess bonus than estimated.
(*iv*) Payment of more overtime premium than estimated.

(*b*) Labour Efficiency or Usage Variance : It refers to that portion of the wage variance which is due to the difference between the standard labour hours specified and the actual labour hours expended. The following formula is used to calculate this variance.

Labour efficiency variance = (Standard hours – Actual hours) × Standard rate

The following factors cause this variance :

(*a*) Use of inferior grade of labour.
(*b*) Lack of good supervision.
(*c*) Use of sub-standard quality of materials.
(*d*) Breakdown of machines during production process.
(*e*) Inadequate working conditions such as poor lighting, lack of ventilation, heating, etc.

(*f*) Lack of proper production organisation involving defective production planning, routing, scheduling, inspection, etc.

B. Idle Time Variance

Sometimes idle time may occur in spite of fixing standard carefully. Such idle time should not be included in efficiency variance but shown separately. Otherwise, employees are made responsible for inefficiency although idle time is beyond their control as for example, breakdown of machine or power supply. The following formula is used to calculate idle time variance :

Idle time variance = Idle hours × Standard rate variance

Idle time variance is always an adverse variance.

C. Labour Mix Variance or Gang Composition Variance

Sometimes employees of different grade may have to be used in place of specific grade because of shortage of labourers. In such a situtation a labour mix variance is calculated to show management how much of labour cost variance is due to change in labour force. It is defined as the portion of the wage variance which is due to the difference between the standard labour grades specified and the actual grades utilised. It arises under two situations.

(*a*) Where Standard composition of labour force if revised owing to shortage of a particular type of labour but the total labour time spent is equal to the total standard time. The following formula is used :

Labour mix variance = (Revised std. mix or time – Actual mix or time) × Std. wage rate per hour

Note : The revised standard mix is the same as the standard mix or time.

(*b*) Where the standard composition of labour force is revised due to shortage of a particular type of labour and total actual time of labour differs from total standard time of labour. The following formula is used :

Labour mix variance = (Revised std. mix – Actual std. mix or time) × Std. wage rate per hour

Where,

$$\text{Revised standard mix or time} = \frac{\text{Total time of actual mix of workers}}{\text{Total time of std. mix of workers}} \times \text{Std. time of the respective category of workers}$$

Problem 15 : The standard and actual figures of Ashok Metal Works are as under :

Standard time for the job	1,000 hours
Standard rate per hour	Re. 0.50
Actual time taken	900 hours
Actual wages paid	Rs. 360

Compute (*i*) Labour rate variance, (*ii*) Labour efficiency variance and (*iii*) Labour cost variance

Solution : Calculation of standard cost = 1,000 hrs. × 0.50 = 500

$$\text{Calculation of actual rate per hour} = \frac{\text{Rs. } 360}{900} = 0.40$$

(*i*) Labour rate variance = (Standard rate – Actual rate) × Actual hrs.
= (0.50 – 0.40) × 900 = Rs. 90 (*F*)

(*ii*) Labour efficiency variance = (Standard hours – Actual hrs.) × Standard rate
= (1,000 – 900) × 0.50 = Rs. 50 (*F*)

(*iii*) Labour cost variance = Standard labour cost – Actual labour cost
= (500 – 360) = 140 (*F*)

Problem 16 : From the following particulars calculate (1) Labour rate variance, (2) Labour mix variance, (3) Labour efficiency variance and (4) Labour cost variance.

	Skilled	*Semi-skilled*	*Unskilled*
No. in std. gang	16	6	3
Standard rate per hour	3	2	1
Actual number in the gang	14	9	2
Actual rate of pay	4	3	2

In a 40-hours week the gang as a whole produced 900 standard hours.

Solution : Calculation of standard hours

In a 40-hour week, the standard gang should have produced 1,000 standard hours as shown below :

Skilled	16 × 40	=	640
Semi-skilled	3 × 40	=	240
Unskilled	3 × 40	=	120
			1,000

But the actual output is 900 standard hours. Hence to find out the total labour cost variance the standard cost or cost charged to production is to be computed with reference to 900 standard hours. This is shown in the following statement.

Statement showing the standard cost actual cost and standard cost of actual gang for actual output, *i.e.,* 900 standard hours :

Gang	*Standard cost*			*Actual cost*			*Standard cost of actual gang*		
	Hrs.	*Rate*	*Amt.*	*Hrs.*	*Rate*	*Amt.*	*Hrs.*	*Rate*	*Amt.*
Skilled $\frac{640}{1,000} \times 900$	576	3	1,728	14 × 40 = 560	4	2,240	560	3	1,680
Semi-skilled $\frac{240}{1,000} \times 900$	216	2	432	9 × 40 = 360	3	1,080	360	2	720
Unskilled $\frac{120}{1,000} \times 900$	108	1	108	2 × 40 = 80	2	160	80	1	80
	900	2.52	2,268	1,000	3.84	3,480	1,000	2.48	2,480

(1) Labour rate variance = (Standard rate – Actual rate) × Actual hours
= (3 – 4) × 1,000 = 1,000 (*A*)

(2) Labour mix variance = (Std. rate of std. gang or mix – Std. rate of actual gang or mix) × Actual hours
= (2.52 – 2.48) × 1,000 = 40 (*F*)

(3) Labour efficiency variance = (Standard hours – Actual hours) × Std. rate
= (900 – 1,000) × 2.52 = 252 (*A*)

(4) Labour cost variance = (Standard labour cost – Actual labour cost)
= (2,268 – 3,480) = 1,212 (*A*)

Problem 17 : From the following particulars relating to Karnataka Toys Co. Ltd. calculate (1) Wage rate variance, (2) Labour efficiency variance, (3) Abnormal idle time variance and (4) Total labour cost variance.

Standard time per unit	2.5 hours
Actaul hours worked	2,000 hours
Standard rate of pay	Rs. 2 per hour

25% of the actual hours has been lost as abnormal idle time.

Actual output	1,000 units
Actual wages	Rs. 4,500

Solution : Calculation of standard cost charged to

Production = 1,000 units × 2.5 hrs. × Rs. 2 = Rs. 5,000

Actual wages paid = Rs. 4,500

Actual wage rate per hour = $\frac{4,500}{2,000}$ = 2.25

Standard wage rate per hour = 2.00

Abnormal idle time = $\frac{25}{100}$ × 2,000 = 500 hrs.

(1) Wage rate variance = (Standard rate – Actual rate) × Actual hours

= (2 – 2.25) × 2,000 = 500 (*A*)

(2) Labour efficiency variance = (Standard hours – Actual hours) × Standard rate

= (2,500 – 1,500) × 2 = 2,00 (*F*)

Standard hrs. = Std. time per unit × Actual output

= (2.5 × 1,000) = hrs. 2,500

(3) Abnormal idle time variance = Idle time × Standard rate

= 500 × Rs. 2 = Rs. 1,000 (*A*)

(4) Total labour cost variance = Standard labour cost – Actual labour cost

= 5,000 – 4,500 = 500 (*F*)

Problem 18 : Quality Ice-cream factory works for 50 hours a week and employs 100 workers on production. The standard rate is Re. 1 an hour and standard output is 200 units per gang hour.

During the week, 10 employees were paid at 80 paise an hour and 5 at Re. 1.20 an hour. Rest of the employees were paid at the standard rate.

Actual number of units produced were 10,200.

Calculate (1) Labour cost variance, (2) Labour rate variance, (3) Labour efficiency variance, (4) Labour yield variance.

Solution :

Calculation of actual cost

		Rs.
85 Workers for 50 hrs. @ Re. 1 per hour	=	4,250
10 Workers for 50 hrs. @ 0.80 p per hour	=	400
5 Workers for 50 hrs @ Rs. 1.20 per hour	=	300
Total actual cost		4,950

Calculation of standard rate

$$\frac{\text{Standard cost (per gang hour)}}{\text{Standard production (per gang hour)}}$$

$$\frac{100 \text{ workers} \times 1 \text{ Re.}}{200 \text{ units}} \quad \text{or} \quad \frac{\text{Rs. } 100}{200} = 0.50 \text{ per unit}$$

Calculation of standard cost

Actual production × Standard rate

10,200 units × 0.50 per unit = Rs. 5,100

(1) Labour cost variance = Standard cost – Actual cost

= 5,100 – 4,950 = Rs. 150 (*F*)

(2) Labour rate variance = (Std. rate – Actual rate) × Actual hours

As the actual wage rate has deviated from the standard in respect of only 15 workers from out of a total of 100 workers, wage rate variance would be calculated only in respect of these 15 workers. Actual hours for 10 workers for 50 hrs. will be 500 hrs. and 5 workers for 50 hrs. will be 250 hrs.

= (0.80 – Re. 1) × 500 = Rs. 100 (*F*)

= (1.20 – Re. 1) × 250 = Rs. 50 (*A*)

(3) Labour efficiency variance = (Standard hours – Actual hours) × Standard rate
= (5,100 – 5,000) × 1 = 100 (*F*)

$$\text{Standard hours} = \frac{\text{Actual production}}{\text{Std. production per hr.}} \times \text{No. of workers}$$

$$= \frac{10{,}200 \text{ units}}{200 \text{ units}} \times 100 = 5{,}100 \text{ hrs.}$$

(4) Labour yield variance = (Std. yield – Actual yield) × Std. labour cost per unit
= (10,000 – 10,200) × 0.50 = 100 (*F*)

Std. yield = 200 units × 50 hrs. = 10,000

Problem 19 : Compute labour variance from the following data of a ship building company.

The particulars of labour force engaged on job on. 777, scheduled to be completed in 30 weeks are :

Category	*Standard*		*Actual*	
	Number	*Wage rate* (Rs.)	*Number*	*Wage rate* (Rs.)
Skilled	75	60	70	70
Semi-skilled	45	40	30	50
Unskilled	60	30	80	20

The actual time taken is 32 weeks. (*Nagarjuna University, M.Com., March 1992*)

Solution :

Category	*Standard*			*Actual*		
	*Weeks**	*Rate*	*Amt.*	*Weeks**	*Rate*	*Amt.*
Skilled	2,250	60	1,35,000	2,240	70	1,56,800
Semi-skilled	1,350	40	54,000	960	50	48,000
Unskilled	1,800	30	54,000	2,560	20	51,200
	5,400		2,43,000	5,760		2,56,000

*Total weeks = No. of workers × No. of weeks

(1) Labour cost variance = Standard cost – Actual cost
= 2,43,000 – 2,56,000
= Rs. 13,000 (*A*)

(2) Labour rate variance = (Standard rate – Actual rate) × Actual hours

Skilled	= (60 – 70) × 2,240	=	22,400 (*A*)
Semi-skilled	= (40 – 50) × 960	=	9,600 (*A*)
Unskilled	= (30 – 20) × 2,560	=	25,600 (*F*)
		=	6,400 (*F*)

(3) Labour efficiency variance = (Standard hours – Actual hours) × Standard rate

Skilled	= (2,250 – 2,240) × 60	=	600 (*F*)
Semi-skilled	= (1,350 – 960) × 40	=	15,600 (*F*)
Unskilled	= (1,800 – 2,560) × 30	=	22,800 (*A*)
Total labour efficiency variance			6,600 (*A*)

Varification :

Labour cost variance = Labour rate variance + Labour efficiency variance
13,000 (*A*) = 6,400 (*A*) + 6,600a(*A*)

(4) Labour mix variance = (Revised std. time* – Actual time) × Std. rate

$$\text{Revised std. time} = \frac{\text{Actual mix}}{\text{Std. mix}} \times \text{Std. time}$$

Skilled $= \frac{5,760}{5,400} \times 2,250$ = 2,400

Semi-skilled $= \frac{5,760}{5,400} \times 1,350$ = 1,440

Unskilled $= \frac{5,760}{5,400} \times 1,800$ = 1,920

Skilled	= (2,400 – 2,240) × 60	=	9,600 (*F*)
Semi-skilled	= (1,440 – 960) × 40	=	19,200 (*F*)
Unskilled	= (1,920 – 2,560) × 30	=	19,200 (*A*)
	Labour mix variance		9,600 (*F*)

Revised labour efficiency variance = (Std. time – Revised std. time) × Std. rate

Skilled	= (2,250 – 2,400) × 60	=	9,000 (*A*)
Semi-skilled	= (1,350 – 1,440) × 40	=	3,600 (*A*)
Unskilled	= (1,800 – 1,920) × 30	=	3,600 (A)
		=	16,200 (*A*)

Verification :

Labour efficiency variance = (Labour mix variance + Revised labour efficiency variance)

6,600 (*A*) = (9,600 (*F*) + 16,200 (*A*)

Problem 20 : 100 skilled workmen, 40 semi-skilled workmen and 60 unskilled workmen were to work for 30 weeks to get a contract job completed. The standard weekly wages were Rs. 60, Rs. 36 and Rs. 24, respectively. The job was actually completed in 32 weeks by 80 skilled, 50 semi-skilled and 70 unskilled workmen who were paid Rs. 65, Rs. 40 and Rs. 20 respectively as weekly wages.

Find out the labour cost variance labour rate variance, labour mix variance and labour efficiency variance.

(*ICWA, Inter, June 1992*)

Solution :

Calculation of standard cost

	Rs.
100 skilled workmen @ Rs. 60 per week	6,000
40 semi-skilled workmen @ Rs. 36 per week	1,440
60 unskilled workmen @ Rs. 24 per week	1,440
	8,880

Calculation of actual cost

80 skilled workmen @ Rs. 65 per week	5,200
50 semi-skilled workmen @ Rs. 40 per week	2,000
70 unskilled workmen @ Rs. 20 per week	1,400
	8,600

Standard wages	=	8,800 × 30	=	2,66,400
Actual wages	=	8,600 × 32	=	2,75,200
1. Labour cost variance	=	Standard wages – Actual wages		
	=	2,66,400 – 2,75,200	=	8,800 (*A*)
2. Labour rate variance per week	=	(Std. rate – Actual rate) × Actual hrs.		
Skilled	=	(60 – 65) × 80 × 32	=	12,800 (*A*)
Semi-skilled	=	(36 – 40) × 50 × 32	=	6,400 (*A*)
Unskilled	=	(24 – 20) × 70 × 32	=	8,960 (*F*)
				10,240 (*A*)

3. Labour mix variance per week

Category	Std. mix	Actual mix	Qty. variance	Std. rate	Variance amt.
Skilled	100	80	20 (*F*)	60	1,200 (*F*)
Semi-skilled	40	50	10 (*A*)	36	360 (*A*)
Unskilled	60	70	10 (*A*)	24	240 (*A*)
					600 (*F*)

For 32 weeks = 600 × 32 = Rs. 19,200 (*F*)

4. Labour efficiency variance =
Week lost 2
Std. weekly cost = Rs. 8,800
Labour efficiency variance = 8,800 × 2 = 17,760 (*A*)
Verification :
Labour cost variance = Labour rate variance + Labour mix variance + Labour efficiency variance
8,800 (*A*) = 10,240 (*A*) + 19,200 (*F*) + 17,760 (*A*)

Problem 21 : The standard output of product 'EXE' is 25 units per hour in manufacturing department of a company employing 100 workers. The standard wage rate per labour hour is Rs. 6.

In a 42 hour week, the department produced 1,040 units of 'EXE' despite 5% of the time paid was lost due to an abnormal reason. The hourly wage rate actually paid were Rs. 6.20, Rs. 6 and Rs. 5.70 respectively to 10, 30 and 60 of the workers.

Compute relevant variance. (*CA, Inter May 1997*)

Solution : *Working Note :*

Calculation of standard non-hours

When 100 worker work for 1 hr. — The std. output is 25 units

Std. man hour per unit $= \frac{100 \text{ hrs}}{25 \text{ units}} = 4$ hrs.

Calculation of std. man hours for actual output :

1,040 units × 4 hrs. = 4,160

Standard data			*Actual data*					
Std. man hours for actual output	*Rate per hour*	*Amount*	*No. of workers*	*Actual hours paid*	*Idle time hrs.*	*Production hours*	*Rate per hr.*	*Amt. paid*
4,160	6	24,960	10	420	21	399	6.20	2,604
			30	1,260	63	1,197	6.00	7,560
			60	2,520	126	2,394	5.70	14,364
		24,960	100	4,200	210	3,990		24,528

(1) Labour cost variance = Std. labour cost – Actual labour cost
= 24,960 – 24,528 = 432 *F*

(2) Labour rate variance = (Std. rate – Actual rate) × Actual hrs.
= (6 – 6.20) × 420 = 84 *A*
= (6 – 6) × 1,260 = NIL
= (6 – 5.70) × 2,520 = 756*F*
672 *F*

(3) Labour efficiency variance = (Std. man hours – Actual production hrs.) × Std. rate
= (4,160 – 3,990) × 6
= 170 × 6 = 1,020 (*F*)

(4) Labour Idle time variance = Idle time hrs. × Std. rate
= 210 × 6 = 1,260 (A)

Problem 22 : The following details are available from the records of *ABC* Ltd. engaged in manufacturing article *A* for the week ended 28th Feb.

The standard labour hours and rates of payment per article *A* were as follows :

	Hours	*Rate per hour*	*Total*
Skilled labour	10	3	30
Semi-skilled labour	8	1.50	12
Unskilled labour	16	1.00	16

The actual production was 1,000 articles *A* for which the actual hours worked and rates are given below :

	Hours	*Rate per hour*	*Total*
Skilled labour	9,000	4	36,000
Semi-skilled labour	8,400	1.50	12,600
Unskilled labour	20,000	0.90	18,000
			66,600

From the above set of data, you are asked to calculate :

(1) Labour cost variance.
(2) Labour rate variance.
(3) Labour efficiency variance.
(4) Labour mix variance.

(CS, Inter, December 1994)

Solution :

	Std. data			*Actual data*		
	Hrs.	*Rate*	*Amt.*	*Hrs.*	*Rate*	*Amt.*
Skilled	10,000	3	30,000	9,000	4	36,000
Semi-skilled	8,000	1.50	12,000	8,400	1.50	12,600
Unskilled	16,000	1.00	16,000	20,000	0.90	18,000
	34,000		58,000	37,400		66,600

(1) Labour cost variance = Std. cost – Actual cost
= 58,000 – 66,600 = 8,600 *A*

(2) Labour rate variance = (Std. rate – Actual rate) × Actual hrs.

Skilled = (3 – 4) × 9,000 = 9,000 *A*

Semi-skilled = (1.50 – 1.50) × 8,400 = NIL

Unskilled = (1 – 0.90) × 20,000 = 2,000 F

7,000 *A*

(3) Labour efficiency variance = (Std. hours – Actual hrs.) × Std. rate

Skilled = (10,000 – 9,000) × 3
= 1,000 × 3 = 3,000 *F*

Semi-skilled = (8,000 – 8,400) × 1.50
= 400 × 1.50 = 600 *A*

Unskilled = (16,000 – 20,000) × 1
= 4,000 × 1 = 4,000 *A*

1,600 *A*

Calculation of revised std. time

$$\text{Revised std. time} = \frac{\text{Actual Mix}}{\text{Std. Mix}} \times \text{Std. time}$$

$$\text{Skilled} = \frac{37,400}{34,000} \times 10,000 = 11,000$$

$$\text{Semi-skilled} = \frac{37,400}{34,000} \times 8,000 = 8,800$$

$$\text{Unskilled} = \frac{37,400}{34,000} \times 16,000 = 17,600$$

Labour mix variance	=	(Revised std. time – Actual time) × Std. rate		
Skilled	=	(11,000 – 9,000) × 3		
	=	2,000 × 3	=	6,000 *F*
Semi-skilled	=	(8,800 – 8,400) × 1.50		
	=	400 × 1.50	=	600 *F*
Unskilled	=	(17,600 – 20,000) × 1		
	=	2,400 × 1	=	2,400 *A*
				4,200 *F*

Problem 23 (Material and labour cost variance) : The following standards have been set to manufacture a product.

Direct material :	Rs.
2 Units of *A* at Rs. 4 per unit	8
3 Units of *B* at Rs. 3 per unit	9
15 Units of *C* at Re. 1 per unit	15
	32
Direct labour 3 hours @ Rs. 8 per hr.	24
Total standard prime cost	56

The company manufactured and sold 6,000 units of the product during the year. Direct material costs were as follows :

12,500 units of *A* at Rs. 4.40 per unit
18,000 units of *B* at Rs. 2.80 per unit
88,500 units of *C* at Rs. 1.20 per unit.

The company worked 17,500 direct labour hours during the year. For 2,500 of these hours the company paid at Rs. 12 per hour while for the remaining the wages were paid at the standard rate. Calculate material price and usage variance and labour rate and efficiency variances. (*University of Delhi, B.Com. (Hons.), 1988*)

Solution :

1. Material price variance	=	(Std. price – Actual price) × Actual qty.		
A	=	(4 – 4.40) × 12,500	=	5,000 (*A*)
B	=	(3 – 2.80) × 18,000	=	3,600 (*F*)
C	=	(1 – 1.20) × 88,500	=	17,700 (*A*)
Total				19,100 (*A*)
2. Material usage variance	=	(Std. qty. – Actual qty.) × Std. price		
A	=	(12,000 – 12,500) × 4	=	2,000 (*A*)
B	=	(18,000 – 18,000) × 3	=	NIL
C	=	(90,000 – 88,500) × 1	=	1,500 (*F*)
				500 (*A*)
3. Labour rate variance	=	(Std. rate – Actual rate) × Actual hours		
A	=	(8 – 12) × 2,500	=	10,000 (*A*)
B	=	(8 – 8) × 1,500	=	NIL
				10,000 (*A*)
4. Labour efficiency variance	=	(Std. hrs. – Actual hrs.) × Std. rate		
	=	18,000 – 17,500 × 8	=	Rs. 4,000 (*F*)
	=	6,000 units × 3 hrs.	=	18,000 hrs.

Problem 24 : The following particulars are available in respect of a particular product :

Quantity of material purchased	6,000 kg.
Value of purchases	Rs. 18,000
Closing stock of materials	500 kg.

Total wage cost	Rs. 14,000
Actual hours	7,000 hrs.
Standard price of materials	Rs. 2.80 per kg.
Standard rate of wages	Rs. 2.50 per kg.
Standard time per unit	2 hrs.
Standard quantity per unit	1.50 kg.
Units produced	3,000 units
Idle time	500 hrs.

You are required to calculate :

(*a*) Total direct material cost variance analysed into price variance and wage variance.

(*b*) Total direct labour cost variance analysed to rate variance, idle time variance and efficiency variance.

Solution : 1. Standard quantity for actual production = 3,000 × 1.50 kg. = 4,500 kg.

2. Standard price = Rs. 2.80 per kg.
3. Actual quantity consumed = 6,000 kg. – 500 kg. = 5,500 kg.
4. Actual price = $\frac{\text{Rs. } 18,000}{6,000}$ = Rs. 3 per kg.
5. Standard time for actual production = 3,000 × 3 = 6,000 hrs.
6. Standard rate = Rs. 2.50 per hour
7. Time booked = 7,000 hrs. – 500 hrs. = 6,500 hrs.
8. Actual time = 7,000 hours
9. Actual rate = $\frac{14,000}{7,000}$ = Rs. 2 per hour

1. Total direct material cost variance = (Std. qty. × Std. price) – (Actual qty. × Actual price)
   = (4,500 × 2.80) – (5,500 × 3)
   = 12,600 – 16,500 = 3,900 (*A*)
2. Material price variance = (Std. price – Actual price) × Actual qty.
   = (2.80 – 3) × 5,500 = 1,100(*A*)
3. Material usage variance = (Std. qty. – Actual qty.) × Std. price
   = (4,500 – 5,500) × 2.80 = 2,800 (*A*)
4. Labour rate variance = (Std. rate – Actual rate) × Actual hrs.
   = (2.50 – 2) × 7,000 = 3,500 (*F*)
5. Idle time variance = (Idle hours × Std. rate)
   = 500 × 2.50= 1,250 (*A*)
6. Labour efficiency variance = (Std. hrs. – Actual hrs.) × Std. rate
   = (6,000 – 7,000) × 2.50= 2,500 (*A*)

Problem 25 : From the following data prepare a unit cost statement showing the prime cost of products *A* and *B* together with anlysis of variance :

		Product A	*Product B*
Material :	Standard	600 kg @ Rs. 5	90 kg. @ Rs. 3.00
	Actual	580 kg. @ Rs. 5.50	100 kg. @ Rs. 2.80
Labour :	Standard	80 hrs. @ Rs. 2	16 hrs. @ Rs. 2.80
	Actual	92 hrs. @ Rs. 1.75	14 hrs. @ Rs. 2.60

(*ICWA, Inter, June 1998*)

Solution :

Unit cost statement

	Product A		*Product B*	
Material :	600 kgs. @ Rs. 5	3,000	90 kg. @ Rs. 3	270
Labour	80 hrs. @ Rs. 2	160	16 hrs. @ Rs. 2.80	44.80
	Std. prime cost	3,160		314.80

Material : 580 kgs. @ Rs. 5.50	3,190	100 kgs. @ Rs. 2.80		280
Labour : 92 kgs. @ Rs. 1.75	161	14 hrs. @ Rs. 2.60		36.40
Actual prime cost	3,351			316.40
Total cost variance	191 (*A*)			1.60 (*A*)

Material price variance	=	(5.00 – 5.50) × 580	(3 – 2.80) × 100
(SP – AP) SQ	=	290 *A*	= 20 *F*
Material usage variance	=		
(SQ – AQ) SP	=	(600 – 580) × 5	(90 – 100) × 3
	=	100 (*F*)	= 30 (*A*)
Material cost variance	=		
MPV + MUV	=	290 (*A*) – 100 (*F*)	20 (*F*) + 30 (*A*)
	=	190 (*A*)	= 10 (*A*)
Labour rate variance	=	(2 – 1.75) × 92	(2.80 – 2.60) × 14
(SR – AR) × AH	=	23 (*F*)	= 2.80 F
Labour efficiency variance	=	(80 – 92) × 2	(16 – 14) × 2.80
(SH – AH) SR		= 24 (*A*)	= 5.60 (*F*)
Labour cost variance	=	23 (*F*) + 24 (*A*)	2.80 (*F*) + 5.60 (*F*)
L.R.V. + L.E.V.	=	1 *A*	= 8.40 *F*

Problem 26 : The following information is available from the cost records of Novell & Co. for the month of March 1994

	Rs.
Materials purchased 20,000 units	88,000
Materials consumed 19,000 units	
Actual wages paid for 4,950 hrs.	24,750
Units produced 1,800 units	
Standard rates and pieces are :	
Direct material rate is Rs. 4 per unit	
Standard output is 10 number for one unit	
Direct labour rate is Rs. 4.00 per hour	
Standard requirement is 2.5 hours per unit.	

You are required to compute all material and labour variances for the month. (*CA, Inter, June 1995*)

Solution :

Material variances

Material cost variance = (Std. qty. for actual output × Std. price) – (Actual qty. × Actual price)
= (18,000 × 4) – (19,000 × 4.40
= 72,000 – 83,600 = 11,600 (*A*)

Note : *Calculation of std. qty. for actual output*

1,800 × 10 = 18,000 units

(2) Material price variance = (Std. price – Actual price) × Actual qty.
= (4 – 4.40) × 19,000
= 0.40 × 19,000 = 7,600 (*A*)

(3) Material usage variance = (Std. qty. – Actual qty) × Std. rate
= (18,000 – 19,000) × 4
= 1,000 × 4 = 4,000 (*A*)

Labour variances :

Labour cost variance = Std. hours for actual output × Std. rate – Actual wages
= 4,500 × 4 – 24,750
= 18,000 – 24,750 = 6,750 (*A*)

Note : *Calculation of std. hours for actual output*

1,800 × 2.5 = 4,500 hrs.

Labour rate variance = (Std. rate – Actual rate) × Actual hrs.
= (4 – 5) × 4,950 = 4,950 (*A*)

Labour efficiency variance = (Std. hrs. for actual output – Actual hrs.) × Std. rate
= (4,500 – 4,950) × 4 = 1,800 *A*

3. Overhead Variance

Overhead variances arise on account of difference between actual overhead and absorbed overheads. In order to calculate overhead variance it is necessary to know the actual and absorbed overheads. The absorbed overhead rates are also known as the standard overhead recovery rate or standard overhead absorption rate. It is calculated by applying the following steps :

(*a*) To make the estimate of probable overheads to be incurred for each department for the next year.

(*b*) This estimated overhead is to be classified into fixed and variable overheads.

(*c*) The capacity utilisation either in terms of machine hours or labour hours or production units is to be estimated.

(*d*) Apply the following formula for calculating the standard overhead absorption rate :

$$\text{Standard fixed overhead rate} = \frac{\text{Budgeted fixed overhead}}{\text{Normal volume}}$$

$$\text{Standard variable overhead rate} = \frac{\text{Budgeted variable overhead}}{\text{Normal volume}}$$

(*A*) **Variable overhead cost variance :** It is defined as the difference between the actual variable overheads incurred and the variable overheads absorbed. This variance arises on account of over or under absorption of overheads. Calculation of this variance can be based on either hours or output. The following formula is used :

Variable overhead cost variance = Standard overhead cost recovered – Actual overhead cost

Where Std. overhead cost when overhead rate is per hours

= (Std. hours for actual output × Std. overhead rate per hour)

Standard overhead cost when overhead rate is output

= (Actual output × Std. overhead rate per unit)

(*a*) ***Variable overhead expenditue variance :*** It is defined as the difference between the actual variable overheads incurred and the allowed variable overheads based on the actual hours worked. Calculation of this variance is based on hours or output. The following formula is used :

Based on rate per hour

Variable overhead expenditure variance = (Std. variable overhead absorption rate per hr. × Actual hrs. worked worked) – Actual variable overhead

Based on rate per unit

Variable overhead expenditure variance = (Std. variable overhead absorption rate per unit – Actual variable rate per unit) × Actual output

(*b*) ***Variable overhead efficiency variance :*** This is defined as the difference between the allowed variable overheads and the absorbed variable overhead. The following formula is used to calculate this variance.

Variable overhead efficiency variance = (Actual hours – Std. hours for actual output) × Standard variable overhead absorption rate

or = (Std. qty. of output – Actual qty. of output) × Std. rate per unit.

(*B*) **Fixed overhead variance :** This is defined as the difference between the standard cost of fixed overhead absorbed in the production achieved, whether completed or not, and the fixed overhead attributed and charged to that period. The formula is :

(Std. hrs. for actual output × Std. fixed overhead rate) × Actual fixed overheads

(*a*) ***Fixed overhead expenditure overhead :*** This is defined as the difference between the budget cost allowance for production for a specified control period and the actual fixed expenditure attributed and charged to that period. In other words it represents the difference between the fixed overhead as per budget and the actual fixed overhead incurred. The following formula is used to calculate this variance :

Fixed oh. expenditure variance = (budgeted qty. × Std. fixed oh. rate per unit) – Actual fixed oh.

or = (Budgeted fixed overhead – Actual fixed overhead)

(*b*) ***Fixed overhead volume variance :*** It is that portion of the fixed overhead variance which is the difference between the standard cost of the overhead absorbed in actual output and the standard allowance for that output. In this definition standard allowance means the budgeted overhead. The fixed overhead volume variance arises mainly because of the use of a pre-determined overhead recovery rate based on a normal volume of activity and of the actual level of activity being less or more than the normal volume so selected. The following formula is used to calculate this variance.

Fixed overhead volume variance = (Actual qty. – Budgeted qty.) × Standard rate

of Fixed overhead volume variance = (Std. hours for actual production – Actual hours worked) × Std. fixed overhead rate

(*c*) ***Fixed overhead efficiency variance :*** It is that portion of the volume variance which reflects the increased or reduced output arising from efficiency above or below the standard which is expected. The following formula is used to calculate this variance :

Fixed overhead efficiency variance = (Actual qty. of production – Std. qty. of production for actual capacity) × Std. fixed overhead absorption rate per unit

or = (Std. hours for actual production – Actual hours worked) × Std. fixed overhead rate

(*d*) ***Fixed overhead capacity variance :*** This is defined as that portion of the fixed overhead volume variance which is due to working at higher or lower capacity than standard capacity.

The following formula is used to calculate this variance :

Fixed overhead capacity or usage variance = (Std. qty. of production – Revised budgeted qty. of production) × Std. fixed overhead rate per unit

or = (Std. hours for actual production – Actual hours of the period) × Std. fixed overhead rate per hour

(*e*) ***Calender variance :*** It is that portion of overhead volume variance which is due to the difference between the number of working days in the period to which the budget is applied.

The following formula is used to calculate this variance.

Calender variance = (Standard units – Revised budgeted units) × Std. fixed overhead rate per unit

or = (Std. number of working days or hrs. – Possible number of working days or hours) × Std. fixed overhead rate per day or hour.

Calender variance = (Budgeted hrs. – Actual hrs.) × Std. rate

(*f*) ***Seasonal variance :*** It is that portion of the overhead volume variance which is due to the difference between the seasonally budgeted output and the average output on which standards have been calculated.

The following are the main causes for the overhead volume variance.

Causes Controllable by Management

(*i*) Employees waiting for work.
(*ii*) Avoidable machine breakdown.
(*iii*) Lack of operator.
(*iv*) Lack of tools.
(*v*) Lack of instructions.

Causes Uncontrollable by Management

(*i*) Decrease in customer demand.
(*ii*) Excess plant capacity.

Problem 27 (Overhead variance) : From the following information compute fixed overhead cost, expenditure and volume/capacity variances.

Normal capacity is 5,000 hours.

Budgeted fixed overhead rate is Rs. 10 per standard hour. Actual level of capacity utilised is 4,400 standard hours.

Actual fixed overheads Rs. 52,000. (*University of Delhi, B.Com. (Hons.), 1991*)

Solution :

(1) Fixed overhead variance = Budgeted fixed overhead – Actual fixed overhead
= 44,000 – 52,000 = 8,000 (*A*)

Budgeted fixed overhead = Std. hrs. × Budgeted fixed overhead rate
= 4,400 × Rs. 10 = 44,000

Note : Budgeted fixed overheads are taken at the actual capacity utilised.

(2) Expense variance = Budgeted total factory overhead – Actual fixed factory overhead
= 50,000 – 52,000 = 2,000 (*A*)

(3) Volume/capacity variance = (Actual capacity – Budgeted capacity) × Std. rate
= (4,400 – 5,000) × 10 = 6,000 (*A*)

Verification :

Fixed overhead variance = Expense variance + Volume variance
8,000 (*A*) = 2,000 (*A*) + 6,000 (*A*)

Problem 28 : From the following particulars calculate all variances relating to fixed overheads.

	Budgeted	*Actual*
Fixed overhead for July 1993	Rs. 10,000	Rs. 10,200
Units produced in July 1993	5,000	5,200
Standard for one unit	4 hours	
Actual hours worked		20,100 hours

Solution :

(1) Total fixed overhead variance = Absorbed fixed overhead – Actual fixed overhead
= 10,400 – 10,200 = 200 (*F*)

Absorbed fixed overhead = 5,200 × 2 = 10,400

$$= \frac{\text{Budgeted oh}}{\text{Units}} = \frac{10,000}{5,000} = 2$$

(2) Overhead expenditure variance = Actual overheads – Budgeted overheads
= 10,200 – 10,000 = 200 (*A*)

(3) Overhead volume variance = (Actual qty. – Budgeted qty.) × Std. rate
= (5,200 – 5,000) × 2 = 400 (*F*)

(4) Overhead capacity variance = (Actual hours – Budgeted hours) × Std. hourly rate
= (20,100 – 20,000) × 0.50 = 50 (*F*)

$$\text{Std. hourly rate} = \frac{\text{Rs. 2}}{\text{4 hrs.}} = 0.50$$

(5) Overhead efficiency variance = (Actual hrs. × Standard hour) × Std. rate per hr.
= (21,000 – 20,800) × 0.50 = 350 (*F*)

Standard hours produced = 5,200 × 4 = 20,800

Problem 29 : From the following data calculate the various overhead based on (1) units of production and (2) hours of production.

		Hours	*Units*
(*i*)	Annual budgeted production	50 weeks × 6 days × 8 hrs. = 240 hrs. or 200 hrs. per month	1,80,000 (or 15,000 per month)
(*ii*)	Production standard per hr.		75
(*iii*)	Annual budgeted fixed overhead		Rs. 2,70,000
	Data for June 1993	*Hours*	*Units*
(*i*)	Actual production		14,500
(*ii*)	Actual hours worked	180	
(*iii*)	Budgeted hours	4 weeks × 6 days × 8 hrs. = 192	
(*iv*)	Extra holiday	1½ days = 12 hrs.	

Solution : (A) *Calculation of overhead variance based on units of production*

Calculation of standard overhead rate = $\frac{\text{Rs. } 2,70,000}{1,80,000}$ = Rs. 1.50 per unit

(1) Volume variance = (Actual qty. – Budgeted qty.) × Std. rate
= (14,500 – 15,000) × 1.50 = 750 (*A*)

(2) Overhead capacity variance :
Change in capacity = 200 – 192 hours = 8 hrs.
Loss of output = 8 × 75 units = 600 units
∴ Capacity variance = 1.50 × 600= Rs. 900 (*A*)

or (Standard units ×
Revised budgeted units for revised working hrs.) × Standard rate
(15,000 – 14,400*) × 1.50 = Rs. 900 (*A*)
*192 × 75 = 14,400

(3) Calender variance = Std. rate × Loss of output dut eo extra holiday
Rs. 1.50 × 12 × 75 = Rs. 1,350 (*A*)

(4) Overhead efficiency variance = (Actual units — Std. units) × Std. rate
(14,500 – 13,500)* = Rs. 1,500 (*F*)
Std. units = Actual hrs. worked × Std. units per hrs.
180 × 75 = 13,500

Verification :
Overhead volume variance = Capacity variance + Calender variance + Efficiency variance
75 (A) = 900 (*A*) + 1,350 (*A*) + 1,500 (*F*)

***(B)* Calculation of variance on the basis of hours of production**

Calculation of standard overhead rate = $\frac{\text{Rs. } 2,70,000}{2,400}$ = 112.50 per hour

(1) Overhead volume variance = (Std. hrs. for actual production – Budgeted hrs.) × Std. rate
= (193.125* – 200) × 112.50 = 750 (*A*)

Std. hrs. for actual production = $\frac{14,500}{75}$ = 193.125

(2) Overhead efficiency variance = (Std. hrs. – Actual hrs.) × Std. rate
= (193.125 – 180) × 112.50 = Rs. 1,500 (*F*)

(3) Overhad capacity variance = (Actual hrs. – Revised budgeted hours) × Std. rate
= 8 × 112.50 = 900 (*A*)

(4) Overhead calender variance = (Revised budgeted hours – Seasonal budgeted hrs.) × Std. rate
= 12 × 112.50 = Rs. 1,350 (*A*)

Problem 30 : Assuming the expenses to be fixed, calculate from the following data (*a*) efficiency variance, (*b*) volume variance, (*c*) calender variance, (*d*) expense variance.

	Budget	Actual
No. of working days	20	22
Man hours per day	8,000	8,400
Output per man hour in unit	1.0	1.2
Standard overhead rate per man hour	Rs. 2	
Actual fixed expenses		Rs. 3,25,000

Solution : Actual output = 8,400 hrs. × 22 days × 1.2 units

Per hour = 2,21,760 units

Standard output per man hour = 1

Standard hours produced = 2,21,760 × 1= 2,21,760

Actual hours worked = 8,400 × 22 = 1,84,800

Ooverhead as per budget = 8,000 hrs. × 20 days + Rs. 2 per hour = Rs. 3,20,000

(1) Overhead efficiency overhead = (Actual hours – Std. hours) × Std. rate
= (1,84,800 – 2,21,760) × 2 = 73,920 (*F*)

(2) Capacity variance = (Actual hrs. – (budgeted hrs.) × Std. rate

Actual hrs. = 8,400 × 22 = 1,84,800

Budgeted hrs. in actual days = 8,000 × 22 = 1,76,000
= (1,84,800 – 1,76,000) × 2 = 17,600 (*F*)

(3) Calender variance = (Budgeted hrs. – Actual hrs.) × Std. rate

Budgeted hrs. = 8,000 × 20 = 1,60,000

Actual hrs. = 8,400 × 22 = 1,76,000
= (1,60,000 – 1,76,000) × 2 = 32,000 (*F*)

(4) Volume variance = (Actual qty. – Budgeted qty.) × Std. rate

Actual qty. = 8,400 × 22 × 1.2 = 2,21,760 units.

Budgeted qty. = 8,000 × 20 × 1 = 1,60,000 units
= (2,21,760 – 1,60,000) × 2 = 1,23,520 (F)

(5) Expense variance = Actual overhead cost – Budgeted overhead cost
= 3,25,000 – 3,20,000 = 5,000 (*A*)

Problem 31 : The budget for a period indicates :

	Rs.
Works overhead fixed	50,000
Works overhead variable	1,50,000
Normal activity	100%

During the period the actual activity was only 70% of the normal load for a total expenditure of Rs. 1,50,000. What are the budget and volume variance? *(ICWA, (Inter), Dec. 1990)*

Solution : Budgeted works overhead for actual qty.

		Rs.
Fixed	=	50,000
Variable $\frac{1,50,000}{100} \times 70$	=	1,05,000
		1,55,000
Actual works overhead for actual qty.		1,50,000
Recovered works overhead for actual qty.		
Fixed Variable $\frac{50,000}{100} \times 70$	=	35,000
	=	1,05,000
		1,40,000

(1) Overhead budget variance = Budgeted overhead – Actual overhead
= 1,55,000 – 1,50,000 = 5,000 (*F*)

(2) Overhead volume variance = Recovered overhead – Budgeted overhead
= 1,40,000 – 1,55,000 = 15,000 (*A*)

Problem 32 : Determine the budget and capacity variance from the following data :

Estimated factory overhead	Rs. 25,000
Estimated direct labour hours	5,000
Actual overhead expenses	Rs. 26,500
Applied overhead expenses	Rs. 22,500

(ICWA, Inter, June 1990)

Solution :

Overhead budget variance = Budgeted overhead – Actual overhead
= 25,000 – 26,500 = 1,500 *(A)*

Overhead capacity variance = (Std. hrs. for actual production – Actual hrs.) × Std. overhead rate per hr.
= (4,500 – 5,000) × 5 = 2,500 *(A)*

Problem 33 : The following information is available from the records of a facory

	Budgeted	*Actual*
Fixed overhead for May (Rs.)	5,000	6,000
Production in May (units)	1,000	1,050
Standard time per unit (hrs.)	10	–
Actual hours worked in May	–	11,000

Compute :

(i) Fixed overhead cost variance
(ii) Expenditure variance
(iii) Volume variance
(iv) Capacity variance
(v) Efficiency variance

(CS, Inter, December, 2000)

Solution :

Calculation of Std. overhead rate :

$$= \frac{\text{Budgeted Fixed overhead}}{\text{Budgeted production units}}$$

$$= \frac{5{,}000}{1{,}000} = \text{Rs. } 5$$

Calculation of hourly rate :

$$= \frac{\text{Rs. } 5}{10 \text{ hrs.}} = 0.50$$

(i) Fixed overhead cost variance = Overhead recovered on actual output – Actual fixed overheads
= (1,050 units × Rs. 5) – 6,000
= 5,250 – 6,000 = Rs. 750 *(A)*

(ii) Expenditure variance = Budgeted fixed oh. – Actual fixed oh.
= 5,000 – 6,000 = Rs. 1,000 *(A)*

(iii) Volume variance = (Budgeted output – Actual output) × Std. rate per unit
= (1,000 – 1,050) × 5 = 250 *(F)*

(iv) Capacity variance = (Budgeted hours – Actual hours) × Std. rate per hr.
= (10,000 – 11,000) × 0.50 = 500 *F*

(v) Efficiency variance = (Std. hours for actual output – Actual hours) × Std. rate per unit
= (10,500 – 11,000) × 0.50 = 250 *(A)*

Problem 34 : Adarsh Ltd. has furnished you the following data :

	Budgeted	*Actual for July 1998*
Number of working days	25	27
Production in units	20,000	22,000
Fixed overhead (Rs.)	30,000	31,000

Budgeted fixed overhead rate is Re. 1 per hour. In July 1998, the actual hours worked were 31,500.

Calculate the following variances :

(*i*) Efficiency variance
(*ii*) Capacity variance
(*iii*) Calender variance
(*iv*) Volume variance
(*v*) Expenditure variance
(*vi*) Total overheads variance

(*CS, Inter, June 1999*)

Solution :

Calculation of Budgeted hours

Budgeted overheads Rs. 30,000

Budgeted overhead rate per hour Re. 1

$$\text{Budgeted hours} = \frac{\text{Rs. } 30{,}000}{\text{Re. 1 per hour}} = 30{,}000 \text{ hrs.}$$

Calculation of standard time per unit of output

$$\frac{\text{Budgeted hours}}{\text{Budgeted output}} = \frac{30{,}000}{20{,}000} = 1.5 \text{ hrs.}$$

Calculation of std. hours for actual output

Actual output × Std. time per unit

22,000 × 1.5 = 33,000 hrs.

Calculation of std. rate per unit

Std. rate per unit of output = 1.5 hrs. × Re. 1 per hr.
= Rs. 1.50

(1) Efficiency variance = (Std. hrs. for actual output – Actual hrs.) × Std. rate per hr.
= (33,000 – 31,500) × 1
= 1,500 × 1 = 1,500 *F*

OR

Efficiency variance = (Std. output for actual hrs. – Actual output) × Std. rate per unit
= (21,000 units – 22,000 units) × 1.50
= 1,000 × 1.50 = 1,500 *F*

***Note :** Calculation of std. output for actual hours :*

$$= \frac{\text{Actual Hours}}{\text{Std. time per unit of output}}$$

$$= \frac{31{,}500 \text{ hours}}{1.5 \text{ hours}} = 21{,}000 \text{ units}$$

(2) Capacity variance = (Revised budgeted hours – Actual hours) × Std. Rate per hour
= (32,400 – 31,500) × 1 = 900 *A*

***Note :** Calculation of revised budgeted hours :*

Actual working days × Budgeted hours per day

27 × 1,200 = 32400

(3) Calender variance = (Budgeted no. of working days – Actual *No.* of working days) × Budgeted overheads/ Budgeted working days

$$= (25 - 27) \times \frac{30{,}000}{25}$$

= 2 × 1,200 = 2,400 *F*

(4) Volume variance = (Budgeted output – Actual output) × Std. rate per unit
= (20,000 – 22,000) × 1.50
= 2,000 × 1.50 = 3,000 *F*

(5) Expenditure variance = Budgeted overheads – Actual overheads
= 30,000 – 31,000 = 1,000 (*A*)

(6) Total overhead variance = (Actual output – Std. rate per unit – Actual overheads)
= (22,000 – 1.50 – 31,000)
= 33,000 – 31,000 = 2,000 (*F*)

Problem 35 : A company has a normal capacity of 120 machines, working 8 hours per day of 25 days in a month. The fixed overheads are budgeted at Rs. 1,44,000 per month. The standard time required to manufacture one unit of product is 4 hours.

In April 1998, the company worked 24 days of 840 machine hours per day and produced 5,305 units of output the actual fixed overheads were Rs. 1,42,000.

Compute :

(1) Efficiency variance
(2) Capacity variance
(3) Calender variance
(4) Expense variance
(5) Volume variance
(6) Total fixed overhead variance.

(*CA, Inter, May 1998*)

Solution :

Working Notes :

		Budget	*Actual*
(1)	Fixed overhead for the month	1,44,000	1,42,000
(2)	Working days per month	25	24
(3)	Working hours per month =	(120 machines × 8 hrs. × 25 days) 24,000	840 machine hours × 24 days = 20,160
(4)	Production units per month	$\frac{24,000 \text{ hrs.}}{4 \text{ hrs.}}$ = 6,000	5,305

(5) Standard hours for actual production
= Actual production units × Std. hours per unit
= 5,305 × 4 = 21,220 hrs.

(6) Standard fixed overhead rate per unit :

$= \frac{\text{Rs. } 1,44,000}{6000 \text{ units}}$ = Rs. 24

(7) Standard fixed overhead rate per hour :

$= \frac{\text{Rs. } 1,44,000}{24,000 \text{ hrs.}}$ = Rs. 6

(8) Standard fixed overhead per day :

$\frac{\text{Rs. } 1,44,000}{25 \text{ days}}$ = Rs. 5,760

(1) Efficiency variance = (Std. hrs. for actual production – Actual hrs.) × Std. rate per hr.
= (21,220 – 20,160) × 6 = 6,360 *F*

(2) Capacity variance = (Budgeted hours – Actual hours) × Std. rate per hour
= (24 days × 120 mach. × 8 hrs. – 20,160) × 6
= 17,280 (*A*)

(3) Calender variance = (Budgeted *No.* of days – Actual *No.* of days) × Std. rate per day
= (25 – 24) × 5,760 = 5,760 *A*

(4) Expense variance = (Budgeted fixed oh. – Actual fixed overhead)
= (1,44,000 – 1,42,000) = 2,000 *F*

(5) Volume variance = (Budgeted output – Actual output) × Std. rate per unit
= (5,305 – 6,000) × 24
= 695 × 24 = 16,680 *A*

(6) Total fixed oh. variance = (Fixed oh. for actual output – Actual fixed overheads)
= (5,305 × 24 – 1,42,000)
= 1,27,320 – 1,42,000 = 14,680 *A*

Verification :

Fixed oh. variance = Expenses variance + Volume variance
14,680 *A* = 2,000 *F* + 16,680 *A*

Volume Variance = Efficiency variance + Capacity variance + Calender variance
16,680 *A* = 6,360 *F* + 17,280 *A* + 5,760 *A*

Problem 36 (Variable overhead variances) : The following data is given :

	Budget	*Actuals*
Production (in units)	400	360
Man hours to produce above	8,000	7,000
Variable overheads (in rupees)	10,000	9,150

The standard time to produce one unit of the product is 20 hours
Calculate variable overhead variances. (*CA, Inter, November 1997*)

Solution :

Working Notes :

(1) Calculation of standard variable overhead per unit

$$= \frac{\text{Budgeted variable oh}}{\text{Budgeted production}} = \frac{10,000}{400} = \text{Rs. } 25 \text{ per unit}$$

(2) Calculation of standard variable overhead per hour

$$= \frac{\text{Budgeted variable oh}}{\text{Budgeted man hours}} = \frac{10,000}{8,000} = 1.25 \text{ per hour}$$

(3) Calculation of Std. variable overhead for actual output

Actual output × Std. variable overhead per unit
= 360 units × Rs. 25 = Rs. 9,000

(4) Budgeted variable overhead based on actual hours worked

Actual hours worked × Std. variable overhead per hour
7,000 × 1.25 = Rs. 8,750

(5) Calculation of standard hours for actual output

Actual output × Std. hours per unit
360 units × 20 hours = 7,200 hours

(1) Variable overhead variance = Std. variable oh. – Actual variable oh.
= 9,000 – 9,150 = Rs. 150 *A*

(2) Variable overhead expenditure variable = Budgeted variable oh. – Actual variable oh.
= 8,750 – 9,150 = 400

(3) Variable overhead efficiency variable = (Std. hours for actual output – Actual hours)
× Std. rate per hour
= (7,200 – 7,000) × 1.25
= 250 *F*

Verification :

Variable oh. variance = Variable expenditure variance + Variable overhead efficiency variance
150 (*A*) = 400 *A* + 250 *F*

4. Sales Variance

Sales variance is useful in controlling sales and thereby earn more profit. Sales variances can be calculated on the basis of (1) Sales margin or (2) Turnover.

(*A*) **Sales variances based on sales margin :** Before the various sales margin variances are dicussed, it is better to know the concept of standard sales margin.

Standard sales margin : This refers to the difference between the standard selling price of a product and its standard cost and it is the same as the standard profit for the product. The term 'Standard cost' used above is to indicate 'total standard cost'. It includes both fixed and variable cost. When fixed cost is excluded it becomes standard marginal cost. The difference between standard selling price and standard marginal cost is known as standard sales contribution.

The various sales margin variances are as follows :

(*a*) ***Total sales margin variance :*** This is the difference between the budgeted margin from sales and the actual margin, when the cost of sales is valued at the standard cost of production. The following formula is used to calculate this variance :

Total sales margin variance = Standard margin or profit – Actual margin or profit.

(*b*) ***Sales margin price variance :*** This is that portion of total sales margin variance which is the difference between the standard margin per unit and the actual margin per unit for the number of units sold in the period. The following formula is used to calculate this variance :

Sales margin price variance = (Std. margin per unit – Actual margin per unit) × Actual qty.

(*c*) ***Sales margin quantity variance :*** This is that portion of total sales margin variance which is the difference between the budgeted number of units sold and the actual number sold valued at standard margin per unit. The following formula is used to calculate this variance :

Standard margin qty. variance = (Standard proportion for actual sales × Budgeted qty.)
× Standard profit

When more than one product is sold, sales margin quantity variance is sub-divided into (*a*) Mix variance and (*b*) A volume variance.

(*d*) ***Sales margin mix variance :*** This is that portion of sales margin quantity variance which is the difference between the actual total number of units at the actual mix and the actual total number of units at standard mix valued at the standard margin per unit. The following formula is used to calculate this variance :

Sales margin mix variance = (Actual qty. × Std. proportion for actual sales) × Std. profit

(*e*) ***Sales margin volume variance :*** This is that portion of the sales margin quantity variance which is the difference between the actual total quantity of units sold and the budgeted total number of units at the standard mix valued at the standard margin per unit. The following formula is used to calculat this variance :

Sales margin volume variance = (Budgeted units – Actual units sold) × Std. marginal per unit

(*B*) **Sales variances based on turnover or sales value :** Sales variances based on turnover is used, by those organisations which would like to exercise control on actual sales by comparing it with budgeted sales. The following are the variances based on turnover.

(*a*) ***Sales value variance :*** This refers to the difference between the budgeted sales and the actual sales. The following formula is used to calculated this variance :

Sales value variance = Budgeted sales – Actual sales

(*b*) ***Sales price variance :*** This refers to that portion of the sales variance which is due to the difference between the standard price specified and the actual price charged. The following formula is used to calculate this variance :

Sales price variance = (Actual price – Std. price) × Actual qty.

(*c*) ***Sales volume variance :*** It refers to that portion of the sales value variance which is due to the difference between the budgeted sales and the standard value of actual mix of sales. The following formula is used to calculate this variance :

Sales volume variance = (Std. qty. of sales – Actual qty. of sales) × Std. price

(*d*) ***Sales quantity variance :*** This refers to that portion of sales volume variance which is due to the difference between standard value of actual sales at standard mix and the budgeted sales. The following formula is used to calculate this variance :

Sales quantity variance = Budgeted sales – Revised standard sales

(*e*) ***Sales mix variance :*** This refers to that portion of the sales volume variance which is due to the difference between the standard and the actual composition of the sales mix. It is the difference between the standard value of actual mix and the standard value of actual sales at standard mix. The following formula is used to calculate this variance :

$$\text{Sales mix variance} = \left(\frac{\text{Std. mix}}{\text{Revised std. mix of actual qty. sold}} - \text{Actual mix}\right) \times \text{Std. price}$$

Problem 37 (Sales variances) : Ultra Modern Cassette Ltd. had budgeted the following sales for February 1991.

Casette *A*	1,100 units @ Rs.	50 per unit
Casette *B*	950 units @ Rs.	100 per unit
Casette *C*	1,250 units @ Rs.	80 per unit

As against this, the actual sales were :

Casette *A*	1,300 units @ Rs.	55 per unit
Casette *B*	1,000 units @ Rs.	95 per unit
Casette *C*	1,200 units @ Rs.	78. per unit

The cost per unit of cassette *A*, *B* and *C* was Rs. 45, Rs. 85 and Rs. 70 respectively.

Compute the different variances to explain the difference between the budgeted and actual product.

(*C.A., Inter, June 1992*)

Solution :

	Cassette A	*Cassette B*	*Cassette C*
Standard selling price (*see assumption 1*)	50	100	80
Standard cost (*see assumption 2*)	45	85	70
Standard profit	5	15	10

Assumption 1 : Standard selling price is assumed to be equal to the budgeted selling price.

Assumption 2 : Standard cost is assumed to be equal to actual cost.

Calculation of actual profit

Actual selling price	55	95	78
Actual cost	45	85	70
Actual profit	10	10	8

Actual profit :

Cassette *A*	—	1,300 @ Rs. 10	=	13,000
Cassette *B*	—	1,000 @ Rs. 10	=	10,000
Cassette *C*	—	1,200 @ Rs. 8	=	9,600
		Total	=	32,600

Budgeted profit :

Cassette *A*	—	1,100 @ Rs. 5	=	5,500
Cassette *B*	—	950 @ Rs. 15	=	14,250
Cassette *C*	—	1,250 @ Rs. 10	=	12,500
		Total	=	32,250

(1) Total sales margin variance = (Std. profit or budgeted profit – Actual profit)
(32,250 – 32,600) = 350 (*F*)

(2) Sales margin price variance = (Std. margin per unit – Actual margin per unit) × Actual qty.

Cassette *A*	—	(50 – 55) × 1,300	=	6,500 (*F*)
Cassette *B*	—	(100 – 95) – 1,000	=	5,000 (*A*)
Cassette *C*	—	(80 – 78) × 1,200	=	2,400 (*A*)
			=	900 (*A*)

(3) Sales margin volume variance = (Budgeted sales qty. – Actual qty. sold) × Std. margin per unit

Cassette *A*	—	(1,100 – 1,300) × 5	=	1,000 (*F*)
Cassette *B*	—	(950 – 1,000) × 15	=	750 (*F*)
Cassette *C*	—	(1,250 – 1,200) × 10	=	500 (*A*)
			=	1,250 (*F*)

(4) Sales mix variance = (Actual qty. – Std. proportion for actual sales) × Std. profit

Cassette *A*	—	(1,300 – 1,67) × 5	=	665 (*F*)
Cassette *B*	—	(1,000 – 1,008) × 15	=	120 (*A*)
Cassette *C*	—	(1,200 – 1,325) 10	=	1,250 (*A*)
			=	705 (*A*)

Calculation of standard proportion for actual sales

Cassette *A* = $\frac{3,500}{3,300} \times 1,100$ = 1,167 units

Cassette *B* = $\frac{3,500}{3,300} \times 950$ = 1,008 units

Cassette *C* = $\frac{3,500}{3,300} \times 1,250$ = 1,325 units

3,500 units

(5) Sales margin qty. variance = (Std. proportion for actual sales – Budgeted qty.) × Std. profit

Cassette *A*	—	(1,167 – 1,100) × 5	=	335 (*F*)
Cassette *B*	—	(1,008 – 950) × 15	=	870 (*F*)
Cassette *C*	—	(1,325 – 1,250) × 10	=	750 (*F*)
			=	1,955 (*F*)

Volume variance = Mix variance + Quantity variance
1,250 *F* = 705 (*A*) + 1,955 (*F*)

Profit and loss statement

	Cassette A	*Cassette* B	*Cassette* C
Budgeted Sales	55,000	95,000	1,00,000
Less : Budgeted cost	49,500	80,750	87,500
Budgeted profit	5,500	14,250	12,500

Variances :

Price variance	6,500 (*F*)	5,000 (*A*)	2,400 (*A*)
Mix variance	665 (*F*)	120 (*A*)	1,250 (*A*)
Qty. variance	335 (*F*)	870 (*F*)	750 (*F*)
	13,000	10,000	9,600

Problem 38 : Compute the following variances from the data given below :

(1) Total sales margin variance.
(2) Sales margin volume variance.
(3) Sales margin price variance.
(4) Sales margin mix variance.
(5) Sales margin quantity (sub-volume) variance.

Product	*Budgeted quantity (Units)*	*Actual quantity (Units)*	*Budgeted sales price per unit Rs.)*	*Actual sales price per unit (Rs.)*	*Standard cost per unit (Rs.)*
X	240	400	50	45	30
Y	160	200	25	20	15

(*CA, Inter, May 1992*)

Solution : (1) Total sales margin variance = Actual profit – Budgeted profit
7,000 – 6,400 = 600 (*F*)
(*see working note 2*)

(2) Sales margin volume variance = (Actual qty. – Budgeted qty.) × Budgeted margin per unit
X = (400 – 240) × 20 = 3,200 *F*
Y = (200 – 160) × 10 = 400 *F*
3,600 *F*

(3) Sales margin price variance = (Actual margin per unit – Budgeted margin per unit × Actual Qty.
X = (15 – 20) × 400 = 2,000 (*A*)
Y = (5 – 10) × 200 = 1,000 (*A*)
3,000 (*A*)

(4) Sales margin mix variance = (Budgeted margin per unit on actual mix – Budgeted margin per unit as budgeted mix) × Total actual qty.
(*Refer working note 3*)
= (Rs. 16.666 – 16) × 600 = 400 (*F*)

(5) Sales margin qty. (sub-volume) variance = (Total actual qty. – Total budgeted qty.) × Budgeted margin per unit on budgeted mix
= (600 – 400) × 16 = 3,200 (*F*)
(*Refer working note 3*)

Verification :

Sales margin variance = Sales margin price variance + Sales margin volume variance
600 (*F*) = 3,000 (*A*) + 3,600 (*F*)

Sales margin volume variance = Sales margin mix variance + Sales margin qty. variance
3,600 (*F*) = 400 (*F*) + 3,200 (*F*)

Working Notes :

1. (*a*) Actual margin per unit = (Actual sales prices per unit – Standard cost per unit)
X = (45 – 30) = Rs. 15
Y = (20 – 15) = Rs. 5

(*b*) Budgeted margin per unit = Budgeted sales price per unit – STd. cost per unit
X = (50 – 30) = Rs. 20
Y = (25 – 15) = Rs. 10

2. (*a*) Actual profit = Actual qty. of product unit sold – Actual margin per unit

X	= 400 × 15	=	6,000
Y	= 200 × 5	=	1,000
			7,000

(*b*) Budgeted profit = Budgeted qty. of units to be sold × Budgeted margin per unit

X	= 240 × 20	=	4,800
Y	= 160 × 10	=	1,600
			6,400

3. (*a*) Budgeted margin per unit on actual mix

$$= \frac{20 \times 400 + 10 \times 200}{600}$$

$$= \frac{8,000 + 2,000}{6,000} = 16.666$$

(*b*) Budgeted margin per unit on budgeted mix

$$= \frac{20 \times 240 + 10 \times 160}{400}$$

$$= \frac{4,800 + 1,600}{400} = \frac{6,400}{400} = \text{Rs. } 16$$

Problem 39 : Compute the missing data indicated by the question marks from the following :

	Product R	*Product S*
Sales quantity		
Standard (units)	?	400
Actual (units)	500	?
Price per unit	Rs.	Rs.
Standard	12	15
Actual	15	20
Sales price variance	?	
Sales volume variance	1,200 (*F*)	
Sales value variance	?	

Sales mix variance for both the products together was Rs. 450 *F*. (*CA, Inter, Nov. 1988*)

Solution :

	Std. sales data			*Actual sales data*		
	Sales qty.	*Price per unit*	*Amt.*	*Sales qty.*	*Price per unit*	*Amt.*
R	?	12	?	500	15	7,500
S	400	15	6,000	?	20	?

(1) Product *R* sales price variance = (Std. sales price – Actual sales price) × Actual sales qty.
(12 – 15) × 500 = 1,500 (*F*)

(2) Sales volume variance (assuming std. sales qty. to be *x*) = (Actual sales qty. – Std. sales qty.) × Std. sales price

= 1,200 *F* = (500 – *x*) × 12

On solving this relation we get the value of *x* as 400 units. Hence standard sales quantity is 400 units.

(3) Sales value variance = Sales price variance + Sales volume variance
= 1,500 (*F*) + 1,200 (*F*) = 2,700 *F*

To find the actual sales quantity of product *S*

Sales mix variance (for product *R* and *S* together) = (Std. rate of actual mix – Std. rate of std. mix) × Actual sales qty.

$$450\ F\ \text{(given)} = \frac{6,000 + 15x}{500 + x} - \frac{10,800}{800} \times 500 + x$$

or $(6,000 + 15x) - 13.5\ (500 + x) = 450\ F$

or $15x - 13.5x - 6,750 + 6,000x = 450\ F$

or $1.5\ x = \text{Rs. } 1,200$

$x = 800$ units

Product *S*

Sales volume variance = (Actual sales qty. – Std. sales qty.) × Std. volume variance
= (800 – 400) 15 = 6,000 *F*

Sales price variance = (Actual sale price – Std. sales price) × Actual sales units
= (20 – 15) × 800 = 4,000 (*F*)

Sales value variance = Sales volume variance + Sales price variance
= 6,000 *F* + 4,00 *F* = 10,000 (*F*)

Problem 40 : The following particulars are available in respect of the Sunshine Co. Ltd. for the period 1992 :

	Budgeted sales			*Actual sales*		
	Qt.	*Rate*	*Amt.*	*Qty.*	*Rate*	*Amt.*
X	1,000	2	2,000	1,800	2,50	4,500
Y	3,000	3	9,000	4,200	2,75	11,550
	4,000		11,000	6,000		16,050

You are required to calculate (*a*) Total sales variance, (*b*) Sales price variance, (*c*) Sales mix variance, (*d*) Sales qty. variance.

Solution : Sales value variance = Budgeted sales – Actual sales

X = (2,000 – 4,500) = 2,500 (*F*)

Y = (9,000 – 11,550) = 2,550 (*F*)

Alternatively total sales value variance = Total budgeted sales – Total actual sales
= 11,000 – 16,050 = 5,050 (*F*)

Sales price variance = (Budgeted selling price – Actual selling price) × Actual selling price

X = (2 – 2.50) × 1,800 = 900 (*F*)

Y = (3 – 2.75) × 4,200 = 1,050 (*F*)

150 (*F*)

Sales mix variance = (Revised std. sales mix – Actual sales mix) × Std. selling price

$$\text{Revised std. sales mix} = \frac{\text{Total actual sales mix}}{\text{Total std. sales mix}} \times \text{Std. qty. of sales}$$

$$X = \frac{6,000}{4,000} \times 1,000 = 1,500 \text{ units}$$

$$Y = \frac{6,000}{4,000} \times 3,000 = 4,500 \text{ units}$$

X = (1,500 – 1,800) × 2 = 6,00 (*F*)

Y = (4,500 – 4,200) – 3 = 900 (*F*)

300 (*A*)

Sales quantity variance = (Revised std. qty. – Std. or budgeted qty.) × Std. selling price

X = (1,500 – 1,000) × 2 = 1,000 (*F*)

Y = (4,500 – 3,000) × 3 = 4,500 (*F*)

5,500 (*F*)

Problem 41 : The budgeted and the actual sales for a period in respect of three products are given below :

Budgeted figures

Product	*Quantity*	*Price*	*Value*
A	1,000	5	5,000
B	750	10	7,500
C	500	15	7,500
	2,250		20,000

Actuals

A	1,200	6	7,200
B	700	9	6,300
C	600	14	8,400
	2,500		21,900

Calculate sales variances. (*CA, Inter, November 1998*)

Solution :

Products	*Budgeted*			*Actual*			*Actual qty. × Budgeted price*
	Qty.	*Rate*	*Value*	*Qty.*	*Rate*	*Value*	*Value*
A	1,000	5	5,000	1,200	6	7,200	6,000
B	750	10	7,500	700	9	6,300	7,000
C	500	15	7,500	600	14	8,400	9,000
	2,250		20,000	2,500		21,900	22,000

(1) Sales value variance = Budgeted sales – Actual sales
= 20,000 – 21,900
= 1,900 *F*

(2) Sales price variance = (Budgeted price – Actual price) × Actual qty.

A	=	(6 – 5) × 1,200	=	1,200 *F*
B	=	(10 – 9) × 700	=	700 *A*
C	=	(15 – 14) × 600	=	600 *A*
				100 *A*

(3) Sales volume variance = (Budgeted qty. – Actual qty.) × Budgeted selling price

A	=	(1,000 – 1200) × 5	
	=	1,000 *F*	1,000 *F*
B	=	(750 – 700) × 10	
	=	500 *A*	500 *A*
C	=	(500 – 600) × 15	
	=	1,500 *F*	15,000 *F*
			2,000 *F*

(4) Sales mix variance = (Budgeted price per unit of actual mix – Budgeted price per unit of budgeted mix) × Total actual qty.

$$= \left(\frac{22,000}{2,500} - \frac{20,000}{2,250}\right) \times 2,500$$

= (8.80 – 8.88) × 2,500
= 222 (*A*)

(5) Sales qty. variance = (Total actual qty. – Total budgeted qty.) × Budgeted price per unit of budgeted mix

$$= (2{,}500 - 2{,}250) \times \frac{20{,}000}{2{,}250}$$

$$= 2{,}222\ (F)$$

Problem 42 : The standard cost data of three products *X*, *Y* and *Z* manufactured by a company are given below together with the budgeted sales and unit selling prices for 1995-96 :

	X	*Y*	*Z*
Budgeted sales (unit)	25,000	20,000	15,000
Selling price per unit (Rs.)	40	60	80
Cost per unit (Rs.)	28	48	64

In April 1996, the cost department of the company gathered the following details for 1995-96 :

	X	*Y*	*Z*
Actual Sales (units)	20,000	22,000	16,000
Average sales realisation per unit (Rs.)	42	56	81
Actual cost per unit (Rs.)	30	50	63

You are required to determine :

(*a*) The budgeted profit and the actual profit for 1995-96.

(*b*) The variance in profit analysed into

(*i*) Cost variance.

(*ii*) Sales price variance.

(*iii*) Sales volume variance.

(*ICWA, Inter, June 1996*)

Solution :

	Budgeted profit			Actual profit		
X	(40 – 28) × 25,000	=	3,00,000	(42 – 30) × 20,000	=	2,40,000
Y	(60 – 48) × 20,000	=	2,40,000	(56 – 50) × 22,000	=	1,32,000
Z	(80 – 64) × 15,000	=	2,40,000	(81 – 63) × 16,000	=	2,88,000
			7,80,000			6,60,000

Variance in profit = 7,80,000 – 6,60,000
= 1,20,000 *A*

(1) Cost variance = (Std. cost – Actual cost) × Actual *No.* of units sold

X	=	(28 – 30) × 20,000	=	40,000 *A*
Y	=	(48 – 50) × 22,000	=	44,000 *A*
Z	=	(64 – 63) × 16,000	=	16,000 *F*
				68,000 *A*

(2) Selling price variance= (Std. price – Actual price) × Actual *No.* of units sold

X	=	(40 – 42) × 20,000	=	40,000 *F*
Y	=	(60 – 56) × 22,000	=	88,000 *A*
Z	=	(80 – 81) × 16,000	=	16,000 *F*
				32,000 *A*

(3) Sales volume variance= (Budgeted volume – Actual volume) × Std. profit

X	=	(25,000 – 20,000) × 12	=	60,000 *A*
Y	=	(20,000 – 22,000) × 12	=	24,000 *F*
Z	=	(15,000 – 16,000) × 16	=	16,000 *F*
				20,000 *A*

CONTROL RATIOS

Ratios are often used as a control technique in addition to monetary value of variance. The following ratios are commonly used in indurstries.

Efficiency Ratio

This ratio measures the efficiency at which the factory operates. The ICMA terminology defines efficiency ratio as "the standard hours equivalent to the work produced, expressed as a percentage of the actual hours spent in producing that work. Expressed as a formula :

$$\text{Efficiency ratio} = \frac{\text{Actual production in terms of standard hrs.}}{\text{Actual hours worked}} \times 100$$

Activity Ratio

This ratio measures the level of a activity at which the factory is operating. The ICMA terminology defines it as "the number of standard hours equivalent to the work produced, expressed as a percentage of the budgeted standard hours". Expressed as a formula :

$$\text{Actual ratio} = \frac{\text{Actual production in terms of std. hrs.}}{\text{Budgeted production in terms of std. hrs.}} \times 100$$

Capacity Ratio

The ICMA terminology defines it as "the relationship between the actual number of working hours and the budgeted number". Expressed as a formula :

$$\text{Capacity ratio} = \frac{\text{Actual hours worked}}{\text{Budgeted production in terms of standard hours}} \times 100$$

Problem 43 : In a manufacturing shop, product X required 2.5 man hours and product Y requires 6 man-hours. In a month of 25 working days of 8 hours a day 2,000 units of X and 1,000 units of Y were produced. The company employed 50 workers in the shop and the budgeted man-hours are 1,08,000 for the year. You are required to work out the capacity ratio, activity ratio, and efficiency ratio. *(ICWA, Inter, June 1990)*

Solution : Standard man-hours produced

Product X : 2,000 units @ 2.5 man-hours	=	5,000	man-hours
Product Y : 1,000 units @ 6 man-hours	=	6,000	man-hours
Total		11,000	man-hours

Budgeted standard man-hours per month

$$= \frac{1,08,000}{12} = 9,000 \text{ man-hours}$$

Actual man-hours worked = 50 workers × 25 days × 8 hrs.= 10,000 man-hours

$$\text{(1) Capacity ratio} = \frac{\text{Actual man–hours worked}}{\text{Std. man–hours budgeted}} \times 100$$

$$= \frac{10,000}{9,000} \times 100 = 111.11\%$$

$$\text{(2) Activity ratio} = \frac{\text{Standard man-hours produced}}{\text{Standard man-hours budgeted}} \times 100$$

$$= \frac{11,000}{9,000} \times 100 = 122.22\%$$

$$\text{(3) Efficiency ratio} = \text{Standard man} - \frac{\text{Hours produced}}{\text{Actual man}} - \text{hours worked} \times 100$$

$$= \frac{11,000}{10,000} \times 100 = 110\%$$

Problem 44 : Calculate from the following figures :

(1) Efficiency ratio
(2) Activity ratio
(3) Capacity ratio

Budgeted production	880 units
Standard hours per unit	10
Actual production	750 units
Actual working hours	6,000

(CA, Inter, May 1999)

$$\text{(1) Efficiency ratio} = \frac{\text{Std. hours for actual production}}{\text{Actual hours worked}} \times 100$$

$$= \frac{750 \text{ units} \times 10 \text{ hours}}{6,000} \times 100$$

$$= 125\%$$

$$\text{(2) Activity ratio} = \frac{\text{Std. hours for actual production}}{\text{Budgeted hours}} \times 100$$

$$= \frac{750 \times 10}{880 \text{ units} \times 10 \text{ hours}} \times 100$$

$$= 85.23\%$$

$$\text{(3) Capacity ratio} = \frac{\text{Actual hours worked}}{\text{Budgeted hours}} \times 100$$

$$= \frac{600}{880 \times 10}$$

$$= 68.18\%$$

Problem 45 : If the activity ratio and capacity ratio of a company is 104% and 96% respectively find out its efficiency ratio" *(CA, Inter, May 1997)*

Solution :

$$\text{Activity ratio} = \frac{\text{Std. hours required for actual production}}{\text{Budgeted hours}} \times 100$$

$$\text{Capacity ratio} = \frac{\text{Actual hours worked}}{\text{Budgeted hours}} \times 100$$

$$\text{Efficiency ratio} = \frac{\text{Std. hours required for actual production}}{\text{Actual hours worked}} \times 100$$

From the above ratios it is clear that efficiency ratio can be obtained by dividing activity ratio by capacity ratio

So,

$$\text{Efficiencey ratio} = \frac{\text{Activity Ratio}}{\text{Capacity Ratio}} \times 100$$

(in percentage)

$$= \frac{104}{96} \times 100 = 108.33\%$$

INVESTIGATION OF VARIANCE AND REPORTING TO MANAGEMENT

Investigation of variance enables to take prompt control over the variance. The following benefits are derived by the process of investigating the variance :

(*a*) The person responsible for the variance is revealed.

(*b*) It reveals the accuracy of accounting system.

(*c*) Whether variance is on account of abnormal conditions and if so how to take precautionary measures in such situtation.

(*d*) To appraise the current standard and revise if need be.

Having investigated the variance, it is necessary to prepare variance analysis reports for the sake of submitting to management. In preparing and submitting such reports the following guidelines may be followed :

(*a*) The reports must be prepared and submitted promptly to the management. Otherwise its purpose is lost.

(*b*) Only those reports which are relevant to the persons jurisdiction to exercise control should be sent.

(*c*) Analysis of variance must be based on cost centre.

(*d*) Ratios, percentages, etc. can also be used while reporting in addition to monetary value of variances.

(*e*) The cost accountant should interact with various levels of management in addition to preparation and submission of reports.

The important reports to be sent to various levels of management are (1) Material price variance report, (2) Material usage variance report, (3) Wage rate variance report, (4) Labour efficiency variance report, (5) Sales value variance report.

Based on the reports of variance analysis, the variances are disposed off. One method of treating variance is to transfer it to costing profit and loss account. The second method advocated by some accountants is to properly distribute over closing stock and cost of sales so that both these items can be shown at actual costs in financial statement.

REVISION AND METHODS VARIANCE

Sometimes standards are revised owing to reasons such as change in wage rate, fiscal policy, etc. If such changes are incorporated in the standards, it may affect the variances and controllable factors may escape the attention of executives. Hence any changes in the factors is included in the revised budget but the standard cost is retained as a matter of policy. This process of retaining the basic standards in spite of change in the factors and analysing the variances on the basis of basic standards is known as revision variance.

A method variance refers to the difference between the standard cost of manufacture performed by normal method and the cost of manufacturing by an alternate method.

QUESTIONS

I. Fill in the blanks

1. The system which determines what the cost 'should be' in advance of production is called ________ technique of costing.
2. For labour, the difference between actual hours at actual rate and actual hours at standard rate is called the _____ variance.
3. Gang composition variance is a sub-variance of _____ variance.
4. When the actual cost is less than the standard cost, the difference is known as _____ variance.
5. Overhead variance is the difference between the __________ cost of overhead absorbed in the output and the _______ overhead cost.
6. Material price variance = (Std. price – Actual price) × ______

[***Answer :*** (1) standard costing, (2) labour rate, (3) labour efficiency, (4) favourable, (5) standard, actual, (6) actual quantity]

II. Choose the correct answer

1. The cost of a product as determined under standard costing is
   (*a*) fixed cost (*c*) direct cost
   (*b*) historical cost (*d*) predetermined cost [ ]
2. While evaluating deviations of actual cost from standard cost, the technique used is
   (*a*) regression analysis (*c*) trend analysis
   (*b*) variance analysis (*d*) linear progression [ ]
3. Which one of the following standards can be attained under the most favourable conditions possible?
   (*a*) theoretical standard (*c*) normal standard
   (*b*) expected standard (*d*) basic standard [ ]
4. Standard costs are useful in all of the following except
   (*a*) reducing cost (*c*) establishing records
   (*b*) speeding up preparation of operating reports (*d*) costing inventories [ ]
5. Controllable variance are best disposed of by transferring to
   (*a*) cost of goods sold (*c*) cost of goods sold and inventories
   (*b*) inventories of work-in-progress and finished goods (*d*) costing profit and loss account

[***Answers :*** 1. (*d*), 2. (*b*), 3. (*a*), 4. (*c*), 5. (*d*)]

III. Mark true or false

1. Standard costs are fixed for each industry by the trade association concerned. *T/F*
2. Standards do not allow for any idleness and wastage and are therefore idealistic. *T/F*
3. Standards are arrived at on the basis of past performance. *T/F*
4. Standards represent achievable targets but after a purposeful effort. *T/F*
5. Standards for materials labour and overheads are inter-connected. *T/F*
6. Variance means the difference between the budget and standard costs. *T/F*
7. Favourable variances are those that increase the amounts and unfavourable ones reduce the amounts. *T/F*
8. All variances are transferred to the cost of sales account. *T/F*
9. Standard costing help management by exception by showing up the total difference between actual profit and standard profit. *T/F*
10. Price variances are calculated at actual quantity multiplied by differences in prices. *T/F*
11. Efficiency variances are concerned with quantities used and are calculated as standard quantity multiplied by difference in price. *T/F*
12. Yield variance shows the efficiency of labour. *T/F*

[***Answer :*** True—4, 5, 10, Rest are all False]

IV. Short and long answer questions

1. Explain the term 'variance' under standard costing and discuss its significance. (*University of Kerala, M.Com., May 1992*)
2. Discuss the utility of variance analysis in cost control. What are the major causes for efficiency, volume, capacity and calender variance? (*Calicut University, M.Com., April 1992*)
3. Distinguish between standard costing and budgetary control. Discuss the advantages and disadvantages of standard costing. (*Kakatiya University, M.Com., August 1991*)
4. Distinguish between standard costing and budgetary control. Are both these systems inter-related? (*Bangalore University, M.Com., May 1989*)
5. Define standard costing. Explain the advantages and limitations of standard costing. (*Bangalore University, M.Com., May 1990*)
6. What are the various circumstances under which material price and material usage variances are likely to arise? (*ICWA, Inter, June 1990*)

EXERCISES

Exercise 1 : *SV* Ltd., manufactures *BXE* by mixing three raw materials. For every batch of 100 kgs. of *BXE*, 125 kgs. of raw materials are used. In February 1986, 60 batches were prepared to produce an output of 5,600 kgs. of *BXE*. The standard and actual particulars for February 1986 are as under :

Raw material	Standard Mix %	Standard Price per Kg. (Rs.)	Actual Mix %	Actual Price per Kg.	Quantity of raw materials Purchased Kg.(Rs.)
A	50	20	60	21	5,000
B	30	10	20	8	2,000
C	20	5	20	6	1,200

Calculate :

1. Material cost variance.
2. Material price variance.
3. Material mix variance.
4. Material yield variance.

(*University of Delhi, B.Com. (Hons.) 1986*)

[*Answer :* Material cost variance = Rs. 17,500 (*A*)
Material price variance *A* = 4,500 (*A*)
B = 3,000 (*F*)
C = 1,500 (*A*)
Material mix variance *A* = 15,000 *A*
B = 7,500 F
C = 0
Material yield variance = Rs. 7,000 *F*]

Exercise 2: The standard mix of product A_2 is as follows :

Kgs.	*Materials*	*Price per kg.* (Rs.)
45	*X*	6.00
25	*Y*	4.50
30	*Z*	9.50

The standard loss in production is 10% of input. There is no scrap value. Actual production for a month was 7,425 kgs. of A_2 from 80 mixes. Actual purchases and consumption of materials during the month were :

Kgs.	*Material*	*Price per kg. (Rs.)*
4,200	*X*	6.50
1,700	*Y*	4.25
2,600	*Z*	9.75

You are required to calculate the following variances for presentation to the management :

1. Material cost variance.
2. Material price variance.
3. Material mix variance.
4. Material yield variance.

(*C.S., Inter, Dec. 1998*)

[*Answer :* Material price variance *X* = 2,100 (*A*)
Material price variance *Y* = 425 (*F*)
Material price variance *Z* = 650 (*A*)
Material mix variance *X* = 2,250 (*A*)
Material mix variance *Y* = 1,912.50 (*F*)
Material mix variance *Z* = 475 (A)
Material yield variance *X* = 675 (*A*)
Material yield variance *Y* = 281.25 (*A*)
Material yield variance *Z* = 712.50 (*A*)
Material cost variance *X* = 5,025 (*A*)
Material cost variance *Y* = 2,056.25 (*A*)
Material cost variance *Z* = 1,837,50 (A)]

Exercise 3 : Gemini Chemical Industries provide the following information from their records :
For making 10 kgs. of Gemco the standard material requirement is.

Material	*Qty. (Kgs.)*	*Rate per kg. (Rs.)*
A	8	6.00
B	4	4.00

During April 1988, 1,000 kgs. of Gemco were produced. The actual consumption of material is as under :

Material	*Qty. (Kgs.)*	*Rate per kg. (Rs.)*
A	750	7
B	500	5

Calculate : (*a*) Material cost variance, (*b*) Material price variance, (*c*) Material usage variance.

(*CA, Inter, May 1989*)

[*Answer :* Total material cost Variance = 1,350 (*A*)
Total material price variance = 1,250 (*A*)
Total material usage variance = 100 (*A*)]

Exercise 4 : A company manufacturing 'distempers' operates a costing system. The standard cost for one of the products of the company shows the following materials standards :

Material	*Quantity*	*Standard price per kg.*	*Total (Rs.)*
A	40 kg.	75	3,000
B	10 kg.	50	500
C	50 kg.	20	1,000
		Material cost per units	4,500

The standard input mix is 200 kg. and the standard output of the finished product is 90 kg.
The actual results for a period are :

Material used *A* = 2,40,000 kg. @ Rs. 80 per kg.
B = 40,000 kg. @ Rs. 52 per kg.
C = 2,20,000 kg. @ Rs. 21 per kg.

Actual output of the finished product = 4,20,000 kg.
You are required to calculate the material price, mix, yield, usage and cost variance.

(*ICWA, Inter, Dec. 1989*)

[*Answer :* Material price variance = 15,00,000
Material mix variance = 19,00,000
Material yield variance = 15,00,000
Material usage variance = 34,00,000
Material cost variance = 4,90,000]

Exercise 5 (Labour cost variance) : The standard labour component and the actual labour component engaged in a week for a job are as under :

	Skilled workers	*Semi-skilled workers*	*Unskilled workers*
(*a*) Standard number of workers in the gang	32	12	6
(*b*) Standard wage rate per hour (Rs.)	3	2	1
(*c*) Actual number of workers employed in the gang during the week	28	18	4
(*d*) Actual wage rate per hour (Rs.)	4	3	2

During the 40-hour working week, the gang produced 1,800 standard labour hours of work. Calculate the difference labour variance. (*University of Delhi, B.Com. (Hons.) 1987*)

[*Answer :*
Labour rate—Skilled = 1,120 (*A*)
Labour rate variance—Semi-skilled = 720 (*A*)
Labour rate variance—Unskilled = 160 (*A*)
Labour efficiency variance—Skilled = 96 (*F*)
Labour efficiency variance—Semi-skilled = 576 (*A*)
Labour efficiency variance—Unskilled = 56 (*F*)
424 (*A*)
Labour mix variance—Skilled = 480 (*F*)
Labour mix variance—Semi-skilled = 480 (*A*)
Labour mix variance—Unskilled = 80 (*F*)
Labour revised efficiency variance—Skilled = 384 (*A*)
Labour revised efficiency variance—Semi-skilled = 96 (*A*)
Labour revised efficiency variance—Unskilled = 24 (*A*)
Total labour cost variance = 2,424 (*A*)]

Exercise 6 : A gang of workers normally consists of 30 men, 15 women and 10 boys. They are paid at standard hourly rates as under :

Men	Re. 0.80
Women	Re. 0.60
Boys	Re. 0.40

In a normal working week of 40 hours, the gang is expected to produce, 2,000 units of output.

During the week ended 31st Dec., 1977, the gang consisted of 40 men, 10 women and 5 boys. The actual wages paid were @ 0.70 Re. 0.65 and Re. 0.30, respectively 4 hours were lost due to abnormal idle time and 1,600 units were produced.

Calculate (1) wage variance, (2) wage rate variance, (3) labour efficiency variance, (4) gang composition variance and (5) labour idle time variance. *(CA, (Final), May 1978)*

[*Answer :*

Labour cost variance	=	256 (*A*)
Wage rate variance—Men	=	160 (*F*)
Wage rate variance—Women	=	20 (*A*)
Wage rate variance—Boys	=	20 (*F*)
Labour efficiency variance—Men	=	512 (*A*)
Labour efficiency variance—Women	=	48 (*F*)
Labour efficiency variance—Boys	=	48 (*F*)
Idle time variance—Men	=	128
Idle time variance—Women	=	24
Idle time variance—Boys	=	8
Labour efficiency variance—Men (after segregeting idle time variance)	=	384 (*A*)
Labour efficiency variance—Women	=	72 (*F*)
Labour efficiency variance—Boys	=	56 (*F*)
Labour mix variance—Men	=	288 (*A*)
Labour mix variance—Women	=	108 (*F*)
Labour mix variance—Boys	=	72 (*F*)
Labour yield variance	=	148 (*A*)]

Exercise 7 : Using the following information calculate labour cost variance, labour rate variance, labour efficiency variance and idle time variance.

Standard hours	:	5,000
Standard wage rate	:	Rs. 4 per hour
Actual hours	:	6,000
Actual wage rate	:	Rs. 3.50 per hr.
Time cost on account of machine breakdown	:	300 hrs.

(Calicut University, B.Com., April 1986)

[*Answer :*

Labour cost variance	=	Rs. 1,000 (*A*)
Labour rate variance	=	Rs. 3,000 (*F*)
Labour efficiency variance	=	Rs, 2,800 (*A*)
Idle time variance	=	Rs. 1,200 (*A*)]

Exercise 8 (Material and labour cost variance) : The standard costs on materials and labour for the making of unit of certain product are estimated as under :

Material—80 kg. at Rs. 1.50 per kg.

Wages—18 hrs. at Rs. 1.25 per kg.

On completion of unit of the product, it was found that 75 kg. of material costing Rs. 1.75 per kg. has been consumed and the time taken was 16 hours, the wages being Rs. 1.50 per hour.

Calculate the material and labour variances. *(Bharathidasan University, B.Sc., April 1988)*

[*Answer :*

Material cost variance	=	Rs. 11.25 (*A*)
Material price variance	=	Rs. 18.75 (*A*)
Material usage variance	=	Rs. 7.50 (*F*)
Labour cost variance	=	Rs. 1.50 (*F*)
Labour rate variance	=	Rs. 4 (*A*)
Labour efficiency variance	=	Rs. 2.50 (*F*)]

Exercise 9 (Overhead variance) : Following information is available from the records of a factory :

	Budget	*Actual*
Fixed overhead for June	Rs. 10,000	Rs. 12,000
Production in June (units)	2,000	2,100
Standard time per unit (hrs.)	10	
Actual hours worked in June		220.00

Compute (*i*) Fixed overhead cost variance, (*ii*) Expenditure variance, (*iii*) Volume variance, (*iv*) Capacity variance, (*v*) Efficiency variance. (*CA, Inter, Nov. 1989*)

[*Answer :* Fixed overhead expenditure variance = 2,000 (*A*)
Fixed overhead capacity variance = 1,000 (*F*)
Fixed overhead efficiency variance = 500 (*A*)
Fixed overhead volume variance = 500 (*F*)
Fixed overhead cost variance = 1,500 (*A*)]

Exercise 10 : A cost accountant of company was given the following information regarding the overhead for February 1987 :

(*a*) Overhead cost variance Rs. 1,400 adverse.
(*b*) Overhead volume variance Rs. 1,000 adverse.
(*c*) Budgeted hours for February 1987, 1,200 hrs.
(*d*) Budgeted overheads for February 1987, Rs. 6,000.
(*e*) Actual rate of recovery of overheads Rs. 8 per hour.

You are required to assist him in computing the following for Feb. 1987 : (1) overhead expenditure variance, (2) actual overhead incurred, (3) actual hours for actual production, (4) overheads capacity variance, (5) overheads efficiency variance and (6) standard hours for actual production. (*CA, Inter, May 1987*)

[*Answer :* (1) 400 (*A*), (2) Rs. 6,400, (3) 800 hrs., (4) 2,000 (*A*), (5) 1,000 (*F*), (6) 1,000 hrs.]

Exercise 11 (Sales variance) : *X* Ltd. operates a budgetary control and standard costing system. From the following data calculate (*i*) sales variance, (*ii*) sales volume variance, (*iii*) sales price variance.

Product	*Budgeted*		*Actual*	
	Unit to be sold	*Sales value* (Rs.)	*Units sold*	*Sales value* (Rs.)
A	100	1,200	100	1,100
B	50	600	50	600
C	100	900	200	1,700
D	75	450	50	300
	325	3,150	400	3,700

(*CS, (Final), June 1987*)

[*Answer :* Sales volume variance = Rs. 200 (*A*)
Sales price variance = Rs. 750 (*F*)
Sales variance = Rs. 550 (*F*)]

Exercise 12 : Budgeted and actual sales for the month of December 1984 of two products *A* and *B* of M/s. *XY* Ltd. were as follows :

Product	*Budgeted sales*		*Actual sales*	
	Units	*Price per unit*	*Units*	*Price per unit*
A	6,000	5	5,000	5.00
			1,500	4.75
B	10,000	2	7,500	2.00
			1,750	1.90

Budgeted cost for products *A* and *B* were Rs. 4 and Rs. 1.50 per unit respectively. Work out from the above data the following variances :

(*i*) Sales value variance.
(*ii*) Sales volume variance.
(*iii*) Sales price variance.

(*iv*) Sales mix variance.

(*v*) Sales quantity variance.

(*ICWA, (Inter), June 1985*)

[*Answer :*				
	Sales value price variance	=	Rs. 550	(*A*)
	Sales mix variance	=	1,781	(*F*)
	Sales qty. variance	=	781	(*A*)
	Sales volume variance	=	1,000	(*F*)]
	Sales value variance	=	450	(*F*)]

Exercise 13 (Ratios) : From the following particulars calculate :
(*a*) Capacity usage ratio, (*b*) Activity ratio and (*c*) Efficiency ratio :

	Budget	*Actual*
Direct labour hours	10,000	9,600
Number of units	5,000	5,200
Fixed overhead	Rs. 2,500	Rs. 2,600

[*Answer :*			
	Capacity usage ratio	=	96%
	Activity ratio	=	104%
	Efficiency ratio	=	108.5%]

12

REPORTING TO MANAGEMENT

INTRODUCTION

The term 'reporting' conveys different meanings under different circumstances. In a narrow sense it meant supplying facts and figures. Where a committee is appointed to study a problem, a report is taken to mean review of certain matter with its pros and cons and offering suggestions. In case of dealing with routine matters, a report refers to supplying the information at regular intervals in standardised forms. In this chapter reporting is taken to mean furnishing of cost accounting information to management. A report is a means of communication which is in written form and is meant for use of management for the purpose of planning decision-making and controlling. Simply stated it is a communication of result by a subordinate to superior. It serves as a feedback to the management. The contents of report, the details of the data reported and the method of presentation depend upon the size and type of the business enterprise, extent of power delegated to subordinates and the existence of various levels of management for whom information is meant.

IMPORTANCE

Cost accounting embraces three important divisions, *viz.*, cost ascertainment, cost presentation and cost control. Cost presentation serves as a link between cost ascertainment and cost control. The management of every organisation is interested in maximisation of profit through minimisation of wastages, losses and ultimately cost. So management will have to be furnished with frequent reports on all functional areas of business to achieve these objectives. One of the important functions of cost accounting is to provide the required information to all levels of management at the appropriate time. The various aspects of reporting such as nature of reports to be prepared, the details of information to be included and mode of presentation are all decided at the time of installation of cost accounting system. In fact, cost ascertainment and cost control are designed in such a way that they suit the scheme of information to be presented so that they serve all levels of management but not the other way round.

REQUISITES OF A GOOD REPORT

A good report should satisfy the following requisities in order to enable the receiver of report to understand and get interested in the report.

(*a*) **Title :** This contains the subject-matter of the report. It should be brief but not vague. Where a lengthy report is to be prepared the subject-matter is to be presented in various paragraphs under different sub-titles.

(*b*) **Period :** It should mention the duration covered by the report.

(*c*) **Units of measurement :** In case of quantitative information is to be reported the units in which quantities are expressed should be clear. For example, production in tonnes, sales in lakh rupees, idle time in hours.

(*d*) **Date :** The date on which the report is presented is to be mentioned. This helps receiver of the report to know what changes must have occurred during the time lag of period covered under the report and date of presentation of report.

(*e*) **Name :** The report must contain the name of the person by whom a report is prepared, the name of person to whom it is meant and the names of those for whom copies are sent.

(*f*) **Standard :** The reports prepared must meet the standard expected by its receiver. Use of highly technical words may by readily understood by lower level management.

(*g*) **Use of diagrams :** Wherever possible the reports must be illustrated by diagrams and charts in addition to description of the report. This facilitates ready understanding.

(*h*) **Recommendations :** Recommendations are to be offered to facilitate the reader as to what course of action is to be taken to set right the defects.

(*i*) **Promptness :** The reports should be prepared periodically and submitted to all levels of management promptly. It is said that report delayed is report denied. If the time lag between the period of preparation and period of submission is more it may give rise to wrong decisions.

(*j*) **Accuracy :** The information furnished in the report must be accurate. It is important to avoid furnishing unnecessary details in the report.

(*k*) **Comparison :** A comparative study must be incorporated in the report so as to facilitate the receiver of the report to know the progress and prospects of the performance. Comparison can be based on past performance or predetermined performance.

(*l*) **Economy :** The expenses incurred in maintaining reporting system must be less than the benfits derived therefrom or loss sustained by not reporting.

(*m*) **Simplicity :** The report should be brief, clear and simple to understand. The form of report should be designed to suit different levels of management. Where it is inevitable to prepare a lengthy report, a brief synopsis should precede the report.

(*n*) **Controllability :** Where variances are incorporated it is essential to stress on controllable aspects and to drop out uncontrollable element. But this depends upon the circumstance under which the report is prepared.

(*o*) **Source of information :** The source of information must be included in the report.

TYPES OF REPORTS

Reports are classified into different types according to different bases. This is shown in the following chart :

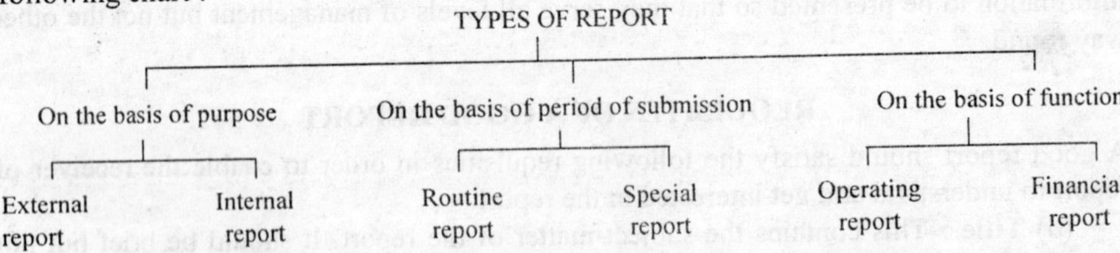

I. On the Basis of Purpose

On the basis of purpose, reports can be classified into two types, *viz.*, (*a*) External report and (*b*) Internal report.

(*a*) **External report :** External report is prepared for meeting the requirements of persons outside the business, such as shareholders, creditors, bankers, government, stock exchange and so on. An example of external report is the published accounts, *viz.*, profit and loss account and balance sheet. External report is brief in size as compared to internal report and they are prepared as per the statutory requirements.

(*b*) **Internal report :** Internal report is meant for different levels of management. This can again be classified into three types : (*a*) Report meant for top level management, (*b*) Report meant for middle level management and (*c*) Report meant for lower level management. Report to top level management should be in summary form giving an overall view of the performance of the business. Whereas external reports are prepared annually, internal reports are prepared frequently to serve the needs of management. Internal report need not conform to any standard form as it is not statutorily required to be prepared.

II. On the Basis of Period of Submission

According to this basis, reports can be classified into two types, *viz.*, (1) Routine reports, and (2) Special reports.

(*a*) **Routine reports :** They are prepared periodically to cover normal activities of the business. They are submitted to different levels of management according to a time schedule fixed. While some reports are prepared and submitted at a very short intervals, some are prepared and submitted at a long interval of time. Some examples of routine reports relate to monthly profit and loss account, monthly balance sheets, monthly production, purchases, sales etc.

(*b*) **Special reports :** Special reports are prepared to cover specific or special matters concerning the business. Most of the special reports are prepared after investigation or survey. There is no standard form used for submitting this report. Some of the matters which are covered by special reports are : causes for production delays, labour disputes, effects of machine breakdown, problems involved in capital expenditure, make or buy problems, purchase or hire of fixed assets, price fixation problems, closing down or continuation of certain departments, cost reduction schemes, etc.

III. On the Basis of Function

According to the purpose served by the reports, it can be classified into two types, *viz.*, (*a*) operating report and (*b*) financial report.

(*a*) **Operating report :** These reports are prepared to reveal the various functional results. These reports can again be classified into three types, *viz.*, (*a*) Control reports, which are prepared to exercise control over various operation of business, (*b*) Information report which are prepared for facilitating planning and policy formulation in a business, (*c*) Venture measurement report which is prepared to show the result of a specific venture undertaken as for example a new product line introduced.

(*b*) **Financial report :** Such reports provide information about financial position of the undertaking. These reports may be prepared annually to show the financial position for the year as in the case of balance sheet or periodically to show the cash position for a given period as in the case of fund flow analysis and cash flow analysis.

FORMS OF REPORT

Reporting of information to management takes different forms. They are explained below :

(*A*) Oral Report

An oral report is not very popular as it does not serve any evidence and cannot be referred to in future. Oral report may take the form of a meeting with individuals or a conference.

(*B*) Descriptive Reports

These are written in narrative style. They are frequently supported by tables and charts to illustrate certain points covered in the report. One important point that must be considered in drafting this form of report is the language. The language used must be simple, easy to understand and lucid. Where the report is very long, it must be suitably divided into paragraphs with headings. They must cover all the principles of good report discussed earlier.

(*C*) Comparative Statement

This form of report is used for preparing the routine report. Under this method the particulars of information are shown in a comparative form, *i.e.*, the actual results are compared with planned results and the deviations between the two are indicated. The various tools used to prepare this form of report are comparative financial statements, ratio analysis, fund flow analysis and so on.

(*D*) Diagrammatic and Graphic Representation

This is more popular form of preparing reports. They occupy lesser space and gives at a glance the whole picture about a particular aspect of study. They also facilitate the comparative study and shows the trend over a period of time. This form of report can be used where a report contains presentation of statistical numbers and other facts and figures. It overcomes the language barrier and is very easily understood by everyone. Of course when large numbers are involved, it is to be reduced by selecting a convenient scale. Diagrammatic representation involves the following forms :

(*a*) **Bar diagram :** They make use of horizontal and veritcal axes to sho.v the magnitude of values, quantity and period. Bar diagrams are of the following types.

(*i*) ***Simple bar diagram :*** These are most popularly used in preparing reports. They consider only length but not the width to indicate the change. Information relating to volume of production, cost of production sales, etc. for different years can be shown under this form.

(*ii*) ***Multiple bar diagram :*** This type of diagram is used to report related matters such as production and sales, sales and profit, advertisement and sales and so on.

(*iii*) ***Sub-divided bar diagram :*** This form of diagram is used to report matters which involve different component parts as for example, the components of total cost of production such as prime cost, factory cost, office cost, cost of sales.

(*iv*) ***Percentage bar diagrams :*** These diagrams depict the information on a percentage basis.

(*b*) **Pie-diagram :** They take the form of circles instead of bars. They facilitate comparison besides depicting the actual information under review.

(*E*) Break-even Chart

This type of chart is prepared to show the relationship between variable and fixed cost and sales. It shows the point of no-profit and no-loss or where total cost equals total revenue received.

(*F*) Gantt Chart

This chart was first introduced by Henry L. Gantt. It is a special type of bar diagram under which bars are drawn horizontally. This chart shows the bars of planned schedule and attained performance. They are largely used to denote utilisation of machine capacity.

REPORTS SUBMITTED TO VARIOUS LEVELS OF MANAGEMENT

1. Top Level Management

The top level management comprises of board of directors, managing director and other executives who are concerned with determination of objectives and formulation of policies. Top management is to be furnished with reports at regular intervals in order to enable them to exercise control over the activities of the business. The following are some of the matters to be reported to board of directors.

(*a*) Master budget which convers all functional budgets for taking remedial actions where there are significant deviations from budgeted figures.

(*b*) Various functional budgets prepared by various departmental managers for holding departmental managers for any shortfall in their performance.

(*c*) Capital expenditure budget and cash budget to know the extent of variances for taking remedial measures.

(*d*) Reports relating to production and sales, which shows the trend of the performance of business.

(*e*) Report covering important ratios such as stock turnover ratio, fixed assets turnover ratio, liquidity ratio, solvency ratio, profitability ratios, etc. to know the improvement in business.

(*f*) Appraisal of various projects undertaken by the organisation.

2. Middle Level Management

It comprises of different department managers such as production manager, purchase manager, sales manager, chief accountant, etc. These managers require reports to improve the efficiency of their respective departments. The following are some of the matters reported to production manager :

(*a*) Report relating to actual capacity utilised as compared to budgeted capacity.

(*b*) Report relating to actual output as against standard output.

(*c*) Labour and machine capacity utilised.

(*d*) Idle time lost.

(*e*) Report on scraps, wastages and losses in production.

(*f*) Report relating to stock of raw materials, work-in-progress and finished goods.

(*g*) Report relating to cost of production, operation of different departments.

The following are some of the matters reported to sales manager :

(*a*) Report relating to number of orders executed, orders received and orders on hand.

(*b*) Report relating to actual sales and budgeted sales and actual selling and distribution expenses and budgeted selling and distribution expenses.

(*c*) Summary of selling expenses incurred in different territories and their corresponding sales.

(*d*) Gross profit earned on different products and in different areas.

(*e*) Market survey reports.

(*f*) Report relating to present and potential demand.

The following are some of the matters reported to financial manager :

(*a*) Report relating to cash position.

(*b*) Summary of receipts and payments.

(*c*) Report relating to outstanding debts on credits sales.
(*d*) Report on debts due on credit purchases.
(*e*) Monthly profit and loss account.
(*f*) Quarterly report on capital expenditure.

3. Lower Level Management

The lower level management include supervisors, forement and inspectors who are concerned with the operations of the factory. They are interested in increasing the efficiency of the production departments. The reports that are to be sent to them are variances relating to planned and actual performance. The report must also emphasise cost control aspects.

Illustration-1

The profit of Bhaskar Ltd. is declining year after year. You, as a Management Accountant of that company, draft a report to the management exploring the reasons for the declining profits and suggesting corrective measures :

Answer :

From

The Management Accountant

....

....

To

The Managing Director

....

....

Dear Sir,

In pursuance of your instructions for ascertaining the reasons for declining profits year after year I submit hereunder my observations and suggestions.

OBSERVATIONS

Profit is basically the difference between the selling price of the products and their costs. Thus, lower the sales or higher the costs, any of them or both of them can be the cause of lower profits. Lower sales may be due to lower selling price or lower volume of sales. Lower selling price may have to be kept on account of market competition or inadequate demand for the goods. Lower volume of sales may be due to tough market competition, in sufficient sales promotion activities, short fall in output, customer dissatisfaction due to inferior quality of goods, non-fulfillment of delivery promises, etc. Cost of production may be higher because of under-utilisation of resources, inadequate control measures leading to more waste of materials, labour, etc., lack of coordination, motivation or incentive among employees, inflationary market conditions resulting in rise in the cost of material, labour and overheads.

CAUSES

In our company the prime causes of declining profits can be summarised as follows :

(1) Lower sales : The sales figure are constantly declining both in terms of quantity and value. Over a period of 5 years from 1995 to 1999, the sales have almost been reduced to one half. Fall in sales is partly due to more competition and partly due to poor quality of our products.

(2) Higher costs : Lower sales have resulted in considerable under utilisation of factory's capacity. As compared to that in 1995 in 1999 about 50% of the factory's capacity is lying idle. However the fixed costs have remained constant. In other words, the fixed cost per unit have gone up resulting in lower profits. Besides, the company has to pay penal interest on borrowings from banks on account of non-payment of loan instalment on time.

(3) Faculty product mix : At present, the company is manufacturing four products A, B, C and D. Products A, B and C are giving contribution of Rs. 4, Rs. 6 and Rs. 2 respectivly. However, product D is giving a loss of Rs. 3 per unit. The company manufactured 10,000 units of each of these products in the year 1999. This means that manufacture of product 'D' alone has resulted in an avoidable loss of Rs. 30,000 in 1999.

(4) Faulty dividend policy : In spite of the fact that the profits of the company are declining every year, the company is paying dividend almost at uniform rate of 15% p.a for the last five years to its equity shareholders. This has resulted in almost negligible ploughing back of profits in the company's business.

SUGGESTIONS

(1) Improving Sales : The company has to push up its sales. This will require improving the quality of the company's products and intensive publicity compaign highlighting the quality, utility and reliability of the company's products.

(2) Full Utilisation of company's capacity : Till the sales of the company picks up requiring full installed capacity of the company, the extra capacity of the company may be hired out. This will result in partial recovery of fixed costs and improving the profitability of the company.

(3) Change in product mix : The product mix requires a change. The production of product D should be discontinued. The company should use the capital rendered surplus for manufacturing other products in the prority order of B, A and C subject to the overall market demand. The company can also think of diversifying into new areas.

(4) Review dividend policy : The dividend policy of the company is to be reviewed. The dividends are to be paid only when there are profits. Moreover sound financial planning requires that company should not go for 100% distribution of its profits. A part of the profits of the company to the extent required and feasible should be retained by the company with itself. This will considerably strengthen the financial resources of the company. It will also help the company in the payment of loan instalments in time, thus resulting in saving of penal interest charged by the bankers.

Illustration-2

The production Manager of Raju Co. Ltd is experiencing difficultes like power shortage, high labour absenteeism and non-availability of raw-materials on time. These have caused decline in production. You as a management consultant of the company, make an indepth study of the problems and report to the management suggesting suitable solution :

Answer :

From

The Management Consultant

....

....

To,

The Managing Director

Raju Co. Ltd.

....

Dear Sir,

Sub : Report suggesting solutions. to problems owing to power shortage, high labour absenteeism and non-availability of raw-materials on time.

With reference to your letter no. ...... dated ...... assigning me the task of recommending solutions for the problems relating to shortage of power and raw-materials and labour absenteeism, I wish to report as under.

The reason for shortage of power supply is mainly due to failure of monsoon. Due to non-availability of sufficient water, the hydro-power generation and supply is insufficient to meet the ever increasing demands of the industry. Same is the case in the thermal power sector where coal is insufficient for generating the required units of electricity.

There is increasing rate of labour absenteeism which adds to the agony. The labourers who feel their work is not sufficiently rewarded feel it is same as staying at home. Due to power breakdown many labourers are sent home due to stoppage in work.

Due to the increased number of firms and failure of monsoon the basic raw-material production is very low, again leading to stoppage in work. Even the materials that are procured are at a high cost.

RECOMMENDATIONS

1. Planning the production schedule in advance and preparation of material procurrent budge, labour requirement budget and proper projection of power requirements would go a long way in eliminating or at least in minimising the problem.
2. Construction of self-generating power supply plants like solar power plants, wind mill etc., would curb the problem. We could also try to store the power when available for future use. Hence if the company could prepare project feasibility report on these matters it would be possible to ascertain whether these can solve our power problems or not. Acquiring power from private sector can also solve the problem.
3. As far as labour absenteeism is concerned, providing them adequate monetary and non-monetary benefits would reduce the turnover and absenteeism. Fringe benefits and retirement benefits provided would go a long way to reduce the rate of absenteeism.
4. Raw-materials supply can be properly regulated by inviting tenders and choosing the price that would be most favourable for us. Centralised purchases would eliminate unnecessary cost involved if any. Dividing the entire loss into most economic order quantities and placing them with different suppliers would give us the twin benefits of cost reduction and uninterrupted supply. Proper material control system should be formulated.

If we try these, I have no doubt, that we shall minimise the problems which we are experiencing at present.

Yours truly

Sd /- Production Manager

Illustration-3

The Directors of Anita Steels Ltd. are facing the problem of working capital. They are not in a position to coordinate the inflow and outflow of cash. Examine the existing management of working capital and submit a report to the management on your findings and recommendations to correct the situation.

Answer :

The Board of Directors
Anita Steel Ltd.
....
....

Sir,

Sub : Problem of working capital management.

With reference to your letter no. .... dated .... assigning me the task of studying the working capital management and suggesting ways and means to improve them, I wish to report as under :

1. The main reason for the inadequacy of working capital is the lack of coordination between cash inflows and outflows. The liquidity management should be sound. Then only coordination is possible in any organisation.
2. Only when the credit management is efficient the inflow of cash would be sound. In our organisation, the credit management is very weak.

3. In addition to credit management, management of inventory also is our important area which will boost the cash inflow. The inventory of finished goods are on the higher side which is due to the ineffective and poor selling line.
4. The cash inflow management is not sound enough in our organisation to monitor and to meet the regular payment to our suppliers, our organisation is not a prompt and regular payer to our suppliers and we never get the discounts and allowances.

SUGGESTIONS

1. The credit collection policy should be streamilined in order to collect promptly from our debtors and bills receivable.
2. Our selling force must be motivated and to provide more concessions and discounts to our distribution network and also to customers which will pave the way for minimum inventory of finished goods.
3. The improvement of credit collection and selling will boost our sales and minimise our inventory and both will reward us with sound cash inflow management.
4. The effective and efficient cash flow will provide us opportunity to coordinate with cash outflow and obtain concessions and discounts from our suppliers.
5. Proper coordinated cash inflow and outflow management will maintain sound and better working capital management. The above recommended line of action will provide us fruitful results in our working capital management.

Yours truly

Sd / Finanace Manager

Illustration-4

ABC Company is facing the problem of raw-materials shortage. As a production manager, you are required to draft a report suggesting reformulation of purchase policy to have uninterrupted supply of raw-materials.

Answer :

The Managing Director

ABC Co. Ltd.

....

....

Dear Sir,

Sub : Interrupted supply of raw-materials — Reformaulation of purchase policy.

With reference to your letter no. .... dated .... assigning me the task of reformulation of purchase policy to have uninterrupted supply of raw-materials, I wish to report as under :

The main reason for delay in supply has been due to lack of alertness of the stores department which has led to a fall in the stock level below danger level interrupting production. This has occured more than once.

There is a boom in demand for the goods continuously in the market and this particular product line where we specialise has given profits to producers which as usual has brought a number of new entrants as our competitors. Unfortunately, the basic raw-materials production has not increased proportionately. Thus dividing total available raw-materials among many has led to shortage in availability and has failed to cater to the needs of the industry.

RECOMMENDATIONS

1. Formulation of a policy to limit the disadvantages of shortage is to begin with proper coordination between the purchase and stores department.
2. The stores department should continuously evaluate the needs in accordance with the production schedule which is available with any department well in advance. Timely requisitions given would lead to easy procurement at the most favourable prices.
3. Proper materials management should be devised by adopting ABC analysis and VED (Vital, Essential, Desinable) analysis that could lead to avoidance of unnecessary procurement and wastage.
4. As far as the general scarcity in the market is concerned, this is a situation which would fade away once the new firms leave the market in the long run. But as far as the present time is concerned, we could

invite tenders from suppliers from other states and if found favourable, orders could be placed with them to be sure of supply which would however be difficult from our old suppliers due to the market conditions.

If we try these, I have no doubt that we shall be able to overcome the challange and survive in this market.

Yours Truly

Sd /- Production Manager

QUESTIONS

Long Answer Questions

1. What do you understand by the term 'reporting to management'. Discuss briefly the matters that you would deal with while reporting to the board of directors.
2. Discuss the general principles to be observed while preparing reports.
3. Describe the various forms of reporting to management.
4. Distinguish between routine and special reports state. The various matters which are sent to management under routine and special reports.
5. Explain different types of reports submitted to the management of an organisation.
6. Explain the information submitted to different levels of management.

Exercise-1 : The profits of XC Co. are declining year by year. As the management Accountant of the company. Draft a report to the management exploring the possible reasons with recommendation.

13

INFLATION ACCOUNTING (ACCOUNTING FOR PRICE LEVEL CHANGES)

INTRODUCTION

Inflation is a state in which purchasing power of money goes down or conversely, there is more money in circulation than is justified by goods and services. The effect of inflation is that the prices of assets go up and the accounts prepared on the basis of conventional accounting system present very distorted figures to the users of accounts.

Inflation Accounting is a method derised to show the effect of changing cost and prices on affairs of a company during course of relative accounting period. It is not a panacea for difficulties confronted by a company during period of inflation but it provides a leeway to see in right perspective the inpact of inflation on the company's operation during the course of relative accounting period.

Accounting for price level changes (popularly known as inflation accounting) has recently been seriously engaging the attention of accountants. So far accountants have been measuring business transactions in terms of monetary units, *i.e.*, rupees. etc. but this standard of measurment is highly unstable and keeps on changing in value particularly on the high side due to inflation almost all over the world.

Features of Inflation Account

(*a*) It is assumed that the unit of measurement is not stable

(*b*) The procedure of recording is automatic

(*c*) All elements of the financial statements are taken into account

(*d*) Realisation principles are not followed strictly, e.g. fixed assets and long term loans are recorded at their current values.

Objectives of Inflation Accounting

1. It portrays the real profit or loss for the period under consideration as against the profit or loss on the basis of historical cost. Inflation accounting shows the true picture of profitablility of the business. In cases when prices have substantially risen, the profit and loss account prepared on the basis of historical cost does not show the proper appraisal of the performance of the organisation. This is because of the fact that though sales revenue is recorded in terms of current rupees, some of important charges (say depreciation) against the revenue are in terms of historical cost.
2. It sets out the real financial position in present day terms rather then conventional position on historical cost basis and indicates the real capital employed. As a result of inflation the value of various assets and liabilities may vary, the same can be represented only by inflation accounting.
3. It ensures that sufficient funds will be available to replace the various assets when the replacement becomes due. At the time of replacement of assets huge

funds are required on account of inflationary condition and if historical method of a ccounting is followed the concern will be experiencing scarcity of funds to replace the assets. If assets are not replaced in time it willl adversely affect the operational efficiency of the organisation.

4. It indicates the profits in constant rupees, *i.e.*, having regard to the general movement in prices for the reference of shareholders as well as the management. The price level adjusted accounts provide the basis for rational appraisal of managerial effectiveness in terms of preservation of the current rupee equivalent of capital invested in the business. The management would greatly benefit by such accounts for the determination of management policies with respect to pricing, credit, dividend, expansion, etc.

A number of studies established that many companies had been taking unsound financial policy decisions because of their sole reliance on accounting statements based on historical costs. The growth rate in real terms was lower than shown and the profit increase in real terms was much less than what is was supposed to be earlier.

A committee under the chairmanship of F.E.P. Sandilands was set up in U.K. in January, 1974 to study the effects of inflation on accounts and suggest remedial measures. The committee presented its report to the British Parliament in September, 1975 which spot lighted certain concepts very dominantly. Among the many recommendations of Sandilands Committee, the following are the important ones.

(1) Definitions

A company's gains (or losses) may be classified into a number of categories.

***(a)* Holding gains:** A holding gain is the difference between the measured value to a company of an asset at any point of time and the original cost incurred by the company in purchasing that asset. Such gains may be either realised or unrealised. This value to the business of an asset on a particular point of time will be arrived at in the light of guidelines set by management after due deliberations.

***(b)* Operating gain:** An operating gain is the difference between the amount realised for a company's output (its earnings from goods or services provided) and the 'value to the business' of the inputs used by the company in generating those amounts. A company's profit should be equated with its operating gains.

***(c)* Extraordinary gains:** An extraordinary gain is the difference between the amounts realised for items which do not form part of a company's normal output and their value to the company at the time of disposal. The distinction between operative and extraordinary gains is essential for their adjustment and operation at the time of presentation.

***(d)* Realised gains:** Total gain may be either realised or unrealised during the year. A realised gain is a gain arising from sale or disposal by the company of any kind of goods, services, assets or liabilities.

***(e)* Unrealised gains:** 'Unrealised gain' arise, when measured value of any asset held by company increase during the life time of the company and the asset is still retained by the company.

(2) Limitations of Historical Costing

Historical costing is more useful where it is desired to measure a company's performance in terms of cost incurred and when prices are stable. But its utility is reduced during a period of inflation. This is because of its limitations which are as follows :

(*a*) Historical cost accounts in their basic form do not recognise unrealised holding gains. Assets are shown in the accounts at cost less depreciation and as such the unrealised holding gains arising from the increase in monetary value of assets due to inflation are not shown. This deprives the shareholders, employees, creditors, etc. from getting useful information on a type of gain which is increasingly important during the time of inflation.

(*b*) Under the historical cost accounting realised holding gains are usually included together with operations gains as profit for the year. When due to inflation, holding gains are large, this factor reduce the usefulness of historical cost accounts since they do not give the correct information required by the users of accounts. This results in exaggerated profit being shown by historical accounting method due to the valuation of the same quantities of closing stocks at higher level in successive years of inflation. If for example, a company maintains a consistent stock which was valued at Rs. 1 lakh at the end of one of the past years and which due to progressive inflation during last several years now stands valued at Rs. 8 lakhs, this will have an important and major impact. This progressive valuation of closing stock at higher amounts will result in acute shortage of funds, and profit shown will not be there in real terms.

(*c*) The aim of calculating and charging depreciation under historical cost accounting is to spread the cost of an asset over its useful life. The depreciation so charged is inadequate because it does not take into account the changes in the replacement value of the fixed assets under inflationary conditions. The depreciation provided for at a reduced rate may be totally inadequate to purchase a new machine the cost of which would have appreciably gone up. It follows that the profits shown by the company during this period were over-stated and that they did not truly reflect the surpluses from the business activities after maintaining the capital assets in tact.

TECHNIQUES OF INFLATION ACCOUNTING

The two techniques used for presenting correct accounts during inflation are as follows :

(1) Current Purchasing Power Method

This method is also known as general purchasing power method. It seeks to show the affairs of an enterprise in terms of a unit of measurement of constant value where costs and prices are changing. According to this method all items in the financial statements are to be restated for changes in the general price level for this purpose any approved price index is used to convert the various items of the balance sheet and the profit and loss account. This method eliminates the effects on account of changes in the value of money. It should be noted that under this method only the changes in general purchasing power of money is taken into account. It does not consider the changes in the value of individuals assets. Since the conversion of each figure in terms of index number of the date of transactions is practically very difficult, it is assumed that all operating trnasactions take place evenly throughout the year. Moreover in respect of monetary terms purchasing power gain or loss is computed.

The system of adjustment underlying the current purchasing power method may be presented under the following three heads.

(a) Common Features

(*i*) All items in the balance sheet and the income statement are adjusted in terms of current rupees.

(*ii*) Items appearing in historical cost accounts are classified into monetary and non-monetary groups. Monetary items are simply related in current rupees; they do not require adjustment. Non-monetary items on the other hand are adjusted in accordance with changes in the purchasing power of money.

(*iii*) Transactions, both capital and revenue are assumed to have taken place evenly throughout the year at the average price level of the year.

(b) Adjustment of Profit and Loss Account

(*i*) Items such as sales, purchases, expenses, taxes, dividends etc. are adjusted in terms of the year and rupee by applying the average index for the year.

(*ii*) Opening and closing stock are adjusted by the price index of the average date of their acquisition.

(*iii*) For computing adjusted depreciation, the fixed assets are first aged and grouped according to the date of their acquisition and then their cost, in current rupees is obtained. The depreciation charges are computed with reference to such adjusted cost either by applying regular rates of depreciation or on a proportionate basis.

(c) Adjustment of Balance Sheet

(*i*) Fixed assets are adjusted in accordance with the index numbers of the dates of their acquisition or if deemed satisfactory, with reference to the index number of the average date of their acquisition.

(*ii*) The method of conversion of inventory is the same as stated above in 2 (*ii*)

(*iii*) The remaining current assets and all liabilities (*i.e.*, monetary assets and liabilities) need no adjustment as they are already stated in current rupees.

(*iv*) The index number at the date of issue or if deemed satisfactory, the average index of the year; is used to adjust equity capital. The preference capital is treated as a monetary item and is simply restated.

Limitations of Current Purchasing Powers

(*a*) In the long run, the CPP method does not remedy the deficiencies of historic cost accounting and so it does not provide the best long term solution to the problem of accounting for inflation.

(*b*) The retail price index is an index of prices of wide range of goods and services purchased by domestic consumers. In many cases, such an index will give a misleading indication of the effects of inflation on individual companies.

(*c*) The method introduces a new set of problems by expressing company accounts in a new unit of measurement, viz. units of current purchasing power, instead of monetary units. The unit of current purchasing power is likely to be conceptually difficult for most users of accounts to understand.

(*d*) The recommendation that CPP statements should be supplementary to the basic accounts weakens their impact.

(2) Current Cost Accounting Method

Current cost accounting is a system of inflation accounting in which each item of financial statements is restated in terms of current value of that item. This method recognises the changes in the prices of individual assets irrespective of the quantum and direction of changes in the general price level. It takes into account the price changes relevant to particular firm or industry rather than the economy as a whole. This method seeks to ensure that adequate provisions or adjustments are made for the maintenance and replacement of the operating assets of the company. Assets are shown in terms of what such assets whould currently cost. Similarly, profits are computed on the basis of what the cost would currently cost. Similarly, profits are computed on thę basis of what the cost would have been at the date of sale rather then the actual amount paid. In other words, it seeks to arrive at a profit which can be safely distributed as dividend without impairing the operational capacity of the firm. In addition to adjustment for depreciation and cost of sales, it deals with the working capital and also loan raised.

Features of Current Cost Accounting Technique

(*a*) The accounts will continue as at present to be drawn-up in terms of monetary units.

(*b*) The accounts should show the value to the business of the company's assets at the balance sheet date.

(*c*) It measures the income after matching current costs with current revenues. It is based on the concept of operational capability. This method seeks to achieve this by substituting the current cost of assets consumed in place of corresponding historical cost.

(*d*) Depreciation for the year is to be calculated on the current value of the relevant fixed assets.

(*e*) The cost of stock consumed during the year is to be calculated on the value of the stock of business at the date of consumption and not at the date of purchase.

(*f*) The effects of loss or gain from loans will be computed and set-off against interest.

(*g*) The current cost operating profit is arrived at by making three adjustments to trading profits before interest is calculated on historical cost basis, *i.e.*, depreciation adjustment, cost of sales adjustment and monetary working capital adjustment. The current cost attributable to shareholders is obtained by making gearing adjustment.

(*h*) Profit for the year should consists of the company's operating gains, and should exclude all holding gains.

(*i*) The current cost balance sheet includes a new reserve 'current cost reserve', which is created to take the credits relating to the revaluation of fixed assets and stock as also those relating to the depreciation adjustment, cost of sales adjustment, the working capital adjustment and the gearing adjustment.

Advantages

(*a*) The principle of showing assets and liabilities at their 'value to the business' will enable the comparative returns on capital employed of different companies to be assessed in a more useful way during a time of inflation that is possible with existing accounting convention.

(*b*) The clear separation in the accounts of holding, operating and extraordinary gains will lead to clear distinction being made between gains which due to a company's productive efforts and gains due to luck or skill in the timing of purchases of assets during a period of inflation. Such accounting presentation will enable the performance of companies to be assessed and compared in a more useful way than with existing methods which do not make such distinction. It is also particularly important for internal management purposes during a period of inflation to have information which clearly distinguishes between operating and holding gain.

(*c*) The principle of current cost accounting are developments of accounting techniques already in use by number of companies. For example, the revaluation of properly assets in company accounts is already widespread and the principle underlying the 'cost of sales adjustment' forms the basis of the 'base stock' method of accounting for stock. Current cost accounting is an evolutionary rather than a revolutionary system of accounting.

QUESTIONS

Simple Questions

1. What do you mean by inflation accounting?
2. State the features of inflation accounting.
3. State the objectives of inflation accounting.
4. What do you mean by holding gain?
5. What do you mean by operating gain?
6. What do you mean by extraordinary gain?
7. State the limitations of historical costing.

Short Answer Questions

1. Explain current purchasing power as a technique of inflation accounting.
2. Explain the current cost accounting as a technique of inflation accounting.

14

RESPONSIBILITY ACCOUNTING

INTRODUCTION

Responsibility accounting is one of the technique of Management Accounting which is used for managerial control. Whole other techniques are used to control the organisation as a whole, responsibility accounting is used to appraise the performance of various segments of an organisation. These segments are called by responsibility centres. This technique is also known as profitability accounting.

Definition

"Responsibility accounting is concerned with collecting and reporting planned and actual accounting information about the inputs and outputs of responsibility centres."

An analysis of the above definition reveals the following features of responsibility accounting.

(*a*) Input and output: Input and output constitutes the basis for responsibility accounting. The input used in an organisation is in the form of physical resources and it takes the form of raw-materials consumed, hours of labour expended and so on. These resources are expressed in monetary terms and is referred to as cost. Similarly, the output when expressed in monetary term is known as revenue. Responsibility accounting is based on cost and revenue data which is also known as financial information.

(*b*) Planned and actual data: In order to facilitate managerial control, financial information is needed both in respect of planned and actual. Actual data is compared with planned or budgeted data and in case of adverse variations the management can focus its attention on the causes responsible for such variation.

(c) Fixation of responsibility: Responsibility accounting centres around the organisation structure of an enterprise. If involves fixation of responsibilities among the superiors and subordinates. Though authrority can be delegated, responsibility can never be delegated. However authority must be coupled with responsibility as without responsibility a person cannot discharge his duties satisfactorily. For the successful functioning of responsibility accounting a clear cut authority and responsibility is to be laid down. The performance of an individual can be evaluated based on the authority and responsibility assigned.

(*d*) Responsibility centres: The establishment of responsibility centre is the nucleus of responsibility accounting. The entire organisation is divided into various segments in such a way that the person who is in-charge of that segment is responsible for the success or failure of that segment. Responsibility centres are classified into three types based on control exercised, *viz*.

(*i*) ***Cost centre***: Under this type the person in-charge is responsible for cost incurred in that centre. In other words, he is responsible only for the cost incurred for input but not for output. The record maintained in the cost centre records only the cost incurred but excludes the revenue earned (*i.e.*, output value). Thus it is clear that a cost centre is a segment whose financial performance is measured in terms of cost. The performance of managers is evaluated by comparing the cost incurred and the estimated cost. The focus of the management is only to exercise control over cost.

(ii) ***Profit centre***: Under this type the manager is responsibile for cost (input), revenue (output) and the profit (*i.e.*, excess of revenue over cost). Where cost exceed revenue it results in a loss. Though, according to generally accepted accounting principle, revenue is recognised only when goods are sold to external parties, for evaluating profit centre, revenue represents a monetary measure of output, irrespective of whether the revenue is realised or not. The underlying principle is that a department has output representing goods and services which are capable of monetary measurement. Profit for the sake of evaluation of profit centre is taken as pre-tax profit. The Manager's performance is decided by the profit earned by that profit centre.

(iii) ***Investment centre***: Under this type the manager is responsible for cost, revenue, and investments made on assets of a responsibility centre. The basis for evaluating the performance of a manager is not by the profit earned by that centre, but on the return on investment. One of the popular tool for reporting performance of an investment centre is the rate of return on investment in assets. Symbollically

$$\text{RoI} = \frac{\text{Net Income}}{\text{Total Assets}}$$

15

FINANCIAL MANAGEMENT : EVOLUTION OF FINANCIAL MANAGEMENT

The term 'Financial Management' refers to corporation finance. At the turn of the previous century corporation finance emerged as a distinct field of study. In the earlier days its evolution was broadly analysed into (*i*) traditional phase; (*ii*) transitional phase and (*iii*) modern phase. Traditional phase lasted for about four decades. As its features, it referred to certain episodic events in the life cycle of the firm, particularly about the formation of the company. It also focussed on the issue of capital, its broad expansion programme and highlighted on mergers, reorganisation and liquidation. The discussions turned out to be more historical descriptive and institutional. The second phase, *i.e.*, transitional phase began arround fourties and continued upto the fifties. This was more or less similar to the traditional phase but with the current problematic views of the managers of finance in the areas of finds analysis, planning and control. The third phase, *i.e.*, the modern phase started in mid fifties, and has witnessed an accelerated pace of development. Economic theories have incorporated these finance ideas and attempted to develop quantitative techniques in explaning these ideas. Attempts are made to rationally match the funds in their uses in the light of appropriate decision criteria. The dominance of the financial decision, maker in his decision making is brought about. Its outlook is insider's view point.

Definition of Finance Function

Finance function involves procurement of funds and their effective utilisation in the business. There are, thus, two aspects of finance function, *viz.* (*a*) procurrement of funds and (*b*) an effective use of these funds in the business.

Funds can be procured from various sources, each having different characteristics in terms of risk, control and cost. From risk point of view equity share capital is considered as best as there is no obligation to return the funds during the course of existing of business. But from the point of view of cost it is considered to be most expensive. Thus is because dividend expectations of the shareholders are higher than interest rate. Debentures as a source of funds is cheaper as the interest rate is not very high. But debentures entail a high degree of risk as they have to be repaid as per the terms of agreement. Further interest payment has to be made whether or not the company earns profit. There are thus risk, cost and control consideration which a finance manager must consider while procuring funds.

The second aspect of finance function is effective utilisation of funds. The finance manager must look into the situation where funds lye idle or where a proper use of funds is not being made. If the funds are not utilised so as to generate income higher than the cost of procuring them, there is no point in running the business. The finance manager must also ensure that finance decisions in respect of fixed assets are properly analysed. This requires knowledge about capital budgeting. He must also keep in view the needs of working capital and ensure that while the firm enjoy an optimum level of working capital, they do not keep too much funds blocked in inventories, book debts and cash.

Definition of Financial Management

In the words of phillppatos "Financial Management' is concerned with the management decisions that result in the acquisition and financing of long-term and short-term assets for the firm. As such, it deals with situations that require the selection of specific assets or combination of assets, the selection of specific liabilities or combination of liabilities, as well as with the problems of size, and growth of enterprise. The analysis of these decisions is based upon the expected inflows and outflows of funds and their effect upon stated managerial objectives."

SCOPE OF FINANCIAL MANAGEMENT

Financial Management is broadly concerned with the acquisition and use of funds by a business firm. Its scope may be defined in terms of the following questions:

- How large should the firm be and how fast it should grow?
- What should be the compostion of the firms assets?
- What should be the mix of the firm's financing?
- How should the firm analyse, plan and control its financial affairs?

The important tasks of financial management may be outlines as follows :

(A) Financial Analysis, Planning and Control

- Analysis of financial condition and performance
- Profit planning
- Financial forecasting
- Financial control

(B) Investing

- Management of current assets (cash, marketable securities, receivables, and inventories
- Capital budgeting (identification, selection and implementation of capital projects)
- Management of mergers, reorganisations and disinvestments

(C) Financing

- Identification of sources of finance and determination of financing mix
- Identifying sources of funds and raising funds
- Disposition of profits between dividends and retained carrings

Scope of financial management for purposes of exposition is divided into two broad categories : (*a*) traditional approach and (*b*) modern approach

(a) Traditional approach: This refers to its subject matter in the academic literature in the initial stages of its evolution as a separate branch of academic study. The term 'corporation finance' was used to describe what is now known in the academic world as 'financial management'. The field of study dealing with finance was treated as encompassing three inter-related aspects of raising and administering resources from outside : (*a*) the institutional arrangement in the form of financial institutions which comprise the organisation of capital market; (*b*) financial instruments through which funds were raised from the capital markets and the related aspects of practices and the procedural aspects of the capital market and; (*c*) the legal and accounting relationships between a firm and its sources of funds.

Limitation of traditional approach: This dominated the seene during 1920s and 1930s. This is now discarded due to the following weaknesses : (*i*) those relating to the basic conceptual and analystical frame work of the definitions and (*ii*) those relating to the treatment of various topics and the emphasis attached to them. The traditional treatment was the outsider-looking-in approach. The second ground of criticism was that the focus was on financing problems of corporate enterprises whereas non-corporate organisations lay outside its scope. Further as a logical corollary, the day-to-day financial problems of a normal company did not receive any attention.

(b) Modern Approach: This approach views the term financial management in a broad sense and provides a conceptual and analytical outlook. In fact, it provides an analytical framework for financial decision making. According to it, the finance function covers both acquisition of funds and allocation too.

Thus, apart from the issues involved in acquiring external funds, the main concern of financial management is the efficient and wise allocation of funds to various uses. The new approach is an analytical way of viewing the financial problems of the firm. Some interpretation considered in the modern context are :

(1) *Finance means cash only*: It must be noted that at this stage, the meaning of finance is described to mean cash only. This meant only liquidity and financing of the firm.

(2) *Finance is raising of funds*: Firstly, this approach amphasised the perspective of an outside lender. It covers instruments and institutions of credit and also practices which encouraged raising of funds. This stressed upon long term finance. However, one cannot ignore the importance of short-term finance, *viz.*, working capital.

(3) *Finance relates to the raising and utilisation of funds*: This relates to modern approach. This approach is concerned not only with raising funds but also their proper utilisation too. This determines the total amount of funds required by the firm. It also allocates these funds efficiently to the various assets. It also obtains the best mix of financing *viz.*, type and amount of corporate securities and finally the use of financial tools to ensure proper and efficient use of funds.

Business activities presuppose both the procurement and utilisation of funds. Thus business finance is the process of raising, providing, and managing of all the funds to be used in connection with the business activities. Thus business activities are more concerned with planning, raising, controlling and administering funds used in the business.

SCOPE OF FINANACE FUNCTION

Finance function deals with procurement and effective use of finds. Therefore the decision which concern management of funds are the subject matter of finance function. It may be seen that all decisions involve management of funds and are therefore, a part of financial management. Some of these decisions are as follows :

(1) Investment Decision

This decision involves the proper selection of assets in which funds will be invested by the firm. Assets normally comprises of long-term assets which will yield return over a period of time in future. Secondly, there are short-term or current assets. These assets in the normal course convert the business into cash within a year. In the case of long term assets, it is capital budgeting. The aspect of financial decision making with reference to current assets or short-term assets is popalarly known as working capital management.

(*a*) Capital budgeting: This is the long-term investment decision—most probably a very crucial final decision of the firm. It relates to the selection of an asset or investment proposal or course of action whose benefits are likely to be available in future over the life time of the project. The first aspect of the capital budgeting decision relates to the choice of the new asset out of the alternative available or the re-allocation of capital when existing assets fail to justify the funds committed. The second aspect of the capital budgeting decision is the analysis of risk and uncertainty. Since the benefits from the investment proposals extend over the future, there accrual is uncertain. They have to be estimated under various assumptions of the physical volume of sale and the level of prices. Finally, the evaluation of the worth of a long-term project implies a certain norm or standard against which the benefits are to be judged. In brief, the main elements of the capital budgeting decisions are : (*i*) the total assets and their compositions; (*ii*) the business risk complexion of the firm; and (*iii*) concept and measurement of the cost of capital.

(*b*) Working capital management: This is concerned with the management of the current assets. As short-term survival is a pre-requisite to a long-term success, this forms an integral part of financial management. There is conflict between profitability and liquidity. If a firm does not have adequate working capital, *i.e.*, it does not invest sufficient funds in current assets, it may become illiquid and consequently may not have the ability to meet its current obligations and thus invite the risk of bankruptcy. If the current assets are too large, the profitability is adversely affected. To summarise, the management of working capital has two basic ingredients, *viz.*, (*a*) an overview of working capital management as a whole and; (*b*) efficient management of the individual current assets such as cash, receivables and inventory.

(2) Finance Decision

This is an important function to be performed by the finance manager. Broadly, he must decide when, where and how to acquire funds to meet the firm's investment needs. The central issue before him is to determine the proportion of equity and debt. The mix of debt and equity is known as the firm's capital structure. The finance manager must strive to obtain the best financing mix or optimum capital structure for his firm. The firm's capital structure is optimum when the market value of shares is maximised. The use of debt affects the return on equity funds but it always increases risk. A proper balance will have to be struck between return and risk. When the shareholder's return is maximised with minimum risk, the market value per share will be maximised and the firm's capital structure would be optimum. Once the finance manager is able to determine the best combination of debt and equity, he must raise the appropriate amount through the best available sources.

(3) Dividend Decision

Dividend decision is the third major financial decision. The finance manager must decide whether the firm should distribute all profits or retain them or distribute a portion and retain, the balance. Like the debt policy, the dividend policy should be determined in terms of its impact on the shareholder's value. The optimum dividend policy is one which maximises the market value of the firm's share. Thus, if shareholders are not indifferent to the firm's dividend policy, the finance manager must determine the optimum dividend-payout ratio. The dividend pay-out ratio is equal to the percentage of dividends distributed to earnings available to shareholders. The finance manager should also consider the question of dividend stability, bonus shares and cash dividends.

Functions of Finance Manager

The principle functions of a finance manager relate to decisions regarding procurement, investment and dividends. However, the finance manager also undertakes the following subsidiary functions.

(*a*) **Supply of funds to all parts of the organisation**: The finance manager must ensure that all branches, departments and units of the organisation are supplied with adequate funds. Those sections which have an excess of funds have to contribute to the central pool for use in other sections which need funds. An adequate supply of cash at all points of time is absolutely essential for smooth flow of operation. Cash management should also ensure that there is no excessive cash.

(*b*) **Evaluation of financial performance**: Management control systems are often based upon financial analysis. Analysis of the financial performance helps the management in seeing how the funds have been utilised in various divisions and what can be done to improve it.

(*c*) **Financial negotiations**: A large part of the time of the finance manager is utilised in carrying out negotiations with the financial institutions, banks, underwrites and public depositors etc. He has to furnish a lot of information to these institutions and persons and has to see that raising of funds is within the various statutes like Companies Act etc. Negotiations for outside financing often require specialised skills.

(*d*) **Keeping track of stock exchange quotations and behaviour of share prices**: This involves analysis of major trends in the stock market and judging their impact on the prices of the shares of the company.

Importance of Financial Management

The importance of financial management cannot be over emphasised. Some people think that a financial manager is useful only in private enterprise. But is can be said that sound financial management is essential in all organisations—profit or non-profit—where funds are involved. Commercial history is replete with examples where firms have been liquidated not because their technology was obsolete or because their products had no demand or because their labour was not skilled but because there was a complete mismanagement of financial affairs.

Financial management essentially optimises the output from the given input of funds. It attempts to use the funds in the most productive manner. In a country like India, where resources are scarce and the demand on funds are many, the need for financial manager is emormous. If proper financial management techniques are used, most of our enterprises can reduce their capital employed and improve their return on investment.

Financial management is very important in the case of non-profit organisation also. In our country it is seen that most non-profit organisations do not pay any attention to financial management. Even a simple transaction like depositing the cheques the same day they are received, is not undertaken. Such organisations pay heavy interest charges on borrowed funds, yet they are tardy in realising their own debtors. All this arises because one has no realisation of the time value of money. It is not appreciated that each rupee has to be made use of and that it has a direct cost of utilisation. It has to be realised that keeping a rupee idle even for a day involves costs. A non-profit making organisation may not be keen to make profit, in the traditional sense of the term, but surely, it needs to cut down its cost and use the funds at its disposal to their optimum capacity. A sound sense of financial management has therefore to be cultivated among own bureaucrats, administrators, engineers and educationists. Unless this is done, the colossal wastage of the slender capital resources of own country cannot be stopped.

Objectives of Financial Amanagement

It has traditionally been argued that the objective of a company is to earn profit. Hence the objective of financial management is also profit maximisation. This implies that the finance manager has to take his decisions in a manner that the profits are maximised. Each alternative, therefore is to be seen as to whether or not it gives maximum profit.

(1) Profit maximisation as an object of financial management: Profit cannot be the sole objective of a business. It is at best a limited objective. If profit is given undue importance, the following problems will arise :

(*a*) Profit maximisation has to be tempered with a realisation of risks involved. There is a direct relationship between risk and profit. Many risky propositions yield high profit. Higher the risk, higher is the possibility of profits. If profit maximisation is the only goal, then risk factor is altogether ignored. This implies that finance manager will accept highly risky proposals; if they give high priority to profit. In practice, risk is a very important consideration and has to be balanced with the profit objective.

(*b*) Profit maximisation as an objective does not take into account the time pattern of returns. For example, proposal 'A', may give a higher amount of profit as compared to proposal 'B'. Yet, if the returns begin to flow say 10 years later, proposal 'B' may be preferred which may have lower overall profits but the returns flow is more quick.

(*c*) Profit maximisation as an objective is too narrow. It fails to take into account the social responsibilities to various groups of people such as Investers, employees and customers. It these group of people are ignored, a company cannot survive for long.

(2) Wealth maximisation as an object of financial management: According to some thinkers on financial management they consider wealth maximisation and value of shares as an important objective of financial management. The value of share of a company gives an indication to its shareholders the worth of such a company. The value of shares is determined by two factors, *viz*.

(*a*) The earning per share of the company

(*b*) The capitalisation rate.

The earning per share depends upon the assessment as to how profitably a company is going to operate in the future or what it is likely to earn against each of its ordinary shares. For example, if a company is likely to earn annually Rs. 5 on its share of Rs. 10, its share will have a higher market value than a company which earns Rs. 4 for its Rs. 10 share each year, presuming that other factors remain the some earning per share is an important factor considered by the shareholders in valuing a company.

The capitalisation rate reflects the liking of the investor for a company. If a company earns a high rate of earnings per share through risky operations or risky financing pattern, the investors, will not look upon its share with favour. To that extent, the market value of shares of such a company will be low. An easy way to determine the capitalisation rate is to start with fixed deposit interest rate of banks. An investor may get say 7% interest (it may vary from time to time) from bank on a one year fixed deposit. However, if he has to invest in shares, he may want a higher return in view of the risks involved. How much higher would be his expectations would depend upon the risk involved in the particular share which in turn depends on company policies, past records, the type of business etc. Thus capitalisation rate is the cumulative result of the assessment of the various shareholders regarding the risk and other qualitative factors of a company. If a company invests its funds in risky ventures, the investors will put in their money only if they get higher return as compared to that from a low risk share.

The market value of a share is thus a function of the earnings per share and the capitalisation rate. Suppose the earnings per share are expected to be Rs. 6 for a share (the face value really does not matter in this regard). If the capitalisation rate expected by the share-holders is 20%, the market value of the share is likely to be $\frac{100 \times 6}{20}$ = Rs. 30

This is so because at this price, the investors have an earning of 20% something which they expect from a company with this degree of risk.

The finance manager has to ensure that his decisions are such that the market value of the shares of the company is maximum in the long run. This implies that the financial policy has to be such that it optimises the earnings per share keeping in view the risk and other factors in mind. Wealth maximisation is, therefore, a better objective for a commercial undertaking, since it represents both return and risk.

QUESTIONS

Simple Questions

1. What do you mean by finance function?
2. Define financial management.
3. List out the four main financial decision.
4. What do you mean by wealth maximisation goal of financial management?
5. What do you mean by profit maximisation goal of financial management?
6. What do you mean by Investment decision?
7. What is meant by capital budgeting?
8. What do you mean by financing decision?
9. What do you mean by dividend policy decision?

Short Answer Questions

1. "The importance of finance function as a management activity has increased in modern time." Explain.
2. "Financial Management is more than mere procurement of funds". Explain the other functions of finance manager.
3. Discuss the scope of financial management.

Long Anwer Questions

1. Discuss the goals of financial management.
2. Explain the various finance decisions invloved in an organisation.

16

CAPITAL STRUCTURE

PLANNING THE CAPITAL STRUCTURE

The term capital structure referes to the proportions of different types of financing used by the firm. By capital structure, we mean the kinds of securities and their proportionate amounts that make up the capitalisation. In simple words capital structure is the composition or the make up of the capital. While capitalisation relates to the decisions about the amount of securities to be issued, capital structure relates to the decisions as to the kinds of securities to be issued.

Some Authors on financial management believe that 'capital structure' is tantamount to 'financial structure' and hence it represents both long-term and short term sources of funds under capital structure. Broadly speaking, capital structure is composed of owned funds and borrowed funds. While owned funds include share capital and free reserves and surplus, borrowed funds represent debenture loan and long-term loans provided by term finacing institutions.

Pattern of Capital Structure

Broadly speaking, there may be three fundamental patterns of capital structure in a new concern.

1. A company may issue only equity shares when regular earning or income is not quite certain.
2. When the average earnings are rather good, even through annual earnings may not be quite certain, preference shares may be issued.
3. A company which expects to have a stable and reasonably good income to pay the fixed interest, may issue debentures.

The general principles do not in practice become operative because these principles are militant to each other. A company usually resorts to the issue of all the three types of securities. It is the gearing that is really of importance in capital structure and hence, we will do well to consider the principles present in the decision of the capital structure.

Principles that determine the Capital Structure

There are at least five important principles that determine proper capital structure of any company. They are : (*i*) cost principle; (*ii*) risk principle; (*iii*) control principle; (*iv*) flexibility principle; (*v*) timing principle.

Capital structure or compsotion of capital pattern of securities or the security mix is the second important aspect of financial planning. Once the financial manager has determined the firm's financial requirements, his next task is to see that these funds are on hand. This capital comes in many forms—long-term and short-term debts secured and unsecured debts, preference shares, equity shares, retained earnings and other sources of finance. To decide upon the rates of these securities in the total capitalisation is to decide the capital structure. So in simple words capital structure is the form of capital. According to Weston and Brigham,

"Capital structure is the permanent financing of the firm, represented by long-term debts, preferred stock and net worth." Net worth is the equity shareholder's equity capital and includes reserves and surpluses, retained earnings and net worth reserves.

Other interpretations of capital structure involve the investment decisions of the firm; the optimal use of leverage, the timing of the pricing of issues as well as determining the acceptable level of risk and liquidity. The basic patterns of capital structure may take any of these forms :

1. Equity shares only
2. Equity shares and preference shares
3. Equity shares and debentures
4. Equity shares, preference shares and debentures

There are no hard and fast rules to indicate what patterns would be ideal under what circumstances and what percentage of capitalisation should be represented by equity shares, preference shares or debentures. If may differ from industry to industry, from trade to trade, from company to company and so on. But whatever decision is taken in evolving the capital structure of a company, two basic principles must be observed. First of all, the ratio of funded debts of equity should always be geared to the degrees of stability of earnings. Secondly, the capital strucuture must be balanced with adequate 'equity cushion' to absorb the shocks of the business cycles and to afford flexibility.

Factors that determine the Capital Structure

To design a suitable pattern of capital structure for the company, a satisfactory compromise among various conflicting factors of cost, risk, control, flexibility and timing should be arrived at. Having studied the principles of capital structure it is important to analyse the factors which determine the ideal financial leverage of a company. The following factors generally determine the capital gearing of the composition of the financial plan of the company.

(1) Trading on equity: Trading on equity is also known as financial leverage. It refers to an arrangement where the borrowing programme is so arranged as to secure a fairly high return on the equity shares. Trading on equity is the financial process of resorting borrowing to generate gain for the residual owner. The practice is known as 'Trading on equity' because it is the equity shareholders who have an interest or equity in the business income. The term owes its name also to the fact that the creditors are willing to advance funds on the strength of the equity supplied by the owners. It is based on the theory that there is a difference among the rates of returns on the different types of securities issued by a company. By issuing debentures and preference shares with a fixed rates of returns, the rate of dividend on equity share is raised. If, On the other hand, the entire capital is raised by issue of equity shares, the rate of dividend will get reduced. Trading on equity acts as a lever to magnify the influence of fluctuations in earnings. Any fluctiations in earnings before interest and taxes (EBIT) is magnified on the earnings per share (EPS) by operation of equity. The larger the magnitude of debt in capital structure, the higher is the variation in EPS given any variation in EBIT.

The concept has got serious implications and limitations.

Firstly, a concern should have stable earnings, as for example, profit with little variations. With a large amount of indebtedness it is under constant pressure to earn a return sufficient to cover the interest cost of such funds. Its products should not have high elasticity of demand, otherwise the earning capacity is likely to be adversely affected.

Secondly it should have large investments in fixed assets because they constitute an important adjunct for borrowing money, since they give the lender a feeling of security, the stable earnings and a huge investment in fixed assets.

Thirdly, the field of operations for such an enterprise should be an established and a non-speculative one.

High gearing of capital exists when the proportion of equity capital to the total capital is small; and in case of low gearing the reverse is true. The higher the gear is, the more speculative the ordinary shares will be. With the increase in the gearing of capital, the value of both the prority rights and equity shares decrease and so does the credit of the company.

(2) Characteristics of the company: Peculiar characteristics of the company affect the factors influencing the choice of different sources of funds. Accordingly weights are assigned to different principles of manoeuvrability, cost, risk, control and timing in the light of the peculiar features of the compamy.

(a) ***Size of the business***: Smaller companies confront tremendous problems in assembling funds because of their poor credit worthiness. Investors feel bad in investing their money in securities cf these firms. Lenders prescribe highly restrictive terms in lending. Hence special attention should be paid to flexibility principle for obtaining funds in future. Again control aspect should also be given special consideration, otherwise large concerns may buy a controlling interest. Larger concerns have to employ different types of securities to procure desired amount of funds at reasonable cost because they find it very difficult to raise huge capital at reasonable cost if demand for funds is restricted to a single source. They should also insist on flexibility principle. In medium sized companies, leverage principle should be given greater consideration so as to mimimise the cost of capital.

(b) ***Form of business organisation***: Control principle carries higher weightage in private limited companies where ownership is 'closely held' by a few shareholders when compared with public limited companies. In partnership or sole proprietorship form, manoeuvrability factor is not helpful owing to limited access to the capital market. Control is undoubtedly an important consideration in such organisations.

(c) ***Stability of earnings***: A company can insist on leverage principle if it has greater stability in sales and earnings and as such the fixed obligation debt with loss risk may be undertaken. A company with irregular earnings should pay greater attention to the risk principle, depending upon the sale of stock to raise capital. If should reduce debt capital because of fixed burden on interest.

(d) ***Asset structure***: A company having major investment in fixed assets and greater stability in sales can pay greater attention to leverage principle to take advantage of cheaper source. Otherwise, risk principle should be given greater weightage than leverage.

(e) ***Age of the company***: Established companies with good earnings should adopt leverage principle since they are in comfortable position to raise capital from whatever sources, they like. New companies should give more weightage to flexibility factor so as to have as many alternatives opened as possible in future to meet their growth requirements.

(f) ***Credit standing***: A company with high credit standing should pay attention to flexibility factor since it can adjust sources of funds upwards or downwards in response to major changes in need for funds than one with poor credit standing.

(g) ***Attitude of management***: Where management has strong desire for assured and exclusive control, preference will have to be given to borrowing for raising capital in order to be assured of continued control. If the management's chief aim is to stay in office they would insist on risk principle or else they would prefer to insist on the leverage principles.

(3) Policy of term financing institution: If the financial institutions adopt harsh poliy of lending and prescribe highly restrictive terms, management must give more significance to the flexibility principle and abstain from borrowing from those institutions to preserve the company's flexibility in capital funds. However, if funds are obtained in desired quantity and on early terms from the financial institutions, the management may assign more weightage to the cost principle and obtain funds from them.

Factors which Influence Planning of Capital Structure in Practice

The various factors which influence planning of capital structure in practice are as follows :

(1) Internal Factors: Some of the internal factors which are to be considered in planning the capital structure are as follows :

(a) *Cost of Capital*: The current and future cost of each potential source of capital should be estimated and compared.

(b) *Risk*: Ordinarily, debt securities increase the risk. While equity securities reduce it, Risk can be measured to some extent by the use of ratios measuring gearing and time-interest earned.

(c) *Dilution of Value*: A company should not issue any shares which will have the effect of removing or diluting the value of the shares by the existing shareholders.

(d) *Acceptability*: A company can borrow only if investors are willing to lend. Few companies can afford the luxury of the capital structure which is unacceptable to financial institutions.

(e) *Transferability*: Many companies put their securities for quotation on the stock exchange quotations and improve the transferability of the shares.

(f) *Matching fluctuating needs against short-term source*: Where needs are fluctiating, a firm may prefer to borrow short-term loans from commercial banks.

(g) *Increasing owner's profits*: Profits of the owners can be increased by relying more and more on debt financing.

(2) External Factors:

(a) *General level of Business activity :* Where the overall level of business activity is rising, a firm would want to expand its operations.

(b) *Level of interest Rates :* If interest rates become excessive, firms will delay debt financing.

(c) *Availability of funds in the money market :* The availability of funds in the money market affects a firm's ability to offer debt and equity securities.

(d) *Tax policy on interest and dividends :* Although each management makes its own decisions on its capital sources, there are certain general factors which seem to influence the overall capital structure.

(3) General Factors: This include the following :

(a) *Size of the business and character of capital requirements*: New and big firms are conservatively financed. But they are likely to issue new securities to the public. If an enterprise is especially successful, it grows rapidly and may issue bonds and prefereed stock without diluting equity stock interests. For companies which expand rapidly, even through their current earnings are low; the sale of equity stock is not desirable. However if assets are plentiful borrowing is possible.

The practice of issuing mortgage bonds encourage borrowing by those firms that have a heavy investment in fixed assets. In some industries, very large quantities of current assets account for a bigger proportion of the total assets.

(*b*) *Operational characteristics*: Businesses differ in their operational characteristics and their need for funds. Merchandising firms operate on a small margin of gross profit, mainly with current assets. Public utilities, on the other hand, have small gross income relative to there capital and require extensive capital.

(*c*) *Continuity of earnings*: A firm must have stable earnings in order to handle recurring fixed charges. Non-durable consumer goods enjoy stability of demand and rigidity in prices is compared to durable consumer goods. The capital structure of all firms in the industries should be more conservative than that of industries which are stable.

(*d*) *Marketability*: The financial management of a corporation watches changes in market psychology and considers them carefully in planning new security offerings. General economic conditions develop new attitudes in the market.

(*e*) *Government influence*: Taxes exercise a major influence on the capital structure of the business. Corporate income-tax has reduced the net earnings of companies. Debt financing is encouraged because of income-tax leverage.

(*f*) *Financial leverage*: Unfavourable financial leverage indicates a low level of profitability and makes borrowings more costly than the returns on investment. It is very difficult for a firm to issue additions stock when profit are low.

CAPITAL STRUCTURE THEORIES

The following are the various capital structure theories:

(1) Traditonal Approach

The crux of the traditional view relating to leverage and valuation is through judicious use of debt-equity proportions, a firm can increase its total value and thereby reduce the overall cost of capital. The rationable behind this view is that debt is relatively cheaper source of funds as compared to equity shares with a change in the leverage, *i.e.*, using more debt in the place of equity, a relatively cheaper source of funds replace a source of funds which involves a relatively higher cost. This obviously causes a decline in the overall cost of capital. It the debt-equity ratio is raised further, the firm would become financially more risky to the investors who would penalise, the firm by demanding a higher equity capitalisation (Kc) But the increase in Kc may not be so high as to neutralise the benefit of using cheaper debt. In other words the advantages arising out of the use of debt is so large that, even after allowing for higher Kc the benefits of the use of the cheaper source of funds are still available. If, however, the amount of debt is increased further, two things are likely to happen; (*i*) owing to increased financial risk, Kc will record a substantial rise; (*ii*) the firm would become very risky to the creditors who would like to be compensated by a higher return such that Kc will rise. The use of debt beyond a certain point will, therefore, have the effect of raising the weighted average cost of capital and conversely the total value of the firm. Thus, upto a point or degree of leverage, the use of debt will adversely affect it. At that level of debt-equity ratio, the capital structure is an optimal capital structure. At the optinum capital structure the marginal real cost of debt, defined to include both implicit and explicits, will be equal to the real cost of equity. For a debt-equity ratio before that level, the marginal real cost of debt would be less than that of equity capital, while beyond that level of leverage, the marginal real cost of debt would exceed that of equity. Thus, there would be an optimal structure according to the traditional view. Of course, there are variations to the traditional approach. According to one of these, the equity capitalisation rate (Kc) rises only after a certain level of leverage and not before, so that the use of debt does not necessary increase the Kc. This happens only after a certain degree of leverage. The implication is that firm can reduce its cost of capital significantly with the initial use of leverage.

Criticism of the traditional view: The validity of the traditional position has been questioned on the ground that the market value of the firm depends on its net operating income and risk attached to it. The form of financing can neither change the net operating income nor the risk attached to it. It can simply change the way in which net operating income and risk attached to it are distributed between equity and debt holders. Therefore, firms with identical net operating income and risk, but differing in their modes of financing should have same total value. The traditional view is criticised because it implies that totality of risk incurred by all security holders of a firm can be altered by changing the way in which this totality of risk is distributed among the various classes of securities. However, the argument of the traditional theorists that an optimum capital structure exists can be supported on two counts; the tax deductibility of interest charges and market imperfections. Modigliani and Miller also do not agree with the traditional view. They criticise the assumption that the cost of equity remains unaffected by leverage upto some reasonable limit. They assert that sufficient justification does not exist for such an assumption. They do not also accept the contention that moderate amounts of debt in 'sound' firms do not really add very much to the 'riskiness' of the shares.

(2) Net Income Approach

This is suggested by Mr. D. Durand. According to him, the capital structure decision is relevant to the valuation of the firm. In other words, a change in the capital structure financial leverage will lead to a corresponding change in the overall cost of capital as well as the total value of the firm. Therefore, if the degree of financial leverage as measured by the ratio of debt to equity is increased, the weighted average cost of capital will decline both in the value of the firm as well as the market price of equity shares. The net income approach to valuation is based on three assumptions; first, there are no taxes; second, that the cost of debt is less than equity capitalisation rate or the cost of equity; third, that the use of debt does not change the risk-perception of the investors. That the financial risk-perception of the investors does not change with the introduction of debt or change in leverage implies that due to change in leverage, there is no change in either the cost of debt or the cost of equity. The implication of the three assumptions underlying the net income approach is that as the degree of leverage increases, the proportion of an inexpensive source of funds *i.e.*, debt in the capital structure increases. As a result of the above, the weighted average cost of capital tends to decline; leading to an increase in the total value of the firm. Thus, with the cost of debt and the cost of equity, being constant, the increased use of debt (increase in leverage), will magnify the shareholder's earnings and thereby, the market value of the equity shares. The financial leverage is an important variable in the capital structure decision of a firm. With a judicions mixture of debt and equity, a firm can evolve an optimum capital structure which will be the one at which value of the firm is the highest and the overall cost of capital lowest. At that structure the market price per share would be the maximum. If the firm uses no debt or if the financial leverage is zero, the overall cost of capital will be equal to the equity-capitalisation rate. The weighted average cost of capital will decline and will approach the cost of debt as the degree of leverage reaches one.

(3) Net Operating Income (NOI) Approach

Another theory of capital structure, suggested by Durand, is the net operating income (NOI) approach. This is diametrically opposite to the net income approach. The essence of this approach is that the leverage/capital structure decision of the firm is irrelevant. Any change in leverage will not lead to any change in the total value of the firm, and the market price of the shares, on the overall cost of capital is independent of the degree of leverage.

Overall Cost of Capital/Capitalisation Rate (Ko) is Constant

The NOI approach to valuation argues that the overall capitalisation rate of the firm remains constant for all classes of leverages. The valuation of the firm, given the level of EBIT (Earnings before Interest and Tax) is determined as follows:

$$V = \frac{EBIT}{Ko}$$

In otherwords, the market evaluates the firm as a whole. The split of the capitalisation between debt and equity is therefore, not significant.

Residual Value of Equity

Value is residual in the case of equity which is determined by deducting the total value of debt (B) from the total value of the firm (V). Symbollically:

Total market value of equity capital (S) = V – B

Changes in Cost of Equity Capital

The equity-capitalisation rate/cost of equity capital (Ko) increases with the degree of leverage. The increase in the proposition of debt in the capital structure relatively to equity shares would lead to an increase in the financial risk to the ordinary shareholders. To compensate for the increased risk, the shareholder would expect a higher rate of return on their investments. The increase in the equity-capitalisation rate (or the lowering of the price-earning ratio, i.e., P/E ratio) would match the increase in the debt equity ratio. The Ko would be :

$$= Ko + (Ko - Kc)\left(\frac{B}{S}\right)$$

Cost of Debt

The cost of debt (Ki) has two parts : (a) Explicit cost represented by the rate of interest. Irrespective of the degree of leverage, the firm is assumed to be able to borrows at a given rate of interest. This implies that the increasing proportion of debt in the financial structure does not affect the financial risk of the lenders, and they do not penalise the firm by charging higher interest. (b) Implicit or 'hidden cost', as shown in the assumption relating to the changes in Ko, increase in the degree of leverage of the proportion of debt to equity canses an increase in the cost of equity capital. This increase in Kc being attributable to the increase in debt, in the implicit of Ki.

Thus the advantage associated with the use of debt, supposed to be a 'cheaper' source of funds in terms of the explicit cost is exactly neutralised by the implicit cost represented by the increase in Kc. As a result, the real cost of debt and the real cost of equity, according to the NOI approach are the same and equal.

Optimum Capital Structure

The total value of the firm is unaffected by its capital structure. No matter what the degree of leverage is, the total value of the firm will remain constant. The market price of the shares will also not change with the change in the debt-equity ratio. There is nothing such as an 'optimum capital structure'. Any capital structure is optimum, according to the NOI approach.

(4) Miller and Modigliani Position

Modigliani and Miller supplied rigorous challange to the traditional view. Thus approach closely resembles with NOI approach. According to this approach, cost of capital and so also value of firm remains unaffected by leverage employed by the firm. Thus, Modigliani and miller argued that any rational choice of debt and equity results in the same cost of capital under there assumptions and that there is no optimal mix of debt and equity financing. The independence of cost of capital argument is based on the hypothesis that regardless of the effect of leverage on interest rates, the equity capitalisation rate will rise by an amount sufficient to offset any possible savings from the use of low-cost debt. They contend that cost of capital is equal to the capitalisation rate of a pure equity stream of income and the market value is ascertained by capitalising its expected income at the appropriate discount rate for its risk class. So long as the business risk remains the same, the capitalisation rate (cost of capital) will remain constant. Hence, as the firm increases the amount of leverage in its capital structure, the cost of debt capital remaining constant, the capitalisation rate (cost of equity capital) will rise just enough to offset the gains resulting from applications of low-cost debt.

Thus, the essence of M-M approach is that for firms in the same risk class, the total value of the firm and the overall cost of capital are not depondent upon degree of financial leverage. The K and U remain constant for all degrees of financial leverage and value of the firm is found out by capitalising the expected flow of operating income at a discount rate appropriate for its risk class.

M-M's argument is based on a simple switching mechanism what is called 'arbitrage'. We shall, therefore, explain arbitrage process in detail.

Arbitrage Process

M-M's approach holds the view that the market value of two firms which are identical in all respects except for the difference in the pattern of financing, will not vary because arbitrage process will drive the total values of the firms together. Rational investors, according to M-M, will use arbitrage in the market to present the existence of the two assets in the same class and with same expected returns from selling at different prices.

The arbitrage process is an act of buying an asset in one market and selling it in another to take advantage of price differentials in the two markets. This process is essentially a balancing operation which would not allow the securities of the identical quality being sold at different prices in two markets. M-M applied the 'arbitrage' argument to explain their view. According to them, because of the operation of the arbitrage process the total value of two firms which are similar in all respects expect that one firm is levered and the other is unlevered, will not be different. The investors of the levered firm, whose value is higher, will liquidate their holdings and buy the shares of investors because they will be able to earn the same return with same perceived risk at relatively lower outlary. This behaviour of the investors will result in rise in the share prices of the firm whose shares are being sold. This process will continue till the market prices of the two homogeneous firms become identical. The investors are as indicated above, assured of the same return with identical risks but at lower outlays by the arbitrage process. This is possible because the investors would borrow in the proportion of the degree of leverage present in the firm. The use of debt by the investor for arbitrage is called 'home-made' or 'personal' leverage.

The counter arguments are as follows :

(*i*) The assumption that firms and individuals can borrow and lend at the same rate of interest does not hold good in practice.

(*ii*) It is incorrect to assume the 'personal' (home-made) leverage 'is a perfect substitute for' corporate leverage.

(*iii*) The existence of transaction costs also interferes with the working of the arbitrage.

(*iv*) Institutional restrictions also impede the working of arbitrage.

(*v*) M-M's conclusions will be frustrated by the incorporate of corporate income taxes.

QUESTIONS

Simple Questions

(*a*) What do you mean by capital structure?

(*b*) List out the principles that determine the capital structure of a company.

Long Answer Questions

1. Explain the factors that determine the capital structure.
2. Explain the (*a*) traditional approach; (*b*) net income approach and (*c*) net operating income approach theory of capital structure.
3. Discuss the M-M proposition on the influence of capital structure on the value of the firm. What are the countee arguments?

17

SOURCES OF FINANCE

INTRODUCTION

After assessing and estimating total capital requirements of an enterprise, the next important problem of management is to decide about the methods and sources of raising necessary funds to finance different kinds of capital requirements. But the methods of raising finance are linked with the period for which funds are needed. From this point of view funds may be classified into the following three heads.

(a) Short-term finance: Funds required for a period of upto one year form short-term finances of a company such funds are usually needed to meet seasonal working capital requirements or special needs for working capital.

(b) Medium-term finance: Funds that are needed for a period from one to five years are often classified as medium term finance. This kind of finance is generally needed to provide funds for permanent working capital or normal extensions and replacement of fixed assets.

(c) Long-term finance: Funds which are needed for a period of more than five years constitute long-term finances of the company. Long-term finance is generally required for permanent investment in fixed assets of the firm. Modernisation and major expansion programmes also give rise to the need for long-term finance.

Since sources of medium-term finance and long-term finance are virtually, the same, the problem of methods and sources of raising funds can broadly be divided into : (*a*) long-term source and (*b*) short-term source.

(1) LONG-TERM SOURCES OF FINANCE

The important sources of raising long-term funds are as follows :

(A) Equity Shares

The Companies Act 1956, defines equity shares as those which are not preference shares. Thus, to better understand the meaning of equity shares, one should know what are preference shares. Shares that carry preferential rights with regard to payment of dividend so long as company exists, and repayment of capital when company is would up, are known as preference shares. This means that dividend on equity shares is paid after disbursing a fixed rate of dividend on preference shares. Rate of equity dividend is not fixed and its payment depends upon profit available for payment of dividend and also intentions of the board of directors. When the company goes into liquidation, equity shares capital is repaid only after all other claims, including those of preference shares, have been fully settled and paid. Equity shareholders control the company by virtue of their entitlement to vote at the general meetings of the company. These shares have the chance of earning high dividends and also face the risk of earning nothing. Investors who are bold enough to take risks purchase equity shares. For this reason equity share capital is also known as venture capital. Equity shareholders also enjoy maximum possibility of capital appreciation.

Advantages of Equity Shares

(*a*) Payment of equity dividend is not binding upon the company, nor is the rate of equity dividend fixed. The result is that equity shares do not impose any fixed burden on company's financial resources. Dividend is paid if profits are available and directors deem it fit.

(*b*) Raising funds by issue of equity shares does not create any charge on assets of the company.

(*c*) Equity shares offer financial flexibility to the company in so far as neither rate nor payment of dividend is legally binding upon the company.

(*d*) Equity shares offer cushion to senior securities like preference shares and debentures and thus provide the company with a wide base to raise additional funds with these senior securities.

(*e*) Equity shares offer maximum opportunity of capital appreciation to investors.

Drawbacks of Equity Shares

(*a*) Equity shares are the most risky security from the point of view of investors with the result that equity dividend is generally higher than preference dividend or interest on debentures. Thus it is more costly to finance with equity shares than with other securities.

(*b*) Control of the company may be manipulated by certain groups of equity shareholders for their personal gains and even at the cost of company's interest.

(*c*) To the extent equity shares are issued, company losses the opportunity to trade on equity.

(*d*) Equity shares provide greater scope for speculation over stock exchanges than any other securities.

Equity shares are indispensable as a method of raising long-term funds by corporate entities. These shares provide the base upon which capital structure of the company is built.

(B) Preference Shares

Shares that enjoy preference over equity shares with regard to payment of dividend when company exists, and return of capitals, when the company is wound up, are known as preference shares. Rate of dividend payable on preference shares is fixed though its payment is not legally binding. However, when directors resolve to pay dividend, preference dividend is to be paid first.

Types of Preference Shares

On the basis of whether preference shares are entitled or not to share in the profit of the company remaining after payment of equity divident, preference shares may be divided into participating preference shares and non-participating preference shares. If nothing is mentioned, preference shares are assumed to be participating.

Preference shares may also be classified into cumulative preference shares and non-cumulative preference shares. When arrears of preference dividend must be paid first before payment of any dividend in future such shares are known as cumulative preference shares. If preference shares are not entitled to arrears of preference dividend, while paying dividend in future, these are known as non-cumulative preference shares.

A company may also issue redeemable preference shares when it undertakes to redeem the amount of preference shares under certain conditions. But the intention to redeem the preference shares must be made clear at the time of issue of such shares. However, preference shares can be redeemed subject to provisions of the companies Act. Thus, only fully paid preference shares can be redeemed, and redemption can be made out of divisible profits or out of proceeds of fresh issue of shares made for this purpose.

Advantages of Preference Shares

(*a*) Preference shares do not place a burden on finances of the company in case profits are inadequate.

(*b*) Issue of preference shares does not create any charge on assets of the company.

(*c*) Preference shares carry fixed rate of dividend and thus facilitate trading on equity by the company.

(*d*) From company's view point, cost of capital raised by issue of preference shares is less than the cost of equity capital.

(*e*) Preference shares appeal to cautious investors who want to earn higher income but prefer to take very less risks.

(*f*) Preference shares are especially useful when existing assets of the company are inadequate to be accepted as collateral security for purpose of issue of debentures or raising term loans.

(*g*) Unlike equity shares, preference shares offer facility of redemption during life time of the company.

Drawbacks of Preference Shares

(*a*) It is more costly to finance with preference shares than with debentures. The point becomes more obvious when it is remembered that dividend on preference shares is not a deductible item of expense for income tax purpose as interest on debenture is.

(*b*) Restrictive convenants often forming part of the terms and conditions of issue of preference shares tend to restrict flexibility of company management with regard to financial matters. Thus, convenants like instituting a skinking fund for redemption of preference shares or requirement that their consent must be obtained before incurring any further liability in future, tend to restrict management flexibility.

(*c*) Preference shares dilute claims of equity shareholders of the company over its assets.

(C) Debentures

Debenture is an acknowledgement of debt under seal of the company. Since those holding debentures are creditors of the company, debentures are also referred to as creditorship security. Evelyin Thomas defines debentures as a "document under the company's seal which provides for the payment of a principal sum and interest there on at regular intervals, which is usually secured by a fixed or floating charge on the company's property or undertakings, and which acknowledges loan of the company."

The following are the important features of debentures :

(*i*) Debentures carry interest at a fixed rate.

(*ii*) Interest on debentures must be paid even if there are no profits, and interest on debenture is a deductible expense for income tax purposes.

(*iii*) Amount of debentures must be redeemed as per terms of agreement.

(*iv*) Debentures are generally secured by charge on the assets of the company.
(*v*) Debentures are creditors and thus sue the company for unpaid dues.
(*vi*) In India, debentures do not enjoy voting rights.

Types of Debentures

Debentures may broadly be classified into the following categories :

(i) Registered or Bearer Debentures: Debentures that are recorded in the Register of Debenture-holders are known as registered debentures. Debenture-holders whose names appear in this register are entitled to periodic payment of interest and redumption of sum due on debentures. Mere delivery is not enough for transfer of registered debentures. These can be transfered by following the given procedure as laid down in the articles of association of the company. Bearer debentures on the other hand, are those debentures for which no register is maintained by the company and which are transferable by mere delivery without any intimation to the company.

(ii) Secured or Unsecured Debentures: When debentures are secured by mortgage or creating charge on assets of the company, these are known as secured debentures. Charge created on assets of the company may be fixed or floating. Such charge is required to be registered with the Registrar of companies. In case of default, debt due by the company can be recovered from the assets duly mortgaged in favour of debenture-holders. When debentures are not secured and thus rank as ordinary unsecured creditors for purpose of repayment of sums due by the company, these are known as simple, naked or unsecured debentures.

(*iii*) Redeemable or Irredeemable Debentures: When debentures are issued subject to redemption on certain terms as specified at the time of issue, such debentures are known as redeemable debentures. Conditions of issue may provide for redemption of debentures in lump sum after a given period of time or on demand by debenture-holders or by draw of lots a certain percentage of debentures each year or at company's discretion. Where no time is fixed in which the company is bound to pay, the debentures are known as irredeemable or perpetual. The debenture holders cannot demand payment as long as the company is a going concern and does not make default in payment of interest, although the company may payback at any time it chooses.

(*iv*) Convertible Debentures: Debentures may also be issued on the condition that these will be converted into equity shares after a given period of time instead of being redeemed by cash payment. These debentures are known as convertible debentures.

(*v*) First and Second Debentures: These may be preferred or ordinary debentures. Preferred, also known as first debentures are those which are to be paid first in case of winding up of the company, while ordinary or second debentures are those which are paid after first debentures have been fully paid off.

Merits of Debentures

(*a*) Company can issue debentures without diluting any control to their holders.
(*b*) Debentures help the company to trade on equity and thus attempt to increase rate of equity dividend.
(*c*) Since debentures are for a specific period, company may adjust its financial plan accordingly.
(*d*) Rate of interest payable on debentures is fixed and generally less than the rate of dividend payable on preference or equity shares.

(*e*) Debentures appeal to cantious and institutional investors who prefer stable rate of return on their investment with minimum or no risk.

(*f*) Funds raised by issue of debentures can be redeemed when these are no longer needed. This helps the company avoid unfortunate situation of over-capitalisation.

Drawbacks of Debenture Finance

(*a*) Issue of Debentures often results in creating charge on assets of the company.

(*b*) Issue of debentures may be based upon such convenants as tend to limit financial flexibility of the enterprise. Thus, provisions regarding creating sinking fund for debenture redemption or creating trust in favour of debenture-holders, tend to limit flexibility of the company.

(*c*) From company's point of view, debentures are the riskiest source of raising funds. Default in payment of interest or redemption of debentures as and when due may invite winding up of the company.

(*d*) Investors who purchase debentures of the company are denied the right of control. This also weakens safety of their capital.

(D) Ploughing Back of Profits

Companies save a part of their profits from distribution to shareholders as dividends use the same to meet financial requirements of business. This process of creating reserves by a company out of its profits and utilising the same for meeting financial requirements of the business from time to time is known as ploughing back of profits. In other words, retaining part of the profits and reinvesting the same into the business is known as ploughing back of earnings. Since in this case company depends on internal resources for meeting its capital requirements, ploughing back of profit is also known as 'internal financing' or 'self-financing'

Merits

(*a*) It is a good business policy not to distribute all the profits and save a part of them for future use by the company.

(*b*) Reserves built during the years of prosperity can be used to effectively fight out unfavourable business situation arising on account of depression or other risk factors.

(*c*) Self-financing is ideally suited for financing expansion and modernisation programmes of the company.

(*d*) Retained earnings are more definite as a source of financing business operations. Internal financing does not make the enterprise become dependent upon market considerations or investors.

(*e*) Though retained earnings are not cost free source of finance company is under no legal or contractual obligation to pay any return to any outside partly when it reinvests its own profits into the business.

Demerits

(*a*) Continuous and excessive ploughing back of profits over a long period of time may canse a company become a monopoly organisation.

(*b*) Management may consider retained profits as cost-free source of financing capital requirements of the enterprise and thus may not always utilise them efficiently and for the best advantage of shareholders.

(*c*) Excessive ploughing back may tempt management of the company to manipulate share prices. By declaring dividends at very high or very low rates, management may cause share prices to change in the direction so as to serve vested interests.

(*d*) The policy of excessive ploughing back of profits withholds flow of funds to capital market and thus does not allow allocation of resources to different companies based upon market forces. In other words, ploughing back of profits makes capital market become inactive and also distorts allocation of resources.

(*e*) Use of accumulated profits for issue of bonus shares may cause a company become over-capitalised.

(E) Specialised Financial Institutions

Faced with the objective of encouraging industrial development in the country through cheap industrial finance, the Government of India established a number of specialised financial instituions to provide cheap financial assistance to business enterprises. Industrial finance corporation of India was the first such financial institution established after independence in 1948. Industrial credit and investment corporation, Industrial Development Bank of India and State Financial Corporations are the important finance institutions providing assistance to industrial undertakings. The assistance from these institutions constitute an important source of finance for meeting the requirements of new as well as already established concerns. The assistance from these financial institutions takes the form of direct subscription to securities of companies, underwriting of securities, grant of loans, guaranteeing loans and debentures and guaranteeing of deferred payments against import of capital goods. These institutions also provide expert advice to industrial enterprises for planning and execution of projects. These institutions also ensure that assistance provided by them is effectively utilised for the purpose for which such assistance is granted.

SHORT-TERM SOURCES OF FINANCE

Short-term funds are needed to finance special and seasonal working capital requirements. Following are the important sources of short-term finance.

(1) Trade Credit

In a number of cases trade credit is the single most important source of short-term funds. Since it is a usual trade practice in many cases to allow credit to reliable purchasers of materials and other items, trade credit is often described as the self-generating source of short-term finance. Credit standards as imposed by sellers are generally not very rigid, and the firms enjoying reputation in the market are able to purchase their requirements of stock on credit as a matter of routine. Willingness of the supplier to permit delay in payment and buyers' need for it largely determine the extent to which trade credit is to be used to finance short-term requirements of funds. Moreover, reputation of the buyer for prompt and timely payments also enhances buying firm's ability to get more trade credit.

Trade credit may be allowed to the buyer either on open account or on the basis of exchange of commercial papers between the parties. Trade credit does not create any charge on assets of the purchasing firm.

Importance of trade credit as source of short-term finance is largely determined by the following factors :

(*i*) Terms and conditions at which trade credit is available.
(*ii*) Payment record of the borrowing firms.
(*iii*) Financial position of the supplier.
(*iv*) Volume and amount of purchases to be made by the borrowing firm.

(2) Commercial Banks

Bank credit is another important source of short-term finance. Traditionally, banks in India have refrained from providing long-term assistance to business enterprise. Consideration of liquidity, safety of investment and availability of expertise in evaluating proposals for short-term assistance are the basic factors that make commercial banks to confine their assistance to business largely for short-term purposes.

Commercial banks meet short-term requirements of finance of business undertakings in the following ways :

(*a*) By discounting of bills and other commercial papers.
(*b*) By accepting or endorsing bills on behalf of customers.
(*c*) By granting loans, overdrafts, and cash credits.

(3) Public Deposits

Public deposits arise when company invites general public to deposit their savings for a certain period of time and at a given rate of interest. Public deposits are external source of finance and thus form part of loan capital of the company. Since public deposits can be upto a period of three years and deposits that fall due for payment can be renewed, these can be used to finance working capital requirements and also serve as source of intermediate financing.

Merits

(*a*) The method of raising funds through public deposits is simple and does not entail any complicated formalities.
(*b*) It is relatively less costly method of raising short-term and intermediate funds.
(*c*) Public deposits are usually unsecured and thus create no charge on assets of the company.
(*d*) Since rate of interest payable on them is fixed, public deposits enable the company to trade on equity and thus increase rate of equity dividend.

Demerits

(*a*) Public deposits are highly unrealiable and uncertain source of finance. For a flourishing company enjoying good reputation, deposits pour in. During depression or financial stringency, this source dries up. Even a slight rumour about financial position of the company makes this source highly unpredictable.
(*b*) The system is also injurious to proper growth of capital market. Use of public deposits as source of intermediate financing may adversely affect supply of funds for industrial securities, more particularly preference shares and debentures.

(4) Advances from Customers

Contractors and producers of costly goods with a considerable length of manufacturing period often demand advance money from their customers while accepting orders for executing the contract or supply of goods. Where acceptance of advances from customers is an accepted business practice, prepayments by clients become a useful source of short-term finance.

NEW FINANCIAL INSTRUMENTS AND INSTITUTIONS

(1) Certificate of Deposit

Certificate of Deposit is a term deposits with a bank to be paid after certain period with guaranteed rate of interest. This deposit is evidenced by a certificate issued by a bank and hence is popularly known as certificate of deposit. The rate of interest agreed to be paid by the bank is dependent on the cash requirement of the bank and the prevalent rate of interest in market. During the conditions of tight money, bank may offer high rates depending upon its own needs of cash. A certificate of deposit is a negotiable instrument. The holder of certificate of deposit can sell the same by delivery in the market and get payment earlier than maturity. The risk of default in the case of certificate of deposit is comparatively less as it is issued by a bank.

In India, certificate of deposit is issued by banks for a period of 91 days to one year with the minimum amount of Rs. 10 lakhs. A certificate of deposit is issued at a discount and the face value is payable at maturity by the issuing bank. The rates of discount keep on varying depending upon cash supply in the money market and bank's own requirement of cash. At times the rates of interest offered by the bank may be 4% to 5% more than the rate for fixed deposit of the identical period. A certificate of deposit is transferable by endorsement and delivery after 45 days of issue. However, in the absence of developed secondary market for certificate of deposits in India, the holder has to reconcile for keeping the same with himself till its maturity.

(2) Commercial paper

Commercial paper is a short-term negotiable money market instrument, consisting of unsecured promissory notes. It is issued in a bearer form with a fixed maturity, typically between 7 days and 3 months. Issues can be made on an occassional basis or more generally, under a medium term revolving programme. Commercial papers may be issued by many types of borrowers including industrial and commercial companies. It is sold either directly by the issuers to investors or placed by intermediary bank or security dealers to investors like insurance companies, pension and provident funds, mutual funds etc.

Advantages of Commercial Papers

The advantage of commercial paper lies in its simplicity. There is hardly any documentation, between the issuer and the investor and there is a flexibility with regard to the maturity of the instrument which can be tailored to the needs of both the issuer and the investor. A well rated company can diversify its sources of finance and raise short-term funds at some what cheaper rates than from banks. This is more true of a financial system where reserve requirements of banks are compulsory. Investors can earn higher returns than what is obtainable from the banking system or a treasury bills. It also provides an incentive to the issuing companies to remain financially strong and efficient as it reduces the cost of borrowing. It also helps companies in raising long-term funds by becoming better known in the financial world. In the Indian context, commercial papers have another advantage of raising funds from the inter-corporate market, which are, at present, not under the control of monetary authorities.

Eligibility for Issue of Commercial Paper

The Reserve Bank guidelines are aimed at ensuring that only first class corporates enter the commercial paper market. Some of the more important guidelines are :

(*a*) A minimum tangible networth of Rs. 10 crores as per the latest audited balance sheet, a working capital limit of Rs. 15 crores or above, listing on one or more stock exchange, ap_1+ rating from CRISIL and a minimum current ratio of 1.33.

(*b*) Commercial paper maturity has to be minumum 3 months and maximum 6 months from the date of issue.

(*c*) Each issue of commercial paper requires the approval of the RBI.

(*d*) The commercial paper may be issued in multiples of Rs. 25 lakhs, but the minimum amount to be invested by a single investor in the primary market shall be Rs. 1 crore of face value.

(*e*) The aggregate amount to be raised by issue of commercial paper is limited to 20% of the company's working capital limit.

(*f*) Commercial paper is in the form of usance promissory notes, negotiable by endorsement and delivery, and issued at a discount to reflect the interest; the discount rate is to be freely determined by the issuing company. The company issuing commercial paper has also to bear the expenses of the issue, including stamp duty, dealer fee, rating agency fee etc.

(*g*) Commercial papers will be issued to any person or corporate bodies (including banks) registered or incorporated in India as well as incorporated bodies.

(*h*) The issue of commercial paper cannot be underwritten or co-accepted in any manner.

A general permission has been granted by the reserve bank to all companies governed by the Foreign Exchange Regulation Act 1973 (now Foreign Exchange Management Act), to raise deposits by issue of commercial paper.

(3) Mutual Funds

A mutual fund is a professionally managed company that pools the funds of investors to invest in a diversified portfolio of securities. The mutual fund invests in various types of securities after careful research and analysis. It offers the individual saver advantages of reasonable dividends and capital appreciation coupled with safety and liquidity. Mutual funds offer the golden mean between slow growing bank deposits and high-risk high-yield corporate securities.

(4) Stock Invest

This is an instrument newly designed by the banks to avoid the difficulties faced by the investors in company securities. This is an instrument which provides special payment system for investors in the primary capital issues in the last decade. Every public issue of joint stock company is oversubscribed by the investing class. This has resulted delay in the allotment process, refund of application money in case of non-allotment, thus causing hardship and loss of interest to the investors. To overcome these difficulties, a new payment instrument called 'stock invest' was designed by the State Bank of India in collaboration with the securities and exchange Board of India and obtained the permission from RBI to introduce this instruments.

With the introduction of stock-invest, oversubscription of public issues and the resulting refund have been simplified. The refunding of money to the non-allottees for whom (the companies) the oversubscription was a nightmare, the stock invest made the companies to have a sigh of relief.

As far as investor is concerned, he was not getting any interest on the money he paid along with the application upto the date of allotment or rejection. This created float funds for the company which could be used for three months without paying any interest on it. Because of scarce resources and high interest rates some companies were tempted to capitalise float funds.

These funds earned upto 20% interest and this interest was used to meet the expenses in returning the non-allotees.

(5) Zero-Interest Bonds (ZIB)

Zero-Interest bonds means bonds which are sold at a discount from their eventual maturity value and have zero interest rate.

ZIB is a good instrument for the investors who are ready to wait till the bond is matured. Investors fnd ZIBs attractive because of low investment cost. Moreover, these bonds mean good tax planning because the bonds do not carry any interest, which is otherwise taxable. Another advantage from the investor's point of view is that it eliminates reinvestment risk. For the institutional investors, who are looking for safe and good returns, ZIB's are the bet option. Companies also find ZIB's quite attractive to issue because there is no immediate interest commitment on maturity, the bonds can be converted into equity shares or non-convertible debentures, depending upon the requirement of capital structure of the company. ZIBs are best suited for companies with long gestation period as the interest service date is much later.

(6) Zero-coupon Bond

It is a process which requires separation of the principal part and interest part of an ordinary bond, and selling them separately to the investors. This process is known as stripping or just strips. This stripping results in two securities, one for the principal part and the other for the interest part which is known as strip. The principal part is stated as a Zero Coupon Bond (ZCB) which is issued and traded at a discount and redeemed at its face value at the maturity. One of the prominent example of ZCB is the IDBI flexibond which would pay Rs. 2 lakhs after 25 years in return for a deposit of Rs. 5300. Essentially, a ZCB is a non-interest bearing instrument that promises a fixed amount upon redemption, which would be higher than the issue price.

QUESTIONS

Simple Questions

1. Define Debentures.
2. What do you mean by Trade credit?
3. What do you mean by certificate of deposit?
4. What do you mean by commercial paper?
5. What is a mutual fund?
6. What is meant by stock invest?
7. What do you mean by zero-interest bond?
8. What do you mean by zero-coupon bond?

Short Answer Questions

1. State the advantages and disadvantages of equity shares capital.
2. Explain the different types of preference shares.
3. State the advantages and disadvantages of preference shares.
4. Explain the different types of Debentures.
5. State the advantages and disadvantages of Debentures.
6. State the advantages and disadvantages of ploughing back of profit.
7. Explain the various sources of short-term source of finance to a business.
8. Explain the various so new financial instruments which enable a company in raising funds.

18

WORKING CAPITAL MANAGEMENT

INTRODUCTION

In practice, a firm has also to employ short-term assets, and short-term sources of financing. The management of such assets described as working capital management is an integral part of the over-all financial management. To that extent, it is similar to the long-term decision-making process because both entail an analysis of the effects of risk and profitability. The problems involved in the management of working capital differ from those in fixed assets. Probably, the most notable feature of such assets, from the point of view of financial analysis is the time dimension. The operational implication is that discounting and compounding techniques to adjust the value of benefits accuring from such assets over time play a fairly significant role in financial management. In contrast, the stock-in-trade of working capital management, by definition, is short-term assets which lose their identity fairly quickly, usually within a year. Therefore, in the management of working capital, the time factor is not crucial as a decision-variable. Yet another notable feature of short-term assets is the question of profitability versus liquidity and the related aspect of risk. If the size of such assets is large, the liquidity position would improve, but profitability would be adversely affected as funds will remain idle; conversely, if the holdings of such assets are relatively small, the overall profitability will no doubt increase, but it will have an adverse effect on the liquidity position and make the firm more risky. Working capital management should, therefore, aim at striking a balance such that there is an optimum amount of short-term assets.

DEFINITION AND TYPES OF WORKING CAPITAL

Working capital is that form of capital which flows and changes constantly from one form to another. It is for this reason it is also known as circulating capital. According to Gerstenberg, "circulating capital means current assets of a company that are changed in the ordinary course of business from one form to another, as for example, from cash to inventories, investories to receivables, receivables into cash.

Gross and Net Working Capital

The total of current assets is known as gross working capital. The excess of current assets over current liabilities is known as net working capital.

Permanent and Variable Working Capital

That irreducible minimum amount of working capital which must remain permanently invested in different current assets of the enterprise is known as permanent working capital. Thus, so long as business is to exist and run, the firm must always maintain some minimum amount of cash, stock and accounts receivables. Such minimum amount of funds as is permanently locked up in current assets of a business should be regarded as permanent working capital and financed out of long term sources. Permanent working capital is also known as regular working capital.

Working capital requirements of a business firm may increase because of seasonal swings or special needs of the business. Such additional working capital as is required to meet seasonal or special needs of the business is known as variable or irregular working capital.

Significance of Adequate Working Capital

Adequate working capital is significant because of its following advantages :

(*a*) Adequate working capital provides sufficient liquidity to the enterprise and thus ensures its solvency.

(*b*) It adds to credit-worthiness and reputation of the enterprise by ensuring prompt payments to suppliers of raw-materials and other creditors of the firm.

(*c*) Firms maintaining adequate working capital can avail of cash discount and thus add to earnings of their business.

(*d*) Banks and other short-term lenders of money base their decisions for lending short-term loans to the enterprise on the basis of analysis of its working capital. Such analysis is designed to test repaying capacity and liquidity position of the borrowing enterprise.

(*e*) At times, the business may face situation when it needs additional funds to save itself from disaster. Adequate working capital also ensures availability of emergency capital and thus helps the enterprise face such situations more successfully.

(*f*) Earning of profits is not a sufficient guarantee that the company can pay dividend in cash. Adequate working capital ensures that dividends are paid regularly.

(*g*) A firm maintaining adequate working capital can afford to buy raw-materials and other accessories as and when needed. This ensures uninterrupted flow of production. Adequate working capital, therefore, contributes to fuller utilisation of resources of the enterprise.

(*h*) An enterprise maintaining adequate working capital can afford to hold up its stock of finished goods and wait for better marketing apportunities.

Factors Determining the Amount of Working Capital

(a) *Nature of business*: A trading company requires large working capital. Industrial concern may require lower working capital. A banking company of course, requires maximum amount of working capital. Basic and key industries, public utilities, etc. require low working capital because they have a steady demand and continuous cash-inflow to meet current liabilities.

(b) *Size of the business unit:* The amount of working capital depends directly upon the volume of business. The greater the size of a business unit, the larger will be the requirements of working capital.

(c) *Terms of purchase and terms of sale*: Use of trade credit may lead to lower working capital, while cash purchases will demand larger working capital. Similarly, credit sales will require larger working capital, while cash sales will require lower working capital.

(d) *Turnover of inventories:* If inventories are large and their turnover is slow, we shall require larger capital but if inventories are small and their turnover is quick, we shall require lower working capital.

(e) *Process of manufacture*: Long period, complex and round about process of production will require larger working capital, while simple, short period process of production will require lower working capital.

(f) Importance of labour: Capital intensive industries, *i.e.*, mechanised and automated industries will require lower working capital, while labour intensive industries such as small-scale and cottage industries will require larger working capital.

(g) Cash requirements: If a company has demand for larger cash needs, it requires a larger working capital e.g. at the time of dividend payment, taxation, interest charges, wages and salaries.

(h) Seasonal variation: During the busy season, a business requires larger working capital while during the stock season a company requires lower working capital.

Estimation of Working Capital Requirements

Adequate amount of working capital is essential for the smooth running of a business enterprise. The finance manager should forecast working capital requirements carefully to determine an optimum level of in working capital. While forecasting working capital requirements, it should be borne in mind that working capital requirements are to be determined on an average basis and not on any specific point of time. The estimate of future working capital can be made if the amount of current assets and current liabilities can be estimated.

Problem 1 : ABC Ltd. provides you with the following information with the request to prepare a statement of working capital:

(A) Cost Records

Total cost of product is Rs. 10 per unit of which 50% is accounted by materials, overheads are $\frac{2}{3}$ of the labour cost per unit.

(B) Sales Target (Annual)

	Rs.	*Terms*
Zone A — (cost + 50%	6,00,000	cash
Zone B — (cost + 25%)	5,00,000	1 month credit
Zone C — (cost + 20%)	1,92,000	2 months credit

(C) Other Details

(*i*) Stocks of both Raw-materials and finished goods are to be kept for 2 months, while processing takes one month.

(*ii*) 20% of supplies of materials are ensured on cash payment, 20% of supplies are taken on advance payment for 15 day's and remaining suppliers have agreed to extend one month credit.

(D) Time lag in payment of wages and overheads is ½ month.

(E) Debtors are valued at cost.

(F) Cash balance is always kept at 10% of net working capital inclusive of cash.

(*University of Bombay, B.Com., April 1999*)

Solution :

Working note:

(1) Calculation of Selling Price Per Unit

Zone A	Cost price per unit	10
	Add : Profit – 50% of 10	5
		15
Zone B	Cost price per unit	10
	Add : Profit – 25% of 10	2.50
		12.50

Zone C	Cost price per unit	10
	Add : profit – 20% of 10	2
		12

(2) Calculation of Annual Units

	SP	*Sale Value*	*Units Annual*
Zone A	15	6,00,000	40,000
Zone B	12.50	5,00,000	40,000
Zone C	12.10	1,92,000	16,000
			96,000

(3) Calculation of Units Per Month

$$\frac{96{,}000 \text{ units}}{12 \text{ months}} = 8{,}000 \text{ units per month}$$

(4) Monthly Cost Sheet

		8,000 Units
Materials	8,000 @ Rs. 5 per unit	40,000
Labour	8,000 @ Rs. 3 per unit	24,000
Ob	8,000 @ Rs. 2 per unit	16,000
	Total cost	80,000

Statement of Working Capital

(1) Raw-materials – 2 months × Rs. 40,000 — 80,000

(2) Work-in-progress (1 month)

Material – 1 Month × 40,000 = 40,000

$$\text{Labour} - 1 \text{ Month} \times 24{,}000 \times \frac{50}{100} = 12{,}000$$

$$\text{Overheads} - 1 \text{ Month} \times 16{,}000 \times \frac{50}{100} = 8{,}000$$

60,000

(3) Finished Goods (2 months) — 1,60,000

(4) Debtors at cost

$$\text{Zone B} \quad \frac{40{,}000 \text{ units} \times \text{Rs } 10}{12} = 33{,}333$$

$$\text{Zone C} \quad \frac{16{,}000 \times \text{Rs}10 \times 2\text{M}}{12} = 26{,}667$$

60,000

(5) Advance to suppliers

$$40{,}000 \times \frac{20}{100} \times \frac{1}{2} \text{ month}$$

4,000

(6) Cash in Hand

$$\frac{1}{9}\,(3{,}64{,}000 - 44{,}000)$$

$$\frac{1}{9} \times 3{,}20{,}000$$

35,556

3,99,556

Less : Current Liabilities

$$(a) \quad \text{Creditors} \quad 40{,}000 \times \frac{60}{100} \times 1 \text{ month} = 24{,}000$$

(b) Labour	$24,000 \times \frac{1}{2}$ month	=	12,000
(c) Overhead	$16,000 \times \frac{1}{2}$ month	=	8,000
			44,000
Net working capital			3,55,556

Problem 2 : The management of German Collaboration Limited has called for a statement showing the working capital needed to finance a level of activity of 3,00,000 units output for the year. The cost structure for the company's product for the said activity is detailed below :

	Cost per unit (Rs.)
Raw-materials	20
Direct labour	5
Overhead	15
Total cost	40
Profit	10
Selling price	50

1. Past trend indicate that raw-material are held in stock on an average for two months.
2. Work-in-progress will approximate to half a months production.
3. Finished goods remain in warehouse on average for a month.
4. Suppliers of materials extend a month's credit.
5. Two month's credit is normally allowed to debtores.
6. A minimum cash balance of Rs. 25,000 is expected to be maintained.

The production pattern is assumed to be even during the year.
Prepare the statement of working capital determination.

(*University of Bombay, B.Com., October 1998*)

Solution :

Statement of Estimated Working Capital

Current assets			
(1) Stock			
(a) Raw-materials : $5,00,000 \times 2$ months		10,00,000	
(b) Work-in-progress :			
(i) Raw-materials $5,00,000 \times \frac{1}{2}$ m	2,50,000		
(ii) Direct labour $1,25,000 \times \frac{1}{2}$ m $\times \frac{50}{100}$	3,125		
(iii) Overheads $3,75,000 \times \frac{1}{2}$ m $\times \frac{50}{100}$	93,750		
		3,75,000	
(c) Finished goods $10,00,000 \times 1$ M		10,00,000	
			13,75,000
(2) Sundry Debtors $12,50,000 \times 2$ M			25,00,000
(3) Cash			25,000
			49,00,000

Less : Current Liabilities	
Creditors 5,00,000 × 1 M	5,00,000
	44,00,000
Add : Safety margin (10%)	4,40,000
Required working capital	48,40,000

Problem 3 : A Company Plans to manufacture and sell 400 units of a domestic appliance per month at a price of Rs. 600 each. The ratio of costs to selling price are as follows :

	% of Selling Price
Raw-materials	30%
Packing materials	10%
Direct labour	15%
Direct expenses	5%

Fixed overheads are estimated at Rs. 4,32,000 per annum.

The following norms are maintained for inventory management

Raw-materials	30 days
Packing materials	15 days
Finished goods	200 units
Work-in-progess	7 days

Other particulars are given below :

(*a*) Credit sales represent 80% of total sales and the dealers enjoy 30 working days credit. Balance 20% are cash sales.

(*b*) Creditors allow 21 working days credit for payment.

(*c*) Lag in payment of overheads and expenses is 15 working days.

(*d*) Cash requirements to be 12% of net working capital.

(*e*) Working days in a year are taken as 300 for budgeting purpose.

Prepare working capital requirement forecast for the budget year. (*ICWA, Inter, June 2001*)

Solution :

Cost Sheet

Raw-materials $\frac{30}{100} \times 600$	180
Packing materials $\frac{10}{100} \times 600$	60
Direct labour $\frac{15}{100} \times 600$	90
Direct expenses $\frac{5}{100} \times 600$	30
Fixed overhead $\frac{4,32,000}{400 \times 12}$	90
Total cost	450
Profit	150
Selling price	600

Production Details

Production per month	400 units
Production per year 400 × 12	4,800 units
Production per day $\frac{4,800}{300}$	16 units

Statement showing working capital requirement

Particulars	*No. of units per day*	*Requirements in No. of working days*	*Total requirement in units*	*Cost per unit*	*Amt.*
Raw-materials	16	30	480	180	86,400
Packing materials	16	15	240	60	14,400
WIP	16	7	112	285	31,920
Finished goods	-	-	200	450	90,000
Debtors $\frac{80}{100} \times 16$	12.8	30	384	600	2,30,400
				Total (A)	4,53,120
Less : Credits					
For raw-materials from suppliers	16	21	336	180	60,480
For packing materials	16	21	336	60	20,160
For overheads and expenses	16	15	240	120	28,800
				Total (B)	1,09,440
Net working capital (A–B)					3,43,680
Add : Cash required at 12% of net working capital					41,242
Total working capital required					3,84,922

Problem 4 : The following are the extracts from the balance sheet of a company as on 31.3.1999. Compute the additional working capital required by the company for the year ending 31.3.2000.

Balance Sheet (Extracts only) as on 31.3.1999

	Rs.	*Rs.*	*Rs.*
Fixed assets :			
Land & Building	5,00,000		
Plant & Machinery	3,00,000		8,00,000
Working capital :			
Current assets :			
Stock	8,00,000		
Debtors	3,00,000		
Cash & Bank	2,00,000		
		13,00,000	
Less : Current liabilities :			
Creditors	3,40,000		
Taxation	80,000		
Bank overdraft	1,40,000		
Bills payable	1,60,000		
		7,20,000	
			5,80,000
			13,80,000

Additional Information

1. It is estimated that sale will increase by 25% next year.
2. Maximum amount of overdraft that can be availed will be only Rs. 1,60,000.
3. There will be no increase in the liability due to increase in exports
4. Period of credit allowed to customers and stock turnover will remain unaltered.
5. Period of credit allowed by creditors and that for bills payable will remain the same.
6. There will be no increase in total amount of cash and bank balance. *(ICWA, Inter, June 2000)*

Solution : **Statement showing additional working capital requirement**

	Current level	*Estimated increase*	*Requirement for next year*
(A) Current assets :			
Stock	8,00,000	2,00,000	10,00,000
Debtors	3,00,000	75,000	3,75,000
Cash & bank balance	2,00,000	–	2,00,000
	13,00,000	2,75,000	15,75,000
(B) Current liabilities			
Creditors	3,40,000	85,000	4,25,000
Taxation	80,000	–	80,000
Bank overdraft	1,40,000	20,000	1,60,000
Bills payable	1,60,000	40,000	2,00,000
	7,20,000	1,45,000	8,65,000
(C) Working capital (A–B)	5,80,000	1,30,000	7,10,000

Additional working capital required :

= 7,10,000 – 5,80,000 = Rs. 1,30,000

Problem 5 : A company has prepared its annual budget, relevant details of which are reproduced below :

(*i*) Sales, Rs. 46.80 Lakhs : 78,000 units
25% cash sales and balance on credit

(*ii*) Raw-material cost : 60% of sales value

(*iii*) Labour cost : Rs. 6 per unit

(*iv*) Variable overheads : Rs. 1 per unit

(*v*) Fixed overheads : Rs. 5 lakhs
(Including Rs. 1,10,000 as depreciation)

(*vi*) Budgeted stock level :
Raw-materials : 3 weeks
Work-in-progress : 1 week (material 100%, labour and overheads approximately 50%)
Finished goods : 2 weeks

(*vii*) Debtors are allowed credit for 4 weeks

(*viii*) Creditors allow 4 weeks credit

(*ix*) Wages are paid bimonthly, i.e., by the 3rd week and by the 5th week for the Ist and 2nd weeks and 3rd and 4th weeks respectively.

(*x*) Lag in payment of overheads : 2 weeks

(*xi*) Cash in hand required : Rs. 50,000

Prepare the working capital budget for a year for the company, making whatever assumptions that you may find necessary. *(ICWA, Inter, June 1998)*

Solution :

Cost Sheet

Raw-materials	36
Labour	6
Variable overheads	1
Fixed overhead (excluding depreciation)	5
Total cost	48
Profit	12
Selling price	60

Statement Showing working capital required

Current Assets	*Duration of period*	*Total No. of units*	*Cost per unit*	*Total cost*
Raw-materials	3 weeks	4,500	Rs. 36	1,62,000
Work-in-progress	1 week	1,500	Rs. 42	63,000
Finished goods	2 weeks	3,000	Rs. 48	1,44,000
Debtors	4 weeks	4,500	Rs. 48	2,16,000
Cash in hand				50,000
			Total (A)	6,35,000
Current liabilities				
Creditors	4 weeks	6,000	Rs. 36	2,16,000
Lag in wages	2 weeks			18,000
Lag in payment of overheads	2 weeks			18,000
			Total (B)	2,52,000
Net working capital (A–B)				3,83,000

Working Notes :

1. Total sales for 4 weeks is 6,000 units excluding 25% cash sales, credit amounts to 4,500 units.
2. One year is assumed to be 52 weeks.
3. Lag in wages $\frac{2}{52} \times 78{,}000 \times \text{Rs. } 6 = 18{,}000$
4. Lag in payment of overheads $\frac{2}{52} \times 78{,}000 \times \text{Rs. } 6 = 18{,}000$

Problem 6 : From the following data, prepare a statement showing working capital requirements for the year 1998 :

(*a*) Estimated activity/operations for the year 1,30,000 units (52 weeks)

(*b*) Stock of raw-materials 2 weeks and material in process for 2 weeks, 50% of wages and overheads are incurred.

(*c*) Finished goods 2 weeks storage

(*d*) Creditors 2 weeks

(*e*) Debtors 4 weeks

(*f*) Outstanding wages and overheads 2 weeks each

(*g*) Seling price per unit Rs. 15

(*h*) Analysis of cost per unit is as follows:

(*i*) Raw-materials $33\frac{1}{3}$% of sales

(*ii*) Labour and overheads are in the ratio of 6 : 4 per unit

(*iii*) Profit is at Rs. 5 per unit

Assume that operations are evenly spread through the year.

(*University of Bombay, B.Com., April 1988*)

Solution :

Cost sheet for the week

	Per Unit	*Cost per week*
Raw-materials	5.00	12,500
Labour	3.00	7,500
Overheads	2.00	5,000
Total cost	10.00	25,000
Profit	5.00	12,500
	15.00	37,500

Statement showing estimated working capital for 1998

Current Assets				
(i) Raw-materials stock		= 12,500 × 2		25,000
(ii) *Work-in-progress* :				
Material 12,500 × 2		=	25,000	
Labour 7,500 × 2 × $\frac{1}{2}$		=	7,500	
Overheads 5,000 × 2 × $\frac{1}{2}$		=	5,000	
				37,500
(iii) Finished goods (12,500 + 7,500 + 5,000) × 2				50,000
(iv) Debtors 37,500 × 4				1,50,000
				2,62,500
Less : Current liabilities :				
Creditors -	12,500 × 2	=	25,000	
O/s wages -	7,500 × 2	=	15,000	
O/s overheads -	5,000 × 2	=	10,000	
				50,000
working capital				2,12,500

Management of Cash

Management of cash is an important function of the finance manager. The modern day business comprises numerous units spread over vast geographical areas. It is the duty of the finance manager to provide adequate cash to each of the units. For the survival of the business, it is absolutely essential that there should be adequate cash. It is the duty of the financial manager to have liquidity at all parts of the organisation while managing cash. On the other hand, he has also to ensure that there are no funds blocked in idle cash. Idle cash resources entail a great deal of cost in terms of interest charges and in terms of opportunities lost. Hence, the question of cost of idle cash must also be kept in mind by the finance manager. A cash management scheme, therefore, is a delicate balance between the twin objectives of liquidity and cost.

Need for Cash

Cash is required to meet three motives. They are as follows :

(*a*) *Transaction motive*—Cash is required to meet day-to-day expenses and other payments on due dates. For this reason, inflow of cash from operations should be sufficient.

But sometimes this inflow may be temporarily blocked. In such cases, it is only the reserve cash balance that can enable the firm to make its payments in time.

(*b*) *Speculative motive*: It implies ability to take advantage of profitable opportunities that may present themselves which may be lost for want of ready settlement.

(*c*) *Precautionary motive:* Cash is required to meet contingent events both arising in short run and long run period.

Estimation of Cash Requirement

The first step in cash management is to estimate the requirements of cash. For this purpose cash flow statements and cash budgets are required to be prepared.

The term 'cash flow' depicts the flow of liquid funds as a result of business activites. A cash flow statement records and reflects the quantum and the nature of inflow and outflow of liquid funds. It can either be a projected statement which acts as a guideline for management or a record of actual performance analysing the strength and the weakness of the short-term financial position. It is thus a vital tool for providing data for a number of managerial decisions.

From the conventional profit and loss account, the management does not know its cash position. It might so happen that, in spite of a big profit, as revealed by the profit and loss account, the company may not have sufficient funds to pay even salaries. This is because adequate profits do not necessarily ensure adequate cash resources. A cash flow statement is actually the summarised form of cash book in which the actual receipts and payments are sectionalised. It shows the sources from where the funds were obtained and the uses to which they were put. Sometimes it is also referred to as 'how come, where gone' statement, because it explains how the funds came and where they have gone.

Cash flow statements can be prepared in the following two ways : (*i*) showing in detail each item of inflow or outflow of cash irrespective of whether it is capital or revenue in nature; or (*ii*) showing the net inflows/outflows from revenue operations as one consolidated figure and inflows/outflows of capital nature separately.

The preparation of cash flow statement offers the following advantages :

(*a*) It tells the management when to plan and for what amount of liquid funds. Profit is not cash and an increase in profit is not necessarily a comfortable cash situation. The increased inflow from profit may have gone into the financing of stocks and debtors or utilised to acquire fixed assets or repayment of long-term liabilities.

(*b*) It shows the amount of natural accruals, management can assess how much is needed for increase in working capital, and how much can be spared for capital expenditure etc.

(*c*) It reveals the estimated availability of cash, so that advance planning of cash, utilisation becomes possible.

(*d*) It reveals the need for additional cash requirements in advance so that negotiation for obtaining loans could be started in time.

It is because of all these advantages that financial institutions insist on projected cash flows statement for 5-10 years before entertaining loan applications. From the cash flow statement, the financial institutions try to form an idea whether the firm to be financed would be able to generate sufficient cash to pay the interest and instalments in time after meeting their own needs. Recently, for the same reason, banks have also started insisting on projected cash flow statement before granting loans for working capital, although the period covered in this case is much shorter.

Cash Budgets for Short Period

Preparation of cash budget month by month would involve making the following estimates :

(a) As regards receipts :

(*i*) Receipts from debtors

(*ii*) Cash sales, and

(*iii*) Any other sources of receipts of cash (say, dividend from a subsidiary company)

(b) As regards payments :

(*i*) Payment to be made for purchases

(*ii*) Payments to be made for expense

(*iii*) Payments that are made periodically but not every month :

1. Debenture interest
2. Income tax paid in advance
3. Sales tax etc.

(*iv*) Special payment to be made in a particular month, for example, dividends to shareholders, redemption of debentures or repayments of loan etc.

Long-range Cash Forecasts

Long-range cash forecasts often resemble the projected source and application of funds statement. The following procedure may be adopted to prepare long-range cash forecasts.

(*i*) Take the cash at bank and in hand in the beginning of the year

(*ii*) *Add*: (*a*) Trading profit (before tax) expected to be earned

(*b*) Depreciation and other development expenses incurred to be written off

(*c*) Sale proceeds of assets

(*d*) Proceeds of fresh issue of shares or debentures; and

(*e*) reduction in working capital, *i.e.*, current assets (except cash) less current liabilities.

(*iii*) *Deduct*: (*a*) Dividends to be paid

(*b*) Cost of assets to be purchased

(*c*) Taxes to be paid

(*d*) Debentures or shares to be redeemed

(*e*) Increase in working capital.

Management of Sundry Debtors

The basic objective of management of Sundry Debtors is to optimise the return on investment on this asset. It is obvious that if there are large amounts tied up on sundry debtors, working capital requirements and consequently interest charges will be high. Also, in such a case, the bad debts and the cost of collection of debts would be high. On the other hand, if the investment in sundry debtors is low, the sales may be restricted, since the competitors may offer more liberal credit terms. Therefore, management of sundry debtors is an important issue and requires proper policies and efficient execution of such policies.

There are basically three aspects of management of sundry debtors. Firstly, the credit policy is to be determined. This involves a trade off between the profits on additional sales that arise due to credit being extended on the one hand and the cost of carrying those debtors and bad debts loss on the other. The second aspect of management of sundry debtors is credit analysis, where by the financial manager determines as to how risky it is to advance credit to a particular party. The third aspect is follow up of debtors and credit collection. Thus, management of sundry debtors involves both laying down credit policies and execution of such policies.

(1) Credit policy: The credit policy of a firm involves a number of decisions like terms of trade discount, length of the credit period, cash discount and other special terms. These decisions in turn determine investments in sundry debtors, average collection period and bad debt losses. Credit policy involves the following considerations.

What should be the credit period? If the demand of a product is inelastic, the credit period may be small. However, if the product has an elastic demand, the credit period will determine the quantum of sales. The credit period is also dependent on the custom in the industry and the practice followed by various competitors. The availability of funds and the credit risk involved also determine the credit period.

Another important factor in determining the credit period is the possibility of bad debts. It is obvious that this possibility will increase, in case the credit period is too long.

A firm cannot determine the credit period once for all, since the situation in the market keeps on changing. Also, a firm may have a policy of allowing different credit periods to different customers.

(2) Discount policy: Discounts are normally given to speed up the collection of debts. A cash discount is a means of improving the liquidity of the seller. The rate of discount to be given should depend upon the cost of carrying debts. Suppose, a firm has an annual sales of Rs. 3 crores and an average collection period of two months. It is obvious that at a given point of time the firm will carry debtors amounting to Rs. 50 lakhs. Suppose, it is decided that a 3% cash discount may be offered to customers who pay cash immediately. Suppose further that the return on investment of this particular firm is 30%, it is obvious that the firm will gain 30% of 25 lakhs (or Rs. 7.5 lakhs) which can be invested in the expansion programme, etc. Since the firm would spend about Rs. 4.5 lakhs by way of cash discount it makes an overall gain of Rs. 3 lakhs. It is obvious that a scheme of cash discount in such a case would be beneficial to the concern.

Credit information is one of the essential aspect of management of debtors. The credit manager has to refer to a number of sources to obtain credit information. The following are the important sources :

(*a*) *Trade Reference*: The prospective customer may be required to give two or three trade references. Thus, the customer may give a list of personal acquaintances or some other existing creditworthy customers. The credit manager can send a short questionnaire to the referees seeking the relevant information.

(*b*) *Bank References*: Sometime the customer is asked to request the banker to provide the required information. However, bankers in India normally refuse to give detailed and unqualified credit reference.

(*c*) *Credit Bureau Reports*: In some cases the association for specific industries maintain credit bureau which provide useful and anthentic credit information for their members.

(*d*) *Past experience*: In case of an existing customer, the past experience of his account would be a valuable source of essential data for scrutiny and interpretation. A shrewd manager can look into the account carefully and try to find out the credit risk involved.

(*e*) *Published Financial Statement*: Sometimes the published financial statements can be examined to see the credit-worthiness of a customer. Further, if a customer's name appears in the list of approved suppliers of a government agency or other reputed organisations, it can be taken as a plus point.

(*f*) *Salesman's interriers and reports*: First hand information through personal contact can also aid in judging the credit rating of a customer. Many companies evaluate the creditworthiness of their customers by consulting salesmen or sales representatives. For proper determination of the limit of the customer the salesman should also ascertain the potential sales which the customer can effect to the ultimate customers.

Once the creditworthiness of a client is ascertained, the next question to resolve is to set a limit on the credit. In all such enquires, the credit manager must be discrete and should always have the interest of high sales in view.

(3) Credit Collection : Efficient and timely collection of debtors ensures that the bad debt losses are reduced to the minimum and the average collection period is shorter. If a firm expends more resources on collection of debts, it is likely to have smaller bad debts. Thus a firm must work out the optimum amount that it should spend on collection of debtors. This involves a trade off between the level of expenditure on the one hand and the decrease in bad debts and investments in debtors on the other.

The collection cell of a firm has to work in a manner, that it does not create too much resentment amongst the customers. On the other hand, it has to keep the amount of outstandings under check. It is important that clear-cut procedures regarding credit collection are set up. Such procedures must answer questions like the following:

(*a*) How long should a debtor balance be allowed to exist before collection procedures are started?

(*b*) What should be the procedure of following up defaulting customers? How reminders are to be sent and how should each successive reminder be drafted?

(*c*) Should there be a collection machinery whereby personal calls by company's representatives are made?

(*d*) What should be the procedure for dealing with doubtful accounts? Is legal action to be instituted? How should the account be handled.

Management of Inventory

Inventories constitute a major element of working capital. Therefore it is important that investment in inventory is properly controlled. Inventory management covers a large number of problems including fixation of minimum and maximum levels, determining the size of inventory to be carried, deciding about the issues, receipts and inspection procedures, determining the economic order quantity, providing proper storage facilities, keeping check over obsolescence and ensuring control over movement of inventories.

Like management of sundry debtors, management of inventories also involves a trade off between the carrying costs and the cost of reduction in sales pursuant to non-availability of inventories for an uninterrupted production programme. Thus, on the one hand, if inventories are kept at a high level, certain costs are incurred like interest lost on money blocked in inventories, cost of storage, cost of obsolescence and other storage losses and cost of maintaining documents concerning the inventories. On the other hand, if inventories are maintained at a low level, there may be interruptions in the production schedule resulting in under-utilisation of capacity and lesser sales. Therefore it is important that inventories are kept at optimum levels and a constant check is kept on the various inventory levels.

QUESTIONS

Simple Questions

1. Define working capital.
2. Distinguish between gross and working capital.
3. Distinguish between permanent and variable working capital.

Short Answer Questions

1. Explain the significance of adequate working capital in a business.
2. Explain the factors which determine the amount of working capital in a business.
3. Explain the techniques of cash management.
4. Explain the various aspects of management of sundry debtors.
5. Write an analytical note on management of inventory.

Exercise 1 : Germini Industrial Enterprise propose to manufacture a cosmetic product which has been developed by its research and development. The cost of production is estimated as follows :

	Cost per unit
Raw-materials	Rs. 80
Direct labour	40
Overheads	40
	160

The new product will be sold at Rs. 200 per unit. For the 1st year, sales are estimated at 1,04,000 units. The company is a going concern with its marketing network and it thinks that the maximum credit to be allowed to the customers will be 8 weeks. Other relevant data are given below :

Raw-materials stock required	4 weeks
Processing time (WIP stage)	2 weeks
Finished goods stock	6 weeks
Credit allowed by suppliers	4 weeks
Cash and bank balance required	Rs. 50,000

Prepare a statement showing the amount of working capital required by the company. You may make assumptions that may be necessary. *(ICWA, Inter, June 1996)*

[*Answer* : Total amount of working capital required; Rs. 56.50 (in lakhs)]

Exercise 2 : Maneklal Ltd. newly commercing business in 1997 has the following projected profit and loss account.

	Rs.	*Rs.*
Sales		42,00,000
Less : Cost of goods sold		30,60,000
Gross profi		11,40,000
Administrative expenses		2,80,000
Selling price	2,60,000	5,40,000
Profit before tax		6,00,000

The cost of goods sold is arrived at as follows

	Rs.
Materials used	16,80,000
Wages and manufacturing expenses	12,50,000
Hire charges of machinery	4,70,000
	34,00,000
Less : Stock of finished goods (10% of goods produced not yet sold)	3,40,000
	30,60,000

The figures given above relate only to finished goods and not to work-in-progress

Goods equal to 15% of the year's production (in terms of physical units) will be in process on the average requiring full materials but only 40% of the other expenses.

The company keeps materials equivalent to 2 months consumption in stock.

All expenses will be paid one month in arrear.

Suppliers of materials will extend 1½ months credit whereas credit of 2 months is allowed to customers.

Cash and credit sales are in the ratio of 1:4 respectively.

The company wishes to maintain cash balance for contingencies of 10% of the working capital excluding such cash balance.

Prepare an estimate of the requirement of working capital considering investment in debtors at book value.

(University of Bombay, B.Com., October 1997)

[*Answer* : Working capital required Rs. 12,50,553]

Exercise 3 : Power Link Ltd. furnishes the following information and requests you to prepare statement showing the requirements of working capital for the year 1998.

	Budget for 1998
Production capacity for the year	20,000 units
Production	90%
Cost structure :	
Crude materials	Rs. 30 per unit
Other direct materials	Rs. 20 per unit
Wages	Rs. 25 per unit
Overhead-Fixed	Rs. 9,000 and Rs. 15 variable per unit
Profit	20% on sales

Other information :

1. Crude material remains in stock for 2 months.
2. Other direct material remains in stock for 1 month.
3. Finished goods remains in stock for 2 months (to be valued at direct cost)
4. The production process takes place 1 month WIP valuation to be made crude material plus direct material at cost : plus 50% of wages and variable overheads.
5. Time lag in payment of wages 1 month and variable overheads half month.
6. Fixed overheads payable quarterly in advance.
7. Crude material purchased from suppliers against advance payment of two months and other direct material suppliers allows credit of 1 month.
8. Credit allowed to customers as under : (Valued at sales price)
   (*a*) 50% of invoice price against acceptance of bill for 4 months.
   (*b*) 25% of invoice price time lag 2 months.
9. Bank balance to be maintained Rs. 50,000.
10. Production and sales take place evenly throughout the year.

(University of Bombay, B.Com., April 1997)

[*Answer* : Estimated working capital Rs. 9,88,250]

Exercise 4 : Modern carry on Ltd., manufactured and sold 1,200 TV sets in the year 1995. The production cost per unit was as under :

		Rs.
Materials		5,000
Labour		2,000
Overheads		1,000
	Total cost	8,000
	Profit	2,000
	Selling price	10,000

For the year 1996, it is estimated that :

1. The output and sales will be 1,800 T.V. Sets
2. Price of materials will rise by 20%
3. Wages rate will rise by 25%
4. Overheads will increase by 50%
5. Selling price per unit will be Rs. 12,000

It is also estimated that :

(*a*) Raw-materials remain in stock for half month before issue to production.

(*b*) Finished goods will remain in godown for one month before sale.

(*c*) All sales will be on credit and credit allowed to customers will be as follows :

(*i*) Acceptance of Bills of exchange for three months against 60% of sales.

(*ii*) 40% of sales one month credit

(*d*) 60% of Raw-materials requirements will be obtained from the suppliers from Japan by making 3 months advance payments.

(*e*) Wages and overheads are paid one month in arrears.

(*f*) Materials will be in process (valued at cost of Raw-materials.

(*University of Bombay, B.Com., October 1996*)

[*Answer* : Estimated working capital Rs. 75,80,000]

FINANCING DECISION—COST OF CAPITAL

MEANING AND SIGNIFICANCE OF COST OF CAPITAL

The term 'cost of capital' means the rate of acquiring the total amount of all funds used within a firm. In the words of Van Horne, "The explicit cost of source of financing may be defined as the discount rate that equates the present value of the funds received by the firm net of underwriting and other cost with the present value of expected outflows. These outflows may be the interest payment, repayment of principal or dividends." To measure the total cost of all funds used by the firm, it is necessary to assess 'cost' of each source. That is to ascertain the cost of funds received from long and short-term debt and all types of share capital.

Therefore, each type of capital, *i.e.*, debentures, share capital and retained profits has its own cost. Equity capital can be obtained from internal as well as external sources and cost of each is calculated differently.

The main object of calculating cost of capital is to ensure that the return on all funds invested exceeds the cost of capital.

Cost of capital is a very important concept in capital structure though it is of recent origin (say since 1965). It has received much attention especially in the advanced countries. It helps the finance manager to determine whether a particular investment will be profitable or not.

The actual measurement of cost of capital is subject to wide margin of error and there is no accuracy about it. Therefore, the 'computed value' of it can be regarded as approximation. In spite of enormous study and research, no perfection has been attained so far.

The cost of debt capital is different from the cost of equity capital which is different from cost of retained profits.

Cost of capital is widely used as a criteria in capital budgeting. A proposal for investment is accepted only when it has a positive 'net present value' when discounted over and above cost of capital. In this sense, the cost of capital is the 'discount rate' used in evaluating the yield from an investment. It will be accepted if it has a rate of return higher than the cost of capital. In this sense, cost of capital is the minimum rate of return expected from an investment.

The concept of cost of capital is very useful for designing optimum capital structure and thereby reduce cost of capital to the minimum for determining the proper method of financing and for retaining control or avoiding risk. This is because heavy equity capital will help management to retain control over the business and avoid risk, whereas heavier doses of equity capital and lower doses of debt capital will lead to loss of control over business by a few shareholders and perhaps to greater risk. This concept can also be used to evaluate performance of top management. Finally, it is used in many other decision making areas such as dividend and working capital. Thus cost of capital is of great utility in financial decision, *i.e.*, designing 'optimum capital structure' and in using capital in maximising wealth which was discussed earlier.

TECHNIQUES OF DETERMINING COST OF CAPITAL

There are many refined mathematical techniques to determine cost of capital-cost of share capital, cost of debt capital and cost of retained profit (or dividend).

As prof, Pandey Observes, "In financial decision making, the term cost of capital is used in a composite or overall sense. In the past it was frequently used to refer to the cost of specific sources of capital such as cost of debt, cost of equity etc. It has been recently recognised that this position is fallacious. A firms decision to use debt capital to finance its projects not only adversely affects its potential for using low cost debt in future, but also makes the position of the existing shareholders moie risky. The increased risk to the shareholders will increase the cost of equity. Similarly the firm's decision to use equity capital to finance its projects would enlarge its potential for borrowings in the future. Because of this connection between the methods of financing and their costs, the term 'cost of capital' should be used in the composite sense. The composite or overall cost of capital is the 'weighted average of the costs' of various sources of funds, weights being the proportion of each source of funds in the capital structure.

Calculation of Cost of Equity Capital

Cost of capital is calculated by using sophisticated techniques. Let us consider here a simple technique. Let us assume that in the case of 'cost of equity capital', the shareholder expects a return which is an 'opportunity cost' of investing in one company rather than in another company. According to prof, Kuchal, a return of 5.5% in 'real terms' before personal taxes, requires a company to earn 35% 'in money terms' before tax if we assume a rate of inflation of 8% per year and corporation tax of 60% and dividend of 5% as the following example shows :

	Rs.
On Rs. 1,000 invested the company earns profit of	350
Less : Corporation tax (60%)	210
	140
Dividend (5%) $\frac{5}{100} \times 1{,}000$	50
Retained profits	90

The shareholders will earn wealth of Rs. 1,000 + 50 + 90 = Rs. 1,140 at the end of the year; but since prices are going up by 8%, they get only Rs. $\frac{1{,}140}{1.08}$ = Rs. 1,055 in 'real terms' and so they would have earned 5.5% on the original investment. It (5.5%) depends on (*a*) rate of dividend, (*b*) rate of tax, (*c*) rate of inflation.

According to prof Kuchal there are four approaches or methods for estimating the cost of equity :

(*a*) $\frac{D}{P}$, *i.e.*, $= \frac{\text{Dividend}}{\text{Price}}$ ratio :

(*b*) $\frac{E}{P}$, *i.e.*, $= \frac{\text{Earnings}}{\text{Price}}$ ratio (*c*) $\frac{D}{P} + g$ *i.e.,* $\frac{\text{Dividend}}{\text{Price}}$ + Growth rate of earnings

(*d*) Realised yield approach.

Briefly stated, the first one means that return is calculated on the basis of what shareholders expect at market price for a share by capitalising a set of dividend which is fixed for all time. It ignores what the company will earn on the 'retained earnings' and what effect the retained earnings will have on shares value.

The second method means that the shareholders will capitalise a definite level of earnings by capitalising the rate of E/P to judge their holding. The selection of market price to which they relate their expected earning involves 'value judgement'. This approach is not satisfactory because not all earnings are received directly by shareholders by way of dividends and earnings cannot be expected to be constant and share value does not remain constant.

The third method means that the focus is on what the shareholder actually receives, *i.e.*, dividend + rate of growth in dividend. The rate of growth of dividend is assumed to be equal to the rate of growth of 'earnings per share', *i.e.*, if earnings grow at 5% per year, and if dividends are constant portion of the earnings, then the rate of growth of dividend is equal to the rate of growth of earnings per share. It is said by proponents of this approach that it is a more accurate way of estimating the future return which shareholders will receive assuming that the 'future price-earnings ratio' is the same as 'current price-earning ratio' and earnings and dividend increase—at the same level (or rate). However, there are many difficulties in applying this in practice because of inflation and uncertainty.

The fourth approach means that in order to remove uncertainty about future dividend and share value, the rate of return actually received by shareholders in a given company is a better one to determine the cost of capital. For example, if they buy shares of a certain company (X), at Rs. 240 on 1.1.1990, and hold it for 5 years and sell it at Rs. 300 in early 1995, and receive dividend of Rs. 14 in 1990 and 1991 and Rs. 14.50 from 1992-1994, his rate of return, *i.e.*, 'discounted each flow' as follows :

Year	*Dividend* *Rs.*	*Sale Price* *Rs.*	*Discount factor at 10%*	*1.1.1980 value* *Rs.*
1990 ending	14.00	—	0.909	12.7
1991	14.00	—	0.826	11.6
1992	14.50	—	0.751	10.9
1993	14.50	—	0.683	9.9
1994	14.50	—	0.621	9.0
1995 (beginning)		800	0.621	186.3
				240.4

The above table shows that as the proponents of this approach say, that the historic realised rate of return "is an appropriate index of expected shareholder's required future rate of return." It is true that realised return varies according to good and bad years, but over a long period, there is 'control tendency' of realised return over a long period can be determined. This approach tells us as to the shareholders 'required rate of return' assuming the same risk and same 'apportunity cost'.

Hence to determine cost of equity capital it is essential to classify companies on the basis of (*a*) income, (*b*) cyclical characteristics, (*c*) growth characteristics.

Once the quantum of capital that is required is determined, the main consideration are income (cost) risk and control. These arise out of sources of capital, the percentage of each source in the total, the cost, the risk to shareholders and control over the management, *i.e.*, capital structure.

WEIGHTED AVERAGE COST OF CAPITAL

A firm does not finance all its projects with only one source. On the other hand, it uses number of sources-equity shares, preference shares, and debt capital. However, the main objects of issuing both equity and debentures is to strike a balance in the capital structure and secondly, to increase the return to equity shareholders. Thus, the earnings per share can be increased only when firm's average cost of financing comes lower in comparison to its total income. Hence, it is quite essential to compute the average cost of capital.

The cost of capital otherwise expressed as a composite or overall cost of capital is the weighted average of the costs of various sources of funds, weights being the proportion of each source of funds in the capital structure.

Weighted average cost, as the name implies, is an average of the costs of specific source of capital employed in a business properly weighted by the proportion, they hold in the firm's capital structure.

Though the concept of weighted average cost of capital is very simple, yet there are problems in the way of its calculations. Its computation requires :

(*a*) computation of weights to be assigned to each type of funds, and

(*b*) assignment of costs to various sources of capital.

Once these values are known, the calculation of weighted average cost becomes very simple. It may be obtained by adding up the products of specific cost of all types of capital multiplied by their appropriate weights.

In financial decision making, the cost of capital should be calculated on after tax basis. Therefore, the component costs to be used to measure the weighted cost of capital should be after tax costs.

Computation of Weights

The assignment of weights to specific sources of funds is a difficult task. Several approaches are followed in this regard but two of them are commonly used, *i.e.*, book value approach and market value approach. As the cost of capital is used as a cut-off rate for investment projects, the market value approach is considered better because of the following reasons : (*i*) it evaluates the profitability as well as the long-term financial position of the firm, (*ii*) the investors always consider the committing of his funds to an enterprise and an adequate return on his investment. In such cases, book values are of little significance, (*iii*) it does not indicate the true economic value of the concern, (*iv*) it considers price level changes.

The next problem in calculating the weighted average cost is the selection of capital structure from which the weights are obtained. There may be several possibilities, *i.e.*, (*a*) current capital structure either before or after the projected new financing, (*b*) marginal capital structure, *i.e.*, proportion of various types of capital in total of additional funds to be raised at a certain time and (*c*) optimal capital structure. All may agree that firms do seek optimum capital structure, *i.e.*, the capital structure that minimises the average cost of capital. Unless we have reasons to believe that the current structure deviates substantially from the optimum capital structure, we may assume that the current capital structure is the optimal structure and use it in the assignment of weights. The marginal capital structure is irrelevant here.

Illustration

The following is the capital structure and the explicit after tax costs for each component :

Debt	Rs. 15 lakhs	4%
Preference shares	Rs. 5 lakhs	8%
Equity shares	Rs. 10 lakhs	11%
Retained earnings	Rs. 20 lakhs	10%
	50 lakhs	

Source of capital	*Proportion to total capital (W)*	*Specific cost (C)*	*Product (W×C)*
Debt	0.3	4	1.2
Preference share	0.1	8	0.8
Equity share	0.2	11	2.2
Retained earnings	0.4	10	4.0
Weighted average cost of capital			8.2%

If there is no weighted average cost of capital, there is no way of estimating total cost. Weight of each source of capital is very much essential from the view point of future profitability of the concern.

Moreover, it also helps the management in devising the optimal capital structure policy. Suppose, if debt-capital ratio measures say from 40% to 60%, the required rate of return for the equity shareholders must increase because the risk element increases for them in the sense that large portion of earnings go to debenture holders and less will be left to them. As a result their dividends decrease. Therefore, efforts should be made to arrive at a optimal capital structure. So that the shareholder's wealth and market value of the firm are maximised. This is possible only when the concern is able to ascertain the weighted average cost of capital.

Cost of Preference Capital

Preference shares are usually fixed cost bearing securities. Their rate of dividend is fixed well in advance at the time of their issue. So, the cost of preference capital is equal to the ratio of annual dividend income per share to the current market price of the preference shares. This ratio is often called a current dividend yield.

For instance, if 9% preference shares (par value Rs. 100) are sold at Rs. 105 per share and issue expenses incurred by the company amount to Rs. 2 per share; then, the cost of preference shares will be as follows :

$$Cp = \frac{9}{105-2} = \frac{9}{103} \text{ of } 8.738\%$$

Therefore, the formula for calculating cost of preference share capital, in case of preference shares having specific maturity date is :

$$Kp = \frac{d}{po(1-f)}$$

Where Kp = cost of preference shares
d = constant annual dividend
Po = Expected sales price of preference shares
f = Flotation costs

In the case of redeemable ones :

$$Po\,(1-f) = \frac{d_1}{(1+k_i)^1} + \frac{d_2}{(1+k_1)^2} + \frac{d_n}{(1+kp)^n} + \frac{P_n}{(1+kp)^n}$$

$$\sum_{t=1}^{n} = \frac{dt}{(1+kp)^t} + \frac{pn}{(1+kp)^n}$$

Where Po = Expected sale price of preference shares
f = floatation costs as percentage of Po
d = dividend paid on preference shares
Pn = Repayment of preference capital amount.

COST OF DEBT

The cost of debt is defined as the rate of return that must be earned on debt-financial investment in order to keep unchanged the earnings available to equity shareholders. Therefore, the rate of return that the debt-financial investment must yield to prevent damage to the stock holder's position can also be called as cost of debt.

It is easy to calculate cost of debt. The cost of funds raised through debt in the form of debentures or loans from financial institution can be determined explicitly as follows :

Calculation of net income

	I situation Rs.	*II situation* Rs.
EBIT	1,00,000	1,00,000
Less : Interest	10,000	Nil
	90,000	1,00,000
Less : Taxes (55%)	49,500	55,000
Net Income	40,500	45,000

We are able to see the difference between the net incomes reported under 2 situations. It is Rs. 4,500 more when interest is not paid. Thus, we can generalise for any tax rate 'T' and any interest payment 'I', the after tax-interest payment is I, that is interest. Even for this (*i*) net cash proceeds from specific source of debt (cash inflows), (*ii*) the amount of periodic payment of interest and repayment of principal in the year of maturity, are important.

Cash Inflow

The net proceeds from long-term loans and debentures are equal to the issue price of the debentures minus all floatation costs that have been paid. The debenture can be issued : (*i*) at par, (*ii*) at a premium and (*iii*) at a premium. The floatation costs consists of the following expenses—printing of prospectus, advertisement, underwriting and brokerage and so on.

Cash Outflow

These are payments to debenture holders and consists of two kinds of payment (*i*) interest payment and (*ii*) repayment of principal. These two components have different tax treatment and therefore, are separately discussed. Interest payments made by a firm on debt issues qualify as a tax deduction in determining net tax income.

The repayment of principal do not qualify for tax deduction in determining the net taxable income. Therefore, in their case, cash outflows are equivalent to repayments of principal sum and do not require any adjustment for taxes. The mathematical formulation of explicit cost of debt would be :

$$D_o(I - f) = \frac{C_O I_1}{(1+k_1)^1} + \frac{C_O I_2}{(1+k_1)^2} + \ldots\ldots \frac{C_O In + C_O P_n}{(1+k_1)^n}$$

Where D_o = Expected sale price per debenture

f = Total floatation costs expressed as a percentage of D_o

$C_oI_1 + C_oI_2 + C_o$ In = cash outflow of interest in time period 1, 2, and the year of maturity

C_oP_n = Principal repayment in the year of maturity

K_1 = cost of debt.

The before-tax cost of debt, K_1 should be converted into an after tax cost of debt Kd.

$$Kd = K_1(1-t)$$

If the repayment of debt is in a number of instalments instead of one lumpsum payment made at the end of the year, then the equation would be :

$$D_o(I - f) = \frac{C_O I_1 + C_O F_1}{(1+k_1)^1} + \frac{C_O I_2 + C_O P_2}{(1+k_1)^2} + \ldots\ldots \frac{C_O In + C_O Pn}{(1+k_1)^n}$$

$$= \sum_{t=1}^{n} \frac{CoIt + CoPt}{(1+k_1)^t}$$

Where Col + CoP refer to interest payments plus principall repayment. The foregoing demonstrates the computation of cost of debt in different situation.

Cost of Perpetual Debt

The interest yield or the market yield on debt can be said to represent an approximation of the cost of the debt.

$$Kt = \frac{1}{SV}$$

$$Kd = \frac{1}{SV}(I - t)$$

Where : K_1 = Before tax cost of debt

Kd = Tax adjusted cost of debt

I = Annual Interest Payment

Sv = Sales value of the debenture

t = tax rate

Problem 1 : A company is considering the following options to raise additional capital for its expansion schemes :

Equity (% of total capital)	*Debt (% of tatal capital)*	*Cost of equity*	*Cost of debt (pre-tax)*
75	25	16%	12%
50	50	18%	14%
25	75	24%	18%

Tax rate is 50%. Which option would you recommend? Show workings. (*ICWA, Inter, June 2001*)

Solution : **Weighted average cost of capital is worked out for each option**

Option I : $(16 \times 0.75) + (6 \times 0.25)$

= $12 + 1.5$ = 13.5%

Option II : $(18 \times 0.5) + (7 \times 0.5)$

= $9 + 3.5$ = 12.5%

Option III : $(24 \times 0.25) + (9 \times 0.75)$

= $6 + 6.75$ = 12.75%

Thus, option II is best as the cost of capital in this option is lowest.

Problem 2 : AB Ltd. estimates the cost of equity and debt components of its capital for different levels of debt; equity mix is as follows :

Debt as % of total capital	*Cost of equity*	*Cost of debt (before tax)*
0	16%	12%
20%	16%	12%
40%	20%	16%
60%	25%	20%

Suggest the best debt : equity mix for the company. Tax rate applicable to the company is 50%. Show workings. (*ICWA, Inter, June 2000*)

Solution : **Statement showing weighted average cost of capital**

% of Debt to total capital	*Cost of equity*	*After tax cost of debt*	*Weighted Average cost of capital*	
0	16%	6%		= 16%
20	16%	6%	$(0.2 \times 6) + (0.8 \times 16)$	= 14%
40	20%	8%	$(0.4 \times 8) + (0.6 \times 20)$	= 15.2%
60	24%	10%	$(0.6 \times 10) + (0.4 \times 24)$	= 15.6%

Weighted average cost of capital is lowest when debt is 20% of total capital.

Problem 3 : Calculate the approximate cost of a company's debenture capital, when it decides to issue 10,000 nos. of 14% non-convertible debenture, each of face value Rs. 100, at par. The debentures are redeemed at a premium of 10% after 10 years. The average realisation is expected to be Rs. 92 per debenture and the tax rate applicable to the company is 40%. (*ICWA, Inter, December 2000*)

Solution :

$$Kd = \frac{C(1-T) + \frac{F-P}{n}}{\left(\frac{F+P}{2}\right)}$$

Where P = net amount realised

C = annual interest payable

T = tax rate

F = redemption price

n = maturity period

$$= \frac{14(1-0.4)+\frac{(110-92)}{10}}{\frac{110+92}{2}} = 10.099\%$$

Problem 4 : Calculate the cost of capital in the following cases :

(*i*) X Ltd. issues 12% debentures of face value Rs. 100 each and realises Rs. 95 per debenture. The debentures are redeemable after 10 years at a premium of 10%.

(*ii*) Y Ltd issues preference shares of face value Rs. 100 each earning 14% dividend and realises Rs. 92 per share. The shares are repayable after 12 years at par. *(ICWA, Inter, June 1998)*

Solution :

(I) $$Kd = \frac{C(1-T)+\frac{F-P}{n}}{\frac{(P+F)}{2}}$$

$$= \frac{12(1-0.5)+\frac{(110-95)}{10}}{\frac{110+95}{2}}$$

$$= \frac{6+1.5}{102.50} = 7.32\%$$

(II) $$Kp = \frac{D+\frac{F-P}{n}}{\frac{P+F}{2}}$$

$$= \frac{14+\frac{(100-92)}{12}}{\frac{100+92}{2}}$$

$$= \frac{14+0.67}{96} = 15.28\%$$

OPERATING AND FINANCIAL LEVERAGE

Operating leverage—Leverage may be defined as the ability of an enterprise to use fixed operating costs to increase the effect of changes in sales on its operating profits. It signifies the use of assets with fixed costs in the anticipation of earning sales revenues more than sufficient to meet the total costs including fixed costs. It exists when a change in sales revenue produces more than proportionate change in the operating profit, (*i.e.*, earnings before interest and taxes). It is determined by the sales, variable cost and fixed cost. Thus it is expressed in the form of the following formula

$$\frac{\text{Contribution}}{\text{Operating profit or EBIT}}$$

Illustration

Sales	Rs. 4,000
Variable cost	Rs. 2,000
Fixed cost	Rs. 600

In the above example, the contribution is 2,000 (sales of Rs. 4,000 minus variable cost of Rs. 2,000) and operating profit is Rs. 1,400 as shown below :

Sales	4,000
Less : Variable cost	2,000

Contribution	2,000
Less : Fixed cost	600
Operating profit	1,400

$$\text{Operating leverage} = \frac{\text{Contribution}}{\text{Operating profit}}$$

$$= \frac{2{,}000}{1{,}400} = 1.429$$

This means that a 1% increase in sales would result in a 1.429% increase in operating profit. Similarly, a 10% decrease in sales would result in a 14.29% decrease in operating profit. Suppose sales increase to Rs. 5,000. This 25% increase in sales would result in 35.725% increase in operating profit. Hence the new operating profit would be Rs. 1,900. However, it may be noted that operting leverage is calculated at one level of sales. It will change at another level of sales.

It is risky to have a high operating leverage since a slight fall in sales would result in a disproportionately larger fall in profits. If operating leverage is high, it automatically means that the break even point would also be reached at a high level of sales. Further, in the case of a high operating leverage, the margin of safety ratio would be low.

Financial leverage: Financial leverage also known as trading on equity means the use of fixed interest bearing long-term debts like debentures and other long-term borrowings and/or fixed dividend bearing prference shares capital along with equity share capital with a view to produce more gains for the equity share-holders.

Financial leverage is expressed in the form of formula which is as follows :

$$\frac{\text{Earning before Interest and Tax (EBIT)}}{\text{Profit Before Tax (PBT)}}$$

Illustration

	Rs.
Ordinary shares	1,000
Long-term loans	3,000
Earning Before Interest & Tax	600
Interest at 10%	300
Earning Before Tax	300

$$\text{Financial leverage} = \frac{\text{Earning before Interest and Tax (EBIT)}}{\text{Profit Before Tax (PBT)}}$$

$$= \frac{600}{300} = 2$$

This means that if the operating profit goes up by 100%, the earnings before tax (the shareholder's income) would go up by 200%. Thus, if EBIT is Rs. 1,200, Rs. 300 will have to be paid to the suppliers of long-term funds. This leaves Rs. 900 as residual earning before tax for shareholders. This represents an increase of 200% on the previous figure of Rs. 300. Therefore, it is obvious that the shareholders gain in a situation where a company has a high rate of return and pays a lower rate of interest to the suppliers of long-term funds. The difference obviously accrues to the shareholders. However, where the rate of return on investment falls below the rate of interest, the shareholders suffer because their earnings fall more sharply than the fall in the return on investment. Financial leverage thus accelerates the impact of a rise or fall in the EBIT on shareholder's income. A company must, therefore, carefully consider its likely profitability position before deciding upon the critical mix. Many companies often commit the mistake of having a very high debt equity ratio in times of prosperity. This gives their shareholders a high rate of return. However, since the period of abnormal profits is necessarily a short one, the company may, in depressed condition, have to pay very high rates of interest leaving even negative returns for the shareholders.

The impact of financial leverage gets accentuated because of the incidence of taxation also. We know that interest is allowed as a charge before tax and, therefore, this gain also accrues to the shareholders.

QUESTIONS

Simple Questions

1. What do you mean by cost of capital?
2. What do you mean by operating leverage?
3. What do you mean by financial leverage?

Short Answer Questions

1. Explain the method of calculating cost of equity capital.
2. Explain the method of calculating cost of preference share capital.
3. Explain the method of calculating cost of debt capital.
4. Explain the significance of (*a*) operating leverage, (*b*) financial leverage.

Exercise 1 : The capital structure of Hindustan Traders Ltd. as on 31.3.1996 is as follows :

Equity capital; 100 lakh equity shares of Rs. 10 each	Rs. 10 crores
Reserves	Rs. 2 crores
14% Debentures of Rs. 100 each	Rs. 3 crores

For the year ended 31.3.1996 the company has paid equity dividend at 20%. As the company is a market leader with good future, dividend is likely to grow by 5% every year. The equity shares are now traded at Rs. 80 per share in the stock exchange. Income-tax rate applicable to the company is 50%.

Required :

(*a*) The current weighted cost of capital.

(*b*) The company has plans to raise a further Rs. 5 crores by way of long-term loan at 16% interest. When this takes place the market value of the equity shares is expected to fall to Rs. 50 per share. What will be the new weighted average cost of capital of the company. (*ICWA, Inter, December 1996*)

[*Answer :* Weighted Average cost of capital = 7.4%
New weighted average cost of capital = 8.45%]

20

INVESTMENT DECISION

CAPITAL BUDGETING

Capital budgeting means long-term budgeting for the company as a whole. It is more important than revenue budgeting or financial budgeting since it focuses on the future opportunities and threats of the changing environment on future technological changes, future products and future markets. It involves a period of 7 to 15 years. One of the major functions of top management is to adopt capital budgeting and ensure that the long-term funds are spent wisely.

Equipment, machinery, building, plant, technology etc., have 'economic life' of investment and cash flows from it is spread over a period of years. It differs from 'physical life' in the sense that it refers to risk of diminishing value of cash flow, whereas physical life refers to the number of years the machinery will provide service before it wears out. It may be longer than economic life which is more useful since it helps to scrap old machinery and instal latest one in order to cope with competition or changes in demand. If these are not met, economic life is lost and the company faces crisis even though machinery may still have 'physical life'. Such a dynamic factor must form part of capital budgeting.

'Capital expenditure' is cost of acquiring and installing fixed assets. They are different from cost of capital. As they are amortised they become expenditure over a period and so they are 'long-term costs'.

Capital bedgeting includes not merely modernisation, upgradation of technology, expansion and diversification but also research and development and human resource accounting. The latter are more or less qualitative, but produce great impact on the corporate performance. As such capital budgeting is different from 'investment' because the latter is just physical capital and does not involve budgeting which seem to extract a definite predetermined rate of return on investment by various methods. Moreover, it includes not merely long-term cost such as plant capacity expansion, and kind of plant, but also future cost such as R & D, HRA, new processes, new materials, etc. So. capital budgeting must be planned for a number of years and there is a long 'gestation period' between the time when plant/project is planned and the time when it becomes a fruition.

Financial management must focus on capital budgeting in order to achieve its objectives. Otherwise the firm will become sick in course of time.

The proposed investment must be based on careful analysis of future yield or return. In other words 'capital productivity' must be measured by the earnings over the whole life of the asset from which cost of investment or cost of capital is deducted. The estimated earnings must take into consideration risk and uncertainty and indirect effects.

Capital budgeting assumes special significance because of the sophisticated tools or techniques used for evaluating the expected future cash flow so that sound decision will be made as to whether the proposed investment is worthwhile. Since it involves serveral crores of rupees depending upon the nature of technology, size of investment and complexity of the new process and product involved, it is necessary to appraise the proposal very rigorously to ensure that the expected cash flow is higher than cost of capital. If cost of capital is higher than the cash flow, the proposal should be rejected. Otherwise the company will become sick as it takes in more capital than what it generates. No business firm should ignore this fundamental principle. It is here that cost of capital becomes a very important component of capital budgeting. The importance of capital budgeting as Dr. Weston and Bringham point out, lies in the fact that it ensures survival and growth of a business enterprise. In a competitive environment it can't survive unless equipment, machinery and technology are modernised and upgraded. The future well being of the firm depends on how well this is dóne and how well it is done better than the competitors. A firm, which lags behind others is bound to become sick. Second, expansion of plant capacity and diversification are essential to achieve economies of scale and higher rate of profit and growth. This is possible when capital is adopted effectively. Third, new buildings and new facilities require capital budgeting. Fourth, research and development and human resources accounting requires capital budgeting.

TECHNIQUES OF CAPITAL BUDGETING

A capital budgeting decision may be defined as the firm's decision to invest its current funds most efficiently in the long-term assets in anticipation of an expected flow of benefits over a series of years. A number of capital budgeting techniques are in use in practice. They are grouped under the following two categories.

(1) Non-discounted cash flow or Traditional Technique

- (*a*) Payback period
- (*b*) Accounting Rate of Return

(2) Discounted Cash Flow Criteria

- (*a*) Net present value
- (*b*) Internal Rate of Return
- (*c*) Profitability Index

I. TRADITIONAL TECHNIQUES

(*a*) Payback Period

This is one of the traditional methods very much widely employed. It is defined as the number of years required to recover the original cash outlay invested in a project. This is a quantitative method for appraising capital expenditure decisions. This method answers the question; "How many years will it take for the cash benefits to pay the original cost of an investment, normally disregarding salvage value." Cash benefits represent CFAT (Cash Flows After Tax). Thus pay back measures the number of years required for the CFAT to payback the original outlay required in an investment proposal. There are two ways of calculating the payback period. The first method is applied when the cash flow stream is in the nature of annuity for each year of projects life, *i.e.*, CFAT are uniform. In such a situation, the initial cost of investment is divided by the constant annual cash flow :

$$PB = \frac{\text{Cash outlay (Investment)}}{\text{Annual cash inflow}}$$

For example, an investment of Rs. 40,000 on a machine is expected to produce CFAT of Rs. 8,000 for 10 years, then

$$PB = \frac{Rs\,40{,}000}{Rs\,8{,}000} = 5 \text{ years}$$

The payback period of 5 years signifies that the investment in the purchase of the machine will be recovered in 5 years. In other words, 20% of capital invested in the zero time period is recovered every year.

Computation of Payback when a Project's Cash Flows are Unequal

The second method is used when cash flows are not equal but vary from year to year. In such a situation, payback is calculated by the process of cumulating cash flows till the time when cumulative cash flows become equal to the original investment outlay. The following table evaluates an investment proposal which costs Rs. 50,000 and yields CFAT of Rs. 8,000, Rs. 12,000, Rs. 15,000, Rs 20,000, Rs. 21,000 and Rs. 24,000 in years from 1 to 6 respectively :

TABLE

Year (1)	Annual CFAT (2)	Cumulative CFAT (3)
1	8,000	8,000
2	12,000	20,000
3	15,000	35,000
4	20,000	55,000
5	21,000	76,000
6	24,000	1,00,000

From the table, it is apparent that the payback period would lie between the 3rd and the 4th year. The cumulative figure at the end of 3rd year is Rs. 35,000; whereas at the end of fourth year is Rs. 55,000; whereas the initial cost of investment is Rs. 50,000 which is Rs. 15,000 over the cumulative figure at the end of the 3rd year. The cash flow for the 4th year is Rs. 20,000. Thus the payback fraction is 0.75, $\left(i.e.\ \frac{Rs.\,15{,}000}{Rs.\,20{,}000}\right)$.

Therefore the payback period for the project is 3.75 years.

Limitations

(*a*) The first shortcoming of the payback method is that it completely ignores all cash inflows after the payback period. This could be very misleading in capital budgeting evaluations :

Example

TABLE

	Project X	*Project Y*
Total cost of the project	Rs. 15,000	Rs. 15,000
CFAT (Cash in flows)		
year 1	5,000	4,000
2	6,000	5,000
3	4,000	6,000
4	0	6,000
5	0	3,000
6	0	3,000
Payback period	3 years	3 years

In the above table the projects differ widely in respect of cash inflows generated after the payback period. The cash flow for project X stops at the end of the third year while that of Y continues for a further period upto the sixth year. In project Y, the cash inflows of Rs. 12,000, continues from 4th year to 6th year, whereas project X does not yield any cash inflow after the 3rd year. Under payback method, however, both the projects would be given equal rankings, which is apparently incorrect. Therefore, it cannot be regarded as a measure of profitability. Its failure lies in the fact that it does not consider the total benefits accuring from the project.

(*b*) Another deficiency of the payback technique is that it does not measure correctly even the cash flows expected to be received correctly. It considers only the recovery period as a whole. This happens because it does not discount the future cash inflows but rather treats a rupee received in the second or third year as valuable as a rupee received in the first year. In other words, to that extent the payback method fails to consider the pattern of cash inflows. It ignores the time value of money.

(*c*) Another flaw of the payback method is that it does not take into consideration the entire life of the project during which cash flows are generated. As a result, projects with large cash inflows in the latter part of their lives may be rejected in favour of less profitable projects which happen to generate a larger proportion of their cash inflows in the earlier part of their lives.

Problem 1 : ITC Ltd., have decided to purchase a machine to augment the company's installed capacity to meet the growing demand for its products. There are three machines under consideration of the management. The relevant details including estimated yearly expenditure and sales are given below. All sales are on cash. Corporate income tax rate is 40%. Interest on capital may be assumed to be 10%

	Machines		
	1	2	3
	Rs.	*Rs.*	*Rs.*
Initial investment required	3,00,000	3,00,000	3,00,000
Estimated annual sales	5,00,000	4,00,000	4,50,000
Cost of production : (estimated)			
Direct materials	40,000	50,000	48,000
Direct labour	50,000	30,000	36,000
Factory overheads	60,000	50,000	58,000
Administration costs	20,000	10,000	15,000
Selling and distribution costs	10,000	10,000	10,000

The economic life of machine 1 is 2 years, while it is 3 years for the other two. The scrap values are Rs. 40,000, Rs. 25,000 and Rs. 30,000 respectively.

You are required to find out the most profitable investment based on 'pay back method'.

(*ICWA, Inter, June 1997*)

Solution : **Statement showing payback period of the three machines**

	Machine I		*Machine II*		*Machine III*	
Initial investment required		3,00,000		3,00,000		3,00,000
Annual sales expected		5,00,000		4,00,000		4,50,000
Less : Cost of sales :						
Direct materials	40,000		50,000		48,000	
Direct labour	50,000		30,000		36,000	
Factory overhead	60,000		50,000		58,000	

Cost of production	1,50,000		1,30,000		1,42,000	
Depreciation	1,30,000		91,667		90,000	
Adm. cost	20,000		10,000		15,000	
Selling & Distribution	10,000		10,000		10,000	
Interest on capital	30,000		30,000		30,000	
		3,40,000		2,71,667		2,87,000
Profit before tax		1,60,000		1,28,333		1,63,000
Less : Tax @ 40%		64,000		51,333		65,200
Profit after tax		96,000		77,000		97,800
Add : Depreciation		1,30,000		91,667		90,000
Net cash flow		2,26,000		1,68,667		1,87,800
Payback period = $\frac{\text{Initial investement}}{\text{Net Annual Cash flow}}$		1.33		1.78		1.60

Machine I is the most profitable as it has the lowest payback period.

(2) Average Rate of Return

The other traditional method of evaluating proposed capital expenditure is also known as the accounting rate of return method. It represents the ratio of the average annual profits after taxes to the average investment in the project. It is based upon accounting information, rather than cash flow. There is no unaminity regarding the definition of the rate of return. There are a number of alternative methods for calculating the ARR. The most common usage of the average rate of return expresses it as follows :

$$\text{ARR} = \frac{\text{Average annual Profits after taxes}}{\text{Average investment over life of the project}} \times 10$$

The average profits after taxes are determined by adding up the after tax profits expected for each year of the project's life and dividing the result by the number of years. In the case of annunity, the average after tax profits are equal to any year's profits.

The average investment is determined by dividing the investment by two. The averaging process assumes that the firm is using straight line method of depreciation, in which case the book value of the asset declines at a constant rate from its purchase price to zero at the end of its depreciable life. This means, that on the average, firms will have, one-half of its initial purchase price in the books. Consequently, if the machine has salvage value, then only the depreciable cost (cost-salvage value) of the machine should be divided by two in order to ascertain the average net investment, as the salvage money will be recovered at the end of the life of the project. Therefore, an amount equivalent to the salvage value remains tied up in the project throughout its life time. Hence, no adjustment is required to the sum of the salvage value to determine the average investment. Likewise, if any additional net working capital is required in the initial year of the project life which is likely to be released at the end of the projects life, the full amount of working capital should be taken in determining the relevant investment for the purpose of calculating ARR. Thus, the average investment consists of the following :

$$\text{Net working capital} + \text{Salvage value} + \frac{1}{2}\ (\text{Intial cost of machine} - \text{Salvage value})$$

Example :

Initial investment	Rs. 11,000
Salvage value	1,000
Working capital	2,000
Service life	5 years

The straight line method of depreciation is adopted

Solution :

Average investment

$$= 2{,}000 + 1{,}000 + \frac{1}{2}\,(11{,}000 - 1{,}000)$$

$$= \text{Rs. } 8{,}000$$

Limitations

(*a*) The earnings calculations ignore the re-investment potential, and hence the total benefits of the project. This drawback can be overcome by using the modified AR approach which involves average cash flows instead of the average profits.

(*b*) It does not take into account the time value of money. Normally, benefits in the earlier years and later years cannot be valued at par.

(*c*) The ARR criterion of measuring the worth of investment does not differentiate between the size of the investment required for each project competing investment proposals may have the same ARR, but may require different average investment.

(*d*) This method does not take into consideration any benefits which can accrue to the firm from the sale or abandonement of equipment which is replaced by the new investment.

Problem 2 : X Ltd. intends to acquire a new machine and finds the following alternatives :

	Machine 'A'	*Machine 'B'*
Cost	Rs. 10,00,000	Rs. 1,00,000
Estimated residual Value	–	–
Estimated life	4 years	4 years
Estimated future profits (before depreciation)		
year 1	50,000	20,000
2	50,000	30,000
3	30,000	50,000
4	10,000	50,000

Based on, accounting rate of return method which of the two machines should be acquired?

Solution :

	Machine 'A'	*Machine 'B'*
	Rs.	*Rs.*
Total profit before depreciation	1,40,000	1,50,000
Total profit after depreciation	40,000	50,000
Accounting rate of return	$= \frac{40{,}000}{1{,}00{,}000}$	$\frac{50{,}000}{1{,}00{,}000}$
	= 40%	= 50%
Average profit after depreciation	10,000	12,500
Average return on investment	10%	12.5%
Return on average investment	$= \frac{40{,}000}{50{,}000}$	$\frac{50{,}000}{50{,}000}$
	= 80%	= 100%

Average return on average investment $= \frac{10,000}{50,000}$ $\frac{12,500}{50,000}$

$= 20\%$ $= 25\%$

$$\left(\text{Average Investment} = \frac{1,00,000 + 0}{2}\right)$$

$= 50,000$

Machine 'B' yielding higher return on investment should be acquired.

II. DISCOUNTED CASH FLOW OR TIME ADJUSTED TECHNIQUES

This takes into consideration the time value of money while evaluating the costs and benefits of a project. The discounted cash flows are popularly known as cost of capital. This is defined as the minimum discount rate that must be earned on a project that leaves the firm's market value unchanged. Another important feature of this is that it takes into consideration all benefits and costs occuring during the entire life of the project.

(a) Net Present Value (NPV) Method

The best method for investment proposal is the NPV method or the discounted cash flow method. This method takes into account the time value of money. This method involves the following steps.

(*i*) *Determine the Cash Outflow:* Each project will involve certain investment of cash at certain point of time. For example a project which requires an initial investment of Rs. 10 lakhs has an outflow of Rs. 10 lakhs.

(*ii*) *Determine the Cash Inflow:* This can be calculated by adding depreciation to profit after tax arising out of that particular project.

Example

For calculating the NPV, let us imagine that a project under consideration will give the following inflows :

Year end	*Cash inflows*
1	2,30,000
2	2,28,000
3	2,78,000
4	2,83,000
5	2,33,000
6	80,000 (Scrap value)

(*iii*) To discount each cash inflow and work out its present value :

For this purpose, the discounting rate must be determined. Normally, the discounting rate equals the cost of capital, since a project must earn at least that much as is paid out on the funds blocked in the project.

The concept of present value can be explained by considering an example. We know that a rupee received this year is not equal to a rupee received next year. This is because the rupee can be deposited in a bank, say at 6% and it becomes Rs. 1.06 next year. Therefore, if somebody offers to give a rupee next year in exchange for a rupee this year, we would ask him to give us 1.06 next year or Re. 1 now. In other words, Rs. 1.06 is the future value of Re 1 at the rate of 6% for one year. or Re. 1 is the present value of Rs. 1.06 at the rate of 6% for one year.

To calculate the present value of various inflows we should refer to the present value table. With the help of this table we can work out the present value of each cash inflow. The present value of Rs. 2,30,000 received after one year at the rate of 6% can be calculated by referring to the 6% column of the table corresponding to year 1. We find a discount factor of 0.943. Thus the present value is Rs. 2.30, 000 × 0.943 = 2,16,890. In other words, Rs. 2,16,890 received now or Rs. 2,30,000 received after a year are equal, provided we can invest the monies received now @ 6% p.a.

Similarly, the present value for other cash inflows would be as follows :

Year end	*Cash inflow*	*Discount factor 6%*	*Present value*
1	2,30,000	0.943	2,16,890
2	2,28,000	0.890	2,02,920
3	2,78,000	0.840	2,33,520
4	2,83,000	0,792	2,24,136
5	2,33,000	0.747	1,74,051
6	80,000	0.705	56,400

The total present value of all cash inflows is Rs. 11,07,917 as compared to the total cash outflows of Rs. 10,00,000. Hence Rs. 1,07,917 is the net present value, *i.e.*, the difference between the total of discounted cash inflows and the discounted cash outflows. There is no need to discount the cash outflows in this case since the money is immediately spent. Comparing the two, we know that the present-value of inflows is higher than the present value of outflow at 6%.

Problem 3 : A Ltd. installed a machine with an estimated life of 5 years and used it for 3 years. The initial cost including installation charges amounted to Rs. 80 lakhs. According to current assessment, the machine can be used for another 4 years. The company has just received an offer of Rs. 50 lakhs for the machine. It is unlikely that a similar offer will be received in the near future. The machine is used for manufacturing a product which has a falling demand. Losses are anticipated over the next two years. Details of profitability projections for the next 4 years are as follows :

	Years			
	1	*2*	*3*	*4*
	(in lakhs of rupees)			
Sales	50	45	40	35
Less : Variable cost	27	24.50	23	18
Fixed cost (allocated)	8	7.50	6.50	6
Depreciation	16	16	-	-
Net profit/(loss)	(1)	(3)	10.50	11

As the estimated working results are not very good and as the company has got a very good offer for the machine, the managing director feels that the machine should be sold immediately.

What is your advice to the managing director? Support your answer with workings.

Cost of capital of the company is 15%. Ignore tax.

Note : Present value of rupee 1 at 15%

At the end of year	*Present value*
1	0.8696
2	0.7561
3	0.6574
4	0.5717

(*ICWA, Inter, December 1998*)

Solution :

Statement Showing NPV

Year	*Cash flow (Sales – V.C) (See note) (in lakhs)*	*Discount Factor 15%*	*Present Value (in lakhs)*
1	23.00	0.8696	20.00
2	20.50	0.7561	15.50
3	17.00	0.6574	11.18
4	17.00	0.5717	9.72
	Present value of the option of retaining the machine		56.40

Present value of the offer received : Rs. 50 lakhs.

Hence it is better to retain the machine and use it for another 4 years.

Note : Allocated fixed costs and depreciation are not relevant costs as they are past cost, irrespective of the decision taken.

Problem 4 : National Electronics Ltd., an electronic goods manufacturing company, is producing a large range of electrical goods. It has under consideration two projects 'X' and 'Y' cash costing Rs. 120 lakhs. The projects are mutually exclusive and the company is considering the question of selecting one of the two. Cash flows have been worked out for both the projects and the details are given below 'X' has a life of 8 years and 'Y' has a life of 6 years. Both will have zero salvage value at the end of their operational lives. The company is already making profits and its tax rate in 50% the cost of capital of the company is 15%.

Net Cash Inflow

At the end of the year	*Project 'X'*	*Project 'Y' (in lakh rupees)*	*Present value of rupee at 15%*
1	25	40	0.870
2	35	60	0.756
3	45	80	0.685
4	65	50	0.572
5	65	30	0.497
6	55	20	0.432
7	35	–	0.372
8	15	–	0.327

The company follows straight line method of depreciating assets. Advise the company regarding the selection of the project. *(ICWA, Inter, June, 1996)*

Solution :

Statement showing net present value of projects

(Rs. in lakhs)

Project 'X'

End of year	*Cash flow*	*Depreciation*	*PBT*	*Tax*	*PAT*	*Net C.F. (PAT+Dep.)*	*Discount factor*	*PV*
1	25	15	10	5	5	20	0.870	17.40
2	35	15	20	10	10	25	0.756	18.90
3	45	15	30	15	15	30	0.658	19.74
4	65	15	50	25	25	40	0.572	22.88
5	65	15	50	25	25	40	0.497	19.88
6	55	15	40	20	20	35	0.432	15.12
7	35	15	20	10	10	25	0.376	9.40
8	15	15	–	–	–	15	0.327	4.91
						P.V of cash inflows		128.23
						Less : Initial investment		120.00
						Net present value		8.23

Project 'Y'

1	40	20	20	10	10	30	0.870	26.10
2	60	20	40	20	20	40	0.756	30.24
3	80	20	60	30	30	50	0.658	32.90
4	50	20	30	15	15	35	0.572	20.02
5	30	20	10	5	5	25	0.497	12.43
6	20	20	–	–	–	20	0.432	8.64
				P.V. of cash inflows				130.33
				Less : Initial investment				120.00
				Net present value				10.33

As project 'Y' has a higher net present value, it has to be taken up.

Problem 5 : A company is considering whether it should spend Rs. 4 lakhs on a project to manufacture and sell a new product. The unit variable cost of the product is Rs. 6. It is expected that the new product can be sold at Rs. 10 per unit. The annual fixed costs (only cash) will be Rs. 20,000. The project will have a life of six years with a scrap value of Rs. 20,000. The cost of capital of the company is 15%. The only uncertain factor is the volume of sales. To start with the company expects to sell at least 40,000 units during the first year.

Required :

(*a*) Net present value of the project based on the sales expected during the first year and on the assumption that it will continue at the same level during the remaining years.

(*b*) The minimum volume of sales required to justify the project.

[**Note :** Annurity of Re. 1 at 15% for 6 years has a present value of Rs. 3.7845 and present value of Re. 1 received at the end of sixth year at 15% is Rs. 0.4323] *(ICWA, Inter, December 1997)*

Solution :

(i) Selling price per unit		Rs. 10
Varialbe cost per unit		6
Contribution per unit		4
Total contribution per year @ Rs. 4 per unit for 40,000 units	=	1,60,000
Less : Cash outflow as fixed cost		20,000
Net cash inflow per year		1,40,000
Total cash inflow at present value for 6 years = 1,40,000 × 3,7845	=	5,29,830
PV of scrap value of Rs. 20,000 at the end of 6th year = 20,000 × 0.4323	=	8,646
		5,38,476
Less : Initial investment		4,00,000
Net present value of the project		1,38,476

(ii) Let x be the number of units to be sold to justify the project

Present value of x units @ Rs. 4 contribution per unit and Rs. 20,000 as fixed cost

= (4x – 20,000) 3.7845

Present value of scrap at the end of 6th year = Rs. 8,646

To justify the project its net present value should be positive.

Hence, [(4x – 20,000) × 3.7845 + 8,646] – 4,00,000

x = 30,853 units

(b) Internal Rate of Return (IRR) Method

The internal rate of return is the rate which equates the present value of cash inflows with the present value of cash out-flows of an investment. In other words, it is the rate at which the net present value of the investment is zero. It is called the internal rate because it is solely dependent on the outlay and proceeds associated with the project and not on any rate determined outside the investment. If the calculated present value of the expected cash inflows is lower than the present value of cash outflows, a lower rate should be tried. On the other hand, a higher rate should be tried where the present value of inflows is higher than the present value of outflows. This process will be repeated unless the net present value becomes zero. Alternatively, internal rate can be obtained by interpolation method when we come across two rates—one with positive NPV and the other with negative NPV. The Internal rate of return is considered as the highest rate of interest which a business is able to pay on the funds borrowed to finance the project out of cash inflows generated by the project. It is also referred to as the 'break-even' rate of borrowing from the bank.

Example

An investment of Rs. 1,38,500 yield the following cash inflows (profit before depreciation but after tax)

Year	*Rs.*
1	30,000
2	40,000
3	60,000
4	30,000
5	20,000

Let us first discount the various cash inflows at 6% to see whether that is the internal rate of return.

Year	*Amount*	*6% factor*	*Discounted value*
1	30,000	0.943	28,290
2	40,000	0.890	35,600
3	60,000	0.840	50,400
4	30,000	0.792	23,760
5	20,000	0.747	14,940
			Rs. 1,52,900

Since our cash outflow is 1,38,500 and our total discounted cash inflow is much higher than that, it is apparent that the internal rate of return is higher than 6%. Let us try 12% as the discounting rate.

Year	*Amount*	*12% factor*	*Discounted value*
1	30,000	0.893	26,790
2	40,000	0.797	31,880
3	60,000	0.712	42,720
4	30,000	0.636	19,080
5	20,000	0.567	11,340
			Rs. 1,31,810

This time the total discounted cash inflow (Rs. 1,31,810) is lower than the cash outflow (1,38,500). Hence a lower rate than 12% is the internal rate of return. Let us try 10%

Year	*Amount*	*10% factor*	*Discounted value*
1	30,000	0.909	27,270
2	40,000	0.826	33,040
3	60,000	0.751	45,060
4	30,000	0.683	20,490
5	20,000	0.621	12,420
			1,38,280

At 10% discounting rate, the sum of the present value of cash inflows is more or less equal to the cash outflow. Hence the internal rate of return is 10%.

Merits

(*a*) This takes into account, the time value of money.
(*b*) The cash flow stream is considered in its entirety by this technique.
(*c*) This technique is more meaningful and acceptable to users because it satisfies them in terms of the rate of return on capital.

Limitation

1. The IRR is difficult to understand and involves complicated computational problems.
2. It may yield results inconsistent with the NPV method if the projects differ in their expected lives; cash outlays or timing of cash flows.
3. If may yield negative or multiple rates under certain circumstances.

Problem 6 : United Industries Ltd., has an investment budget of Rs. 100 lakhs for 2001-02. It has short listed two projects A and B after completing the market and technical appraisal. The management wants to complete the financial appraisal before making the investment. Further particulars regarding the two projects are given below :

	A	*B*
	(In lakhs of rupees)	
Investment required	100	90
Average Annual cash inflow before depreciation and tax (estimated)	28	24

Salvage Value : Nil for both projects
Estimated Life : 10 years for both projects.
The company follows straight line method of charging depreciation. Its tax rate is 50%
You are required to calculate :
(*a*) payback period; and
(*b*) IRR of the two projects

Note : P.V. of an annuity of Re. 1 for 10 years at different discount rates is given below :

Rate (%)	*Annuity value for 10 years*
10	6.1446
11	5.8992
12	5.6502
13	5.4262
14	5.2161
15	5.0188

(ICWA, ,Inter, June 2001)

Solution : **Statement Showing Payback Period**

	Project 'A' *(Rs. in lakhs)*	*Project 'B'* *(Rs. in lakhs)*
Cash flow p.a before depreciation & tax	28	24
Less : Depreciation	10	9
Profit before tax	18	15
Less : Tax @ 50%	9	7.50
Profit after tax	9	7.50
Add : Depreciation	10	9.00
Post tax cash flow	19	16.50

$$\text{Payback period} = \frac{\text{Investment}}{\text{Post-tax annual cash flow}} \qquad = \frac{100}{19} \qquad \frac{90}{16.5}$$

$$= 5.26 \text{ yrs.} \qquad = 5.45 \text{ yrs.}$$

Internal Rate of Return

Present value of cash inflow and NPV

Project A

	12%	*13%*	*14%*
Cash inflow	107.35	103.10	99.11
Less : Investment	100.00	100.00	100.00
	7.35	3.10	(–) 0.89

$$\text{IRR} = 13\% + \frac{3.10}{(3.10+0.89)}$$

$$= 13 + 0.775 = 13.78\%$$

Project B

	12%	*13%*	*14%*
Cash inflow	93.23	89.53	
Less : Investment	90.00	90.00	
	3.23	(–) 00.47	

$$\text{IRR} = 12\% + \frac{3.23}{3.23+0.47}$$

$$= 12\% + 0.87 = 12.87\%$$

Project 'A' is better of the two, although the difference is not very substantial. If may be desirable to assess the risk and locate the vulnerable aspects of the two projects, by using other techniques before taking the final decision.

Problem 7 : Orient Enterprises Ltd. have under consideration two projects A and B for the present, it wants to take up only one of the two projects and not both. The details regarding the two projects are given below.

	Project A	*Project B*
	(in lakhs of rupees)	
Investment required	95	200
Estimated net cash flow (PAT+Depr.) at the end of year 1,	40	80
Estimated net cash flow (PAT+Depr.) at the end of year 2,	40	80
Estimated net cash flow (PAT+Depr.) at the end of year 3,	45	120

The cost of capital of the company is 12%. Using NPV method, which project would you recommend? Also calculate the internal rate of return of the two projects.

Note **:** Present value of Re. 1 at the end of each year during the three year period at various rates of discount are given below :

Year	*Discount rate*								
	10%	*11%*	*12%*	*13%*	*14%*	*15%*	*16%*	*17%*	*18%*
1	0.9091	0.9009	0.8929	0.8850	0.8772	0.8696	0.8621	0.8547	0.8475
2	0.8265	0.8116	0.7972	0.7832	0.7695	0.7561	0.7432	0.7305	0.7182
3	0.7513	0.7312	0.7118	0.6931	0.6750	0.6575	0.6407	0.6244	0.6086

(ICWA, Inter, December 1999)

Solution : **Net present value of projects with cash flows discounted at 12%**

(Rs. in Lakhs)

		Project A		*Project B*	
Year	*P.V factor at 12%*	*Cash flows*	*Present value*	*Cash flows*	*Present value*
0	1.0000	(–)95	(–) 95	(–) 200	(–) 200
1	0.8929	40	35.72	80	71.43
2	0.7972	40	31.89	80	63.78
3	0.7118	45	32.03	120	85.42
			NPV (+) 4.64		NPV (+) 20.63

Internal rate of return of project A

(Rs. in Lakhs)

Year	*Cash flows*	*NPV at 14% Discount factor* *P.V. factor*	*P.V*	*NPV at 15% Discount factor* *P.V factor*	*P.V*
0	–95	1.0000	–95	1.000	–95
1	40	0.8772	35.09	0.8696	34.78
2	40	0.7695	30.78	0.7561	30.24
3	45	0.6750	30.38	0.6750	29.59
			NPV (+) 1.25		NPV (–) 0.39

$$\text{IRR of Project 'A'} = 14\% + \frac{1.25}{(1.25+0.39)} \times 1\% = 14.76\%$$

Internal rate of return (IRR) of project B (Rs. in Lakhs)

Year	*Cash flows*	*NPV (at 17% Discount factor)* *P.V factor*	*P.V*	*(NPV at 18% Discount factor)* *P.V. factor*	*P.V*
0	(–) 200	1.0000	(–) 200	1.0000	(–) 200
1	80	0.8547	68.38	0.8475	67.80
2	80	0.7305	58.44	0.7182	57.46
3	120	0.6244	74.93	0.6086	73.03
			NPV 1.75		NPV (–) 1.71

$$\text{IRR of Project B} = 17\% + \frac{1.75}{(1.75+1.71)} \times 1\%$$

$$= 17.51\%$$

As there is no capital Rationing it is more profitable to take up Project B.

(c) Profitability index or desirability factor: Profitability Index is the ratio of the present value of future cash benefits, at the required rate of return to the initial cash outflow of the investment. Expressed in the form of a formula :

$$\text{Profitability index} = \frac{\text{PV of cash outflow}}{\text{Initial cash outlay}}$$

Suppose, we have three projects in view, each involving discounted cash outflow of Rs. 5,50,000; 75,000 and 1,00,20,000. Suppose further that the sum of discounted cash inflows for these projects are Rs. 6,50,000, 95,000 and 1,00,30,000. The profitability index for the three projects would be as follows :

(*a*) $\frac{6,50,000}{5,50,000} = 1.18$

(*b*) $\frac{95,000}{75,000} = 1.27$

(c) $\frac{1,00,30,000}{1,00,20,000} = 1.001$

It would be seen that in absolute terms project (c) gives the highest cash inflow, yet its profitability index is low. This is because the outflow is very high also. This factor helps in ranking the various projects.

Problem 8 : Three independent projects which are not mutually connected and any of them can be independently considered and any of them can be selected. The overall cost of capital of the company is 10% and the expected cash flows from the projects are given :

Cash flows (income)

Project No.	*Investment required now*	*Year 1*	*Year 2*	*Year 3*	*Year 4*	*Year 5*
I	10,000	12,000	3,000	–	–	–
II	14,000	–	–	10,000	5,000	7,000
III	9,000	–	4,000	5,000	5,000	2,000

You are required to advise the management about the choice of the project.

Solution :

Year	*Discount factor @ 10%*	*Project I* cash flow	P.V.	*Project II* Cash flow	P.V.	*Project III* Cash flow	P.V.
1	0.909	12,000	10,908	–	–	–	–
2	0.826	3,000	2,478	–	–	4,000	3,304
3	0.751	–	–	10,000	7,510	5,000	3,755
4	0.683			5,000	3,415	5,000	3,415
5	0.621			7,000	4,347	2,000	1,242
		15,000	13,386	22,000	15,272	16,000	11,716

As the investment required for each project is different profitability index is the best.

$$\text{P.I.} = \frac{\text{Sum of discounted cash inflows}}{\text{Sum of discounted cash outflows}}$$

Project I $= \frac{\text{Rs } 13,386}{\text{Rs } 10,000} = 1.339$

Project II $= \frac{\text{Rs } 15,272}{\text{Rs } 14,000} = 1.091$

Project III $= \frac{\text{Rs } 11,716}{\text{Rs } 9,000} = 1.302$

Since project I is the hightest, project I is preferable.

Relationship between Risk and Return

In the techniques explained earlier it was assured that cash flow—both inflows and outflows—accrue as a result of the various capital expenditure proposals can be known with certainty. This assumption is not realistic in actual circumstances. We must realise that evaluation of capital expenditure proposals involves projections of the future. Future is always uncertain. No body can say with certainty about the quantum and frequency of the future cash flows. In other words, the assumption that the cash flows are certain and, therefore, deterministic in nature is not a realistic assumption. The estimates of cash inflows and outflows can only be what may be termed as probability estimates, *i.e.*, they represent only likely happenings. We must appreciate that there are too many unknown and uncertain factors which influence cash flows and, therefore, it is important to recognise that each cash inflow or outflow is only a probable figure.

Therefore a more realistic approach for capital budgeting would be to recognise that the cash flows are generally probabilistic in nature and in most circumstances only random variables, *i.e.*, they may happen or they may not happen. This approach highlights the need for considering the question of risk and uncertainty while carrying out the capital budgeting exercise.

Actually, if risk and uncertainty factors are not taken into account, there is always a danger that the capital expenditure evaluation may produce misleading results. This is because we know that risk and return have a direct relationship. Higher the return from a project, higher would be the risk normally. Similarly, lower the return, lower would be the risk. Now, if we use the net present value method or the IRR method or any such method which evaluates only the return aspect, there is every possibility that we shall end up in selecting projects with higher risk. In other words, the tendency to ignore risk and uncertainty factors and to rely only on measures of profitability—whether time adjusted or not—can result in accepting highly risky projects. It is therefore, necessary that the capital budgeting exercise should attempt to optimise both, the return and risk factor.

The following are the various methods of accounting for risk.

(1) Application of various possibilities to the cash flows: Under this method the management has to work out the various possible cash flows in different years. Thus, the management by keeping in view the key factors which would affect the future cash flows may work out not a single set of cash flows but a multiple set of possible cash flows which may arise out of the given capital expenditure proposal. The next step would be to estimate the probabilities attached to each cash flow. From this the expected cash flows can be calculated.

Suppose there are 2 projects A & B each requiring an initial investment of Rs. 15 lakhs and having 5 years life. Suppose further that the cash flows from the two projects and their probabilities are as follows :

Project A

Probability weights	0.20	0.20	0.40	1.10	0.10
Years1 (*Rs. in lakhs*)	3	5	6.5	7.5	8
2	3	4	5.5	7.0	8
3	3	4	4.5	5.0	6
4	1	2	3.2	4.0	5
5	1	2	2.2	4.0	5

In otherwords, in the first year the probability of earning Rs. 3 lakhs is 0.2, of earnings Rs. 5 lakhs is also 0.2, of earnings Rs. 6.5 lakhs is 0.4 and so on

Project B

Probability	*Cash flows in each of the five years (Rs. in lakhs)*
0.10	3.0
0.20	3.5
0.40	4.5
0.20	5.5
0.10	6.0

The expected cash flows in each of the five years for project A can be calculated by taking the weighted average as below :

Year 1

0.20 (3) + 0.20 (5) + 0.40 (6.5) + 0.10 (7.5) + 0.10 (8) = 5.75 lakhs

Year 2

0.20 (3) 0.20 (4) + 0.40 (5.5) + 0.10 (7) + 0.10 (8) = Rs. 5.10 lakhs

Year 3

0.20 (3) + 0.20 (4) + 0.40 (4.5) + 0.10 (5) + 0.10 (6) = 4.3 lakhs

Year 4

0.20 (1) + 0.20 (2) + 0.40 (3.2) + 0.10 (4) + 0.10 (5) = 2.78 lakhs

Year 5

0.20 (1) + 0.20 (2) + 0.40 (3.2) + 0.10 (4) + 0.10 (5) = 2.78 lakhs

Similarly the expected cash flows for each of the five years for project B will be :

0.10 (3) + 0.20 (3.5) + 0.40 (4.5) + 0.20 (5.5) + 0.10 (6) = 4.50 lakhs

If we calculate internal rate of return for the above projects on the basis of expected cash flows, IRR for project A would be 14% and for project B, it would be 15%. However, if we calculate internal rates of return on the basis of most likely or model cash flows without applying probability weights, *i.e.*, the cash flows with the greatest probability of recurring, they would be 17.3% and 15.2% for projects A and B respectively.

It is clear from the above that when model cash flows are taken into account, project A will be prefered but when expected cash flows are taken into account, it is the project B which should be preferred. It is because of the fact that cash inflows from project A vary from year to year whereas in the case of project B they are stable. Since the expected value take into account all the cash flows and their probabilities they are better indicator of the risk involved.

(2) Varying the discounting rate: Under this method a higher rate of discount is adopted for projects which are considered more risky. Conversely, lower, discount rate is applied for less risky projects. In the above example, a glance on the cash flows of project A and B would indicate that project A is comparatively more risky, than project B because the distribution of cash flows of project A is negatively skewed whereas that of project B is normal.

As such the management may decide to discount the cash flows of Project A by 15% and those of project B by 10%. It may be noted that it is a difficult task to ascertain the extent of riskiness of different projects and then make adjustments in discount rate. Although with the help of standard deviation and coefficient of variation techniques one may be able to determine which project is more risky but the determination of discounting rates may remain to be a subjective decision.

(3) Adjusting the cash flows: Under this method, risk element is compensated by adjusting cash inflows rather than adjusting the discount rate. Expected cash flows are converted into certain cash flows by applying certainty-equivalent coefficients, depending on the degree of risk inherent in cash flows. To the cash flows having higher degree of certainty, higher certainty-equivalent co-efficient is applied and for cash flows having low degree of certainty, lower certainty-equivalent co-efficient is used. For evaluation of various projects cash flows so adjusted are discounted by a risk free rate.

QUESTIONS

Simple Questions

1. What do you mean by capital budgeting?
2. List out the various techniques of capital budgeting?
3. What do you mean by payback period?
4. What do you mean by Accounting Rate of Return.
5. What is NPV?
6. What is IRR?
7. What is profitability index?

Short Answer Questions

1. Explain payback period technique of capital budgeting.
2. Explain ARR technique of capital budgeting.
3. Explain NPV technique of capital budgeting.
4. Explain IRR technique of capital budgeting.
5. Explain the relationship between risk and return.

Exercise 1 : A company is considering to expand its production. It can go in either for an automatic machine costing Rs. 2,24,000 with an estimate life of 5½ years or an ordinary machine costing Rs. 60,000 having an estimated life of 8 years. The annual sales and costs are estimated as follows.

	Automatic machine Rs.	*Ordinary machine Rs.*
Sales (Goods)	1,50,000	1,50,000
Costs :		
Materials	50,000	50,000
Labour	12,000	60,000
Variable overheads	24,000	20,000

Compute the comparative profitability of the proposals under pay-back period.

(*University of Madras, B.Com., March 1994*)

[*Answer :* Automatic 3.5 years Ordinary 3 years]

As payback period in case of ordinary machinery is shorter, it is to be preferred.

Exercise 2 : Modern Electronics Ltd. is considering the purchase of a machine. Two machines A and B are available each costing Rs. 50,000. In compairing the profitability of these machines a discounted rate of 10% is to be used. Earnings are expected to be as follows :

Year	*Machine A cash inflow Rs.*	*Machine B cash inflow Rs.*
1	15,000	5,000
2	20,000	15,000
3	25,000	20,000
4	15,000	30,000
5	10,000	20,000

You are given the following data :

Year :	1	2	3	4	5
P.V. of Re. 1 @ 10% Discount :	0.909	0.826	0.751	0.683	0.621

Evaluate the project under :

(*a*) payback period

(*b*) Net present value

(*University of Madras, B.Com., September 1994*)

[*Answer :* (*a*) Payback period -A 2.6 years

-B 3.33 years

Machine 'A' is preferable since its payback period is shorter :

(b) NPV of machine A - 15,385
NPV of machine B - 14,865
Machine 'B' is preferable since NPV of machine 'A' is higher]

Exercise 3 : A Ltd. is considering the question of taking up a new project which requires an investment of Rs. 200 lakhs on machinery and other assets. The projects is expected to yield the following gross profit. (before depreciation and tax) over the next five years :

Year	*Gross profit (in lakhs of rupees)*
1	80
2	80
3	90
4	90
5	75

The cost of raising the additional capital is 12% and the assets have to be depreciated at 20% on 'written down value' basis. The scrap value at the end of the five-year period may be taken as zero. Income tax applicable to the company is 50%.

Calculate the NPV of the project and advise the management whether the project has to be implemented. Also calculate the internal rate of return of the project.

Note : Present value of Re. 1 at different rates are as follows :

Present Values

Year	*10%*	*12%*	*14%*	*16%*
1	0.91	0.89	0.88	0.56
2	0.83	0.80	0.77	0.74
3	0.75	0.71	0.67	0.67
4	0.68	0.64	0.59	0.59
5	0.62	0.57	0.52	0.52

(ICWA, Inter, June 1998)

[*Answer :* NPV at 12% = Rs. 19.31 lakhs
IRR = 15.6%]

Exercise 4 : XYZ has decided to diversify its production and wants to unverst its surplus funds on the most profitable project. It has under consideration only two projects 'A' and 'B'. The cost of project 'A' is Rs. 100 lakhs and that of 'B' is Rs. 150 lakhs. Both projects are expected to have a life of 8 years only and at the end of this period 'A' will have a salvage value of Rs. 4 lakhs and 'B' Rs. 14 lakhs. The running expenses of 'A' will be Rs. 35 lakhs per year and that of 'B' Rs. 20 lakhs per year. In either case the company expects a rate of return of 10%. The company's tax rate is 50%. Depreciation is charged on straight line basis. Which project should the company take up?

Note : Present value of annuity of Re 1 for 8 years at 10% is 5.335 and present value of Re. 1 received at the end of the 8 year is 0.467.

(ICWA, Inter, December 1995)

[*Answer :* Project B is more profitable than project A, the increase in profit being Rs. 8.020 lakhs (27.258 – 19.238). Hence, project B should be taken up.]